THE BIRDS
OF VANCOUVER ISLAND'S
WEST COAST

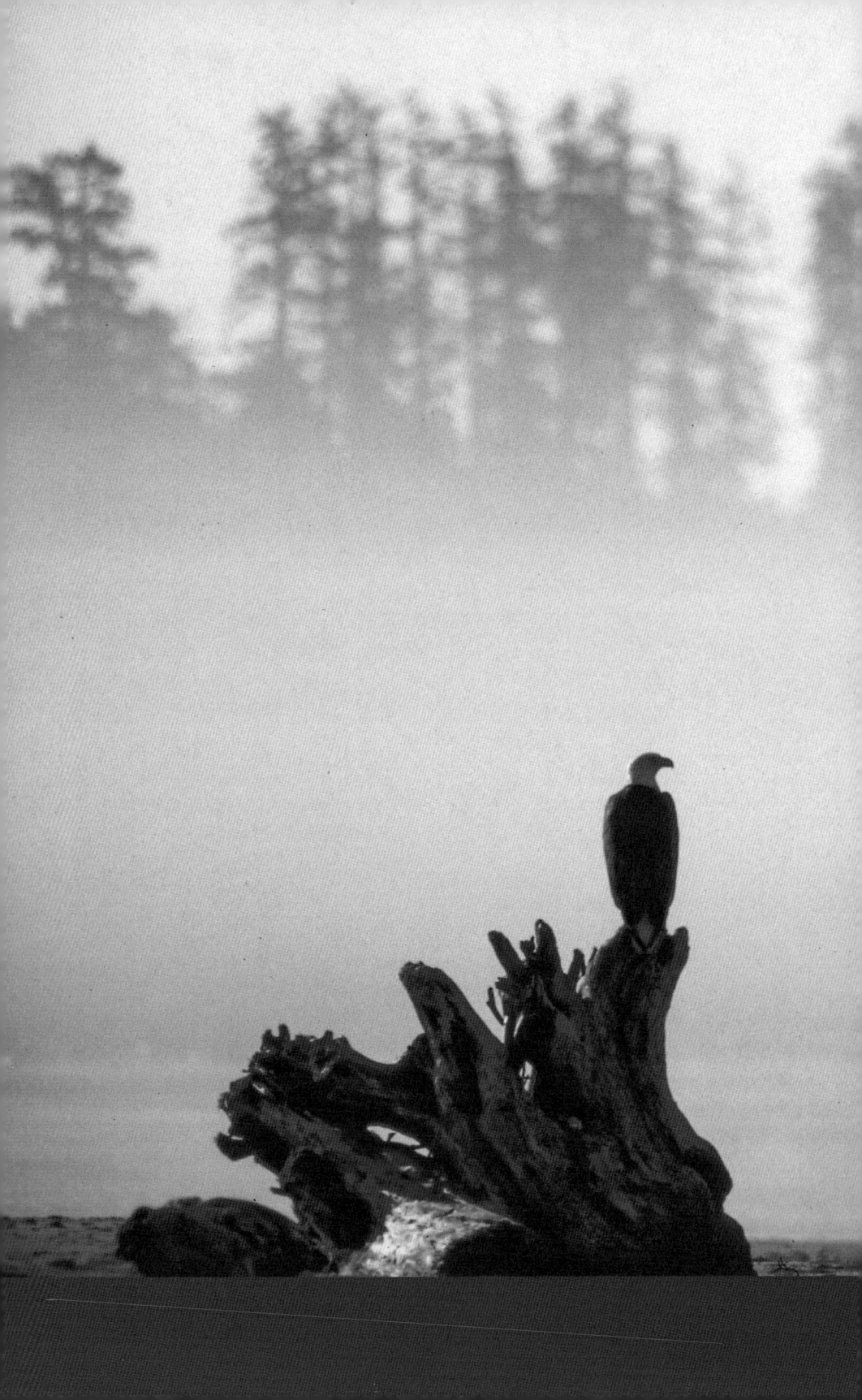

ADRIAN DORST

The Birds of Vancouver Island's West Coast

On Point Press | a UBC Press imprint
Vancouver · Toronto

© On Point Press, an imprint of UBC Press, 2018

All rights reserved. No part of this publication may be reproduced, stored in a retrieval system, or transmitted, in any form or by any means, without prior written permission of the publisher, or, in Canada, in the case of photocopying or other reprographic copying, a licence from Access Copyright, www.accesscopyright.ca.

27 26 25 24 23 22 21 20 19 18   5 4 3 2 1

Printed in Canada.

ISBN 978-0-7748-9010-6 (hardcover); ISBN 978-0-7748-9012-0 (PDF)

Cataloguing-in-publication data is available from Library and Archives Canada.

UBC Press gratefully acknowledges the financial support for our publishing program of the Government of Canada (through the Canada Book Fund), the Canada Council for the Arts, and the British Columbia Arts Council.

UBC Press
The University of British Columbia
2029 West Mall
Vancouver, BC V6T 1Z2
www.ubcpress.ca

PAGES 2-3: A Bald Eagle surveys its domain from a driftwood tree root on Long Beach.

PAGES 4-5: Canada Geese arrive at Jensen's Bay, Tofino.

CONTENTS

12 Preface

16 Acknowledgments

21 Abbreviations

22 Map of Vancouver Island's West Coast

24 Introduction

42 REGULAR SPECIES ....

494 ACCIDENTAL SPECIES ....

524 HYPOTHETICAL SPECIES ....

526 References

548 Index

42 REGULAR SPECIES

Order Anseriformes
Ducks, Geese, and Swans
(Family Anatidae)
- 43 Snow Goose
- 45 Ross's Goose
- 46 Emperor Goose
- 46 Greater White-fronted Goose
- 50 Brant
- 53 Cackling Goose
- 57 Canada Goose
- 61 Trumpeter Swan
- 63 Tundra Swan
- 64 Wood Duck
- 65 Blue-winged Teal
- 67 Cinnamon Teal
- 68 Northern Shoveler
- 70 Gadwall
- 71 Eurasian Wigeon
- 72 American Wigeon
- 73 Mallard
- 74 Northern Pintail
- 77 Green-winged Teal
- 79 Canvasback
- 80 Redhead
- 81 Ring-necked Duck
- 83 Greater Scaup
- 84 Lesser Scaup
- 86 King Eider
- 86 Harlequin Duck
- 88 Surf Scoter
- 90 White-winged Scoter
- 92 Black Scoter
- 93 Long-tailed Duck
- 95 Bufflehead
- 96 Common Goldeneye
- 98 Barrow's Goldeneye
- 100 Hooded Merganser
- 102 Common Merganser
- 105 Red-breasted Merganser
- 106 Ruddy Duck

Order Galliformes
New World Quail
(Family Odontophoridae)
- 107 California Quail

Grouse and Ptarmigan
(Family Phasianidae)
- 108 Ruffed Grouse
- 110 Sooty Grouse
- 111 White-tailed Ptarmigan

Order Gaviiformes
Loons
(Family Gaviidae)
- 113 Red-throated Loon
- 115 Pacific Loon
- 117 Common Loon
- 119 Yellow-billed Loon

Order Podicipediformes
Grebes
(Family Podicipedidae)
- 120 Pied-billed Grebe
- 122 Horned Grebe
- 123 Red-necked Grebe
- 124 Eared Grebe
- 125 Western Grebe
- 127 Clark's Grebe

Order Procellariiformes
Albatrosses
(Family Diomedeidae)
- 128 Laysan Albatross
- 130 Black-footed Albatross
- 133 Short-tailed Albatross

Shearwaters and Petrels
(Family Procellariidae)
- 134 Northern Fulmar
- 136 Murphy's Petrel
- 137 Mottled Petrel
- 138 Pink-footed Shearwater
- 139 Flesh-footed Shearwater
- 140 Great Shearwater
- 141 Buller's Shearwater
- 142 Sooty Shearwater
- 144 Short-tailed Shearwater
- 146 Manx Shearwater
- 147 Black-vented Shearwater

Storm-Petrels
(Family Hydrobatidae)
- 148 Fork-tailed Storm-Petrel

150 Leach's Storm-Petrel

Order Pelecaniformes

Boobies and Gannets
(Family Sulidae)
151 Brown Booby

Cormorants
(Family Phalacrocoracidae)
152 Brandt's Cormorant
154 Double-crested Cormorant
155 Pelagic Cormorant

Pelicans
(Family Pelecanidae)
157 American White Pelican
159 Brown Pelican

Order Ciconiiformes

Herons and Egrets
(Family Ardeidae)
161 Great Blue Heron
163 Great Egret
164 Cattle Egret
165 Green Heron

Order Accipitriformes

New World Vultures
(Family Cathartidae)
165 Turkey Vulture

Ospreys, Eagles, and Hawks
(Family Accipitridae)
167 Osprey
169 Golden Eagle
170 Northern Harrier
172 Sharp-shinned Hawk
174 Cooper's Hawk
175 Northern Goshawk
177 Bald Eagle
181 Red-tailed Hawk
184 Rough-legged Hawk

Order Gruiformes

Rails and Coots
(Family Rallidae)
185 Virginia Rail
186 Sora
188 American Coot

Cranes
(Family Gruidae)
189 Sandhill Crane

Order Charadriiformes

Stilts and Avocets
(Family Recurvirostridae)
192 American Avocet

Oystercatchers
(Family Haematopodidae)
192 Black Oystercatcher

Plovers
(Family Charadriidae)
195 Black-bellied Plover
196 American Golden-Plover
197 Pacific Golden-Plover
200 Snowy Plover
201 Semipalmated Plover
203 Killdeer

Sandpipers and Phalaropes
(Family Scolopacidae)
205 Upland Sandpiper
205 Whimbrel
208 Long-billed Curlew
209 Hudsonian Godwit
210 Bar-tailed Godwit
211 Marbled Godwit
214 Ruddy Turnstone
215 Black Turnstone
216 Red Knot
218 Surfbird
220 Ruff
221 Sharp-tailed Sandpiper
222 Stilt Sandpiper
223 Sanderling
225 Dunlin
226 Rock Sandpiper
228 Baird's Sandpiper
229 Least Sandpiper
230 Buff-breasted Sandpiper
232 Pectoral Sandpiper
234 Semipalmated Sandpiper
235 Western Sandpiper
238 Short-billed Dowitcher
240 Long-billed Dowitcher
242 Wilson's Snipe

244 Wilson's Phalarope
245 Red-necked Phalarope
247 Red Phalarope
250 Spotted Sandpiper
251 Solitary Sandpiper
252 Wandering Tattler
254 Greater Yellowlegs
255 Willet
256 Lesser Yellowlegs

Skuas and Jaegers
(Family Stercorariidae)
257 South Polar Skua
258 Pomarine Jaeger
260 Parasitic Jaeger
261 Long-tailed Jaeger

Murres, Auks, and Puffins
(Family Alcidae)
262 Common Murre
265 Thick-billed Murre
266 Pigeon Guillemot
267 Marbled Murrelet
270 Scripps's Murrelet
272 Ancient Murrelet
274 Cassin's Auklet
275 Parakeet Auklet
276 Rhinoceros Auklet
278 Horned Puffin
279 Tufted Puffin

Gulls and Terns
(Family Laridae)
281 Black-legged Kittiwake
283 Sabine's Gull
284 Bonaparte's Gull
286 Franklin's Gull
287 Heermann's Gull
289 Mew Gull
290 Ring-billed Gull
291 Western Gull
293 California Gull
294 Herring Gull
296 Iceland Gull
297 Slaty-backed Gull
298 Glaucous-winged Gull
299 Glaucous Gull
301 Caspian Tern
302 Common Tern
303 Arctic Tern

Order Columbiformes

Pigeons and Doves
(Family Columbidae)
305 Rock Pigeon
306 Band-tailed Pigeon
307 Eurasian Collared-Dove
309 White-winged Dove
310 Mourning Dove

Order Strigiformes

Owls
(Family Strigidae)
311 Western Screech-Owl
314 Great Horned Owl
316 Snowy Owl
317 Northern Pygmy-Owl
319 Barred Owl
320 Short-eared Owl
321 Boreal Owl
322 Northern Saw-whet Owl

Order Caprimulgiformes

Nightjars
(Family Caprimulgidae)
324 Common Nighthawk

Order Apodiformes

Swifts
(Family Apodidae)
325 Black Swift
327 Vaux's Swift

Hummingbirds
(Family Trochilidae)
329 Anna's Hummingbird
330 Rufous Hummingbird

Order Coraciiformes

Kingfishers
(Family Alcedinidae)
333 Belted Kingfisher

Order Piciformes

Woodpeckers
(Family Picidae)
335 Red-breasted Sapsucker
336 Downy Woodpecker

337 Hairy Woodpecker
340 Northern Flicker
342 Pileated Woodpecker

Order Falconiformes

Falcons
(Family Falconidae)
344 American Kestrel
345 Merlin
346 Gyrfalcon
347 Peregrine Falcon

Order Passeriformes

Tyrant Flycatchers
(Family Tyrannidae)
350 Olive-sided Flycatcher
352 Western Wood-Pewee
353 Willow Flycatcher
354 Hammond's Flycatcher
355 Pacific-slope Flycatcher
357 Say's Phoebe
357 Ash-throated Flycatcher
358 Tropical Kingbird
360 Western Kingbird
361 Eastern Kingbird
361 Scissor-tailed Flycatcher

Shrikes
(Family Laniidae)
363 Northern Shrike

Vireos
(Family Vireonidae)
365 Cassin's Vireo
366 Hutton's Vireo
367 Warbling Vireo
368 Red-eyed Vireo

Jays, Magpies, Crows, and Ravens
(Family Corvidae)
369 Gray Jay
370 Steller's Jay
372 Blue Jay
373 Black-billed Magpie
373 Clark's Nutcracker
374 Northwestern Crow
376 Common Raven

Larks
(Family Alaudidae)
378 Horned Lark

Swallows and Martins
(Family Hirundinidae)
380 Northern Rough-winged Swallow
381 Purple Martin
382 Tree Swallow
384 Violet-green Swallow
386 Bank Swallow
387 Barn Swallow
389 Cliff Swallow

Chickadees
(Family Paridae)
390 Chestnut-backed Chickadee

Long-tailed Tits
(Family Aegithalidae)
392 Bushtit

Nuthatches
(Family Sittidae)
393 Red-breasted Nuthatch

Creepers
(Family Certhiidae)
394 Brown Creeper

Wrens
(Family Troglodytidae)
395 House Wren
396 Pacific Wren
398 Marsh Wren
399 Bewick's Wren

Dippers
(Family Cinclidae)
400 American Dipper

Kinglets
(Family Regulidae)
401 Golden-crowned Kinglet
403 Ruby-crowned Kinglet

Thrushes
(Family Turdidae)
405 Western Bluebird
405 Mountain Bluebird
406 Townsend's Solitaire
407 Swainson's Thrush
409 Hermit Thrush
410 American Robin
412 Varied Thrush

Catbirds, Thrashers, and Mockingbirds
(Family Mimidae)
414 Gray Catbird

- 415 Brown Thrasher
- 416 Sage Thrasher
- 416 Northern Mockingbird

Starlings
(Family Sturnidae)
- 418 European Starling

Wagtails and Pipits
(Family Motacillidae)
- 419 White Wagtail
- 420 American Pipit

Waxwings
(Family Bombycillidae)
- 422 Bohemian Waxwing
- 423 Cedar Waxwing

Longspurs and Snow Buntings
(Family Calcariidae)
- 425 Lapland Longspur
- 426 Snow Bunting

Wood-Warblers
(Family Parulidae)
- 427 Tennessee Warbler
- 428 Orange-crowned Warbler
- 429 Nashville Warbler
- 430 MacGillivray's Warbler
- 432 Common Yellowthroat
- 433 American Redstart
- 433 Yellow Warbler
- 436 Chestnut-sided Warbler
- 436 Blackpoll Warbler
- 437 Palm Warbler
- 438 Yellow-rumped Warbler
- 440 Black-throated Gray Warbler
- 441 Townsend's Warbler
- 443 Wilson's Warbler

Sparrows and Towhees
(Family Passerellidae)
- 444 American Tree Sparrow
- 445 Chipping Sparrow
- 446 Clay-colored Sparrow
- 446 Lark Sparrow
- 447 Lark Bunting
- 448 Fox Sparrow
- 450 Dark-eyed Junco
- 451 White-crowned Sparrow
- 453 Golden-crowned Sparrow
- 456 Harris's Sparrow
- 456 White-throated Sparrow
- 457 Vesper Sparrow
- 458 Savannah Sparrow
- 460 Song Sparrow
- 462 Lincoln's Sparrow
- 463 Swamp Sparrow
- 464 Spotted Towhee

Tanagers
(Family Thraupidae)
- 465 Western Tanager

Cardinals, Grosbeaks, and Allies
(Family Cardinalidae)
- 467 Rose-breasted Grosbeak
- 467 Black-headed Grosbeak
- 468 Lazuli Bunting
- 469 Indigo Bunting
- 470 Dickcissel

Blackbirds, Orioles, and Allies
(Family Icteridae)
- 470 Yellow-headed Blackbird
- 471 Western Meadowlark
- 472 Bullock's Oriole
- 473 Red-winged Blackbird
- 475 Brown-headed Cowbird
- 477 Rusty Blackbird
- 477 Brewer's Blackbird
- 478 Common Grackle

Finches and Allies
(Family Fringillidae)
- 479 Brambling
- 480 Evening Grosbeak
- 480 Pine Grosbeak
- 481 Gray-crowned Rosy-Finch
- 482 House Finch
- 484 Purple Finch
- 485 Common Redpoll
- 486 Red Crossbill
- 488 White-winged Crossbill
- 489 Pine Siskin
- 491 American Goldfinch

Old World Sparrows
(Family Passeridae)
- 492 House Sparrow

494 ACCIDENTAL SPECIES
- 495 Falcated Duck
- 495 Tufted Duck
- 496 Arctic Loon
- 496 Solander's Petrel
- 497 Magnificent Frigatebird
- 498 Snowy Egret
- 498 American Bittern
- 499 Black-crowned Night-Heron
- 499 Black-necked Stilt
- 500 Bristle-thighed Curlew
- 501 Curlew Sandpiper
- 501 Crested Auklet
- 502 Black Tern
- 503 Oriental Turtle-Dove
- 504 Yellow-billed Cuckoo
- 504 Black-billed Cuckoo
- 505 Barn Owl
- 505 Burrowing Owl
- 506 Great Gray Owl
- 507 Lesser Nighthawk
- 507 Eastern Whip-poor-will
- 509 Black-chinned Hummingbird
- 509 Costa's Hummingbird
- 509 Black Phoebe
- 510 Great Crested Flycatcher
- 511 Gray Kingbird
- 511 Philadelphia Vireo
- 511 Eurasian Skylark
- 512 Blue-gray Gnatcatcher
- 512 Siberian Accentor
- 513 Gray Wagtail
- 513 Chestnut-collared Longspur
- 514 Smith's Longspur
- 514 McKay's Bunting
- 515 Northern Waterthrush
- 515 Black-and-white Warbler
- 515 Prothonotary Warbler
- 516 Connecticut Warbler
- 516 Hooded Warbler
- 517 Northern Parula
- 517 Bay-breasted Warbler
- 518 Prairie Warbler
- 519 Canada Warbler
- 519 Grasshopper Sparrow
- 520 Yellow-breasted Chat
- 520 Rustic Bunting
- 521 Painted Bunting
- 521 Bobolink
- 522 Orchard Oriole
- 522 Baltimore Oriole

524 HYPOTHETICAL SPECIES

PREFACE

Two young Short-billed Dowitchers pause in their southbound flight to rest and feed on a beach pool.

In 1978, the British Columbia Provincial Museum (now the Royal British Columbia Museum) published a pioneering book on west coast birds called *Birds of Pacific Rim National Park*.[1] It was authored by David F. Hatler (PhD student), R. Wayne Campbell (Curator, Vertebrate Museum, Department of Zoology, University of British Columbia), and Adrian Dorst (naturalist/birder). The book listed 231 species confirmed for Pacific Rim National Park, a 511-square-kilometre (197-square-mile) region that encompasses Long Beach, the Broken Group (Islands), and the West Coast Trail. A few records from other areas of the west coast region were also included. Today, 39 years later, the number of species for the west coast region stands at 360, a gain of 129 species. Just as important is that the status of many species has been clarified. For instance, in 1978 the status of the Palm Warbler, with only one record, was considered accidental, but today, with 55 additional sightings, it is considered a rare fall migrant. The Northern Shoveler, then listed as an uncommon migrant, is today considered common. A change in status of this sort can be attributed either to an increase in sightings due to natural changes in range or to more observations in the field. In the case of the Palm Warbler, it is likely due to the latter, whereas in the case of the Northern Shoveler, it is due primarily to range expansion.

I had contemplated writing this book for years without any serious effort to actually begin, knowing it would be a huge amount of work with little or no reward. In the end, I decided that after all the years spent recording the comings and goings of birds on this coast, I couldn't allow myself not do it. Tackling the project would of course require still more fieldwork to fill in some of the gaps in information. Not that I needed any additional excuse to drop everything to go birding, my philosophy long having been that if it's sunny, it's too nice to work, and if it's wet and stormy, well, one just has to go out to see what the storm blew in.

As it turned out, I was wrong about there being no reward. The reward has been in the research, the writing, and the additional fieldwork, all of which have taught me so much more. Had I not taken on this project, I would not have learned of the discovery of an isolated population of Marbled Godwits in Alaska, or of the longevity of the Manx Shearwater (50 years), or that a female Laysan Albatross can lay eggs and raise chicks for 62 years, or that the multitude of Savannah Sparrows we see on our beaches in fall have just made a 2,600-kilometre ocean crossing from Unalaska Island. These things I learned, and much, much more.

The records in this book have been extracted from various sources, including two Vancouver Island–based birding websites, scientific papers and government reports, the four volumes of *The Birds of British Columbia* by R. Wayne Campbell and colleagues (Royal BC Museum and UBC Press), and of course from *Birds of Pacific Rim National Park* (BC Provincial Museum), the foundation on which this work is built. My search for important records that I may have missed led to Keith Taylor's online *Birds of Vancouver Island*, as well as the online list *Rare Birds of Vancouver Island*, by Rick Toochin, Paul Levesque, and Jaimie Fenneman. Although the latter was useful for tracking down records of vagrants, it unfortunately contains serious errors. An additional source of information was the publication *Wildlife Afield: A Journal of British Columbia Natural History*, published by the Biodiversity Centre for Wildlife Studies (BCFWS) in Victoria. Breeding records came from various sources, including the BC Nest Record Scheme (BCNRS) and the *Atlas of the Breeding Birds of British Columbia* (edited by P.J.A. Davidson, R.J. Cannings, A.R. Couturier, D. Lepage, and C.M. Di Corrado). To determine the migration periods and status of many species on the west coast, I relied largely on the more than 35,000 records in my own files, readily accessible through eBird. Sponsored by Cornell University and Bird Studies Canada, eBird, with the help of thousands of contributors, is revolutionizing knowledge about the distribution of birds in North America and elsewhere. Valuable records have also been gleaned from residents of Tofino and Ucluelet.

Given that much of the west coast region is thinly populated and difficult to reach, if not downright remote, the bulk of the records found in this book originate from the central west coast between Barkley Sound and Clayoquot Sound. However, records from all regions of the coast have been used whenever available. The results presented in this book, I believe, give an accurate representation of which species occur in the west coast region as a whole, their status, and their times of arrival and departure.

Because Jordan River straddles the boundary separating the west coast region from southern Vancouver Island, records from that location should probably be viewed in a somewhat different light. Nevertheless, this location is frequently visited by birders who submit year-round sight records, thereby providing valuable information on migrants passing through our region's southernmost extremity. It would be wise for readers to keep in mind, however, that sightings from that location may not be typical for the region as a whole.

This book was written with the aim of building upon and expanding on the original work of 40 years ago. If I have succeeded in doing the subject justice, it is in no small part due to the diligence of hundreds of enthusiastic birders who have taken the time to record their sightings in the public domain. I hope all of you enjoy this book, in which you played a part.

ACKNOWLEDGMENTS

A beach-walker stops to admire a flock of Alaska-bound Marbled Godwits feeding on Long Beach.

In recognition of the vital role that birders play in our understanding of the distribution of birds, I have endeavoured to give credit within the species accounts to all those who have made particularly noteworthy or significant observations. Often, however, the names of observers were not available in the literature, and sometimes editorial considerations made it impractical to include them. Such being the case, wherever possible and practical I have included the names of the observers of birds in the *casual* and *accidental* categories, and occasionally for other sightings that were particularly noteworthy. Before listing all of the contributors whose records have found a place in this book, there are a few people I wish to mention in particular. Special thanks go to David F. Hatler and R. Wayne Campbell for bringing me to the west coast in the first place, so many years ago, to conduct bird surveys in the newly proclaimed Pacific Rim National Park. Without their faith in the ability of a newcomer from eastern Canada, I might never have taken up residence on the west coast of Vancouver Island. In addition, as science editor for this work 45 years later, Wayne Campbell selflessly contributed a great deal of time and effort in adding records and information of which I had no knowledge.

Special thanks also go out to Rod Palm for inviting me along on many cold and bumpy pelagic trips, and for making available the data from 65 pelagic bird and mammal surveys. Thanks also to Jerry Etzkorn, who, as assistant lighthouse keeper at Carmanah Point, kept detailed records for a number of years of the birds he saw there, many of which he kindly copied and sent my way, contributing a great number of important sightings. Thanks to Mark Hobson for giving me access to his detailed notes from Lemmens Inlet, near Tofino, and to George and Sylvia Bradd for their counts of Sandhill Cranes passing over their home near Port Alberni. Thanks too to Ian Cruickshank for all his contributions during the final summer of this project. And thanks, finally, to three Tofino residents – retired Tofino fisherman "Extraordinary Ralph" Crombie, retired commercial pilot Doug Banks, and Arthur Ahier – all of whom kept me informed about sightings at the Jensen's Bay mudflats and elsewhere.

I am grateful to Michael Rodway, Wayne Campbell, and Moira Lemon for permission to extract information on the current distribution and populations of seabird colonies along the west coast area from a pre-publication draft of their updated seabird catalogue for British Columbia. Thanks also to Randy Schmidt and Holly Keller at UBC Press, and to copy editor Frank Chow, typesetter Irma Rodriguez, and cartographer Eric Leinberger.

Listed below in alphabetical order are the names of people whose records were incorporated into this book. To anyone I may have missed, my sincere apologies. Some contributors I missed may be mentioned in the text. Thanks to all of the following:

Ryan Abbot, Christine Adkins, Arthur Ahier, David Allinson, Christine Anderson, John Anderson, Ted Ardley, Dorothy Arnet, Roland Arnet, Petra Arnold, Christian Artuso, Bill Asteriades, Brian Avent, Joseph Baier, David Baird, Christine Ball, Dan Banks, Doug Banks, James Barber, Erica Barkley, Wayne Barnes, Karen Barry, Avery Bartels, Sam Barwick, Joseph Bear, Barbara Beasley, Garrett Beisel, Jur Bekker, S. Benoit, Michael Bentley, Mary Bewick, Paul Bewick, Lynn Bieber-Weir, Brian Bielfelt, Jim Biggar, Randy Bjorklund, Barbara Blackie, Alan Blair, Adam Blake, Peter Blancher, Peter Boon, Sandy Bowie, George Bradd, Sylvia Bradd, James Bradley, Jenny Bradshaw, Ewen Brittain, Nick Brooks, Marylin Buckle, Alan E. Burger, Claudia Burns, Mike Burrell, Roger Burrows, Michael Butler, Robert W. Butler, Warren Cairo, Marcie Callewaert, Barbara Campbell, Barry Campbell, R. Wayne Campbell, Peter Candido, Richard J. Cannings, Robert A. Cannings, Russel Cannings, G. Clifford Carl, Cathy Carlson, Harry R. Carter, Don Cecile, Karen Charleson, Steve Charleson, Barbara N. Charlton, Richard Chiovitti, Michael Church, Randy Churchill, Chris Chutter, Richard Clarke, Peter Clarkeson, Helene Clay, Brooke Clibbon, Paul R. Clyne, Aziza Cooper, Merrily Corder, Dominic Cormier, Doug Cowell, Catherine Craig, David Crocker, Susan Crocker, Ralph Crombie, Ed Crooks, Ian Cruikshank, Michael Currens, John Cyrus, Paul de Niverville, Eric Demers, Sergey Dereliev, Christopher Di Corrado, Andreas Deissner, Matt Dil, Daniel Donnecke, Robert Dovos, Rudolf H. Drent, Randy Dzenkiw, Jerry Etzkorn, Jason Feaber, Jaimie Fenneman, Karen Ferguson, Susan Fleck, Mark Fortune, Dudley Foskett, J. Bristol Foster, Leslie Fox, David F. Fraser, Jan Fries, Marcel Gahbauer, Shantel Gamon, John Garret, Jerremy Gatten, Pierre Geofray, David Gibson, Jack Gillie, Jeff Gilligan, M.E. (Peggy) Goodwill, J.E. Victor Goodwill, Max B. Gotz, Glen Gould, Wesley

Greentree, Brian Grisborne, Sarah Groves, Jean Sebasian Guenette, Charles J. Guiguet, James Hamilton, Bob Hanson, Anne Harfenist, Alexis Harrington, Christopher Harris, Michael Harrison, David F. Hatler, Louise Haviland, James Headrick, Harvey Henderson, Nathan Hentze, Debra Herst, Jerry Herst, Denise Herzberg, Brendan Higgins, Christmas Ho, Mark Hobson, Kathleen Horn, Roger Horn, Barrie Hotchkiss, Neil Hughes, Pamela Hunt, Robert Huxley, Rad Icenoggle, Doug Innes, Marian Innes, Nigel Jackett, Alana Janisse, Juka Jantunen, Daryl Johnson, Devon Johnson, Ryan Johnston, Ian Jones, Edward Joran, Brian Keating, Daryl Keeble, Steve Kelling, Christian Kelly, Jeremiah Kennedy, Ken Kennedy, Michael Kennedy, Jeremy Kimm, Robin Kite, Alexa Klinka, Michael Klotz, Steve Knight, Daniel Konig, Heidi Krawjewsky, Michael Lanzone, Orin Lawson, Paul Lehman, Jan Leina, Moira J.F. Lemon, Denis Lepage, Paul Levesque, Dan Lewis, Eric Lofroth, Gail Loughridge, Chris Lowther, Rob Lyske, Jeff MacAdams, Stuart Mackenzie, Lisa Madry, Mark Maftei, Art Martell, Adrianne Mason, Tom Maxie, Arlene McGinnis, William (Bill) E. McIntyre, Darryn McKonkey, Martin K. McNichol, Sandy McRuer, Ian McTaggart-Cowan, Guy McWethy, Charles Meints, T. Melling, Mitch Meredith, Ryan Merrill, G. Scott Mills, John Mills, Daniel Mitchell, Peter Mitchell, Dale G. Mjertaas, Guy Monty, Ken Morgan, Phillip Morrison, Michael Mullin, Colleen Murchison, Andy Murray, Wayne Neily, Anne Nightingale, Andrea Norris, Mark Nyhof, George Olioso, Marie O'Shaughnessy, Doug Palfrey, Roderick Palm, Larry Peavier, Ed Pellizzon, Frank Pinilla, David Pitt-Brooke, Claudette Poirier, Terry Poulton, Ilya Povalyaev, Jennifer Provencher, Caleb Putman, Kenneth Racey, Mary Rae, Lea Ramsea, Keith Riding, Jeanine Randall, Wayne Raud, Margaret Reine, Robert Repenning, John Reynolds, Julie Reynolds, Noella Rickaby, June Ryder, Mark Robbins, Mary Robichaud, Brad Robinson, Michael S. Rodway, Gerald Romachuck, Ron Ronconi, Ben Ronnenbergh, Donna Ross, Richard Rowlett, Mathew Sadler, Dan Salisbury, Dan Sandri, Ron Satterfield, Chris Saunders, Joan Saunders, Owen Schmidt, Barbara Schramm, Bernard Schroeder, Peter Schultz, Jim Schwarz, Spencer G. Sealy, Tanya Seebacher, Brian Self, Nimali Seneviratne, Michael G. Shepard, David Shipway, Christopher Siddle, George P. Sirk, Arnold Skei, Brian Slater, George Smith, Ken Sole, John Spahr, Simon Starr, Ed Stedman, Andy Stepniewski, Tom Stere, Brian Sterenberg, John Sterling, Bob Steventon, Anne Stewart, Joanna Streetly, David Stirling, Ken R. Summers, Douglas Tate, Keith Taylor, Rick Taylor, James Telford, Marcel Theriault, Toby Theriault, James Thompson, Erin Thomsin, Camilla Thorogood, Allyson Timmermans, Mike Toochin, Rick Toochin, Sharon Toochin, Jared

Towers, Andy Tuecher, Eric Tull, Laurence Turney, Bill Tweit, Mike Tyne, Brian Uher-Koch, Iwan Van Veen, Linda Vaxvick, Dan Vedova, William Verbrugge, Kees Vermeer, Wim Vesseur, Lena Ware, Jody Wells, Rob Werona, Mike Wesbrook, Pam White, Peg Whittington, Fred Wickens, Magil Wieber, Jennifer Wilcox, David Willard, Helen Williams, Megan Willie, Jacqueline Windh, John G. Woods, Mike Woods, Mike Yip, and Yuri Zharikov.

Finally, I would like to thank Hiroshi Hasegawa, who photographed and kindly gave me permission to use the image of the adult Short-tailed Albatross on the cover of this book. A species once common off our shores, this bird was hunted to near-extinction for its feathers on the Japanese islands where it breeds. Today it is making a remarkable comeback, thanks to protective laws and human stewardship, and it is once again being seen over our offshore waters. It seemed appropriate to use a photo of this species on the cover because this bird symbolizes humanity's ability to do both good and harm. With continued stewardship and protection it is likely only a matter of time before this handsome, long-winged glider is once again the most common albatross over west coast waters.

ABBREVIATIONS

AOS	American Ornithological Society
AOU	American Ornithologists' Union
BC Photo	A photograph in the collection of the BCFWS
BCFWS	Biodiversity Centre for Wildlife Studies
BCNRS	British Columbia Nest Record Scheme
BCPM	British Columbia Provincial Museum
CBC	Christmas Bird Count
COSEWIC	Committee on the Status of Endangered Wildlife in Canada
CVMUBC	Cowan Vertebrate Museum, University of British Columbia
CWS	Canadian Wildlife Service
IUCN	International Union for Conservation of Nature and Natural Resources
MVZ	Museum of Vertebrate Zoology (Berkeley)
NM	nautical mile
NMC	National Museums of Canada
PRNP	Pacific Rim National Park
RBCM	Royal British Columbia Museum
UBC	University of British Columbia
UBCBBM	Formerly in the collection of UBC, now at the Beaty Biodiversity Museum

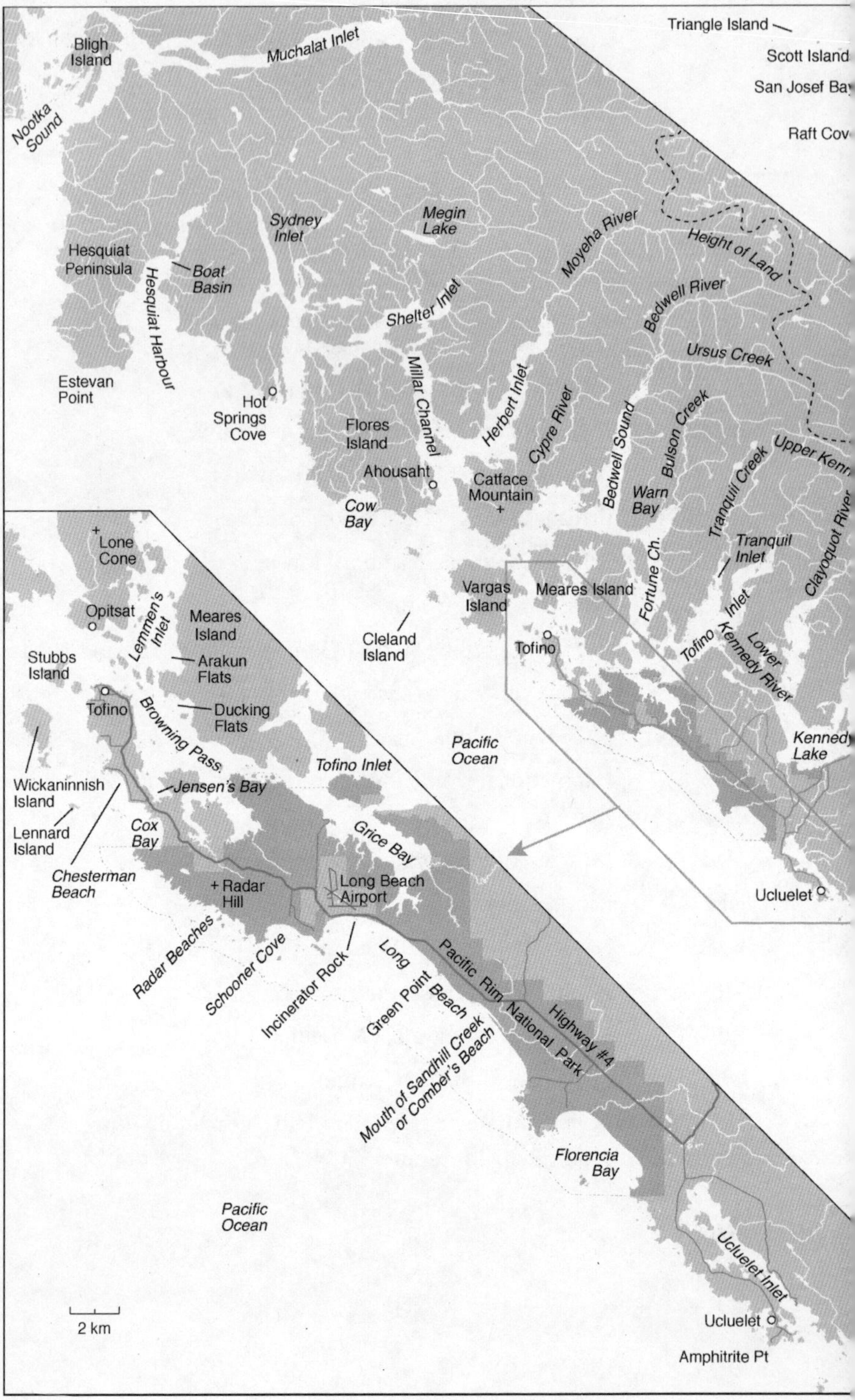

Triangle Island
Scott Island
San Josef Bay
Raft Cove
Bligh Island
Muchalat Inlet
Nootka Sound
Sydney Inlet
Megin Lake
Moyeha River
Height of Land
Hesquiat Peninsula
Hesquiat Harbour
Boat Basin
Shelter Inlet
Bedwell River
Ursus Creek
Estevan Point
Hot Springs Cove
Millar Channel
Herbert Inlet
Cypre River
Bedwell Sound
Bulson Creek
Flores Island
Ahousaht
Catface Mountain
Cow Bay
Warn Bay
Tranquil Creek
Upper Kennedy
Clayoquot River
Tranquil Inlet
Fortune Ch.
Vargas Island
Meares Island
Cleland Island
Tofino
Tofino Inlet
Lower Kennedy River
Kennedy Lake
Pacific Ocean
Ucluelet
Lone Cone
Opitsat
Lemmen's Inlet
Meares Island
Arakun Flats
Stubbs Island
Tofino
Browning Pass
Ducking Flats
Tofino Inlet
Wickaninnish Island
Jensen's Bay
Lennard Island
Cox Bay
Chesterman Beach
Radar Hill
Grice Bay
Long Beach Airport
Radar Beaches
Schooner Cove
Incinerator Rock
Long Beach
Green Point
Pacific Rim National Park
Highway #4
Mouth of Sandhill Creek or Comber's Beach
Florencia Bay
Pacific Ocean
Ucluelet Inlet
Ucluelet
Amphitrite Pt
2 km

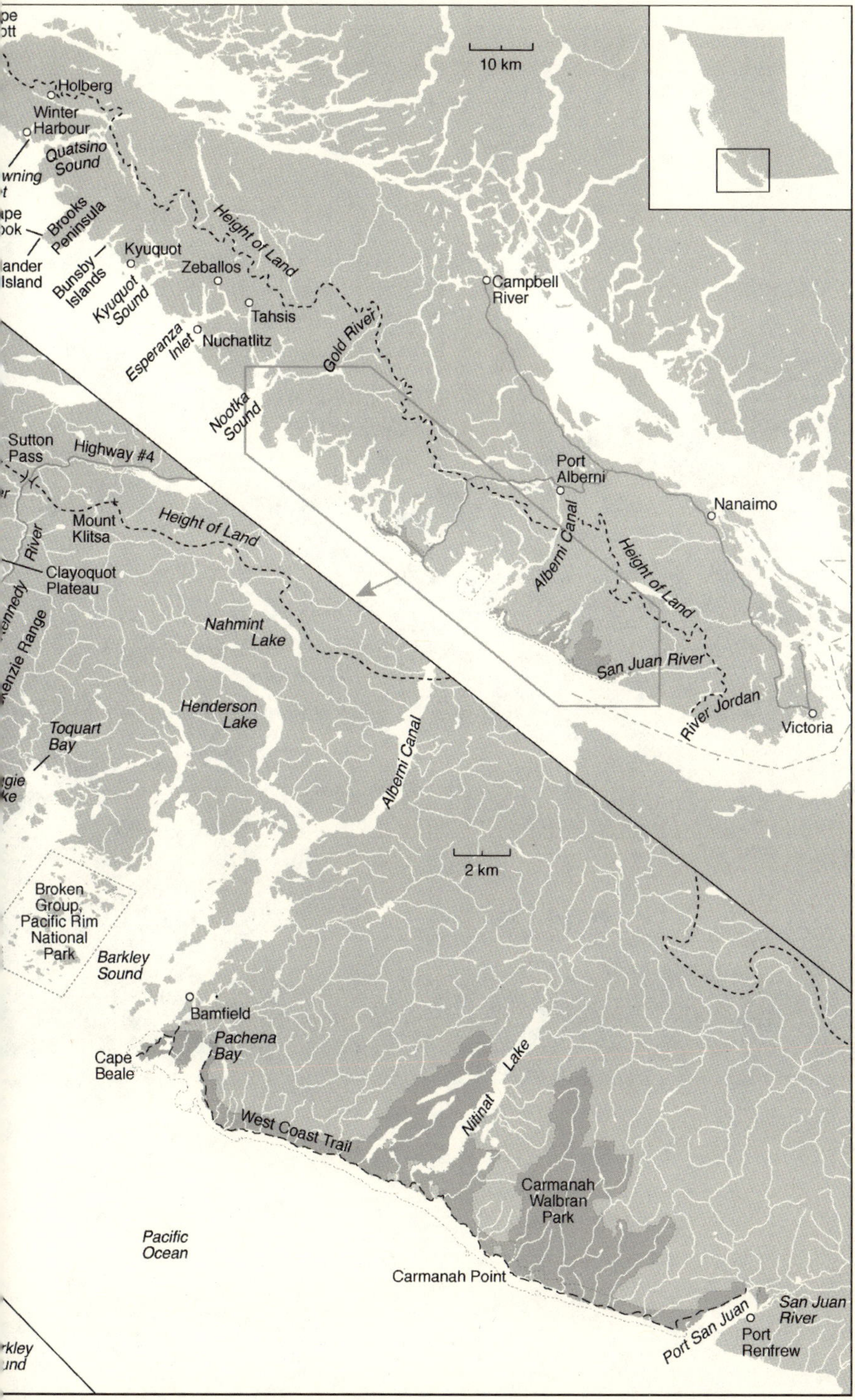

10 km
Holberg
Winter Harbour
Quatsino Sound
Brooks Peninsula
Island
Bunsby Islands
Kyuquot
Kyuquot Sound
Zeballos
Tahsis
Height of Land
Esperanza Inlet
Nuchatlitz
Gold River
Nootka Sound
Campbell River
Port Alberni
Nanaimo
Alberni Canal
Height of Land
San Juan River
River Jordan
Victoria
Sutton Pass
Highway #4
Mount Klitsa
Height of Land
River
Clayoquot Plateau
Nahmint Lake
Henderson Lake
Toquart Bay
Alberni Canal
2 km
Broken Group, Pacific Rim National Park
Barkley Sound
Bamfield
Pachena Bay
Cape Beale
Nitinat Lake
West Coast Trail
Carmanah Walbran Park
Pacific Ocean
Carmanah Point
Port San Juan
San Juan River
Port Renfrew

INTRODUCTION

Breaking surf, Cox Bay, Tofino

The west coast of Vancouver Island has been luring visitors to its shores for at least 7,000 years. Cross the island's height of land, which separates the more developed eastern half from the wild western half, and you enter a region that is shaped by the Pacific, an ocean that covers some 40% of the planet. Sail directly away from Long Beach in a southwesterly direction and you will not see land until you hit the beaches of Australia, 11,000 kilometres (6,835 miles) away. Sail in a northwesterly direction and you will arrive in Tokyo by the shortest route, having travelled some 7,400 kilometres (4,600 miles).

The west coast of the island is distinctive in both geography and climate. Facing seaward, it bears the brunt of the gales and storms and torrential downpours that are spawned over the immense ocean, and even in summer the west coast climate is tempered by fog and temperatures that are often 10°C cooler than those on the sheltered side of the island. In winter, on the other hand, the west coast basks in a climate that is often the mildest in Canada, albeit wet.

If the climate is distinctive, so are many of the birds that visit the region – oceanic birds, including shearwaters, albatrosses, and storm-petrels. These are birds adapted to pelagic waters, and for the most part they rarely venture near shore except for breeding. Great multitudes of shorebirds and waterfowl follow the coast north and south each year along the great aerial freeway known as the Pacific Flyway. At the peak of the season, birds such as Pacific Loons and Surf Scoters pass by at a rate of thousands of individuals per day, while flocks of Western Sandpipers containing as many as 20,000 birds are observed over the mudflats near Tofino.

Passerines of many kinds and in large number likewise follow the coast on their great journey north and south. On one occasion, radar tracking conducted at night near the north end of the island during the peak of the migration revealed 20,000 passerines flying overhead in a period of several hours. While migrants pass over unseen in fair weather, when inclement weather strikes unexpectedly, birds, unable to navigate without the sun or stars as guide, are forced to the ground in large numbers. Birders lucky enough to be in the area during such a fallout can rejoice in their good fortune.

Geography and Climate

The west coast region, as defined here, stretches from Jordan River in the south to Cape Scott in the north, and includes the Scott Islands and Triangle Island. The dividing line between western Vancouver Island and eastern Vancouver Island is the height of land from which water drains in opposite directions. The region includes the villages and communities of River Jordan (usually referred to as Jordan River), Port Renfrew, Ucluelet, Tofino, Ahousat, Gold River, Tahsis, Zeballos, Kyuquot, Port Alice, Winter Harbour, Quatsino, Coal Harbour, and Holberg at the northern tip of the island. The highest point on the island is a mountain called Golden Hinde, which straddles the divide at 2,200 metres (7,219 feet) elevation. The only area draining westward that is excluded from the west coast region is the Alberni Valley area, including Sproat Lake and Great Central Lake. With an average annual rainfall of 1,907

A sea of mountains, Clayoquot Sound

millimetres (75.1 inches) for Port Alberni, and with midsummer temperatures averaging 6°C degrees higher than Tofino (more in August), that area belongs, climatically and biologically, to eastern Vancouver Island. The dividing line, therefore, has been drawn through upper Alberni Inlet, just above Mactush Creek and Franklin River. Seaward, the region extends outward for a distance of 100 kilometres from shore. Although arbitrary, this figure seemed to me to be a reasonable distance for including offshore waters that can still considered part of the west coast region.

As with eastern Vancouver Island, the west coast's topography consists largely of mountains and valleys, with a lowland coastal plain near the sea. Where the west coast region differs radically from the east side is in its coastline, which is broken by numerous sounds and inlets. By my count, there are five sounds and 30 inlets on the west coast, with each sound having its own unique character. Whereas Barkley Sound is open and studded with small islands, Clayoquot Sound is distinguished by three large ones. Nootka Sound and Kyuquot Sound are dominated by a single large island, while Quatsino Sound has only a few small ones.

The west coast's mountainous terrain, combined with the broken coastline, limited or prevented road building and accessibility to much of the region for many years. This discouraged settlement by non-natives and delayed resource extraction (logging), which effectively preserved the land in a wild state for longer than elsewhere on the island. Even today, the region is often referred to as "the wild west coast," and, indeed, thanks to the environmental battles of the 1980s and 1990s, large tracts of undisturbed rainforest remain. All of the remaining intact wilderness valleys on Vancouver Island are found on the west coast, most of them in Clayoquot Sound. Access into much of the region remains difficult and is often limited to travelling by boat, by floatplane, or on foot.

Facing the open ocean, the west coast region receives prodigious amounts of rain. Gold River receives 2,851 millimetres (112.2 inches), while Port Renfrew and Tofino, both of which are located on the outer coast, receive an annual average of 3,505 millimetres (138 inches) and 3,271 millimetres (128.8 inches), respectively. Compare this with Victoria's 926 millimetres (36.5 inches)! Yet the rainfall in Tofino is relatively moderate for the west coast. Far more rain falls in the mountains. In the Clayoquot Valley, which lies just north of Kennedy Lake, 8,220 millimetres (323.6 inches) of rain was once recorded in a single year. Henderson Lake, north of Barkley Sound, topped that in 1997 with 9,307 millimetres (366 inches), breaking all records and making this the wettest spot in North America. That amount translates to 30.5 feet, or 10 times the average annual rainfall for Victoria.

Forest Cover

The west coast's high precipitation nurtures coniferous woodlands that are classified as true temperate rainforest. In their climax state, these forests are dominated by western redcedar (an arborvitae) and western hemlock. In prime growing sites, amabilis fir may also be found. Sitka spruce often dominates in valley bottoms and as fringe forest in the ocean-spray zone along the outer coast. Douglas-fir, which was the dominant tree species throughout the island during a 3,000-year-long drier and warmer period beginning several millennia after the last ice age, now occurs in the west coast region as a minority tree, and is largely restricted to well-drained areas, most often on steep mountain slopes. These trees can often be identified at a great distance because they protrude above the forest canopy and have broad rather than pointed tops. Only in a few locations in the west coast region does this species still dominate, among them the upper Kennedy River, the Namint Valley, and formerly the San Juan River Valley. Shore pine survive in some of the most challenging environments, such as bogs and on rocky hills with little soil, while yellow cedars may be found in bogs, as well as at higher elevation in the mountains. In the subalpine zone, mountain hemlock dominates. As with most rules, there are exceptions. In at least one location – Sydney Inlet – mountain hemlock may be found growing at sea level. Subalpine fir is found only at the higher elevations in Strathcona Park.

Deciduous trees are in a minority in the west coast region. Three of the most common are bigleaf maple, Douglas maple, and red alder. Maple trees grow in some valleys, sparsely in others, and not at all in still others. They are not usually found near the outer coast. Red alders, on the other hand, can be found almost everywhere except at high elevations. They often border the forest on shorelines and river courses and quickly take hold wherever there is disturbance, such as a landslide, or where logging has taken place. This fast-growing tree stabilizes the soil after disturbance and restores nitrogen. Red alders attract specific bird species, particularly passerines, during migration. Due to the extensive logging that has taken place over the past half-century, deciduous habitat is far more common today than in the past.

Bird Habitats

Some of our small passerines seek out dense shrubbery and places with substantial understorey for breeding. Among them are three wood-warblers –

Orange-crowned, MacGillivray's, and Wilson's warblers. Prevalence of such vegetation is closely related to the availability of light. Salmonberry bushes, which provide food for a number of bird species during the nesting season, are likewise dependent on an abundance of light in order to flourish. And as with other forest shrubs, more light results in more berries.

There is considerable variability in forest types, and each variation has an influence on which birds may be present. As a general rule, expect more birds in an open forest with a lot of understorey, and fewer in a closed-canopy forest with little understorey. Few birds inhabit closed-canopy tree plantations where light is at a premium, and these areas are also devoid of dead snags. Snags are a vital component of a healthy forest environment, providing nesting cavities for Wood Ducks, Hooded Mergansers, woodpeckers, owls, chickadees, and some swallows and swifts. Snags, of course, are absent from areas that have been clearcut, but today logging companies are sometimes required to leave a few older trees and snags.

The west coast region has numerous lakes, the largest being Kennedy Lake and Nitinat Lake, both of which were saltwater inlets long ago. Other sizable lakes include Henderson, Nahmint, Victoria, Hesquiat, Crawfish, and Muchalat Lake. If we include all lakes, from the largest to the smallest, both at low and high elevation, they add up to well over 300 in number. It is safe to say that many of these lakes have never been visited by birders or by biologists, and some are so remote and inaccessible it is doubtful that human feet have ever trod their shores. Red-throated and Common loons and Mew Gulls are known to nest on some of the deeper lakes, while shallow ones that allow aquatic vegetation to flourish provide suitable habitat for birds such as Wood Ducks, Mallards, Hooded Mergansers, and Pied-billed Grebes. A few small lakes are also known to provide a resting place, watering hole, and preening ground for hundreds of ducks at night.

The region's convoluted coastline, about 420 kilometres (260 miles) long as the crow flies, would easily be three or four times as long if one were to trace the shore through each sound, inlet, cove, and island. Small offshore islands provide breeding grounds for a variety of seabirds and Black Oystercatchers. The most important of these is Triangle Island, followed by Solander, Cleland, Seabird Rocks, and Sea Lion Rocks. There are also several treed islands on which Leach's Storm-Petrels breed.

Much of the coast consists of a rocky shoreline. Whereas in protected waters the rocky shore is usually an unproductive habitat for birds, the reverse is true along the outer coast. There the biologically rich intertidal zone provides foraging habitat for shorebirds such as oystercatchers, turnstones, Surfbirds, and Wandering Tattlers. In spring and summer, sandy beaches such as Long Beach provide food for an even greater number, consisting of thousands of sandpipers and plovers that feed on red worms living just beneath the surface. In winter, numerous estuaries provide important feeding grounds for waterfowl, including Trumpeter Swans, Common and Barrow's goldeneyes, and Common and Hooded mergansers. Mudflats, however, comprise the most important habitat for migratory and wintering birds.

The largest and most significant mudflats on the west coast, and indeed the whole island, are located in southern Clayoquot Sound, near Tofino. Here, hundreds of geese, thousands of ducks, and tens of thousands of shorebirds visit each year. Indeed, these mudflats are the most important stopover on Vancouver Island for Western Sandpipers and Short-billed Dowitchers, and the only major stopover in the province for Whimbrels. In all, 43 species of waders have been recorded in the west coast region. Many other birds, such as cormorants, loons, herons, and eagles, also convene here to partake in the rich bounty. Mudflats are also found in Ucluelet Inlet, at Browning Inlet, northwest of Quatsino Sound, and at Hansen Bay in Cape Scott Park.

There are at least six notable categories of human-altered landscapes in the west coast region that influence the presence of birds. The first comprises logged areas, which usually have been clearcut. This type of habitat can range from little more than a field of stumps to being densely covered in native shrubbery, young alders, or even Scotch broom, a foreign invasive species. The second category consists of forests where red alders dominate. These are usually locations that previously were clearcut but never replanted. In a few locations the trees are now close to a hundred years old.

Closed-canopy monoculture tree plantations make up a third category. These are areas previously logged and then replanted with seedlings of one or more species of conifer that have attained a height and density that shut out the sun, resulting in a forest floor with little or no vegetation. Such forests provide very poor habitat for bird life.

Town sites are a fourth category. Villages, because they provide open spaces, lawns, gardens, and groves of deciduous trees, offer a surprising amount of biodiversity, and are therefore often a haven for certain species. The presence of backyard feeders is an additional attraction.

The fifth category consists of roads. I include this as a category because roadsides often have prolific deciduous growth, creating habitat for passerines such as American Robins, Wilson's Warblers, and Swainson's Thrushes.

The sixth and final category includes airports and golf courses, or rather *the* airport and *the* golf course at Long Beach, since there is only one of each. Built during the Second World War to prevent the Japanese military from landing and getting lost in our dense west coast rainforest, the airport is used and maintained to the present day. Because of active vegetation suppression around the runways, the airport acts as a magnet for migratory birds that prefer open country such as grasslands and tundra, or dense shrubbery, which is found on the periphery. The golf course provides extensive lawns, shrubbery, and scattered trees. Long is the list of birds that have been seen there, including some that are rarely seen elsewhere. At the airport, a long pond dug as a landing strip for float planes attracts both ducks and shorebirds.

Please note that the airport has restricted access and there are no-trespassing signs on the perimeter. Anyone contemplating birding there is well advised to stay away, particularly during the busy summer season, when passenger jets take off and land frequently. I would advise anyone who is determined to enter the airport grounds in violation of the directive to go early or late in the day, wearing inconspicuous clothing and staying on the periphery, well away from any runways. At the golf course, large areas can now be viewed from McLean Point Road and there is no need to enter the grounds.

Most birding is done on or near the outer coast, and much has yet to be learned about birds in the mountains, particularly at higher elevation. The status of high-elevation breeders, such as American Pipit and Townsend's Solitaire, still needs to be clarified. Only recently has Barrow's Goldeneye been found breeding. Surprises undoubtedly still await the mountain hiker.

Using This Book

Names of Birds

Species are listed in taxonomic order, based on the eBird/Clements Checklist (now maintained by the Cornell Lab of Ornithology), with the Latin name following the official English name for each species. Periodically, name changes are made or species are split by the American Ornithological Society (AOS), creating two or more out of one. For North American birds, the Clements Checklist largely defers to the North American Classification Committee of the AOS. Names in older books may therefore differ from those in the latest publications. For example, Pacific Wren was Winter Wren before it was split, and Cackling Goose was created from the Canada Goose. Bullock's Oriole was split from Northern Oriole, Red-breasted Sapsucker from Yellow-bellied

Vancouver Island's west coast is interrupted by five sounds. One of the two largest is Barkley Sound, with the Broken Group Islands of Pacific Rim National Park seen below.

Like ocean tentacles, some 30 inlets penetrate the west coast, the longest for over 30 kilometres. Here I am shown paddling on Shelter Inlet in the mid-1980s.

The west coast region was once cloaked in old-growth rainforest. Much of what remains is in Clayoquot Sound. Ursus Creek lies below, while Bulson Valley lies over the saddle.

To visit the Megin River is to enter a primeval world unaltered by modern humans. Seen here is the upper river. The Megin is now protected as part of Strathcona Provincial Park.

Pacific rainforest is highly variable, depending on the growing site. In these rocky hills, dominated by shore pine, expect to hear the ethereal song of the Hermit Thrush.

Old-growth lowland rainforest bordering streams is often dominated by Sitka spruce, which are fertilized by salmon carcasses following spawning. Note the dense understorey.

Introduction 35

A hiker enjoys the view from Steamboat Mountain on the Clayoquot Plateau. More than 300 lakes dot the region, providing nesting habitat for Red-throated Loons and other birds.

Alpine and subalpine zones remain far from thoroughly explored, and much remains to be learned about birds in the high country. This view looks south from Nine Peaks.

36 *Introduction*

The mudflats of southern Clayoquot Sound provide habitat for thousands of waterfowl and shorebirds. Jensen's Bay is seen on the far side, while Cox Bay lies behind the peninsula.

Beaches, such as Chesterman Beach and Cox Bay, seen here, are vital feeding grounds for migratory shorebirds.

Dune grass on Stubbs Island, near Tofino, attracts hundreds of migrant Savannah Sparrows each fall, after their long ocean flight from the Alaska Peninsula.

Once an ice age refugium, the northwest slope of Brooks Peninsula is now characterized by open glades and stunted forest, providing habitat for birds such as Sooty Grouse.

Remotely located on the northwestern tip of Vancouver Island, Cape Scott Provincial Park is visited by birders only occasionally. Seen here are the dunes at Guise Bay.

Estuaries are important feeding areas for waterfowl such as Trumpeter Swans, dabbling and diving ducks, as well as shorebirds. Seen here is the estuary of the Zeballos River.

Sapsucker, and Sooty Grouse from Blue Grouse. Western Flycatcher in British Columbia became Pacific-slope Flycatcher, and the western version of the Rufous-sided Towhee became Spotted Towhee.

Sometimes names were changed to more accurately reflect a bird's family or generic status. Going back a long way, Sparrow Hawk, not being a hawk at all but a falcon, became American Kestrel. Likewise, the falcons known as Pigeon Hawk and Duck Hawk became Merlin and Peregrine Falcon, respectively, the AOU having adopted the British names for these birds. Marsh Hawk became Northern Harrier. The diving duck known in North America as Oldsquaw was given the British name of Long-tailed Duck, and Red-backed Sandpiper became Dunlin.

Names have occasionally been changed from "common" to "northern," as with the Northern Flicker, or from "northern" to "common," as with the Common Raven. American Merganser was changed to Common Merganser, though in Britain it is still known as Goosander. Common Scoter was changed to Black Scoter in North America when the species was split from the Eurasian form, which remains the Common Scoter.

One might conclude from the above that name changing has been rampant. A perusal of the 1941 edition of Roger Tory Peterson's *A Field Guide to Western Birds* shows that there have indeed been many changes over the past half-century, although most have remained the same. Interestingly, Bullock's Oriole, Red-breasted Sapsucker, and Spotted Towhee were considered full species at the time, before being lumped and then split again. With the advent of DNA sequencing, such determinations are now somewhat easier to make.

There may well be a further split in future if the four currently recognized subspecies of the Fox Sparrow are given full species status. Three of the four occur in British Columbia, and all three have been recorded in the west coast region of Vancouver Island.

Status
Abundance and season are indicated in the status bar at the top of each species account. Relative abundance is designated as follows:

- abundant – easily found and often in large numbers
- common – easy to find and seen on many or most outings
- fairly common – not seen on most outings but usually not hard to find
- uncommon – present in the region but often hard to find
- rare – seen only occasionally in most years

- casual – very rare; recorded three times or more, but less than once a year on average
- accidental – out of normal range and usually far from home; recorded only once or twice.

Seasons

The seasons are defined as follows: winter includes January, February, and March; spring includes April, May, and the first half of June; summer runs from mid-June to mid-September; and fall runs from mid-September to the end of December.

Confusion can result from misunderstanding of the terms "spring migrant" and "fall migrant." Although for most migrants the spring migration period occurs in April or May, some birds migrate as early as March. And although for most birds the migration is over well before the end of May, for a few species the spring migration continues into June. For some birds, the southbound or "fall" migration begins as early as late June, and for a few it can continue through November and December. It is therefore best to regard these terms flexibly, with the northbound migration usually being synonymous with spring migration, and the southbound migration meaning fall migration, regardless of the month in which it takes place. Birds seen in January, February, and March are generally considered winter visitors, although even in the first half of January some birds may still depart for points further south.

The breeding season varies considerably for different species. Bald Eagles and Great Horned Owls may begin nesting as early as February, whereas Pacific Wrens begin nesting in April. Birds such as swifts and nighthawks may not breed until well into June. Overall, birds have a higher probability of being breeding birds in June than in any other month.

Range and Distribution

Most species accounts in this book begin with a description of the bird's geographical range and distribution. For information within the borders of British Columbia, including pelagic waters, I relied in most cases on the four volumes of *The Birds of British Columbia* (1990–2001) by R. Wayne Campbell and colleagues. When applicable, updated distributions from new literature were included. For regions in North America but outside the province, I relied on maps in popular guides such as *The Sibley Guide to Birds* (2000–08) by David Sibley, and the *National Geographic Field Guide to the Birds of North America* (2006–08), edited by Jon L. Dunn and Jonathan Alderfer; the maps in the latter are particularly accurate, in my estimation. For bird distribution outside North America, if any, maps shown on Birdlife International websites were consulted, as well as *A Guide to the Birds of Mexico and Northern Central America* (1995) by Steve N.G. Howell and Sophie Webb. For shorebirds, various sources were used, including *Shorebirds: A Complete Guide to Their Behaviour and Migration* (1988) by Alan Richards, and *The Shorebird Guide* (2006) by Michael O'Brien, Richard Crossley, and Kevin Karlson.

REGULAR SPECIES

This section of species accounts includes all birds that occur regularly in the west coast region and those that have occurred often enough (3 times or more) and are expected again. Birds of rare and casual occurrence are therefore also included here, though not those of accidental occurrence (2 times).

Red-breasted Sapsucker

ORDER ANSERIFORMES

Ducks, Geese, and Swans   *Family Anatidae*

SNOW GOOSE
Anser caerulescens

STATUS: Uncommon fall migrant, casual in spring.

Small numbers of Snow Geese are sometimes seen in fall at the Long Beach Golf Course. Shown here are adults and juveniles.

Flying high above the earth against a clear blue sky, a skein of these white geese with black wingtips can be a dazzling sight, capturing our imagination as we see them arriving from a distant land, several thousand kilometres away. Snow Geese breed from the shores of Hudson Bay north to the Arctic regions of Canada and Alaska, including the High Arctic islands. They winter in numerous regions of the United States and Mexico. The birds we see on the Pacific coast, however, belong to a population that breeds outside North America, on Russia's Wrangel Island and the adjacent mainland of eastern Siberia. They winter from California to Washington and southwestern mainland British Columbia. The more northerly wintering birds divide their time between the Skagit Valley and the Fraser River delta, where they gather by the tens of thousands. The Wrangel Island population has increased from a low of 47,000 in 1976 to over 100,000 in 2006 and 228,500 in 2015.[2] The primary migration corridor for birds wintering in the Fraser-Skagit region is along the mainland coast and over the Strait of Georgia.

On Vancouver Island's west coast, Snow Geese are normally seen infrequently. In 1978, *Birds of Pacific Rim National Park* listed only seven records, although the text mentions that local residents said they were once common in fall.[1] Overlooked was a record of a bird that spent the winter of 1973/74 at Hansen Lagoon in Cape Scott Park.[4] Between 1981 and 2014, there were 48 additional sightings, most of those involving from 1 to 6 birds on the ground at the airport and golf course. All birds seen on our coast were recorded in fall except on four occasions: on 18 April 2004, 54 birds were seen passing over Tofino; on 30 April 1988, a single bird was seen at Stubbs Island; on 30 March 2012, 200 birds were seen over Long Beach; and on 15 April 2014, a single bird was also seen over Long Beach. Most of our fall sightings were recorded between 28 September and 30 October. Records outside this period are few, although in 2014 a small flock was seen at Jensen's Bay until late November. The earliest fall sighting involved a single bird at Long Beach on 11 September 1992. There are also a handful of records for early November, with the latest date being the 20th of the month in 2014.

Large flocks are seen passing over periodically. Besides the sighting in 2012, flocks have been seen passing over the central west coast as follows: 220 birds on 6 October 1982, 200 on 30 October 1987, 90 on 28 September 2004, 73 on 5 October 2011, and 95 on 30 September 2013. As well, a flock of 50 birds was seen offshore during a pelagic bird survey on 12 October 1993. The largest number seen on the ground prior to 2016 was 33 birds on 22 and 24 October 2010, at the Long Beach Airport and the adjacent golf course.

More flocks were seen in October 2016 than in any other year. This was due to a series of severe storms that rolled in from the Pacific. Many locals reported seeing Snow Geese passing over around this period. On 24 October, 210 birds were grounded in Jensen's Bay, Tofino, due to gale-force winds, and a flock of 15 birds was present at the golf course on 20 October. By 26 October the flock had grown to 30 birds, and by 29 October to 85 birds. A flock of 26 birds was seen as late as 12 November, and a flock of 12 birds on 24 November. On 8 December, 2 birds were spotted at the airport. Most of the birds we see on the ground in our area are ones that have been separated from a larger flock, or, as in 2016, blown off course by a storm. The occasional high-flying birds seen coming in from the west are presumably taking a direct route over the ocean from the Alaska Peninsula.

Snow Geese that breed in Arctic Canada and that normally migrate south over the Great Plains very occasionally stray into our region. We know this only because of the occurrence of a dark-morph Snow Goose on the Tofino mudflats on 11 October 1972. These dark birds were at one time thought to be a separate species, called the Blue Goose. Dark-morph birds do not occur in the Pacific population.

ROSS'S GOOSE
Anser rossii

STATUS: Casual spring transient.

This diminutive white goose, only slightly heavier than a Mallard, is North America's smallest. It breeds in the northern regions of Canada, along the shores of Hudson Bay in Ontario, Manitoba, and northern and eastern Nunavut, east to southwestern Baffin Island, and west to the Amundsen Gulf. The species winters at numerous locations in the southern United States. In the west, it winters primarily in southern Oregon and California, and further east from western Texas and New Mexico into northern Mexico. Most of the eastern population migrates through the Prairie provinces and the US Midwest, while California-bound birds take a route further west through Alberta.

In British Columbia, this species occurs only sporadically, but it has been reported from many localities over the years, both on the coast and in the interior of the province. Sightings are usually of a single individual travelling with geese of other species. The largest number ever recorded in British Columbia was seven individuals reported near Powell River on 11 October 1981.

For our west coast region, we have three records, all in April, and a new distribution record for British Columbia. On 16 April 1998, a lone bird was seen and photographed among a flock of Brant at the edge of Browning Passage, Tofino. The following day, it was seen again on the Stubbs Island sandspit. There were no further sightings until 30 April 2012, when a Ross's Goose was spotted at the Long Beach Airport in the middle of a very large flock of Greater White-fronted Geese, grounded due to a strong headwind. The third sighting occurred a year later, on 6 April 2013, when two birds were seen among a flock of Dusky Canada Geese passing over Green Point at Long Beach. From their small size compared with the much larger Canada Geese it was evident they were Ross's Geese and not the larger Snow Geese.

EMPEROR GOOSE
Anser canagicus

STATUS: Casual vagrant in winter and spring.

This species breeds in northeastern Siberia and western Alaska, and winters primarily in the Aleutian Islands and the Alaska Peninsula. It is seen irregularly along the Pacific coast, south to central and coastal California. In British Columbia, there have been numerous records since 1894, with 26 of those from Vancouver Island. It is seen mostly between mid-November and the end of May.

In the west coast region, we have five records. The first dates from December 1912, one male collected at Goose Lagoon, Cape Scott (UBCBBM B003344). The second sighting involved six birds at Estevan Point on 30 December 1930, one of which was collected (RBCM 4966). On 8 December 1982, three birds were observed at Cleland Island, with one bird staying until 26 May 1983.[2] The third sighting was a well-described single bird seen with six Glaucous-winged Gulls on rocks by a lighthouse keeper on Kains Island, Quatsino Sound, on 19 December 1990. There were no further records until 14 December 1996, when Don Cecile, who was driving into Tofino for a day of birding, was startled to see an Emperor Goose standing on the highway, apparently having mistaken the rain-slicked pavement for a river. It flew off over Tofino with Don in hot pursuit and disappeared to the northwest.

Between 1964 and 1986, the Emperor Goose population suffered a 70% decline, plunging from 139,000 birds to 42,000. With tightened hunting regulations imposed in Alaska, and with the US Department of Fish and Wildlife aiming to restore the population to historical levels, the population had risen to 98,200 birds (spring count) by 2015.[2]

GREATER WHITE-FRONTED GOOSE
Anser albifrons

STATUS: Abundant spring migrant and common to abundant fall transient. Casual in summer. Uncommon in winter.

This goose is known to older locals and hunters as "California Red Legs" or "Speckle Belly." It breeds in northern Eurasia, Alaska, the Canadian Arctic, and western Greenland. It can be divided into five subspecies, three of them in

Greater White-fronted Geese often land in fall at the Long Beach Golf Course and airport. This bird is an adult.

North America. These three populations are sometimes referred to as Midcontinent, Pacific, and Tule. The population known as Midcontinent (*A. a. gambelli*) breeds from northern and central Alaska east through Arctic Canada to the region west of Hudson Bay. It migrates over the Great Plains to winter in the Mississippi valley, along the Gulf Coast, and in northeastern Mexico. It is segregated in winter from birds from the Pacific Flyway. The Pacific population (*A. a. sponsa*) breeds in western Alaska and migrates over the eastern Pacific to winter in California and northwestern Mexico, and to a lesser extent in southeastern Oregon. The Tule Goose (*A. a. elgasi*) breeds in Cook Inlet, Alaska, and migrates over the eastern Pacific to winter mainly in the Sacramento Valley in California.

In 1978, *Birds of Pacific Rim National Park* listed the Greater White-fronted Goose as an uncommon spring and fall migrant.[1] That is certainly not the case today. In late April of any given year, large numbers may be seen passing over the west coast. On 28 April 1993, a total of 3,175 birds were counted passing over Tofino, and on 30 April 2012, an estimated 2,300 were seen resting on the tarmac of the Long Beach Airport after a sudden change in wind direction grounded the birds. The largest movement recorded so far took place on 28 April 2011, when a remarkable 26,850 geese were counted passing over the Long Beach coastal plain, the vast majority of them Greater White-fronted Geese.

It is worth noting that the Pacific population has undergone a dramatic increase in North America since falling to a low of 73,100 birds in 1979, down from 480,000 birds in the period from 1966 to 1968. With careful management, the population had increased to 433,400 by 2001, and was estimated at 479,100 birds in 2015.[2]

During spring passage, birds will often pass over at the end of a southeasterly weather system using a tail wind to their advantage, and it is not unusual for them to intermingle with flocks of Cackling Goose, making it difficult to determine the relative numbers of each. When the weather is clear and calm, they tend to avoid the coastal plain altogether and instead fly over the open ocean several kilometres or more out to sea. At such times most birds pass by unseen.

The first flocks begin arriving in early to mid-April. The earliest arrival dates were 6 April in 1993 and 4 April in 2009. Spring passage usually peaks during the last few days of April or the first few days of May at the latest. Most birds pass through in a one- or two-day period, after which the movement abruptly drops off, with the exception of a few laggard flocks that may be seen for an additional week or two. Birds have been seen as late as June on two occasions. On 1 June 2008, 15 birds were seen at Tofino, and on 2 June 2010, a single bird was seen at the airport. There is a single record of birds lingering into the summer. A flock of 10 birds was seen and photographed on the beach at Stubbs Island on 9 July 2010.

The southward migration begins in late August. The earliest date recorded thus far is 22 August in 2012, when a flock was heard over Tofino during inclement weather. In 2001, 20 birds were seen at the Long Beach Airport on 23 August, and in 2014, 4 birds were observed on 30 August. Given that the movement is already under way in late August, one might expect a surge in numbers in September. However, between 1983 and 2014, there were only 14 records for that month. Birds presumably pass by unseen, far offshore. Occasionally, during an early autumn gale when birds face a stiff headwind, they are pushed to shore, as happened on 27 September 2013, when 200 birds were seen passing low over Green Point, Long Beach.

In September 2014, the west coast experienced a gale from the southeast for four days in a row. Southbound birds flying over the ocean must have been taken by surprise. On 22 September, Guy Monty reported 4,500 birds passing over the Bamfield area, and scattered flocks were seen at Tofino and Long Beach the following day. On 24 September, 150 birds were recorded on the ground at the Long Beach Golf Course among a much larger contingent of Cackling Geese. The following day, a survey of the airport next door produced a count of 2,200 Greater White-fronted Geese, with the majority on the ground and the rest passing over. An estimated 850 birds were still present on 26 September; the wind had abated but the rain persisted. As late as 17 October, 156 birds remained at the golf course.

In most years, fall transients are seen primarily in October, although not in numbers comparable to spring. A notable exception occurred on 4 October 2008, when 1,600 birds were found on the ground at the Long Beach Golf Course and another 600 landed at the nearby airport due to sudden strong headwinds. This storm also resulted in 43 birds choosing to overwinter in the Tofino area for the first time, far north of their usual wintering grounds in California and southern Oregon. Birds continued to overwinter in Tofino during the following three years, with 20 individuals in the second winter, 39 in the third winter, and 20 in the winter of 2011/12. No birds stayed the following winter, but in 2014/15, a flock of 38 birds once again overwintered in Tofino. In May, the flock gradually dissolved, with small groups breaking off from the main flock and leaving, rather than all departing at once.

While residing in Tofino, these birds performed a community service by keeping village lawns well clipped and fertilized, and entertaining locals and visitors alike by bedding down in the middle of the street, bathing in large puddles, stopping traffic by languidly strolling across the street, crosswalk or not, and loitering on the police station lawn.

Curiously, flocks choosing to overwinter here are sometimes composed entirely of young birds of the year, and not birds from the previous winter as one might expect. These overwintering birds are believed to belong to the Pacific population, which has two breeding populations, one at Bristol Bay and the other further north in western Alaska. The Bristol Bay population winters primarily in central Mexico, and those from further north winter in central California and Oregon. It is likely, therefore, that our overwintering birds belong to the latter group.

The Tule Goose has a population numbering between 5,000 and 10,000 birds, compared with 479,100 for the Pacific population in 2015.[3] Tule Geese are said to be larger and darker, with a larger bill, longer legs, and a sparsely streaked breast. They breed around Cook Inlet, Alaska, and winter mainly in the Sacramento Valley of California, where they are adapted to feeding in marshes. Although Tule Geese may well pass through the west coast region, thus far no birds seen on the ground have been identified as such.

That adult Greater White-fronted Geese are very devoted to their young was demonstrated by an incident that occurred in September 2011. At the Long Beach Airport, I observed two adult geese circling several times, calling all the while, then disappearing to the south. A short while later, a juvenile also circled the airport, calling repeatedly. It wasn't hard to put two and two together. The young bird had become separated from its parents and they were searching for each other.

Three days later, at the north end of Chesterman Beach, two Greater White-fronted Geese passed overhead, calling. Suddenly, from the end of the beach we heard the frantic honking of a juvenile bird (I'm convinced it was the same one), which flew past us as fast as its wings could propel it. It had recognized the voices of its parents. The adult birds must have heard the youngster, because they changed course and did a slow circle, allowing it to catch up. It was a touching moment to see the family reunited and disappear towards the south. That these geese would delay their journey and spend days searching for their youngster demonstrates, I think, a level of devotion we rarely attribute to birds.

BRANT
Branta bernicla

STATUS: Common to abundant spring migrant; rare in summer, fall, and winter.

This small goose has a broad distribution in the northern hemisphere. It breeds in northern Siberia, in the Baltic Sea region of Europe, and in Arctic Canada and Alaska. North American Brant consist of three subspecies comprising four populations: Eastern High-Arctic Brant (*B. b. hrota*, also known as Light-bellied Brant), which breeds in the eastern High Arctic and migrates to winter in Ireland via Greenland and Iceland; Atlantic Brant (*B. b. hrota*, also known as Light-bellied Brant), which breeds in the eastern low Arctic and migrates to the US Atlantic coast; Western High-Arctic Brant (intermediate between *hrota* and *nigricans*, also known as Gray-bellied Brant), which winters in Padilla Bay and two other bays in Puget Sound; and Black Brant (*B. b. nigricans*), which winters from southwestern British Columbia along the Pacific coast to northwestern Mexico. A small number of this group winters in Haida Gwaii.[5]

The wintering population in the Salish Sea (formerly Strait of Georgia, Strait of Juan de Fuca, and Puget Sound) has declined drastically since the late 1800s, largely due to market hunting in the 1890s and early 20th century.[6] Today, most of the population bypasses British Columbia entirely in fall, passing by offshore to winter in Mexico, particularly at two large lagoons in Baja California. During the spring migration, large numbers stop along the eastern shore of Vancouver Island to rest and feed; a portion of the population passes by the west coast, many stopping over at Tofino. Here they often seek shelter in protected waters where food is available in the form of eelgrass and sea lettuce (*Ulva* sp.), which form most of their diet.

On Vancouver Island's west coast, Brant have been recorded in every month of the year, although rarely in summer, fall, and winter. Occasionally from 1 to 3 birds are present in June and July on offshore islands. In 1969, 2 to 3 birds remained on Cleland Island from 2 to 6 June, and in 1970, 1 to 2 birds were present from 1 June to 20 July, although 21 and 20 birds (likely late migrants) were recorded on 13 and 16 June, respectively (BCFWS). Most of the spring movement occurs in April and May. Brant rest and feed at two locations near Tofino – in the waters surrounding Stubbs Island and in Browning Passage, where they rest and feed along the edge of the mudflats near Laddie Island. I had never seen Brant at the latter location until the spring of 1992, though I have been assured by locals that they have done this in the past. Since 1992, they have used this area on many other occasions, though not every year. Greatly increased boat traffic and low-flying aircraft near Stubbs Island in recent years may well have had an influence on this move to a quieter location.

The number of Brant stopping at Tofino varies significantly from year to year, and this may be influenced by weather and sea conditions. Rafts of Brant have also been noted resting on the ocean two or more kilometres offshore. Most of these birds do not bother to enter Clayoquot Sound. Birds have also been observed in kelp beds off the south end of Vargas Island, where they fed on *Ulva*, an alga also known as sea lettuce, growing on bull kelp. Peak numbers for the spring season at Tofino in the past 25 years have ranged from as low as 550 birds on 26 May 2009 to 2,600 birds on 3 May 2002 and 3,000 birds on 2 May 2010.

It is difficult to establish the exact timetable for spring migration, although it appears that birds begin arriving by mid to late March. There are several records for that month: 17 birds at Stubbs Island on 20 March 2011; 20 birds seen offshore on 25 March 1996; and 60 birds off Vargas Island on 26 March 1994. In 1978, *Birds of Pacific Rim National Park* mentioned that in the past there was a substantial movement through the area during March, but that this was no longer true.[1]

By early April, Brant begin to rapidly increase in numbers, reaching a peak by early May. Migrants continue to be seen throughout the month of May and well into June. Surveys at Long Beach in recent years have revealed birds passing by until about mid-June. The year 2010 was unusual in that stragglers continued throughout all of June and small numbers persisted through July and even August.

On 1 June that year, 105 birds were still at Browning Passage; on 18 June, 46 birds lingered at Stubbs Island; on 27 June, 75 Brant were seen passing by Green Point at Long Beach; on 18 July, 10 birds were at Stubbs Island; and on 11 August, 5 birds were present at Chesterman Beach. Presumably, birds seen after mid-June are nonbreeding laggards. There have been July occurrences in a few other years as well.

In fall, Brant do not follow the spring route south along the eastern Pacific coast. Instead, nearly the entire population, estimated in 2015 at 136,500 birds, first gathers at Izembek Lagoon on the Alaska Peninsula, then takes a direct route over the ocean to the lagoons of Baja California. Puget Sound birds would, of course, choose a separate route and some may pass our shores en route to the Strait of Juan de Fuca, though this remains unproven. A flock of 25 birds seen passing Amphitrite Point on 26 November 2009 could well have been from this population.

There are 17 winter records from Tofino that so far defy explanation. All of these are of single birds or small flocks. Dates range from 18 December to 14 February. Most December records involve single birds. Some January dates at Tofino are as follows: 17 birds on 9 January 2007; 10 on 16 January 1999; 40 on 23 January 1997; and 26 on 31 January 2011. There have been additional January and February sightings recorded offshore. On 22 January, 30 birds were recorded 4.4 NM southwest of Tofino, and on 14 February 1996, 37 Brant were counted. These ranged from 4.6 NM from shore to 10.9 NM out.

Birds seen in during the winter months were clearly passing through and not wintering here. The question is, where were they bound? According to Tofino resident Rolley Arnet, in the 1950s locals hunted Brant from November through January. Asked in which direction he thought these birds were moving, he said that the consensus among hunters at the time was that they were travelling south.

Hunting of Brant is now rare in Clayoquot Sound. The only instance in recent years that I know of occurred on 14 May 2007, at Stubbs Island, when a flock of 135 birds were shot at by local hunters from the Tle-o-quot band. When the shooting stopped, 25 birds were down. Police arrived on the scene, but departed after being told by the hunters that they were exercising their legal right to hunt as First Nations members.

Counts of Western High-Arctic Brant (Gray-bellied) wintering in Puget Sound in January 2015 numbered under 6,000 birds,[2] and the hunting season remained closed. Until recently, all Brant seen in the Tofino area were Black Brant. An exception occurred on 1 June 2015, when 3 Western High-Arctic Brant were reported at Stubbs Island by Arthur Ahier. It is worth noting that moulting Black Brant, occasionally seen in summer, can have pale bellies. However, all birds seen at the beginning of June should be in fresh plumage.

CACKLING GOOSE
Branta hutchinsii

STATUS: Abundant spring migrant, common and sometimes abundant fall migrant, casual in winter.

Cackling Goose: subspecies *B. h. minima,* foreground; *B. h. taverneri,* back centre, and *B. h. leucopareia* on the left and right.

The Cackling Goose is named for its high-pitched voice. In appearance, it is very similar to the Canada Goose, complete with black neck stocking and white "chin strap." However, it is smaller and has a shorter neck and stubbier bill. Overall size is variable, depending on which population an individual belongs to. Until 2004, when it was recognized as a separate species by the American Ornithologists' Union (AOU), the four populations that make up the Cackling Goose were considered to be merely subspecies of the Canada Goose. The

Cackling Goose breeds from northern Baffin Island and the Keewatin region, westward through the Canadian Arctic to the north slope of Alaska, western Alaska, and the Aleutians.

Of the four populations, or subspecies, Richardson's Cackling Goose (*B. h. hutchinsii*), also known as Hutchins's Goose, breeds furthest east in the Canadian Arctic and follows a migratory route west of Hudson Bay, through Nunavut, the Canadian Prairie provinces, and the American Midwest. The other three subspecies migrate west of the Rocky Mountains. Taverner's Cackling Goose (*B. h. taverneri*) migrates through the BC interior, while the small Cackling Goose (*B. h. minima*) and Aleutian Cackling Goose (*B. h. leucopareia*) migrate over the Pacific Ocean and along the coast. The English name associated with the subspecies *B. h. minima* is Ridgway's Cackling Goose, although this name is not yet commonly used in Canada.[7]

In our west coast region, large numbers of Cackling Geese are seen passing over each spring. Nearly all are believed to be *B. h. minima*. The earliest migrants are usually seen around mid-April or shortly thereafter. In 2012, a flock of 80 birds was seen as early as 6 April, and in 2013, a flock of 4 was seen on 10 April. There are only two records of birds passing over in March. In 1992, a small flock was seen travelling with Canada Geese on the 22nd of the month, and in 2008, a flock of 30 birds was seen passing over Tofino on 20 March.

There is a gradual increase in numbers during the second half of April, with peak days usually producing counts of 5,000 or more birds. As early as 1972, David F. Hatler recorded 6,500 geese passing over Turtle Island, Barkley Sound, on 2 May and he thought they were *B. h. minima*.[1]

Today there is no doubt that they were Cackling Geese. Dates in subsequent years on which 5,000 or more birds have been recorded are as follows: 28 April 2008 – 5,000 birds; 27 April 2009 – 5,600; 2 May 2011 – 6,045; and 27 April 2013 – 5,000. After the big day, a few flocks of stragglers bring up the rear. On rare occasions, we see a flock or two after the first week of May. By mid-May, and sometimes well before, virtually all birds have passed through.

As can be deduced from the above, the peak day of the migration occurs during a very short window, usually from 27 April to 2 or 3 May. However, large numbers are sometimes seen well before this. In 2007, 2,000 birds were recorded as early as 16 April, and the following year, 1,800 birds were counted on 19 April. In 2014, 1,825 were observed on 22 April.

In autumn, the first migrants are usually seen in the first or second week of October, although they are already passing by offshore in the last 10 days of September. We know this because of occasions when adverse weather conditions such as rain, fog, or strong headwinds force birds to shore. In recent years, birds have been recorded several times in September on the central west coast. A flock of 16 Cackling Geese was seen at the Long Beach Airport on 25 September 2011, 10 were seen there on 27 September 2012, 11 on 24 September 2013, and a single bird on 19 and 27 September 2016.

On 22 September 2014, a very large weather front over the Pacific generated strong southeasterly winds. The first indication that this would bring geese ashore occurred at Jensen's Bay, when 6 Cackling Geese were seen beating their way into a strong headwind in the direction of the airport. The following morning, 145 birds were counted passing over Chesterman Beach, and 510 birds were already on the ground at the airport. On 24 September, with no let-up in the gale-force winds, parts of the Long Beach Golf Course were covered in Cackling Geese. A census over the entire grounds produced an estimate of 900 birds. On 26 September, 800 birds were counted, and 295 birds were still present as late as 17 October.

The other two subspecies that pass through our region are seen only occasionally. Taverner's Cackling Goose (*B. h. taverneri*) normally migrates over the BC interior. This subspecies is larger than *B. h. minima*, with a longer neck, and looks virtually identical to the Lesser Canada Goose (*Branta canadensis parvipes*), which migrates over the Great Plains.[8] Birds believed to have been this subspecies were seen at the Long Beach Golf Course in 1997, 1998, 2012, 2014, and 2016. They are not recorded at all in most years, but there was a veritable invasion in 2012. The first bird, a lone individual in the company of 10 smaller birds (*B. h. minima*), was recorded on Stubbs Island on 27 September. Nearly a month later, on 24 October, 45 more birds were seen at the Long Beach Airport. On 31 October, 102 birds were counted there, and on 12 November 130 birds. Taverner's Cackling Goose was seen through most of December, with 23 birds at Tofino on 23 December, and 7 birds remaining until 27 December. A flock of 23 birds was again seen locally in 2014, this time at the golf course on 19 November. A flock of 13 remained in Tofino until late December. In 2016 a flock of 16 birds was seen and photographed at the golf course on 5 November.

The Aleutian Cackling Goose (*B. h. leucopareia*) is larger than *B. h. minima* and is usually pale-breasted, lacking the glossy dark breast that the smaller bird often has. The neck rings on this population are usually wider, and a high percentage of birds have them. They formerly bred on the Aleutian Islands until Russian fur traders introduced arctic foxes. Predation by foxes on the eggs and young resulted in the elimination of geese throughout the archipelago except on three islands. In 1967 the population was estimated at fewer than 1,000 individulas.[2] The foxes were eventually trapped in a control program and the subspecies was reintroduced. By 2015 the population was estimated at 189,000 birds.[2]

This subspecies winters primarily in the central valley of California, with a smaller number on the state's northwest coast. In migration they take a direct route over the ocean and make landfall in northern California. However, birds occasionally make it to our region in fall due to adverse weather, notably on 22 October 2009, when a flock of 35 Cackling Geese landed on a street in Tofino during heavy overcast and rain. This flock marched merrily down the middle of the street to a nearby park and settled in. Some members of the flock had the characteristics mentioned previously and clearly belonged to the Aleutian population; they stayed for nearly two weeks, feeding on lawns in the village. On 24 October that same year, 54 Aleutian Cackling Geese were seen at the airport, and on 3 November, 32 birds were still lingering in Tofino. In 2012, 18 Aleutian Cackling Geese were seen at the airport on 1 November, with half the birds having wide neck rings. In the fall of 2014, birds were again seen at the airport, with 4 out of the 6 having neck rings.

A very rare spring sighting occurred on 3 June 2016, when 3 birds were found at the Long Beach Golf Course during inclement weather. A blue neck collar on one of the birds confirmed that it was indeed of the Aleutian population. It had been banded in Manteca, Stanislaus County, California. On 14 October that same year, 35 birds were found at the Long Beach Golf Course after an intense storm. The flock had swelled in size to 126 birds by 18 October, and to 140 birds by 23 October. On 26 October, 325 birds were counted, although by now many in the flock were Ridgway's Geese (*B. h. minima*). Two flocks of Aleutians remained in the area as late as 26 November.

Identifying the subspecies that a flock of birds belongs to has little value except to provide evidence of their origin and destination. Keep in mind that some cross-breeding is reported to occur among different subspecies due to intermingling on the winter range.

Ridgway's Cackling Goose (*B. h. minima*) winters in the Willamette Valley and Lower Columbia River Valley of Oregon and Washington. While some may linger on the central west coast through November and well into December, there were no records of overwintering birds until 2008/09, when a single individual was seen throughout January and February at Stubbs Island. It was last seen at the Long Beach Airport on 27 March. Two individuals overwintered in the Tofino area in the next two years, and one individual in 2014/15, always in the company of a flock of Greater White-fronted Geese.

CANADA GOOSE
Branta canadensis

STATUS: A common, sometimes abundant migrant in spring and fall, locally common in winter. Rare breeder.

Four subspecies of Canada Geese occur in the region. These very dark birds are believed to be of the coastal race, *B. c. fulva*.

The Canada Goose may be seen as either a breeding bird, a migrant, or a wintering bird, in virtually all areas of the continent north of Mexico, with the exception of the High Arctic. In the past, about 10 geographical populations or subspecies were recognized. Following further research, the species was split into Canada Goose and Cackling Goose. Today, Canada Geese are divided into 7 subspecies, 5 of which occur in British Columbia, with 4 of those in our region.

On Vancouver Island's west coast, the most commonly occurring Canada Goose is the subspecies *B. c. occidentalis,* also known as the Dusky Canada Goose, which breeds in the Copper River Delta of Alaska, on islands in Prince William Sound, and in the Gulf of Alaska. Although it may be a cliché, old-timers in Tofino tell of geese in such numbers that they darkened the sky. Sadly, that is no longer the case. Charles Guiget, who visited the area in the fall of 1950, estimated 5,000 Canada Geese, although he covered only one-third of the area. The *Vancouver Sun* outdoor writer Lee Straight, visiting Tofino in 1953, estimated that there were about 10,000 geese present.[9] Although those numbers sound impressive today, local hunters were already concerned about the declining numbers by the late 1950s, if not earlier. Some attributed the decline to the introduction of outboard motors, which gave hunters greater mobility and resulted in greater disturbance, even if it did not result in greater mortality for the birds. A few hunters even lobbied federal and provincial governments to bring in restrictions, but to no avail. While the provincial government created a Tofino waterfowl management reserve in the 1950s, it was set up largely for the benefit of hunters, not birds, according to David F. Hatler.

In his Canadian Wildlife Service report on the waterfowl of Clayoquot Sound, Hatler listed some of the maximum estimates and counts made in later years:[9] 10 November 1959 – 7,660 birds; 16 November 1960 – 3,467; 11 November 1961 – 4,810; and 16 November 1967 – 1,725. A very thorough census of birds in the fall of 1972 found a maximum of 1,974 birds on 1 November. If the 1950 estimates were reasonably accurate, there was an 80% decline in just 20 years.

Nor did the decline end there. A decade later, on 18 November 1982, the season peaked at 550 birds, and on 26 October 1985, a maximum of 300 birds were tallied. An effort on my part to arouse the concern of the British Columbia Fish and Wildlife Branch about the declining numbers got nowhere. It was made abundantly clear by the head of the regional office that his only concern was that hunting should continue without any added restrictions.

During the 1980s and 1990s, goose numbers at Tofino were not closely monitored, although enough counts were made to show that maximum numbers rarely exceeded 300 birds, and in some years did not exceed 200. Surveys were stepped up beginning in 2007. On 20 December that year, birds peaked at 305, and the following year at 351. In 2010 goose numbers hit rock-bottom, with a mere 128 birds counted. On 13 November 2011, 540 birds were tallied, and on 9 November 2012, a more respectable 800 birds. In 2013, the count was a more modest 533. Still, there are now hopeful signs that Canada Goose numbers are increasing on the mudflats of Clayoquot Sound.

This increase may be partly due to Jensen's Bay's becoming a de facto sanctuary after the village of Tofino extended its boundary further south in 1980. Hunting is not allowed in or near the village. It took local waterfowl many years to realize they were safe there, but now ducks gather in Jensen's Bay by the thousands and Canada Geese by the hundreds each fall and winter. Recommendations for such a sanctuary were first made in Hatler's 1973 report, and these were largely supported by local hunters. However, the recommendations were never acted upon by the provincial government.

Grice Bay, which became a sanctuary when Pacific Rim National Park was created, is said by locals to have once been a site where thousands of Canada Geese gathered to feed. That was no longer the case by 1967 and possibly much earlier, leading Hatler to conclude that something drastic had happened to the eelgrass beds between the 1930s and 1967. He suspected that siltation from logging activity, carried into the bay by Kootowas Creek, buried the eelgrass beds in silt and raised the mudflats to a level the eelgrass could not tolerate. By the time the national park reserve was established, protecting the bay "for all time," the damage had already been done.[9] Today the extensive mudflats of the bay are barren, with eelgrass remaining only in deeper water. Geese do enter the bay, but largely to find sanctuary and rest.

Could an overall decline be responsible for the collapse of the population in our west coast region? Most Duskies nest in the Copper River Delta of Alaska. In March 1964, an earthquake lifted the entire delta two to six feet, changing it from tidal wetlands to drier uplands. Initially this benefited the goose population, which increased to about 25,500 birds in 1979. It is interesting to note, however, that at the same time, Duskies were seriously dwindling at Tofino. Because of the uplift in the Copper River Delta, shrubs and trees gradually invaded. This in turn brought in predators such as brown bears, wolves, coyotes, foxes, and Bald Eagles, which fed on the birds and their eggs, bringing about a downward trend. By the mid-1990s, the population had declined to only 12,000 to 14,000 birds. An experimental program to remove predatory brown bears failed as foxes moved in to take their place. Middleton Island, located about 60 mi offshore in the Gulf of Alaska, and home to about 1,500 Duskies, was not affected by the quake lift and habitat change.[2]

US federal and state wildlife managers have been exemplary in managing geese, on both the breeding grounds and winter range. Large areas in the Willamette Valley were set aside to protect geese, which now number 250,000 birds, among them Dusky Canada Geese, which in 2015 were estimated at 17,700 breeding birds.[2]

In spring, Canada Geese begin to depart from the Clayoquot Sound mudflats in late March, just as the first flocks of migrating Canada Geese pass over from points south. While it is difficult to determine with certainty the identity of birds passing overhead, viewing them through a spotting scope has revealed that nearly all are Duskies, and thus we know their origin and destination. It appears that a substantial part of the Dusky population passes along the west coast of the island, with the peak of the migration being in the middle of April. The earliest dates I have for migrants passing over at Tofino are 22 March 1992 with 200 birds, and 24 March 1994 with 545 birds. There have been numerous observations of 450 and 500 birds passing over, but also occasions with considerably more. On 13 April 1997, and again on 3 April 1999, 1,150 birds were recorded at Tofino, and on 15 April 2000, 2,730 Canada Geese were counted passing by Long Beach. The highest spring count occurred on 16 April 1997, with 6,500 Canada Geese passing over Tofino. By the time the big passage of Greater White-fronted Geese and Cackling Geese occurs at the end of April, most of the "Duskies" have passed through. In 1996, 200 birds were seen as late as 3 May, but that was unusual. Nearly all migrating birds pass over the outer coast or over the ocean. It was a surprise, therefore, to find a flock of 120 birds on the water at the mouth of the Tahsish/Kwois River, deep in Kyuquot Sound, on 23 April 1990.

In spring and autumn migration, Sea Otter Cove and Hansen Lagoon, in Cape Scott Park about 250 km northwest of Tofino, are major stopover sites where thousands of birds rest and feed. Up to 10,000 geese have been reported here in May, and in fall these sites represent the first suitable resting and feeding areas for birds having departed Haida Gwaii.[4]

Besides the Dusky Canada Goose, several other subspecies have been recorded in our region. The Vancouver Canada Goose, *B. c. fulva*, is darker and decidedly browner than the former, as well as somewhat larger. It breeds from the northern mainland coast of British Columbia north through southeast Alaska. This is a largely sedentary population and only a small number reach our region, a few making it as far south as Washington. It was first recorded in our west coast region during intensive waterfowl surveys in 1972 by Hatler et al., and large, dark birds believed to belong to this population continue to be seen occasionally.[9] On 24 October and again on 12 November 2016, 10 birds were seen in Jensen's Bay, Tofino, and five days later 32 large, dark birds were seen and photographed at the Long Beach Golf Course.

A third subspecies found here is the Western Canada Goose, *B. c. moffetti*, which is roughly the same size as *B. c. occidentalis* but is pale-breasted and grey overall, with a shorter neck than *B. c. maxima*. Small numbers are seen at Tofino fairly regularly, and some occasionally overwinter.

Birds believed to be the Giant Canada Goose, *B. c. maxima*, occur only occasionally. Weighing from 15 to 19 pounds, this species was originally found only on the Great Plains, and for a period of over 30 years was believed extinct. It was rediscovered in Minnesota in 1963,[10] and subsequent breeding and introduction programs have distributed the birds far and wide, often in city parks. Large, grey plumaged, long-necked birds believed to be this subspecies have occasionally turned up at the Tofino mudflats, at the airport, and once at Schooner Cove in July. There are several breeding records for the Canada Goose in the west coast region, but it is unclear which subspecies was involved.

TRUMPETER SWAN
Cygnus buccinator

STATUS: Fairly common in fall, winter, and early spring. Very rare in summer.

This family group of Trumpeter Swans, adults and juveniles, was photographed at Sandhill Creek, Long Beach.

Trumpeter Swans weigh as much as 13.5 kg and are the heaviest flying birds in North America. This bird's numbers were greatly reduced by hunting in the 19th and early 20th centuries, and for a considerable time it was on the endangered species list. With protection, numbers have greatly increased. Birds have also been reintroduced into parts of the range they formerly occupied. Today they breed locally from James Bay, eastern Ontario, and the Great Lakes westward through the Great Plains region to several localities in Nevada and Oregon. The primary breeding area lies far to the north and extends from northwestern Alberta, northeastern British Columbia, and the western Northwest Territories to the Yukon and Alaska. The bulk of the population winters in British Columbia and Washington, mostly on the coast.

On Vancouver Island's west coast, we normally see Trumpeter Swans only as a winter visitor, and possible as a transient. While the species is seen in large numbers at several locations on the east side of the island, on the west coast they appear in more modest numbers, rarely exceeding 35 birds to a flock. Indeed, most counts are well below that number. The highest count ever recorded at one location was 49 birds on 3 January 1995 at Grice Bay. Provincial biologist Ian Smith counted 203 swans on aerial surveys between Tofino and Port Renfrew in February 1971, with 68 of those reported in Pacific Rim National Park.[1] On-the-ground surveys have never matched that number, however. It seems likely that his figures included birds in the Nitinat region.

In most years birds begin arriving in late October or the first half of November. There are three very early records. On 23 September 1980, a single bird was seen near Tofino, and on 6 October 1982, 6 birds were seen at Sandhill Creek, Long Beach. On 8 October 1992, a single bird was observed at the Long Beach Airport. On the central west coast, Trumpeter Swans are seen most often at two locations, Grice Bay and Sandhill Creek, though less so at the latter location than formerly. At Grice Bay, the preferred location is at the head of the bay, near the mouth of Kootowis Creek. Birds may also be seen on the water at the Tofino mudflats on occasion. As well, small flocks visit the river mouths far up the inlets of Clayoquot Sound, including Tranquil Creek and the Cypre, Bedwell, and Moyeha rivers. In addition, there are numerous remote lakes on the west coast that are likely used by swans. Aerial surveys conducted in winter from 1968 to 1973 found swans on Kichla Lake, Keecha Meadows, Hobiton Lake, and Cheewhat Lake.[1] Birds have also been seen on Mallard Lake, near Tofino, and on a flooded bog on Vargas Island.

In spring, departures may commence as early as February, though it appears that most depart during the month of March. At Grice Bay, 16 birds were recorded on 18 March 2008, 5 on 4 March 2009, 9 on 19 March 2011, and 15 on 18 March 2012. In 2014, 39 birds were recorded there on 20 March. Exactly one week later, 29 birds remained. Two days later, all were gone. By April, sightings are few. On 23 April 1990, 4 birds were recorded at the mouth of the Tahsish/Kwois River in Kyuquot Sound, and on 28 April 2012 at Grice Bay. On 24 April the following year, 2 birds were again recorded at Grice Bay. By 7 May, a single bird remained. Such late birds are likely nonbreeding individuals.

There are three summer records involving nonbreeding birds. On 10 June 1973, two birds were present on Perry Lake near Tahsis Inlet, and in 1987 a juvenile lingered at Swan Lake until at least 2 July. It appeared to be quite content, feeding among the densely packed pond lilies of the shallow lake. In 2014, a single bird was recorded in the estuary of the Cypre River in Clayoquot Sound on 13 August. That observer informed me that the bird had already been seen there a week or so earlier.

TUNDRA SWAN
Cygnus columbianus

STATUS: Casual migrant in spring and fall.

Formerly known as Whistling Swan, this is one of only two swans native to North America. It breeds in Arctic Canada and northern and western Alaska. A subspecies with a partially yellow bill known as Bewick's Swan (*C. c. bewickii*) breeds throughout northern Siberia. Canadian birds winter on the Atlantic coast from Maryland to North and South Carolina. Birds from western Alaska winter from Utah, Nevada, and northern California north along the coast to Washington and southern British Columbia. In the southern interior of the province, the species is regarded as "uncommon to locally abundant in winter," and "locally uncommon to common in winter along the coast." As a migrant, it is considered fairly common to common on the coast.[6]

Its status on the west coast differs considerably from that in the interior and the Salish Sea basin. In 1978, *Birds of Pacific Rim National Park* listed only two records that were considered reliable. On 9 April 1969, 31 birds were seen and heard flying over Vargas Island, and on 12 November 1973, 34 birds were seen and heard passing over Ucluelet. In the four decades since then, only nine additional records, listed below, have been added. A single adult spent most of the winter of 1973/74 on Hansen Lagoon in Cape Scott Park.[4] On 27 March 1980, 50 birds were seen and heard passing over Tofino, and on 7 February 1989 a Tundra Swan was found dead at Grice Bay. On 5 April 2005, and again on 24 March 2007, flocks of Tundra Swans were heard passing over Tofino during the night, though the number could not be determined. On 14 November 2012, 19 Tundra Swans were reported from Ucluelet Inlet.

The latest sightings occurred in 2014 and 2015. On 10 and 11 November 2014, a single bird was seen resting on the water at Jensen's Bay, Tofino. The following year, on 2 November, a family group of six birds was observed on the ground at the airport. Four days later, on 6 November, airport employee Chantel Gamon found that one juvenile had been killed by a predator, presumably an eagle, and one of the adults had been injured and could no longer fly. One of the adults had departed with two of the young, leaving one youngster behind with the remaining adult. Both birds were captured by airport staff and volunteers the following day and transported to a wildlife rehabilitation centre. Although we have only eight reliable records of their passage through our region, Tundra Swans probably occur here more often than records indicate. Two of those records involved birds heard passing over at night. One might well wonder how many birds pass over without being heard. Nor can all flocks of swans be identified. A flock of 85 birds seen passing over Tofino on 19 March 2004 was suspected of being this species but was not positively identified.

WOOD DUCK
Aix sponsa

STATUS: Locally fairly common in spring, summer, and early fall. Breeds.

Few birds in the Northern Hemisphere equal the male Wood Duck's splendour in plumage, so we are most fortunate in having this species on our coast. It breeds throughout the eastern half of the United States and the Midwest, north into Manitoba and southeastern Canada. In the western United States, it is found in Montana, Idaho, Washington, Oregon, and California, and locally elsewhere. In the Canadian west, it breeds only in southern Alberta and British Columbia. In British Columbia, it breeds in the southern one-third of the province east of the Coast Mountains. On the coast, it breeds only in the Fraser Valley, the Salish Sea basin, and the southern half of Vancouver Island.[6]

Its preferred habitat consist of ponds and lakes in wooded areas, especially when pond lilies are present, and slow-flowing rivers with trees along the banks. Because this species nests in tree cavities, a shortage of natural nesting sites inspired a major effort in the Fraser Valley in the late 1960s and early 1970s to put up nesting boxes in appropriate habitat. This resulted in a major surge in the population there, and may have contributed to an upsurge in numbers on Vancouver Island, including the west coast. In 1978, *Birds of Pacific Rim National Park* mentioned four locations where Wood Ducks were seen from 1970 to 1972 – Swan Lake, near the Tofino/Ucluelet Junction, Kennedy River, Turtle Island in Barkley Sound, and near Sarita Bay, east of Bamfield.[1] Birds were known to breed at the first and last of these locations.

Wood Ducks continue to breed at Swan Lake. On 22 August 2010, 1 adult and 5 young were present, and on 11 August 2013, 5 young and an adult male were seen. The species undoubtedly breeds on the lower Kennedy River as well, as adults have been seen there with fledged young in late summer. Birds are also seen at sewage ponds at Ucluelet and in Pacific Rim National Park, where on 15 June 2006, an adult with several young were seen by George Bradd. As many as 13 adults were observed at the latter location on 20 May 2010.

There appears to be some good habitat for Wood Ducks on the lower Kennedy River, and birds are often seen there. Shallow waters choked with pond lilies may also be found at a few remote locations such as Kanim Lake near Stewardson Inlet, and at a lake near Hesquiat village. These latter two locations have never been investigated, as far as I know. A female with four small ducklings (about two to three days old) was found on Pachena Lake, 8 km east of Bamfield, on 13 June 1973 by William Verbruggue (BCNRS files) and a pair of birds was found on 15 May 2008 at Frederick Lake, due north of the previous location. If birds breed occasionally at some of these locations, the population on our west coast could be somewhat larger than is currently known. Most Wood Duck records are from the central west coast and thus far only one that I know of has been recorded north of Tofino. On 22 September 1992, a young male was seen on Megin Lake, 25 mi northwest of Tofino.

In spring, birds begin arriving in early to mid-April. The earliest date is 2 April in 2008, though most birds arrive considerably later. Just when birds depart in fall is difficult to determine, though it is likely to be in the month of September, for which there are 11 records. Indeed, one of the largest flocks on record – 23 birds – was seen on 25 September 2008 at the sewage pond in Pacific Rim Provincial Park. The largest flock ever reported, containing 35 birds, was seen at the same location on 13 September 2013.

By October nearly all birds have departed. On 8 October 2004, eight birds were still present at the sewage pond in Ucluelet, and on 11 October 2010, two birds were seen at the Long Beach Airport. There is only a single November record. On 22 November 2013, a single bird was observed at the Long Beach Airport.

BLUE-WINGED TEAL
Spatula discors

STATUS: Uncommon spring migrant. Casual fall transient.

Like the Cinnamon Teal, to which it is closely related, this dabbling duck shows a marked preference for ponds, shallow lakes, and marshes, and does not spend

These Blue-winged Teal are taking a much-needed rest at Sandhill Creek, Long Beach, during spring migration.

much time in the marine environment, other than resting occasionally during migration. It is widely distributed throughout North America, and can be found in most regions except for the treeless north. In Canada it breeds from the Maritimes to British Columbia, and north to the Northwest Territories and Yukon. It winters from the southeastern United States and the California coast south to Mexico, Central America, and northern South America. In British Columbia, it breeds in much of the province east of the Coast Mountains, as well as in the Fraser Valley and southeastern Vancouver Island.

Records for the west coast go back to 1968, when Richardson saw two birds at Browning Inlet on northwestern Vancouver Island in the second week of September, and again in the third week of October. In 1978, *Birds of Pacific Rim National Park* listed only 3 additional records, all in spring.[1] One of these involved a male seen at Swan Lake from 19 June to 5 July 1972. The species was then considered a "very rare migrant." Since that time, its status has changed considerably, with 56 records since 1980. This increase is perhaps not surprising, given the fact that the estimated breeding population in North America is currently estimated at 8.5 million birds, or 73% above the 60-year average.[2]

The overwhelming majority of sightings have been in spring, between mid-May and 10 June. Most sightings have involved from 1 to 4 individuals, but 9 birds were recorded on four occasions, and flocks of 10, 12, and 15 birds have also been seen. There are five dates earlier than mid-May, with the two earliest arrival dates being 29 April and 6 May. The latest spring date is 21 June 2002, when a pair was seen at Tofino. A record of a male near Cleland Island on 17 June 1970 is noteworthy (BCFWS). The species has also been seen further north in spring and fall. On 29 May 1973, two males were seen in a small bay off Clerke Point, Brooks Peninsula,[13] and a male was seen on Hansen Lagoon in Cape Scott Park in October 1973.[4] The only July record is the one in 1972 mentioned above. Aside from the two birds seen at Browning Inlet in 1968, there is only a single additional record for the autumn migration period. On 22 August 2009, 11 Blue-winged Teal were seen at Jensen's Bay, Tofino.

On the central west coast, the three locations where this species has been seen most often are Jensen's Bay, the ponds at the Long Beach Airport, and the lower Kennedy River. Birds may also be seen occasionally flying by along the outer coast.

CINNAMON TEAL
Spatula cyanoptera

STATUS: Casual transient in spring and summer.

This handsome duck is a bird of the west, with only sporadic occurrences in eastern North America. Its breeding range covers the western half of the United States, extending into central Mexico in the south and into southern Saskatchewan, southern Alberta, and British Columbia in the north. In British Columbia, it breeds across the southern third of the province, including the Fraser Lowlands. On the coast, it is considered an "uncommon to fairly common migrant and summer visitant" to the Salish Sea basin, including southeastern Vancouver Island, where it breeds. The species has occurred in most other regions of the province as a vagrant.[6]

On Vancouver Island's west coast, we know it only as a sporadic transient. In 1978, *Birds of Pacific Rim National Park* listed only two occurrences.[1] The first was a pair seen on 20 May 1972 in Barkley Sound, and the second involved a sighting of six birds on 23 August 1972 along the West Coast Trail. Since then there have been 13 additional sightings involving singles and pairs. Locations where birds have been seen include Cleland Island, the Tofino mudflats, the sewage pond in Pacific Rim National Park, off the north end of Long Beach, and at the airport. All 13 sightings occurred in the spring migration period from April to June. The earliest spring record is of a pair seen on 8 April 2012, at the floatplane pond at the airport. These birds stayed until at least 22 April. The latest spring record is of a single bird seen on 10 June 2011, also at the airport.

NORTHERN SHOVELER
Spatula clypeata

STATUS: Common migrant in spring, late summer, and fall. Uncommon in winter.

Northern Shovelers in breeding plumage rest on the Stubbs Island spit near Tofino. A Caspian Tern is seen on the left.

This handsome dabbling duck with its outsized bill breeds extensively throughout much of the Northern Hemisphere, from Europe east to Kamchatka, and in North America from Alaska to western Ontario and the Great Lakes, south through the Midwest to New Mexico, sporadically in the Northeast. In British Columbia, it breeds in the southern half of the province, the Peace River region, and in the far north of the province. In southwestern British Columbia, it breeds in the Fraser Valley and has bred on southeastern Vancouver Island. The species winters along the Atlantic coast, in the southern United States, and in Mexico. In the west, birds winter north to Washington and extreme southern British Columbia. On the coast, they winter on the Fraser River delta and on southeastern Vancouver Island.

This species has seen a dramatic increase in breeding numbers in North America, with a 75% rise over the long-term average to 4.4 million birds in 2015.[2] A large increase has also occurred on the west coast. Indeed, here the rise in numbers is even more dramatic. In 1978, *Birds of Pacific Rim National Park* listed a mere 13 records.[1] That number has grown to well over 300 today. The following examples of high counts at Tofino over the past 30 years illustrate an incremental increase: 8 birds on 8 October 1982; 20 on 22 September 1983; 25 on 28 April 1993; 70 on 26 April 1996; 110 on 8 October 2008; 175 on 25 August 2009; and 196 on 1 May 2015. It is worth noting that Hatler et al. mentioned that most sightings involved single birds or pairs, though one observation involved 30 birds in a lagoon on Vargas Island on 8 May 1971.[1]

The start of the spring migration can be gauged by an abrupt rise in numbers on the mudflats near Tofino in late April in most years. The earliest spring arrivals in 2013 were recorded on 10 April, with 160 birds. In all other years, first arrivals occurred after mid-April at the earliest. Some birds are still seen passing by until late May. By June the spring passage is over. I have only a single record for that month – 2 birds on 12 June 1987, at Stubbs Island.

The southbound migration usually begins in the second half of August. The two earliest dates both occurred in 2015, the first on 3 August, when a single bird was seen at the Long Beach Airport, and the other on 8 August, when 9 birds were seen at Chesterman Beach by Cathy Carlson. In 2001, the earliest date was 18 August, and in 1993 and 2009 it was 22 August. A flock of 175 birds seen at Jensen's Bay on 25 August 2009 is an unusually high number, especially so early in the season. The migration continues throughout September and into October. To determine when the fall migration ends, I had to peruse older records before birds began overwintering. I found two records as late as 8 October, and one on 14 October, leading to the conclusion that by mid-October the autumn passage is probably at an end.

Winter birds were first recorded at the Tofino mudflats in 2001, with 3 birds seen on 5 January and 1 bird on 22 February. No other birds were recorded in winter until 2007/08, when 35 birds were seen on 7 December, 21 birds on 31 December, 8 birds on 18 January, and 11 birds on 16 February. Since then, a small but variable number have overwintered in four of the following five years: 4 birds on 4 February 2009; 7 on 3 January 2010; 6 on 22 January 2011; and 15 on 5 January 2013. No further winter sightings occurred after this date.

During the peak of the migration in spring, it is not unusual to observe Northern Shovelers over the ocean, winging their way north, often in the company of other ducks. Good observation spots are Incinerator Rock at Long Beach, Box Island at Schooner Cove, and Amphitrite Point, Ucluelet. A good location to view these birds close-up is the viewing platform at the end of Sharp Road in Tofino, although timing is everything.

GADWALL
Mareca strepera

STATUS: Uncommon to rare migrant. Locally common winter resident.

Largely grey with black hindquarters, Gadwall drakes are far from showy. Nevertheless, they have a beauty of a subtler sort. Few people can remain unimpressed by this bird once they are afforded a close-up look. East of the Rockies, it breeds from northern Texas to northern Alberta, east to the Great Lakes region and into Quebec. West of the Rocky Mountains, it breeds from northern California to southern British Columbia. *The Birds of British Columbia* considered it to be a "locally common to abundant migrant on the southwest coast," and in winter "locally fairly common to abundant on southern Vancouver Island."[6]

On the west coast, the oldest record dates from 13 September 1968, when 12 birds were seen on a brackish lagoon on Vargas Island.[1] Five more records followed, up to the end of 1972, when it was considered a rare migrant. Since then, there has been a gradual increase in both the number of sightings and the number of birds in the Tofino area. This is not surprising, given that Gadwalls have been increasing in numbers and expanding their range in North America for the past half-century. The species first nested in the Fraser River delta in 1966 and 1967. Supplemented by the importation of eggs by game-bird breeder Richard Trethewey in Pitt Meadows, by 1990 they were fairly common breeders there (R. Wayne Campbell, personal communication). Some maximum numbers recorded near Tofino over the years demonstrate the increase in our region: 17 birds on 15 April 1993; 31 on 16 January 1996; 56 on 19 December 2006; and 98 on 11 December 2012.

First fall arrival dates are highly variable. The two earliest records are 18 September 2010 and 24 August 2001, but these are exceptional, with most first arrival dates much later. Nearly all observations have been made in Jensen's Bay or from the end of Sharp Road nearby. I have a single record of eight birds seen at Grice Bay. The spring movement away from the west coast occurs primarily in April. By early May, numbers have dwindled significantly, although a few may linger well into the month and sometimes even to the end of the month. The latest spring record I can find is 1 June 2010.

The breeding population for North America in 2015 was estimated to be 3,834,000 birds, which is well above the long-term average of 1.9 million birds since 1955.[2]

EURASIAN WIGEON
Mareca penelope

STATUS: Generally rare, but locally uncommon in fall, winter, and spring.

This species is the Eurasian counterpart to the American Wigeon. It has a very extensive breeding distribution throughout much of Asia and Europe and, like the American Wigeon, migrates further south after the breeding season. In North America, it is a regular winter visitor, primarily on the Atlantic and Pacific coasts. In British Columbia, it is considered an uncommon to fairly common winter visitor on the south coast, where numbers of records increased twentyfold between 1965 and 1981.[11]

Eurasian Wigeons are usually seen among flocks of American Wigeon. The mudflats of southern Clayoquot Sound near Tofino are home to thousands of American Wigeons in fall, winter, and spring, and the Eurasian species is usually found among them in small numbers. In 1978, *Birds of Pacific Rim National Park* listed nine records, all of them from 1972. The largest number recorded was 4 individuals. More than 200 additional sightings have been recorded since 1995. Although most counts involve 5 birds or less, there are many counts higher than 10. Some of the largest numbers are 17 birds on 6 February 2001 and 17 November 2009, and 25 birds on 30 November 2007 and 30 November 2008.

The foregoing counts involved mainly males. Females were included only very occasionally, as they are very difficult to distinguish from female American Wigeons. Nearly all records are from the end of Sharp Road and Jensen's Bay in Tofino. The two species hybridize occasionally, suggesting that small numbers of Eurasian Wigeons probably breed in western Alaska and perhaps elsewhere in North America, including British Columbia. As many as three hybrid males have been observed in a single flock of American Wigeon.

Birds usually arrive in October and November. Earliest fall dates are 18 September 2008 – 1; 30 September 2012 – 1; and 9 October 2011 – 3. As we saw previously, the highest numbers are usually seen in November and December, though once in February. It appears that some birds move further south as winter progresses. In spring, records suggest that birds head north as early as March. The highest number ever recorded in April was 5 birds. One or two birds may occasionally linger into May, but there are no records for June, July, and August.

AMERICAN WIGEON
Mareca americana

STATUS: Common fall migrant and locally abundant visitor in fall, winter, and spring.

With its bold green eye stripe and white forehead and crown, the male of the species is indeed a handsome bird. For many decades it was known as Baldpate, the "bald" apparently derived from the old English word "balde," meaning white.

The range of the American Wigeon stretches from the Maritimes across southern Quebec, all of Ontario, and nearly all of western Canada and Alaska. It also breeds throughout much of the northwestern United States, south to northern Nevada and Colorado, though it does not breed in western Oregon and only rarely in western Washington.[12] In British Columbia, it breeds in the eastern and central interior, in the Peace River region, and in the far north. It breeds sparingly in the Salish Sea basin, including southeastern Vancouver Island. The winter range stretches from the Atlantic coast westward across the southern half of the United States, south to Mexico, Central America, and northern South America. Along the Pacific coast, it winters north to the Copper River Delta in Alaska.

In our west coast region, the largest numbers congregate on the mudflats of southern Clayoquot Sound, near Tofino, where they may be seen in rafts containing thousands of birds. Fall migrants begin arriving from early to late September, depending on the year. Earliest arrival dates were 2 September in 1982, 2009, 2013, and 2017, and 29 August in 2008. In 2011 the first birds were not seen until 22 September.

The pace of new arrivals picks up through October, and by mid-month substantial flocks may already be present. Birds usually reach their maximum number for the year at some point in November. Following are some high counts made since the year 2000: 1 January 2001 – 4,000 birds; 4 December 2004 – 2,800; 1 November 2007 – 4,500; 2 November 2008 – 5,000; 16 November 2008 – 8,000; 25 December 2008 – 3,500; 1 January 2010 – 2,800; and 9 November 2012 – 3,000.

Although numbers diminish somewhat after November, substantial numbers may still be encountered into February in some years. On both 6 February 2001 and 15 February 2009, 3,000 birds were counted. Although at times American Wigeons congregate in large rafts containing only their own species, often they are intermingled with other dabbling ducks, making accurate counts a challenge.

Spring departures begin in March, with numbers gradually decreasing as the season progresses. By April the decrease is obvious, and by May numbers are getting very low. A few birds may persist until mid-month or even late May, but I can find no June records.

Breeding waterfowl numbers in North America are monitored from year to year, primarily to maintain a large population for sport hunting. In 2015 the American Wigeon breeding population was estimated at about 3 million birds, 17% above the long-term average since 1955.[2] In Clayoquot Sound, duck hunting has decreased in the past 30 years, which may have contributed to the somewhat higher numbers of American Wigeon we have been seeing. And because the village of Tofino now extends to Jensen's Bay, that area has become a de facto sanctuary where birds are safe from hunters, if not from disturbance by paddleboarders.

MALLARD
Anas platyrhynchos

STATUS: Common to locally abundant spring and fall migrant. Locally common to abundant in winter. Uncommon in summer. Breeds.

Mention the word "duck" and the image that comes to mind for many people is that of a Mallard, for this species is probably the quintessential duck in the Northern Hemisphere. With the North American population estimated at 11.6 million birds in 2015, it is also the most abundant of waterfowl.[2] Mallards breed from Virginia and southern Quebec west to the US Pacific states, British Columbia, and Alaska. In the north, its range extends to the mouth of the Mackenzie River. In British Columbia, it breeds in virtually all regions of the province below 1,300 m elevation.

In our west coast region, we find the largest numbers congregating on the mudflats of southern Clayoquot Sound near Tofino in autumn, winter, and spring. Migrant Mallards usually begin arriving in October, but first arrival dates vary considerably from year to year. Small flocks or single birds seen in August and September are usually local birds. There are two exceptions. On 24 August 2003, 40 birds were seen at the Tofino mudflats, and on 27 September 2008, 50 birds were counted there. All other first arrival dates are from the month of October. Some early dates at Tofino, though not necessarily first arrivals, are: 24 October 2000 – 20 birds; 29 October 2007 – 250; 10 October 2010 – 25; 19 October 2011 – 250; and 24 October 2013 – 210.

Peak numbers occur from mid-November to mid-January, and these tend to range from 500 to 700 birds. On both 12 January 1995 and 5 January 2001, 700 birds were counted. On 27 December 2009, an estimated 600 were present. On 13 November 2011, there was a count of 1,200 birds. The highest count ever recorded was made during a Christmas Bird Count involving multiple participants, with a total count of 1,733 birds, though some duplication cannot be ruled out. By mid to late January, the population has dwindled considerably, usually ranging from 200 to 400 individuals. In 2014, 675 birds were counted on 5 January, and 470 birds on 17 March.

There is generally no noticeable upsurge in numbers in spring. Instead, the population gradually dissipates during April and early May. After mid-May, only a few laggards remain. Birds seen later than this are usually found on bodies of fresh water, where they breed. Mallards have been seen through June, July, and August at a number of locations, including at a sewage pond in Pacific Rim National Park, at a pond at the airport, at Swan Lake, and on the lower Kennedy River, where on 12 July 2002, a female with five young was seen, and on 9 June 2014, a female with three young. Hatler et al. mentioned birds nesting at Swan Lake, on Vargas Island, and possibly at Mallard Lake.[1] A Mallard with young has also been seen at a small unnamed lake southeast of Tofino Inlet.

During the winter months in the Tofino area, Mallards disperse over the mudflats to feed at low tide, and at high tide congregate in a small cove in Jensen's Bay to rest and preen, often onshore. It is interesting to note that Mallards, unlike most ducks, do not usually feel threatened by an approaching Bald Eagle. Instead of taking to the air in alarm, they stay put. Bald Eagles are able to differentiate between species and are well aware of the Mallard's ability to launch itself straight into the air.

NORTHERN PINTAIL
Anas acuta

STATUS: Common to abundant migrant in spring, late summer, and fall. Locally common in winter.

Very handsome in its breeding plumage, the male Northern Pintail cannot be well described without using the word "elegant." Even when passing high overhead, birds of both sexes can often be distinguished from other dabblers by their slender profile with long necks and pointed tails. The species has an extensive breeding range that covers most of Eurasia and much of northern

The Northern Pintail can be identified by its very long neck. This juvenile was photographed in late summer.

North America, particularly the western half. Birds winter along the Atlantic seaboard, the southern United States, and much of the western United States, south to the Caribbean, Central America, and Colombia. Along the Pacific coast, they winter north to southeast Alaska.

This fleet-winged bird can cover a lot of ground. Part of the population nesting in eastern Siberia flies south to winter in Japan, while others cross the Bering Strait and fly south to winter in California, having passed by our west coast region. Strings of Northern Pintails have often been noted far offshore during pelagic bird and mammal surveys, winging their way southward in late summer and fall. Birds banded in Japan have been recovered in six US states, as far east as Mississippi.[14] At least 16 Japanese-banded birds have been recovered in California since 1977.[15] Data collected over many years reveal that birds begin arriving at the Tofino mudflats in late August. The earliest date for Tofino, with one exception, was 17 August in 2000, when 35 birds were observed on the water. The exception occurred in 2012, when on 10 August 40 birds were seen. Sizable flocks may already congregate during the last week of August, with 400 birds on 24 August 2001 and 690 birds on 25 August 2009. First migrants, however, may appear in early August. On Cleland Island, 3 birds flew southeast over the island on 6 August 1969, and in 1970 2 birds were first seen on 1 August (BCFSW).

In the late summer and early fall of 1972, Northern Pintails were the second most common dabbler on the Tofino mudflats. Such is not the case today, though it may be true if birds travelling offshore are taken into account. That large numbers travel offshore is supported by observations made on 29 August 2012, when an estimated 2,800 birds were seen on the water at Tofino during inclement weather that forced birds off the ocean. Long strings of Northern Pintails have also been observed passing overhead on pelagic bird surveys far offshore. Hatler et al. believed that the bulk of the southward migration occurs in August,[1] but I would now extend that period through September. As late as 8 October in 1984, 1,000 birds were seen flying past Long Beach, driven close to shore by what were described in my notes as "foggy conditions."

On the Tofino mudflats, numbers appear to peak in October at close to 600 to 800 birds, which often stay until the end of December. By early January numbers are declining, and by February are lower still. Winter highs include 300 birds on 5 January 2001; 50 on 19 January 2008; 408 on 3 January 2010; 75 on 15 February 2009; 220 on 4 February 2010; and 76 on 13 February 2011. Note that numbers are still declining in early January, and by February rarely exceed 200 birds.

The spring migration is not nearly as pronounced as the fall movement, partly because of the presence of wintering birds, but mostly because the majority of birds pass by offshore without stopping. In some years, records show a slight to moderate increase in the local population, beginning in late March and continuing through April. In other years, there is no evidence of an increase at all. On occasions when a stiff headwind is blowing, forcing birds closer to shore, observations at Incinerator Rock, Long Beach, show that large numbers pass by offshore. On 20 April 2013, 382 birds were counted in a one-hour period, and an additional 125 in the following half-hour period. A week later, on 27 April, a flock of 80 birds was observed passing Long Beach, again during a brisk northwesterly. And on 8 April 2014, during a brisk headwind, a one-hour count from Incinerator Rock tallied 1,965 Northern Pintails passing by. The earliest observation of birds flying north was on 2 April in 2016, when a flock of 45 was seen accompanied by Surf Scoters. Migrants may linger into June. On Cleland Island, one circled the island on 25 June 1969 and a male with two females flew low over the island on 25 June 1970 (BCFWS). On Brooks Peninsula, 3 birds flew over on 9 June and 40 on 16 June, both in 1973.[13]

Northern Pintails have undergone a 77% decline in breeding numbers in North America over the past 40 years. This might explain the discrepancy between its status in 1972 and its status here today. At the end of 2015, the world breeding population stood at roughly 5.3 million birds, with 3 million of those in North America.[2]

GREEN-WINGED TEAL
Anas crecca

STATUS: Common to abundant in fall. Common to uncommon in winter. Common in spring, rare in summer. Rare breeder.

This is the smallest of the dabblers. It has a very broad breeding range that covers much of northern Eurasia and northern North America. On this continent, it breeds throughout Canada except for the northern tundra regions and southernmost Quebec. In the United States, it breeds in the New England states, and from the Great Lakes region through the more northerly midwestern states and in most of the west except for the southwest. In British Columbia, it breeds throughout the province, including the coast, though not in the Coast Mountains. The species winters from the southern half of the United States south to Mexico. Birds winter further north along the Atlantic and in the west. On the Pacific coast, birds winter north to the Alaska Peninsula.

On Vancouver Island's west coast, Green-winged Teal begin arriving in late August or early September. The earliest dates for the Tofino area are 15 birds on 13 August 2010, and 18 birds on 18 August 2001. Several July records at the Long Beach Airport may represent breeding birds. *Birds of Pacific Rim National Park* mentioned flocks seen flying with Northern Pintails as early as 8 and 9 August in 1972.[1] In 2001, 200 birds had already arrived at Tofino on 24 August. In contrast, in 2008 it was 27 September before as many as 200 birds were seen. Birds increase very gradually throughout September, and only by October or November do they reach maximum numbers.

On the central west coast, they are found primarily on the mudflats, frequently intermingling with other dabblers. Local resident and artist Mark Hobson found that they also make use of several of the small lakes on Meares Island. On 21 and 23 September 2008, he observed 1,200 Green-winged Teal at one of the lakes, and also more than 100 among other dabblers at Summit Lake on 21 August 2008. The importance of freshwater bodies to dabblers during the nonbreeding season has perhaps been overlooked.

In 1972, the Northern Pintail was the second most common dabbler in the Tofino area, after the American Wigeon. However, it was the Green-winged

Teal that held that title in later years, with maximum numbers at the Tofino mudflats reaching 3,000 birds on 1 January 2001 and 3,500 birds on 24 November 2008. The North American breeding population was estimated at 3 million birds at the end of 2015, which is 98% above the long-term average.[2] That might explain the increase in numbers in our region since the 1970s.

After maximum numbers are reached in November, they usually begin to decline shortly thereafter. Fall numbers can fluctuate greatly from year to year. In the fall of 2010, numbers were extremely low, peaking at 135 birds on 14 November. In 2014, numbers were lower still, with a maximum of 50 birds on 9 November.

Wintering birds too can vary greatly in numbers. Some maximum winter counts are: 13 February 2002 – 600 birds; 17 February 2008 – 480; 15 February 2009 – 700; 13 January 2010 – 250 birds. In 2011 and 2012, winter numbers were extremely low, with highs of 28 birds recorded on 7 February 2011 and 30 birds on 7 January 2012. In 2015, only a single bird was recorded in January, February, and March. It should be noted that they normally reach their lowest numbers in February and March.

The spring movement, unlike in fall, is not particularly noticeable at the Tofino mudflats. Green-winged Teal may be observed passing north along the outside coast, however. It is not at all unusual to see small flocks of teal flying by, mixed with other dabblers, or resting on a creek or secluded cove. On 11 May 2011, a raft of 1,000 birds was seen resting on the water in the shelter of Box Island at Long Beach, and on 1 May 2015, a raft of 400 birds was seen at the same location. Occasionally single birds are reported in June, such as on 10 June 1969 and 13 June 1970 on Cleland Island (BCFWS).

Nesting on the west coast is rare, though the species has nested in the vicinity of the West Coast Trail.[6] Summer records from the Long Beach Airport, particularly in 2010, suggest that birds may occasionally nest there. On 2 June, a single bird was seen on the floatplane pond. On 6 July, two birds were seen there, and on 13 July 2010, six birds were recorded. There are a number of shallow ponds at the airport that may provide breeding habitat for this species. Birds have also been seen occasionally in summer at Swan Lake, near the Pacific Rim Highway junction.

The Common Teal of Eurasia is currently considered a subspecies of the Green-winged Teal, though it can be readily distinguished in the field by the horizontal white bar located just above the sides, rather than the vertical stripe on the sides of the American bird. Some authorities, particularly in Europe, regard the two as separate species. This split may well be adopted by the American Ornithological Society in the future. The Common Teal is a rare but regular winter visitor to southwestern British Columbia. The only sighting in our west coast region was recorded on 29 November 1972, at the mouth of Maltby Slough, near Tofino.

CANVASBACK
Aythya valisineria

STATUS: Uncommon to rare visitor in fall and winter. Very rare in spring.

This handsome duck, with its sloping red head, white body, and black breast, is the largest in its genus. Its Latin name refers to one of its favourite winter foods in the east – wild celery (*Vallisneria americana*). It breeds in the western United States, from Washington and Oregon east to western Minnesota, north through the Canadian Prairie provinces and interior British Columbia to the Northwest Territories, Yukon, and Alaska. In British Columbia, it breeds in the south-central interior north to the vicinity of Prince George, in the Peace Lowland in the Boreal Plains Ecoprovince, and rarely in the far northwest corner of the province. It is considered a fairly common to very common migrant through most of the southern interior of the province.[6] It winters in the Atlantic states, the southern United States, and Mexico. Along the Pacific coast, it winters north to southwestern British Columbia.

The Canvasback was blue-listed in the period from 1975 to 1981, after which it was still considered a "species of concern" for some time. The population has since been relatively stable at a long-term level of 560,000 birds. By the end of 2015, the estimate for North America was up to 800,000 birds, 30% above the long-term average.[2] In Louisiana, winter congregations of up to 70,000 birds have been recorded.

On our coast, Canvasbacks have declined significantly as a winter visitor. In 1978, *Birds of Pacific Rim National Park* listed 25 records.[1] Since then, 72 records have been added, though there have been far fewer birds. The largest flock ever recorded on the central west coast was 400 birds on 7 December 1969.[1] In 1981, the number peaked at 101 birds on 22 November. Flocks of 50 or so birds continued to be seen until 31 January 1996, when a high of 57 birds was recorded. After this, numbers greatly declined. No flock of more than 15 birds was ever recorded again up to the present time. All records are from the mudflats of southern Clayoquot Sound, and from Grice Bay, where they feed in the submerged eelgrass beds located off Indian Island. Canvasbacks usually arrive after mid-October or in November, and depart in late February. There are several records for March and two in April. A bird seen off Stubbs Island on 27 April 1984 was extremely late.

The reason for the decline of this species on the west coast is unknown. It is interesting that the increase in numbers elsewhere has not translated into more visitations to the west coast region.

REDHEAD
Aythya americana

STATUS: Casual visitor in spring, fall, and winter.

This diving duck is somewhat similar in appearance to the Canvasback, but the drake's body is pale grey rather than white, and it has a round head rather than a sloping one. This species breeds in much of the western United States and the Canadian Prairie provinces, north through Alberta to the Northwest Territories. It breeds also in central Alaska and the southern interior of British Columbia. Its wintering grounds are largely in southern regions of the United States, south through Mexico to Guatemala and parts of the Caribbean. In the United States, it winters along the Atlantic coast north to Massachusetts, and in the west, north to Washington and southern BC.

On the south coast of British Columbia, this duck is considered rare, and in our region even more so. In 1978, *Birds of Pacific Rim National Park* listed only a single record for the west coast – a sighting by Richardson of a flock of 8 birds in early May 1968, at Grant Bay, just above Quatsino Sound.[16] Since then, there have been nine additional sightings, three of which likely involve the same individuals. Those records are: 23 January 1995, Tofino – 1; 26 January 1995, Grice Bay – 2; 29 January 1995, Grice Bay – 1; 29 December 2001, Tofino – 1; 24 November 2002, Tofino – 12; 27 January 2007, Tofino – 1; 7 October 2008, Jensen's Bay, Tofino – 2; 17 January 2015, Ucluelet Inlet – 2; 29 October 2015, Long Beach Airport – 1 female or juvenile (photo).

Overall in North America, the Redhead is considerably more numerous than the preceding species, and its population is considered stable. In 2015, the population was estimated at 1.2 million birds, which is 71% above the long-term average.[2] On our coast, the Redhead is clearly outside its normal range and will be seen only as a very occasional visitor.

RING-NECKED DUCK
Aythya collaris

STATUS: Uncommon transient in spring and fall. Rare in winter.

Ring-necked Ducks are usually seen on fresh water and only rarely on marine waters. This bird is either a female or a juvenile.

This diving duck is named, curiously, for one of its least salient features, the ring around its neck, which is barely visible. Other features, however, make this bird easy enough to identify, particularly the males. During migration, it is most often seen on freshwater bodies, such as lakes, ponds, sloughs, and marshes, where it may be found seen singly, in pairs, or occasionally congregating in flocks. To a lesser extent, it also uses sheltered bays in the marine environment, particularly in autumn.

Ring-necked Ducks are largely restricted to North America. They breed in the forest regions of the northeastern United States and Canada, from Newfoundland and the Maritimes west to British Columbia and Alaska. They also breed in the Rocky Mountain region of the United States, and in the westernmost states from northeastern California to British Columbia. The species winters in the southern half of United States, south to Mexico and Central America. On the Pacific coast, birds winter as far north as Juneau, Alaska.

In British Columbia, the species breeds throughout much of the province east of the Coast Mountains, particularly the southern half, the Peace River region, and the far northeast of the province. It breeds or has bred locally in the Fraser Valley and on southeastern Vancouver Island. Some birds winter in

British Columbia, particularly in the Okanagan Valley, the Fraser Valley, and the Salish Sea basin.[6]

In the west coast region, Ring-necked Ducks occur primarily as migrants. In most years, first arrivals are seen in April or May, although *Birds of Pacific Rim National Park* listed three March records.[1] Since then there has been only one additional record for that month. There are six first arrival dates in April, with the earliest recorded on 2 April 2008 at the Pacific Rim National Park sewage pond, when nine birds were sighted, and 14 April 1994, when five birds were seen at the same location. Of 79 records in total, 28 were recorded in spring. The monthly breakdown in spring is 4 sightings in March, 11 in April, and 13 in May. By mid-month the spring passage, though small, is usually over. There are two late records. On 24 May 2003, a pair was seen at the Pacific Rim National Park sewage pond, and on 26 May 2009 a single bird was present at the airport. I can find only one summer record. On 23 July 2014, a male was seen on the lower Kennedy River.

The fall movement begins in late September, with the earliest sighting recorded on 19 September in 2004, when a single bird was observed at the airport. While there are only 5 records for September, there are 16 for October and 10 for November, indicating that the bulk of the migration occurs in October. A few migrants persist into December, with 7 records for that month.

There are six records for January. Indeed, the very first sighting for the west coast region was recorded on 11 January 1970 on upper Kennedy Lake, and another was recorded on 14 January 2009 at the Tofino mudflats. On 2 January 2008, five birds were observed at a bog on Meares Island, and two birds were recorded at the same location on 21 and 27 January 2010. On 17 January 2015, three males were found on a pond at the Long Beach Golf Course. While these records certainly qualify as winter occurrences, they are not necessarily proof of birds overwintering. Elsewhere on Vancouver Island, the species winters on southeastern and southern portions of the island, where there are also several breeding records (BCNRS). There are, however, two records that are much later than that. On 26 February 2008, four Ring-necked Ducks were observed by Mark Hobson at a bog on Meares Island, just west of Lemmens Inlet, and three birds were still there on the first day of March.

The largest number ever recorded in our region was 19 birds found among Lesser Scaup on 7 November 2013 at Grice Bay. Other small flocks that were recorded are as follows: 15 birds on 5 December 2005 at Grice Bay; 12 on 15 October 2004 at Swan Lake; 11 on 3 April 2008 at the Pacific Rim National Park sewage pond; 9 on 20 October 2007 at a Meares Island bog; and 7 on 27 October 2008 at the floatplane pond at the Long Beach Airport.

In 2015, the total population for this species in North America was estimated at 500,000 birds.[2]

GREATER SCAUP
Aythya marila

STATUS: Common spring and fall migrant. In winter, uncommon, though fairly common locally. Casual in summer.

The Greater Scaup breeds mostly on lakes in the boreal forest zone and on the tundra, where it nests on small islands on lakes. Its breeding range stretches from northern Eurasia west to Iceland, and in North America from Hudson Bay west to the Yukon and Alaska. A disjunct breeding population exists south of Ungava Bay in Quebec and Labrador. The species winters along the Atlantic coast from the Maritimes south to northern Florida and the Gulf of Mexico, and along the entire Pacific coast from the Aleutians and Gulf of Alaska south to Baja California. It also winters locally inland, including the interior of Washington state and British Columbia's Okanagan Valley. In our province, this species is a widespread and common migrant in spring and fall, and is a common winter visitor to the coast.

This is the most numerous duck in the genus *Aythya* in our west coast region. In 1978, *Birds of Pacific Rim National Park* mentioned flocks of 300 to 350 in southern Clayoquot Sound.[1] Since then, there has been only one record of a flock of comparable size: on 24 September 1982, 300 birds were seen at Chesterman Beach. Greater Scaup began to decline in numbers in North America in the early 1980s, and this is reflected in the numbers recorded on the west coast. They reached a record low of 3.47 million birds in 1998, which is considered to be a 57% decline over a 25-year period.[2] The largest number recorded here since that decline was 220 birds on 25 September 2011, at Tofino. Numbers recorded in late fall and winter are inevitably lower, suggesting that birds seen in September are migrants passing through, and not wintering birds.

As suggested by the figures already mentioned, Greater Scaup begin arriving in mid-September or slightly earlier. We have one very early date of 2 birds at Tofino on 4 August in 2001. By early to mid-November, the fall movement is likely over. The species overwinters here in small to modest numbers. While numbers remain fairly stable from December through February, they fluctuate considerably from year to year. In the winter of 1994/95, Greater Scaup peaked at 50 birds, and in 2001/02 at 80 birds. For the next eight years, all winter counts remained below 30. On 16 December 2009, a flock of 67 was tallied at Stubbs Island, increasing to 93 birds by 31 January. For the next few years, winter numbers were again rather low, with a slight rise in 2014/15. On 19 January 2016, numbers at Grice Bay peaked at 69 birds.

The exact timing of the spring movement is difficult to determine, but appears to begin from early to mid-March. In 2011 at Tofino, birds increased from a winter population of only 13 all the way up to 80 birds on 20 March. By 5 April numbers had risen to 127, by 30 April to 165, and by 8 May to 207. After that, numbers dropped sharply. Nevertheless, 46 birds were observed there on 17 May. In 2013, from a winter high of 23 birds, the population had increased to 30 birds by 8 March and 144 birds by 24 March. The migration is usually over by late May, although in some years migrants are still passing through in June. In 1987, 39 birds were recorded at Tofino on 13 June, and 7 birds as late as 27 June. In 2011, 21 birds were counted on 9 June. Summer records in July and August are few and would have to represent nonbreeding birds. Further north, during migration watches from Clerke Point on Brooks Peninsula in the spring of 1973, 97 Greater Scaup were counted between 14 and 31 May, and an additional 19 birds on the first two days of June.[13]

Wintering Greater Scaup appear to favour waters above submerged eelgrass beds (as opposed to beds that are exposed at low tide). Favoured locations on the central west coast are at Grice Bay, Browning Passage (particularly near Laddie Island), the Stubbs Island area, the west side of Father Charles Channel, and, according to Hatler, the head of Ucluelet Inlet.[1]

The trend of somewhat low scaup numbers continues for North America, with a combined Lesser and Greater Scaup estimate for 2015 of 4.4 million birds, which is 13% below the long-term average.[2]

LESSER SCAUP
Aythya affinis

STATUS: Uncommon fall migrant and winter visitor. Casual spring migrant.

This is a smaller version of the previous species and care must be taken in the identification. The Lesser Scaup's breeding range covers a much larger area than that of the Greater Scaup, extending from eastern Manitoba and western

Minnesota westward to Alaska, British Columbia, and large parts of the northwestern United States. In British Columbia, it is a widespread breeder east of the Coast Mountains. The species winters in much of the eastern United States, as well as the southwestern United States south through Mexico, Central America, and the Caribbean. On the Pacific coast, it winters as far north as Washington, southwestern British Columbia, and the south-central part of the province. It is considered an uncommon to very common winter visitor on southeastern Vancouver Island.

In our west coast region, the Lesser Scaup occurs much less frequently than its larger cousin. In 1978, *Birds of Pacific Rim National Park* listed only 5 records, all reported in 1971 and 1972, and considered it a rare migrant.[1] For the period after 1990, there are an additional 65 records, mostly involving single birds, pairs, or small flocks of fewer than 10 birds, but on occasion larger numbers were recorded. The highest counts were 26 birds on 3 February 1995 at Tofino; 48 on 7 October 2008 at Grice Bay; 145 on 18 November 2008 at Grice Bay; 150 on 3 April 2009 at Arakun mudflats; 195 on 7 November 2013 at Grice Bay; and 99 on 28 November 2014, also at Grice Bay.

The overwhelming majority of records are from the fall and winter period, though an occasional flock may pass through in spring. Birds arrive as early as late September, though most of the movement is later than that. The earliest sighting on record was on 21 September in 2013 at Jensen's Bay, Tofino, when a single individual was seen. The month of October has 12 records, and November and December have 9 records each. January has the most, with 13 records, and February has 6. Spring records are remarkably scarce, with a total of only 9 records for the months of March, April, and May combined. The latest spring date was 14 May in 2009, when 19 birds were seen near Tofino.

The three locations where most birds have been seen are Browning Passage, Grice Bay, and the waters around Stubbs Island. Occasionally one or two birds will also be found on a pond at the Long Beach Airport. Lesser Scaup do occasionally fraternize with Greater Scaup and some may therefore be overlooked, particularly when viewed at a distance. As well, ducks of many species migrate over the open ocean, even many miles offshore. It seems possible, therefore, that significant numbers of this species pass by undetected.

Lesser Scaup have the largest population of any diving duck in North America. However, overall numbers on the continent can fluctuate greatly from year to year. For example, in 2012 North American numbers were close to their long-term average, but a year later the combined total for the two species was 20% lower.[2]

KING EIDER
Somateria spectabilis
STATUS: Casual winter visitor.

The King Eider nests in the Arctic regions of northern Siberia, from the Chukotka Peninsula west to the Taimyr Peninsula, in northern Greenland, and throughout much of Arctic Canada and Alaska. On the Atlantic coast, birds winter in eastern Canada south to the New England states. On the Pacific coast, they winter from the Aleutians to Yakutat in the Gulf of Alaska. A small number winter further south, sporadically along the BC and US coast to Los Angeles and San Diego.

In British Columbia, there are records of wintering birds from Haida Gwaii (Queen Charlotte Islands) to Iona Island (Greater Vancouver) and the east side of Vancouver Island. It is regarded as a very rare vagrant along the coast.[6]

On 8 January 1994, I found two female King Eiders off Stubbs Island, Tofino.[17] These were subsequently verified by others. The birds remained at that location until at least 5 February. On 26 March, only a single bird was located, and it remained until 26 April. Because the species is to be expected again, albeit rarely, the King Eider is considered casual in our west coast region.

HARLEQUIN DUCK
Histrionicus histrionicus
STATUS: Common in spring, summer, and fall. Uncommon in winter. Breeds.

The Harlequin Duck is named for its bold-patterned plumage reminiscent of a clown or jester. This little duck of fast-moving streams and turbulent marine waters breeds throughout northern Siberia, Iceland, Greenland, and both coasts of North America. The eastern population breeds from eastern Quebec and Labrador to southern Baffin Island. In the west, it breeds from the Bering Sea and Aleutian Islands throughout much of interior Alaska, the Yukon, most of British Columbia, including Vancouver Island and Haida Gwaii, and western Alberta. In the United States, it breeds in the northern Rocky Mountains and in the Cascades of Washington and Oregon. The species winters along the Pacific coast from the Alaska Peninsula to northern California. Nonbreeders spend summers feeding and roosting on rocky islands along the entire BC coast.[6]

Harlequin Ducks are found almost exclusively among the reefs and islets of the outer coast and are rarely seen on inlets.

In our west coast region, this handsome little duck is seen most often in summer. We have records from the entire length of the coast, from Port Renfrew to Triangle Island. In April or May, birds depart for breeding territories on fast-flowing streams and rivers. After breeding, males return to the ocean, where food is abundant, leaving more food available for the females and young. Males gather on the outside coast to take advantage of the abundance of molluscs and crustaceans, and to go through a moult that results in an eclipse plumage that looks similar to that of females but with the addition of white tertials, which females lack. Flocks consist primarily of postnuptial and nonbreeding males, but a small percentage of nonbreeding females can also be found in the mix.

A major moulting site on the west coast is found on the seaward side of Vargas Island in Clayoquot Sound. It consist of two archipelagos made up of reefs and islets known as Wilf Rocks and the La Croix Group. Harlequin Ducks move freely anywhere within this area and also to Cleland Island to the northwest. In 1969 moulting birds (3) arrived on Cleland Island on 15 May, increased to 19 birds (16♂, 3♀) between 31 May and 2 June, and peaked at 20 birds on 25 June. The latest record was a lone female on 22 August. In 1970, the first moulting Harlequins arrived on 11 May; increased to 29 birds (28♂, 1♀) on 15 May, 58 birds (54♂, 4♀) on 16 June, and 91 birds on 22 June; peaked at 115 birds on 26 June; and decreased steadily to 4 birds on 20 August, when records ceased (BCFWS). Although the size of moulting populations varies along the entire west coast, patterns are similar. For example, 180 km north,

156 Harlequin Ducks (139 ♂, 17 ♀) were present during August 1981, in the vicinity of Brooks Peninsula.[13]

Usually they are scattered in small groups throughout this area, but occasionally they will all gather in a very large flock. Eighty-five birds were counted from Medallion Beach, Vargas Island, on 22 July 1988, and 75 at that location on 2 July 2001. On 27 May 2003, there were 200 birds at Cleland Island, and 200 birds again a year later, on 29 May 2004. On 10 June, 150 were still at Cleland Island, and on 27 June, what was probably the entire population in the area, an estimated 250 birds, congregated in a marine pool at Medallion Beach. A few days later, on 1 July, 200 birds were back at Cleland Island. Those were the largest numbers ever recorded here. More modest numbers were found in 2011, with 45 birds recorded on 9 June.

Not much is known about winter numbers for the simple reason that sea conditions in most years discourage travel on the outer coast. Harlequin Ducks avoid protected inside waters, though they do seek out quieter waters on the outer coast, for example, in the lee of islands. Birds have also been seen at Sea Lion Rocks and in the semi-sheltered waters at the south end of Long Beach, near the park interpretive centre. On 12 December 2016, eight males were observed there. During the 1970s, birds could often be found in Florencia Bay, but rarely since then. Very occasionally, birds may be seen in Tofino harbour and at Stubbs Island.

Harlequin Ducks breed on some of the streams and rivers that empty into the sea between Pachena Bay and Port San Juan. The distribution map in *The Birds of British Columbia* shows two other breeding records for our region, one in the Barkley Sound area and one in Kyuquot Sound.[6] Two birds recorded on the Tahsis River on 17 April 1979 were probably there as breeding birds. It is likely that they breed on other rivers throughout the region as well. The source of moulting birds on our west coast is unknown.

SURF SCOTER
Melanitta perspicillata

STATUS: Common year-round. Abundant migrant in spring.

The Surf Scoter is our most common sea duck. It breeds on ponds and lakes in the boreal forest from Labrador to Alaska. This is one of the least studied ducks in North America, and even its breeding range is not well defined, with significant discrepancies appearing on maps found in different field guides.

The US Fish and Wildlife Service (Western Division) and the Canadian Wildlife Service are attempting to answer these and other questions through a project called Sea Duck Joint Venture. Surf Scoters winter along the Atlantic coast from Nova Scotia to Florida, and on the Pacific coast from the Aleutian Islands to Baja California.

Not for nothing are these birds called Surf Scoters. In our region, birds may be seen on the open ocean off Long Beach throughout the spring, summer, and fall. In fall and winter, when sea conditions are often severe, Surf Scoters frequently seek shelter in the protected waters of sounds and inlets. In marine waters, these birds feed largely on molluscs and crustaceans obtained by diving. The greatest concentrations occur at Pacific herring spawning beds, where scoters feed on the eggs. On 26 March 1990, a flock estimated at 12,000 to 15,000 birds was found near the north shore of Barkley Sound close to a herring spawning area. Similarly, in the spring of 1993, while flying low over Hesquiat Harbour in a floatplane, I was struck by the large number of Surf Scoters on the water below. Although no count was made, they were certainly there by the thousands. In 1978, *Birds of Pacific Rim National Park* mentioned 4,000 birds near Stubbs Island on 25 March 1971, during a herring spawn, and on 13 March 1973 there was a concentration of "several thousand" birds in Barkley Sound, "the majority of which appeared to be Surf Scoters."[1]

Herring no longer spawn near Stubbs Island due to one too many ill-advised fisheries, nor do they spawn at dozens of other locations on the BC coast where herring fisheries took place.[18] This raises the question of whether there could be a link between the reduction of this annual food bonanza and the decline in numbers of this species.

Because significant numbers of Surf Scoters are present year-round, it is difficult to determine the beginning and end of the spring movement. A one-hour survey conducted at Incinerator Rock, Long Beach, on 20 April 2013, recorded 1,720 Surf Scoters passing by. A day earlier, 1,300 were recorded in the span of an hour. On 21 April, 435 passed by in a one-hour period. Significant numbers were still passing by Long Beach on 25 April. It is tempting to conclude that this was the height of the spring migration in 2013, although birds were seen travelling north long after these dates.

In June and July, flocks of from 50 to 200 birds can usually be found on the water off Long Beach and Vargas Island as summer residents. The highest number recorded in summer off the central west coast was on 12 June 2016, with a combined total of 2,350 birds at Long Beach and Florencia Bay. Based on the plumage of the males, these were all immature birds from the previous year. Flock size in July of most years is usually under 100 birds. In 2014, it was lower than usual, with numbers off Long Beach not exceeding 20 birds. In the vicinity of Brooks Peninsula, small flocks of 10 to 75 Surf Scoters are present throughout the year, with up to 200 birds reported in winter. During spring migration watches at Clerke Point on Brooks Peninsula in 1973, 6,525 Surf and White-winged scoters were counted in May, and another 2,673 in June. The net northward movement of scoters was 28,600 in May and 15,400 in June. Seventy percent of June migrants had passed by mid-month.[13]

As is the case in spring, it is difficult to determine the beginning of the autumn movement. In 1968, Campbell et al. (1990) believed that numbers increased as the summer progressed,[6] and in 1978, Hatler et al. said there was fairly good evidence that the main fall movement begins in August.[1] I have seen no evidence for either. In 2000 there was an increase in numbers off Vargas Island in mid-September, and in 2012 there was an increase off Stubbs Island in late September. In other years this increase may not occur until early to mid-October. It appears to this observer that the fall movement begins in late September in most years.

There has been a general decline in the scoter population since the 1950s, but the reason for this remains unknown. Currently, the North American population is estimated at 700,000 birds, and the Pacific population at 225,000.[2] Numbers are declining in some areas, though the wintering population on the southwest coast of our province was considered stable in the period from 1999 to 2012.[19]

WHITE-WINGED SCOTER
Melanitta deglandi

STATUS: Common migrant in spring and fall, and fairly common in summer. Uncommon in winter, though fairly common locally.

At 1,670 g (3.7 lbs), this is the largest of our ducks. Only the King Eider, very rare here, is as large. The breeding range of the White-winged Scoter spans the Prairie provinces, interior British Columbia, the Northwest Territories, the Yukon, and interior Alaska. The species winters on the Atlantic coast from Newfoundland to Georgia, and on the Pacific coast from the Alaska Peninsula south to northern Baja California.

White-winged Scoters are seen regularly along our coast. Indeed, they have occurred in every month of the year, and are often found in proximity to Surf Scoters, which usually outnumber them considerably. The most frequent sightings occur over the open Pacific during the spring and fall migration periods. When the bird migration was particularly closely monitored in the years from 2008 to 2016, modest numbers were recorded off Long Beach throughout the months of April, May, and June. Birds seen in the latter half of June are probably nonbreeding birds, with small flocks often persisting throughout July and August.

In some other locations on the BC coast, large rafts of several thousand birds have been recorded, but that is not often the case off our shores. The largest movement was recorded on 3 August 1968, when David Hatler observed 2,000 birds moving south in Barkley Sound. He believed that this was the beginning of the fall movement. This conjecture seemed to be supported by a record of 400 or more White-winged Scoters in Florencia Bay on 24 July 1972.[1] These may have been newly arrived males that left the breeding territory early. Likewise, a modest influx was noted on 2 August 2013, when 113 birds were spotted from Incinerator Rock, Long Beach.

No such large numbers have been seen since Hatler's observation of 2,000 birds in 1968. The largest flock recorded in subsequent years was a flock of 500 birds near Stubbs Island on 25 March 1971, and 800 birds in Hesquiat Harbour on 7 March 1976. The latter were likely there to feed on herring spawn. These represent the largest numbers thus far recorded off our west coast, though it's worth noting that large areas of the west coast are only rarely visited by birders.

Spring migration begins in late March or early April. At Incinerator Rock, 29 birds were recorded on 30 March 2013, 90 birds on 1 April 2015, and 123 birds on 30 March 2016. On 17 May 2016, 225 were counted off Incinerator Rock. Flocks continue to be recorded throughout May and June, though usually in far smaller numbers than Surf Scoters. In June, birds are usually seen on the water rather than passing by, and it isn't clear when the northward movement ends. In 2014, 40 birds were seen passing Long Beach as late as 25 May, though it is not unusual to see small flocks in west coast waters throughout the summer. In June 2016, larger numbers than usual were counted off Long Beach and in Florencia Bay, with combined totals of 375 birds on 10 June and 310 birds on 22 June. As with Surf Scoters, these are presumed to be mostly nonbreeding immatures hatched the previous year.

In late fall and winter, when savage storms cause severe sea conditions, White-winged Scoters spend their time feeding in protected waters, usually in small flocks but sometimes in larger groups. In Clayoquot Sound, 69 birds were recorded at the mouth of Cypre River on 30 January 1989, 150 birds at Yellow Bank on 3 November 1998, and 150 birds off Stubbs Island on 7 October

1999. The latter two records probably involved birds still in transit rather than wintering birds.

In *Birds of Pacific Rim National Park,* David Hatler speculated cautiously that White-winged Scoters preferred deeper water than Surf Scoters.[1] Years of observations off Long Beach have shed no further light on that idea. At times, Surf Scoters are seen in shallower water, at other times White-winged Scoters. Off the south end of Long Beach, flocks of scoters often contain members of both species, although White-winged Scoters are almost always greatly outnumbered by Surf Scoters.

This scoter was recently split into three species, one in Europe, one in eastern Siberia, and one in North America. The Velvet Scoter of Europe retains the Latin name *M. fusca,* while the American bird is *M. deglandi* and the Siberian bird is *M. stejnegeri.* The last is casual in Alaska and could very well turn up in our west coast region. A very good look at the bill will be needed, however, to distinguish it from the American bird.[20]

BLACK SCOTER
Melanitta americana

STATUS: Uncommon spring and fall migrant and winter visitor.

The Black Scoter has two disjunct populations, one breeding in the east and the other in the west. Eastern birds breed in northern Quebec and western Labrador, and along the shores of Hudson Bay in Ontario and Manitoba. They winter along the Atlantic coast. The western population breeds only in Alaska. This population winters along the Pacific coast, from the Aleutian Islands south to southern California.

In British Columbia, this bird is mainly restricted to the coast, with a few widely scattered records inland. On the coast, it is seen primarily during the spring and fall migration and in winter. Its status ranges from uncommon to locally very common. It is reported to feed primarily on molluscs and to some extent on other aquatic invertebrates, and prefers waters less than 11 m in depth. In the Salish Sea region, the species is sometimes seen in flocks consisting of hundreds of birds.[6]

On Vancouver Island's west coast, this species is by far the least common of the scoters. In 1978, *Birds of Pacific Rim National Park* listed 33 records, with the largest flock made up of 13 birds.[1] Since then, 70 additional records have been added, with 15 of those from the years 2012 and 2013. Consistent with the findings of Hatler et al., flock size was almost always fewer than 12, and often sightings involved just 1 or 2 birds.[1] Of interest, therefore, is a count of 53 birds on the water at the south end of Long Beach on 24 December 2012, and 50 birds at Cleland Island on 14 March 2014. The birds at Long Beach were closely associated with Surf Scoters, which on this occasion they outnumbered. Those two counts are the highest numbers thus far recorded in our region. Although the species may be encountered in all months of the year, records suggest that the spring movement occurs from mid-March to mid-May, while the autumn movement occurs from mid-October through December. The only two sightings in January and February were recorded in 2013. Summer records are rare. Single birds were recorded off Long Beach on 22 June and 31 July 2014, and 26 July 2015. A pair was seen in Florencia Bay on 22 June 2016.

Although Black Scoters prefer somewhat sheltered waters, in the west coast region nearly all sightings have been along the outer coast, with only a handful of records from inside Barkley Sound. In Clayoquot Sound, most records are from Stubbs Island. On the central west coast, the location where this species has been found most often is at the south end of Long Beach.

Overall, the Pacific population of Black Scoters appears little changed over the past 20 years, with an estimate of approximately 40,000 birds in 2015.[2] It should be noted, however, that the US Fish and Wildlife Service itself does not consider its population estimates for scoters to be highly accurate.

The Common Scoter (*M. nigra*) is the Black Scoter's Eurasian counterpart. In appearance the two species are nearly identical except that the Eurasian bird has a grey knob on the bill, rather than a yellow one. In February 2015, the first one ever recorded on this continent was photographed in California,[21] and in November 2016, one was found off Oregon.[22] It therefore is a bird to watch for in our region.

LONG-TAILED DUCK
Clangula hyemalis
STATUS: A fairly common migrant and winter visitor.

Formerly known in North America by the name "Oldsquaw," this attractive little duck with its haunting call is always a treat to see and hear. It has a circumpolar breeding range from the tundra regions of Siberia to Canada, Greenland,

and Norway. In North America, it breeds from Labrador to northern Quebec, north to the High Arctic islands and west throughout the tundra regions of Canada and Alaska. Eastern birds winter along the Atlantic coast and on the Great Lakes. In the west, birds winter along the Pacific coast as far south as California.

On the central west coast of Vancouver Island, Long-tailed Ducks begin arriving from mid to late October. The earliest recorded fall arrival was on 8 October 2012. Most birds don't arrive until November. They are often seen in the winter months in Father Charles Channel and at Stubbs Island, near Tofino. They usually occur in small numbers, but up to 45 birds have been seen there in recent years.

Larger numbers were reported in the early 1970s, when flocks totalling up to 200 birds were recorded.[1] There is also a record of 60 birds at Tofino Inlet on 2 May 1976, and 155 birds seen off Meares Island on 9 November 1981. The location of this last record is somewhat unclear as Meares Island has many miles of shoreline.

There were no further records of large flocks until 1 and 4 May 2011, when 75 birds were counted off Long Beach, 1 to 2 km from shore. On 11 December 2011, 150 birds were seen at that same location, and a year later, on 24 December 2012, 77 birds were counted there. Birds off Long Beach are usually seen on the water in very tightly knit flocks. On 15 February 2013, numbers totalled 240 birds in two flocks. Birds off Long Beach had been overlooked primarily because sea conditions in winter are often severe, which prevents spotting of birds on the water. Birds have continued to be seen there in fairly large numbers in subsequent years.

In spring most birds have departed by late April. In the years that birds were recorded in May, most were seen in the first week of the month, with 2 birds on 4 May 1996; 75 birds on 4 May 2011; 2 on 5 May 2013; and 43 on 6 May 2014. The latest spring records involve single individuals and likely nonbreeders, occurring on 29 May 1969, 30 May 1970, 24 May 2016, and 26 May 2017.

While the species has declined in Europe, the population is believed to have remained relatively stable in North America since the early 1990s, according to the Canadian Wildlife Service, which states that "it remains the most abundant Arctic sea duck in North America."[23] The breeding population of this species is difficult to monitor since large areas of its nesting grounds are not covered by aerial surveys and it mostly winters offshore in the Pacific. The North American population has been "crudely" estimated at one million birds.[2]

BUFFLEHEAD
Bucephala albeola
STATUS: Common to abundant in fall, winter, and spring.

Although closely related to goldeneyes, this little duck is less than half the weight of the other two species in the genus *Bucephala*. Indeed, at 380 g (13 oz), it is the smallest of all the diving ducks. It breeds from northeastern Ontario west to British Columbia, the Northwest Territories, the Yukon, and Alaska. It also breeds locally in the western United States. In British Columbia, it has a widespread breeding distribution east of the Coast Mountains, where it nests in tree cavities, usually those made by Northern Flickers. It has bred in the Fraser Valley and at least once on central Vancouver Island. On the Pacific coast, the species winters north to the Alaska Peninsula and south to central Mexico.

"The Bufflehead is our most abundant diving duck." So begins the text for this species in *Birds of Pacific Rim National Park* (1978).[1] That statement is no less true today. However, it is worth noting that Surf Scoters often exceed it in numbers during Pacific herring spawning events, and during migration. Buffleheads usually begin arriving on our coast during the second half of October. First arrival dates for ten separate years were all in the second half of October with one exception; 4 birds were seen at Grice Bay on 11 October 2009. Most birds, however, arrive in November and December. They reach their maximum numbers sometime in late November or December, depending on the year, after which some, or many, of the birds disappear. Further north, flocks of up to 40 birds winter each year from November through March in Johnson's Lagoon, in the Nasparti River estuary, and at the mouth of the Klaskish River.[13]

Until recently, the three highest counts recorded on our coast occurred during the 1970s and 1980s. On 12 April 1972, at least 1,000 were seen at Grice Bay; on 25 March 1984, 1,300 birds were counted at Stubbs Island;[1] and on 4 April 1989, 1,500 birds were recorded on the eelgrass beds northeast of Vargas Island. The latter two counts were made during a Pacific herring spawning event. Although 500 sightings have been recorded since then, none approached these numbers until recently, when 640 birds were counted at Grice Bay on 18 December 2012. Not until the fall of 2014 did numbers match or exceed those seen in the 1970s. On 8 November of that year, 625 birds were counted at Grice Bay. On 12 November numbers were up to 1,350 birds, and by 22 November had soared to a remarkable 2,500 birds. After that date, numbers began to decline.

In spring, Buffleheads depart throughout the month of April, with only small numbers remaining by the end of the month. Exceptions occurred on 4 May 2008, when 213 birds were still in Grice Bay, and on 30 April 2011, when 88 birds were counted at Stubbs Island. In 2011, 16 birds remained on 8 May. The latest spring date was 16 May in 2010. *Birds of Pacific Rim National Park* mentioned two spring dates that were later – 19 May in 1972 and 30 May in 1971.[1] There are no records between May and October. Males, it should be noted, depart before the females. Of the 213 birds counted at Grice Bay on 4 May 2008, only 4 were males.

During the winter of 2015/16, numbers at Grice Bay were unusually low, with as few as 17 birds counted on 7 January and 20 birds on 13 January. This trend continued into the autumn of 2016, when numbers at Grice Bay peaked at a mere 35 birds on 21 November. Birds were almost nonexistent in the following winter.

COMMON GOLDENEYE
Bucephala clangula

STATUS: A common migrant in spring and fall, common in winter. Rare breeder.

Goldeneyes are handsome diving ducks, sometimes known as "whistlers," after the sound of their wings in flight. This species has an extensive breeding range in both North America and Eurasia. On this continent, it is found throughout most of Canada except for the northern tundra regions. In the United States, it breeds in the New England states, the Great Lakes region, the northern Rocky Mountains, and Alaska. In British Columbia, it breeds east of the Coast Mountains and on the southwest mainland coast and Vancouver Island. It does not breed on Haida Gwaii.[24] It winters from southern Canada to northern Mexico. On the Pacific coast, it winters from the Aleutian Islands south to the Sea of Cortez, Mexico.

In our west coast region, Common Goldeneyes arrive very late in the fall. They are said to linger on lakes in the interior and at higher elevation until those waters threaten to freeze over. Records indicate that most birds arrive here in late November or December. There are few records before mid-November. On 14 November 2003, three birds were seen near Tofino, and on

1 November 2007, a single bird was found at Grice Bay. One of only two records I have that are earlier than November occurred on 11 October 2009, with two birds at Grice Bay. A young bird seen on a pond at the Long Beach Airport on 24 and 27 August 2014 was so early as to be anomalous, and may have been a bird hatched on Vancouver Island.

Counts conducted at Grice Bay show that numbers stay relatively stable during the winter and begin to increase after mid-February with an influx of birds from further south. In 2008, this happened as early as 17 February. In other years, this may not occur until well into March. In 2008, numbers peaked at 36 birds on 30 March, and in 2009 at 36 birds on 4 March. In 2010, numbers peaked at 59 birds on 21 March. In 2011, Common Goldeneye numbers went from a wintertime maximum of 12 birds to 38 on 17 March, 44 on 19 March, 61 on 27 March, and 86 on 30 March. By 4 April, numbers had plummeted to only 11 birds as most had left for their breeding grounds in the north or in the interior. In the following year, 30 birds were still present on 5 April, but by 24 April only 6 remained. By May, all birds have usually gone. The increase in springtime numbers recorded at Grice Bay are consistent with two reports from Barkley Sound, where Richard Cannings recorded 40 birds on 27 March 1993 and 100 birds on 1 April 1989, at the mouth of Maggie River.

Ian McTaggart-Cowan reported in 1931 that the species was common in the Tofino area in early May, and in 1978, Hatler et al. listed one sighting in that month.[1] However, during the past decade, when birds were very closely monitored, only two May sightings were recorded. A lone bird was seen at Grice Bay on 4 May 2008 and also on 2 May 2010.

Common Goldeneyes were thought to rarely breed on the coast, with volume 1 of *The Birds of British Columbia* listing only a single breeding record for Vancouver Island.[6] Recently, 22 additional breeding records were unearthed.[24] While nearly all island records were from east of the divide, 4 of the sightings were recorded in the west coast region. In a rather strange coincidence, the first two breeding records for the west coast region were both recorded on the same day at separate locations by different people. On 6 July 1974, a female with a brood of seven young was found on Megin Lake by Leslie Fox and Susan Fleck; 30 km by air to the east-southeast, on a small high-elevation lake in the Bedwell River drainage, a female with six young was found by Ian D. Smith.

There were no further records for our region until 27 July 1986, when I found a female with a single young on a small lake at 1,025 m elevation on Mount Klitsa. Eight years later, an adult female with a single young was seen on Crest Lake by Doug and Marian Innes. Crest Lake is located 14 km northeast of Gold River, beside Highway 28. It is interesting to note that two of our four breeding records were located on the height of land separating eastern and western Vancouver Island. Given that there are hundreds of lakes west of the divide, most of them rarely, if ever, visited by humans, it seems likely that Common Goldeneyes nest in our region more frequently than is currently recognized.

While most records of Common Goldeneyes outside the summer period are from locations near the outer coast, winter surveys were also conducted on river estuaries in Clayoquot Sound during the 1980s. Unfortunately, those results are in the hands of a government agency and are not available. That significant numbers of Common Goldeneyes do occur up the inlets at river mouths in winter is supported by the results of two surveys that are available. Those counts were conducted on 30 January 1989 at the mouth of Cypre River (28 birds) and at the mouth of Bedwell River (36 birds), for a total of 64 birds that day.

BARROW'S GOLDENEYE
Bucephala islandica

STATUS: Common in protected inlets and estuaries in fall, winter, and spring. Rare in summer. Rare breeder.

This diving duck is named for the British arctic explorer John Barrow. It is primarily a North American bird, although with four separate populations, one of them outside the continent on Iceland, hence the Latin name. In eastern Canada, the species breeds in southern Quebec and northern Labrador. The bulk of the population breeds in the west, from Alaska and the Yukon through British Columbia east of the Coast Mountains and locally on eastern Vancouver Island (BCNRS), through the Cascade Mountains of Washington and Oregon, and the Rocky Mountains from Alberta to northwestern Wyoming. Over 60% of the world population is believed to breed in our province. Numbering about 200,000 birds, most of the western population winters along the Pacific coast, from Prince William Sound and Kodiak Island, Alaska, to California's Big Sur coast. On southeastern Vancouver Island, it is a very common migrant and winter visitor.

With only 13 records for the west coast region up to 1978, *Birds of Pacific Rim National Park* listed this bird's status as a "rare winter species."[1] It is evident today that Barrow's Goldeneyes are considerably more common than that away from the outer coast. They prefer sheltered waters, particularly sheltered coves and estuaries, and many locations in Clayoquot Sound provide exactly those conditions. Visit places such as Lemmens Inlet, Warn Bay, and Tranquil Inlet in season, and chances are that you'll find them, sometimes in considerable numbers. At Tranquil Inlet, 121 birds were present on 28 April 1989, and 80 birds on 13 November 2015. On waterfowl surveys conducted during winter in the early 1980s, I found birds at these and other locations, though unfortunately those records are archived by a government agency and are not accessible.

That Barrow's Goldeneyes prefer these locations is said to be due to their preference for waters with lower salinity. Their preferred food is small mussels, which thrive at Pacific oyster farms. This likely explains their prevalence in Lemmens Inlet, where local resident Mark Hobson has recorded concentrations numbering more than 200 birds, and where flocks of 50 or 60 birds are not unusual. On 6 November 2009, Hobson counted 240 birds, and two days later a remarkable 320 birds. In recent years, Barrow's Goldeneyes have also been seen at a more accessible location along the shores of Indian Island in Grice Bay. When seen at this location, they usually number only a handful, but on 17 March 2012, a flock of 38 was observed. Birds have also been reported at a few locations in Barkley Sound, Ucluelet Inlet, Toquart Bay, Pachena Bay, and Port San Juan. It seems likely, therefore, that Barrow's Goldeneye will also be found in other sounds and inlets in our west coast region.

Times of arrival and departure in spring and fall are difficult to determine with any accuracy. Hobson recorded only small numbers in Lemmens Inlet in April. As mentioned above, we know that 121 birds were present at Tranquil Creek as late as 28 April in 1989, and 66 birds on 25 April in 2015. However, these could have been southern birds passing through, rather than local wintering birds, and the same could have been true of the 38 birds at Grice Bay on 17 March 2012. Based on the records we have, birds begin arriving in October and depart before the end of April.

A sighting recorded by Nigel Jackett in 2008 seems rather curious. On 28 September he found a Barrow's Goldeneye at one of the small high-elevation lakes on the Clayoquot Plateau. This bird must have been either lingering after breeding there, or in transit.

Since the publication of volume 1 of *The Birds of British Columbia* in 1990, small numbers of Barrow's Goldeneye have been found breeding on Vancouver Island, mainly in Strathcona Park (BCNRS). Guy Monty has also reported seeing the species on a number of high-elevation lakes on the island during the breeding season.[25] The possibility of breeding in our region was first raised by Hatler et al. after a male was seen on Kennedy Lake on 17 July 1967.[1] A male reported by Hobson in Lemmens Inlet, near Tofino, on 10 June 2009 was also intriguing. There is also a record of a bird seen in the Franklin River estuary on 11 June 2005. Breeding was not confirmed until 26 June 2014, when a female Barrow's Goldeneye accompanied by two young was found by Art Martell on Crest Lake, which is located on the divide beside Highway 28. This was followed on 15 July 2014 by Michael Shepard's finding of a female with three young on Sarita Lake. With more than 300 lakes of various sizes in the west coast region, most of them in remote locations, this species could well be a regular, if uncommon, breeding bird.

HOODED MERGANSER
Lophodytes cucullatus

STATUS: Resident. Fairly common in fall, winter, and spring. Uncommon in summer. Breeds.

Hooded Mergansers breed locally on ponds and small lakes and spend the winter in protected marine waters.

With its bold markings and black-and-white hood, the adult male of this species is exceedingly handsome. This is our smallest merganser, and the only member of its genus. Unlike Common and Red-breasted mergansers, which are found also in Eurasia, the Hooded Merganser is exclusively a North

American bird. It has a discontinuous breeding range, an eastern and a western one. In the east, it breeds from Nova Scotia west to Saskatchewan and south to Louisiana and Mississippi. In the west, the breeding range extends from northern California, western Oregon, Washington, Idaho and western Montana, western Alberta, and most of British Columbia north on the coast to at least Juneau, Alaska.[26]

Hooded Mergansers use tree cavities and crevices for nesting, and will also use nest boxes made for that purpose. They breed close to freshwater ponds, lakes, rivers, streams, and marshes. That they breed on the west coast is supported by 22 breeding records consisting of broods observed in the company of females (BCNRS). A brood of three or four was reported south of Bamfield as early as 21 August in 1943 by T. Pearse.[6] Hatler et al. described an observation on a lake on Effingham Island involving an adult female with three very small young on 9 July 1972.[1] Adults with broods have also been found at Swan Lake in 1984, Calamity Lake, near Bamfield, in 1979 and 1989, and in and around Lemmen's Inlet, near Tofino, periodically from 1996 up to the present by Mark Hobson. A female with young was also found at Kennedy Lake in 2005 by the Victoria Natural History Society, and on a pond near the Highway 4 junction on 17 May 2016 by Ian Cruickshank.

Also notable is an observation on 16 June 2014 of 3 eclipse males found lounging on a shallow lake in the Kennedy River valley, one with many dead trees surrounding it, which likely provide suitable cavities for nesting. Although breeding records are lacking for northern areas of our region, it is likely that Hooded Mergansers breed in isolated locations throughout the west coast region. On Brooks Peninsula, a flock of 6 male and 2 female adults was seen on a large lake on 23 May 1978.[13]

Birds leave marine waters for freshwater ponds and lakes mostly in April. Dwindling counts there and an observation of an adult male at Swan Lake on 17 April 1994 support this. Of more than 360 records, only 8 were seen in May, and only 2 of those were on marine waters. Young birds capable of flight have been observed as early as late June. The earliest record involved 3 flying young on a pond at the Long Beach Airport on 25 June in 2016, though in most years the first young are seen in early July. By October, Hooded Mergansers are beginning to show up in the marine environment at locations such as the Jensen's Bay mudflats near Tofino, and at Grice Bay. Throughout the fall and winter, they may be seen in small groups of usually 6 or fewer birds, but sometimes up to 10 or 12 individuals. On 30 November 2014, a flock of 15 birds was seen from the Sharp Road observation platform at Tofino.

COMMON MERGANSER
Mergus merganser

STATUS: Common to locally abundant in spring and fall, uncommon to locally common in summer and winter. Breeds.

In fall and in winter, Common Mergansers gather in flocks up to 600-strong, dispersing to breeding territories in spring.

This is the largest of our three mergansers. In older books it may be listed as "American Merganser," while in Britain it is called "Goosander." These birds will commonly swim with their heads partially submerged in order to look for small fish beneath the surface, the only ducks that are known to do this. In fall, they gather in large, tightly knit flocks containing hundreds of birds in order to pursue their prey, diving and surfacing and diving again. Pity the poor fish that try to escape such a mob! Common Mergansers occasionally engage in the unusual practice of feeding in the shallow water between the beach and the surf zone at Long Beach.

Common Mergansers breed throughout much of the Northern Hemisphere. The species' preferred breeding habitat is lakes and rivers, where it feeds on small fishes and other aquatic life. In Canada its breeding range covers nearly the entire country except for the prairie grasslands and the northernmost tundra regions. In the United States, it breeds in the New England states and in most forested regions of the western states. In fall, these birds migrate to ice-free waters, wintering throughout much of the United States except for the southeast and the coldest regions of the northern Midwest. On the Pacific coast, Common Mergansers winter from southern California north as far as Prince William Sound, Alaska.

In British Columbia, Common Mergansers breed throughout the province wherever suitable habitat is found, mostly rivers and lakes, but some are reported to nest along the marine shore, in large natural tree cavities on Haida Gwaii and among the islands of Barkley Sound (BCNRS). Paddle any river on Vancouver Island's west coast in June or July and you will likely encounter females with young. Males may already have departed in order to moult elsewhere, leaving more food available for the female and her young. Young may be seen as early as late May and early June in Barkley Sound (BCNRS). On the lower Kennedy River, I observed two females with young as early as 30 May in 2015, while in the summer of 1985 a female with downy young was seen on the Megin River as late as mid-July. In wide streams such as the lower Kennedy River, families stay close to shore for safety, but as the young mature they venture further from shore. On 30 June 2015, a female and seven half-grown, flightless young were seen diving in the middle of Kennedy Lake, at least a kilometre from the nearest shore, and on 25 July 2016, a female was observed leading her half-grown young across Sydney Inlet. Both the young and the female were still flightless at this time. Family groups with flightless young have also been reported from Winter Harbour, Mahatta River, the mouth of Nasparti Inlet,[13] Chekleset Bay, Zeballos, Bamfield, Nitinat Lake, and Port Renfrew (BCNRS).

As with other ducks, males go through a moult that replaces their breeding plumage with an eclipse plumage resembling that of the female. Only by viewing the white in the wing is the male readily distinguishable from the female. Not until late October or November do males regain their white, black, and green breeding plumage.

Where males spend the summer months after breeding remained somewhat of a mystery until 13 males were observed at the head of Sydney Inlet on 28 June 2000, and 30 males were observed at the mouth of Kootowas Creek at the head of Grice Bay on 29 July 2003. The following year, on 24 July, 12 males were seen off Medallion Beach, Vargas Island. There are no further July records until 2010, when 25 birds were spotted at Stubbs Island on 18 July. At the mouth of the Sydney River, 10 males were found on 6 July 2015 and again on 24 July a year later. We can conclude from this that after breeding, males gather in small flocks and disperse into the marine environment.

By September, birds from further afield begin to join local birds. In 2010, 160 birds were seen in Grice Bay on 10 September, and in 2012, 190 birds were observed at Stubbs Island on 20 September. In 2014, 49 birds were first found at Stubbs Island on 3 September; by 13 September the number had increased to 145 birds. By 22 September there were at least 200 birds, and by 28 September, 327 birds. Numbers may peak as early as mid-October, after which there is a gradual decline. However, flocks of 200 and 300 birds have been seen to mid-November and beyond. High counts in fall were 530 birds on 13 October 2008 and 600 birds on 15 October 2009, both at Tofino.

To support such large numbers requires an abundance of small fishes, which these birds find in the shallow waters over the mudflats of southern Clayoquot Sound. Rarely do Common Mergansers frequent deeper waters or the exposed outside coast, although on 2 December 2014, during a spell of unusually placid seas, a flock of 52 birds was seen feeding on the outer coast in Florencia Bay.

In southern Clayoquot Sound, Common Mergansers also make use of lakes. Tofino resident Mark Hobson reports that in late summer and fall, large numbers gather at a lake on Meares Island. In 2008, Hobson recorded 160 birds on the lake on 18 September, 200 birds on 19 September, 150 birds on 21 September, 352 birds on 11 October, and between 500 and 600 birds on 12 October. This closely parallels counts made during the day in marine waters from Stubbs Island to Grice Bay. Hobson reports that they usually arrive at dusk or just before, and immediately begin drinking fresh water and preening. After spending the night on the lake, they depart in the morning for the marine environment.

Large flocks may persist in the Tofino area into late fall and early winter. On 10 December 1992, 450 birds were seen on Father Charles Channel near Tofino, and 130 birds were recorded at Jensen's Bay, Tofino, as late as 1 January in 2001. That Common Mergansers overwinter in moderate numbers, at least in some years, is demonstrated by records in January and February. On 21 January 2013, 73 birds were seen at Tofino, and on 7 February 2013, 95 birds were recorded at Grice Bay. A flock of 81 birds sighted on 12 March 2011 was probably a wintering flock rather than new arrivals.

In the 1970s, the total wintering population along North America's Pacific coast was estimated at 24,000 birds.[27] Accurate information about the current population and trends is lacking. The North American population as a whole is roughly estimated at 1.2 million birds.[2]

The spring movement begins in late April, but most of the increase is seen in May. At Jensen's Bay, maximum spring counts in five successive years were 248 birds on 21 May 2011; 240 on 19 May 2012; 231 on 10 May 2013; 113 on 2 May 2014; and 205 on 28 April 2015. As late as 3 June 2015, 55 birds were still present, 10 of them females.

RED-BREASTED MERGANSER
Mergus serrator

STATUS: Common in spring and fall, locally fairly common in winter. Rare in summer.

Like the previous species, the Red-breasted Merganser has a long beak with a serrated edge designed to grasp fish, and like the other mergansers, it is an accomplished fisher. As a group, mergansers are sometimes referred to as "sawbills." This species has a global breeding range roughly equal to that of the Common Merganser, though it extends further north than the latter, and not as far south. On this continent, it breeds throughout much of the boreal forest and tundra regions of Canada, with the exception of British Columbia and northwestern Alberta. In the contiguous United States, it breeds only in northern Maine and the Great Lakes region. In British Columbia, it has been found nesting only on Haida Gwaii and in the extreme northwest corner of the province in the vicinity of Atlin Lake (BCNRS). The western population spends the winter on the Pacific coast, from the Alaska Peninsula south to southern Baja California, Mexico.

On Vancouver Island's central west coast, the first Red-breasted Mergansers usually begin arriving in the first half of October. The first arrival date in 2003 was 11 October. First arrival dates for other years were 15 October 2004, 13 October 2008, and 4 October 2009. The two earliest arrivals were both on 26 September, with 4 birds at Stubbs Island, Tofino, in 2010, and 25 birds at Port San Juan in 2013. There is an even earlier record of 9 birds on 4 September 2001 at Stubbs Island, but these may have been nonbreeding birds that spent the summer here. There is a precedent for this. In 1978, *Birds of Pacific Rim National Park* reported six records of birds seen from June through September that were believed to be nonbreeding summer residents.[1] A flock of 7 birds off Jacobson Point, Brooks Peninsula, on 26 June 1975 were also considered nonbreeders,[13] as was a female at Cleland Island from 2 June to 6 July 1970 (BCFWS).

In southern Clayoquot Sound, numbers increase through fall, with the largest numbers recorded in November and December. Some of the highest counts were as follows: 240 birds on 7 November 1994; 250 on 10 November 1996; 90 on 21 November 2000; 65 on 11 November 2008 and 2 November 2009; 118 on 1 December 2013; and 133 on 9 November 2015. Note that this last figure was the highest number recorded since 1996. A review of all records over the past three decades shows a marked decline in numbers since the mid-1990s. Only in 2013 did numbers rise to half of the level of 1994.

By late December or January, most birds have passed through and those that remain are small in number, with counts in January and February usually under 20 birds. An exception occurred in 2016, when 48 birds were counted at Grice Bay on 13 January and 38 on 28 January. By March, new birds begin arriving from the south. The spring movement is not nearly as pronounced as the fall movement, however, and birds appear to stay around for a long time. Maximum counts in spring do not usually exceed 30 birds. An exception was 49 birds on 13 March 2015. An increase to 28 birds as early as 6 March in 2013 suggests the arrival of birds from elsewhere. It is worth noting that numbers at Grice Bay stay fairly constant from mid-March until the beginning of May.

By mid-May all birds have normally departed. Only two records are later than that. On 16 May 2008, seven birds were seen at the Tofino mudflats, and on 1 June 1999, two birds were recorded at Tofino. Summer records are very rare, but in 2016 a very drab nonbreeding bird was seen periodically at the north end of Long Beach from 27 June to mid-September.

RUDDY DUCK
Oxyura jamaicensis
STATUS: Rare fall migrant. Casual in spring and winter.

The Ruddy Duck is only an occasional visitor to our region, and when seen here is usually in juvenile or nonbreeding plumage.

This small diving duck breeds throughout much of western North America, from the Northwest Territories and the Yukon through the American west and Midwest to southern Mexico. In British Columbia, it breeds widely in the south-central interior, the West and East Kootenays, and the Peace River region (BCNRS). On the coast, it has been found breeding near Vancouver[28] and in the Fraser Valley, and occasionally on southeastern Vancouver Island. It winters in the southern United States and Mexico, and along the Pacific coast to southwestern British Columbia.

Whereas the Ruddy Duck is a common migrant on the southeast side of Vancouver Island, in 1978, *Birds of Pacific Rim National Park* did not list it as occurring in the west coast region. Since the year 2000, however, Ruddy Ducks have been recorded in 10 separate years. That they are being seen now may be due to new habitat in the form of a sewage pond near Long Beach and a landing pond for floatplanes at the Long Beach Airport. Most records have been from these two locations, with others from Grice Bay and one from Stubbs Island.

Most sightings occur in autumn, with the earliest arrival date being 14 October in 2001. Birds have been seen to the end of November and into December. As late as 18 December in 2009, three birds were seen at Grice Bay, and on 23 December 2012, two birds were observed at that location. All records, except for the one mentioned above, have involved one or two individuals. Most individuals have been juveniles.

There are only three spring records. Two birds were seen from 12 to 25 April 2003, and one on 25 April 2012, all at the sewage pond near Long Beach. On 18 March 2013, a bird was seen at Grice Bay.

ORDER GALLIFORMES

New World Quail   *Family Odontophoridae*

CALIFORNIA QUAIL
Callipepla californica

STATUS: Casual south of Port Renfrew. Fairly common only at Jordan River.

This small, attractive quail was first introduced to British Columbia near Victoria in the late 1860s.[6] It is a resident from Baja California north to southern British Columbia, including southern and southeastern Vancouver Island. It is properly not a bird of Vancouver Island's west coast region and has been recorded only at the very southern edge of our region at Jordan River. The earliest record is a sighting of a single bird on 8 April 1973. Additional records followed from 1991 onward. As many as 20 birds were recorded at Jordan River on 19 September 2010, 29 September 2013, and on 26 October 2013. There is one record of a bird seen elsewhere. A single bird was seen on 19 December 2010, some miles to the northwest of Jordan River. It seems likely that, lacking suitable habitat on the west coast, this quail will be largely restricted to the extreme southern part of our region.

Grouse and Ptarmigan   Family Phasianidae

RUFFED GROUSE
Bonasa umbellus

STATUS: Uncommon resident to at times fairly common locally. Breeds.

Ruffed Grouse can be found in nearly all forested areas of Canada from coast to coast. In the United States, they are found in the Northeast from Maine to the Carolinas, and in the West from Wyoming and western Montana to Idaho. It also inhabits western parts of the Pacific states, from northern California to the Canadian border. In British Columbia, it is found in forested areas throughout the province, east of the Coast Mountains, as well as on the southwest mainland coast, including Vancouver Island. It is absent from Haida Gwaii and from larger forested islands off the mainland coast, probably because these birds are designed for an abrupt, short flight, not a prolonged one over water.

In our region, this grouse is often seen on roadsides. In late spring and early summer, it may be heard drumming, a sound created by pumping its wings. This is quite helpful in determining whether members of the species are in a given area. On an excursion to the lower Kennedy River, I once inadvertently parked for the night beside a Ruffed Grouse drumming log, to be rudely awoken very early in the morning by drumming so loud it had me wondering if the bird was using the roof of my van as its drumming station.

In the west coast region, this is a year-round resident. In 1978, *Birds of Pacific Rim National Park* listed 77 records.[1] From 2008 to the end of 2012, during a period of intensive birding on the central west coast, I recorded birds only 12 times. This suggested that the species was not as common as previously. However, in the 2013-14 period, the species was recorded 16 times in just two years. Ruffed Grouse are subject to periodic fluctuations in population, and the disparity in sightings between the three periods may have resulted from that. As well, some prime habitat was lost along McLean Point Road years ago, when the area was cleared for a golf course. These birds are also vulnerable to automobile traffic, with road-killed birds seen on a number of occasions.

While birds can be hard to find near the outer coast, a one-day bird survey around the lower Kennedy River on 8 June 2013 logged three males drumming and a hen followed by five newly hatched chicks crossing the road, suggesting that it is fairly common in disturbed habitats. Likewise, a female with young was found in a logged area overgrown with Scotch broom (*Cytisus scoparius*) and berry bushes in the Kennedy Lake lowlands on 15 June 2014. Birds were also seen on an excursion across Vargas Island in the summer of 2014, with as many as five dust-baths found on the trail, with a considerable distance between them, suggesting that birds were common there.

This species inhabits a variety of forest types and has been seen and heard at numerous locations, including some of the intact wilderness valleys in Clayoquot Sound. In the summer of 1989, it was heard in the Clayoquot River valley, and on 26 May 1994, three males were heard drumming in the Ursus Creek drainage. Birds have also been seen and heard at Florencia Bay, at Green Point, and along a logging road leading to South Bay, near Tofino. Occasionally, birds can still be seen along McLean Point Road, beside the golf course. They are fairly common along a seldom-used logging road in the Cypre River area of Clayoquot Sound, as well as in the upper Kennedy River valley near Sutton Pass. The breeding bird mapping project resulted in records from numerous outlying locations in the west coast region, as far north as Cape Scott and as far south as Jordan River. The evidence, then, is that Ruffed Grouse are found at low elevation throughout the west coast region. Published records have single birds seen in Cape Scott Park between 17 and 25 May 1974,[4] and on Brooks Peninsula the grouse was considered a possible resident with a brood of three young seen on 22 August 1981.[13] There are breeding records for 14 scattered locations along the entire west coast (BCNRS).

This species comes in two colour morphs, grey and red. Whereas Hatler et al. reported more greys than reds 40 years ago,[1] red birds are much more common today, at least on the central coast. Greys appear to be rather rare. A grey morph bird was recorded near Cypre River on 14 July 2013.

SOOTY GROUSE
Dendragapus fuliginosus

STATUS: Uncommon to locally common resident. Breeds.

On their subalpine breeding territory, male Sooty Grouse perform an impressive display during the mating season.

This bird was formerly known as Blue Grouse. When the species was split, birds in the interior were named Dusky Grouse (*D. obscurus*) and coastal birds became Sooty Grouse. Sooty Grouse occur from the Sierra Mountains and north coast of California north though western Oregon, western Washington, and coastal British Columbia to southeast Alaska. In many areas, Sooty Grouse spend the winter months in trees at high elevation and move down the mountain in early spring. In our west coast region, birds are usually found at higher elevation even in summer. The best time of year to find Sooty Grouse is late spring and early summer, when males are on territory, vocalizing with low, booming hoots repeated five or six times.

Sooty Grouse are sometimes found at low elevation in bogs. In the summer of 1980, a bird was found hooting from a copse of trees in a large bog at Cape Scott Provincial Park, and birds were seen beside the highway in boggy areas of Pacific Rim National Park in the 1970s, though rarely in recent years. These were likely young males born in a logged-off area nearby, looking for a territory of their own. Birds have also been recorded from the hills and low mountains southeast of Barkley Sound in recent years, which is not surprising in a landscape altered by logging activity. In the early 1970s, three males were heard vocalizing in logging slash near Lost Shoe Creek in what is now Pacific Rim National Park.[3] This species is resident on Brooks Peninsula, and females with one or two young were found in August 1981. On 6 May 1976, an adult female was seen on Solander Island, 1.7 km west of the peninsula.[13]

As a logged-off area becomes a young forest, it becomes unsuitable habitat for this species. Lacking clearcuts, however, birds may be encountered at higher elevation, such as at the top of Lone Cone on Meares Island, at the top of Radar Hill near Cox Bay, and on ridges where forest cover is sparse. For example, Sooty Grouse are often heard hooting on the mountain ridges high above the mouth of the Sydney River estuary, where bare areas devoid of trees are scarce, and they may be heard in the high country near the lower Kennedy River.

The following records show that birds are also found in the subalpine zone of the higher mountains. On 27 July 1986, two birds were encountered at high elevation on Mount Klitsa, and on 13 August 2008, six birds were found there. On 27 August 1990, a bird was found in the subalpine zone of Steamboat Mountain (Clayoquot Plateau), and on 1 September 2008, three birds were found on Halfpipe South.

Sooty Grouse also frequent mountain slopes at lower elevation when open areas are present. During a birding expedition on Adder Mountain on 2 October 2016, a total of 10 birds were flushed from the ground in such habitat above 750 m (2,460 ft) elevation.

WHITE-TAILED PTARMIGAN
Lagopus leucura

STATUS: Uncommon resident at high elevation. Breeds.

Ptarmigan are grouse that inhabit treeless barrens, be they in the far north or at high elevation above the treeline in more southern latitudes. In winter they turn entirely white in order to become invisible against the snow. In summer, their plumage is designed to blend in with the rocks and low vegetation, which it does superbly. White-tailed Ptarmigan inhabit high elevations throughout much of interior British Columbia, the Yukon, and Alaska. There is a population on Vancouver Island that is isolated from the mainland. These are considered a separate subspecies with the name Vancouver Island White-tailed Ptarmigan (*L. l. saxatilis*).

The White-tailed Ptarmigan inhabits alpine regions such as Steamboat Mountain (Clayoquot Plateau), where this bird was found.

The breeding distribution of White-tailed Ptarmigan on Vancouver Island covers the central region of the island and historically has changed very little, ranging from Mount Brenton in the south to as far north as Tsitika Mountain.[29] They are also found in the west coast region on mountain peaks on both sides of Highway 4, north and northeast of Kennedy Lake. On a solo climb to the summit of Canoe Peak in the Mackenzie Range on 25 August 1973, I had my first memorable encounter with this species when I found a female with young at the edge of a snowfield. So fearless are these birds when it comes to interactions with humans that they sometimes allow one to approach within an arm's length. Fourteen years later, on 27 July 1987, I had a second encounter, this one on Steamboat Mountain on the Clayoquot Plateau. Like the first, this bird was entirely unafraid and was perfectly camouflaged against the grey rock. It was detected only because a hiking partner heard the "clacking of its feet" on the rocks while resting. Despite my having made a good number of climbs and seeing evidence of their presence in the form of scat, these were my only visual encounters with the species in the west coast region.

In 2008, the BC Conservation Corps, in partnership with the BC Ministry of Environment, conducted a survey in the west coast region between Sproat Lake and Kennedy Lake. The search team found 14 adults and 13 juveniles, and/or evidence of their presence at the following locations: Steamboat, Pogo, Adder, Klitsa, Half Pipe, Jack's Peak, 5040, Nahmint, Hall, Canoe, and Triple Peak.[30]

There are numerous other peaks and ranges in our west coast region high enough to potentially support this species, although its presence has not been confirmed at those locations.

Anyone searching for this bird without the aid of a helicopter will need a great deal of stamina and a very sharp eye. It is worth noting that during the breeding season this ptarmigan feeds on two plants: white mountain-heather (*Cassiope mertensiana*) and pink mountain-heather (*Phyllodoce empetriformis*). It also prefers to be close to pools of water, a snowfield, or both, in order to regulate body temperature during the warm summer. In winter, birds are said to move down into the subalpine Mountain Hemlock Zone and the adjacent upper montane forest. Because of its unique subspecies status and low population on Vancouver Island, the species is on the provincial Blue List.

The White-tailed Ptarmigan population has almost certainly been affected, for better or for worse, by the decrease in ice and snow in alpine areas of the west coast region over the past 40 years. On my excursion to the top of the Mackenzie Range in August 1973, I estimated the snowfield to be 15 to 20 feet deep. By the late 1980s, that same slope was entirely bare by late July due to the current warm trend.

ORDER GAVIIFORMES

Loons   *Family Gaviidae*

RED-THROATED LOON
Gavia stellata

STATUS: Uncommon in summer, fairly common in fall, winter, and spring. Breeds.

Loons belong to an ancient family of diving birds well adapted to catching fish. Scientists tell us they have a lineage going back 70 million years. They appear somewhat peculiar, having their legs placed well back near the transom, so to speak, a fact that makes them very efficient swimmers but awkward on land. They are superb divers, and in Britain they are known as divers rather than loons. There are four species of loons in British Columbia, three of which occur regularly on Vancouver Island's west coast.

In all plumages the Red-throated Loon may be distinguished from other loons by its small size and its slender, upturned bill, which it holds slightly aloft. It is also the shiest of the loons. Where other loons dive in response to boat traffic on marine waters, members of this species usually take wing far ahead of any advancing boat. Indeed, it is also the only loon capable of rising from the water with little effort. This fact makes it highly susceptible to disturbance by boat traffic.

Its breeding range extends across northern Eurasia, Greenland, and northern Canada, from Labrador to Alaska and coastal British Columbia. There are breeding records from many locations along the BC coast, particularly Haida Gwaii but also in our region. At least two pairs breed on Brooks Peninsula, on Menziesia and Ledum lakes, the most northerly location for the west coast of Vancouver Island.[13] On 23 July 1970, a pair was found nesting on a small mountain lake called Larry Lake, beside Highway 4, above Kennedy Lake. Since then, adults in breeding plumage have been observed there in other years. As recently as the summer of 2014, one and two birds were seen there on several occasions. Unlike other loons breeding in the province, the Red-throated Loon flies to the nearby ocean to obtain food for its young.[31] Therefore the presence of Red-throated Loons off Long Beach throughout the summer suggests that they probably breed on some of the other high-elevation lakes in the mountains. A bird observed in Sulphur Passage on 23 July 2000, and also on 26 July 2016, plus an adult in breeding plumage at Sydney Inlet on 26 July 2014, suggests that the species may nest nearby on one or more of the numerous upland lakes surrounding the Megin River. This species is known to commute between its lakeside nest site and the marine waters where it feeds.

Red-throated Loons may be seen in any month of the year, although in larger numbers in fall, winter, and spring, when they are found mostly in protected waters. An examination of more than 200 records since 1982 shows a barely discernible pattern of increasing numbers, beginning in September and decreasing in May, which is what one might expect. Some high numbers are: 25 birds on 19 December 1990, Tofino; 26 on 19 December 1996, Tofino; 36 on 13 January 2003, Tofino; 18 on 13 September 2012, south end of Long Beach; and 59 on 19 October 2013, in Wickaninnish Bay. The 59 were counted from three separate locations at Long Beach. Small numbers continue to be seen off Long Beach in June and July. Particularly interesting is a count of 21 birds at Cox Bay on 13 July 2012. Some were in breeding plumage and some were not, suggesting that this group comprised adults with young.

With the exception of the count at Cox Bay, the Tofino area counts cited previously were nearly all in Browning Passage, which often attracts higher numbers and where birds are prone to being disturbed by frequent boat traffic. As with other loons, this species moves to more sheltered waters during heavy seas.

Red-throated Loons occasionally exploit a niche into which other birds rarely venture – the waters inside the surf zone on sandy beaches, where they will pursue fishes in as little as a foot or two of water. Only Common Mergansers are also known to do this.

PACIFIC LOON
Gavia pacifica

STATUS: An abundant migrant in both spring and fall, common in summer. In winter, fairly common but sometimes hard to find.

Pacific Loons migrate through our region in very large numbers in spring. Seen here is a juvenile in winter.

This exceedingly handsome loon was formerly considered conspecific with the Arctic Loon, which is why you will not find it in older books. It breeds from southern Baffin Island and the western shores of Hudson Bay west to the Yukon, Alaska, and eastern Siberia. In British Columbia, it breeds in the far north of the province and has bred as far south as Embryo Lake at the south end of Takla Lake.[32]

Pacific Loons winter along the Pacific coast from Prince William Sound, Alaska, to Baja California, Mexico. They are then abundant in many places on the BC coast and formerly in Active Pass during the winter season, when hundreds could be seen from the ferry. On Vancouver Island's west coast, they are also present in winter but in much more modest numbers. They are abundant as migrants, however.

In spring they begin passing by our shores as early as March, and by late April the northward movement is well under way. Based on many counts conducted for half-hour periods at Incinerator Rock, several thousand birds may pass by per day during the peak period in May. On 4 May 2013, birds were passing by Long Beach at a rate of about 400 per hour, and on 7 May 2014, at a rate of 1,400 per hour. On 3 May 2016, birds passed by at 1,758 per hour. As late as 25 May in 2014, birds were recorded passing by at a rate of 750 birds per hour. It should be noted, however, that the rate can fluctuate considerably over any given day and throughout any given week. It is somewhat puzzling that on days with seemingly ideal flying conditions, few birds may be seen, while on days with a stiff headwind, many are recorded. It may be that on fair days birds are passing by far offshore.

Towards the end of May, numbers drop off, but smaller numbers continue passing by throughout most of June. A count made from Vargas Island on 11 June 1999 determined that birds were still passing by at a rate of 20 per hour. Observations made from Incinerator Rock at Long Beach show that in the second half of June there are gradually more birds on the water than are passing by. However, on 25 June 2012, of 25 birds seen, "most were flying north," and as late as 28 June in 2009 some birds were still flying north. By July, the migration is over.

About 190 km north of Long Beach, at-sea migration counts were conducted from Clerke Point on Brooks Peninsula between 14 May and 27 June 1973. A total of 47,081 Pacific Loons were counted. The day of heaviest migration was 21 May. The estimated net northward movement during the period was 153,900 in May and 25,800 in June, for a total of 179,700 Pacific Loons.[13]

Nonbreeding birds continue to be seen throughout July and August. Some high numbers are: 145 birds on 9 July 1983, Vargas Island; 39 on 6 July 2010, Long Beach; 208 on 11 July 2012, Long Beach; and 37 on 6 August 2009, Long Beach.

The beginning of the southward movement is somewhat unclear, probably because rough sea conditions make counting difficult on outside waters after September, but there does seem to be an increase by late September. By October there is a noticeable increase. A few counts are: 400 birds on 14 October 1983, Chesterman Beach; 400 on 27 October 2001, Father Charles Channel; and 230 on 4 October 2012, Long Beach. By November, numbers are higher still. Two examples are: 2,000 birds on 2 November 1983, on the water at Chesterman Beach; and 500 on 19 November 2011, Chesterman Beach.

Counts of 97 and 110 birds during the first week of December in 2009 may still be late migrants.

In 2014, I was surprised to see flights of birds headed in a southerly direction as late as 24 December. Thirty minutes of counting produced a total of 332 birds passing by. Sightings in January and February usually consist of 5 birds or less, although occasionally larger flocks are seen. On 11 February 2013, 24 birds were seen off Stubbs Island, and on 15 February 2013, 250 birds were seen off Long Beach.

The Pacific Loon population has undergone a rather dramatic increase of approximately 148% over the last 40 years. The global population was estimated at between 930,000 and 1,600,000 individuals in 2006.[33]

COMMON LOON
Gavia immer

STATUS: Common spring and fall migrant and common winter visitor. Fairly common in summer. Breeds.

With its image engraved on our one-dollar coin, this handsome bird is familiar to Canadians from coast to coast. Its haunting cry has come to represent the vast northern forests with their multitude of lakes. Indeed, with 95% of its world population breeding in this country, the Common Loon could reasonably be considered our bird. Its breeding range covers nearly all of Canada, except for the High Arctic. It breeds as well in Alaska, Greenland, and Iceland. In Britain, where Iceland birds winter, it is known as the Great Northern Diver. In North America, the species winters on the Atlantic coast from Newfoundland south to the Gulf of Mexico. On the Pacific coast, it winters from the Alaska Peninsula to central Mexico.

In British Columbia, Common Loons nest on lakes in most regions of the province. In late summer and in fall, most birds vacate the interior lakes for a winter spent on the coast. This is both to avoid freeze-over and to go where food is most abundant.[34] In our west coast region, Common Loons can be found year-round, although they are somewhat less common in summer. We know them primarily as migrants and winter visitors. Most commonly we see them either as single birds, in pairs, or in small groups. Very occasionally, Common Loons are reported in larger numbers. In 1978, *Birds of Pacific Rim National Park* mentioned a concentration of 61 birds at Toquart Bay in Barkley Sound on 18 June 1971, and 30+ birds near Vargas Island in September 1970.[1] A report of 100+ birds near Lennard Island on 15 May 1977 would almost certainly have involved Pacific Loons, and not this species. Pacific Loons often gather in large, tightly knit flocks, while Common Loons rarely, if ever, do. Among more than 725 records collected since 1980, the overwhelming majority consist of 5 birds or less. The largest count was 53 birds recorded on 10 August 2014, at Incinerator Rock, Long Beach, and these were spread over a large area.

During the summer months, when quiet waters prevail, Common Loons are frequently seen on outside waters, such as off Long Beach. Birds seen in June and July may represent nonbreeding birds, but probably also birds that nest on area lakes. When autumn storms blow in, resulting in heavy seas, Common Loons move to more sheltered waters in the sounds and inlets. In Clayoquot Sound, the locations most often frequented by Common Loons are places where there are large eelgrass beds, particularly those not exposed at high tide, such as near Indian Island in Grice Bay, Elbow Bank in Maurus Channel, Father Charles Channel, and the Tofino waterfront. In the Barkley Sound region, favoured areas include Toquart Bay and Pachena Bay. In waters around Brooks Peninsula, protected waters in Brooks Bay and Checleset Bay are used by Common Loons.[34]

Spring and autumn movements are difficult to ascertain, but likely parallel those elsewhere on the coast. According to a paper on Common Loons by Campbell et al. (2008) birds begin arriving on coastal and interior lakes from late March to mid-April, depending on the location.[34] The average arrival date in most locations is in fact the first half of April. Birds seen passing Long Beach in May are likely travelling to the far northern parts of the Common Loon's breeding range.

There is plenty of evidence (e.g., adults in summer) that Common Loons breed in our west coast region, although the only confirmed breeding records I could find were as follows: 27 July 1970, an adult and a flightless young seen on Sugsaw Lake, near Bamfield;[1] a one-week old young with two adults on Clayoquot Arm of Kennedy Lake on 19 June 1969, and a large young (same record) with one adult on 19 August 1969[35] (BCNRS); and two records at Lizard Lake near Port Renfrew on 20 May 1979 (nest on small islet with broken egg) and 18 May 1981 (one egg with two adults) (BCNRS). Most of the evidence consists of adult birds seen in summer on freshwater lakes and on sheltered marine waters near lakes. Birds have been seen in June on Nitinat Lake, Sarita Lake, Rosseau Lake, Kennedy Lake, Spire Lake, and Shelter Inlet in Clayoquot Sound. Birds seen at Shelter Inlet in summer are believed to nest at one or more of the many small upland lakes to the north of that inlet. An observation of two birds in Sulphur Passage near Shelter Inlet on 27 June 2000 is also noteworthy. On 29 June 2014, an adult accompanied by a full-sized juvenile was seen on Kennedy Lake, and again on 30 June of the following year. On that occasion, three other Common Loons were seen on the lake, and one flying overhead. Birds also make use of the slow-flowing lower Kennedy River in summer.

The fall migration runs from late August until November.

YELLOW-BILLED LOON
Gavia adamsii

STATUS: Rare visitor in fall, winter, and spring. Casual in summer.

The Yellow-billed Loon is a rare visitor to west coast waters, primarily in winter. This juvenile was found in Grice Bay.

This is the largest of our loons. Its breeding range extends across the northern tundra of Canada, west of Hudson Bay to northern and western Alaska, and large areas of northern Siberia. Asian birds winter in the Yellow Sea and the waters off Japan, as well as off Norway. North American birds winter primarily along the Gulf of Alaska, but they also venture south in small numbers to California and Baja California. In *The Birds of British Columbia*, the Yellow-billed Loon is considered an uncommon migrant and rare winter and summer visitor along the BC coast.[6] In Haida Gwaii, birds are not all that rare even in the summer months.

On the west coast of Vancouver Island, Yellow-billed Loons were recorded 6 times up to the end of 1974.[1] Since then, the species has been recorded 35 more times, with all but one sighting logged on the central west coast. Those 35 sightings likely involved 29 different individuals. The species occurs primarily from October to the end of April, although birds have been recorded in every month of the year except February. Its absence in February can be explained by the lack of observers on the water at that time of year. On several occasions, birds have been seen in summer in full breeding plumage. The hundreds of kilometres of coastline in our region are not well travelled in summer, let alone in the winter months. It therefore seems likely that Yellow-billed Loons are present in the west coast region in most winters in small numbers. In 2016, 4 separate individuals were recorded on the central west coast.

The global population is estimated at between 16,000 and 32,000 individuals, with 3,000 to 4,000 in Alaska and up to 20,000 in Canada.[33]

ORDER PODICIPEDIFORMES

Grebes *Family Podicipedidae*

PIED-BILLED GREBE
Podilymbus podiceps
STATUS: Uncommon resident. Breeds.

Like loons, grebes are superbly adapted to the aquatic environment, with legs placed well back on the body, which aids in underwater propulsion. Unlike loons, grebes have flat, lobed toes rather than webbed feet, which serve as paddles in the water and, in flight, compensate for the absence of a tail.

During the breeding season, this species is widely distributed in North America, nesting throughout the United States, much of the Prairie provinces and Ontario, and east to Nova Scotia. In British Columbia, Pied-billed Grebes nest in the southern half of the province, east of the Coast Mountains, including Vancouver Island, as well as in the Peace River region. They breed on permanent ponds, marshes, shallow lakes, and the backwaters of slow-flowing rivers, particularly if such waters have an abundance of aquatic plants. This species has the unusual ability to sink beneath the surface with just its head above the water like a periscope.

In our region, the species is known to breed at three locations, all on the central coast (BCNRS).[36] These include five young, about a week old, swimming

Pied-billed Grebes nest on small, shallow lakes and depart for marine waters after breeding. Shown here is a bird in winter garb.

with an adult on Swan Lake near the junction of Highway 4, on Kennedy Lake on 5 July 1972; a nearly full-grown young raised on a bog near the head of Lemmens Inlet on 31 August 2004; and an adult incubating on a nest on a small lake near the Kennedy River on 28 July 2001. On a survey of the lower Kennedy River on 5 July 2013, birds were heard at three separate locations, suggesting the presence of at least three breeding pairs. It seems likely that the species is more widespread than is currently recognized, as there are other small bodies of fresh water scattered along the coast that have never been surveyed. When birds are present during the breeding season, they may be located by their loud vocalizations, aptly described by David Sibley as a "throaty bark."[37]

Adults brood their chicks for about three weeks and may feed them for up to another six weeks before they become independent. Soon after, adults leave the nest site.[38] At Swan Lake in 2010, young were already left to fend for themselves on 3 August, when they were still far from being able to fly. The young were last seen on 22 August. Upon leaving the breeding area, birds head for the marine environment, where they prefer the sheltered waters of coves and inlets, usually near the shore. Records of birds on salt water range from 25 September to 25 March, and they are usually seen as singles or in pairs. There are also several records of birds on a freshwater pond at the Long Beach Airport from early September to late October.

Numbers present in the region can vary considerably from year to year. In 2013, not a single bird could be found on marine waters during fall, winter, and spring. Two years later, on 9 November, no fewer than five birds were found at Grice Bay.

HORNED GREBE
Podiceps auritus

STATUS: Common spring and fall migrant and winter visitor. Casual in summer.

This small grebe breeds from northern Ontario west throughout the Prairie provinces, the Northwest Territories, the Yukon, Alaska, and interior British Columbia. In the United States, it breeds in the Dakotas and northern Montana. It winters along the Atlantic coast from Nova Scotia south to Florida and the Gulf States, and along the Pacific Coast from the Alaska Peninsula to central Baja California. In British Columbia, the species breeds primarily in the south-central interior, the Peace River region, and scattered locations in northern parts of the province. A spotty distribution elsewhere in the province suggests that its breeding range may include most of the province east of the Coast Mountains. *The Birds of British Columbia* considers it common to very common as a migrant throughout the province, and common to very common as a winter visitor on the coast.[6]

In the west coast region, we see Horned Grebes almost solely as migrants and winter visitors, usually as single birds, pairs, or small groups. They begin arriving in September, though in some years the first birds are seen in late August. The earliest fall arrival ever recorded was a single bird seen on 14 August 2017, from Incinerator Rock. Other early arrivals occurred on 19 August 1971 at Logan Creek and 20 August in 1972 at Port San Juan.[1] There have been several other August records since then. Maximum numbers are reached by late October or early November. At Grice Bay, numbers between 10 and 25 are commonly seen, spread out over a large area. On 3 November 2011, a maximum of 62 were counted there. An even larger number was recorded in the waters surrounding Stubbs Island on 23 October 2011, when 69 birds were tallied.

The largest numbers of all, surprisingly, come from the open ocean as much as a kilometre or two off Long Beach. I say "surprisingly" because sea conditions are often severe in winter and I had been under the impression that the species prefers protected waters. Horned Grebes were first noted off Long Beach on 10 December 2011, when a tightly knit flock of 70 birds was observed from Incinerator Rock using a spotting scope. On 30 December 2012, two flocks added up to 125 birds in total. Even larger numbers were recorded in 2013, when an estimated 250 birds were seen off Green Point on 17 February, and 245 were counted there on 10 November. The largest count yet was made on 3 December 2014, during a period of unusually placid seas when three large flocks, as well as a number of smaller ones, totalled 550 birds. When sea conditions are rough, these birds are clustered together in tightly knit flocks, but when sea conditions are calm they tend to disperse over a larger area. On this occasion, most birds remained in tightly knit flocks.

In late March and April, birds begin to moult into their breeding plumage. It is difficult to determine just how early birds begin to depart for their breeding territories, but numbers decline noticeably during the month of April. By the end of the month, few are left. The latest spring dates are 1 May 2011, with 24 birds off Long Beach, and 8 May 2010, when a single bird was seen at Stubbs Island, Tofino. There is one later date. Hatler mentioned that on 9 May 1972 he observed 16 birds at Turtle Island in Barkley Sound.[1]

Summer sightings are rare. Of more than 500 records since 1980, only 1 is in June and 2 are in July. In 1978, on the other hand, *Birds of Pacific Rim National Park* listed 12 records for June and 2 for July.[1] Records in June and early July are undoubtedly nonbreeding birds.

RED-NECKED GREBE
Podiceps grisegena

STATUS: Common spring and fall migrant. Common in winter, rare in summer.

The Red-necked Grebe in breeding plumage is a striking bird. However, for most of its stay on our coast, the red neck is absent. While similar in profile to the Horned Grebe, it can be readily distinguished from it, even at a great distance, by its larger size and comparatively robust bill. Its breeding range extends from the boreal forest region of western Quebec through Ontario north of the Great Lakes, through Minnesota and North Dakota, and through the Prairie provinces to British Columbia, the Yukon, and Alaska. In British Columbia, it breeds in much of the interior of the province, except for the north-central region. There is one breeding record for Vancouver Island, two half-grown young on Cowichan Lake on 14 August 1935.[39] We normally see Red-necked Grebes only as a spring and fall migrant and winter visitor. It is considered a common migrant and winter visitor on the BC coast.

On Vancouver Island's west coast, Red-necked Grebes have been seen in every month of the year, though rarely in June and July. The very first birds begin arriving from the breeding grounds during the first week of August or shortly thereafter. In 2014, the first arrival was in fact seen on 29 July, and in 2016, 5 birds were seen on 31 July. Both these records are unusually early. In late summer, birds are still in breeding dress. Numbers tend to stay small in August, but increase rapidly in the second half of September as migrants pass through. These birds clearly prefer protected waters for feeding, though they are sometimes seen in numbers off the exposed coast, particularly during the migration period or when waters are calm. On 5 May 2013, 47 birds were seen off Incinerator Rock, Long Beach. Occasionally 2 or 3 birds are seen there in winter, braving rougher waters.

Red-necked Grebes are not usually seen in large flocks, but may converge on an area, creating a loosely knit aggregation of birds. Some of the largest counts have been made in late September and early October, with 50 birds seen on 21 September 1983 off Chesterman Beach; 90 on 7 October 1998 at Stubbs Island; 43 on 27 September 2008 at Stubbs Island; and 83 on 30 September 2012 on Father Charles Channel (east of Vargas Island).

After the main migration period has passed, numbers stabilize at somewhat lower levels for the rest of the winter period, although occasionally up to 40 and 50 birds have been counted. At Ucluelet, 34 birds were seen on 3 January 1976, and 35 birds at Amphitrite Point on 16 February 2010.

By late March, birds are beginning to moult into their breeding plumage once again and we begin to see birds with red necks. Particularly close monitoring of birds in the spring of 2012 revealed an increase in numbers in April, presumably due to migrants arriving from further south. Numbers dropped off abruptly during the last week of the month, and by early May only a few scattered individuals remained.

EARED GREBE
Podiceps nigricollis

STATUS: Casual vagrant in summer, fall, and winter.

Eared Grebes breed throughout much of the western United States, except for the most southern areas and the western halves of the coastal states. In Canada, they breed from southern Manitoba to British Columbia. In British Columbia, Eared Grebes breed in the southern half of the province east of the Coast

Mountains and in the Peace River region. The species is considered a rare to fairly common migrant and winter resident in the coastal waters of the Salish Sea and Strait of Juan de Fuca.[6]

On the west coast, with four "unconfirmed" reports, occurrence was considered hypothetical by Hatler et al. in *Birds of Pacific Rim National Park*.[1] Such a cautious approach is sensible, given that Horned Grebes are sometimes mistakenly identified as this species. Indeed, given what we now know, some doubt is thrown on a record from our region going back to 4 May 1931, when five birds were reported at Tofino. By this time of year, however, birds should be in breeding plumage, making misidentification unlikely. At least one other record mentioned in *Birds of Pacific Rim National Park* has a high chance of being valid. In January 1974, a bird was reported from Jordan River, a location that is close to the south end of the island, where birds are somewhat more common.

At this writing, 11 additional records have been accepted for this publication. The first confirmed sighting of an Eared Grebe occurred in 1996, when from 2 to 26 January an individual was seen repeatedly near Tofino. Other sightings are as follows: 25 September 2000, Ucluelet – 1; 17 September 2001, Stubbs Island, Tofino – 1; 19 January 2002, Jordan River – 1; 27 January 2007, Grice Bay – 2; 11 October 2008, Port San Juan – 1; 1 to 15 January 2010, Grice Bay – 1; 25 February 2010, Grice Bay – 1; 18 January to 13 March 2011, Grice Bay – 1; 25 February 2015, Amphitrite Point, Ucluelet – 2; and 22 July to 10 August 2015, south end of Long Beach – 1 in breeding plumage.

Note that most sightings have occurred in January and February. The summer sightings recorded in 2015 likely involved a very early southbound migrant. The fact that four of our records are from Grice Bay is also interesting, as this location is favoured by the other four species of grebes. On two occasions, five of the six species of grebes that occur in British Columbia were recorded from the Grice Bay boat launch during a single count.

WESTERN GREBE
Aechmorphorus occidentalis

STATUS: Uncommon to locally common migrant and winter visitor. Rare in summer.

The word "elegant" readily comes to mind when attempting to describe this grebe, with its swanlike neck and contrasting pattern of white and dark. This combination makes the bird easy to identify even at a great distance. This species breeds throughout much of the western United States, from Minnesota to California, north to southeastern Oregon and eastern Washington. A breeding population also exists in Mexico. In Canada it breeds in large areas of the Prairie provinces west to northern Alberta and British Columbia. In British Columbia, it breeds at a few locations on shallow lakes in the southern interior. The number of breeding pairs is said to be under 200. However, up to 100,000 Western Grebes have wintered on the BC coast, particularly in southern areas of the Salish Sea, where they are sometimes seen in rafts of thousands. These birds arrive not only from the BC interior but also from the Prairie provinces and the northwestern United States.[40]

In our west coast region, Western Grebes are seen in small to moderate numbers from September to early May, when they seem to prefer deepwater inlets. Such habitats are rarely surveyed and there may be pockets of significant aggregations distributed along the west coast. For example, 100 birds were estimated in Klaskish Inlet on 12 March 1976.[13] Their distribution in Barkley Sound and Clayoquot Sound is not well known, as these waters are not often travelled during the winter months. Records from accessible areas near Tofino suggest that arrival and departure dates for this species are similar to those of the Red-necked Grebe, though perhaps somewhat later than the latter. Earliest arrival dates were 16 August in 2002, 18 August in 2012, and 19 August in 2014. Numbers increase gradually through September, October, and November. In April they begin to decline, and by the end of the month the birds are largely gone, though a few may linger into May.

Summer records are few. I have only 1 for June and 2 for July, both off Long Beach. *Birds of Pacific Rim National Park,* on the other hand, lists 16 records for June and 12 for July.[1] As many as 140 birds were seen off Baeria Rocks in Barkley Sound in June 1970, and 44 birds on 22 June 1972. These were almost certainly nonbreeders. Fewer than 10 Western Grebes spend the summer off Brooks Peninsula.[13]

The largest numbers recorded on the west coast that I know of were 1,705 birds at Hesquiat Harbour on 5 October 1972[6] and 3,000 birds in Barkley Sound on 5 March 1976. The largest numbers recorded in Clayoquot Sound in later years are as follows: 55 birds at Tofino on 29 December 1987; 290 at Tranquil Inlet on 28 April 1989; 65 at Grice Bay on 29 January 1995; and 40 at that location on 29 December 1998. Of more than 150 personal records from the central west coast between 1998 and 2016, only two sightings involved more than 20 birds, suggesting that a significant decline has occurred. Those two exceptions involved 22 birds on 19 January 2013 and 58 birds off the south end of Long Beach on 19 October 2013.

No surveys have been conducted in recent years in remote areas of Tofino Inlet where large flocks used to reside, such as Fortune Channel and Tranquil Inlet. However, a flock of 500 birds was reported wintering at the north end of Millar Channel during the winter of 2016/17, by Arthur Ahier. The flock's size may have reached 700 birds, but was down to 76 individuals by 8 April. In addition, tour-boat operator Michael Mullin reported 100 or more birds off Rafael Point, Flores Island, on 5 February 2015, and again on 8 April.

There is concern about this species, which has declined locally in the Salish Sea by 95% since 1975. Off coastal California, on the other hand, there was an increase of 300%, indicating that the winter range has shifted south to adapt to food availability. Based on Audubon Christmas Bird Count data, the population in North America has declined overall by 52%.[41]

In Barkley Sound in recent years, there have been several counts of 100 birds or more. At the McKenzie Anchorage, northwest of Bamfield, 365 birds were tallied by Anne Stewart on 6 March 2011, and 122 birds on 11 January 2012. To the south, at Port San Juan, 100 birds were reported by Jeremy Kimm on 26 October 2013. Nevertheless, these numbers are a far cry from the 3,000 birds reported in 1976.

In the Clayoquot Sound region, given the inaccessibility of much of the coast, it may well be that large flocks are present elsewhere but are just not being seen.

CLARK'S GREBE
Aechmophorus clarkii
STATUS: Casual vagrant in spring and summer.

Clark's Grebe was considered a species distinct from the Western Grebe as early as 1858. However, after the early 1880s, based on the scientific opinion of the time, it was considered merely a pale morph of that species. A century later, in 1985, its status as a separate species was finally restored. The breeding range of the Clark's Grebe in the United States and Mexico covers much of the same region as the previous species, though it does not extend north of Wyoming and Oregon except in eastern Washington. Only there does its breeding range extend to the Canadian border. In British Columbia, it has nested only at Salmon Arm, though there have been confirmed sightings at 35 locations in the province between 1981 and 2009.[6] The species winters in California, Arizona, and Mexico.

Since 1981 there have been 14 confirmed records of the Clark's Grebe on Vancouver Island, including a bird photographed in Port Alberni on 8 April 1988 (BC Photo 1229).[42] In our west coast region, there have been 6 reports since 1990. Given the similarity of this species to the Western Grebe in winter, and the possibility of hybrids, only records supported with photo-documentation have been accepted here. On 16-18 August 2007, a bird was seen and photographed at Port Renfrew by Roger Taylor for a first verified record for our region. Eight months earlier, on 27 December 2006, a bird believed to be a Clark's × Western Grebe hybrid was seen in Tofino harbour by several observers.

ORDER PROCELLARIIFORMES

Albatrosses Family Diomedeidae

LAYSAN ALBATROSS
Phoebastria immutabilis

STATUS: Rare visitor in late winter, spring, and fall. No records in April, July, and November.

This distinctive albatross with its white body and dark mantle derives its name from the place where it was first discovered, a small island located some 1,750 km northwest of the big island of Hawaii. The vast majority of the population breeds here in the northwestern Hawaiian Islands, but there is also a small colony off Mexico and another off Japan. Its population is currently estimated at 1.18 million birds,[43] with 457,451 breeding pairs on the three islands of the Midway Atoll in 2016.[43] As with many other seabirds, Laysan Albatrosses disperse across the northern Pacific Ocean after breeding.

This species was not recorded in Canadian waters until September 1968, when one was reported at La Perouse Bank off Vancouver Island's west coast.[45] A second bird was reported on 17 August 1970, 40 km off Ucluelet.[6] However, without a specimen or a photograph, neither of these records would likely have been accepted. The first proven Canadian record occurred on 24 February 1971, when a bird was photographed by R. Wayne Campbell 40 km west of Estevan Point (BC Photo 149).[6] *Birds of Pacific Rim National Park* (1978) listed only this one record for our waters, and considered it a "very rare winter visitor."[1]

Volume 1 of *The Birds of British Columbia* (1990) considered it a "very rare vagrant," and listed 11 records up to the end of 1986 for our west coast region, two of them as specimens.[6] One of these was brought ashore in March 1986 after being caught on a halibut longline 16 km west of Hotsprings Cove. The person in possession of this bird, the late Norma Baillie, donated it to the Royal BC Museum upon learning of its significance.

Since 1986, sightings of the Laysan Albatross have increased. At this writing, there have been at least 50 sightings in offshore waters within the 100 km limit, recorded in all months of the year except for April, July, and November. Out of 65 marine bird and mammal surveys conducted by Strawberry Island Research out of Tofino to a distance of 35 NM offshore, this species was encountered seven times. However, more than one bird was recorded on three of those occasions. On 5 March 1998, two birds were seen, and on 19 October 1999, an astonishing total of nine birds were recorded on a single trip, with eight of the birds congregating near a dragger. Just four months later, on 12 February 2000, five birds were recorded. There is one nearshore occurrence for the west coast. Gale-force winds on 29 October 1973 may have forced a bird into Brooks Bay, north of Brooks Peninsula, the following day.[13]

Not surprisingly, many sightings go unreported. But ask an offshore fisherman if he has seen a white albatross with dark wings, and chances are he will answer in the affirmative. Ucluelet fisherman Mike Tyne reported seeing a Laysan Albatross 25 mi southwest of Ucluelet on 15 August 2008, while he was skipper on the fishing vessel *FV Royal Mariner*. Likewise, former commercial fisherman Ralph Crombie remembers seeing this bird occasionally during his years of fishing.

There have also been sightings on organized pelagic birding trips. Most sightings involved single birds, but two birds were seen off Tofino on both 11 and 14 September 2013, three birds were seen off Tofino on 16 September 2016, and four birds on 8 May 2017. One of the two birds recorded in September 2013 was a banded bird that was tracked back to the banding location through the band number. It turned out that this bird had been hatched earlier that year on Guadalupe Island, off the coast of Mexico, and banded four months later, on 10 May. Perhaps birds of Mexican origin account for the increase in sightings off our shores. The Guadalupe Island colony became established only in 1986 and now has 400 or more birds.

The following is a breakdown of 33 occurrences in our west coast waters by month: January – 1, February – 2, March – 3, April – 0, May – 2, June – 5, July – 0, August – 4, September – 10, October – 5, November – 0, December – 1. Keep in mind that observers tend to be on the water from May to October, and that few venture out during the winter months. In contrast to these figures, Kenyon et al. reported that further offshore this species was seen most often during the month of February. Closer to shore, results were somewhat different. Within the 100 km limit, Kenyon listed 29 records in total, with 9 of those in winter, 19 in spring, and 1 in summer.[46]

Threats to this species are many. Laysan Albatrosses were killed in large numbers for their eggs and feathers in the late 1800s and early 1900s. Although they have gradually rebounded, they have not reached historical levels of abundance. Between 1978 and 1992, thousands died due to driftnet fishing, until it was banned in 1993. In 1990 alone, 17,500 are believed to have perished due to this practice. Longlining also took its toll, with an estimated 5,000 to 18,000 birds killed annually. That number has since decreased due to preventive measures.[47]

In 2011, the Japanese tsunami also took its toll, killing an estimated 110,000 Laysan Albatross chicks and 2,000 adults on Midway Atoll. Other threats remain. The most serious may be ocean warming and acidification, followed by the ingestion of plastic by chicks. Many young currently die because of this. It also remains to be seen what effect the radioactive water leaking into the Pacific Ocean from the Fukushima meltdowns will have on marine life.

On the positive side, these birds are closely monitored and protected on their Hawaiian breeding grounds, and improved fishing methods have reduced the death toll. Some progress has been made. One of this bird's great strengths is its remarkable longevity. One Laysan Albatross female nesting on Midway is known to be at least 62 years old, and was still producing chicks in February 2013.

BLACK-FOOTED ALBATROSS
Phoebastria nigripes

STATUS: Uncommon to common in offshore waters from March to November. Rare in winter.

This is one of three albatrosses that roam the North Pacific Ocean, and of the three it is by far the most common in Canadian coastal waters. It breeds in 14 locations, from the northwestern Hawaiian Islands to several islands off Japan and islands off Mexico, primarily Guadalupe. The Hawaiian Islands are by far the most important, with 97.5% of the population breeding there, particularly on Midway Atoll, with 24,000 breeding pairs, and Laysan Island, with

The Black-footed Albatross is the most common albatross over offshore waters, with occasional counts of 50 or more birds.

21,000 pairs.[5] After breeding, and while reaching sexual maturity for four years, birds disperse to roam the ocean for food, particularly the northeastern Pacific and off North American shores. It was determined from an analysis of stomach contents that the diet contained oil (10%), eggs of flying fishes (50%), squid (32%), crustaceans (5%), and some indigestible material that included plastics.[48]

Black-footed Albatrosses have been recorded in our offshore waters in all months of the year. They begin arriving in early spring. The earliest record we have is 10 March in 1994, when 18 birds were counted offshore from Tofino. Sightings become more frequent as the season progresses. Most sightings are of single birds passing by. Occasionally, small flocks may be found sitting on the water during calm weather. The largest congregations occur around fishing boats, particularly draggers, where these birds scavenge offal. Concentrations of 50 birds or more have been recorded offshore from Tofino in June, July, September, and October. Sporadically, small numbers venture into large open bays along the coast. On 7 September 1973, the late Pat Martin saw three birds in Brooks Bay.[13]

Martin and Myres (1969) stated that numbers increase as the summer progresses into autumn.[49] However, data collected on 65 offshore bird and mammal surveys out of Tofino by Strawberry Island Research shows an increase initially and then a decline late in July and August. Larger numbers are again seen in September and October. Maximum numbers recorded on a single day during the following months are as follows: 18 birds in March, 40 in April, 27 in May, 80 in June, 50 in July, 15 in August, 21 in September, and 60 in October. These totals are much higher than recorded during six pelagic day trips (three in May and three in September) 50 mi off Tofino in 1969 and 1970. From 1 to 16 albatrosses were seen on five trips.[49] It is worth keeping in mind that a major factor in finding high numbers of birds is the presence or absence of a fishing boat along the route, and that food is patchily distributed in the ocean environment, both of which vary considerably from year to year.

The Black-footed Albatross was seen on 52 of the 61 fully completed pelagic bird and mammal surveys out of Tofino. Months in which no birds were seen were most likely to be in the period from January to the end of June. Of 4 surveys conducted in February, only 1 found a bird. Somewhat surprisingly, of 8 surveys conducted in June, 2 produced no birds, 1 found a single bird, and 1 found 50 birds. One June survey found 50 birds.

The highest numbers have been reported on pelagic birding trips off Tofino, although I am in no position to vouch for the accuracy of the estimates. On 20 September 2014, 65 birds were reported; on 14 September 2013, 130 birds; and on 12 September 2010, 300 birds. A whopping 600 birds were estimated on 8 May 2017.

By November, numbers have decreased, although we do have a record of 12 birds as late as 7 November in 1998. After that, only single birds have been recorded. Lone birds were seen on 20 December 1998, on 24 December 1999, on 22 January 2000, and on 12 February 2000, all off the central coast. This clearly indicates that a few birds linger through the winter. *The Birds of British Columbia* listed only three winter records for the province.[6]

The Black-footed Albatross faces a number of human-based threats. It first suffered large population declines in the 19th and early 20th centuries due to feather and egg collecting. When that practice ended and breeding colonies were protected, numbers rebounded. In the late 20th century, a new threat was posed by driftnet fisheries, which caused the deaths of large numbers of birds until they were outlawed. No sooner was one threat eliminated than another arose, this time in the form of longline fishing. In 2003, it was estimated that 2,000 birds were caught annually in the US-based fishery and 6,000 in the Japanese/Taiwanese fisheries.[50] By using seabird bycatch prevention measures, the toll in the US fishery has been greatly reduced. Nevertheless, based on mortality from the longline fleets, and in the absence of better fishing methods, the population is projected to decline by 60% over a period of three generations. The population estimate from three major nesting colonies is 64,500 breeding pairs.[51] Nonbreeding birds are not included.

SHORT-TAILED ALBATROSS
Phoebastria albatrus
STATUS: Casual visitor in offshore waters.

This handsome seabird was one of three albatross species found regularly off our shores in the past. That they were once abundant is supported by the fact that large numbers of their bones have turned up in native middens from California to the Aleutians, including at the village of Yuquot on our west coast.[6]

This species nested on 12 islands off the coast of Japan and Taiwan but was intensely hunted in the late 19th century for the feather trade. With the population decimated by the 1930s, the species was finally protected in 1933. For years there were no nests to be found, and by 1949 the Short-tailed Albatross was believed to be extinct.

Miraculously, that "extinction" was short-lived, for in 1951 the species was rediscovered. An estimated 50 juveniles had survived far out at sea, and when they matured they returned to the island of Tori-shima to nest. The first egg was laid in 1954. By 1980 they had increased to nearly 100 pairs, and by 2014 to 609 pairs.[52] Because other islands had by now also been recolonized, the global population was estimated at 4,354 individuals. The prognosis for this species therefore seems good, even if its genetic diversity was greatly reduced.

Postbreeding, Short-tailed Albatrosses roam widely over the North Pacific Ocean, particularly off the Aleutian Islands. The first specimen taken off the west coast of North America was collected in Washington waters in 1854 or 1855. An adult collected near Victoria by J. Hepburn in May 1862 represents the first confirmed record for British Columbia and for Canada. This specimen is found in the University Museum of Zoology, Cambridge, UK.[52] In the years between 1862 and 1896, there were 14 sightings involving 20 individuals, all of them in the Strait of Juan de Fuca region.[52] However, there is a complete absence of records from British Columbia waters in the years from 1907 to 1940, a reflection of the species' decimation in its breeding range. It is highly probable that it was sporadic in occurrence in our region well before 1907, probably by the mid-1890s at the latest.

The first confirmed sighting of a Short-tailed Albatross in BC waters since 1907 occurred on 11 June 1960, when an immature was photographed 64 km west of Vancouver Island by G. Clifford Carl.[6] According to Kenyon et al. (2009), there have been 30 sightings within the Canadian 200 NM exclusive economic zone (EEZ) off our shores, all but one since 1996.[46] Eight of those were off

Vancouver Island within the 100 km limit adopted for this book. The species was recorded in all months of the year except December (few surveys were conducted during that month), and birds showed a distinct preference for feeding over the continental shelf break.[46] Additionally, a radio-tagged individual was tracked in our west coast offshore waters from 11 to 19 November 2003,[53] and another from 12 September to 1 November 2006. Radio tracking has revealed that birds travelling to North American waters are likely to be males or juveniles. Females remain in the western Pacific.

The three most recent sightings are as follows. On 8 March 2011, Barrie Hotchkiss photographed a bird 20 km off Ucluelet,[54] and on 13 May 2017, two immatures were photographed off Tofino from the fishing vessel *FV Nordic Pearl* by Lindsay Dealy. This was followed by a sighting on 1 June, when a single immature was seen 56 km off Tofino by numerous observers on a birding excursion.

Shearwaters and Petrels *Family Procellariidae*

NORTHERN FULMAR
Fulmarus glacialis

STATUS: Uncommon in spring, common in summer and fall in offshore waters.

With a population of 15 to 30 million birds, this is one of the most common seabirds in the world. It is distributed over marine waters throughout most of the Northern Hemisphere, and it breeds at numerous locations. In the Pacific Ocean, it breeds in the Aleutians and on islands in the Bering Sea. In British Columbia, a few birds nested or attempted to nest off Vancouver Island's west coast at Triangle Island in June 1976. The species winters in more southern waters.[54]

In the west coast region, Northern Fulmars may be seen in offshore waters from March to the end of November. The earliest record I could find occurred on 10 March (1994), when 5 birds were seen. There is also a record of 12 birds seen on 25 March 1946 at La Perouse Bank.[54] Numbers tend to be small in spring but increase during the summer. In waters offshore from Tofino in 2002, 20 birds were recorded on 21 June, 50 birds on 16 July, and 65 birds on 15 August. Much larger numbers have been recorded elsewhere in August. On 9 August

Most Northern Fulmars in the eastern Pacific are dark morph birds, such as this one, with light birds occurring as a minority.

1970, 500 birds were reported over Barkley Canyon, and on 22 August 2009, 1,500 birds were reported at the Swiftsure Bank on a pelagic trip.[26]

The largest numbers have been reported near the end of August and in September. Figures of 2,000 or more were reported on 9 September 1983, 12 September 2010, and 14 September 2013. The largest number yet reported occurred on 28 August 1985, on a pelagic trip out of Bamfield, with an estimate of 10,000 birds.[26] More modest numbers are seen through October and sometimes into November.

Most of our November records come from Amphitrite Point, where in 2009 birds were first seen from shore on the fifth of the month, though no numbers were given. On 20 November, 150 birds were seen, and on 26 November, 27 birds. Two years later, on 8 November, 300 birds were reported from the same location. Foul weather and heavy seas appear to be factors in bringing birds so close to shore.

Birds have also been seen at Long Beach on rare occasions. In November 2003, a half-dozen birds were picked up in weakened condition on the southern part of the beach during a time of heavy seas; likewise on 18 October 2016, when three birds were found. It appears these birds cannot find adequate food when the ocean is in turmoil. Aside from the sightings from Amphitrite Point and Long Beach mentioned above, Northern Fulmars are rarely seen from shore. However, Don Cecile once saw many birds passing by Cape Scott, and there is a record of three birds in Esperanza Inlet on 8 June 2012.

There are three plumage variations: a light morph, one that is all dark, and an intermediate. In the eastern Pacific, most birds are dark, though some light and intermediate birds are seen as well.

MURPHY'S PETREL
Pterodroma ultima

STATUS: Casual in pelagic waters, particularly further offshore.

This gadfly petrel was first described in 1949 by seabird biologist Robert Murphy. It nests on rocky islets around South Pacific Islands. After the breeding season, it disperses north and east over the Pacific Ocean. Murphy's Petrels were first spotted off the west coast of the United States in 1981, and the first record for the waters off the state of Washington occurred on 25 April 1992.[55] Many more sightings have been made since then, and at times it appears that this species is far from being rare. In May 2009, for example, 33 birds were reported on a pelagic cruise off the Oregon coast; in the following year, 46 birds were reported on another trip. On a cruise from San Diego to Vancouver in early May 2015, birders spotted a total of 123 Murphy's Petrels in American waters.[56]

In BC waters, this species has been somewhat more elusive. Although birds had periodically been reported very far offshore by seabird researchers, no sightings were supported by photographic evidence. That changed in 2014 when Paul Lehman and Bruce Rideout saw and photographed a bird 258 km southwest of Tofino. This sighting was subsequently accepted by the BC Bird Record Committee as the first substantiated occurrence for the province. This sighting was well outside the 100 km limit used in this book, but there have been at least two records in recent years of birds well within the 100 km limit. On 20 August 2010, a Murphy's Petrel was reported 16.5 km (9 NM) off Triangle Island by Russel Cannings, and on 4 April 2014, a bird was reported 29 km (18 mi) west of Cape Cook by Oscar Camino.

Given the frequency of sightings off the American coast,[57] and given the fact that birds are also reported off our shores, even if mostly outside the 100 km limit, it is evident that Murphy's Petrels are not "accidental" and will be seen here again. It is therefore considered as a casual species in our region.

MOTTLED PETREL
Pterodroma inexpectata
STATUS: Casual transient in pelagic waters in all months. More likely in winter and spring.

The Mottled Petrel, formerly known as Scaled Petrel, is a distinctively marked seabird belonging to the family of gadfly petrels. Currently there are 35 species worldwide, some of which are under taxonomic review. Mottled Petrels breed on islands off New Zealand, and after the breeding season disperse north over the Pacific Ocean, including the waters off North America and the Aleutian Islands. Aside from when they return to their breeding colonies, these birds rarely stray anywhere near land.

The first known sighting in British Columbia occurred in the waters of our west coast region on 24 February 1971, when a bird was found on board the ship MV *CNAV Endeavour* 24 km off Flores Island.[45] The bird was photographed and released. Fifteen years later, on 16 June 1986, a second bird was seen 19 km southwest of Flores Island.[6] There are also records of birds much further from shore, beyond the 100 km limit. Three of those sightings fall between late February and late April, and the fourth occurred in June.

There have been at least eight additional sightings in our offshore waters within the 100 km limit. Kenyon et al. recorded the species on five occasions, all of them beyond the continental shelf break in winter.[46] Ryan Merrill and John Mills recorded a bird 26.5 km (14.3 NM) off Carmanah Point on 21 February 2012. Ten days later, on 3 March, a bird was seen and photographed 53.7 km (29 NM) off Carmanah Point. Another was found 75 km (40 NM) off Carmanah Point. Also that day, the same observers saw three additional birds in nearby Washington waters.[58]

Given the fact that few birders engage in pelagic birding in February and March, these last observations raise the tantalizing possibility that this species visits our west coast waters considerably more often than records indicate. Although this species rarely approaches land, as mentioned earlier, it is worth noting that in Washington birds were reliably observed from land on two occasions. In late February 1976, a single bird was seen from a jetty at Ocean Shores, and in late November 2002, during severe weather, numerous Mottled Petrels were observed from the same location.[59]

PINK-FOOTED SHEARWATER
Ardenna creatopus
STATUS: Rare spring migrant, common in summer and fall.

The Pink-footed Shearwater is the largest of the region's shearwaters and is usually common in summer and fall.

This white-bellied shearwater breeds in the southeastern Pacific Ocean, on islands off the coast of Chile. Compared with the Sooty Shearwater, its population is not large, with an estimated 56,000 breeding pairs.[60] After the breeding season, which runs from late October to April or May, Pink-footed Shearwaters leave the breeding colonies and wing their way to the North Pacific Ocean and British Columbia.

Unlike Sooty Shearwaters, this species is rarely seen from land, although there is a littoral record of 6 birds with a large flock of Sooty Shearwaters near Solander Island on 27 August 1967.[13] Travel 15 or 20 km out to sea, however, and they soon begin to appear. In the waters off Vancouver Island, the earliest records are in late April and May, and usually involve sightings of a single bird. An exception occurred on a pelagic birding trip out of Tofino on 8 May 2017, when a remarkable 200 birds were reported near fishing vessels. Birds have been recorded as early as late April. In 1940, a bird was recorded as early as 28 April off Kyuquot, and in 1974 on 26 April, off Cape Beale.[6] While small numbers are seen in May, we usually begin to see this species in larger numbers only by the second half of June. In 2001, 12 birds were seen on 19 June, and in 2002, 8 birds on 21 June.

Numbers continue to increase through July and August, and into September. The largest counts usually range up to several hundred birds spread over a large area in late August and early September. An early noteworthy record was of 125 birds off Tofino on 13 September 1969.[48] An unusually large number was recorded on 14 September 2013 by birders on a pelagic birding trip out of Tofino. Estimates ranged from 2,500 to 5,000 birds, making this the largest number ever recorded off our shores. Numbers begin to decline by late September, and most birds have gone by mid-October. It seems likely that the very large numbers seen on 14 September 2013 represented a major southward movement. The latest fall records I could find, both from offshore Tofino, are of 10 birds on 12 October 1993, and 30 birds on 15 October 2002.

Although in no immediate danger, this species faces numerous threats, primarily on the islands where they breed. These include threats from cats, dogs, coatis, rats, and cattle. In addition, there is danger to their nesting burrows from erosion caused by goats and rabbits, from the harvesting of chicks, and from commercial fishing.[61] In 2013, it was estimated that a minimum of 400,000 seabirds of all kinds were killed around the world each year due to gillnet fishing, with an additional 160,000 killed through other methods, including longline fishing.[62]

FLESH-FOOTED SHEARWATER
Ardenna carneipes

STATUS: Uncommon to rare summer and fall transient. Casual in spring.

This all-dark shearwater with pink bill and pale feet is said to be closely related to the Pink-footed Shearwater. It was formerly called Pale-footed Shearwater (*Puffinus carneipes*) and recently was removed from the genus *Puffinus*.[63] Although it weighs less than a Sooty Shearwater, its wings are broader and it looks larger. It breeds primarily in the southwest Pacific on Lord Howe Island, New Zealand, and in West Australia. There is also an outlier colony in the Indian Ocean.

The Flesh-footed Shearwater was first recorded off British Columbia in 1937.[64] There are records from our region dating back to 1940 and 1946. *Birds of Pacific Rim National Park* listed 17 sightings up to 1978, recorded from 2 May to 26 September.[48] An additional 22 sightings have been reported since then. Combining all records, the breakdown by month is as follows: May – 1 record,

June – 3, July – 6, August – 8, September – 15, and October – 4. October sightings were all near the middle of the month.

Most sightings are of 1 or 2 birds, but on pelagic trips out of Tofino, 5 were seen on 26 September 2000, and 4 on 14 September 2014. The first Pacific sighting in North America occurred on 28 September 2008, when 12 to 15 birds were reported on the Swiftsure Bank among many thousands of seabirds. Far larger numbers have been reported well north of our region at the Goose Island Group banks.[6] The global population is estimated at 74,000 breeding pairs and is believed to have declined by 20 to 30% over three generations, causing some concern.[65]

GREAT SHEARWATER
Ardenna gravis
STATUS: Casual in late summer.

This large and distinctive shearwater is a bird of the Atlantic Ocean. It breeds primarily on two islands in the Tristan da Cunha Island group, southwest of Cape Town, South Africa. A very small population breeds on Kidney Island near the Falkland Islands in the southwestern Atlantic. The entire population is estimated at 15 million birds.[66]

In recent decades, Great Shearwaters have been recorded in a number of locations in the Pacific Ocean, including Australia, New Zealand, and Chile. The first North American sighting occurred in Monterey Bay, California, on 24 February 1979.[67] Another sighting followed in 1994 and two more in 2001, all off California. There was also a sighting in Alaska on 3 August 2001.[68] On 24 August 2002, a bird was recorded for the first time just south of us, in Washington.[69]

A Great Shearwater was recorded amid great excitement on 20 September 2010, during a pelagic birding trip out of Tofino, when a bird was observed at close range by all on board and photographed by Sergey Dereliev.[70] For birders it doesn't get much better than finding a new bird for the province. Ironically, for two European birders on board, this shearwater was of little interest as they had seen them before off their home shores.

Unknown to those on board, a Great Shearwater had already been reported in British Columbia waters by three American birders 10 years earlier. On 24 June 2000, a bird was seen 28 NM southwest of Pachena Point by Richard

Rowlett, G. Scott Mills, and Barbara Blackie. Based on field notes and drawings made at the time, this record was accepted by the BC Bird Records Committee.

On 5 August 2013, a bird was once again seen and photographed in offshore waters, this time from a cruise ship northwest of Vancouver Island by Oregon residents Jeff Gilligan, Paul Lehman, and Owen Schmidt. Coordinates for that sighting are latitude 51°22′9.2″N, longitude 129°46′46.6″W, or about 110 km northwest of Triangle Island.[71] While this sighting was somewhat outside the region as defined in this book, it remains an interesting and significant observation. It is apparent that this species is likely to be seen again in our waters, and it is therefore considered as casual rather than accidental.

BULLER'S SHEARWATER
Ardenna bulleri

STATUS: Uncommon to fairly common migrant in fall.

With its white underside and distinctive pattern on the upper side of the wings, Buller's Shearwater, previously known as New Zealand Shearwater, is easy to distinguish from other shearwaters. The species breeds only on two islands and surrounding islets off the north coast of New Zealand. After pigs were eliminated on the island of Aorangi in 1936, the population increased from 200 in 1938 to 200,000 pairs by 1981.[72] After the breeding season, which runs from October to April, the entire population disperses into the vast Pacific Ocean in search of food.

Although first reported off the north end of Vancouver Island on 7 August 1926,[73] this species was not accepted as occurring in Canadian waters until a specimen was collected on 26 September 1970, 40 km west of Tofino (UBC 13571).[74] Since then, there have been numerous sightings from early August to early November.

Among the earliest dates ever reported were sightings in the first week of July from west of Cape Beale and west of Kyuquot in 1971. Single birds were also recorded north of Vancouver Island on 17 July and again on 29 July by Roger Burrows. The earliest date that birds were recorded by Strawberry Island Research, out of Tofino, was 20 August in 2001, when five birds were seen.

While numbers have ranged from 1 to 8 birds on pelagic bird and mammal surveys out of Tofino, larger numbers have been reported on occasion. A total of 25 birds were seen 64 km west of Tofino on 26 September 1970,[48] and 33 birds on a pelagic birding trip off Tofino on 7 September 2014. An even larger number, 95 birds, was recorded on 1 October 1977 at La Perouse Bank. The largest count was made on a pelagic trip out of Ucluelet on 16 October 1992, when a remarkable 225 birds were reported by Brian Self.[26]

It is interesting to note that the two records with the largest numbers were both in October, at a time when the southbound movement is believed to be winding down. Our latest dates are 21 October in 2004, with eight birds, and 7 November in 1998, with two birds. The latest date we have is 8 November in 1986, at La Perouse Bank, also with two birds.[6]

The world population was estimated at 2.5 million birds in 1990, but this is now considered too high.[75] Although population numbers are considered healthy, the species is considered vulnerable because breeding is restricted to a very small area.[76]

SOOTY SHEARWATER
Ardenna grisea

STATUS: Common and often abundant migrant in spring and fall. Common in summer. Very rare in winter.

Sooty Shearwaters are usually the most abundant tubenose in offshore waters and may sometimes be seen from shore.

With a population estimated at 20 million birds,[66] the Sooty Shearwater is one of the most abundant seabirds in the world. It nests in burrows on islands in the southern oceans, notably around New Zealand, but also off Chile, the Falkland Islands, Tasmania, and New South Wales. After the breeding season, which ends in March, birds from Australasia head for the North Pacific Ocean in one of the longest migrations in the world. Radio-tagged individuals have revealed that they travel up to 64,000 km (nearly 40,000 mi) annually.[77] Some will travel to the waters off Asia, while others travel east to North America. It is not yet clear where birds that breed in Chile go.

In spring the very first birds may arrive off our coast as early as February. On 12 February 2000, 3 birds were seen off Tofino on a bird and mammal survey by Strawberry Island Research. Several trips in March found no birds, but 2 birds were seen offshore from Tofino on 10 March 1994. On 19 March 1946, "a few" birds were reported off Ucluelet, and on 26 March 1995, 33 were counted on a pelagic bird and mammal survey out of Tofino.

Numbers increase considerably during the month of April. On 17 April 1994, 800 birds were counted on a pelagic bird survey. This just happens to be the largest number counted on any of the Strawberry Island Research bird surveys out of Tofino over the past 20 years or so, although many counts approached that number. This pales in comparison with the more than 10,000 birds reported 29 km west of Tofino on 8 May 1977. The largest number ever recorded in spring occurred six days later, on 14 May 1977, when 50,000 birds were estimated 40 km off Ucluelet, and another 50,000 the same day 20 km further out. Truly astounding numbers have been observed off Haida Gwaii, with 250,000 to 500,000 reported on 14 May 1985.[8]

During 36 days of migration counts from Clerke Point on Brooks Peninsula in May and June 1973, a total of 33,949 Sooty Shearwaters were counted. Of these, 18,680 were counted during 16 days in the last half of May and 15,269 during 20 days in June. The estimated net northward movement in late May was 56,000 in late May and 89,800 birds in June. The day of heaviest movement was 21 May, when 2,000 shearwaters passed by each hour. Coincidentally the passage coincided with two low-pressure frontal systems converging on the coast. Also, flocks of up to 450 Sooty Shearwaters were frequently seen foraging in Brooks and Checleset bays in May and June.[13]

Throughout the spring and summer months, small to moderate numbers may be seen from shore at Long beach or, better yet, scoping from a headland. A few examples are: 600 birds on 13 May 2009 from Vargas Island; 350 on 19 June 2009 from Incinerator Rock, Long Beach; and 157 on 23 September 2000 from Incinerator Rock. By October, numbers are greatly diminished, even far offshore. The largest number recorded during that month was 200 birds on 21 October 2004, during an offshore trip. A dwindling number of birds pass by in November, and by December records are very scarce. Twelve birds reported on 18 December 1993 on a pelagic bird and mammal survey out of Tofino could possibly have been Short-tailed Shearwaters as winter records are fairly rare. *The Birds of British Columbia* lists a record of 2 birds seen off Long Beach on 28 February 1978, and 3 birds were seen off Tofino on 12 February 2000. It seems possible that February records involve very early spring arrivals.

Sooty Shearwaters have been undergoing a decline. In the California Current System, numbers declined by as much as 90% between the late 1970s and the 1990s.[78] This decline has been blamed on a concurrent rise in sea surface temperatures and is therefore not a local phenomenon. This probably explains the discrepancy in numbers off our shores between the 1970s and more recent years. Despite their large population globally, Sooty Shearwaters face other threats. In the recent past, high seas driftnet fisheries killed an estimated 350,000 birds per year.[79] Although that fishery has been curtailed, the US Fish and Wildlife Service has stated that "the effects on shearwaters and the magnitude of the by-catch from ongoing fisheries are largely unknown." Nor are Sooty Shearwaters entirely safe on their breeding grounds. In New Zealand, native Maori take 250,000 chicks annually for food, oils, and fat, including for commercial sale. In Tasmania, the Palawa people likewise harvest this species for food.[63] The greatest threat facing Sooty Shearwaters and many other seabirds may be the current warming of the ocean, as well as increased ocean acidification. We need only remember the Passenger Pigeon and Great Auk to know that a large population does not guarantee the survival of a species.

SHORT-TAILED SHEARWATER
Ardenna tenuirostris

STATUS: Irregular. Generally uncommon to rare in spring, summer, and fall. Sometimes locally abundant. Casual in winter.

This species can be difficult to distinguish from the Sooty Shearwater with certainty except under favourable conditions. In flight, the underwings tend to have less white than the Sooty and the head has a more tucked-in look. Field marks include a somewhat shorter, slighter bill, and, when seen up close, the plumage appears pale grey on the throat and front of the neck. Overall this species has a tidier look than the Sooty. It is advisable to use caution in identification as mistakes are easily made.

Short-tailed Shearwaters breed on islands off southern and eastern Australia. After the breeding season, which ends in late April and May, birds disperse northward to the North Pacific Ocean and the Bering Sea. Some venture even further afield into the Arctic Ocean. They are often highly gregarious, and have been reported to gather in feeding flocks of 20,000 birds or more (see below). Short-tailed Shearwaters feed primarily by diving, and can reach a depth of 70 m in search of fish, cephalopods, and crustaceans.

Although it has been recorded in every month of the year, *The Birds of British Columbia* considers this species to be of irregular occurrence in BC waters.[6] It is considered very rare in spring and fairly common in summer and autumn. In winter it is considered casual. The species can be locally abundant at times, though nearly 90% of all records are of individuals or of flocks of less than 10 birds.

That the species is indeed irregular is supported by observations made on 65 pelagic bird and mammal surveys off Tofino, during which the species was recorded only 7 times in the 14 years they were conducted. Four of the 7 sightings were in 1994, and 3 of those occurred in winter and spring. Two birds were seen on 8 February, 3 birds on 10 March, and 45 on 17 April. No Short-tailed Shearwaters were seen again until 17 June 2003, nine years later, when a single bird was observed. We also have 3 records in autumn, all from offshore Tofino: 12 October 1993 – 10 (photos); 11 September 1994 – 1; and 21 October 2004 – 1. It should be pointed out that the species is easily overlooked among the many Sooty Shearwaters.

Ironically, the month of May, in which no Short-tailed Shearwaters were seen on any of the bird and mammal surveys out of Tofino, produced the greatest abundance ever reported off our shores. On 19 May 1972, a concentration on the Swiftsure Banks was said to be at least 24 km across, and was estimated by observer P.W. Martin to contain "hundreds of thousands" of birds.[80] A specimen was collected (RBCM 11905).

Although this species has been reported on rare occasions in the Salish Sea in winter, I could find no winter records for our region other than on 8 February 1994, off Tofino. On one occasion during the month of December, while photographing ocean waves at Box Island, Long Beach, I inadvertently captured shearwaters on film, flying close to shore. These may well have been Short-tailed Shearwaters.

Threats to this species are probably the same as for Sooty Shearwaters. On their breeding grounds off Australia, Short-tailed Shearwater chicks, called "muttonbirds," are still commercially harvested for food, feathers, and oil, and are killed by being thrown into vats of boiling water. Some 200,000 chicks are "harvested" under licence annually.[81] Despite the harvest and other threats at sea, the population remained at an estimated 23 million birds in 2004.[66]

MANX SHEARWATER
Puffinus puffinus

STATUS: Casual visitor in spring, summer, and early fall.

This smallish shearwater with white underparts is a bird of the North Atlantic Ocean, breeding primarily in the west of Britain and Ireland. There are small breeding colonies in the Canary Islands, the Azores, Brittany, Iceland, Newfoundland, and Massachusetts. In winter it flies south to the waters off southwest Africa and the southeast coast of South America. Large numbers have been seen off Tierra del Fuego and even in the Strait of Magellan, making it not entirely surprising that the species has increasingly been turning up in the Pacific Ocean, from Australia and New Zealand to the west coast of North America.

The first verified record for the state of Washington occurred in 1992,[82] and the first verified record for California was on 25 July 1993.[7] By October 2010, there were more than 100 accepted records for the state of California and 64 reports for the neighbouring state of Oregon. On 4 August 2009, a photo of two birds taken at Icy Bay became the first solid evidence for the presence of the species in Alaskan waters,[83] although there had been reports as far back as 1975.

In July 1994, two researchers, Ian Jones and Christine Adkins, working on Triangle Island, off Cape Scott, heard and recorded an unfamiliar sound emanating from a burrow. They were eventually convinced that the sound came from a Manx Shearwater, raising the possibility of attempted breeding even before the species was confirmed for the province. Four years later, on 18 May 1998, Michael Bentley reported a bird off Triangle Island, and on 4 May 2002, Ken Morgan reported one north of Triangle Island.[46] A bird was also seen at Cape Scott on 16 June 2004.[46] Two years later, the first photograph of a Manx Shearwater in British Columbia waters was taken on 8 August 2004 when Jukka Jantunen and six members of the Rocky Point Bird Observatory observed a bird at close range at Race Rocks, just south of our region.[84]

There have been further sightings in the west coast region. On 2 June 2005, a Manx Shearwater was reported off the West Coast Trail by Nathan Hentze, and on 18 September 2011, a bird was reported 65 km (35 NM) off Quatsino Sound by Mike and Sharon Toochin. On 29 April 2012, photos were taken of a bird 16.5 km (9 NM) off Ucluelet by Peter Candido, and on 20 June 2012, a bird was photographed 5.5 km west of Nootka Island by Jared Towers. Several others have been reliably reported recently, including one on 18 October 2015 off Amphitrite Point, Ucluelet, by Guy Monty et al.

The now numerous sightings of Manx Shearwaters along North America's Pacific coast raises the possibility that this species may be nesting somewhere on the west coast. It may also throw doubt on earlier sight records of the Black-vented Shearwater, dating back as far as the 1960s, including my sighting of a small shearwater with white underparts flying by on stiff wings west of Cleland Island on 15 June 1999, and again on 5 September 2012, south of Vargas Island.

Manx Shearwaters number about one million birds and are extremely long-lived, with one female living to the ripe old age of 52 years. She was banded on an island off the north coast of Wales at an estimated age of five years in 1957, and was recaptured in 2003. She was still breeding at that advanced age.[85]

BLACK-VENTED SHEARWATER
Puffinus opisthomelas
STATUS: Unclear. Casual in summer, fall, and winter.

The Black-vented Shearwater looks somewhat like a Pink-footed Shearwater, but is considerably smaller and does not have a pink bill. It breeds only on six islands off the coast of Mexico and has a population estimated in 2016 at 82,000 mature individuals, down from the 80,000 breeding pairs estimated in 1998-99.[86] The previous estimate, however, is now believed to have been inaccurate. After the breeding season, which differs from that of shearwaters in the Southern Hemisphere by beginning in March and probably ending in August or September, birds disperse over the eastern Pacific from southern Mexico to Oregon. They are occasionally seen further north to the waters off Washington, and rarely to British Columbia. In our province, the Black-vented Shearwater was first recorded south of our region at Albert Head in 1891, when two specimens were taken. Another bird was collected at that location in 1885.[6]

For our west coast region, we have 11 records. The first bird was reported on 15 July 1940,[46] west of Cape Scott, and on 3 July 1954, a second bird was reported off Solander Island (Cape Cook). On 24 July 1967, a bird was reported from southwest of Cleland Island.[87] In September 1982, single birds were reported off our shores at four locations.[46] Then in two consecutive years, single birds were reported from Amphitrite Point, Ucluelet, on 28 September 1986[13] and on 7 September 1987. There were two more reports in 1988, with one at Brooks Peninsula on 9 August and another on the continental shelf break on the northern edge of American waters.[13]

My use of the word "reported" is deliberate because of the possibility of mistaking the Manx Shearwater for the Black-vented Shearwater. The two can be easily misidentified unless the observer is afforded a good look and knows exactly how to distinguish between the two. In the past, the Manx Shearwater was not expected in our waters and any smaller white-breasted shearwater would likely have been presumed to be a Black-vented Shearwater.

Postbreeding birds usually do not arrive off Monterey, California, until mid-October or November. Two of the birds collected at Albert Head were taken in late October and November, and the third in February. Any summer sightings in our waters would be nonbreeding birds. Reports of this species should probably be treated with utmost caution unless accompanied by a photograph.

Storm-Petrels   Family Hydrobatidae

FORK-TAILED STORM-PETREL
Oceanodroma furcata

STATUS: Fairly common in pelagic waters from May to October. Locally abundant. Rarely seen inshore. Breeds.

Storm-petrels are another of the tubenose families. To fishermen around the world, they are often known as "sea swallows." Four genera have been reported off the shores of North America, and two species in the genus *Oceanodroma* are found on our coast. The Fork-tailed Storm-Petrel nests on islands from the Kuril Islands in Russia, the Aleutians, and the Gulf of Alaska through British Columbia and northern California. In British Columbia, at least 327,404 birds breed at 47 sites, particularly on Haida Gwaii (17%), Queen Charlotte Strait (37%), and Vancouver Island (28%).[88]

In our west coast region, at least 92,040 Fork-tailed Storm-Petrels breed at six sites from Triangle Island in the Scott Islands to Seabird Rocks in the south near Pachena Bay.[88] On the central west coast, a small number breed on

Cleland Island, which is where I was first shown a bird on a nest beneath a chunk of driftwood in 1971. The bird was light grey and soft to the touch. It had a dovelike head with a small tube on its bill, and exuded the distinctive pungent odour characteristic of all tube-nosed swimmers.

This species enters and leaves its nesting site under cover of darkness and is therefore only normally seen many miles offshore. Between 1993 and 2008, on 65 pelagic bird and mammal surveys by Strawberry Island Research out of Tofino, numbers seen varied from 1 to 100 birds. Larger numbers have been seen elsewhere. On 21 August 1949, 500 were seen at La Perouse Bank, and on 1 September 1985, more than 1,400 were seen at the same location.[6] On 14 September 2013, Tofino resident Arthur Ahier took a photo of a flock far offshore, and a count made later revealed more than 700 birds in the photo. A far larger number was reported somewhat outside our area, 110 km NNW of Triangle Island by Paul Lehman et al. (personal communication) on a *Wings* birding tour. On 5 August 2013, Lehman et al. estimated as many as 10,000 Fork-tailed Storm-Petrels and a similar number of Leach's Storm-Petrels.

Only occasionally are Fork-tailed Storm-Petrels seen near shore, for example, when lost in thick fog. In the late 1960s, the species was regularly seen feeding in the evening under fish-processing plants in Tofino (R.W. Campbell, personal communication). In March 1993, a bird spent two days flying around Tofino harbour under cloudless skies. The largest number recorded on inshore waters was 300 birds in Ucluelet Inlet on 7 March 1985,[6] though this was highly unusual.

The Birds of British Columbia states that Fork-tailed Storm-Petrels are believed to arrive in the breeding area from early March to April, but "specific details are lacking." Other than the March record mentioned above, the earliest record I could find was a bird seen at the entrance to Shelter Inlet on 7 April 1985. By May, birds are seen more often. They are most common in August and September, as indicated above. On surveys conducted by Strawberry Island Research, the species was not recorded in October, although there is a record from Bamfield for 1 October 1977, when 107 birds were reported. That some birds may persist into November is indicated by a record of 6 birds reported off Victoria on 19 November 1983. A handful of winter records have come from elsewhere in BC waters.[6]

Fork-tailed Storm-Petrels are reported to feed on small fishes, squid, and planktonic crustaceans. The world population was estimated at 6 million birds and is currently expanding.[89]

LEACH'S STORM-PETREL
Oceanodroma leucorhoa

STATUS: Common over pelagic waters in spring and summer. Rarely seen in daylight hours except beyond the continental shelf. Very rare on inside waters. Breeds.

Leach's Storm-Petrels have a broad distribution, and are found in both the Atlantic and Pacific oceans. In the Pacific, they range largely north of the equator. In North America, the species breeds in colonies on offshore islands from the Baja California peninsula to the Aleutian Islands. In winter the species ranges south to the latitude of Ecuador. The population is large, with an estimated 6.7 to 8.3 million breeding pairs worldwide in 2016.[90] A 30% decline over three generations has been noted, primarily in the Atlantic Ocean.

In British Columbia, the species breeds at 42 sites. About 32% of the provincial population of 1,040,790 Leach's Storm-Petrels breed on the west coast of Vancouver Island. The largest colonies (553,200 birds, 53% of BC population) are located in Queen Charlotte Strait.[88]

Leach's Storm-Petrels are burrow nesters. Adults excavate a burrow in the soft earth, usually under a log or tree root or at the base of a clump of grass. When these are not available, such as on parts of Cleland Island, birds dig into the earth among the waist-high vegetation. In such locations, burrows can be easily damaged by human traffic, making it important to limit or restrict such visitations. To lessen predation by hawks or falcons, nesting birds wait until nightfall to leave the burrow, a practice that is usually successful. However, at a colony located on a treed island near Kyuquot Sound, a Western Screech-Owl took advantage of this practice by pouncing on incoming birds in the dead of night. The main mammalian predators, day or night, are Northern River Otters and Northern Raccoons.

Leach's Storm-Petrels travel many miles offshore to reach warmer waters of 14°C or higher to feed. Off the central west coast, this means travelling some 30 km or more offshore, beyond the continental shelf. Very rarely, when birds have become lost in heavy fog, they may be seen close to shore or even on inside waters. On one such occasion, birds were reported from Shelter Inlet. Fog was certainly not the cause on 26 August 1989, when a bird was observed at Grice Bay on a clear day under sunny skies. A bird was seen under similar conditions at Stubbs Island on 18 August 1991. Single birds were observed from shore at the south side of Vargas Island on 24 June 2000 and 3 August 2008, though notes from the time do not mention weather conditions.

A few birds winter off the British Columbia coast, though the northward movement is believed to commence in April, with most birds arriving in May. Nests with eggs have been recorded from 14 May to 20 August, with a single egg being the norm. After an incubation period of 41 or 42 days, the young are fed for 40 days, then abandoned. They are then forced to live off their fat reserves for another 25 to 36 days, after which they abandon the burrow for the sea. The latest date a young bird was found in a burrow was 26 October.[6] Such late departures of young from their burrows could explain a sighting in Millar Channel on 27 October 2016 by Arthur Ahier.

ORDER PELECANIFORMES

Boobies and Gannets   Family Sulidae

BROWN BOOBY
Sula leucogaster

STATUS: Casual fall visitor.

Related to Northern Gannets, boobies are birds of the tropics and subtropics that feed on fish by plunging into the water. The Brown Booby is found from the Caribbean to South America, Africa, India, Australasia, and the South Pacific. In the eastern Pacific, it breeds only in the Sea of Cortez, and from there wanders the ocean off Mexico and Central America. It is seen occasionally off southern California.

Given its normal range, one would not expect to see this bird in BC waters. However, on 18 October 1997, a bird was seen very close to the province at Protection Island, Washington.[91] Eleven years later, on 20 October 2008, a Brown Booby landed on a fishing boat near the eastern end of Dixon Entrance on the north coast for a first record for British Columbia.[92] The following year, on 29 August, the first sighting for Vancouver Island occurred when a bird was seen off Tower Point near Metchosin.[93]

The first sighting in the west coast region occurred on 4 September 2013, when a Brown Booby was spotted and photographed from a cruise ship 32 km (20 NM) northwest of Nootka Island by Mike and Sharon Toochin, and Meg Brown.[94] Two months later, on 12 November, a bird landed aboard a fishing vessel about 5.5 km (3 NM) off Ucluelet, where it was photographed by the skipper, Robbie Heggelund. It stayed aboard his boat until the following day, when it abandoned the vessel off Carmanah Point.[94] On 20 September 2014, an adult Brown Booby was seen and photographed 57.5 km (31 NM) west of Tofino by a group of 10 birders on a pelagic birding excursion. Fifteen months later, on 20 October 2015, yet another bird was found, this time about 9 km (5.6 mi) west of Cape Beale, by observers aboard a US National Oceanic and Atmospheric Administration (NOAA) research vessel.[84]

With four sightings in three consecutive years, this bird's status can for now be considered casual rather than accidental. However, when the pendulum swings back again and the ocean cools, its status may well revert back to being extremely rare.

Cormorants   Family Phalacrocoracidae

BRANDT'S CORMORANT
Phalacrocorax penicillatus

STATUS: Common spring and fall migrant. Fairly common in summer and winter. Former breeder.

This cormorant was named after German naturalist Johann Friedrich von Brandt, who first described it from specimens collected on the Pacific coast by Russian explorers. It breeds from British Columbia south to northwestern Mexico. There have been six intermittent breeding colonies off the west coast of Vancouver Island in the past and, surprisingly, two as far north as southeast Alaska.[95] In British Columbia, we see Brandt's Cormorants almost entirely as a result of postbreeding dispersal, when birds nesting along the US Pacific coast migrate north for the remainder of the year to take advantage of more productive feeding areas.

On Vancouver Island's west coast, this cormorant may be seen in every month of the year, though certainly not in equal numbers. In spring, primarily in April and May, but possibly as early as March, resident wintering birds head south to colonies in Washington, Oregon, and California. As late as 17 May in 2013, flocks of Brandt's Cormorants totalling 350 birds were seen flying in a southerly direction past Cleland Island, indicating that the southward movement had not yet ended. A small number of birds persist in our area throughout the summer.

The exact start of the northward movement is difficult to determine. As early as 20 July in 2010, a group of 25 birds was observed at South Beach in

Brandt's Cormorants arrive from their breeding grounds in the United States in large numbers in late summer. Seen here is a juvenile.

Pacific Rim National Park. It is uncertain whether these were nonbreeding summer residents or new postbreeding arrivals. Certainly by early to mid-August, postbreeding Brandt's Cormorants are beginning to pass by Long Beach. On 6 August 2009, 27 birds were counted from Incinerator Rock, Long Beach, and 12 birds were counted from the same location on 9 August 2011. On 14 August 2011, 35 birds were seen west of Tofino. By September, the increase in numbers is considerably more noticeable. On 10 September 1996, an estimated 320 birds were observed on Monk's Rock, northwest of Vargas Island, and on 22 September, 100 birds were seen passing by the south end of Vargas Island.

In winter, Brandt's Cormorants prefer the more protected waters away from the outer coast. In southern Clayoquot Sound, birds can be seen throughout the winter, gathering with other cormorants on "shag rocks" in Tofino harbour. In the evening they depart to roost on rocky islands on the exposed outer coast. Presumably this is done to avoid predators. Winter numbers are not large, at least not in Clayoquot Sound, with Brandt's Cormorants being outnumbered by Double-crested Cormorants and usually by Pelagic Cormorants.

In 1965, Brandt's Cormorants were found breeding in the province for the first time at Sea Lion Rocks, off Long Beach.[96] They later established other small colonies on White Island, Great Bear Rock, and Starlight Reef, reaching a maximum population of 150 pairs in 1970.[1] By 1982, numbers had dwindled to 50 birds, and in 1989 the last breeding record for the west coast of Vancouver

Island involved 51 pairs nesting on Starlight Reef.[88] In 1987, 3 nests were found outside our region on Race Rocks in the Strait of Juan de Fuca,[6] and it was reported that some Brandt's Cormorants may also have nested on Sartine Island off the northwest tip of Vancouver Island in 1975. None were nesting here in 1987, but in 1989, 39 nests with young were counted.[88] Although searches have been carried out by the staff of Pacific Rim National Park, no nests have been found in the park since 1989. In 2013 and 2014, several pairs nested outside our region on Mandarte Island.[97] Those were the only known nesting Brandt's Cormorants remaining in British Columbia.

DOUBLE-CRESTED CORMORANT
Phalacrocorax auritus

STATUS: Common to locally abundant in fall. Common in winter and spring. Rare in summer.

Although it appears to be the largest of the three common "shags" on our coast, and has the largest wingspan, this cormorant averages nearly a pound lighter than the Brandt's Cormorant. Nevertheless, its size alone is a good indicator of which species you are observing. Size, thick curved neck, orange colour at the base of the bill, and a tendency to fly at higher altitudes are all good clues to its identity.

Double-crested Cormorants breed from Cuba and Florida north along the Atlantic coast to the Maritimes, west to the Great Lakes, the Canadian Prairie provinces, and the US Midwest, to Montana, southern Idaho, and northern Utah, and locally elsewhere. On the Pacific coast, it breeds from southwestern Alaska south locally to British Columbia, Washington, Oregon, and northwestern Mexico. On the Pacific coast, it has a remarkably long winter range, stretching from the Alaska Peninsula in the north to the Sea of Cortez, Mexico.

In British Columbia, this species was first reported breeding on Mandarte (Bare) Island in the Salish Sea in 1927.[98] The entire population, which breeds only in the Strait of Georgia, peaked at 2,032 pairs in 1986-87 at 15 sites, and by 1990 the population had decreased to 1,729 pairs at 14 sites.[88] Bones found in archaeological sites show that this species has been present in this region for the past 5,000 years,[6] thus in 1927 it was apparently re-establishing itself.

In the west coast region, the nonbreeding population has increased greatly in recent decades, probably due to the increase in Washington state after the removal of predators and cessation of egg collecting on nesting colonies, and the programs to release hatchery-raised prey.[99] Although *Birds of Pacific Rim National Park* listed 85 records for the west coast region, the largest number recorded at one time was 12 birds on 2 May 1970, at Tofino.[1] The species was listed as uncommon. More than 500 records have been gathered since then. These show a striking increase in numbers beginning in the mid-1990s. High numbers recorded at Tofino demonstrate this increase: 35 birds recorded on 9 November 1996; 105 on 13 November 1997; 110 on 26 November 1998; 178 on 27 October 2001; and 270 on 5 November 2007.

This last record was the highest ever. After that date, numbers appear to have levelled off. Still, there are three additional counts of over 200 birds: 225 birds were recorded on 22 November 2009; 212 on 29 December 2012; and 220 on 20 October 2014. This species has recently increased in numbers in British Columbia, Washington, Oregon, and California (72% from 1987-92 to circa 2009) as well as the interior of the continent.[100]

Birds usually begin to trickle into our region in early September, with the influx gradually gaining momentum throughout the rest of the month and through October and November. That some of our highest numbers have been recorded in late October and November suggests that the population peaks at that time. A few individuals have been seen as early as August. The earliest record I have is of a single bird at Cleland Island on 14 August 2002. I have no records for July, although Hatler et al. list one for that month.[1] In spring it appears that birds depart largely in April, though some may already do so in March. By May, few birds remain, although a handful may be seen up to late May, as well as an occasional straggler into June.

Double-crested Cormorants are voracious eaters of small fishes, and unlike their two more ocean-dwelling cousins, they rarely feed in exposed outside waters. Watching a tightly knit flock of 200 or more birds diving for food over an eelgrass bed in Clayoquot Sound, one can only wonder to what extent the increase in population has affected other diving birds with which Double-crested Cormorants apparently compete for food.

PELAGIC CORMORANT
Phalacrocorax pelagicus
STATUS: Common resident. Breeds.

This is our smallest cormorant. In breeding plumage, white flank patches make it easy to distinguish from other cormorants. At other times, small size

The Pelagic Cormorant is a common breeding bird on Vancouver Island's west coast, where it nests on sea cliffs and sometimes in caves.

combined with a thin neck and bill are helpful field marks at a distance. Its breeding range stretches from the Kuril Islands in east-central Asia to northeastern Siberia, the Aleutian Islands, the Bering Sea, and along the entire Pacific coast of North America, south to northern Baja California. There is some migratory movement from northern areas, though most appear to be year-round residents.

An estimated 4,495 pairs of Pelagic Cormorants currently breed at 85 sites on rocky headlands, islands, and cliff faces, including at times in surge channels and even sea caves. About 52% breed in the Strait of Georgia and 26% on the west side of Vancouver Island. Of 144 confirmed historical breeding sites in the province, 56% occur in the Salish Sea and 35% on the west coast of Vancouver Island.[88] The largest colony in our region is located on Solander Island, off Cape Cook, with 464 nests counted in 1988.[6] Numbers and site occupancy vary from year to year.

Nesting on the outer coast can be hazardous. An unseasonal storm during the breeding season can wipe out nests, as has been observed in a surge channel at Fletcher's Beach, near Ucluelet. Birds may also abandon a site for unknown reasons, only to recolonize at a later date. Populations can fluctuate a great deal. Triangle Island had 1,200 pairs in 1949, but only 33 nests were counted in 1984. One year later, the number had jumped to 144 nests.[6] In Barkley Sound, there was an 85% decline in the nesting population between 1969 and 2006-07, with many colonies abandoned between 1982 and 1989.[101]

Locations where Pelagic Cormorants nest or have nested in the past are numerous. For example, there are 32 known or suspected breeding colonies in Barkley Sound alone.[101] Most are on the outer coast, exposed to the ocean swells, including at Sea Lion Rocks off Long Beach. They also nest on islands in Barkley Sound, on White Island off Portland Point, Cape Beale, Quisitis Point, and Florencia Island. There are no known nesting sites in the protected waters of Clayoquot Sound.

In fall and winter, when sea conditions are often severe, cormorants gather at more sheltered locations such as southern Clayoquot Sound, Monk's Rock, Stubbs Island, and three "shag rocks" in Tofino harbour that are used as daytime roosts. The birds use these as a base from which to launch foraging expeditions in the surrounding waters. Long periods are spent resting, preening, and drying their plumage. With the approach of dusk, birds depart for unknown roosts closer to the exposed outside coast, probably as protection from potential predators. To see 50 or more birds in Tofino harbour is common. A high count was 86 birds on 18 November 2009. A one-man Christmas count in the Tofino area on 26 December 1982 produced 169 birds, and another on 29 December 1987 produced 155. By late April, most birds have departed for breeding locations along the BC coast, and they are generally scarce or absent in protected waters locally until their return in late September or October. Sea conditions likely play an important role in the timing of this movement.

Pelicans   Family Pelecanidae

AMERICAN WHITE PELICAN
Pelecanus erythrorhynchos
STATUS: Casual summer visitor.

With its white plumage, black flight feathers, and large orange bill, the American White Pelican is unmistakable. Twice the weight of a Brown Pelican, it tips the scales at 7.5 kg (16.5 lbs). The species breeds on inland lakes in colonies containing hundreds of birds, sometimes thousands. Its breeding range extends locally throughout much of the American west and north into the Canadian Prairie provinces. Roughly two-thirds of the world population breeds in Canada. Birds have nested as far east as Ontario, and north to the southern boundary of the Northwest Territories. In British Columbia, the only known extant breeding colony is at Stum Lake on the Chilcotin Plateau

This flock of American White Pelicans, very rare on the west coast, spent hours resting and preening at Jensen's Bay, Tofino.

of the interior, although it has recently been found breeding at Puntzi Lake (BCNRS files, R.W. Campbell, personal communication). The species winters in the southern United States and Mexico, south to Guatemala and El Salvador on the Pacific coast and Nicaragua on the Atlantic side. This species has increased by 456% in 40 years, with the population currently estimated at over 180,000 birds.[102]

Vancouver Island's west coast is far removed from this bird's interior migration corridor and it is therefore not a bird one would expect to see here. However, on three consecutive days in 2014, a flock (or flocks) of American White Pelicans was reported near Tofino. A flock estimated at 30 birds was first spotted on 1 July by whaleboat skipper Marcel Theriault, flying in "V" formation at the mouth of Father Charles Channel. Then, in typical fashion for this species, they proceeded to circle and soar. The following day, a large flock was seen at Chesterman Beach by two observers from Nanaimo. A large flock was also seen flying west over Browning Passage by Jack Gillie and Alexa Klinka, though they were uncertain of the exact date. They believed it was 3 July. Fifteen days later, on 18 July, 2 birds were reported over Long Beach.

These occurrences did not come entirely out of the blue, so to speak. Flocks of American White Pelicans were also reported from Bellingham, Washington, from Squamish and Victoria, and from Brunswick Point in the Fraser River delta. Two years later, on 13 June 2016, Marcel Theriault, accompanied by Tom Stere, once again spotted White Pelicans in Clayoquot Sound, this time a flock of 44 birds soaring and wheeling over Millar Channel, north of the village of Ahousaht. A flock of 58 birds was seen the following day over Ucluelet Inlet, over Long Beach, and over Tofino, and another flock was seen over Tofino on 16 June. The latest sightings occurred in 2017, when a flock of 16 birds was seen and photographed at Tofino on 7 and 8 June.

In view of the multiple sightings in our region in three separate years, and considering the expanding population, this species is considered casual in occurrence.

BROWN PELICAN
Pelecanus occidentalis

STATUS: Formerly a casual visitor in spring, summer, and fall. Now a fairly common visitor in some years. Absent or rare in most years.

Brown Pelicans are large birds adapted to catching fish by plunging into the ocean from as high as 20 m (65 ft) above the surface. A flexible pouch beneath the bill balloons underwater and acts as a net to catch the fish. Anyone who has spent time on the coast of the southern United States or Mexico will have seen flocks of these birds flying low over the water, one behind the other. I recall a pescador in Baja California gesturing to a squadron of pelicans skimming by us. "Mexican Air Force," he offered.

On the Atlantic coast, Brown Pelicans breed from Virginia to northern South America. On the Pacific coast, they breed from southern California to Chile. Nonbreeding birds normally venture as far north as the mouth of the Columbia River. British Columbia, therefore, lies well outside the normal range for this species. The first Brown Pelican recorded in BC waters was seen at Burrard Inlet in 1880.[103] During the next 100 years, the species was recorded in the province 15 additional times.[6]

In the west coast region, surprisingly, I could find only a single record prior to the 1980s, and the Brown Pelican was not listed at all in *Birds of Pacific Rim National Park* in 1978. The first record for the region is of a single bird seen at Long Beach on 28 July 1979.[6] However, the status of this species on our coast was about to change quite dramatically, beginning with an El Niño event in 1983. On 23 August of that year, a flock of 24 birds was seen at Port Renfrew, and on 29 August, a single bird was seen off Cape Beale. As late as 11 November of that year, 15 birds were observed off Carmanah Point. More observations followed in 1985, with 16 birds seen at Port Renfrew on 3 August, and 6 birds at Bamfield on 29 August.[6]

Since 1985, Brown Pelicans have been seen in at least 17 separate years up to 2014. In 1997, assistant lighthouse keeper Jerry Etzkorn recorded numerous flocks passing by Carmanah Point from 5 September to 19 October. He recorded a flock of 76 birds on 15 September and two flocks of more than 70 birds each on 19 September. From 2000 to 2016, birds have been recorded in our region in every year except 2003 and 2015. The largest numbers are seen south of Barkley Sound, off the West Coast Trail. On 29 August 2006, as many as 200 birds were recorded off Port San Juan by John Reynolds.

While the species is not as numerous on the central west coast north of Barkley Sound, there have nevertheless been numerous sightings off Long Beach and Clayoquot Sound. Besides the record from 1978, there were sightings in 1993, 1997, 1998, and 1999. On 7 June 2006, a flock of 35 was seen off the south end of Long Beach, and on 8 June 2009, 29 birds were seen from Incinerator Rock. It does not appear that birds often venture past Estevan Point, although there is at least one sight record off Kyuquot Sound. Birds have also been seen by tour-boat operators along the central coast, though these sightings were not recorded.

Brown Pelicans have been recorded from May to December. On several occasions during the months of November and December, when sea conditions on the outside are fierce, Brown Pelicans have sought refuge in Tofino harbour. In 2012, a bird with a head wound was captured by locals and transported to a wildlife facility for treatment.

In the late 1960s and early 1970s, the widely used pesticide DDT was found to cause thinning of the eggshells of Brown Pelicans and other birds, resulting in nesting failure.[104] This deadly pesticide was subsequently banned in the United States in 1972, and the population gradually recovered. Population recovery and expansion, combined with a trend of slightly warmer ocean water, is believed to be responsible for the northward expansion of this grand bird in recent years. In 2014, Brown Pelicans nested for the first time on an island in the Columbia River, thereby expanding their breeding range northward by hundreds of miles.[105]

ORDER CICONIIFORMES

Herons and Egrets *Family Ardeidae*

GREAT BLUE HERON
Ardea herodias

STATUS: Common resident in summer, fall, and winter. Uncommon in spring. Rare local breeder.

A Great Blue Heron fishes in a shallow lagoon. The showy plumes on this bird demonstrate that it is an adult.

The Great Blue Heron weighs remarkably little for such a large bird, reaching a mere 2.4 kg (5.3 lbs). This explains why these birds appear able to walk on water in a bed of bull kelp. The long legs are designed for standing in the water and spearing small fish, which they do by catapulting the head forward at lightning speed.

This heron is found across much of the United States and Canada from Atlantic to Pacific, though not in the far north. On the Pacific coast, its range extends north to Kodiak Island, Alaska. In British Columbia, it breeds in colonies in the southern interior, the Fraser Valley, the Salish Sea basin, Haida Gwaii, and Prince Rupert. Colonies exist on the east side of Vancouver Island as well as on the Gulf Islands. The Great Blue Heron is a common bird on the BC coast, including in our west coast region. Coastal birds belong to the subspecies *A. h. fannini*, while interior birds are of the subspecies *A. h. herodias*. While Great Blue Herons may be seen in suitable habitat almost anywhere along our coast, the largest numbers may be found on mudflats, especially where eelgrass beds are present.

Birds in the Clayoquot Sound area do not breed on the west coast but depart for colonies elsewhere on the island. The only rookery found on the west side of the island thus far was at Tahsis, where a colony containing nine nests was found in May 1989. Also intriguing is a report by Chris Chutter of 20 birds seen at Sea Otter Cove, Cape Scott Provincial Park, on 14 June 2014, raising the possibility of a rookery nearby.[106]

In Clayoquot Sound, herons are scarce in April, May, and June, and reappear usually beginning in early July. Birds may then be seen spiralling down from high in the air to land on the mudflats at the edge of Browning Passage, a rendezvous point apparently engraved on a mental map. The early returnees are always young birds that arrive without help from adults, the adults showing up much later. These young birds line up along the passage, forming a ragged line that stretches for 3 km (2 mi) and including as many as 70 or 80 birds. The chronology of their return was recorded for a number of years beginning in 1999. For the year 2000, the count results were as follows: 15 July – 9 birds; 17 July – 22; 18 July – 33; 3 August – 39; and 13 August – 53. In 2001, birds arrived slightly earlier and the count results were as follows: 10 July – 9 birds; 11 July – 18; 20 July – 30; 22 July – 50; 26 July – 56; and 6 August – 73 birds. In 2002, the first 13 herons arrived on schedule on 10 July, and numbers increased at a very similar rate to 2001, peaking at 81 birds on 12 August.

In 2003, the first birds arrived very early, with 12 birds on 1 July, and apparently peaked at 75 birds on 30 July. The following year, first arrivals were two weeks earlier still, with 34 birds counted on 13 June and 51 on 18 July. The highest count on the mudflats of southern Clayoquot Sound was made in the early 1980s, when 97 birds were tallied, though the exact date was lost. That count included the Arakun Flats. While herons often roost in trees on the Arakun Islands, there is no rookery there, as was suspected by Hatler et al.[1]

After numbers peak in August, herons begin to disperse and the number of birds inhabiting the mudflats on the Tofino side decreases significantly. Instead of 60 or 70 birds, 20 may be the norm. High numbers recorded from the end of Sharp Road late in the year were 20 birds on 6 December 2007, 18 on 16 November 2010, and 22 on 6 December 2013.

Small numbers, usually one or two birds, can be encountered along the entire west coast in all four seasons. In spring, single birds have been reported foraging in Cape Scott Park between 16 and 23 May 1974,[4] in the vicinity of Brooks Peninsula on 6 August 1981 and 30 October 1979,[13] and in Bamfield during the winter (BCFWS).

Herons are occasionally taken in their breeding colonies by Bald Eagles, although on the west coast they do not appear to have any other natural enemies and are not normally preyed upon, being able to outmanoeuvre an eagle most of the time. A pair of eagles teaming up may obtain a different result (see under Bald Eagle). Herons are highly territorial when it comes to protecting their preferred fishing spot and will vigorously defend it from others. When disturbed or surprised, herons emit a loud, harsh vocal protest that would befit a pterodactyl.

GREAT EGRET
Ardea alba

STATUS: Casual vagrant in spring and fall.

Formerly known as the Common Egret, the Great Egret has a strong association with the tropics and subtropics. It breeds from India and Southeast Asia to Australia, and in most of South America, Central America, and the southern United States. In the United States, they push north in spring to breed along Atlantic shores north to New England, and in the Mississippi Valley to southern Minnesota and Wisconsin. In Canada, they nest in southern Ontario and in Manitoba. In the American west, the species breeds north to the southern half of Idaho and Oregon, with an outlying colony in southern interior Washington. Birds are often seen well outside the breeding range.

In British Columbia, the first sighting occurred on 9 September 1970,[107] and there have been many occurrences since.[6] On Vancouver Island's west coast, we have five records. The first was a bird seen and photographed at the Long Beach Airport on the improbable date of 22 November 1992. A second bird was recorded at Jensen's Bay, Tofino, from 27 August to 30 September 2001. On 29 October 2006, a Great Egret was reported from the south end of Long Beach, and in 2011, a Great Egret was found at Jensen's Bay on 16 April. This individual stayed until 3 June, during which time it was seen by numerous residents and visitors alike, at times being accompanied by its smaller cousin the Snowy Egret (see under Accidentals). The fifth record occurred on 22 August 2017, when a bird was photographed at Nels Bight, Cape Scott Provincial Park.

CATTLE EGRET
Bubulcus ibis

STATUS: Casual visitor in spring, fall, and winter.

This small white heron is named for its association with cattle and other hoofed animals. In fact, it originates in the African savannah, where it is adapted to feeding on insects stirred up by the feet of grazing mammals. It was first discovered in North America in 1953 but, unknown to ornithologists, was already established in Florida as early as 1941. It apparently arrived in South America in 1877 or just before that, a flock of birds having apparently flown across the Atlantic Ocean on its own. It may not have become established there until much later, however.

Since the 1950s, the species has taken the southern United States by storm and it now breeds in numerous southeastern states and at a number of locations in the western United States as well. As a wanderer it has been seen in all Canadian provinces, including British Columbia. In this country, it breeds, or has bred, only in southern Saskatchewan, Manitoba, and southern Ontario.

A Cattle Egret was first reported in British Columbia near Victoria on 26 November 1970, although the first verified sighting was not recorded until November 1973, near Sooke.[108] The first occurrence for the west coast region happened just a month later at Tofino, and may have involved the same bird.[1] More sightings followed, with observations in at least 13 separate years. There are eight records for November, six for December, and two for October. The two spring sightings occurred on 9 May 1981 and 11 March 2016. Most sightings have been in the Tofino area, but also at the Pachena (BC Photo 372) and Carmanah lighthouses, at Hotsprings Cove, and at the Long Beach Airport. There is a single record from the southern tip of Brooks Peninsula on 26 November 1974.[13]

Most sightings have involved from 1 to 4 birds, though a flock seen at Port Renfrew on 8 December 1984 contained 11 birds. After 1999, occurrences greatly decreased, with only three additional records up to the present. A single bird was seen at Ucluelet on 29 October 2006, and again eight years later, on 8 November 2014. On 11 March 2016, a bird was photographed on the Tofino Hospital grounds. I recently heard of additional sightings in the Tofino area since 1999, but lack specific dates. It may be that the population expanded to its maximum extent in North America during the 1980s or 1990s, and has since contracted somewhat.

GREEN HERON
Butorides virescens
STATUS: Casual vagrant in spring, summer, and fall.

This small, colourful heron frequents brushy banks on slow-flowing rivers, ponds, lakes, and sloughs. Its breeding range covers much of Mexico, the eastern United States, and the Pacific coast to southern British Columbia. It winters from California south to Mexico and Central America. The species did not appear in British Columbia until 1 October 1953.[109] Since then it has expanded its range and today is considered an uncommon breeder in the Fraser Valley and on southeastern Vancouver Island to Courtenay and Port Alberni.[110] There is one extralimital breeding record from Green Lake, near Whistler.[111]

In the west coast region, we have eight records. They include 18 September 1971, Tofino – 1; 13 June 1994, Schooner Cove parking lot – 1; 18 July to 9 August 1996, at pond beside the Long Beach Golf Course – 1; April 2002, Tofino-Ucluelet Airport – 1; 27 April 2008, Grice Bay – 1; 3 December 2011, San Juan River near Port Renfrew – 1; and 3 July 2013, Morpheus Island, Tofino – 1. There is also one record from Klaskish River on 22 May 1978 that extends the range about 180 km northward from the Tofino area.[13]

ORDER ACCIPITRIFORMES
New World Vultures   Family Cathartidae

TURKEY VULTURE
Cathartes aura
STATUS: Uncommon visitor in spring, summer, and fall.

Turkey Vultures are sometimes erroneously referred to as "Turkey Buzzards." However, buzzards are large hawks in the genus *Buteo*, while Turkey Vultures belong to the family of New World vultures. The species feeds largely on carrion, although it is also known to prey on snakes and even young birds. It has

Two Turkey Vultures perch in an ancient western redcedar snag. This species has become much more common in recent years.

the unusual characteristic among birds of having an acute sense of smell, which it uses to detect dead animals hidden from sight beneath the forest canopy. While members of this family are generally associated with warmer climates, Turkey Vultures are found from southern South America to southern Canada. In British Columbia, they breed in the Okanagan Valley, Shuswap Lake region, and Creston Valley.[112] On the coast, the species breeds in the Salish Sea basin, including eastern Vancouver Island and the Sunshine Coast, where the species is a common summer visitor.[112]

In our west coast region, Turkey Vultures were unknown until 1974, when on 25 May a bird was observed at the San Josef River near Cape Scott Provincial Park.[113] The first known sighting on the central west coast occurred on 20 May 1979, at Cox Bay, near Tofino. On 22 June 1995, two birds were seen feeding on a sea lion carcass at Long Beach. Then in 2002, single birds were recorded over Tofino on three occasions – 19 April, 28 April, and 24 September. Birds were also seen at two other locations on the west coast that year.

Disregarding sightings from Jordan River on our southern boundary, where birds are more common, Turkey Vultures have been recorded in every year since 2001 except 2007, with multiple sightings in most years. In 2014 there were already seven sightings before the end of June. Most records have involved single birds, but on several occasions two and three birds were recorded. On

29 August 2006, six birds were reported over Juan de Fuca Provincial Park, and on 11 June 2016, five birds were seen over the Long Beach Airport. As far back as the 1980s there was a reliable report of a kettle of a dozen birds over Tofino.

Spring records begin as early as late April. In 2011, a very early sighting occurred on 8 April, with a bird seen over the airport at Long Beach. Birds may be seen throughout the summer to the end of September. The latest sighting ever recorded was on 29 October in 2013, when a bird was observed feeding on a sea lion carcass at Long Beach.

An inexperienced observer may mistake a distant soaring Turkey Vulture for an eagle, but note how the wings bend upward in a dihedral and how the bird sways from side to side. When the bird is directly overhead, you may see the naked red head of adults. As it is now being seen multiple times each year, this is a bird to watch for in our region.

Ospreys, Eagles, and Hawks   *Family Accipitridae*

OSPREY
Pandion haliaetus

STATUS: Common spring and summer visitor. Uncommon to rare fall migrant. Breeds.

The Osprey is a specialist, feeding almost entirely on fish captured beneath the surface of the water and occasionally capturing small mammals.[114] Upon spotting a fish, it dives from a height and plunges into the water, feet first, gripping the fish with its talons. To prevent fish from escaping, it has barbed pads on the soles of its feet to aid in holding its prey. Upon surfacing, the Osprey will shake itself like a dog in order to rid itself of excess water. Flying to a perch or to its nest to consume its catch, it always carries the fish head first to overcome wind resistance, and must evade any Bald Eagles in the area that may attempt to steal it, a not unusual occurrence. If the fish is large, such as a moderate-sized salmon, the Osprey may have difficulty gaining altitude and its flight will be laboured.

Ospreys have a wide distribution and are found in much of the world, either as breeding birds, migrants, or wintering birds. In Canada, with the exception of the Great Plains and the tundra regions of the north, they breed on lakes and rivers and other wetlands throughout the country. Although birds are residents in some southern regions such as Florida and Baja California, Canadian Ospreys and those from Alaska and the northern states arrive in

Because of access to both protected and outside waters, the Osprey is a common breeding bird in southern Clayoquot Sound.

spring and, after breeding, migrate south in late summer and fall. While some birds winter in California, most travel to Mexico, Central America, and South America, as far south as northern Argentina. In British Columbia, they breed throughout most of the province except Haida Gwaii.[111]

Ospreys do not breed in all areas of the west coast region. Rather, they tend to breed only in the most favourable locations with both outside and inside waters available. At such locations, when sea conditions on the exposed coast make it difficult to see fish beneath the surface, such as during an unseasonable storm or strong westerly winds, birds can turn to calm inside waters. They also favour areas with sandy beaches, where the shallow water makes it easier to spot fish. The most favourable location on the west coast appears to be southern Clayoquot Sound, where in most years there are believed to be three or four active nests within a 6.43 km (4 mi) radius of Tofino. These are usually located in a dead snag. In the late 1960s, Hatler et al. believed there were at least three nests on Vargas Island alone.[1] While three nests were indeed located in later years, it is unlikely that all three are occupied in any given year.

Other locations where nests currently exist, or can be deduced to exist based on sight records during the breeding season, are Port San Juan, Pachena Bay, on or near Dodd Island in Barkley Sound, Ucluelet Inlet, Long Beach, and Boat Basin. Hatler also mentioned a pair taking up residence on Turtle Island in the Broken Group in 1973, though he saw no evidence for nesting elsewhere in that region.[1] There are few nesting records for northern areas. Three areas that may have the conditions favoured by this species are the Bunsby Islands, Whyat, and possibly Cape Scott. The most northerly breeding record is just west of the mouth of the Klaskish River, near the east end of Brooks Bay, where a nest contained two large young on 14 August 1981.[13]

In spring, birds usually arrive on our coast between 14 and 18 April. During a 16-year period when first arrival dates were tracked, there were three earlier records, with an extremely early date of 1 April in 1994. In the vicinity of Brooks Peninsula, Ospreys have been recorded from 8 April (1973) to 27 August (1981).[13]

The fall movement begins with local birds departing in late August and September, probably shortly after the young have fledged and have learned to fly. By early October, only stragglers remain, though these are probably birds from further north passing through. Few birds are seen in late October and even fewer into November. On 5 November 2007, a bird was seen passing over Tofino, and on 6 November 2009, a bird was seen at the Long Beach Airport. Surprisingly, there are two records for December. On 5 December 1995, an Osprey was recorded at Chesterman Beach, Tofino, and on 8 and 16 December 2001, a very late bird was observed at Tofino.

Ospreys are usually seen singly or in pairs, but on occasion four or more have been recorded simultaneously. At Jensen's Bay, Tofino, as many as six birds have been seen flying overhead, not just at the end of the breeding season but in spring.

GOLDEN EAGLE
Aquila chrysaetos
STATUS: Rare visitor.

The Golden Eagle has an extensive range in the Northern Hemisphere, breeding in large areas of Asia, eastern and northern Europe, Spain, and western North America. In eastern North America, it breeds sparingly in the northern forests of Labrador, Quebec, and Ontario. In the west, it breeds in mountainous regions from Mexico to Alaska. In British Columbia, it breeds in most suitable areas of the province east of the Coast Mountains. Records are lacking, however, for the central part of the province, where mountain ranges are largely absent. On Vancouver Island, Golden Eagles breed, or have bred, on the southeast side of the island and are seen occasionally in the mountains of the interior of the island.[111]

On the west coast of the island, records are scarce. In 1978, *Birds of Pacific Rim National Park* documented a sighting from just outside our area above Sproat Lake on 13 April 1969.[1] Another bird was observed flying high overhead in the same general area on 25 May 1987. The first sighting fully within our region occurred on 22 July 1978, when an immature bird was identified by Bristol Foster and Trudy Carson soaring low over Brooks Peninsula.[13] On 8 October 1997, one was seen flying over the harbour at Tofino. Another bird, an immature, was seen at Tofino on 21 February 1998.

Periodic reports by local residents of Golden Eagles in or around Tofino have thus far turned out to be juvenile Bald Eagles. There have also been several reports from Tofino that may well be valid, but they lack documentation and are therefore not included here. A report of a bird seen at Mount Klitsa on 13 August 2008, and one seen at Tofino Creek on 4 November 2013, are both considered reliable. In the mountains, away from the coast, Golden Eagles undoubtedly occur more often than records indicate.

NORTHERN HARRIER
Circus hudsonius

STATUS: Uncommon fall transient. Rare in spring and winter, casual in summer.

This is a bird of open fields and marshes, where it hunts by flying low over the terrain and pouncing suddenly on its prey. It has undergone a name change and in older books may be listed as "Marsh Hawk." Its breeding range covers the northern half of the United States and much of Canada, except for the most northern regions and western Alaska. In British Columbia, it is widespread as a breeding resident east of the Coast Mountains. On southeastern Vancouver Island, it is an uncommon to fairly common migrant in spring and fall, rare in summer and uncommon in winter. It is a rare breeder on the island.[111]

For the west coast of the island, *Birds of Pacific Rim National Park* listed 10 records, all of them in autumn, and considered the species a "rare fall bird."[1] Two records were overlooked, however, both from Hansen's Lagoon in Cape Scott Park. A female or immature was seen hunting on 17 May 1974 and a single bird was present around the lagoon from 25 to 28 October 1973.[4] Between 1978 and 2014, there were 89 additional sightings, mostly of juveniles. As was the case prior to 1978, most sightings occur in fall, with the overwhelming majority seen in October. Breaking them down by the month up to the end of

2013, there are 2 records for August, 15 for September, 39 for October, 11 for November, and 5 for December. There is 1 record each for January and February. For the spring period, we have only 14 records, with 10 in April and 4 in May. There is a single record for June and 3 records for July. A bird seen at Cleland Island on 30 July 1987 is difficult to explain, although it may have been a very early fall migrant. Most sightings involved single individuals, but two birds were seen on five occasions.

Records from 2014 onward were excluded from the above breakdown due to the fact that from September 2014 to 10 May 2016, a female is known to have successfully spent two successive winters, and the months in between, in the Tofino/Long Beach area. Including records from those years would have skewed the results. This bird arrived at the Long Beach Airport as a juvenile and departed a year and a half later as an adult, resulting for the first time in records for the species in all months of the year. In the fall of 2016, an adult female, believed to be the same bird, arrived back at the airport in the company of what is believed to be her offspring, and both birds were often seen hunting there in subsequent months.

Northern Harriers are seen most often at the Long Beach Airport, attracted by the open terrain, but they are also seen over tidal meadows and at Stubbs Island. In transit they may of course be seen almost anywhere, and the frequency of sightings naturally depends a lot on the frequency at which observers are present. In 2012, there were 19 sightings by a single observer. This was exceeded in 2015 with 24 sightings. There have also been occasions when two birds were seen on a single bird walk, such as on 2 September 1984, 19 September 2003, 28 September 2012, 19 December 2014, and 16 October and 6 December 2015, all at the airport.

Because there are few small mammals available as prey at the airport, these harriers apparently survive by preying on birds. The birds that are most plentiful in fall in the short-cropped stubble beside the runways are Savannah Sparrows, Wilson's Snipe, and other shorebirds. Harriers have been observed carrying several species of prey, including a snipe, an American Coot, a Northern Pintail, and, on one occasion, a garter snake.

Northern Harriers may in turn fall victim to other raptors, as I discovered in the fall of 2012, when I found the remains of a harrier on the airport tarmac, its body consumed. Both Bald Eagle and Northern Goshawk came to mind as suspects, but a Peregrine Falcon could also have been responsible. In late August 2014, two Peregrine Falcons were observed by Tofino resident Doug Banks making repeated attempts to take a juvenile Northern Harrier at Jensen's Bay. Surprisingly, the harrier proved too elusive even for these fleet-winged raptors.

Also interesting was seeing a juvenile Northern Harrier harassing a Northern Goshawk perched in a tree, by dive-bombing it. This harrier was apparently confident in its ability to elude the large accipiter if necessary.

On 1 February 2015, a juvenile harrier carrying two sticks was observed soaring with an adult Red-tailed Hawk, much like hawks are known to do in courtship. After circling with the *Buteo* for four or five minutes, it broke away, dropped the sticks it had been carrying, folded its wings, and plummeted straight down after them at a speed that would have done a Peregrine Falcon proud. Although I cannot account for such inexplicable behaviour, it certainly increased my respect for the flight capabilities of this species.

SHARP-SHINNED HAWK
Accipiter striatus

STATUS: Uncommon fall transient from August to late December. Rare in winter, spring, and summer.

This small forest hawk preys on small to medium-sized birds. Any small hawk seen in a backyard pursuing small birds at a feeder is likely to be this species. That it can and does take prey nearly as large as itself speaks to its ability as a hunter. I once observed a Sharp-shinned Hawk snatch and immobilize a Northern Flicker by pinning its wings to its body and then flying off with it, a remarkable feat when one considers that the flicker's weight nearly matched that of the little raptor. I have also heard of a Steller's Jay being caught, although in that incident the jay succeeded in breaking free.

Sharp-shinned Hawks breed from the northeastern United States south at higher elevation to Mississippi and Alabama. They also breed in forested areas in much of the American west. In Canada, the breeding range of this species covers forested regions of virtually the entire country, including British Columbia. *The Birds of British Columbia* considers it to be a "common to very common spring and autumn migrant throughout much of the province."[6] It breeds in much of the province and has been known to breed on southeastern Vancouver Island.

In our region, the Sharp-shinned Hawk has been seen in every month of the year, though it is rare in spring, summer, and winter. It is most prevalent as a fall transient. Of 110 records since 1982, 90 sightings occurred during the fall migration period from August to the end of December. August has 8

The small Sharp-shinned Hawk, a bird-hunting accipiter, has been known to capture birds up to its own size and weight.

records and September has 5. This accipiter is more likely to be seen in October than any other month. There are 39 records for that month, followed by November with 17 and December with 21. This closely parallels findings from 1968 to 1974 by Hatler et al.[1] After December, numbers drop off. There are 9 records for January, 3 each for February and March, and 1 record for April. For May there are 5 records.

The decline in numbers in January parallels a decline in passerines, and therefore in the availability of prey, during the same period.

Hatler et al. listed two records for June and six for July, and described compelling evidence through observations by Jim Biggar in 1971 that led him to suspect breeding on islands in Barkley Sound.[1] In the end, he had to conclude that the breeding status of this hawk on the west coast remained speculative. And so it remains today, with only four additional summer records in the many intervening years, two in June and two in July. If it breeds at all in the west coast region, it probably does so only sporadically.

Records from the central west coast reveal that the number of sightings can drop considerably in some years. While I have typically recorded 8 to 12 sightings annually, in 2011 the number dropped to just 4. In 2015, there were only 3 sightings despite a great deal of time spent in the field.

COOPER'S HAWK
Accipiter cooperii

STATUS: Rare transient in fall. Casual visitor in winter, spring, and summer.

The Cooper's Hawk, like the Sharp-shinned Hawk, is a bird hunter. This raptor is much larger than the "Sharpy," however, averaging more than twice the weight of the former. It is therefore capable of taking larger prey. It breeds throughout most of the United States, with the exception of the southern Midwest, southern Florida, and two regions in the Southwest. It also breeds in southern Canada from Atlantic to Pacific. In British Columbia, it is a summer visitor to the southern half of the interior of the province and has bred as far north as Prince George. There are scattered records for coastal areas of Vancouver Island and it is an uncommon resident on southeastern Vancouver Island, where it breeds.[111]

On the west coast of Vancouver Island, the pattern of this bird's occurrence is very similar to that of its cousin the Sharp-shinned Hawk, although Cooper's Hawks are seen much less frequently. In 1978, *Birds of Pacific Rim National Park* listed 14 records and designated it a rare resident.[1] Since then, 30 additional records have been added, bringing the total number of sightings to 45, essentially verifying that the rare designation is correct. Combining all records, the fall season has by far the most, with 22 sightings from the beginning of October to the end of December. October had 12, November had 6. The months of December, January, July, and September had 4 records each. March and May had 3 each, while April and August had 2 each. Nearly all birds were recorded on the central west coast, from Ucluelet to Tofino. There are 3 records from Jordan River, a single record from Hansen's Lagoon in Cape Scott Park on 15 May 1974,[4] and a single record of two birds at Triangle Island. Most records are single observations, but in 1960 a bird was present on Stubbs Island, near Tofino, from 8 July to 9 August.[111]

Which bird species Cooper's Hawks feed on while in our region is largely unknown, though the choice is likely to be varied. In December 2014, one was observed pursuing Eurasian Collared-Doves at a feeder in Tofino and is believed to have caught at least one.

NORTHERN GOSHAWK
Accipiter gentilis
STATUS: Rare resident. Retreats to more remote areas in summer. Breeds.

The Northern Goshawk has a reputation as a fearsome hunter of medium-sized birds and red squirrels. Shown here is a juvenile.

The Northern Goshawk is a superb hunter, inhabiting many forest types and adapted to pursuing its prey even through fairly dense forest vegetation, for this large raptor is remarkably agile. Its breeding range covers forested areas across Canada, Alaska, and the northern and western United States. It is a largely sedentary species on the coast. In the interior, it is reported to move south in large numbers in some years.

Two subspecies occur in British Columbia. *A. g. atricapillus* is found throughout the province east of the Coast Mountains. The subspecies, *A. g. laingi*, also known as the Queen Charlotte Goshawk, inhabits the Pacific coastal rainforest and breeds throughout southeast Alaska, Haida Gwaii, and Vancouver Island.[111] Some authorities include the BC mainland coast in its range, while others do not. Of specimens re-examined, a significant number of coastal individuals were found to have characteristics of both subspecies, even on Vancouver Island.

If we regard birds inhabiting the Pacific rainforest as a distinct population, as does the US Fish and Wildlife Service, there are estimated to be 360 pairs on the BC coast and 300 pairs in southeast Alaska.[115] A population inventory for all of Vancouver Island conducted by the Wildlife Branch of the BC Ministry of the Environment from 1994 to 1998 resulted in 51 goshawk detections and the location of 19 nesting territories. In addition, 16 territories were located by others, bringing the total of known nesting territories on the island to 35.[116] Population estimates are based on such evidence. The Canadian Northern Goshawk Recovery Team estimated that there were 165 breeding pairs on Vancouver Island,[117] not a large number for an island of 32,134 km^2 (12,408 mi^2). The Committee on the Status of Endangered Wildlife in Canada (COSEWIC) stated in its 2013 report that the population of this subspecies in Canada was estimated at just over 1,000 individuals and it was therefore considered threatened. The government of British Columbia has likewise red-listed this subspecies.[118]

Breeding season home ranges for Northern Goshawks may be as large as 4,500 ha for females and 6,000 ha for males. During the breeding season, goshawks are known to hunt Red Squirrels, grouse, ptarmigan, jays, thrushes, woodpeckers, and crows. I could find little information on the specific location of nests on the west coast, other than the fact that nests have been found near Jordan River[119] and in the Walbran Valley.

Because this is a forest hawk that uses stealth in hunting, and because it tends to nest in mature forest far from human habitation, it is rarely seen during the breeding season. Nearly all records we have, therefore, are from the period October to May, after birds have dispersed from their breeding territories to take advantage of a much larger area for hunting. In 1978, Hatler et al. listed 8 records for the west coast region.[1] Today we have 67 records. Most are from the central west coast, but two are from Kyuquot Sound, where, on 25 April 1990 and 15 October 1991, I saw single birds at the mouth of the Tahsish/Kwois River, and another is of an immature perched in a tree in Nasparti Inlet on 7 August 1981.[13]

Most sightings on the west coast occur in fall. There is 1 record for September, 8 records for October, and 14 for November. Sightings drop off somewhat during December, with 7 records, but there are 11 records for January, 6 for February, 8 for March, and 7 for April. In the winter of 2014/15, both a juvenile bird and an adult were seen on a few occasions, and possibly overwintered in the mid-coast region.

We have only two records for May and two for June. A bird was seen on the upper Kennedy River on 1 June 2005, and at Sarita Lake on 9 June 2014. An additional August sighting occurred on the upper Kennedy River on 16 August 2010. Two birds were seen on 29 December 2014, a juvenile on Stubbs Island and an adult at the end of Sharp Road in Tofino. June records are generally very rare, except to researchers trying to determine population numbers on the island, and those results are not readily available.

Three of our observations involved birds with prey. On two occasions, a Northern Goshawk was seen feeding on a freshly caught Northwestern Crow. In the winter of 2012/13, and again in the following two years, both an adult and a juvenile Northern Goshawk were seen repeatedly frequenting an area where Eurasian Collared-Doves congregated at a feeder outside Tofino. In February 2015, an adult was observed nearby, feeding on a chicken. In the past, many birds were undoubtedly shot by rural residents for such behaviour, and this may occur occasionally even today.

The Northern Goshawk on Vancouver Island is seriously threatened by the continued logging of its habitat. A 2007 report commissioned by the US Wildlife Service Alaska Region, the Queen Charlotte Goshawk Status Review, states unreservedly that "clearcut logging significantly degrades habitat by creating large forest openings devoid of prey." Second growth is little better, according to the report. "Dense second-growth stands that follow may be suitable for some prey, but these prey are largely unavailable to goshawks because the stands are too dense for the birds to effectively hunt." On Haida Gwaii, according to the same report, the population is already so precarious it is unlikely to survive. Unfortunately, the practice of leaving some trees surrounding a known nest site and logging the rest is entirely inadequate and is a recipe for the bird's continued decline.[120]

BALD EAGLE
Haliaeetus leucocephalus
STATUS: Common resident. Breeds.

Bald Eagles breed throughout Canada and Alaska, with the exception of the most northern regions and the prairie grasslands. In the United States, it breeds in the Great Lakes region, the Atlantic coast from Maine to Florida, the Gulf Coast, and the Mississippi region. In the west, it breeds from Colorado to Montana and Idaho, and on the Pacific coast from Northern California to the Aleutians. Bald Eagles winter from the Maritimes and Great Lakes region south throughout most of the United States and into northern Mexico.

Beached sea lions are an important food source for Bald Eagles and Northern Ravens during the winter lean period.

In British Columbia, the species winters primarily along the coast, the Fraser Valley, and locally in the southern interior.[111]

Because of the historically abundant food resources of the Pacific coast, especially in British Columbia and Alaska, Bald Eagles are most abundant here, both as breeding birds and in winter. This remains true today for the west coast of Vancouver Island, despite the exploitation of resources over the past century, notably forests, salmon, and Pacific herring. The seasonal migration of salmon to creeks and rivers to spawn has helped sustain a large eagle population for centuries, and presumably for millennia. The spawning of herring at a time of year when food is in short supply has also been important. It is, after all, survival during the lean times of year that determines how large the population will be over the long term.

Bald Eagles are opportunists and do not survive on fish alone. An idea that gained some prominence in the 1960s was that this regal bird was merely a scavenger. That notion is false, however. They are adept hunters and are remarkably agile for such a large raptor, taking birds whenever the opportunity presents itself. When large flocks of gulls are gathered on the shore, it is not unusual to see an eagle do a flyover just to test them. Any bird that is slow or injured will become a target. Nor do eagles confine themselves to gulls. Ducks and geese are also taken, and on rare occasions even swans. Bald Eagles can readily distinguish between those species that are vulnerable and those that are not. Mallards, because of their ability to rise straight out of the water, usually get a free pass. Green-winged Teal are a more likely target, though in no way are they easy. If an eagle can get close enough in direct pursuit to force the bird to take evasive action by plunging into the water, the eagle has a very real chance of tiring it out and capturing it.

Bald Eagles have a special strategy for diving ducks. I observed this strategy in action on a number of occasions at the Tofino mudflats, where a pair of eagles claimed a particular section of water as their hunting territory. Ducks of various species would routinely dive in the shallow water in front of my home at high tide. With numerous individuals underwater at any given time, it was not possible for an eagle to single one out, demonstrating the principle of safety in numbers. However, if an eagle spotted a lone bird that had strayed too far from the rest, it would launch an attack. The duck would then take evasive action by diving. The eagle would hover overhead, aided by the lift provided by a southeast wind, and swoop down whenever the duck surfaced for air, in this way tiring out its prey. This could go on for quite some time, threatening to tire out the eagle before the duck. This is when the eagle's partner would come in and take over. Eventually, the duck would tire and the eagle would descend, plucking the bird from beneath the surface.

Judging by the piles of feathers at the airport and at Jensen's Bay, geese fall prey to eagles rather routinely, mostly Cackling Geese and juvenile Greater White-fronted Geese. The victims are almost always solitary birds that have been separated from their flocks. On one occasion, I watched a lone Cackling Goose fly past a small island containing an eagle nest. The goose was still gaining altitude and so must have been at a disadvantage when an adult eagle launched itself in pursuit and snatched it out of the air.

A pair of eagles that lived at the mouth of Maltby Slough, Tofino mudflats, until the giant western redcedar in which they nested was felled or blown over in a storm are reported to have taken Great Blue Herons from time to time. This pair succeeded by hunting in tandem. Eagles will also steal prey caught or killed by others, such as Ospreys, Peregrine Falcons, and human hunters, particularly those who don't use dogs for retrieval. Eagles are savvy enough to be attracted to an area by gunshots, knowing that easy prey may soon be available. I once watched an eagle retrieve a duck before the hunter could launch his boat to claim it.

At Triangle Island, located 50 km off Cape Scott, Bald Eagles take advantage of the thousands of seabirds that breed there, particularly Common Murres. In the summer of 1995, there were five eyries and no fewer than 23 eagles, according to a bird researcher working there.[121] Even shellfish such as abalone may sometimes be consumed. Beneath an eagle nest near Mosquito Harbour in Clayoquot Sound, I once found cockle shells. A total of 204 prey remains were collected beneath two nests on Brooks Peninsula. They included an unidentified loon (1), Sooty Shearwater (1), Pelagic Cormorant (1), Surf Scoter (2), Bufflehead (1), unidentified gulls (3), Mew Gull (91), Common Murre (92), Rhinoceros Auklet (5), and unidentified fishes (8).[13]

Bald Eagles will also eat carrion such as seals and sea lions that wash up on beaches. The importance of this should not be underestimated. During winter, when food is in short supply and juveniles are vulnerable to starvation, a sea lion carcass can spell the difference between life and death. At the mouth of Sandhill Creek (Combers), it is quite common to see numerous eagles perched in the trees when there is a carcass on the beach. In 1982, at MacKenzie Beach in Tofino, a juvenile eagle claimed a sea lion carcass for itself and refused to relinquish its prize, even when closely approached by humans.

Spawning herring too have traditionally been an important food for eagles at a time of year when other food is scarce. In the late 1970s, herring still spawned on an eelgrass bed across from Tofino harbour in spring. On 12 March 1980, during a spawning event, a total 88 eagles were counted from Main Street in Tofino. Unfortunately for the eagles, that was the last year herring spawned there. The fact that ill-conceived openings for commercial fishing are responsible for the disappearance of herring runs at dozens of locations along the BC coast was not widely publicized though it was well documented by Terry Glavin in an article titled "Red Herring," published in the *Georgia Straight* (27 March–3 April 1997).

Bald Eagles are very territorial and they have a strict protocol of do's and don'ts to be ignored only at their own peril. A mated pair has a specific territory around the nest in which they alone are allowed to hunt, and not necessarily just during the breeding season. Exceptions are made at times for juvenile birds (probably their own) and for birds from neighbouring territories to pass over, provided they do so at a high enough altitude. According to Canada's premier eagle photographer, Tofino resident Wayne Barnes, an eagle that penetrates or crosses another's territory at low altitude is quickly escorted through or out of that territory. Areas far from nests are considered neutral territory. During times of great food abundance, such as a herring spawn, the rules seem to be thrown out the window. At such times, numerous eagles will enter a nesting territory without consequence.

Breaking protocol is serious business. On one occasion, two birds scrapping in mid-air locked their talons into each other and tumbled out of the sky in front of my home. Both birds would have died in this encounter had their talons not been carefully extracted from their deadly grip by human intervention. The birds were promptly released, though it remains unclear whether they survived their wounds. They would certainly have perished if left to cope on their own. More recently, an adult eagle died by flying into a power line in Tofino while attempting to evade an attacker whose territory it had invaded. Such electrocutions are not uncommon.

Eagles will occasionally converge from all the territories in an area to soar together for a short time. After one lengthy period of foul weather, 16 birds were seen to converge and wheel high overhead before dispersing again, as if in celebration of clear skies at last. They also occasionally convene in small groups on the mudflats for no apparent reason. The largest such gathering I have witnessed consisted of 21 individuals that were standing on Long Beach near Sandhill Creek. The fact that 16 of the birds were adults was even stranger, considering that this congregation occurred during the breeding season.

Southern Clayoquot Sound has a particularly high nesting density. Here birds have the benefit of both outside waters and protected inside waters, as well as a large waterfowl population for much of the year. This is particularly advantageous during the long periods of severe weather commonly experienced on the west coast in fall and winter.

RED-TAILED HAWK
Buteo jamaicensis

STATUS: Uncommon visitor in fall, winter, and spring. Rare in summer. Rare breeder.

The Red-tailed Hawk is one of the most common hawks in North America, and has probably been seen by more people than any other raptor. It is often seen soaring above towns and farms across the continent, or perched in trees, on power poles, or on fence posts beside roads and highways. This species breeds in virtually all of North America with the exception of the northern tundra regions, south through Mexico and locally in Central America. Over its large range, it has a number of geographical and morphological variations. On the prairies, there is a very pale form called "Krider's Red-tailed Hawk," and in the Yukon and Alaska there is a very dark population called "Harlan's" Hawk that has also been recorded in British Columbia. In the west, adult Red-tailed Hawks are richly coloured with a rusty hue to the breast feathers, and a minority of birds are all dark with a red tail. A juvenile can be all dark with no red tail. Another variant is mostly dark with a rusty upper breast and a red tail.

In *Birds of Pacific Rim National Park,* Hatler et al. considered this species our most common hawk.[1] Records spanning the many years since 1978 demonstrate that this is indeed the case. Hatler et al. listed 66 records for the Red-tailed Hawk for our region. Most sightings were in fall, winter, and spring, but there were also 5 records in June, 3 in July, and 3 in August. After observing a bird carrying a stick in June, Hatler suspected breeding. However, of 145 sightings recorded since 1978, nearly all are from fall, winter, and spring. Only 6 records are from the summer months, 4 of them from July 2014. It appears that nearly all Red-tailed Hawks vacate the west coast region for the duration of the breeding period.

The preferred prey over most of its range is small mammals, and to a lesser extent medium-sized birds, but these hawks are highly opportunistic and will also feed on carrion and garter snakes. On 25 March 2013, a Red-tailed Hawk was seen flying over the highway near Long Beach Airport with a garter snake in its talons. Townsend's Voles that live on treeless islands and in tidal meadows are another possible source of food but, with meadow voles and rabbits lacking on the west coast, food suitable for this raptor does not seem to be in great supply. I suspect that in our area this raptor survives largely by hunting birds. During salmon spawning, it is also known to feed on fish carcasses.

The Red-tailed Hawk's common hunting method is to perch in a tree, sometimes for hours, and survey its surroundings, usually in semi-open areas or forest edge but occasionally in the forest. Because it has neither the dazzling flight capability of falcons nor the agility of the Northern Goshawk, it relies on taking its prey by stealth. Red-tailed Hawks are nevertheless very capable fliers. I was surprised one day to see one repeatedly doing complete rolls while being harassed by a Common Raven.

As with other raptors, there is a high mortality rate during the first winter. On one occasion, a starving juvenile was brought to me in a cardboard box. After a meal of supermarket burger, the bird recovered its strength overnight and the next morning it was clamoring for freedom. Against my better judgment, I released it behind the house, and it flew off. Two days later, to my great surprise, the bird was back, perched on a low branch near my back door, clearly conveying its desire for more food. So for nearly a week I brought it additional food until it was strong enough to fend for itself. That this bird returned to my back door for help displayed, I thought, a surprising degree of both intelligence and trust.

On the day I am writing this account, a dead adult Red-tailed Hawk was brought to me after it had slammed into a plate glass window surrounding a patio. Sadly, death by flying into windows is one of the great tragedies of modern times, accounting for the loss of tens of millions of birds annually. One study estimates that from 365 million to 988 million birds are window-killed annually in the United States alone.

In fall, Red-tailed Hawks begin returning in late September and early October. There are 4 records from the last few days of September and 18 from October. The months of November and December have similar numbers, but by January we see a noticeable decline, either because some of the birds have moved elsewhere or because of the mortality of young birds unable to compete. A gradual reduction continues through the spring until May, for which there are only 5 records. Thus far, it remains unknown whether all Red-tailed Hawks arrive from elsewhere to winter in our region or whether some birds nest at unknown locations on the west coast. Given that these birds prefer open country and forest edge, there appears to be little suitable nesting habitat on the west coast. Large logged-off areas may provide suitable habitat, but so far there is little evidence that Red-tailed Hawks agree with that assessment. An adult bird seen hunting in semi-open country near the lower Kennedy River on 30 May 2015 was late enough in the season to warrant suspicion it was possibly nesting in the area. There are no confirmed breeding records for Vancouver Island's west coast, although a family group of four was present in the vicinity of Brooks Peninsula from 6 to 14 August 1981 and may have nested.[13] The only confirmed breeding in the west coast region occurred near Gold River, where a nest was found in an old conifer on 1 June 1977 (BCNRS files).

Most birds seen in our region are of the coastal subspecies, *B. j. alescensis*, but the subspecies *B. j. harlani*, or Harlan's Hawk, which breeds primarily in Alaska, has been seen here on two or three occasions. On 19 December 2009, an adult was seen at the Long Beach Airport, and on 2 October 2011, another bird suspected of being a Harlan's Hawk was seen at the same location. A Harlan's Hawk was also seen at Stubbs Island a few years earlier, but a date is lacking.

The Harlan's Hawk was an inhabitant of Beringia during the long Wisconsin glaciation. Isolated during the breeding season from other populations of Red-tailed Hawk by the great ice sheets that blanketed North America, it evolved into its present form over many millennia. Today it breeds in Alaska, and in fall migrates to southern parts of the midwestern United States. Some authorities believe it is a candidate for separate species status. Indeed, after its discovery in 1833, it was considered a distinct species until 1891, when it was demoted to the status of a subspecies of the Red-tailed Hawk. In 1944, the AOU reversed that decision and it became a species once again. By 1972, it was once again regarded as merely a subspecies of the Red-tailed Hawk. Opinions continue to differ as to the classification of this bird.

Care should be taken not to mistake a dark morph Red-tailed Hawk (*B. j. alescensis*) for a Harlan's Hawk, although these dark birds are just as rare in our region as the latter. In January and February 2011, an all-dark juvenile was repeatedly seen in the village of Tofino, and on 12 December 2014, another dark juvenile was photographed on Stubbs Island.

ROUGH-LEGGED HAWK
Buteo lagopus

STATUS: Casual spring and fall transient.

This large *Buteo* is a bird of the far north, where it breeds on treeless tundra from Newfoundland and Labrador to Alaska. While superficially similar in appearance to the Red-tailed Hawk, it weighs less but is somewhat larger. In flight, its wings are slightly longer, as is its overall length. This bird has the ability to hover over one spot, a useful skill on the tundra, where perches are in short supply. The species winters from Nova Scotia and the New England states west to northern New Mexico, northern Arizona, and California in the south, and north to the southern Prairie provinces and southern mainland British Columbia. In British Columbia, it is considered a regular migrant and winter visitor throughout much of the province east of the Coast Mountains, as well as in the Fraser Lowlands and to a lesser extent southeastern Vancouver Island. It is rare to uncommon in winter on southern Vancouver Island.[111]

On Vancouver Island's west coast, sightings are few and far between. Our first record involved a female collected near Tofino on 10 October 1937 (A. Peake, RBCM 52). There were no further sightings for 34 years, until a bird was seen on Ououkinsh Inlet on 26 May 1971. Later that same year, on 15 September, a bird was seen near Tofino.[1] There have been five additional sightings in the mid-coast region: 10 October 1998, Tofino – 1; 20 October 2005, Long Beach Airport – 1; 13 December 2005, Amphitrite Point, Ucluelet – 1 immature; 2 October 2006, Long Beach – 1; and 11 October 2009, Tofino – 1. Two additional reports were omitted due to the possibility of misidentification.

ORDER GRUIFORMES

Rails and Coots   *Family Rallidae*

VIRGINIA RAIL
Rallus limicola

STATUS: Uncommon transient in fall, casual in spring and summer. Breeding suspected but unconfirmed.

Most members of the rail family are notoriously hard to observe and the Virginia Rail is no exception.

This species feeds and breeds in shallow wetlands and marshes dense with vegetation. In the United States, its breeding range covers the Northeast, much of the Midwest, and nearly all the West. In Canada, it breeds from the Maritimes and the southern half of Ontario to the southern half of the Prairie provinces. Further west, its range extends north from Washington state into British Columbia. In British Columbia, it breeds in the central interior north to Williams Lake and Kleena Kleene, the Creston Valley, the Fraser Lowlands, and southeastern Vancouver Island, where it is considered rare to locally fairly common.[111]

On the west coast of Vancouver Island, this species is not often found. In 1978, *Birds of Pacific Rim National Park* listed only nine records,[1] four of which were seen at the same rain pool on Cleland Island in the months of July and August in 1967,[87] and in 1969 and 1970. Richardson had four sightings at Browning Inlet in October and November 1968, and on 6 October 1973, a bird was seen flying low across the highway at Long Beach. Others have been observed doing that since then, and on one occasion resulted in a road-killed bird.

Since 1978, Virginia Rails have been recorded 29 more times, bringing the total number of records up to 38, not a large number from which to draw conclusions about status and distribution. However, with 32 occurrences in fall, it seems safe to say that the Virginia Rail is overwhelmingly a fall transient in our area. To break it down, 6 records were from September, 9 from October, 9 from November, and 8 from December. The earliest fall date was 2 September in 2009, at Jensen's Bay, Tofino. The latest date was 30 December in 2011 at Port Renfrew. Four of the fall records involved three birds and those were all recorded at Stubbs Island, near Tofino.

We have no records for January or February, probably due to the danger of standing water freezing over. On 7 December 2013, a bird was in fact observed at the airport by Doug and Phyllis Banks during a cold spell that froze the water.

It was still very much alive and surviving. We have only one sighting for spring. On 25 March 1984, a bird was heard on Stubbs Island. For many years, this location was the most reliable one I knew of for finding Virginia Rails, having produced 12 of our records, virtually all of them based on vocalizations provoked by hand clapping or other loud noises. Birds have also been seen in the tidal meadows at Jensen's Bay, at the mouth of the Moyeha River, and in sedge-choked drainage ditches at the Long Beach Airport, at nearby Long Beach, and on the outskirts of Tofino.

The Virginia Rail's preferred habitat on the west coast appears to be shallow standing water containing tall sedges, as well as drainage channels in tidal meadows. Because such habitat is common and the birds so secretive, the species is undoubtedly more common than records show.

Virginia Rails are not entirely restricted to such habitat. In September 2014, much to my surprise, three birds were flushed at the airport from an area dominated by heather, broom, and other low vegetation not subject to standing water at any time of year. It was raining at the time, however, and there was a pond not far away.

There is little evidence that the species breeds in the west coast region (BCNRS files), as suitable breeding habitat such as marshes with cattails (*Typha latifolia*) is rare here. On 26 July 2016, however, a Virginia Rail was heard several times in a wet area containing sedge at the Long Beach Airport. Because fall migrants are not expected until September, this midsummer date suggests the possibility of breeding.

SORA
Porzana carolina

STATUS: Rare summer visitor and casual fall migrant. Rare breeder.

Like the previous species, this rail is widespread in North America, breeding from the Maritimes and New England across the continent to parts of all western states and British Columbia, the Northwest Territories, and Nunavut. The species winters in the southern United States, the Caribbean, Mexico, Central America, and northern South America.

The bird's secretive nature and the fact that large areas of British Columbia are remote make determining its exact range difficult. The species apparently breeds in suitable habitat throughout much of British Columbia east of the Coast Mountains. On Vancouver Island, it is known to breed from Victoria

The Sora is rarely seen, even in areas where it is common. This bird was photographed on its winter range in Mexico.

north to Nanaimo. Its preferred breeding habitat is marshes and wetlands containing emergent vegetation such as cattails, bulrushes, and sedges.

On our west coast, the Sora was first recorded on 19 October 1971, when an individual was caught in a mammal trap at the Long Beach Airport. The specimen is now in the Royal BC Museum in Victoria (RBCM 11966). That remained our one and only record until 1983, when a bird was flushed from one of the sedge-filled ponds at the same location. Since then, birds have been seen there on four more occasions. They are also seen or heard periodically along the lower Kennedy River in summer. On 21 June 1998, Ucluelet resident Daryl Keeble photographed an adult along the river, near the bog. They apparently breed there in some years. George Bradd reported seeing an adult with a chick on 28 July 2002.

There are 12 records in all. Two were recorded in June, 2 in July, 5 in September, and 3 in October. Besides the two locations already mentioned, a bird was flushed from a sedge-filled pond at Stubbs Island on 17 September 2004. Records suggest that Soras migrate through our area in fall in small numbers. Given its secretive nature and the fact that not a lot of time has been spent looking for this bird in the sedge wetlands it inhabits during migration, this rail is probably more common than records indicate. No birds have been found in the tall sedge habitats preferred by Virginia Rails.

AMERICAN COOT
Fulica americana
STATUS: Rare fall visitor, casual in winter.

American Coots are occasional winter visitors to protected waters such as Ucluelet Inlet, Grice Bay, and Tofino harbour.

This is the largest North American member of the rail family. It is more often seen riding ducklike on the water than walking along the shore or among marsh vegetation like other rails. In Canada, the species breeds on freshwater ponds, lakes, and marshes throughout most of the west, from British Columbia, the Yukon, and the Northwest Territories east to the Great Lakes region, southern Quebec, and New Brunswick. In the United States, it breeds throughout much of the country but is absent from much of the east. The species breeds through Mexico, Central America, and northern South America. In British Columbia, the American Coot breeds in the Peace River region and in the northeast corner of the province. In the southern half of the province, it breeds widely in the interior and also in the Fraser Valley and on southeastern Vancouver Island, where it is considered a common to abundant migrant and winter visitor.

On Vancouver Island's west coast, the situation is quite different. In 1978, *Birds of Pacific Rim National Park* listed only 17 sightings, mostly from southern Clayoquot Sound, and considered it an uncommon migrant, rare in winter.[1] Thirty-eight years later, with an additional 85 records, its status remains essentially unchanged. It should be noted that a good number of those 85 records involved the same bird or birds seen on multiple occasions. Sightings tend to be few and numbers are small. Flocks of more than 3 birds are fairly rare. Between 1998 and 2015, only 3 sightings exceeded 7 birds – 18 birds at Grice Bay on 5 November 1998, 20 in Ucluelet Inlet on 17 January 2014, and 30 there exactly one year later. Most sighting since 1978 have occurred in the months of October and November, though we also have records from September, December, January, and March. Hatler et al. listed a sighting for April as well.[1] All but three records are from the central west coast from Ucluelet to Tofino. Two exceptions were seen along the south side of Barkley Sound at Bamfield and the Sarita estuary. The most northerly record is from Browning Inlet on 30 October 1968.[16] More sightings were recorded at the Long Beach Airport and at Grice Bay than from any other location.

Cranes   Family Gruidae

SANDHILL CRANE
Antigone canadensis

STATUS: Common spring and fall migrant from Barkley Sound south, rare elsewhere.

Cranes are long-legged and long-necked birds superficially resembling herons. However, cranes do not fold their necks into an "S," and unlike herons they do not spear fish. Instead, cranes have a varied diet that includes vegetable material, insects, amphibians, snails, reptiles, and even small mammals. They are also very distinctive in their behaviour and perform elaborate dance displays as part of their mating ritual. There are 15 species worldwide if we include the two crowned-cranes of Africa. In North America, we have only two species, the Whooping Crane and the Sandhill Crane.

Unlike the endangered Whooping Crane, the Sandhill Crane has a very large population. Indeed, it is the most abundant of any of the world's cranes. At the Platte River in Nebraska, an estimated 600,000 gather every spring on their northward migration.[122] In the east, a population that was nearly extirpated has grown to 80,000 to 100,000 birds.[123]

Currently, six subspecies are recognized in North America, though they are more easily separated as the Greater Sandhill Crane, mostly of the south, and the Lesser Sandhill Crane of the north. The Greater stands 1.37 to 1.52 m

Sandhill Cranes are rare north of Barkley Sound. This Lesser Sandhill Crane was found at the Long Beach Airport.

(4.5 to 5 ft) tall, while the Lesser ranges from 0.91 to 1.06 m (3 to 3.5 ft) high. Two populations, one in Florida and one along the Gulf Coast, are sedentary. The rest migrate north, some as far as western Alaska and eastern Siberia.

In British Columbia, three separate migration routes are recognized, one through northeastern British Columbia, one through the central interior, and one along the coast. Some 3,500 coastal birds pass by Cape Flattery, Washington, each spring, where they cross the Strait of Juan de Fuca to reach the west coast of Vancouver Island.[124] Large numbers have been recorded passing by Carmanah Point by assistant lighthouse keeper Jerry Etzkorn. In 1998, he counted 115 birds on 7 April, 170 on 9 April, and 95 on 15 April. Similarly, he counted 390 birds from 11 to 16 April 2000.

At Ucluelet and Tofino, this species is rarely seen because birds turn north into Barkley Sound and cross the island there, following Alberni Inlet. Surprisingly, there are remarkably few records from Barkley Sound itself. Two are mentioned by Hatler et al.[1] On 16 August 1968, three birds were seen flying over Imperial Eagle Channel, and on 19 April 1971, six birds flew north over the Stopper Islands. There is also a record from Sarita River, where 150 birds were seen on 10 April 1982, and from the mouth of Bamfield harbour, where 50 birds were observed on 14 April 2013. It is possible that most birds make the turn earlier, for example, at Pachena Bay, or even earlier at Clo-oose.

We do know that large numbers pass over the Alberni Valley, just outside our region, particularly the area around Sproat Lake Provincial Park. On 7

April 1985, 55 birds were seen passing over, and on 6 April 2013, 230 birds were observed. The largest numbers were recorded in 2014, when George and Sylvia Bradd counted 328 birds on 9 April, 95 on 10 April, 760 on 15 April, 28 on 18 April, and 75 on 19 April, for a total of 1,286 that month. An additional 206 birds were spotted passing over McCoy Lake on 14 April, by Russel Cannings. It appears that after passing over the Alberni Valley, Sandhill Cranes continue in a northwesterly direction to Comox Lake, staying on the inside of the Beaufort Range to reach the inner coast near Courtenay. There are records from the Courtenay area that support this.

In fall, birds appear to follow the same route in reverse, with many birds again recorded from both the Alberni Valley and Carmanah Point. All fall dates from Carmanah Point fall between 14 and 24 September. While there have been sightings from outside this migration corridor at Ucluelet, the Long Beach Airport, and Tofino, all but four records involved fewer than 5 birds. One sighting occurred in the early morning hours of 19 September 1972, when 18 birds were seen flying southeast over Tofino. The second observation occurred in spring, when a hundred or so birds were reported soaring over Tofino by numerous residents. Unfortunately the date was not recorded. On 18 September 2007, 25 cranes were seen over Ucluelet Inlet. In 2016, 49 Sandhill Cranes landed briefly at Jensen's Bay on 16 April, then continued their journey. Skies were overcast and they may have missed their turn into Barkley Sound.

While the fall records already mentioned occurred during the migration period, most sightings were recorded well after, indicating that birds seen in the Tofino/Long Beach area are wayward birds that have been separated from their flocks and are temporarily lost. One sighting occurred in September and four in October. The latest fall date was 11 November in 2000, and involved three birds. An individual seen on 5 August 1994 also appears rather anomalous, far too early to be a fall migrant.

It is believed that most of the birds passing over Vancouver Island breed in the bogs of the mainland coast of British Columbia, on Haida Gwaii, and in southeast Alaska. On Vancouver Island, birds have been recorded breeding only on the northernmost part of the island in the Nahwitti Bog, just to the east of the west coast region (BCNRS files). Not surprisingly, a pair was recorded nearby at Hansen's Lagoon in Cape Scott Park, from 15 to 21 May 1974.[4]

It remains uncertain which Sandhill Cranes migrate over Vancouver Island, Greater or Lesser, or perhaps both. The small size of a bird photographed at the Long Beach Airport showed that it was clearly a Lesser. However, in 2005, biologists in the state of Oregon planted satellite transmitters on eight Greater Sandhill Cranes captured near Portland. Two of those birds migrated to southeast Alaska, raising the possibility that birds nesting on the BC coast are Greater Sandhill Cranes.[125]

ORDER CHARADRIIFORMES

Stilts and Avocets Family Recurvirostridae

AMERICAN AVOCET
Recurvirostra americana
STATUS: Casual spring vagrant.

This elegant wader nests primarily on the Great Plains, from the Canadian Prairies south to Texas, but also quite widely further west, from central Washington south to Arizona and southern California. It winters from Florida, the Gulf Coast, and coastal California south to Cuba, Mexico, and Guatemala. In British Columbia, it is a rare visitor from April to December but has nested in the province sporadically on Bechers Prairie in the Cariboo (BCNRS), at Alki Lake near Kelowna (BCNRS), Beresford Lake south of Kamloops (BCNRS), and Duck Lake near Creston.[126] In 1988, a pair nested for the first time on the coast at Serpentine Fen in the Fraser River delta. On the south coast, the species occurs sporadically as a rare migrant in spring, summer, and early fall.[7]

On Vancouver Island's west coast, we have four records in three separate years, all from Tofino: 7 May 1987, Tofino area mudflats – 4;[127] 30 June and 1 July 2008, Tofino mudflats – 1; 19-29 April 2011, Tofino mudflats – 1; and 10-12 May 2011, Tofino mudflats – 1. The latter two records may have involved the same individual.

Oystercatchers Family Haematopodidae

BLACK OYSTERCATCHER
Haematopus bachmani
STATUS: Common resident along the outer coast. Breeds.

Two oystercatchers are found in North America, a black-and-white bird known as the American Oystercatcher, and an all-black bird known as the Black

Black Oystercatchers feed on intertidal life, primarily on the rocky outside coast. These birds are foraging on a mussel bed.

Oystercatcher. The American Oystercatcher inhabits Atlantic shores and the west coast of Mexico, while the Black Oystercatcher is a bird of Pacific shores from the Aleutian Islands to central Baja California. Only in Baja do their ranges overlap, and there one may see both birds side by side on the same reef.

Black Oystercatchers feed exclusively on intertidal marine invertebrates, including limpets, mussels, chitons, whelks, and other snails, as well as crabs, soft-shelled clams and oysters, and polychaete worms.[128] Small mussels make up the greater part of their diet. In our west coast region, they nest on rocky islands and headlands and islets along the outer coast, where the female lays her eggs in a depression in the rocks or upper sandy beaches, lined with small bits of marine shell fragments or sometimes pebbles, bits of wood, or the hard parts of gooseneck barnacles.

At Cleland Island, where Glaucous-winged Gulls nest in large numbers, oystercatcher eggs are often subject to predation by that species. Although oystercatchers are reported to vigorously defend their nests, loss of eggs is not unusual. At locations closer to Vancouver Island, additional predators may include mink, northern river otters, Northwestern Crows, and Common Ravens. Occasionally there are additional losses when an unseasonable storm, especially during high tides, sends waves crashing upon the shore. Then, nests located too close to the intertidal zone may be wiped out, which happens periodically on Cleland Island. If this happens early in the season with full clutches (two or three eggs), birds will usually nest a second time.

Young oystercatchers already have well-developed legs when they hatch, and leave the nest not long after hatching. At a command from a parent, they dart into a depression or cavity and freeze. Their ability to blend into the dark rocks and disappear is astounding, though such camouflage is vital if they are to survive their many potential predators. If the young manage to survive the first two weeks, their chances of longer-term survival greatly increase.

Oystercatchers are not often seen on sandy beaches, though at Long Beach they occasionally land on the beach at the mouth of Sandhill Creek (Combers), at Lovekin Rock, and at the north end. They are more often seen on the rocks at the south end of Long Beach, at Green Point, and on Lovekin Rock. Along the West Coast Trail, birds have been seen at numerous locations but are not as common as they are further north. In fall and winter, when severe sea conditions often prevail, birds will abandon the outer coast for more protected waters. Sizable flocks are then seen on the mudflats of Clayoquot Sound at low tide, or resting on rocks in or near Tofino harbour at high tide. They may also be seen flying low over the water between resting and feeding locations. Although oystercatchers rarely venture very far up the inlets, 40 birds were found at the mouth of Cypre River, located north of Meares Island, on 30 January 1989, and a flock was reported in Warn Bay in the fall of 2016. In Barkley Sound, which is more exposed to the open ocean, birds have occasionally been found far within the sound.

Through 1990, at least 2,134 pairs of Black Oystercatchers nested along the BC coast at 315 confirmed sites. Of these, 35% nested along Vancouver Island's west coast.[88] The Western Hemisphere population (Baja California to Aleutian Islands) is estimated at less than 11,000 individuals.[129] There were 29 breeding pairs on the Scott Island group in 1989, 13 pairs in Quatsino Sound in 1988, 9 pairs in the Solander Island/Brooks Bay area of Brooks Peninsula, 23 pairs in Checleset Bay, and 125 pairs in the Kyuquot Sound area.[130] Thanks to surveys done by Pacific Rim National Park personnel in recent years, the estimated breeding population from Cleland Island to Port Renfrew is 320 pairs.[130] Cleland Island has the largest breeding population of any single location, with approximately 44 breeding pairs, while islands and islets in Barkley Sound have about 50 pairs.

Cleland Island is the only location along the west coast where significant numbers of nonbreeding Black Oystercatchers gather each year in summer. Between 16 June and 17 July 1970, an average of 52 birds roosted and fed on the island. The maximum count was 106 birds on 17 July (BCFWS).

Plovers Family Charadriidae

BLACK-BELLIED PLOVER
Pluvialis squatarola

STATUS: Common spring and fall migrant, rare in summer, locally fairly common in winter.

The largest of our plovers, the Black-bellied Plover is strikingly handsome in its contrasting black-and-white breeding plumage. It is conspicuous in both appearance and voice, the latter a rather mournful cry that can be heard from a considerable distance and is unmistakable once you know it. Black-bellied Plovers may be found on mudflats as well as on sandy beaches, and eat a variety of food, including worms, mollusks, crustaceans, and even *Velella* (small jellyfish with sails), which occasionally wash up on beaches in large numbers.

This species has a widespread breeding range in Arctic regions, from Russia and Siberia to western and northern Alaska and Canada. It winters in coastal regions around the world, from Australia and Southeast Asia to Africa and Europe. In the Americas, it winters along both coasts, on the Pacific side from Chile to northern Haida Gwaii in British Columbia. Two subspecies of Black-bellied Plover breed in North America: *P. s. squatarola* in northern Alaska and *P. s. cynosurae* in the Canadian Arctic. The estimated breeding population of the former has increased significantly to 262,700 birds. Estimated numbers for the latter have dropped from 150,000 to 100,000 birds. Combined, the two subspecies are estimated at 362,700 birds.[131]

Although Black-bellied Plovers pass through coastal British Columbia in sizable numbers, on Vancouver Island's west coast they are usually seen in small flocks of up to 30 individuals. Occasionally, concentrations of 50 or more birds are tallied, such as on 25 April 1996, when 73 birds were seen at Incinerator Rock, Long Beach, and on 29 April 1969, when over 100 were estimated on Chesterman Beach.[1] In fall of the same year, 85 birds were counted on the Tofino mudflats on 5 and 19 October. In 2013, 102 birds were counted at the same location on 20 April; a few days later, Tofino resident Arthur Ahier estimated a minimum of 150 birds spread out over a large area along Browning Passage.

Migrants usually begin arriving after mid-April and numbers peak by the end of the month or in early May. By mid-May, numbers have dropped off, although some birds will continue to pass through until the end of the month. There are a surprising number of records of small flocks seen during the last week of May, as a final wave of migrants brings up the rear, for example: 28 May 1996 – 12 birds; 26 May 1999 – 17; 26 May 2009 – 22; 27 May 2010 – 12; and 23 May 2012 – 21. By June only a handful of stragglers remain, presumably nonbreeders. In some years, a few birds linger throughout the entire month of June and into July.

The presence of nonbreeding birds in June and July makes it difficult to determine just when the southward migration begins. The earliest date that appears to involve new arrivals is 27 July in 2000, when 15 birds were seen at Chesterman Beach. There is also a record of 13 birds seen on 2 August 2010, and 8 birds on 7 August 2011. Unlike in spring, the fall movement is far less obvious. Small numbers may occur throughout late summer, and by October and November birds are seen more often. Habitats in which they are seen most often are sandy beaches and mudflats. They are also seen occasionally at the Long Beach Airport.

Birds of Pacific Rim National Park did not list any winter records, although it did list a date of 6 March 1973, which was likely a wintering bird. In the winter of 1992/93, 40 birds were recorded at Chesterman Beach on 12 December, and 31 birds were seen on the Tofino mudflats on 3 January. On 29 January 1995, 41 birds were counted on the Tofino mudflats. Since then, observations of 16 to 22 birds in winter have been fairly frequent, surging to 46 birds on 7 January 2015.

AMERICAN GOLDEN-PLOVER
Pluvialis dominicus

STATUS: Rare transient in late summer and fall.

The American Golden-Plover was for a time known as the Lesser Golden-Plover when it was lumped with what later became the Pacific Golden-Plover. After the species was split in 1993, the American bird was reissued its former name. This species has a widespread breeding range in Canada's Arctic, from Baffin Island and Hudson Bay west to Alaska and the Bering Strait. There are several breeding records from northern British Columbia, and one in the central interior (BCNRS). The species winters in South America, from Paraguay and southern Brazil to northern Argentina.

This species is considered rare to very rare in spring anywhere in the province.[111] Although it is seen more often in fall, the bulk of the population migrates well east of the Rocky Mountains, bypassing British Columbia. A small number of birds are sighted in the interior of the province, while a somewhat larger number use the coast as a migration corridor. Although most reports are of 5 birds or fewer, occasionally larger flocks have been reported, such as 200 birds at the Vancouver International Airport on Sea Island near Vancouver on 16 September 1972,[132] and another 200 south of us at Ocean Shores, Washington, on 18 September 1983.[133] Such large numbers are highly unusual, however.

In our west coast region, we have had 36 sightings since 1982, nearly all of which have involved from 1 to 3 individuals. The largest number recorded was 5 birds at the Long Beach Airport on 23 October 1983. Two birds at Chesterman beach on that same date bring the total for a single day to 7. The earliest date for the fall migration period was of a single bird seen flying over the airport on 19 July in 2013. The next earliest date was recorded on 7 August 1997. There are 2 records in August, 14 in September, and 18 in October. In 1978, *Birds of Pacific Rim National Park* listed 1 record in July, 4 in August, 10 in September, and 2 in October, though no distinction was made, at that time, between the American and Pacific Golden-Plover.[1] The latest date on which the species was recorded was 3 November in 2013, when a single individual was observed and photographed at the Long Beach Airport. Evidence suggests that fall passage occurs primarily from early September to late October.

To date, there are no spring records for the west coast. Although there are several old reports from as far back as 1931, based on what is now known, those were almost certainly Pacific Golden-Plovers. Despite occasional sightings of American Golden-Plovers on the southeast side of Vancouver Island in spring, no bird closely scrutinized in our region has proven to be this species.

PACIFIC GOLDEN-PLOVER
Pluvialis fulva

STATUS: Rare transient in both spring and fall.

The Pacific Golden-Plover breeds across much of northern Siberia, from the Yamal Peninsula in the west to the Bering Strait. In North America, this species breeds only in western Alaska. The winter range extends from Somalia through coastal India, Southeast Asia, Australia, and New Zealand. Most of the Alaskan population makes a direct, nonstop flight to Hawaii, a distance of 4,000 km (2,480 mi), with a small number wintering in southern California. The latter are undoubtedly the birds we see in British Columbia.

Handsome even in juvenile plumage, this Pacific Golden-Plover was found feeding on a Stubbs Island beach near Tofino.

Until 1993, this bird and its American cousin were considered to be conspecific, and the species was then known as Lesser Golden-Plover.[134] Research conducted during the early 1980s in western Alaska, where the ranges overlap, revealed that they did not interbreed. The two subspecies were subsequently given full species status, with the Asian bird designated as Pacific Golden-Plover and the American bird reverting to the name it had until the mid-1970s – American Golden-Plover.

Because little effort had been devoted to distinguishing between the two subspecies in the field, the status of the Pacific Golden-Plover on our coast was unclear. With care, however, the birds can be safely identified. No spring records existed prior to 30 April 1981, when on a rainy day at the west end of Schooner Cove, I found an adult male golden-plover in full breeding plumage feeding on the beach. But why did it have white sides? A detailed written description from that day shows that it was unequivocally a Pacific Golden-Plover.

A decade and a half passed with no further spring records. Then, on a hunch, I decided to check the Long Beach Airport. In a remarkable stroke of luck, I heard a golden-plover calling as soon as I arrived, and a moment later a bird spiralled down from the sky to land beside the runway. It proved to be a male Pacific Golden-Plover in breeding plumage. That sighting occurred on 30 April 1997, 16 years to the day after the first sighting.

Birds were found in all subsequent years that searches were conducted at the airport in spring, demonstrating that a small number pass through our region annually in spring as well as fall. Of 43 spring records, 11 are for April, 29 for May, and 3 in early June. All records fall between 23 April and 3 June. That there are 31 records before 16 May and only 6 after that indicates that most of the spring movement occurs in the first half of the month. Flock size varied from single individuals to family groups of five birds. Based on the information we have today, spring sightings listed in *Birds of Pacific Rim National Park* under American Golden-Plover – five birds on 7 May 1931 at Chesterman Beach, and a single bird on 18-20 May 1974 at Tofino – were almost certainly Pacific Golden-Plovers.

We would not expect to see this species between the end of the first week of June and September. In 2016, however, an apparent female in breeding or transition plumage was observed and photographed on Long Beach from 28 June to 8 July. Apparently too early to be a postbreeding bird, its appearance here at this time of year is difficult to explain unless it was a nonbreeding bird.

For the fall migration period, there are 28 records after 1980, with 14 occurrences in September and 11 in October. On the central west coast, the earliest record was 7 September in 2012, and the latest dates were 26 October in 2001 and 31 October in 2013. There were no August sightings for our region until 12 August 2017, when I observed an adult in nonbreeding plumage on Long Beach. There are August records from Washington, indicating that some pass through earlier.

Habitat preferences for both golden-plover species during migration appear to be identical – treeless spaces such as airports, golf courses, and sandy beaches. Unlike their European counterparts, North American birds rarely convene on mudflats. We have only a single record of a golden-plover at the mudflats, and it flew by without landing. To date, nearly all of our spring records are from the Long Beach Airport and adjacent golf course. In fall, 16 records are from the airport, 9 from beaches, 1 from the rocky shore, and 1 undetermined. Most records are from the central west coast, but there is one from the mouth of the Cheewat River along the West Coast Trail. Virtually all records are of singles, pairs, or family groups. The largest number recorded was 7 birds at the airport on 26 October 2001, and again on 17 September 2011. Though not impossible, a report of 30 birds at Boat Basin in August 2002 is highly unlikely, because of both the high number and the early date. In the absence of photographs or a detailed description, it has been discounted.

SNOWY PLOVER
Charadrius alexandrinus
STATUS: Casual vagrant in spring and early summer. Accidental in winter.

This diminutive sand plover is found in Asia, Africa, and Europe, as well as the United States, the Caribbean, and the Pacific coast of North and South America. It has a predilection for sandy habitats such as ocean beaches and the shores of alkaline lakes in the interior of the continent. On the Pacific coast of North America, it breeds north as far as Ocean Shores Peninsula, Washington.[135]

Although British Columbia lies well north of this bird's normal range, Snowy Plovers are occasional spring and summer visitors. *The Birds of British Columbia* lists 8 occurrences for the province up to the end of 1989.[6] The BC Rare Bird List chronicles 16 records to the end of 2013. For the west coast region, we have records from 10 separate years. All sightings were of single birds, except for one occasion when three birds were seen. Snowy Plovers encountered here likely represent individuals that have overshot their normal range in Washington, perhaps swept up in the wave of Semipalmated Plovers flying north. It is interesting to note, however, that 6 of our sightings have occurred in June, well after Semipalmated Plovers have passed through, suggesting that they may be wandering nonbreeders.

The Snowy Plover was first recorded at Combers Beach on 29 April 1972.[136] A second sighting of probably the same bird occurred on 6 May 1972, also at Long Beach. On 9 June 1972, a third sighting of a Snowy Plover was made at Incinerator Rock, Long Beach.[1] The rest of the records are as follows: 17 July 1973, Chesterman Beach – 1;[136] 2-5 June 1981, Chesterman Beach, Tofino – 1 (BC Photo 697);[41] 7 June 1986, Chesterman Beach, Tofino – 3 (BC Photo 1092); 13, 15, and 16 June 1986, Chesterman Beach – 1; 8 May 1991, Cape Scott Provincial Park – 1;[137] 6 May 1996, Chesterman Beach – 1;[138] 29 April and 6 May 1997, Long Beach – 1; 1 June 1998, Chesterman Beach – 1; 24 May 2010, Long Beach – 1;[139] 18 December 2014, Long Beach – 1;[140] and 18 June 2016, Florencia Bay – 1.[141]

The December record is remarkable for the date. It was a colour-banded bird found by Robin Kite, who subsequently tracked down the bird's origin through the colour combination. Someone from the Point Reyes Bird Observatory in California revealed that the bird was hatched the previous spring in Centerville Beach, Oregon.

The absence of records between 1998 and 2010 is probably due to the decline of the species along the US coast. Because of many factors – including shoreline degradation, urban development, weather, introduced beach grasses, recreational activity, and predation on eggs – Snowy Plovers have been in gradual decline for years. In 1993, the US federal government listed the species as threatened. In the state of Washington, with as few as 20 to 30 nesting birds, the species was listed as endangered. In December 1999, 18,000 acres was set aside as critical habitat, and in 2001 a draft recovery plan was created to restore the species' numbers. From 2006 to 2009, numbers dropped precipitously. By 2013 the population had stabilized somewhat, with 29 nests found and monitored, and 6 additional nests known to exist but never found.[142] On the Oregon coast, birds are doing considerably better. Due entirely to conservation and recovery efforts, the population went from a low of 45 birds in 1993 to 518 resident birds in 2016.[143]

SEMIPALMATED PLOVER
Charadrius semipalmatus
STATUS: Common spring and fall migrant.

This small plover with sand-coloured upper parts and a conspicuous black breast band is a familiar sight on west coast beaches. The word "palmated" refers to webbing between the toes; thus "semipalmated" means that the bird is semi-webbed. This species has a very extensive breeding range from Nova Scotia and Newfoundland to Arctic and subarctic regions of Canada. West of Hudson Bay, it breeds in most regions above 60° latitude, including Alaska, with the exception of the northernmost Canadian islands. It winters on the Atlantic coast from Virginia south to southern Argentina, and on the Pacific coast from Oregon to Chile. In British Columbia, the species is a common breeding bird on the beaches of northern and eastern Haida Gwaii and, to a lesser extent, in the subalpine regions of the Chilkat Pass region in the extreme northwestern portion of the province. There is a single breeding record from Iona Island on the Lower Mainland.[144] Recently the species has been expanding its breeding range into the Chilcotin region of the province.[145]

On Vancouver Island's west coast, these small plovers are seen solely as migrants, but conspicuous ones, as they feed on our beaches in considerable numbers in both spring and summer. Even at a distance, they are easy to distinguish from sandpipers through their habit of standing still then running and tipping forward. Watch closely and you may see a bird standing still with

The small Semipalmated Plover is found on west coast beaches in large numbers in both May and late summer.

one foot caressing the surface of the wet sand. It will then make a sudden dash to pluck a red worm from the sand. This foot action apparently aids the bird in detecting its prey. In late summer and fall, amphipods become an important food source. Infrequently, the species is seen on small sandy beaches on islands and peninsulas during migration, such as 12 birds on Brooks Peninsula on 4 August 1981.[13]

First arrival dates in spring usually occur in the second half of April, with numbers rising rather rapidly in the last week of April and peaking by the last few days of April or the first week of May.[146] On 4 May 1985, 150 birds were counted at Incinerator Rock, Long Beach, and on 1 May 1988 and 25 April 1992, 115 birds were counted there. Flocks of 50 or more birds are quite common. The maximum number recorded from any single location in recent years was 120 birds at the Long Beach Golf Course on 6 May 2009, during a storm. This number still falls well below the maximum number listed in *Birds of Pacific Rim National Park*, which was 400 birds at Long Beach on 8 May 1974.[1] That number presumably resulted from a count over a broad expanse of beach rather than at any single location. Numbers quickly decline after the first week of May, though a few may linger to the end of the month.

The earliest spring date involves a lone bird on Stubbs Island on 12 April in 2010. In 2012, the first two birds arrived on 18 April. June birds are rare and likely involve nonbreeding individuals. Two and three birds were still present at Chesterman Beach on 8 June in 2012 and 2014, and four birds were present on Stubbs Island on 12 June 1987.

The first fall migrants usually appear by about mid-July. However, there are two records as early as late June. In 2008, a bird was seen at Stubbs Island on 30 June, and in 2016 a single individual was seen in the company of newly arrived Western Sandpipers at Long Beach on 23 June. From late July through August, and in some years up to the middle of September, substantial numbers ply our beaches, the adults passing through first, followed by the juveniles. In 2009, the highest number, 57 birds, was recorded on 8 September at Chesterman Beach. In 2011, numbers peaked from 17 August to 22 August, with more than 60 birds counted. October sightings are fairly rare, with only six records. A single bird, seen at the airport on 9 November 1996, is our latest fall record.

Outside our region, highest numbers in spring and fall migration are from Rose Spit, Haida Gwaii, where 2,100 and 1,761 birds, respectively, were reported.[146]

KILLDEER
Charadrius vociferus

STATUS: Generally uncommon, locally common resident. Breeds locally.

This plover with two bold black bands across its breast is well known to farmers across North America, for it most commonly nests in and around farm fields. It is named after its rather loud alarm calls of "killdeer – killdeer." It breeds in suitable habitat throughout almost the entire continent, including Mexico but excluding the northern reaches of Canada and most of Alaska. The species winters throughout the southern United States, but in the west it winters north to western Montana, Washington, and southern British Columbia. On the coast, a few individuals may winter north to Haida Gwaii and even Alaska.

Killdeer inhabit open spaces, but since these are rather rare on the west coast, the habitat we most often find them in are beaches and human-cleared land. On the central west coast, most records by far are from the airport and nearby Long Beach. Nesting may begin as early as late April in some years, and not until well into May in other years. In 2016, a Killdeer was already on the nest incubating four eggs on the remarkably early date of 28 March, although nests with eggs have been found as early as 1 March in the Fraser River delta.[111]

Some birds start late. A nest with four eggs was found at Schooner Cove on 4 July 1967. Another nest was found in the sand dunes near Sandhill Creek in mid-May 1969.[1] Nests have been found at the Long Beach Airport on many occasions, with an estimated three to five pairs of birds nesting there in most years.

The Killdeer scrapes a rudimentary nest on the ground that is little more than a depression in the soil. The eggs are shaped to avoid rolling out of the nest. With tufts of lichen around the nest, the spotted eggs are virtually invisible. Don't expect to spot them in your peripheral vision. Meanwhile, one of the parents is doing a broken-wing act in order to distract you. This is designed to lure predators away from the nest. After hatching, the downy chicks are able to follow the parents on their outsized legs in very short order. At a signal from the mother, they scurry away then freeze. So perfect is their camouflage that you are highly unlikely to find one.

With the young grown up, birds begin to depart in August and September. Sometime in October, numbers increase again, with the apparent arrival of migrants from elsewhere. On 16 October 2009, 24 birds were counted at the airport. On 15 December 2013, there were 20, and on 26 November 2009, there were 35 birds. As late as 1 January 2010, those 35 birds were still present. No further counts were made that year until 4 March, when only a single bird was found. However, it is not unusual to see a small number of overwintering birds in January and February. On 16 January 2016, seemingly out of nowhere, a flock of 16 birds suddenly appeared on the school playground in Tofino. The last sizable flock seen in the Tofino/Long Beach area prior to this had been recorded on 11 November 2015, when 18 birds had been observed at the airport. It seems highly unlikely a flock of this size would have been overlooked for a period of over two months, which strongly suggests that the January birds were migrants passing through. This phenomenon occurred again on 22 December 2016 when 34 birds suddenly appeared at the airport.

Most records are from the central west coast, but there are also records from the north shore of Barkley Sound, Alberni Inlet, the Bamfield area, Juan de Fuca Trail, Jordan River, Boat Basin, Tahsis, Stubbs Island, and Brooks Peninsula. Most records from the last location occurred in September and October and are believed to have involved migrants from further north.

As far as I know, there have been no instances of Killdeer nesting on beaches or in sand dunes since the 1960s. This is probably due to two factors: human traffic is much greater now, and wolves returned to the area in the 1970s. These animals regularly patrol the beaches and dunes on the west coast, as their tracks attest.

Sandpipers and Phalaropes   Family Scolopacidae

UPLAND SANDPIPER
Bartramia longicauda

STATUS: Casual in spring and summer.

This large sandpiper is a bird of the grasslands and, unlike most members of the family, is not closely associated with bodies of water. Its breeding range extends from the Maritimes and the New England states westward to the Midwest, south to northern Oklahoma, and north to the Canadian Prairies. In Canada, its range covers southern Manitoba, southern Saskatchewan, and most of Alberta, and into the Northwest Territories, the Yukon, and Alaska. Like many grassland birds, the species is vulnerable and has declined in many parts of its range. It winters in South America east of the Andes Mountains, from northern Brazil to northern Argentina.

There is a single breeding record, near Chetwynd, in northeastern British Columbia. While the province is normally considered outside the breeding range for this species, birds have been reported from widely separated locations throughout the interior and coastal areas of British Columbia, largely as fall transients. The Upland Sandpiper is a very rare transient in spring east of the Coast Mountains, and rare in fall throughout most of the province. On the coast, it is considered a casual visitor.

We have three records for the west coast region. The first occurred on 3 June 1976, when an individual was seen at Cleland Island. There were no further records until 29 June 2011, when I saw a bird pass almost directly overhead at the Long Beach Airport. The Upland Sandpiper is a species I was very familiar with from my days on the family farm in Ontario, where birds could be seen and heard almost daily in summer in the early 1960s. On 31 August 2016, a bird was once again seen at the airport, this time by Ian Cruickshank, and verified by others the following day.

WHIMBREL
Numenius phaeopus

STATUS: Common spring migrant, uncommon to locally common in summer, rare in fall.

This large shorebird occurs widely throughout the world, nesting in Arctic and subarctic regions of North America, Europe, southern Russia, and Siberia, with

The mudflats of Grice Bay and Jensen's Bay are the most important feeding grounds for migratory Whimbrels in British Columbia.

a different subspecies for each of these regions. The American subspecies, *N. p. hudsonicus,* was originally known as the Hudsonian Curlew until the British name for it was adopted. It breeds south and west of Hudson Bay, in the extreme north of the Northwest Territories, in northern and western Yukon, and in most of Alaska except for southern areas.

Until recent years, it was thought that the north slope of Alaska was populated by birds that migrate along the Pacific coast. In 2008, however, a bird that was radio-tagged in Virginia travelled 5,000 km (3,200 mi) on a nonstop 146-hour flight to the Mackenzie River Delta on her way to the breeding ground on the North Slope of Alaska.[148] It remains a mystery where exactly western migrants nest (perhaps in Alaska's interior?). We do know that they winter along the Pacific coast, from northern California south to southern Chile. Some individuals have wintered as far north as Washington and even British Columbia.

Not all Whimbrels seen on our shores are necessarily western birds. One radio-tagged individual from Alaska's North Slope was tracked crossing Alaska and the Gulf of Alaska, to arrive in Puget Sound, Washington. From there it flew to Grays Harbor, and from there directly east to the Great Lakes and beyond. This was an eastern bird taking a western route for part of the distance.

The most important feeding area for Whimbrels in British Columbia is undoubtedly the mudflats of Clayoquot Sound, near Tofino. Within the sound, the preferred feeding area is Grice Bay at low tide, where birds feed on ghost shrimp on rising and falling tides. As the tide rises, many birds travel to Jensen's Bay, where the mud is exposed for a longer period. At high tide, birds congregate primarily in two rest areas – the spit on Indian Island in Grice Bay, and the tidal meadows in Jensen's Bay. Nights are spent on rocky islets on the outside coast. Whimbrels can often be seen flying west over Chesterman Beach in the evening on their way to Wilf Rocks, islets in the La Croix Group, or Cleland Island. Birds may also feed on sandy beaches and on rocky islets, but to a far lesser extent than on mudflats.

In spring, the first birds usually arrive by mid-April or shortly thereafter. The earliest arrival dates we have are 29 March in 2015, 9 April in 1993, and 8 April in both 2012 and 2014. By the third week of April, Whimbrels have usually begun arriving in flocks, and by the end of April they are present in large flocks, when as many as 100 to 150 birds may be seen at Grice Bay or at the viewing stand at the end of Sharp Road in Tofino. During the first half of May, from 200 to 250 birds have been seen, and in several years they have peaked at 270 birds or more. After mid-May, numbers begin to decline, though smaller flocks are seen throughout the month and well into June. A small number of nonbreeding birds often persist throughout the month of June and into July, making it somewhat difficult to determine first arrival dates for southbound birds.

The southward migration occurs largely in July. First arrivals are usually detected in the first week of July, supplementing birds that have remained throughout the month of June. Even so, in the first week of July, numbers do not exceed 30 birds. In 2002 and 2003, the first detectable increase occurred on 25 June and 27 June, respectively. There is a gradual increase in July, though numbers never approach those seen in spring. High counts of 40 to 60 birds are usually the maximum, but 69 birds were counted on 19 July 2014 and 80 birds on 12 July 2015.

By the last week of the month, most birds have passed through. It appears that the vast majority of birds bypass the area entirely on the southward journey, possibly flying by far out at sea. A few birds are seen on the central west coast in August, for example, 40 birds on 6 August 2000; 17 on 24 August 2001; 26 on 5 August 2002; and 8 on 21 August 2013. A few stragglers may be seen throughout September in most years. For October we have only a single record, with 3 birds seen at Combers Beach on 8 October 1984. The latest sighting ever recorded was on 26 December in 1982, when a single bird was seen at Jensen's Bay, Tofino. There are many records of Whimbrels, from singles to flocks of 20 or so, from April through August on numerous rocks, islets, and islands along the entire west coast of Vancouver Island.[13]

LONG-BILLED CURLEW
Numenius americanus
STATUS: Casual transient in spring, summer, and fall.

The Long-billed Curlew is the largest of all North American shorebirds. It is a bird of the grasslands of the west, where it typically nests on flat or rolling shortgrass prairie in the vicinity of sloughs, ponds, and shallow lakes. In Canada, it breeds in southern Saskatchewan, southern Alberta, and interior British Columbia, where it is found in the Okanagan, Nicola, and Creston valleys and in the Chilcotin-Cariboo and Prince George regions. The species winters on beaches and mudflats, from the Texas Gulf Coast to Mexico, and on the Pacific coast from California to El Salvador. Individuals have wintered as far north as Washington, and at least one individual wintered in British Columbia. It is regarded as a rare spring migrant on the south coast, casual in summer and autumn.[111] Vagrants have been reported on the coast north of Vancouver Island, at Burnett Bay north of Queen Charlotte Strait, Butze Point east of Prince Rupert, and Langara Island on Haida Gwaii.[149]

This species was not listed in *Birds of Pacific Rim National Park*,[1] although the first record for the west coast region occurred on 5 May 1976, before its publication, when a bird was seen at Solander Island, off Cape Cook.[13] Since then, there have been 21 additional sightings in 14 separate years. Of birds recorded in spring, 3 occurred in April, 11 in May, and 2 in June. The earliest spring arrival date was 12 April in 2015, with a bird that lingered on the Clayoquot Sound mudflats for 13 days. The latest spring date was 9 June in both 1993 and 2010. Given that Long-billed Curlews arrive on their breeding grounds by the end of April at the latest, it is interesting to note that all but 4 of our spring records are from May and June. This suggests that most birds we see on our coast are nonbreeders.

The majority of our sightings have involved single birds. However, a pair spent nearly a month in the Clayoquot Sound region in 1993. They were first seen on the Tofino mudflats at Jensen's Bay on 8 May, and again at Cleland Island on 23 May. On 9 June, two individuals were reported at Tree Island near

Vargas Island. While there is no way of knowing for sure, all three records are presumed to be of the same individuals. On 11 May 2005, three birds were recorded at Medallion Beach, Vargas Island. These birds were about to land on the beach when they spotted the observers and continued on their way. The largest number yet recorded was four adults at Chesterman Beach on 6 August 2015. Ten of our records are from mudflats, while most of the rest were seen on sandy beaches. There was also a sighting at the airport.

For the fall migration period, we have 5 records. For more than a week, from 3 to 10 August 2004, two young birds-of-the-year, apparently siblings, wandered and fed unconcerned among strolling tourists on Chesterman Beach, Tofino. The second autumn sighting occurred on 14 August 2005 at Dare Beach, on the West Coast Trail. There was a third fall sighting on 30 September 2006 at Long Beach. The fourth involved the foursome at Chesterman Beach mentioned above, and the fifth was a single individual flying over Chesterman Beach on 15 August 2015. Although Long-billed Curlews remain rare visitors to our region, they have been seen often enough on the central west coast to make this a bird worth watching for.

HUDSONIAN GODWIT
Limosa haemastica
STATUS: Casual migrant in spring, summer, and fall.

This handsome shorebird was decimated by hunting in the late 19th century. The eastern population breeds along the southwestern shore of Hudson Bay and west of James Bay. The western population breeds in the northern Northwest Territories, and in three separate locations in Alaska. Today the population is reported to be at around 77,000 birds and well out of danger.[131] A small number nest in the Chilkat Pass at Mile 75 along the Haines Road of northwestern British Columbia (BC Photo 297).

Like the Bar-tailed Godwit, this species makes a long, nonstop flight during migration. Birds of the eastern population fly for as long as seven days in order to reach their wintering grounds in Argentina and Tierra del Fuego. Western birds fly south to rest and refuel on Amazonian rivers, and then continue to their wintering ground on Isla de Chiloé off the coast of Chile. The return migration corridor runs primarily from the Gulf Coast of Mexico north through the midwestern states, though individuals have been recorded in all states and provinces as occasional transients.

In British Columbia, migrating Hudsonian Godwits have been reported from widely separated locales, although, with the exception of the Peace River region,[150] most reports have been from the coast. In our west coast region, the species has been recorded 10 times in seven separate years, all of them after 1980. It is interesting to note the increasing frequency of occurrences, although this may be attributable in part to closer monitoring of the shorebird migration. Most sightings have involved males in breeding plumage. However, there is one record from 11 August 2004 involving four birds in nonbreeding plumage at Ahouse Bay, Vargas Island. These were observed by local kayak guide Andy Murray, who offered me a very convincing description that appeared to eliminate any other possibility.

All known records are as follows: 30 April 1983, Long Beach – 1;[151] 29 September 1986, Grice Bay – 1;[152] 10 September 1993, Chesterman Beach, Tofino – 1;[153] 24 May 1999, Tofino mudflats – 1 (photo); 2 June 2004, Carmanah Creek (Carmanah Point) – 1 (photo);[154] 11 August 2004, Ahouse Bay, Vargas Island – 4; 27 May – 2 June 2010, Tofino mudflats – 1 (photo);[139] 19-22 May 2012, Tofino mudflats – 1 (photo); 23 May 2012, Tofino mudflats – 2 (photo); 14-17 June 2012, Tofino mudflats – 1.

BAR-TAILED GODWIT
Limosa lapponica

STATUS: Casual vagrant in spring, summer, and fall.

This godwit is largely Eurasian, breeding from northern Europe eastward across northern Siberia to the Bering Strait. In North America, it breeds only in western Alaska. The Eurasian population winters from Africa to Southeast Asia to Australia. The Alaskan population is notable for having the longest nonstop flight of any bird in the world. After breeding in the uplands, birds gather at ocean mudflats to fatten up for the journey south. When sufficiently fuelled up, as much as 55% of a bird's body weight is fat. They are then ready to depart from Alaska to fly nonstop across 11,600 km (7,200 mi) of trackless ocean to New Zealand.[155] The return journey north, by way of China, is even longer, although it is not nonstop.

In North America, birds are seen occasionally along both the Atlantic and Pacific coasts, those on east coast belonging to the European subspecies, while those on the west coast are from the Alaskan population (*L. l. baueri*). In British Columbia, there are nine records prior to 1990, all from the Fraser Lowlands and extreme southern Vancouver Island, where they are occasionally seen during fall migration between early August and late October, when birds are in their drab nonbreeding plumage.[111] It is somewhat surprising, therefore, that half the sightings in the west coast region have been of males in breeding plumage in spring. The sighting of a female in July is very curious and likely represents a nonbreeding wanderer.

Birds of Pacific Rim National Park (1978) did not list the species at all. Since then, we have had 6 sightings, all of them since 1990. Of those, 3 occurred in spring, 1 in summer, and 2 in fall. All of our records are as follows: 3 September 1992, Pachena Bay – 1 (photo); 7 May 1999, Tofino mudflats – 1 male in breeding plumage (photo);[156] 16-19 May 2001, Tofino mudflats – 1 male in breeding plumage (photo);[157] 1-26 September 2006, Port Renfrew – 1 juvenile (photo);[158] 7-11 June 2010, Tofino mudflats – 1 male in breeding plumage (photo);[159] 6 July 2010, Incinerator Point, Long Beach – 1 female (photo).[159] Two additional reports from Tofino lack documentation and have not been included here.

MARBLED GODWIT
Limosa fedoa

STATUS: A fairly common spring migrant. Rare transient in summer and fall.

Marbled Godwits are exclusive to North America and have three widely separated breeding populations. While the bulk of the population breeds on the Great Plains of Canada and the northernmost of the American states, a smaller, disjunct population breeds along the southwestern shore of James Bay in Ontario. A third population nests remotely on the north side of the Alaska Peninsula, nearly 3,000 km (1,864 mi) northwest of its closest neighbours on the Great Plains. The birds we see in our area are from that population. The subspecies winters from southern Washington to Panama.

Although Marbled Godwits were first recorded as occurring in Alaska in 1881, when three birds were shot, breeding was not verified until June 1982, a full century later. Although no nests were found at that time, from 700 to 1,000 birds were observed feeding in Ugashik Bay near suitable habitat during the June breeding season.[160] Further study has revealed that the Alaskan birds are larger than birds elsewhere, but with shorter measurements in tarsi, wing, and bill, and that they winter from southern Washington to the San Francisco Bay area of California. They were subsequently given the subspecies designation

Newly arrived from the breeding grounds on the Alaska Peninsula, a Marbled Godwit feeds at Long Beach in August.

of *L. f. beringiae*.[160] While the name may be new, it is believed that this population was already well established in the region now called Beringia during the last ice age, which ended some 12,000 years ago. The population estimate for this subspecies in 2012 was 2,000 birds, while the estimate for the total population ranges from 140,000 to 200,000.[131]

Marbled Godwits are seen more often on Vancouver Island's west coast than anywhere else in British Columbia. *Birds of Pacific Rim National Park* listed 20 sightings of the Marbled Godwit, recorded from May to October. There was only a single sighting in May, with most occurrences in July and August. Its status was listed as "a very rare migrant."

Much has changed in the intervening years. More birds than were recorded in all of the years up to 1978 may now occur in a single year. In 2012 and 2014, there were more than 30 records of individuals and flocks in each year. My personal records alone add up to more than 300 in the years since 1978. Most sightings occur in spring and involve from one to a handful of birds, but also larger flocks. There are 49 records of flocks of 10 or more birds, while the largest flock, recorded on 30 April 2013 by a former park naturalist, the late Barry Campbell, contained 48 birds. The most prolific spring was in 2001, when 165 individuals in 13 flocks were recorded. The greater number of birds seen annually since the early 1970s, particularly in spring, is probably due to more thorough monitoring in the field rather than an increase in population. Indeed, the population in North America over the past 40 years has remained stable.[161]

The main spring movement is usually brief. The earliest arrival date ever recorded was on 9 March in 2013, nearly a full month earlier than the next earliest date of 4 April in 2006. The first flocks usually begin passing through by about mid-April or shortly thereafter. Exceptions occurred in the years 2007, 2015, and 2016. A flock of 10 birds was seen on 11 April 2007, 15 on 9 April 2015, and 22 on 7 April 2016. The movement peaks by the last week of April or the first week of May at the latest. An occasional flock may be seen later. In 2001, 18 birds were seen as late as 19 May, and 13 birds on 21 May. In 2005, a flock of 16 was still present on 22 May. A few stragglers may be seen until the end of the month.

June sightings were rare prior to 2012, with only four records. In that year, two nonbreeders were present at Jensen's Bay, Tofino, until 17 June. In 2013, two birds appeared on 6 June, and one was seen as late as 30 June. In 2014, nonbreeding birds again showed up in early June, this time three of them. It isn't clear whether birds were previously overlooked in June or whether birds spending the summer is a new phenomenon. I suspect it is the former.

The most reliable location for finding Marbled Godwits in spring, particularly in late April, is the mudflat beside Dead Man Islands, across from Tofino harbour. With the use of a spotting scope, birds may often be found feeding at low tide, directly in front of the island. Marbled Godwits may also be found at Jensen's Bay, at the end of Sharp Road, at Grice Bay, at Chesterman Beach, and at Long Beach, though not as reliably as at the first location.

During the southward movement, the species has been recorded from July to November. Records include 8 sightings in July in six separate years, 3 sightings in August, 14 in September, 12 in October, and 1 in November. Five of the October sightings occurred in 2006. Flock size during the southward migration is much smaller than in spring, with one to three birds being the norm. However, one July sighting involved seven birds, one September sighting eight birds, and one October sighting five birds. In September 2014, two birds spent five days feeding on Chesterman Beach. These birds likely had had a difficult crossing as they appeared emaciated.

The breeding grounds for the Alaskan population are situated about 2,250 km (1,400 mi) northwest of Tofino (or directly west of Sitka, Alaska). The authors of a paper on this subspecies, Daniel D. Gibson and Brina Kessel, speculated that godwits from this population fly a route directly across the ocean, rather than following the shore around the Gulf of Alaska. They offer as supporting evidence the fact that Marbled Godwits are only rarely seen in any coastal areas of Alaska other than the breeding area. This is supported by the paucity of sightings on most of the BC coast as well. The relatively few sightings in our area in fall suggests that most birds bypass the island, making landfall south of us in Washington and Oregon. Fall birds seen on our coast are presumed to be birds that aimed a little too far north, or that were driven to shore by adverse weather.

RUDDY TURNSTONE
Arenaria interpres

STATUS: Uncommon spring and fall transient.

This handsome shorebird with reddish back and bold black-on-white markings is a member of the rock sandpiper group, though this bird is found in a greater variety of habitat than its close relative the Black Turnstone, including pebble beaches, sandy beaches, and even mudflats. Turnstones are named for their habit of overturning pebbles and beach debris in order to feed on what's underneath. The species is circumpolar and widespread, breeding in the High Arctic of Eurasia and North America and wintering over large areas of the world. The species migrates along both the Atlantic and Pacific coasts, and also sparingly overland, where it is seen in a variety of freshwater habitats, including the shores of the Great Lakes.

In British Columbia, this species is very rare inland,[162] but is a regular spring and fall transient on the coast, particularly on the west coast of Vancouver Island. Here it is seen most often in the same habitat where we find its cousin the Black Turnstone – the rocky intertidal zone, especially on reefs, islets, and headlands. Occasionally it is seen on the Tofino mudflats or in the adjacent tidal meadows, or on Long Beach.

The spring migration period is very brief. Birds normally begin arriving in early May, and by mid-month nearly all birds have passed through. For those first two weeks in May we have 32 records, compared with only 5 records for the second half of the month. There is a single record earlier than May. On 27 April 2015, a bird was seen at Incinerator Rock, Long Beach. *Birds of Pacific Rim National Park* mentions 17 records for the whole of May.[1] The earliest arrival date is 4 May in 1989, 1993, and 2001. Hatler et al. mention an early date of 1 May in 1974.[1] A very late bird, seen on Cleland Island from 1 to 6 June 1970, would appear to be a nonbreeding laggard.

The fall migration begins in early to mid-July and ends by mid-September. The earliest record I have is of a bird seen at Cleland Island on 10 July 2004. *Birds of Pacific Rim National Park* lists the earliest fall record as 2 July in 1970, also at Cleland Island.[1] The book lists 30 records for July, 20 for August, and 5 for September. Most of those were likely seen at Cleland Island by graduate students working there. The two latest fall records both occurred on 27 September. In 1972, six birds were seen at the north end of Long Beach, and in 1997 a single bird was recorded at Incinerator Rock, Long Beach.

Unlike Black Turnstones, Ruddy Turnstones are not seen here in large numbers. All but one of 64 sightings recorded since 1980 involved 10 birds or fewer, and most involved 1 or 2 birds. *Birds of Pacific Rim National Park* listed the species as uncommon,[1] and evidence gathered since then supports that designation. There is 1 record of more than 10 birds. On 12 May 2013, 11 birds were seen at Jensen's Bay, Tofino. A flock of 75 birds reported at Lennard Island on 25 April 1977[111] is anomalous, both for the large number and for the early date, and may be a case of mistaken identity.

BLACK TURNSTONE
Arenaria melanocephala

STATUS: Fairly common year-round, but rare in May and June.

Although this turnstone appears black and white at a distance, at close range the careful observer will see that it its upper parts are far from black and instead are mostly dark brown. The Black Turnstone inhabits the reefs, islands, and rocky shores of the Pacific coast, where it feeds mainly on small barnacles and mussels, isopods, and limpets in the intertidal zone.[163] It is often seen in association with Surfbirds.

The Black Turnstone breeds on the coast of western Alaska and the Aleutian Islands, and winters from southeast Alaska south to Baja California and the Sea of Cortez, including coastal Sonora. In British Columbia, it is widely distributed over most coastal areas, including the west coast of Vancouver Island, where it is seen in every month of the year but mainly from July to the end of April. Records suggest that the northward migration occurs largely in late April. *Birds of Pacific Rim National Park* mentioned a concentration of 500 birds near Turtle Island in Barkley Sound on 25 April 1972, and noted that it suggested a spring movement.[1] Sightings made since then in Clayoquot Sound appear to support this, with a sighting of 450 birds on 28 April 1989 at the mouth of Tranquil Creek, and 150 birds on 26 April 1992 at Deer Bay, Tofino Inlet. These also happen to be the largest concentrations we have records of, and it suggests that these locations are staging areas. The latter two places are many kilometres away from the outer coast, which could explain why Hatler et al. did not find a noticeable spring movement through the area.[1] Indeed, aside from the records mentioned above, these birds are not often seen after the month of March.

By early May nearly all birds have departed. The few records for May involve only a few birds. For the month of June, we have only 14 records, but by early July birds begin returning from Alaska. On 6 July 1969, 30 birds, and on 8 July 2003, 45 birds, had already arrived at Cleland Island. Compared with the low number of observations in May and June, there are 126 records for July. Black Turnstones continue to be seen throughout fall, winter, and spring, though never in the large numbers we have recorded in late April. Most flocks contain 60 individuals or fewer. The average flock size for more than 10 birds on Cleland Island for the 34 records in 1969 and 1970 was 35 birds. The largest flock, 150 birds, was seen on 26 July 1970 (BCFWS). The largest flocks seen in late summer and fall were estimated at 200 birds at Cleland Island on 12 August 1973 and a similar number at Chesterman Beach, Tofino, on 31 October 2008.

That Black Turnstones also frequent the estuaries of creeks and rivers, well up the inlets of Clayoquot Sound in fall and winter, is confirmed by the following records at Bedwell River: 45 birds on 18 October 1987; 30 on 30 January 1989; and 40 on 27 October 1989. On 26 December 2012, a flock of 82 birds was seen flying from Long Beach to Tofino Inlet over the airport, very likely en route to Tranquil Creek.

Although Black Turnstones may be encountered anywhere along the rocky shore, a few readily accessible places to look for this species on the central west coast include the Wild Pacific Trail, Ucluelet Inlet, the south end of Long Beach, Green Point, Lovekin Rock, the northwest end of Chesterman Beach, and the foreshore in Tofino harbour.

RED KNOT
Calidris canutus

STATUS: Uncommon spring migrant. Casual in summer.

Red Knots are widespread throughout the world, breeding from northern Siberia to Greenland, west to the High Arctic Canadian islands, and to northwestern Alaska. Wintering birds are found from Australia to Africa, Europe, Great Britain, southern South America, the US Atlantic coast, California and Baja California, and the Gulf of Mexico.

Red Knots have been divided into six subspecies, with birds that transit through British Columbia belonging to the subspecies *C. c. roselaari*, which breeds in northern and western Alaska and Wrangell Island, north of Siberia. There are two other *roselaari*-type populations, one wintering in the southeastern United States and the other in Brazil. The Pacific population winters from California to western Mexico, and possibly further south.[164] I have personally seen them in moderate numbers in the salt marshes at Guerrero Negro, in Baja California.

Grays Harbor and Willapa Bay in Washington are staging areas for the Pacific population, with a high of 6,000 birds counted at the former location in the spring of 1981.[133] Nowhere else on the Pacific coast south of Alaska have Red Knots been seen in such large numbers.

In our west coast region, the Red Knot is primarily a transient during the month of May, with 106 of 141 records during that month. There are only 2 records for April. The earliest spring sighting ever recorded occurred on 30 March in 1984, 27 days later than the earliest record of 4 March for the Fraser River delta (BCFWS). Numbers peak during the second and third week of May, with sightings declining rapidly after that. The latest spring dates are 29 May in 1970 on Cleland Island (BCFWS) and 27 May in 2017 at Jensen's Bay. Most sightings are of single birds, pairs, or flocks of under a dozen, but very occasionally larger flocks are seen. For example, 17 birds were recorded on 9 May 1986; 39 on 8 May 1990; 73 on 14 May 2002; 33 on 19 May 2004; and 31 on 13 May 2012. Most sightings have occurred on the Tofino mudflats, particularly at Jensen's Bay. This is partly due to the fact that this area is the most intensively monitored. Birds are also seen on sandy beaches and on rocky islands such as Cleland.

The southward movement occurs mostly in the second half of July and in August, but there just aren't many records. Since 1982, there have been 3 sightings in July and 8 in August. The latest fall date was 30 August in 2012, when two birds were seen at Long Beach. *Birds of Pacific Rim National Park*, on the other hand, listed 10 records for July, 4 for August, 5 for September, and 2 for October.[1] Some of those July sightings may have involved the same bird.

The largest flock recorded in summer consisted of 36 birds, all adults, seen at Long Beach on 12 July 1972, when inclement weather forced them to the shore. The relatively small number of birds seen here in summer suggests that most birds pass by far out to sea without stopping. In Washington, most birds seen are juveniles, which pass through from mid-August to mid-October. Adults fly south earlier and are not usually seen at any of the Washington locations. There have also been several November records from south of the border, but such late dates are very rare.

Three subspecies of Red Knot breed in North America: *C. c. islandica* in the northeastern Canadian High Arctic, *C. c. rufa* in the central Canadian Arctic (and Greenland), and *C. c. roselaari* in northwestern Alaska (and Wrangel Island, Russia). Breeding populations are estimated at 80,000 birds, 42,000 birds, and 17,000 birds, respectively. The Red Knot population *C. c. rufa*, which migrates through eastern North America, is much lower in numbers than in the 1980s and 1990s. The Pacific population (*C. c. roselaari*), which winters in northwestern Mexico with stopovers in Grays Harbor and Willapa Bay in Washington state, was estimated at 17,000 birds in 2012.[131] Some information suggests a possible decline.

SURFBIRD
Calidris virgata

STATUS: Common to abundant spring and fall migrant. Fairly common in winter. Uncommon in May. Rare in June.

This is another of the rock sandpipers, that small group of shorebirds that live mostly along the rocky shore. Like the Black Turnstone, with which it frequently mingles, this species is also seen on pebble beaches and in estuaries. In protected waters, birds may be seen resting on log booms at high tide, usually in the company of Black Turnstones. Surfbirds earned their name because of their habit of feeding in the surf-washed intertidal zone, where they can be seen evading breaking waves just in the nick of time.

Surfbirds breed in the uplands of the Yukon and Alaska, often far into the interior and away from the ocean. The entire population, estimated at 70,000 to 100,000 birds,[1] winters or migrates along the Pacific coast, from Kodiak Island and Prince William Sound, Alaska, south along the entire length of the Pacific coast to Tierra del Fuego.[165] On our coast, this bird has been recorded in all months of the year, though far less in May and rarely in June. The southward migration begins in the second half of July. Ten birds were recorded at Chesterman Beach on 21 July 2003, and again on 17 July 2010. There is one very early record of 10 birds seen on 29 June 1970 at Cleland Island (BCFWS). In 1970, numbers for July peaked at 100 birds on the 24th of the month. By August, birds are passing through in much larger numbers.

The Surfbird is aptly named for its habit of feeding in the surf zone of the rocky shore. This bird is in juvenile plumage.

There are old records from Barkley Sound of 700 to 1,000 birds at Fleming Island on 10 August 1967 and 2,000 or more on Tzartus Island on 14 August 1968.[1] Most records are of smaller flocks, though some are still of substantial size. A total of 450 birds were seen at the south end of Long Beach on 29 August 2004, and 150 at Sulphur Pass Provincial Park on 18 September 1997. At Tranquil Creek, 137 birds were seen on 23 September 2012, and 245 were present at Green Point on 10 November 2013. The fall movement continues through October, November, and December. There are 16 records for October, 17 for November, and 12 for December. By January, sightings are few in number.

By mid-February we again begin to see an increase in numbers, and by March more so. This is the beginning of the spring movement. On 17 February 2013, 170 birds were recorded at Green Point, Long Beach, and on 8 March 1990, there were 1,500 along the north shore of Barkley Sound. Although there aren't many records for April, the largest flock on record occurred during this month. On 25 April 1972, David F. Hatler estimated 4,500 to 5,000 birds off Turtle Island in Barkley Sound.[1] On 28 April 1974, 300 birds were reported from Ucluelet. It would be interesting to determine whether Barkley Sound is a staging area for this species in spring, as Paulson speculated.[133]

Although *The Birds of British Columbia* states that Surfbirds rarely frequent the heads of inlets,[6] this is not the case in Clayoquot Sound. Here, birds are often found 30 km up Tofino Inlet, roosting on Rankin Rocks (Wayne Barnes, personal communication). It is interesting that two of the sightings occurred during late April, which appears to be the peak migration period in spring. On 26 April 1989, I found 100 birds at Deer Bay, at the head of Tofino Inlet, and on 28 April 1989, I found 350 birds at the mouth of Tranquil Creek in the company of a large number of Black Turnstones.

While *Birds of Pacific Rim National Park* listed eight records for May,[1] the intervening years have produced only one additional sighting in that month, suggesting that by the beginning of May the spring migration is largely over and only stragglers remain. We have three June records, one each on the 10th, 25th, and 29th of that month. The first is almost certainly a nonbreeding bird, while the latter two could be very early southbound migrants.

Surfbirds can be remarkably tolerant of human presence. On one occasion, I was thrilled to find myself sitting on the rocky shore at Chesterman Beach in the midst of hundreds of birds, some of them little more than an arm's length away. On another occasion at Tranquil Creek (28 April 1989), I was able to photograph birds in breeding plumage no farther than 3 m (10 ft) away.

RUFF
Calidris pugnax
STATUS: Casual migrant in spring and fall.

This flamboyant Eurasian species is named for the spectacular ruff on the necks of males in spring, which they display during the breeding season to attract females. These ruffs range from white to black to rufous, or a combination of these colours. In North America, the species is usually seen at a time of year when it lacks the ruff.

The Ruff breeds in the northern half of Europe and east across much of Siberia. Most birds winter in Africa, but some winter eastward to India, the Philippines, and Australia. They frequently wander to the Western Hemisphere. Although rare in North America, the Ruff has been recorded in most states and all Canadian provinces. In British Columbia, it has been recorded primarily in the Fraser River delta and on southern Vancouver Island.

For our west coast we have eight records involving from five to seven individuals, all of them between Tofino and Ucluelet. The first sighting involved a juvenile found by Aziza Cooper on 26 August 1997 at Long Beach.[166] This bird was observed from as close as 5 m, and Cooper's field notes and sketch are convincing. The second was a juvenile male seen on 28 and 30 August 2000 at a sewage pond near Long Beach.[167] This bird was seen by a number of observers and photographed. A third individual was found at Grice Bay on 26 April 2007 by June Ryder and Michael Church, who submitted a detailed description.[168] There were two sightings in 2015. The first was a bird passing over Tofino on 9 September, photographed in flight by T. Melling. The second sighting, by Eric Tull et al. and possibly involving the same bird, occurred at the Long Beach Golf Course on 19 September. On 15 August the following year, a female was observed on the mudflats at the end of Sharp Road by Guy Monty and Anne Nightingale. Ten days later, on 25 August, a female was seen and photographed near the south end of Long Beach by Ian Cruickshank. Six days later, on 31 August, Cruickshank found a bird at the Long Beach Airport that was subsequently seen by others. Although it was likely the same bird as the one seen on the beach, this time it was extremely shy.

It is noteworthy that all fall sightings occurred in the period from mid-August to late September.

SHARP-TAILED SANDPIPER
Calidris acuminata
STATUS: Casual fall transient.

The Sharp-tailed Sandpiper looks very similar to the Pectoral Sandpiper, to which it is closely related. This shorebird, however, breeds exclusively in northeastern Siberia and winters in Australasia, from south China to Southeast Asia, Indonesia, Australia, and New Zealand. A peculiarity of this species is that adults migrate more or less directly south over the Asian continent, while thousands of juveniles take a detour and migrate from 1,200 to 3,000 km due east to the fecund shores of western Alaska, where they fatten up for the long journey south over the Pacific Ocean.[169] For unknown reasons, a small number of juveniles regularly deviate from this route and end up along the Pacific coast of North America. Perhaps they are caught up in the movement of Pectoral Sandpipers migrating in a southeasterly direction.

In our province, the Sharp-tailed Sandpiper is considered an uncommon to locally fairly common autumn transient on the coast by Campbell et al.[111] That is not the case in our region. For Vancouver Island's west coast, *Birds of*

Pacific Rim National Park listed just 3 records: 27 August 1966 at Green Point, Long Beach – 1;[169] 16 September 1972 at Tofino – 1;[1] and 16 October 1972 at South Bay (PRNP) – 1.[1] Since 1982 there have been 13 additional sightings in 10 separate years, with dates ranging from 27 August to 29 October. All records are of single individuals, with the exception of an occurrence on 12 October 2008, when 2 birds landed in front of a large party of birders at Jensens's Bay, Tofino.

Although they are said to prefer fresh or brackish wetlands, most of our records are from the marine environment. Four records are from the Long Beach Airport, where fresh, standing water can be found, four sightings occurred on mudflats, and five birds were seen on beaches.

STILT SANDPIPER
Calidris himantopus
STATUS: Casual transient in spring, summer, and fall.

This long-legged sandpiper breeds in the High Arctic of Alaska, in western Canada, and in the region west of Hudson Bay. It winters largely in central South America, but small numbers winter in southern Florida and the Gulf Coast of Texas. In migration it passes throughout the eastern half of the United States and through Ontario, Manitoba, Saskatchewan, and the northern half of Alberta. In British Columbia, with the exception of the Peace River region, where it is more common,[150] it is a casual transient in spring and rare in autumn. In the Salish Sea basin, it is considered casual in spring and very rare in fall.

On Vancouver Island's west coast, we have eight records: one in spring, six in summer, and one in fall – or, to put it another way, two during the northward migration and six during the southward movement. Southbound birds occurred between 15 July and 4 September.

All records for the west coast region are as follows: 15 July 1960, Stubbs Island – 1; 25 May 1971, Long Beach – 1 in breeding plumage; 8 June 1982, Long Beach – 1 (BC Photo 801); 19-24 August 1989, Tofino mudflats and Chesterman Beach – 1 (photo); 1-4 September 2000, Pacific Rim National Park sewage pond – 1; 5 August 2010, Sandhill Creek, Long Beach – 1 adult, largely in breeding plumage (photo); 18 August 2012, PRNP sewage pond – 1 juvenile; and 8 August 2013, Tofino mudflats – 1 juvenile (photo).

SANDERLING
Calidris alba

STATUS: Common spring and fall migrant. Variable in winter, from uncommon to common, and occasionally abundant.

Flocks of Sanderlings are often seen running in front of an incoming wave. These birds were photographed in early May.

This beach-walker is one of the most cosmopolitan of wading birds and is familiar to most people who have spent some time on sandy ocean beaches. These are the sandpipers that we see marching up the beach like a platoon of soldiers, just ahead of an incoming wave. They breed in the High Arctic of north-central Siberia, northern Greenland, and the Arctic islands of Canada, north to within 800 km (500 mi) of the North Pole. Their winter range extends along coastlines throughout much of the world, with the exception of the most northern areas and eastern Asia. North American Sanderlings winter on beaches throughout much of the Americas, south to Tierra del Fuego.[26]

The species has been recorded in most of British Columbia, including the interior, but it is far more common on the coast. Its preferred habitat appears to be sandy beaches, but in our area they are also seen on mudflats during the winter, often mingling with Dunlin. They are also seen on rocky islets and headlands, where they like to rest at high tide. In winter plumage they appear very white and can be identified from far away. Flocks of birds can sometimes be spotted from Long Beach, resting on Sea Lion Rocks, where they appear as white dots against the black rocks.

Numbers are variable from season to season and year to year. Flock size may not exceed 150 birds in the Tofino/Long Beach area in some winters but may be several times that in others, such as the winter of 2001/02. On 20 November 2001, 575 birds were recorded at Chesterman Beach. On 3 February 2002, 800 birds were seen at Incinerator Rock, Long Beach, and on 15 February, an estimated 1,200 birds were again seen at Incinerator Rock.

According to *The Birds of British Columbia,* the spring movement begins by late March, increases in April, and peaks in late April.[111] This is not in accord with sightings recorded on the central west coast since 1982. Even with 370 records available, it remains very difficult to distinguish between wintering birds and arriving migrants. A surge in numbers at the Tofino mudflats on 11 March 1992, to 800 birds, may be evidence of spring migrants but could still represent wintering birds. A sudden increase in numbers to 600 birds on 24 April 1996, and again on 30 April 1997, almost certainly indicates newly arrived migrants. It is also significant that both these flocks were seen on Long Beach rather than on the mudflats where wintering birds are usually found. Spring passage is most obvious throughout the month of May, when flocks of birds can be seen feeding on Long Beach, many of them changing into breeding plumage. To summarize, it appears that wintering birds depart first, and migrants arrive from further south beginning in late April.

That the migration continues throughout most of the month of May is demonstrated by sightings recorded at Long Beach: 20 birds on 21 May 1996; 185 on 20 May 2009; and 195 on 30 May 2012. In 2015, a large number were still present during the last week of the month, with 305 birds seen near Incinerator Rock on 26 May and 180 birds on 31 May. As late as 3 June, 120 birds were passing through, while on 15 June the last 2 stragglers were seen. In 2016, 335 birds were seen feeding on Long Beach as late as 28 May. It seems likely that the birds that pass through latest are the ones that nest the furthest north.

The fall migration usually begins in mid-July, although the two earliest records are 11 July in 2015 and 6 July in 2016. The numbers passing through in July and August tend to be small, and larger numbers are often not seen until September. There are exceptions. On 14 August 2002, 75 birds were recorded, and on 20 July 2013, 74 birds. In 2014, 137 birds were seen on 29 August, and in 2016, 60 birds were recorded on 20 August. It is worth noting that of 223 birds recorded on Long Beach on 31 August 2017, all were juveniles. Numbers continue to increase during the months of September, October, and November, which is much later than for most shorebirds.

DUNLIN
Calidris alpina
STATUS: Common to abundant migrant and winter visitor. Rare in summer.

With a rusty red back and black belly, the Dunlin in full breeding plumage is a handsome bird, and a far cry from the drab grey fellow we see in winter. Indeed, until the early 1960s, this bird was known in North America as the Red-backed Sandpiper, before the British name was adopted. It breeds in northern regions of Siberia, Iceland, eastern Greenland, and North America, where it breeds from the James Bay and the Hudson Bay regions north and west to western Alaska. On the Pacific coast, the species winters mainly from southern Vancouver Island and the Fraser River delta south to Mexico and sporadically to Central America.

On Vancouver Island's west coast, the Dunlin occurs as both spring and autumn migrants and winter visitors. Unlike most shorebirds, which begin arriving from the north in late June or early July, Dunlin only begin to trickle into our region only after mid-September. In the Tofino area, numbers build up very gradually, and only by late October or early November, depending on the year, do we see large numbers. Then, flocks of more than 1,000 birds are the norm and flocks tend to range from 1,000 to 4,000 birds. For example, 2,450 birds were seen on 18 November 2008; 3,000 on 16 November 2010; 2,800 on 19 December 2009; and 3,500 on 27 March 2009. The three highest estimates were all in January and February, with 4,000 birds on 7 January 2015; 4,500 on 15 February 2009; and 4,000 on 24 February 2010.

During the winter, Dunlin spend most of their time feeding on the mudflats of Clayoquot Sound at low tide. Only occasionally do they feed on beaches in winter, although they do so regularly in spring. In the time period approaching high tide, they depart for a location well away from the mudflats to rest for a few hours. Tofino resident Wayne Barnes has photographed large numbers of Dunlin spending high tide resting on rocky islets far up Tofino Inlet, at the mouth of Tranquil Inlet. They likely do this to elude potential predators such as Peregrine Falcons, which are more prevalent along the outer coast. In winter,

Dunlin are often accompanied by Sanderlings, which can be distinguished by their much paler plumage, though the latter, if present, are usually there in much smaller numbers.

Dunlin numbers begin to decline in March as birds depart for the north, although transients from further south will arrive in late April and pass through until about mid-May, though in reduced numbers. Stragglers may be seen until the end of the month and sometimes into June. More often than not, birds in spring are mixed in with large flocks of Western Sandpipers, with whom they readily fraternize. By May, most birds are either in breeding plumage or in transition.

ROCK SANDPIPER
Calidris ptilocnemis
STATUS: Rare fall transient and winter visitor. Casual in spring.

As its name indicates, this bird frequents the rocky shore, though very occasionally it may be seen on sandy beaches. The Rock Sandpiper is closely related to the Purple Sandpiper of the Atlantic, which is very similar in appearance but has been recorded only once in British Columbia. When seen on our coast, the Rock Sandpiper is often in the company of other dwellers of the rocky shore – Surfbirds and Black Turnstones.

Rock Sandpipers breed in extreme eastern Siberia, the Kuril and Commander Islands off the Kamchatka Peninsula, and the Pribilof Islands. In North America, the species breeds in western Alaska as well as the Aleutian archipelago. Those birds breeding on islands tend to be year-round residents, but birds on the Alaskan mainland migrate south along the coast as far as northern California. In British Columbia, Rock Sandpipers are considerably more common on the north coast than on the south coast. *The Birds of British Columbia* considers it a "fairly common to locally very common" migrant and winter visitor on the north coast, while it is an "uncommon to locally common migrant and winter visitant" on the south coast.[111]

In our west coast region, this bird can be elusive. This is partly due to the inaccessibility of much of the coast. The first documented occurrence was on 9 August 1968 at Tzartus Island in Barkley Sound. *Birds of Pacific Rim National Park* listed 6 records for our region.[1] By late 2016, there was a total of 38 records in 22 separate years, not a large number for a period covering over four and a half decades, though this partly reflects the paucity of observers. Of those

38 sightings, 26 were made during the fall migration period and 6 in winter. There were 8 sightings in October, 10 in November, 5 in December, 4 in January, and 2 in February. Both August and September have a single record. Only the months of April, June, and July have no records at all.

That there have been no sightings in April is particularly curious as this is the month when most Rock Sandpipers are believed to pass through in spring. Indeed, spring sightings are remarkably rare, with only six records. One of those involved a sighting on Trevor Channel in Barkley Sound on 30 March 1985. Another March record involved a bird that overwintered in Tofino Harbour from 30 November 2007 to 27 March 2008. Sighting also occurred on 21 March 2015 and 24 March 2016. The only record of a bird in breeding plumage involved a bird seen on Cleland Island on 9 May 1996.

Paulson mentions high counts in winter outside our region: 70 birds at Victoria on 27 January 1953; 50 at Ocean Shores, Washington, on 26 March 1977; and 90 at Chain Islets, BC, on 27 December 1980.[133] The highest count ever recorded in Victoria was 82 birds on 6 May 1974. Records from the 1980s, however, showed a decline in these southern latitudes.

In our region, the largest flock seen to date contained 20 birds, recorded at Green Point on 3 January and 1 March 1976. We also have a record of 17 birds at Tofino Inlet on 4 October 1972, and 10 birds at Green Point on 22 November 2014. Flocks containing 6 birds were recorded four times: at Cleland Island on 5 January 1989, at Long Beach on 21 January 2001, at Carmanah Point on 1 January 2002, and at Green Point on 24 March 2016.

There are three subspecies in North America and one in eastern Asia. Both *C. p. tschuktschorum* and *C. p. couesi* are believed migrate to British Columbia and Washington. Only close-up photos are likely to resolve the issue of which subspecies visit our shores.

Although Rock Sandpipers are far from common in our region, when this bird is specifically searched for in the right season, one can sometimes get lucky. On the central west coast, accessible locations may be found at the south end of Long Beach, at Green Point, and at the north end of Chesterman Beach. Rock Sandpipers should be looked for among flocks of Surfbirds and Black Turnstones. At Green Point and at Chesterman Beach, the best time is at high tide, when birds are resting.

A food habit study from stomach contents near Vancouver, BC, during the nonbreeding seasons showed the diet, in order of importance, to consist of Acorn Barnacles (*Balanus* spp.), filamentous algae (*Ulothrix* sp.), and limpets (*Littorina* spp.).[163]

BAIRD'S SANDPIPER
Calidris bairdii
STATUS: Uncommon to locally fairly common summer and fall transient. Casual in spring.

This sandpiper is named after the 19th-century American naturalist and ornithologist Spencer Fullerton Baird. It breeds extensively in the High Arctic of eastern Siberia, Alaska, Canada, and western Greenland. Its primary migration route in North America is through the central Great Plains, although individuals, particularly juveniles, may be encountered in all US states and all Canadian provinces and territories. The species winters in South America from Peru to Tierra del Fuego, some having made a one-way journey of 15,000 km (9,330 mi) or more in as little as five weeks.[170] In British Columbia, this species may be seen in appropriate habitat throughout much of the province during both the spring and fall migration periods. It has frequently been found on subalpine and alpine ponds.

Unlike elsewhere on the south coast, Baird's Sandpipers in our region occur almost exclusively during late summer and early fall. I would have said exclusively but for a single record listed for the Tofino waterfront for 2 May 1971 in *Birds of Pacific Rim National Park*, although no details were given. Hatler et al. listed eight July records and gives a date of 13 July 1960 as the earliest occurrence in summer.[1] There are two additional early records, each of a single bird, for Bamfield on 15 July 1979 and Cleland Island on 28 July 1970 (BCFWS). All sightings since then, however, have been recorded between 2 August and 6 October (1982), with birds usually having passed through before the end of September.

Their preferred habitat on our west coast is sandy beaches, where we see them in small numbers, from single individuals to a maximum of 15 recorded at Chesterman Beach on 3 September 1974. Although it is rare to see more than 5 or 6 birds at any one time, on 9 August 2017, a flock of 14 birds was once again recorded at Chesterman Beach. There is a single record from the Long Beach Airport. On 13 September 2014, 4 juveniles were seen feeding at the floatplane pond.

That some birds may spend a considerable amount of time feeding at one location before moving on is demonstrated by observations at Cape Cook lagoon near Brooks Peninsula. A uniquely marked individual Baird's Sandpiper remained feeding with a small flock of Western Sandpipers for 19 days between 6 and 24 August 1981.[13]

LEAST SANDPIPER
Calidris minutilla

STATUS: Common to abundant transient in spring, common transient in summer. Casual in fall and winter.

As the name suggests, this is the smallest of the North American sandpipers. Although it is not conspicuously different in appearance from the Western Sandpiper, with practice it can be readily distinguished from it, even at a distance, by its darker brown upper parts, heavily streaked neck and breast, and yellowish rather than black legs. In flight, its head has a more tucked-in look.

The Least Sandpiper breeds from Newfoundland and Labrador westward across northern Canada to Alaska. In British Columbia, it breeds in the Chilkat Pass area in the northwest corner of the province, on the Spatsizi Plateau, and it has bred at Masset in northern Haida Gwaii.[111] The species winters from the southern United States through Mexico and Central America to the northern half of South America. On the Pacific coast, it winters as far north as central Oregon.

On Vancouver Island's west coast, spring migration begins in late April. While individual birds have been seen as early as mid-month, the first flocks begin arriving by 20 April or shortly thereafter. The earliest recorded arrival of a flock was on 18 April in 2002, when 65 birds were seen on the Tofino mudflats. As with Western Sandpipers, numbers build very rapidly and peak during the last few days of April or the first week of May, after which birds continue to trickle through in greatly reduced numbers until around mid-May. There are a few exceptions. On 24 May 1999, 25 birds were seen at Jensen's Bay, Tofino. Single birds were seen as late as 25 and 31 May in 2001, on 26 May in 2010, and on 26 May in 2002.

Least Sandpipers often mingle with Western Sandpipers, though they may also be seen in separate flocks, particularly early during spring passage. Some of the higher numbers recorded on the central west coast, either as separate flocks or mixed in with other sandpipers, are as follows: 350 birds on 24 April 1984; 700 on 25 April 1988; 250 on 30 April 2000; 300 on 23 April 2001; 450 on 3 May 2011; and 300 on 27 April 2013. A high of 2,500 birds reported from Long Beach in 1983 was almost certainly erroneous and was likely a mixture of the two species.

The southward passage can begin as early as the last week of June. There are June records from the 25th or later in four separate years, and a single record of a bird seen on the 23rd. In most years, the first birds are seen in early July.

Unlike the rapid northward movement in spring, the southward movement is much more gradual, and flock size is much reduced. The migration continues through July and August and into September, although numbers in September are small. An exception was 20 birds at Chesterman Beach on 18 September 2009. There are three October records, two from the beginning of the month and one of a single bird on 27 October 2003.

There were no winter sightings before 2011, when on 12 February six birds were observed resting on Shag Rocks across from Tofino harbour. On 26 December 2012, four birds were observed at the Long Beach Airport, and on 11 January 2013, a single individual was seen at Jensen's Bay. There was also a late fall occurrence, with a lone individual seen at the airport on 14 December 2015.

BUFF-BREASTED SANDPIPER
Calidris subruficollis
STATUS: Casual transient in late summer.

This species once numbered in the hundreds of thousands and possibly millions, but was brought close to extinction in the 1920s by hunting. The current population is estimated at 23,000 to 84,000 individuals, or 15,000 to 56,000 mature individuals.[171] According to the IUCN Red List of Threatened Species, the population is believed to be currently declining.

The Buff-breasted Sandpiper nests in the vegetated uplands of the High Arctic from the north slope of Alaska to the Boothia Peninsula and large Arctic islands of Canada. Like the Upland Sandpiper, it is not as partial to aquatic environments as most other sandpipers. In fall, these birds migrate south over Saskatchewan and Manitoba, then continue through the midwestern states to the Gulf of Mexico and on to their wintering grounds in Paraguay and northern Argentina. Some birds cover nearly 29,000 km (18,000 mi) in their annual movements.[172]

This species displays a penchant for wandering. Although its migration corridor passes through the centre of the continent, it has been seen in every state in the United States and in every province in Canada. Indeed, of all North American birds that make an occasional crossing to the British Isles, this species is the most likely to do so, after the Pectoral Sandpiper. In British Columbia, it has been seen in many widely separated localities, including the interior, though most sightings have been on the coast.

The rare Buff-breasted Sandpiper is seen only occasionally as a solitary individual on a beach. This bird is in juvenile plumage.

For the west coast of Vancouver Island, we have 14 records, all of which fall within the period from 15 August to 9 September, with the exception of a single record on 5 August 2001. This last record is so early as to be anomalous, but it was seen by two observers. Given the fact that 8 sightings occurred in the first nine days of September, this appears to be the optimal time to look for this species. All birds were seen on beaches, with the exception of a sighting at the airport and possibly the one at Grant Bay. Given the narrow time frame in which it passes through, and the paucity of observers on our coast, it is safe to say that the species occurs here much more often than records indicate. Note that all sightings in the west coast region involve single birds with the exception of one sighting of three birds.

All records are as follows: 4 September 1907, "Clayoquot" (most likely Stubbs Island) – 1 collected (NMC 3526);[173] 1 and 2 September 1964, Long Beach – 1 juvenile (BC Photo185);[173] 4 September 1968, Grant Bay – 1 juvenile;[16] early September 1973, Long Beach – 1; 27 August 1975, Nootka Island – 1 juvenile;[174] 15 September 1990, Chesterman Beach – 1 juvenile;[175] 5 August 2001, Chesterman Beach – 1; 9 September 1993, Combers Beach (PRNP) – juvenile;[153] 22 August 2004, Long Beach Airport – 3 juveniles; 1 September 2004, Stubbs Island, Tofino – 1 juvenile; 13 September 2006, Jordan River – 1 juvenile;[158] 9 September 2007, Vargas Island – 1 juvenile (photo); 15 August 2012, Chesterman Beach – 1 juvenile (photo); and 7 September 2012, Incinerator Rock, Long Beach – 1 juvenile.

PECTORAL SANDPIPER
Calidris melanotos

STATUS: Uncommon to locally common transient in spring and fall.

Pectoral Sandpipers are one of the truly long-distance migrants, with some birds travelling from central Siberia to Argentina.

Pectoral Sandpipers have one of the longest annual migrations of any shorebird. Some may exceed even the long flight of the American Golden-Plover. Pectoral Sandpipers breed in the High Arctic, from the shores of Hudson Bay in Canada to Alaska and northern Siberia. Each year it makes the arduous journey to and from southern South America, where it winters. Birds from further west in Siberia travel nearly halfway around the world and back each year, for a flight of up to 32,000 km (20,000 mi) annually. Some Siberian birds are believed to cross the southern Arctic Ocean to Canada and Alaska on their way south.[172]

During the migration period, Pectoral Sandpipers may be seen throughout much of North America, including British Columbia. This species frequents a variety of habitat during transit, including ponds, rivers, tidal meadows, beaches, rocky islets, and wide open spaces such as airports and golf courses. It is often found among short vegetation around ponds, or in vegetated fields away from water. When crouching in low vegetation, it is extremely well camouflaged.

Birds of Pacific Rim National Park regarded the species as rare in spring and uncommon in fall in the west coast region.[1] Observations in recent years have shown that it occurs regularly in spring, however. For example, in 2009 at the Long Beach Airport, 15 birds were recorded on 15 May, 28 on 18 May, and 15 on 20 May. In 2012, 34 individuals were seen at the airport on 21 May, while 52 birds were found feeding at the adjacent golf course, for a total of 86 birds that day. Weather often has a strong influence on numbers seen on the ground, and on this day a low overcast sky with rain prevailed, forcing the birds down. These and other records suggest that a substantial number of birds migrate through our area in spring during a short window, beginning around mid-May. Some of the birds seen here may well be preparing for an ocean crossing, this being the shortest route to western Alaska and eastern Siberia. Our earliest spring arrivals were a single individual on 8 May 2014 at Long Beach, and 7 birds at the Long Beach Golf Course on 10 May 2016. Birds were seen as late as 26 and 27 May in 2009 and 2013, respectively. The latest occurrence was 3 birds on 28 May in 2017, at the airport.

In fall, Pectoral Sandpipers are seen more often than in spring, though flock size is usually smaller. Fall passage usually begins in early August and ends in late October. *Birds of Pacific Rim National Park* listed one July date,[1] and since then there have been two other July sightings, with one bird seen on 23 July 2014 at Chesterman Beach and another on 16 July 2016 at the Long Beach Airport. Bird surveys conducted during adverse weather help in determining just when birds pass through an area, since during fair weather birds tend to pass through without stopping. This applies to Pectoral Sandpipers as well as many other species.

The bulk of the migration occurs in September and early October. The four highest fall counts were 29 birds on 4 October 1996, 23 on 15 September 2010, 12 on 22 September 2011, and 65 on 31 August 2016. In the case of the 2010 date, 12 birds were seen at the airport and 11 at Chesterman Beach. In addition, *Birds of Pacific Rim National Park* listed a sighting of 15 to 20 birds on Vargas Island on 10 September 1972.[1] The latest sightings recorded in fall involved single birds on 26 October in 1991, at Tofino, and on 31 October in 2013, at the airport.

In the summer of 1995, I observed Pectoral Sandpipers on the Koye River, on the BC mainland coast, wading in shallow water and apparently feeding on salmon eggs. If such behaviour also occurs in our region, it has not yet been recorded.

SEMIPALMATED SANDPIPER
Calidris pusilla

STATUS: Uncommon transient in late summer and fall, casual in spring.

This is one of three small North American sandpipers collectively referred to as "peeps." To the novice birder, the three species will be difficult to distinguish from one another at first, but through familiarity with the birds and after learning the field marks, identification can become relatively easy.

This sandpiper is the eastern equivalent of the Western Sandpiper. It breeds in the tundra regions from northern Labrador, Baffin Island, and the Hudson Bay region west through Nunavut and northern Northwest Territories to northern and western Alaska. It migrates through much of North America east of the Rocky Mountains, to winter from the Caribbean and southeastern Mexico south to the northern half of South America, where it can be found on both coasts. In British Columbia, it occurs abundantly during spring and fall migration only in the northeastern parts of the province. It may be very common in spring and locally very common in fall in southern parts of the Salish Sea in some years.[111]

In our west coast region, the species occurs much less frequently. *Birds of Pacific Rim National Park* listed 16 records, with 9 of those occurring in spring. Five of the spring sightings were recorded in 1971 and 1 in 1972. We then have a 40-year gap with no spring sightings until 30 April and 29 May 2012, when single Semipalmated Sandpipers were seen at the Long Beach Airport and at Chesterman Beach, Tofino, respectively. On 3 May 2014, there was an additional sighting at Long Beach. In contrast, during that same 40-year period, there were 53 records during the fall migration period, with birds recorded from 16 July to 26 September. Ten sightings were in July, 35 in August, and 9 in September. Most sightings involved single individuals, though 8 records involved 2 birds and 6 involved counts of 3 birds. There were also single counts of 4, 5, 6, and 8 birds. The two largest counts involved 12 birds on 2 September 2013 at Chesterman Beach, and 20 birds on 2 August 2009 at Nuchatlitz. Of 56 records since 1982, 44 were recorded in the past 10 years.

Nearly all sightings were on sandy beaches, with one sighting at the sewage pond in Pacific Rim National Park and two at the airport. The most favoured locations on the central coast, based on existing records, are Long Beach west of Incinerator Rock, the mouth of Sandhill Creek at Long Beach, Chesterman Beach, and Medallion Beach on Vargas Island. The discrepancy between spring sightings recorded up to 1972 and the three records since then is somewhat puzzling. Hatler et al. raised the possibility of misidentification.[1] Because there are no photos or other documentation from that era, this is possible. However, it is also possible that in some years more birds pass through our region and that 1971 was one of those years. Records suggest that 2012 was another such year.

The world population is estimated at 2.2 million birds.[131]

WESTERN SANDPIPER
Calidris mauri

STATUS: An abundant migrant in spring and summer, rare in June, and rare in fall.

Western Sandpipers are our most abundant shorebird, with flocks of 15,000 to 20,000 birds recorded on occasion.

The Western Sandpiper is another of the three small North American sandpipers collectively called "peeps." Only Western and Least Sandpipers occur in large numbers in the west. The Least Sandpiper is smaller, has darker brown upper parts, and lacks the rufous crown and scapulars of this species in spring. Western Sandpipers breed in western and northern Alaska and across the Bering Strait in extreme eastern Siberia. They migrate southeast to winter along the Atlantic coast from New Jersey to Florida and the Gulf of Mexico, south to French Guiana. Along the Pacific coast, they winter from Washington to southern California, and locally in South America from Colombia to southern Peru.

Western Sandpipers have two migration routes along the BC coast, one on the inside of Vancouver Island, the other on the outside. Far greater numbers use the inside route and feed at Boundary Bay, where as many as 500,000 birds pass through each spring and 1.2 million in fall.[176] As many as half a million birds have been seen in a single day. In the west coast region, the central west coast is particularly important, during both the northward and southward migration. Although the largest numbers are found on the mudflats of southern Clayoquot Sound, many also feed on the red worms found on sandy beaches. In spring, birds often begin at the south end of Long Beach and work their way north, with Least Sandpipers, Dunlin, Semipalmated Plovers, and Sanderlings often intermingled with them.

The very first spring migrants usually begin arriving in the third week of April, with numbers building up rather quickly in the last week of April. In the 13 years that spring numbers were closely monitored at Jensen's Bay, Tofino, numbers almost always peak in the first week of May. In 1997, the high count occurred on 8 May, which was the latest so far recorded. On average, numbers peak on either 3 or 4 May, but on three occasions they peaked as early as 1 May.

At the height of the migration, there are rarely fewer than 10,000 birds present. Flocks of 20,000 birds were recorded on 8 May 1997 and 4 May 2010. A total of 25,000 were recorded on 3 May 2011, and 30,000 were estimated on 4 May 2012. The largest numbers ever recorded in our west coast region came on 6 May 2002, when a massive flight of birds arrived on the same day. The impression was of snowflakes drifting upward as an estimated 50,000 birds were seen lifting off simultaneously to depart for Alaska. Admittedly, to estimate such numbers with any degree of accuracy is daunting, if not impossible. My estimate of 50,000 birds was still 10,000 short of the estimate by another experienced observer present. Impressive as these numbers may be, they still don't come close to rivalling those seen at Boundary Bay.

Western Sandpipers prefer to catch a tailwind to save on time and effort. It has been shown that birds arriving on the nesting grounds with a store of fat remaining have greater reproductive success than those that do not. These birds therefore make use of southeasterly winds whenever possible. The entire population is believed to stop at the Copper River Delta in Alaska. One bird covered the distance between San Francisco Bay and Copper River in a remarkable 42 hours, a distance of 3,250 km (2,000 mi).[177] Most birds, however, make stops along the way, flying from San Francisco Bay to Grays Harbor, Washington, or they continue to Boundary Bay or to the mouth of the Stikine River in southeast Alaska, and finally on to the massive mudflats of the Copper River Delta in Alaska. A minority of birds stop at Tofino.

Generally, birds do not dally long, because it is advantageous for them to catch a supporting wind so they can arrive at the breeding site early. A study using small radio transmitters attached to 58 adult birds revealed that they flew the 3,250 km between San Francisco Bay and the Copper River Delta at an average speed of 422 km per day.[177] Scientists found that the average length of stay at feeding grounds is three days. I believe it is often much shorter at Tofino.

At the mudflats of southern Clayoquot Sound, after the mad rush of birds in the first week of May, the remaining migration continues at a less urgent pace for another week or 10 days with much smaller numbers. At Tofino, numbers may be down to 500 by mid-month. There were 400 birds on 16 May 2008; 800 birds on 15 May 2011; and 675 birds on 15 May 2013. By the third week of May, only small numbers remain, with a few stragglers seen until the end of the month. Occasional laggards are seen into June. In 1999, a small flock of 23 birds was seen as late as 1 June, and 2 birds were present at Chesterman Beach on 9 June 1993.

The southbound migration is much more protracted than in spring, stretching over a period of nearly three months and usually beginning during the last week of June. In some years, less than three weeks have elapsed between the departure from our shores of the very last spring migrants and the arrival of the first southbound migrants. In 2014 and 2016, the first southbound migrants arrived on the central west coast on 23 June, while the earliest summer arrivals ever observed were recorded on 18 June 2017 by Ian Cruickshank. The migration gradually picks up steam through July and into August. It is probably reasonable to say that in late June, migrant numbers are measured in tens, in July by the hundreds, and in August by the thousands.

Adults depart the nesting grounds first, leaving the young behind to fatten up for the journey south and, rather miraculously, to find their own way to wintering grounds they have never seen. The young birds will find and recognize the very beach where their parents traditionally spend the winter. A bird with coloured bands on its legs, photographed in Tofino in spring, was traced to a beach in Ecuador, where it had been banded.

At low tide, birds disperse to feed. At high tide, birds congregate at a limited number of favoured locations to rest, often in very large flocks. At this time, it is not uncommon for them to be attacked by a falcon, either the Merlin or the much larger Peregrine. Despite the momentary chaos, few birds are actually taken successfully (see under Peregrine Falcon and Merlin).

In the Tofino area in spring, Jensen's Bay is by far the most favoured location for resting; in summer, a rock at Arakun Flats and another at the end of the Stubbs Island spit are often used. Chesterman Beach was formerly an important feeding and resting area, particularly in late summer, when flocks of thousands of birds were a fairly common occurrence. On 24 August 1989, a flock of 11,000 birds was recorded resting there, and later that season, 12,000 birds on 9 September. Two years later, on 29 August 1991, 10,500 birds were estimated at the same location. Unfortunately, shorebirds have been increasingly crowded out in recent years by heavy beach use by locals, tourists, surfers, and free-roaming dogs, a mix that makes coexistence very difficult. Dogs are a particular problem.

By mid-September, the fall passage is practically over. Late flocks of from 300 to 400 birds have been recorded up to 22 September, and occasional flocks of up to 25 birds to the end of the first week in October. After that, only a very few small flocks are seen, mostly individual stragglers to the end of October. November birds were not recorded until recent years, with 5 birds at Chesterman Beach on 2 November 2012, and single individuals on 6 November 2012 and 7 November 2013.

SHORT-BILLED DOWITCHER
Limnodromus griseus

STATUS: Common to abundant spring migrant, fairly common in late summer.

This is by far the more common of the two dowitchers that pass through our area. Indeed, the Clayoquot Sound mudflats at Tofino host the largest numbers of Short-billed Dowitchers found anywhere in British Columbia. In our region, they inhabit the marine environment almost exclusively, whereas their long-billed cousin favours fresh water. The species can be divided into three populations, with separate breeding ranges in northern Canada.[178] The eastern subspecies, *L. g. griseus*, breeds from south-central Quebec and central Labrador to James and southern Hudson bays. A second subspecies, *L. g. hendersoni*, breeds from northern Manitoba to western Alberta. A third population, *L. g. caurinus*, breeds across southern Alaska, including the St. Elias Mountains of northwestern British Columbia and just into southern Yukon. *L. g. caurinus* has been recorded breeding as far south as Masset in Haida Gwaii. Short-billed

Short-billed Dowitchers, partial to marine mudflats, pass through our region each spring, sometimes in considerable numbers.

Dowitchers winter along both coasts of the Americas. On the Pacific coast, birds winter from Oregon south to Peru.

On Vancouver Island's west coast, the spring migration occurs largely between mid-April and the end of the first week in May. Earliest arrival dates were 23 March in 2008 and 30 March in 2004. Numbers slowly increase during April, and by about 20 April they build significantly in some years. The migration peaks sometime in the last week of April or the first week in May, depending on the year. Highest numbers recorded on the Tofino mudflats are as follows: 3,600 birds on 28 April 1984; 5,000 on 2 May 1992; 3,500 on 26 April 1996; 4,500 on 3 May 1996; 4,000 on 6 May 2002; and 8,000 on 28 April 2004. No such large numbers have been recorded in recent years.

Numbers on our west coast vary greatly from year to year, as they do in Grays Harbor, Washington.[133] It appears that when weather conditions are particularly favourable for travel, the birds simply keep moving and do not stop to rest or refuel. For example, in Tofino in 2008, numbers for the season peaked at a maximum of 300 birds on 5 May. In 2009, they peaked at 450 birds on 30 April, and in 2011 at 950 on 3 May. In the spring of 2014, the maximum count was a mere 103 birds.

While the largest numbers have usually passed through by the end of the first week of May, if not earlier, smaller numbers continue to be seen until mid to late May. By the last week of the month, nearly all have departed, much earlier in some years. A few nonbreeders may linger into June, or even throughout the entire month. By the beginning of July, the first southbound migrants reappear.

Unlike in spring, fall passage is a long drawn out affair, spanning the months of July, August, and September, and involves far smaller flocks. Most pass through in July and August. For September, I could find only seven records, and for October only five. The latest date was 18 October 2009, with 1 bird in Tofino and 5 at the airport. No flocks containing over 100 birds have been recorded during fall passage. The largest flocks were 92 on 25 July 2002 and 95 on 18 July 2003. Most birds likely pass by far out to sea. To date, we have no records in winter.

While birds passing through our area in spring are predominantly the coastal subspecies, *L. g. caurinus*, photos taken at Tofino show that the Prairie subspecies, *L. g. hendersoni*, also occurs here, both in spring and in late summer.

LONG-BILLED DOWITCHER
Limnodromus scolopaceus

STATUS: Uncommon to locally common transient in spring, late summer, and fall. Casual in winter.

Long-billed Dowitchers feed in shallow freshwater ponds and shun marine tidal flats. In flight, they utter a single note.

The Long-billed Dowitcher breeds in the extreme north of Canada's Northwest Territories, the Yukon, and northern and western Alaska. It winters from North Carolina to Florida west to Texas and south through most of Mexico. On the Pacific coast, it winters from Washington south to El Salvador. Small numbers occasionally winter on the Lower Mainland and on southern Vancouver Island.[111]

On our west coast, this species passes through in far smaller numbers than its short-billed cousin. Because the birds prefer fresh water, nearly all records are from the Long Beach Golf Course and nearby airport, where they frequent ponds and standing water. Earliest spring arrival dates are usually during the last few days of April. Small numbers of from one to a dozen birds may be seen there throughout the month of May. During inclement weather, larger numbers may be seen, such as on 11 May 2017, when 143 birds were counted. In fair weather, birds may be few. The latest spring date was 27 May in 2009, when four birds were seen. By June, the migration has passed.

The southbound migration begins early. Three early dates are 3 July 2011, with six birds; 4 July 2009 with one bird; and 5 July 2015 with six birds, all at the Long Beach Airport. The very earliest record occurred on 24 June 2014, with a single adult at the airport. It had an injured foot and therefore was likely a nonbreeding bird that had failed to make the journey north.

Small numbers pass through during July and August, all of them adults. One of the largest numbers recorded during the southward passage was 45 birds at the golf course on 27 July 2000. Numbers remain low throughout August and September, rarely reaching 20 birds on any given day. The largest number ever recorded in fall was 128 birds at the airport on 25 September 2011. Records suggest that the bulk of the migrants, all juveniles, pass through in late September and October. Surprisingly, 31 birds were seen as late as 26 October in 2010, and 17 birds on 7 November, also in 2010, at the airport. The latest fall date was 18 November in 2008, when a bird was found in the marine environment at Jensen's Bay, Tofino.

There are two winter records, likely involving the same bird. A bird was observed on the Tofino mudflats on 3 January and 11 January 2013, and was seen again in March. Additionally, a bird was recorded at the airport on 7 April 2013. This could be a very early arrival or, more likely, the same overwintering individual.

The Long-billed and Short-billed dowitchers can be difficult to separate in the field, but with care can be distinguished with confidence. Unsurprisingly, the former often has a noticeably longer bill. The surest way to distinguish the two is by voice, the Long-billed Dowitcher uttering a single note in flight, whereas the Short-billed Dowitcher utters multiple notes. When flushed, the Long-billed Dowitcher can also utter multiple notes, however. Habitat is an excellent indicator, as the Long-billed Dowitcher is nearly always found on freshwater ponds and only rarely on marine mudflats. Short-billed Dowitchers, on the other hand, are found almost exclusively in the marine environment.

WILSON'S SNIPE
Gallinago delicata

STATUS: Common spring and fall migrant, locally abundant. Rare in winter. Casual in summer. Breeding suspected but unconfirmed.

Wilson's Snipe feed on worms in damp, leafy ground. When it remains motionless, its plumage renders it very nearly invisible.

Wilson's Snipe, as well as four other North American species with the Wilson's prefix, are named in honour of Scottish-American ornithologist Alexander Wilson, who is often regarded as the father of ornithology in America.

This species is familiar to many west coast residents as the bird with the long, straight bill that is sometimes seen probing for worms in the damp earth of backyard lawns. At the slightest hint of danger, these birds crouch in the grass and, if approached too closely, explode from the ground and vanish in a fast, erratic flight, punctuated by a harsh call. On leafy ground or in a brown-grass environment, the bird's beautifully patterned back camouflages its presence magnificently. So well camouflaged are these birds, in fact, that I once flushed four of them less than 30 feet from where a Merlin had been perched above them moments earlier. The sharp-eyed falcon had failed to spot them as they remained motionless on the ground in plain sight.

This species was for many years lumped with the Eurasian form, *G. gallinago*, and called the Common Snipe, before being split and reverting back to its original name. It is restricted to North America, where it breeds throughout Alaska and nearly all of Canada, with the exception of the most northerly regions. In the United States, it breeds in the northeastern states and throughout much of the West, except for the most southerly areas. In British Columbia, it breeds in suitable habitat in much of the province, including southeastern Vancouver Island. Its preferred habitat is wet meadows, fens, marshy ground, and other generally wet places. On our west coast, where such habitat is scarce or lacking in summer, they are not known to breed. However, on the evening of 26 June 2016, the Wilson's Snipe's characteristic "winnowing" flight was heard over the Clayoquot Bog, adjacent to the lower Kennedy River, suggesting that it breeds there.

The Wilson's Snipe winters in the southern half of the United States, south to Central America and northern South America. In the west, it winters north through Oregon and Washington to southern British Columbia. On the coast, birds occasionally winter north to Haida Gwaii and into southeast Alaska.

Spring migrants arrive here as early as late March, but most birds arrive during the month of April. The three highest spring counts at the Long Beach Airport were all recorded in the last week of April, with 30 birds on 30 April 2000, 22 on 27 April 2008, and 45 on 30 April 2012. There is also a count of 13 birds at the Long Beach Golf Course on 19 April 2009, and 10 birds at the Long Beach Airport on 11 May 2011. It is safe to say that the spring movement occurs largely between mid-April and mid-May, peaking at the end of April.

The fall movement usually begins in early September. The earliest dates thus far recorded were on 29 August in 2013, with 4 birds, and 31 August in 2016, with 3 birds, both at the airport. The fall migration reaches its peak in mid to late October. Because snipe favour open areas with low vegetation, the largest concentrations have been found at the airport, where the vegetation is regularly clipped short. Surveys in October, when the ground is saturated with rain, sometimes produce more than 50 birds. The highest numbers recorded were 110 birds on 11 October 1984, 62 on 18 October 2009, 133 on 26 October 2001, and 76 on 9 November 2016. After October, numbers normally decline, though birds persist in smaller numbers throughout the month of November and into December. However, as many as 33 birds were seen as late as 26 November in 2009, and intense storms delayed many migrants until 9 November in 2016.

A few birds linger into December, and by January only the most persistent birds remain. When temperatures fall below freezing, remaining birds search out the few places where the ground remains free of ice. During a sustained cold spell, even these hardy birds will be forced to depart or perish. In 2015, several individuals survived the winter at the airport, with records through January, February, and March.

WILSON'S PHALAROPE
Phalaropus tricolor

STATUS: Casual vagrant in spring and summer.

Phalaropes are distinct from other shorebirds in that the gender roles are reversed. It is the female that is brightly coloured, and it is the male that is drab and that incubates the eggs and rears the young. Phalaropes are also different in that they habitually land on the water, where they swim in circles in order to bring food to the surface. However, whereas the other two phalarope species spend much of the year on the ocean, the Wilson's Phalarope is much more terrestrial and spends more of its time walking along the shores of ponds and sloughs, although it too can swim on the water.

Unlike Red and Red-necked phalaropes, Wilson's Phalaropes breed only in North America. The breeding range covers much of the American and Canadian west, except for the southwestern United States and the northern forest regions and beyond. There are also a number of disjunct populations far from the main range, such as in southern Ontario and southern Quebec, James Bay, and the Yukon. The species migrates overland to winter primarily on the lakes of the Altiplano in South America and the pampas of Argentina. In British Columbia, the species breeds in the central interior, from the south Okanagan north to Prince George, and also in the Peace River region. In recent decades, it has bred at Iona Island in the Lower Mainland and on southeastern Vancouver Island.[111]

In our west coast region, Wilson's Phalaropes were unknown until 28 July 1996, when a bird was seen at the edge of the sewage pond in Pacific Rim National Park. The second sighting occurred on 9 June 2002 and involved a pair of birds that landed very briefly in shallow water on the mudflats at Tofino before flying off again. The third occurrence was on 30 June 2008, at Jensen's Bay; the bird was seen again on 1 July. On 8 April 2012, a single bird was seen on the floatplane pond at the Long Beach Airport, and on 29 May 2013, a female in full breeding plumage was seen at the sewage pond in Pacific Rim National Park. The sixth and seventh records involved a breeding-plumaged female at the airport on 24 June 2014, and two birds, a male and a female, photographed at the airport on 23 May 2017.

Note that three of our six records occurred in June, and we have one additional record just outside that period, on 29 May. These may be wandering nonbreeding birds. The record in early April is an early spring migrant, and the one on 28 July is most likely a fall transient.

It is interesting to note that Wilson's Phalaropes have been seen on the west coast only in the past 20 years. This is probably due to two reasons: the species has undergone an extension of its breeding range in both North America and British Columbia, and the central west coast has been more intensely monitored during that time.

RED-NECKED PHALAROPE
Phalaropus lobatus

STATUS: Common spring and fall migrant, occasionally abundant. Casual in June.

This species, formerly known as the Northern Phalarope, has a larger breeding range than the Red Phalarope, though it does not breed as far north. It inhabits marshy ponds and wet meadows in the tundra region from northern Europe and Siberia to Alaska and northern Canada, where it is found from the Yukon to Labrador. The North American population winters largely in the eastern Pacific Ocean off South America. This species migrates overland more than the Red Phalarope does, particularly in the west. In the interior of British Columbia, the species is considered an uncommon spring migrant and common to locally abundant autumn migrant. On the coast, the species is considered a very abundant migrant.[111]

In our west coast region, the first migrants begin to arrive after mid-April, with the earliest arrival date being 17 April. By the end of the month or early May, the migration is in full swing. Large flocks have occasionally been reported during the month of May. Flocks of up to 5,000 birds were reported offshore from Ucluelet on 1-4 May 1949.[48] The largest number ever recorded off our

Red-necked Phalaropes feed mostly on marine waters; however, this juvenile was found feeding beside a freshwater pond.

shores was seen on 15 May 1969, when 20,000 birds gathered off Cleland Island. Two days later, 3,000 more were seen, while throughout the day on 18 May "continuous flocks of 100 to 5,000 birds were seen passing on the way north."[1] Observing such large numbers appears to be a rare event, however. The largest number I personally recorded occurred on 8 May 2017, when an estimated 8,000 birds were seen in the shelter of Box Island during inclement weather. Most records involve far fewer birds. An estimated 2,000 birds recorded on a pelagic birding trip out of Bamfield on 9 May 2010 is also noteworthy. Spring dates range from 17 April to 20 May.

Although rare in June, we do have several records for the central coast in that month. On 19 June 2001, two birds were seen offshore from Tofino. On 6 June 2010, 6 June 2014, and from 12 to 16 June 2017, lone birds were seen on a pond at the Long Beach Airport. June birds may be nonbreeding laggards.

The Red-necked Phalarope was the most numerous species observed during at-sea spring migration surveys from Clerke Point on Brooks Peninsula between 14 May and 27 June 1973. The site is about 190 km north of Long Beach. The peak movement occurred during the first two weeks of May, and migration had ceased by mid-June. A total of 43,959 birds were counted in May and 762 in four days in June. An estimated 200,000 Red-necked Phalaropes passed by, of which 4,600 moved northward after the end of May. The peak movement occurred in mid-month (14 May). Martin and Myres[48] recorded 15 May as the peak movement. The nearshore migration counts represent only a small proportion of the actual population moving northward further out to sea.[13]

The fall movement begins in early July with the arrival of females, followed by adult males in late July and early August.[111] Indeed, a bird photographed at the Long Beach Airport on 27 July 2015 appears to be a postbreeding male. The earliest known record for southbound migrants involved 8 birds seen off Cleland Island on 9 July 2004. The following day, 30 birds were seen at the same location. Juveniles arrive much later and pass through until at least late September. A few stragglers may be seen through October and even November. The largest number reported during the southbound migration was 4,500 off Tree Island on 14 July 1975.[111]

Occasionally, severe sea conditions push birds ashore, as occurred in 1982. From 26 October to 20 November that year, small numbers were seen at numerous locations in the Tofino/Long Beach area, including birds photographed walking on the beach. There were eight birds at Incinerator Rock on 28 October, and three birds at Radar Beach on 20 November. The latest fall date recorded was 29 November in 2013, with five birds seen from Incinerator Rock, Long Beach.

RED PHALAROPE
Phalaropus fulicarius

STATUS: A sometimes common transient in offshore waters in spring, summer, and fall. Onshore, casual transient in spring, rare and irregular transient in fall. Casual in winter.

The Red Phalarope is largely a pelagic species, spending much of the year on the ocean and only coming on land to breed. This species has a widespread breeding range, from Iceland, Arctic Canada, and northern Alaska to northern Siberia. It winters in the eastern Atlantic, off the coast of Africa, and in the eastern Pacific Ocean off South America. Some winter as far north as Baja California, Mexico.

In British Columbia, birds are rarely seen on inland waters but migrate north and south over pelagic waters, usually many miles offshore. The species is not encountered in spring on most offshore birding trips, both off the coast of

While Red Phalaropes are usually found many miles offshore, during times of rough seas, individuals may seek relief on land.

British Columbia and off Washington. Trips around mid-May appear to have the greatest chance of success. Martin and Myres reported flocks of up to 50 birds off Ucluelet between 12 and 17 May 1949, during which several birds were collected.[48] More recently, on 15 May 1996, 21 birds were seen offshore from Tofino, and on 13 May 2001, flocks totalling 405 birds were recorded, beginning 36.3 km (19.6 NM) offshore. Birders on a pelagic trip out of Tofino on 8 May 2017 recorded an estimated 800 Red Phalaropes. An even larger number was recorded off Triangle Island on 17 May 1974, with an estimate of 1,000 birds.[179] These numbers appear to support Paulson, who stated that the largest numbers in spring occur in mid-May.[133] *The Birds of British Columbia* listed early and late dates of 30 April and 28 May.[111]

In late summer, birds are again found offshore, beginning in late July. The earliest recorded date of a southbound bird is 16 July 2002. Martin and Myers recorded the species as being numerous far offshore on the tuna fishing grounds between 26 July and 11 August 1946.[48] On late summer trips out of Tofino, 73 birds were counted on 3 August 2005 and 47 birds on 14 August 2010. A report of 300 birds at Long Beach on 27 July 1983 seems doubtful and is far more likely to have involved Red-necked Phalaropes, which are often seen closer to shore.

Red Phalaropes are occasionally encountered on shore, or very close to shore, in fall when sea conditions are severe. The earliest onshore records are 31 August in 2017, when a slightly injured bird was observed on Long Beach, and 19 September in 2003, when a bird was seen on a pond at the Long Beach Airport. There are eight records for October, four for November, four for December, and, surprisingly, five for January. Four of the January sightings occurred in 2003, after multiple sightings from October to December in 2002, when sea conditions were severe and late December birds lingered into January. On 28 December 2002, as many as eight birds were seen near Tofino, and in early January, single birds were seen at four separate locations. We have dates of 2 January at Tofino (two locations), 4 January at the airport, and 5 January at Amphitrite Point, Ucluelet. In addition, 30 Red Phalaropes were reported feeding at a salmon farm in Shelter Inlet at the mouth of Sulphur Passage that same week, with some birds still present on 29 January. It is perhaps significant that the waters in Shelter Inlet have been described by scientists from the University of Washington as having pelagic characteristics.

Several dead birds were found at the airport during this same period, suggesting that many must have perished. The only other January record occurred on 2 January 2006, when two birds were seen at Grice Bay. A record on 7 February 1998 at Tofino is the latest occurrence in winter.

In late December of 2005, birds were again turning up very close to shore on the central west coast. West of Carmanah Point, assistant lighthouse keeper Jerry Etzkorn picked up 10 dead birds on the beach on 23 December. A few locations where birds have been seen from shore or onshore on the central west coast are Grice Bay, Incinerator Rock at Long Beach, Father Charles Channel, Amphitrite Point, the PRNP sewage pond, and the floatplane pond at the airport.

Unlike shorebirds whose males are usually the first to depart from the nesting ground, in this species, because of gender role reversal, it is the females that are the first to leave for marine waters, and it is likely the females we see first in August, followed by the adult males, with the juveniles coming last. The species is said to be most common off the shores of North America between September and December. Outside our area, there is a record of 5,000 birds seen off Victoria on 11 November 1982. This event would almost certainly have been due to heavy weather on the open ocean. Such very large numbers are exceptional for BC waters but have been reported periodically in November and December in Oregon waters.

SPOTTED SANDPIPER
Actitis macularius

STATUS: Uncommon in spring and summer, fairly common in fall. Rare in winter. Breeds.

The Spotted Sandpiper is easy to distinguish from other sandpipers by its diagnostic bobbing motion as it stands or walks along the shore, and by its fluttering flight with the wings below the body. Unlike most sandpipers, which nest in the northern regions, this sandpiper breeds from coast to coast across much of North America, with the exception of Mexico, the southern United States, and the northern tundra regions. The species winters from the southern United States to Brazil and northern Chile. On the Pacific coast, it winters north to Washington and rarely to southwestern British Columbia.

In our region, Spotted Sandpipers nest along river courses, creeks, lakeshores, and occasionally the ocean shore. Birds have been documented nesting at Portland Point, Clayoquot Arm of Kennedy Lake, and the Moyeha River. Additional breeding records in the BC Nest Record Scheme are from Bamfield, Sandhill Creek, Brooks Peninsula, Holberg, and Cape Scott Park. There is also a record of four birds on Ursus Creek on 26 May 1994, and two birds at the mouth of the upper Kennedy River on 10 July 2014. Given that few people visit streams and rivers during the nesting period, birds are usually seen during migration in both spring and late summer. The spring movement occurs primarily in May. Hatler et al. noted that the spring movement was "particularly evident" on several islands in the Broken Group between 10 May and 25 May 1972.[1] That seems to be supported by records in recent years from Jordan River, Sarita Estuary, Pachena Beach, and elsewhere in Barkley Sound. There are also a couple of records from late April.

In summer, single birds were seen regularly in a variety of open marine and freshwater habitats on Brooks Peninsula between 22 May and 21 August, and a nest with four eggs was found on 28 June 1973.[13] The fall movement is much more conspicuous, beginning by about 20 July and continuing through August and most of September. A favoured location in Pacific Rim National Park is a beach at the extreme south end of Long Beach known as Lismer Beach. Here one can often find half a dozen birds in late summer. On 18 August 2012, 15 birds were present. Whether these were local birds or migrants from further north is not known.

Spotted Sandpipers are also fairly common on beaches along the West Coast Trail during the southward migration period. A survey conducted on 13 August 1972 between the Darling and Klanawa Rivers found 17 birds; another 13 were counted between the Darling River and Michigan Creek on the following day.[1] Birds have also been recorded in some of the river valleys. On 12 August 1990, a bird was present in the Clayoquot River valley, and on 28 September 1992, one was seen along the Megin River.

In most years, few birds are seen after September. However, individuals have been known to overwinter in some years, notably the winter of 1972/73, when birds were spotted along the inlet near Tofino in 9 out of 25 weeks between 8 October and 31 March. There are March records from Pachena Point in 1984, from the south end of Long Beach in 1994, and from Jordan River in 2013.

SOLITARY SANDPIPER
Tringa solitaria
STATUS: Casual migrant in spring and fall.

As its name suggests, the Solitary Sandpiper is most often seen singly, though sometimes in pairs. It tends to frequent freshwater ponds, though it will use a variety of habitats during migration, including subalpine regions. It breeds throughout most of the northern forest regions of Canada, from Labrador to the Yukon and into Alaska. In British Columbia, it has been found breeding in a variety of locations in the interior of the province, particularly in the central interior and the northeast. The species winters in Mexico, the Caribbean, and Central and South America. As a migrant, it is considered rare on the south coast, including southeastern Vancouver Island.

Although *Birds of Pacific Rim National Park* did not list the species, the distribution map for the Solitary Sandpiper in *The Birds of British Columbia* shows that the species had occurred on the central west coast before 1990.[111] There were no further records until 27 July 1996, when a bird was seen at the sewage pond in Pacific Rim National Park Reserve. Today, the number of records for the region totals 14. Of the 13 records for which we have dates, 5 were in spring and 8 during the southward migration period. Five of our spring sightings were recorded from 29 April to 16 May, which is the usual time frame reported elsewhere. The sixth sighting was very late, occurring on 23 May in 2009.

As with other shorebirds, the fall migration occurs over a much longer time span. The earliest record occurred on 22 July in 1979 (Calamity Lake east of Bamfield – 1, BCFWS files) and the latest on 1 October in 2001. All were single birds except on 16 September 2001, when two birds were seen. All sightings in both spring and fall were at the sewage pond in Pacific Rim National Park, and at the Long Beach Airport and adjacent golf course. It has not been seen on mudflats or elsewhere in the marine environment.

WANDERING TATTLER
Tringa incana

STATUS: Fairly common migrant in spring, summer, and fall. Rare in June.

Like Black Turnstones and Surfbirds, the Wandering Tattler is a sandpiper of the rocky shore and has a range that is exclusively western. The species breeds in the highlands and alpine zones of Alaska, the Yukon, and extreme northwestern British Columbia, where it lives largely on insects, specifically caddisflies and their larvae, during the breeding season. After breeding, birds return to the coast to feed in the intertidal zone on crustaceans, molluscs, and marine worms. They winter from eastern Australia to islands in the South Seas, and along the American Pacific coast from northern California to Ecuador and the Galapagos Islands.

In British Columbia, this bird largely avoids the protected waters of fjords and inlets in favour of the reefs, islands, and surf-washed rocky shore on the exposed outside coast. Spring passage on the west coast begins in late April, with the earliest bird recorded on 22 April in 2014, at Box Island, Long Beach. Most of the migration takes place during the month of May. The majority of sightings consist of one or two birds, but at Cleland Island, which is a most favourable location for seeing these birds, much larger numbers are sometimes seen. Chronologically, high numbers recorded at Cleland Island are 20 birds on 28 April 1977; 10 on 4 May 1988 and 8 May 1989; 15 on 15 May 1969; 30 on 16 May 1970; and 20 on 19 May 1970 (BCFWS files). The spring passage is over by late May. There are only 12 records for June, all from Cleland Island.

The Wandering Tattler is a bird of the rocky, surf-swept outer coast, but occasionally ventures into protected waters.

In 1970, up to 6 birds were recorded between 1 and 20 June, and 3 birds were seen on 1 June 2002.

The southward movement begins in early to mid-July and comes to an end by about the end of September. The earliest dates, both from Cleland Island, are 4 July of 1970 (1 bird) and 9 July in 2004 (1 bird). The movement peaks in late July or early August, when up to 20 birds have been counted (BCFWS files). I personally counted a dozen birds on Cleland Island on 4 August 2003, and estimated two dozen birds on another occasion. The largest number ever recorded there was 40 birds on 24 July 1967.[111] Only an occasional straggler remains in October. The latest record I could find is of a bird at Green Point, Long Beach, on 22 October 1972. There is also a record of a bird on the beach at the mouth of Sandhill Creek, Long Beach, on 15 October 1975.

As mentioned earlier, this species prefers the outer coast, but it should be noted that there are several records of birds in protected waters. On 26 September 1970, eight birds were reported from Tofino Inlet, though no exact location was given, and on 13 May 2013, three birds were seen at McIntosh Bay, on the north side of Vargas Island. More surprising, on 1 August 1997, two birds were seen at the mouth of Bedwell River, 33.5 km (21 mi) from the outer coast. Half of that distance is up a narrow fjord known as Bedwell Sound. Such inland locations are not often visited by birders, raising the possibility that the species may occur there more often than we currently realize.

GREATER YELLOWLEGS
Tringa melanoleuca

STATUS: Common spring migrant, uncommon to locally common in summer and fall.

The Greater Yellowlegs breeds throughout much of the boreal forest region in Canada, from Newfoundland and Labrador west to the Prairie provinces and through northern parts of British Columbia to southern Alaska. In our province, the species is also known to nest in the Chilcotin-Cariboo, the Nechako Lowlands, and the Peace Lowland (BCNRS). Greater Yellowlegs winter along the Pacific coast from Washington to southern South America. On rare occasions, birds have wintered in the Fraser Lowlands.

This long-legged wader is one of the first migrant shorebirds to arrive in our region in spring, its presence announced with a loud, ringing three- or four-note cry. On the central west coast, they are usually seen in shallow water on the Tofino mudflats or at Grice Bay, often in groups of 6 or a dozen in pursuit of small fish. It is not unusual to see one swim in order to cross deeper water. First arrivals may be seen as early as the first week of April, though usually later. There has been a trend in recent years for birds to arrive much earlier than formerly. Indeed, in four consecutive years, beginning in 2013, first arrivals were seen before the end of March. In 2004, a flock of 5 Greater Yellowlegs was seen on 20 March. By 31 March that number had increased to 15 birds. Although they tend to travel in small flocks, on occasion larger aggregations are seen, such as 38 birds on 1 May 1999; 55 on 29 April 2009; and 76 on 20 April 2003. Gatherings of from 18 to 28 birds have been recorded on numerous occasions. Numbers peak in late April or early May, after which they decline rather quickly. Small numbers continue to be seen throughout May, and even into June in some years.

The southward migration usually begins in early July, although 29 birds were already at Sandhill Creek, Long Beach, on 28 June 1990. Birds were seen at Tofino on 27 June in both 2012 and 2014, and on 24 June 2013. The earliest date ever recorded for southbound birds was 18 June in 2017, at the airport. Most first arrival dates for southbound birds have been in early July and the migration continues throughout the summer to the first half of September. An occasional straggler may be seen in October. There is a record of 13 birds at the Long Beach Airport on 14 October 2012, and 2 birds at the same location on 14 October 2014. The very latest fall bird on record of was seen on 10 November

2004, also at the airport. The latest fall sighting listed in *Birds of Pacific Rim National Park* is 13 November in 1961, at Tofino.[1]

While most sightings of the Greater Yellowlegs have been in shallow water on mudflats, they have also been seen in shallow creeks (Sandhill Creek), beach pools (Chesterman Beach and Vargas Island), shallow lakes (Swan Lake), marine lagoons (Spring Island, Ucluelet), and, rarely, sandy beaches without pools (Long Beach).

Greater Yellowlegs have been found nesting in the Nahwitti Bog at the north end of Vancouver Island, just east of our region.

WILLET
Tringa semipalmata
STATUS: Casual vagrant.

This large shorebird has a peculiar distribution, with two distinct populations that are currently considered subspecies. The eastern population breeds along the Atlantic coast of North America, north to Nova Scotia. The western race breeds on the Great Plains, from Manitoba and North and South Dakota westward in Canada to the Rocky Mountains, and westward in the United States to southern Idaho, Oregon, and Nevada.

Western birds winter along the Pacific coast, principally from California south to Mexico and coastal South America. Small flocks winter north to Willapa Bay, Washington. Although British Columbia is outside the normal range for this species, birds do turn up in our province periodically, mostly on southern Vancouver Island and on Iona Island in the Fraser River delta.

Birds of Pacific Rim National Park did not list the species for our west coast region in 1978.

Today there are three records. The first sighting occurred in 1989, when a bird was seen at the south end of Long Beach on 24 August by Lois Piji. Less than a year later, a bird was seen at Tofino on 20 April 1990 by Rory Paterson. The third sighting occurred on 24 April 2013, when an individual was seen at the south end of Long Beach among Black-bellied Plovers and Whimbrels by a former chief naturalist at Pacific Rim National Park, Barry Campbell.

There was a report of a Willet being seen on Whaler Islet in Clayoquot Sound in the summer of either 1988 or 1989. If it was 1989, it was likely the same bird that was reported by Lois Piji.

LESSER YELLOWLEGS
Tringa flavipes

STATUS: Rare spring transient, uncommon in summer and fall. Very rare in June.

During the migration period, this wader has a widespread distribution, being found in the United States from the Atlantic to the Pacific. Its breeding range stretches from northeastern Ontario and Hudson Bay westward and northward through the boreal forest region to northern British Columbia, the Northwest Territories, the Yukon, and Alaska. In this province, the Lesser Yellowlegs breeds in the northeast and northwest regions. It is fairly common to common in much of the interior as a spring and fall migrant. On the coast, its status ranges from rare to locally very common.

In the west coast region, this bird is considerably less common. *Birds of Pacific Rim National Park* listed only 14 records, all involving southbound birds from July to September.[1] Mentioned in the text, however, were 2 spring records from Browning Inlet in the northern part of our region, one of 10 birds in late April and one from the first week in May. Since *Birds of Pacific Rim National Park* was published in 1978, 130 additional sightings have been recorded, 29 of those in spring, with 10 in April and 19 in May. The earliest spring record was on 9 April in 1996, at the Tofino mudflats, and the latest was on 18 May in 2011, at the Long Beach Airport. Most spring migrants pass through from 20 April to mid-May.

In our region, as in other areas of the coast, this species is much more prevalent during the return migration in summer and fall. Our earliest record of southbound migrants occurred on 28 June 1969, on Cleland Island (BCFWS files). A sighting nearly as early occurred on 29 June in 2010, when 6 birds were seen at Jensen's Bay, Tofino. There was also a sighting at the airport on 5 July 2015. Most of the migration occurs in July and August, and by September birds begin to thin out. Combining all records, old and new, there have been 22 sightings in July, 40 in August, 11 in September, and 2 in October. The latest fall record was of 2 birds at the Long Beach Airport on 17 October in 2003. Most records involve from 1 to 6 birds, but occasionally reach a dozen. The largest number seen was 14 birds at Jensen's Bay, Tofino, on 3 July 2002.

Lesser Yellowlegs are seen in both the marine environment and freshwater ponds and wetlands. Locations where birds have been seen other than those already mentioned include Swan Lake, the sewage pond near Long Beach,

Megin Lake, Long Beach Golf Course, Chesterman Beach, Pachena Bay, San Juan River, Grice Bay tidal meadows, and Sandhill Creek (Combers). There is one record from the northern half of our region. On 27 June 1975, two birds were seen by Charles Guiguet at the mouth of the Klaskish River near Brooks Peninsula.

A word of caution: in summer, juvenile Greater Yellowlegs, which have a shorter bill than adults, are sometimes mistaken for this species, but Lesser Yellowlegs have a finer bill and are considerably smaller, though this is not always apparent unless the two species are side by side.

Skuas and Jaegers   Family Stercorariidae

SOUTH POLAR SKUA
Stercorarius maccormicki

STATUS: Rare in May and June in pelagic waters, uncommon in late summer, becoming rare in fall.

Related to jaegers, the large and robust South Polar Skua is not likely to be mistaken for one of its smaller relatives. It breeds in Antarctica from November to February, and after the breeding season disperses to the North Atlantic and North Pacific. The first record of this bird in BC waters was on the La Perouse Bank on 2 July 1947.[48]

The Birds of British Columbia considered it to be very rare in summer, and a rare autumn transient in offshore waters.[6] *Birds of Pacific Rim National Park*, with only 3 records, considered it very rare in fall off Vancouver Island's west coast.[1] Since then, the total number of records has risen to 39. Although sightings on most birding excursions involve 1 or 2 individuals, 4 birds were seen on six occasions, 5 birds on one occasion, and 6 birds on three occasions. The largest number ever reported on a single trip was 13 individuals on a pelagic birding tour out of Ucluelet on 16 September 2001.

Breaking sightings down by the month, we have 5 records in May, 1 in June, 6 in July, 9 in August, 16 in September, and 1 in October. That last record is from 10 October 1992, when four birds were observed at Barkley Canyon. Keep in mind that pelagic birding trips are done more often in August and September, which partially accounts for the larger numbers seen in those two months. That these birds are not the rarity they were once considered to be now seems evident. In 2002, South Polar Skuas were seen in four consecutive months on marine bird and mammal surveys out of Tofino.

All records are from well offshore, with the exception of one bird seen in the Strait of Juan de Fuca. A report of two birds seen from shore at Botanical Beach, while not impossible, is considered unlikely and, lacking photographic evidence, is not included here.

POMARINE JAEGER
Stercorarius pomarinus

STATUS: Rare spring transient in pelagic waters. Fairly common in late summer and fall.

This is the largest of the three jaegers. The word "jaeger" derives from an old German word meaning hunter, and this seems quite apt. On its arctic breeding grounds, this species preys on lemmings and also takes the eggs and chicks of other birds. Over marine waters, it pirates fish from seabirds and also preys on small birds. The species breeds in northern Siberia, northern Alaska, and large areas of Arctic Canada. After the breeding season, birds migrate to southern oceans. In the Pacific Ocean, birds winter in the Australasia region and off the shores of the Americas, from Washington to southern Chile.

In our west coast region, Pomarine Jaegers are transients, with perhaps some nonbreeders present in summer. In *The Birds of British Columbia*, this species was regarded as an uncommon transient in spring.[6] However, only two spring records were listed for our region, a single individual seen at La Perouse Bank on 16 May 1977,[178] and 10 individuals on 16 May 1985.[180] However, 12 additional sightings are listed elsewhere.[46] The majority of spring sightings occur in the first half of May.

June records are rare. Although a Canadian Wildlife Service (CWS) report states that the species was recorded off southwestern Vancouver Island from June to September, I was able to find only a single record for that month, that of a bird seen on 21 June 2002 on a bird and mammal survey out of Tofino by Strawberry Island Research. For the month of July, there are six records, with the two earliest in mid-July and the others after the 20th of the month. The first two could be nonbreeding birds, while the other three are likely early fall migrants. It is worth noting that in years of low food supply in the north, birds may disperse early.

Like other jaegers, the robust Pomarine Jaeger is parasitic in nature, stealing food from other birds. This is a dark morph bird.

By August, Pomarine Jaegers are seen much more often, and numbers peak in September. Of the seven occasions when 9 or more birds were seen on a single trip, five of those occurred in September and one at the very end of August. On each of four offshore trips, a total of 12 birds were seen. All of those were in September. By October, most birds have passed through. I was able to find only two records for that month, with 3 birds seen on 1 October 1977 and 5 birds recorded on 12 October 1993. Thus far we have only one record after October. On 9 November 1993, a single bird was recorded 20.3 km (11 NM) southwest of Tofino by Rod Palm of Strawberry Island Research.

A CWS report by Kees Vermeer et al. makes the interesting observation that in offshore waters, Pomarine Jaegers harass Sabine's Gulls, whereas the other two jaeger species pursue mostly Arctic Terns, which are found further offshore.[181] This could explain why Pomarine Jaegers are seen more frequently than Parasitic Jaegers. It should be noted, however, that this species also harasses larger birds, such as Herring Gulls and California Gulls, which are commonly seen many miles offshore.

Pomarine Jaegers occur as both a light-morph bird and one that is all dark. Both occur over west coast waters, though I could find no information on the ratio of each.

PARASITIC JAEGER
Stercorarius parasiticus
STATUS: Rare spring transient, uncommon in summer and fall in pelagic waters. Rare in inshore waters.

The Parasitic Jaeger is named for its habit of stealing food from other birds such as terns and gulls. In Britain, it is known as Arctic Skua, for it has a circumpolar breeding distribution extending from Siberia to Europe, Iceland, Greenland, northern Canada, and Alaska. The species winters off New Zealand, Australia, New Guinea, southern Africa, and much of South America. In the eastern Pacific, it winters from Mexico to Tierra del Fuego.

The passage of Parasitic Jaegers through our west coast waters is a bit of a puzzle. *The Birds of British Columbia* states they are an uncommon to fairly common spring transient, rare in summer and a fairly common to common autumn transient.[111] Vermeer et al. stated that during their study in waters offshore from southwestern Vancouver Island, Parasitic Jaegers were recorded from July through October, though no specific dates were given.[181] The latter statement corresponds more closely to the sightings recorded on pelagic birding trips and on marine bird and mammal surveys with Strawberry Island Research out of Tofino. However, eighty Parasitic Jaegers were counted during migration surveys from Clerke Point, Brooks Peninsula, between 14 May and 27 June 1973. A few birds passed by in late May but most were counted in June following days of southeasterly winds.[13] There have also been occasional observations made from shore, notably in June, in Barkley Sound, Brooks Bay, and Checleset Bay, and off Cleland Island.

Records I have access to add up to 86 sightings: 10 in May, 25 in June, 4 in July, 15 in August, 31 in September, and 1 in October. Most sightings involved single birds, but seven birds were seen on 16 July 2002, 60 km (32.4 NM) offshore from Tofino; six on 31 July 1971, near Tofino; and six on 12 September 2010, on an offshore birding trip southwest of Tofino. Birds seen in mid-July and later are likely the vanguard of the fall movement.

The largest number of birds seen in a single day was 17 on 2 September 1984, between Cape Beale and La Perouse Bank, providing evidence that September is the peak migration period for this species in our region. Keep in mind that September is also the most popular month for pelagic birding trips. The single record for October was seen from Incinerator Rock, Long Beach, on 13 October 2009. There have been other land-based sightings in autumn from Cleland Island, Tofino Harbour, Grice Bay, Barkley Sound, Amphitrite Point,

Pachena Bay, Port San Juan, and Jordan River. All but one of these were seen in September.

Outside of the Brooks Peninsula, sightings in spring have been few. The earliest record I could find was of a pair of birds observed off the north end of Vancouver Island on 7 May 2006. Nearly as early was a bird seen on 9 May 1972 southwest of Barkley Sound. With only seven sightings for May, it seems surprising that so few have been seen in spring. However, according to Vermeer et al., Parasitic Jaegers pursue Arctic Terns, which pass by far out to sea.[181] This could account for the paucity of records at this time of year. A map in a paper by Kenyon et al. shows an additional 10 locations where offshore spring sightings have occurred. Six of those sightings were outside the continental shelf break.[46]

LONG-TAILED JAEGER
Stercorarius longicaudus

STATUS: Rare transient in spring and fall in pelagic waters. Casual in June.

This is the smallest of the jaegers and also the most elegant. The species breeds in the High Arctic, further north than any other jaeger. Its breeding range spans northern Siberia, Europe, Greenland, Canada, and Alaska. After the breeding season, which begins in June, Long-tailed Jaegers return to marine waters and fly south. While these birds are highly pelagic, they are sometimes seen on inside waters and even inland on rare occasions. Winters are spent on southern oceans.

The first occurrence of this species off our shores was recorded on 11 May 1891, when two birds were collected (RBCM 1460 and 1461). The second record for the region did not occur until 40 years later, when on 28 May 1931 a bird was seen at Chesterman Beach, Tofino. Five years later, two birds were recorded off Cape Scott on 29 July 1936.[111] Since then, there have been a good number of additional sightings, though very few of them in spring.

The Long-tailed Jaeger is the least common of the three jaegers, according to both Kees Vermeer and Ken Morgan, who have conducted numerous pelagic bird surveys over the past 25 years. This has also been our finding based on numerous pelagic bird and mammal surveys out of Tofino. On 65 surveys, this species was encountered on only 5 occasions. Morgan and Vermeer point out that this species is usually seen seaward of the shelf break. Although this jaeger catches its own food much more than do the other two, it is reported to harass Arctic Terns for food further out to sea.[181] According to Ken Morgan, birds arrive in the first week of May. In fall they are seen until the second week of October. Most are said to occur between mid-August and mid-September.

Of the 6 spring records I know of, dates fall between 11 May and 28 May. A map showing spring sightings in a paper by Kenyon et al. shows the locations of an additional 8 spring sightings, all of them outside the shelf break.[46] I could find no June records for our area, and the only July records are 29 July 1936 (mentioned above) and 16 July 2013. Three of the 11 August records occurred, coincidentally, on the 20th of August in the years 2001, 2002, and 2010. On 21 August 2010, three birds were seen 9 NM southwest of Triangle Island by Russel Cannings, and single birds were recorded at two other locations nearby on the same day. J.E.V. Goodwill recorded a bird near Solander Island on 27 August 1967.[13] Of the 8 September records, 4 were on or before the 15th of the month, one was on the 18th, and the rest were after the 20th. The largest number reported in September was five birds between 21 and 23 September 2006, off southwestern Vancouver Island. We have no November records. However, Long-tailed Jaegers have been recorded in November on the Salish Sea. These likely represent very late birds that have sought out less turbulent waters during a month when sea conditions are often severe on the outside.

Murres, Auks, and Puffins   Family Alcidae

COMMON MURRE
Uria aalge

STATUS: Common to abundant in late summer and fall. Uncommon in winter. Fairly common in spring and early summer. Breeds.

The Common Murre is found in both the Atlantic and Pacific oceans and breeds widely throughout the Northern Hemisphere. In Britain, it is known as Guillemot. On North America's Pacific coast, it breeds from western Alaska and the Aleutians south to the Channel Islands of California. The species winters throughout its breeding range, though there may be large movements within that range. Alaska birds have been recorded in northern British Columbia waters after the breeding season and young hatched in Washington state move into the Strait of Juan de Fuca and along the outer west coast after breeding.

Common Murres, such as the adult shown here, breed on our coast in large numbers and disperse widely after breeding.

Common Murres nest in colonies, which are usually situated on island cliffs and headlands. Birds are often packed close together, and the parents take turns incubating a single egg. During the incubation period, one of the adults goes out to sea to forage for food, often travelling a long distance, although this varies depending on the location. In Alaska, birds usually stay within 60 km of the nest, but in some locations they fly as far as 125 km out to sea. When the chick is old enough to leave the nest, the male calls from the water and the chick drops from the cliff to join its father, sometimes from a height of 1,000 ft. The male then accompanies the chick for up to a month and a half, feeding it until it is able to fly. Common Murres feed on small fishes, krill, and squid, and propel themselves underwater using their wings, essentially flying underwater. In the Atlantic, Common Murres were found to dive as much as 177 m (580 ft) below the surface.[182]

The Common Murre has a global breeding population estimated at 13 to 20.7 million birds,[183] and British Columbia provides a breeding ground for only a small percentage of the world population. Of those, more than 98% nest at Triangle Island, located off the northwestern tip of Vancouver Island.[88] A census conducted there in 1989, found 5,937 birds. In 2003, the count was 4,327 birds, down 25%.[183] (In comparison, the population in Alaska is estimated at

2.8 million birds scattered in 230 colonies.[182] Eagles may be a contributing factor to the decline at Triangle Island. A study conducted by Julia K. Parrish and S.G. Zador[184] found as many as 23 Bald Eagles present on Triangle Island, with five active eyries. Predation on murres was common, with secondary predation on eggs by gulls and crows whenever eagles caused birds to abandon their nests. Somewhat ironically, the presence of another raptor, the Peregrine Falcon, may actually protect Common Murres (see under Peregrine Falcon).

Significant as such predation may be, it pales in comparison to what humans inflicted on a population of Common Murres off the coast of California in the latter half of the 19th century. At the Farallon Islands, millions of eggs were commercially harvested for the San Francisco market during a 40-year period, resulting in a decline in population from between 400,000 and 500,000 birds to only 5,000. Today the population has recovered to the fairly robust level of 170,000.[185]

Common Murres continue to face many dangers, from gillnets to oil spills. In California, gillnets were responsible for the deaths of an estimated 70,000 murres before the practice was stopped. The Nestucca oil spill in 1989 resulted in the deaths of an estimated 30,000 murres off Washington and British Columbia.

Triangle Island supports 98% of the 8,358 birds currently estimated breeding in British Columbia at three sites. Historically the species has occasionally bred elsewhere on our coast. For example, a pair nested on Florencia Island in 1969 and also at Cleland Island the same year.[186] They attempted to nest at Cleland again in subsequent years, and in 1975, eight pairs nested there. A nesting pair was found at Starlight Reef in Barkley Sound in 1975,[1] and two pairs nested there in 1980. None of these breeding sites have remained active.

Common Murres have been recorded in all months of the year. The largest numbers are seen after the breeding season, when they sometimes congregate in very large numbers. On 25 July 1972, 10,000 birds were estimated in Wickaninnish Bay, and on 19 August 1977, 9,000 birds were estimated in Barkley Sound. I could find no records of such large numbers in recent years, although several counts top 1,000 birds. The largest count since the 1970s was made on 14 August 2002, when 2,000 birds were estimated on the water around Cleland Island. On 18 August 2011, 1,330 were counted on the outside of Vargas Island, and on 18 September 2013, 1,015 birds were tallied from Incinerator Rock, Long Beach. In 2015, numbers off the central west coast were extremely low, probably due to an immense zone of unusually warm water offshore.

Although Common Murres are seen mostly on outside waters, a few birds show up on sheltered inlets, sometimes many kilometres from the outside coast.

THICK-BILLED MURRE
Uria lomvia

STATUS: Casual summer vagrant, except for Triangle Island, where it has nested. Rare breeder.

The Thick-billed Murre was formerly known as Brunnich's Murre in North America, and is still known as Brunnich's Guillemot in the United Kingdom. As a breeding bird, it is widely distributed through the Northern Hemisphere, from Siberia, Norway, and Iceland to Greenland and North America. In the west, its breeding range extends along the shores of western Alaska and islands of the Bering Sea to the Aleutian Islands and islands in the northern Gulf of Alaska. The western population winters in the Bering Sea and in the Gulf of Alaska, south to the waters off southeast Alaska. Birds have been seen as far south as California.

The first documented occurrence for this species both in our region and in the province occurred in 1980 when two birds were observed and photographed among Common Murres on Triangle Island. There had, however, been a reliable sighting 10 years earlier outside our region at Langara Island, Haida Gwaii.[111] In 1981, 19 nesting pairs were found at Triangle Island,[187] and in 1982 a total of 70 birds were counted there.[111] In 1989, a maximum of 41 birds were counted, of which 7 appeared to be nesting.[88] It remains the only place in British Columbia where this species is known to nest and is the southernmost known breeding site in the eastern Pacific.

Sightings further south are rare. A bird was reported on the mid-coast at Lennard Island on 10 August 1984, and there is a record of a bird seen 24 km west off Pachena Point on 29 August 1985.[111] *The Atlas of Pelagic Seabirds Off the West Coast of Canada and Adjacent Areas* lists two sightings off Ucluelet, one on 31 October 1984 and one on 24 January 1995.[46] Two additional winter sightings were made off Barkley Sound on 9 and 25 February 1999. A summer sighting was made off Tofino, well beyond the continental shelf break, on 30 June 2002.

Because most observations are made from a distance, and the Common and Thick-billed murres are similar in appearance, Thick-billed Murres may occur more often than records indicate. Identification of fall and winter birds should be made with utmost caution, however, as Common Murres, on rare occasions, have a plumage virtually identical to that of the Thick-billed Murre. One such bird was seen in Tofino harbour on 2 and 3 February 2007. Observing additional field marks such as bill shape, white gape-line, and unstreaked flanks are essential.

PIGEON GUILLEMOT
Cepphus columba

STATUS: Common to locally abundant in spring and summer, uncommon in fall and winter. Breeds.

Pigeon Guillemots breed in clefts and cavities on rocky islets off our outer coast. Shown here is an adult in breeding plumage.

The Pigeon Guillemot is an inhabitant of the North Pacific, from the Kuril Islands and Kamchatka Peninsula in Asia east to the Aleutian Islands and the shores of Alaska and British Columbia, south to southern California. In winter, northern birds move further south to open waters, while birds from California move further north. This guillemot is closely related to the Black Guillemot of the Atlantic and Arctic regions, which it closely resembles. The range of the two species meets in northwestern Alaska.

Pigeon Guillemots will nest in colonies at locations in which there is safety from land-based predators and where adequate nest sites are available, such as on headlands and islands. However, they will not hesitate to nest singly in isolated locations, and are reported to be very flexible in their choice of nest sites. Where soft earth is available, they will dig burrows or take up residence in existing burrows. More often, they will seek a crevice in the rocks or spaces among beached driftwood or large rocks. Even man-made structures are used, including beams under wharves and piers.[187]

Breeding populations have not been determined for British Columbia, but 12,403 birds have been reported from 339 potential nest sites. Of these, 15% (50 sites) occur along the west coast of Vancouver Island.[46] Three locations in the west coast region where significant colonies exist are Triangle Island, Cleland Island, and Seabird Rocks. Take a boat tour to Cleland Island in May or June and you'll see a hundred or more birds sitting on the rocky shore and in the water nearby, their piercing whistles ringing over the sound of breaking surf. This scene is likely to repeat itself at the other colonies.

In spring, birds become more evident in nearshore waters beginning in April, as they prepare for the breeding season. Of 123 records in my personal files, only 2 are in the month of January, 4 in February, and 2 in March. April has 11 records, while May has 22. The first landings in breeding colonies generally occur in the last two weeks of April.[111] At Cleland Island, 208 adults were counted in 1988.[111] At Seabird Rocks, Hatler et al. estimated 50 pairs in 1972.[1] Islands in Barkley Sound provide nesting habitat for an undetermined number of breeding pairs. At Wouwer Island, 30 birds were counted on 17 July 2013, and at Folger Island 60 birds on 2 August 2013.

By late September or early October, birds seek shelter in calmer waters. In Clayoquot Sound, birds are then often found in Father Charles Channel. On 4 October 2001, 30 birds were counted there, and on 30 September 2012, 32 birds. As they disperse, birds are seen less often and in much smaller numbers. On the central west coast, I have 12 records for October, 8 for November, and 7 for December. That pattern seems to hold further south in Barkley Sound, Port San Juan, and Jordan River. A count of 218 birds off Amphitrite Point on 1 September 2012 can probably be explained as an early movement of postbreeding birds en route to their wintering grounds further south, perhaps in the Salish Sea. The winter distribution is apparently not well known.

MARBLED MURRELET
Brachyramphus marmoratus

STATUS: Common, sometimes abundant in spring and summer. Uncommon to rare in fall and winter. Breeds.

The Marbled Murrelet breeds from the Aleutian Islands and the Alaskan Peninsula south through coastal British Columbia, Washington, Oregon, and northern California. This little seabird is named for its brown breeding plumage, which has a marbled look. In fall, birds revert back to their black-and-white winter plumage. Young birds are already thus attired. Fishermen sometimes refer to this bird as a "kiss-my-ass" for its habit of abruptly diving beneath the surface of the ocean, giving the viewer an ever-so-brief glimpse of its rear end.

At a mere 220 g (8 oz) in weight, this seemingly insignificant little bird would not attract much attention from the public were it not for its nesting habits and the subsequent controversy about the destruction of its habitat. For unlike others in its family, which nest in burrows or on the ground on islands, this little auk is known to nest on the ground only in the northern part of its range in Alaska. For over a hundred years, ornithologists were perplexed about just where this bird nested in most of its range. The mystery was solved in 1974, when a maintenance worker in a California park near Santa Cruz discovered a nest while climbing a redwood tree.[188] In British Columbia, the first nest was found in 1990 by John Kelson and Irene Manley high up in a Sitka spruce tree in the Walbran Valley.

Unknown to everyone, a nest had actually been discovered decades earlier when naturalist Glen Ryder found one near Chilliwack in 1955. However, a paper outlining the discovery was not published until 2012.[189] An unusual aspect of this first discovery was the fact that the nest was located not in an old-growth conifer as are most nests but in a bigleaf maple, a deciduous tree.

Today we know that a pair of birds will seek out a moss-covered branch high up in the canopy of the old-growth forest to make their nest. The female will lay only a single egg. After hatching, both parents return to the nest before dawn and after dusk to feed the chick. At a nest under observation at Sechelt, the parents were seen feeding the chick five sand lance in the morning and two at dusk.[190] They choose dawn and dusk in order to avoid tipping off potential predators such as jays, crows, and ravens as to the location of the precious egg. Nests may be located in a river valley as far as 60 km from the ocean. In one instance, birds flew 95 km one way to feed their chick.[190]

Logging is big business on the coast and, naturally enough, with the destruction of the bird's forest habitat, the population suffered a noticeable decline in numbers. Alarm bells went off in the environmental community and the species was listed as threatened in Canada by COSEWIC in 1990[190] and in the United States by the Fish and Wildlife Service in 1992. The BC Ministry of Environment became involved and expended considerable resources on Marbled Murrelet research; at the same time, its sister agency, the BC Forest Service, was working hard to maintain the continued liquidation of old-growth forests.

After Kelson and Manley's nest discovery in 1990, government-funded research teams equipped with mountaineering gear searched through river valleys for additional nests. It was a daunting task that ultimately resulted in 200 nests being found in the province. Radio telemetry was also used to track birds to nesting sites. Murrelet numbers were found to be strongly correlated with the size of the watershed and with mature forest mostly below 600 m elevation, though a nest has been found as high as 1,100 m (3,600 ft) elevation.[190]

Radar was used to determine the number of birds using particular watersheds. Between 1996 and 2013, a total of 946 radar counts were conducted at 58 coastal sites. These revealed hundreds of murrelets flying in and out of watersheds during the predawn hours, where otherwise they would have been invisible. In our west coast region, 11 watersheds were monitored. Numbers varied, of course, but maximum counts were as follows: Bulson Creek – 300 birds; Bedwell River – 400; Power River – 300; and Tahsish – 400. The total recorded at the Klaskish River was a remarkable 900 birds.[191] No significant decline in numbers was noted during this period.

Earlier surveys conducted in Clayoquot Sound between 1982 and 1992 had revealed a 40% decline over a 10-year period. Extensive logging during the 1980s in several valleys that emptied into marine waters likely contributed to this reduction in numbers, although warmer water from an El Niño event could have been a contributing factor.

Much greater declines have been noted along the US coast from Washington to California. In Prince William Sound, Alaska, where significant logging has also taken place, Marbled Murrelets suffered an 89% decline between 1972 and 2004.[192] The estimate for the global population in 2006 was 994,000 birds, with estimates of 88% of the population in Alaska, 10% in British Columbia, and 2% in Washington, Oregon, and California.[192] Based on that estimate, the BC population would have consisted of around 99,000 birds. A COSEWIC estimate for the global population ranged from 236,000 to 841,000 birds, while the BC population was believed to consist of roughly 54,450 to 94,200 adults in 2012.[193]

In our west coast region, Marbled Murrelets may be seen in all months of the year, though they are uncommon in winter. The largest numbers recorded on counts conducted in offshore waters by Strawberry Island Research in the months of December, January, and February were 38 birds seen on 7 February 1994 and 25 birds on 12 February 2000. All other counts produced 4 birds or fewer. Small numbers have also been recorded in protected inside waters in winter, for example, in Tofino harbour and at Grice Bay.

By late March or the beginning of April, paired birds begin to appear on outside waters. At Incinerator Rock, Long Beach, 26 birds were seen on 6 April 2014 and 70 birds on 7 April 2015. On 9 April 2015, 103 birds were counted, all of them still in winter plumage. "Many" murrelets were reported that same day from the outside of Flores Island. By late May or June, hundreds of birds may be counted. During the breeding season in June, a considerable number may also congregate on inside waters, for example, at Browning Passage, which bisects the Tofino mudflats. On 4 June 1993, 116 birds were counted there; on 10 June 1994, 240 birds; and on 18 July 2002, 180 birds.

In 1997, assistant lighthouse keeper Jerry Etzkorn conducted counts on Carmanah Bay. Sightings began on 7 April with a single bird, gradually increasing through the month. On 30 April, 21 birds were counted; on 25 May, 75 birds; and on 10 June, 352 birds. Numbers peaked at 465 birds on 12 June. Significant numbers continued throughout July and into August. A year earlier, birds had peaked on 22 June with a count of 976 birds.

Murrelets also gather on Wickaninnish Bay and can often be seen from Incinerator Rock, Long Beach, using a spotting scope. During June and July, from 100 to 200 birds have been counted there. The largest number recorded thus far from that location was 334 birds on the water on 30 May 2011.

SCRIPPS'S MURRELET
Synthliboramphus scrippsi

STATUS: Casual visitor to marine waters.

This small seabird was known as the Xantus's Murrelet until 2012, when it was split into two species, Scripps's Murrelet and Guadalupe Murrelet. The former is the more northerly of the two. It breeds on islands off the coast of southern California and northern Baja California, Mexico. After breeding, it normally ranges off the coast of southern California, but there are scattered reports of individuals seen further north off the coasts of Oregon and Washington. It was unknown in British Columbia until 25 October 1971, when the first specimen for the province was collected in the waters of Hecate Strait after a female collided with a boat.[194]

Records are sparse for the west coast of Vancouver Island. The earliest reliable report of this species off our shores and within the 100 km limit adopted for this book occurred on 1 August 1981. There were no further records until 27 September 1994, when a bird was sighted off Brooks Peninsula. Other sightings in west coast waters followed on 25 October 1997, 15 September 1998, 8 and 26 August 2000, and 27 August 2001.[10]

In the summer of 2004, tour-boat operator Leigh Hilbert photographed a bird on the water near Tofino that appeared to be this species, probably a juvenile. However, the angle of the shot and the quality were such that its identity was difficult to determine with certainty. The white front of the neck and the lack of a white collar appear to rule out every alcid but the Craveri's and Scripps's murrelets. Weeks later, on 25 September 2004, while on a marine bird and mammal survey with Strawberry Island Research off Tofino, I briefly observed two Scripps's Murrelets on the water.[195] Unfortunately, the birds flew directly away from the boat, and their identity could not be confirmed by others on board the vessel.

Two years later, on 1 October 2006, while en route to Vargas Island by boat, I encountered an unfamiliar alcid on the water at the mouth of Father Charles Channel, near Tofino, only several hundred metres from the nearest land. For reasons too lengthy to go into here, the bird was initially believed to be a Long-billed Murrelet from Asia. Fortunately, photos were taken and after a photo was posted online, two ornithologists who had worked with Scripps's Murrelets off California contacted me and convinced me that it was this species.[196] A copy of that photograph is in the files of the Biodiversity Centre for Wildlife Studies (BC Photo 3524).[41] This was the first verified record of this species in our west coast waters. During this period, there were five additional sightings off our shores that were beyond the 100 km limit. As well, there have been numerous reports from the waters off Washington state, particularly near Grays Harbor. Birds were subsequently recorded off Cape Scott and Port Renfrew in August 2009,[197] and four birds were seen and photographed at the northern edge of Nitinat Canyon on 7 September 2016 by Ryan Merrill and others.

Most sightings thus far recorded in the waters off Vancouver Island's west coast have been in the months of August and September, though two occurred in October and, further offshore, two in July. In Washington waters, there have been a number of sightings as early as late June. Since this species is seen off Oregon and Washington with some regularity, it very likely occurs off our coast more frequently than records indicate.

ANCIENT MURRELET
Synthliboramphus antiquus
STATUS: Irregular. Uncommon in June and July, rare in most other months. Occasionally fairly common in winter.

Ancient Murrelets are found only in the North Pacific, where they breed on islands stretching from British Columbia north to the Aleutian archipelago and the Bering Sea. They also breed in Korea, China, and Russia. They spend the winter in much the same region, but some move southward as far as Oregon, with a few even reaching southern California. The population is believed to number from 1 to 2 million birds,[198] though accurate numbers are lacking from most areas except British Columbia. In this province, an estimated 540,312 birds nest at 31 sites on Haida Gwaii.[88] Ancient Murrelets have disappeared from 7 sites and are known to have declined at 6 others due to introduced rats and raccoons.

On their breeding grounds, these murrelets nest in burrows on the forest floor. Once the young are one to three days old, the adults take to the water and, in the dead of night, call to their young. The young can distinguish their parents' voices from all others and respond by leaving the burrow and using their outsized legs to propel themselves quickly to the water to join their parents. This is a strategy designed to thwart potential predators. In some colonies, the adults escort the little ones to the sea.[199]

Ancient Murrelets have been recorded off the west coast of Vancouver Island in all months of the year. The month of July, with 29 sightings, has had by far the most. June has 10 records while August has 7. September has 8 records, December and February both have 6, and April has 5. All other months have from 1 to 3 records. Most sightings have been made in offshore waters, but occasionally the birds are seen from shore using a spotting scope. Sightings have been made from Incinerator Rock at Long Beach (on 14 occasions) in the months of February, March, June, July, November, and December. Birds have also been seen off Vargas Island, Cleland Island, and Amphitrite Point.

Adults with young have been recorded off the west coast in June on a number of occasions.[200] On 19 June 2001, a family of 2 adults and 1 young were observed 31 NM offshore. In 2014, a family group of 2 adults and 3 young were seen from Incinerator Rock, Long Beach, as early as 6 June, which is shortly after the first young leave the burrows. This raises the question of how they could have travelled over 500 km from Haida Gwaii in such a short period of time. For years there has been speculation that some Ancient Murrelets must nest at an unknown location on Vancouver Island's west coast. Although young birds have been reported to drift a great distance in a short time, it strains one's credulity to imagine these birds drifting over 500 km in just two weeks or less. Two young birds off Tofino looked less than two weeks old.

The Birds of British Columbia considers this species a "common to abundant spring and autumn migrant off the outer coast."[111] The largest number for nearshore regions that I could find prior to 2014 was 10 birds at Triangle Island on 21 June 1978. Very large numbers have been recorded south of us, off Victoria, including 7,000 birds on 2 November 1983 and 13,000 on 19 November 1983. These birds are said to arrive through the Strait of Juan de Fuca, which would of course have taken them through west coast waters. If this is the case, Ancient Murrelets spend most of their time far offshore, for they are rarely seen from shore, though with some notable exceptions.

In the late fall of 2014, during a spell of unusually calm seas, 6 birds were seen from Incinerator Rock, Long Beach, on 30 November, and 99 birds on 2 December. A count at Green Point that same day produced 12 more birds. During the following winter, again during a time of very calm seas, 5 birds were observed from Long Beach on 21 February, and 17 birds the following day. On 29 October 2016, small flocks of 4 to 6 birds, totalling 38 birds, were observed passing by Amphitrite Point.

Further evidence that birds are spread widely over the Pacific comes from pelagic excursions conducted by Strawberry Island Research in winter and early spring. On 7 February 1994, 8 birds were observed 20.9 km (11.3 NM) from shore, and on 9 March, 4 birds were seen 23.7 km (12.8 NM) off Tofino. In 1996, 2 birds were seen on 14 February, 21.5 km (11.6 NM) from shore, and 7 birds in 3 groups on 25 March. The latter ranged from 25 km (13.5 NM) to 57.5 km (30.8 NM) from shore. It appears that Ancient Murrelets disperse in family groups, pairs, and singles over a vast area of ocean. It is worth noting that in Alaska waters, adults have been observed up to 176 km offshore as early as July. That birds sometimes enter the Strait of Juan de Fuca in very large numbers in November and December is likely due to seasonally severe weather, which causes birds to seek calmer, protected waters.

In 2013 and 2014, the National Wildlife Research Centre, based in Ottawa, placed geolocator chips on birds in Haida Gwaii. Three were subsequently recovered, revealing that these birds inexplicably migrated westward across the Pacific to spend the winter in the waters off Japan, making an annual circuitous flight of nearly 16,000 km (9,940 mi).[201] Because there is no obvious reason for them to do this, and because genetic evidence indicates that this species originated in Asia, it is believed that they were retracing their ancestral route back to home waters.

CASSIN'S AUKLET
Ptychoramphus aleuticus
STATUS: Common in pelagic waters in spring, summer, and fall. Casual in winter. Breeds.

Weighing less than 200 g (6 oz), this is the smallest auk normally found in our waters. Cassin's Auklets breed on offshore islands from northern Baja California to the Aleutian Islands. They are colony nesters that nest in burrows in the ground. They come and go from the burrow under cover of darkness to avoid predators and seek food far out to sea. As a result, they are seldom seen from shore or even around their breeding colonies.

In winter, they do not migrate as such but travel further out to sea. British Columbia, with 60 colonies (52 confirmed, 8 unconfirmed or abandoned) of various sizes on its coast and a population of over 2.7 million birds,[88] is home to 80% of a world population estimated at 3.6 million birds.[202] The largest breeding colony in existence, with 550,000 pairs, is found at Triangle Island off Vancouver Island's northwestern tip. Alaska has 53 colonies with an estimated 473,000 birds.[202] Another colony in our region with a sizable population is Solander Island, off Cape Cook, which had a population of 34,000 pairs in 1989. Two small colonies are found further south, at Seabird Rocks and at Cleland Island.

To see Cassin's Auklets, it is advisable to travel offshore to the continental break, where they feed on zooplankton, larval fishes, and cephalopods. At Triangle Island, Cassin's Auklets are reported to fly as far as 90 km from their colony on day flights, and to dive to a maximum depth of 80 m.[203] Off Tofino, the continental break is 39 km from the Cleland Island colony.

On numerous bird and mammal surveys to the continental break with Strawberry Island Research, Cassin's Auklets were seen from April to October. The largest numbers were seen in September and October, with 50 birds on 25 September 2004; 50 on 15 October 2002; 120 on 2 September 2010; and 200 on 21 October 2004. Occasionally very large numbers are seen far offshore. On 1 April 1976, M.G. Shepard counted more than 11,000 birds in 68 groups, 57 km northwest of Cook Bank off Cape Scott. On a trip from Bamfield to La Perouse Bank, on 1 October 1977, 617 birds were counted.[111]

There are few records in the time period from November to the end of January when birds are far out at sea, but by early February birds begin to appear in offshore waters. On 7 February 1994, 78 Cassin's Auklets were recorded southwest of Tofino by Strawberry Island Research, with the first bird seen 20.9 km

(11.3 NM) from shore. On 10 February the following year, 25 birds were seen, beginning 37.5 km (20.3 NM) out, and on 14 February 1996, 20 birds were recorded from 44.5 to 50 km (24 to 27 NM) southwest of Tofino. There is one January record. On 22 January 2000, 5 birds were recorded in the same area.

This species has been seen occasionally in spring and summer on the waters surrounding Cleland Island, and there have been a few sightings from Long Beach using a spotting scope, but land-based sightings are few. On 19 December 2014, however, during a prolonged period of very heavy seas and severe weather, six Cassin's Auklets were observed flying low over Long Beach and landing on the beach, perhaps for relief from being buffeted by heavy surf. Common Ravens saw this as an opportunity for an easy meal, and carried them off. More birds could be seen in the surf. A living bird picked up on the beach in a weakened state appeared otherwise healthy. It is believed that birds were dying of starvation. Thirty dead birds were found the next morning on a 1 km stretch of beach,[204] and birds were subsequently reported washing up dead from California to Haida Gwaii. These totalled at minimum tens of thousands of birds. One seabird ecologist called the scale of the die-off "unprecedented."[205] The population has been declining for some time at a rate believed to be 2% per year, possibly due to ocean warming. Studies have shown that this species can be seriously impacted during an El Niño year.

This auklet is named after John Cassin, an almost forgotten ornithologist of the 19th century, who described for the first time almost 200 birds from around the world. Four other North American birds were also named after him.

PARAKEET AUKLET
Aethia psittacula

STATUS: Casual in offshore waters in fall, rare in winter and spring.

The Parakeet Auklet breeds on islands in the Bering Sea, the Aleutians, Kodiak Island, and islands in Prince William Sound. Its winter range is believed to be largely the same as its breeding range – the Bering Sea and the northern Gulf of Alaska. Vagrant birds are occasionally found as far south as the waters off southern California.

This species was virtually unknown in BC waters until 24 February 1971, when three birds were reliably sighted 15 mi southwest of Estevan Point.[45] Two birds were seen at separate locations in mid-December 1975, from the research vessel *Parizeau*. There is also a record of a bird seen on 18 September 1986 some 65 km southwest of Ucluelet.

On 23 December 1988, a tug towing a barge off Grays Harbor, Washington, accidentally rammed the barge, resulting in the spilling of 87,000 L of bunker C oil. An estimated 56,000 seabirds died as a result, and 3,137 dead birds were recovered on the beaches of the central west coast of Vancouver Island, among them 15 Parakeet Auklets.[206]

Since the *Nestucca* oil spill, as it became known, this auklet has been recorded from pelagic waters off Vancouver Island's west coast on 12 additional occasions, 6 of them within the 100 km limit used here. At least six birds were seen at three separate locations beyond the continental shelf break on 14 February 1997. A bird was also observed off Barkley Sound on 9 February 1999, and a total of five birds were seen at two locations off the central west coast on 1 April 2003.[46] At least two birds, and possibly as many as five, were seen at Clayoquot Canyon on 17 April 2010.[207]

It now appears that the Parakeet Auklet is a regular but rare visitor to offshore waters.

RHINOCEROS AUKLET
Cerorhinca monocerata

STATUS: Common in spring and summer, locally abundant in summer, uncommon in fall and winter. Breeds.

Despite its name, this is considered to be a puffin, the only one with its own genus. The name derives from the horny protrusion at the base of the bill that we see on adults in the breeding season. Like other auks, Rhinoceros Auklets breed on islands, where they dig long burrows for nesting in order to avoid predation of their eggs and chicks. They avoid daytime arrivals and departures for the same reason. Instead, under cover of darkness, birds come rocketing into the nesting area in a barely controlled crash-landing as they hurl themselves into the low vegetation. Only a single egg is laid during a breeding season.

In North America, the Rhinoceros Auklet's breeding range stretches from the Aleutian Islands along the Gulf of Alaska to British Columbia, Washington, Oregon, and California, where it breeds on three offshore islands off the south coast. The species has expanded its range south into Oregon and California only since the 1960s, though it may just have been getting re-established in its former range. It also breeds in Asia, from Japan to islands in the Sea of Okhotsk, although Asian birds were found to be a genetically distinct population.

About 56% of the world's estimated 1.5 million breeding Rhinoceros Auklets are found in British Columbia, and 73% of the breeding population in North America occurs in the province. Nearly 720,000 Rhinoceros Auklets breed in British Columbia at 35 sites.[88] On Vancouver Island's west coast, Rhinoceros Auklets breed at three sites: Triangle Island, Cleland Island, and Seabird Rocks.[208] Surveys conducted on Triangle Island in the 1950s found none breeding there. By 1966, there were an estimated 3,000 breeding pairs, and by 1976, 15,000 breeding pairs. By 1984, the population had risen to 22,000 pairs, and by 1990 to 42,000 pairs.[209] Although Cleland Island, near Tofino, is much smaller, an expansion also took place there. In 1967, there were an estimated 25 pairs breeding.[87] Two years later the population was estimated at 375 to 450 pairs. By 1982, there were 2,700 pairs. Current numbers are unknown, although hundreds of birds can be seen on the water surrounding the island in summer.

Rhinoceros Auklets spend the winter in offshore waters, from southern British Columbia to Baja California, though winter records are few in BC waters. On 13 offshore bird and mammal surveys conducted by Strawberry Island Research in the months of November to the end of March, from 1 to 3 Rhinoceros Auklets were found on all trips with the exception of two, both in March. On 9 March 1994, 14 birds were found, and on 25 March 1996, 10 birds. On 4 offshore surveys conducted in April, there was little increase in the number of birds on 3 of the trips. On the fourth, conducted on 17 April 1994, a total of 23 birds were counted. One notable record is of 100 birds seen in offshore waters by Ryan Merrill as early as 30 March 2009.

Birds are believed to begin returning to the vicinity of the nesting colonies by the end of April and the beginning of May. On 27 April 2009, 17 birds were seen off Vargas Island, and on 21 April 2013, 9 were seen off Long Beach. There are also several late April records from northwest of the Olympic Peninsula. By late May through June, July, and early August, hundreds of birds may be seen on the water near Cleland Island. They forage quite widely for food and may be seen off Long Beach in summer. Although they feed largely on outside waters, some venture into protected waters. On 6 July 2015, 350 birds were seen feeding in the waters off Ahousaht, attracted by an abundance of food. They are also frequently seen in the channel north of Vargas Island and deep into Father Charles Channel, east of Vargas Island, in August.

Birds begin to disperse after the breeding season. Although still plentiful in early August, they have decreased noticeably by mid to late August. Birds are still being seen through September and October, though in gradually decreasing numbers. By November, sightings are scarce. On 4 November 2007, 1 was seen in Tofino Harbour, and on 19 November 2011, 2 birds were seen near Tofino. On 14 November 2012, 2 birds were seen at Amphitrite Point, Ucluelet. Small numbers have also been seen further south, with 6 birds off Jordan River on 19 December 2010 and 18 off Botanical Beach on 30 December 2011.

Despite nesting in burrows, their eggs are not immune to predation. Researchers found that on Triangle Island, a native species of mouse (*Peromyscus keeni*) enters the burrows to feed on the single egg that is laid, taking a significant percentage of them. In one plot, as many as 35% were taken.[210] At Helgesen Island in Haida Gwaii, the arrival of raccoons reduced the population from 13,000 pairs to 2,000 pairs between 1986 and 1993.

The salmon gillnet fishery is also a threat. A study found that nearly one-quarter of all seabirds caught in gillnets are Rhinoceros Auklets. Currently the world breeding population is believed to be in the neighbourhood of 1.5 million birds, with 73% of them breeding in British Columbia, 12% in Alaska, and 13% in Washington. The total number of birds, including nonbreeders, is believed to be somewhere between 2 and 3 million.[211]

HORNED PUFFIN
Fratercula corniculata

STATUS: Casual visitor in summer. Uncommon visitor at Triangle Island. Possibly a rare, local breeder.

This Alaskan puffin is readily distinguishable from the Tufted Puffin by its white breast, larger bill, all-white face, and absence of tufts. The primary breeding range of this species begins at the end of the Aleutian Islands and runs east to Prince William Sound. It also breeds on islands in the Bering Sea and along the shores of western Alaska. The species winters far offshore as far south as California. In British Columbia, it is an uncommon summer visitor to Haida Gwaii, and breeding was confirmed at Anthony Island in 1977.[212]

At least 60 Horned Puffins (30 pairs) have been sighted at 12 sites in British Columbia, of which 4 occur on Vancouver Island's west coast.[88] The Horned Puffin is most frequently seen at Triangle Island, where it is suspected that a few may breed. Birds have been regularly observed from the early 1970s to the present. For example, on 1 August 1977 and from 6 to 21 July 1986, 8 to 10 birds were seen there. Birds have also been observed carrying fish, and in 1976 a

Horned Puffin was seen entering a burrow.[212] Birds have also been recorded at Solander Island, off Cape Cook, and in the Scott Islands.

South of Cape Cook, I know of only 8 records, most of them from the mid-coast region: 20 June 1975, off Long Beach – 1; 16 February 1980, Tofino – 1 dead bird in the harbour; 10 July 1990, Cleland Island – 1; 16 July 1997, off Vargas Island – 1; 8 July 2003, Cleland Island – 1; 13-26 June and 4-6 July 2006, Cleland Island – 1; 29 January 2012, Pachena Bay – 1 dead bird on the beach; 15 August 2016, Barkley Sound, east of Chrow Island – 1 (photo by Jody Wells).

TUFTED PUFFIN
Fratercula cirrhata

STATUS: Uncommon to locally abundant from late spring to late summer. Breeds.

One of the most handsome seabirds on the west coast is the Tufted Puffin, easily identified by its colourful, parrot-like beak.

This is one of three puffins in the genus *Fratercula*, *fratercula* meaning "little brother" in Latin. All three species have a very large bill and a white face, but only the Tufted Puffin has an all-black body. Like other alcids, puffins dive for fish using their wings for propulsion, hence the relatively small wings on a large body. This puffin is restricted to the North Pacific Ocean and the Bering

Sea, with occasional summertime forays into the Beaufort Sea. It breeds on islands stretching from northwestern Japan to the Bering Sea, the Aleutian Islands, and Alaska, south to British Columbia, Washington, Oregon, and northern California. Its population in the western states has been reduced by 85% to 90% in the past 30 years, while in Japan only 10 breeding pairs remain. Large numbers still breed in Alaska and British Columbia and the total population is estimated at nearly 3 million birds, with 80% in North America. In Alaska, there are 693 colonies,[213] and in British Columbia, the Tufted Puffin breeds at 22 confirmed sites. Another 9 sites are unconfirmed.[88]

About 90% of the 78,648 Tufted Puffins currently breeding in British Columbia nest in the Scott Islands,[88] which includes Triangle Island, with as many as 25,000 birds estimated nesting there in 1989.[111] Here they lay their eggs in burrows dug in the soft soil amid large clumps of grass (*Elymus* spp.). Currently about 8% of the population also nests on the steep slopes of Solander Island, off Cape Cook.[88] Up to a dozen pairs historically bred on Cleland Island, 10 miles west of Tofino, but in 1985, 4 decapitated Tufted Puffins suspected to have been killed by mink were found in burrows.[214] A small colony of possibly 20 pairs also bred at Seabird Rocks in the early 1970s,[1] and at least 1 pair was suspected of nesting on Florencia Island in 1969. However, a search of that island in the summer of 1972 failed to find any burrows in the very limited habitat available, though several birds were seen just offshore.

For those wishing to view these birds in the wild, the most accessible colony is that on Cleland Island, near Tofino, where birds can usually be found on the water in the vicinity from mid-May to mid-September. Since the island is a provincial ecological reserve, landing requires a permit. In August, birds are often seen along the southwest side of Vargas Island, and occasionally on the east side in Father Charles Channel, among the many Rhinoceros Auklets that go there to feed. Tufted Puffins are rarely seen from Long Beach or in Barkley Sound. This species is also found in offshore waters and has been seen on many bird surveys and pelagic trips.

Tufted Puffins usually begin arriving in west coast waters in early to mid-May. There are, however, three records from the month of April. On 29 April 2012, a single bird was seen by numerous observers on a pelagic birding trip out of Ucluelet, and on 20 April 1982, a bird was seen at Cleland Island. The earliest recorded date was 17 April in 1994, in offshore waters. After the breeding season, birds begin to depart in late August. By mid-September, they are mostly gone, and sightings later than that are rare. A late bird was seen by many observers on a pelagic birding trip off Ucluelet on 18 September 2011.

The latest date I could find is 25 September 1993, with a bird seen offshore on a bird and mammal survey with Strawberry Island Research out of Tofino. Tufted Puffins are reported to spend the winter in the North Pacific Ocean, far from land.

Gulls and Terns Family Laridae

BLACK-LEGGED KITTIWAKE
Rissa tridactyla

STATUS: Irregular. Varies from uncommon to abundant in offshore waters from March to October. Rare to uncommon in inshore waters. Casual in winter.

Black-legged Kittiwakes are easily distinguished from other gulls. Adults look as though their wing tips were dipped in ink, while juveniles have a bold, black bar diagonally across the upper surface of the wing. This small gull of the open sea is found in both the Atlantic and Pacific oceans. It breeds in the high north of both Eurasia and North America, although in Europe it breeds as far south as Spain and Portugal. Its North American breeding range in the east stretches from the Gulf of St. Lawrence to Labrador and northern Ellesmere Island. In the west, it breeds from northwestern Alaska to the Aleutians, and south to Baranof Island. Alaska has 371 colony sites, with a population estimated at 1,322,000 individuals.[215] There is one small colony in British Columbia on an abandoned lighthouse on Holland Rock, at the entrance to Prince Rupert (BCNRS). After the breeding season, birds may travel as far south as the waters off Baja California.

This is a gull of the offshore waters. Martin and Myers reported them constantly present from the end of March to the end of May.[49] On 12 March 1976, 100 birds were seen off Brooks Peninsula, and on the following day, 200 were estimated off Triangle Island.[111] On 10 March 1994, 250 birds were seen in offshore waters west of Tofino, and on 25 March 1996, 50 birds were recorded there.

More recently, records reveal that birds begin arriving considerably earlier. On 16 February 2010, 175 birds were seen from Amphitrite Point, and on 23 February 2013, 35 birds were recorded at the same location.[26] On 21 February 2012, 129 birds were seen off Carmanah Point. Surprisingly, I could find few records during the month of April anywhere off the BC coast, although *The*

Birds of British Columbia lists a record of 3,000 to 10,000 birds at Reef Island on 22 April 1985.[111] There are numerous records for the month of May, however. On 28 May 1973, during a spring migration survey, 750 birds were counted passing Clerke Point on Brooks Peninsula in 1.5 hours.[13]

Significant numbers of birds, assumed to be nonbreeders and immatures, may be found in foraging flocks or roosting on islands in June and July. On Cleland Island, largest roosting numbers (all immatures) were: 18 May 1969 – 200 birds; 20 May 1970 – 200+ birds; 21 and 23 June 1970 – 300+ birds; 2 July 1970 – 130 birds; 11 July 1970 – 100 birds; 20 and 23 July 1970 – 20 birds; and 11 August 1970 – 5+ birds (BCFWS). Off Brooks Peninsula, roosting flocks estimated at 100 birds have been seen on offshore islands in March, April, and May, with 600 in June and 300 in July.[13] *The Birds of British Columbia* lists several records of large foraging flocks of immatures in late June and July.[111] On 10 July 1973, 1,200 birds were recorded at Imperial Eagle Channel in Barkley Sound, and on 27 June 1975, 550 birds were seen near Solander Island, off Cape Cook. Also in 1975, 300 birds were recorded off Florencia Island on 11 July, and 120 birds off Cleland Island from 12 to 16 July.[111]

Hatler et al. concluded: "It is now evident that the Black-legged Kittiwake varies in its occurrence from year to year."[1] Black-legged Kittiwakes were rarely seen in July on numerous bird and mammal surveys off Tofino with Strawberry Island Research, yet *Birds of Pacific Rim National Park* listed more occurrences for July than any other month.[1] A photo in *The Birds of British Columbia* shows hundreds of Black-legged Kittiwakes roosting on Portland Point on 4 August 1969.[111] According to the caption, they are nonbreeding birds. They are unlikely to be postbreeding birds as the fledging period for the Black-legged Kittiwake is 34 to 58 days and they return to the nest to roost for another several weeks.[216]

For the fall movement, I can offer no better assessment than that offered in *The Birds of British Columbia*, that the fall movement begins in August, peaks in September, and is usually over by late October.[111] A few birds may remain as winter visitors off the outer coast. Sightings recorded in later years appear to support this. We have 11 records for October but only 1 in November. There was also a sighting of 30 birds off Botanical Beach on 30 December 2011,[26] and a record of a single bird off Amphitrite Point on 12 January 2014.

Birds are seen over inshore waters only very occasionally. However, on 30 May 1993, 85 birds were seen at Stubbs Island, just across from Tofino harbour, and on 13 October 2012, 5 birds were seen far from the open ocean at Esperanza. This species may be observed from shore along the outer coast only if one is very lucky. The best chance for a sighting is on a pelagic birding trip.

SABINE'S GULL
Xema sabini

STATUS: Fairly common in spring and fall in offshore waters, occasionally abundant.

For this species to be referred to as a "seagull" is not quite the misnomer it is for most other gulls, for like the kittiwakes, the Sabine's Gull spends most of its life at sea, coming ashore only to breed. Its breeding range is circumpolar, spanning both North America and Eurasia. About half the world population breeds in Canada. On this continent, it breeds mostly north of the Arctic Circle except in eastern Canada and western Alaska, where it breeds also along the entire length of the Aleutian Islands. Although this species is confined largely to the Atlantic and Pacific oceans, some individuals wander overland, having been seen in every province in Canada and every state in the contiguous United States. In the Pacific Ocean, birds spend the winter offshore, from Panama to Chile.

This small gull is very distinctly marked, both as a juvenile and an adult, and is therefore easy to identify. It often congregates in large flocks, feeding by fluttering low over the water. It is seen mostly well offshore in pelagic waters and is rarely spotted from shore. While there are several records for March, such early observations are rare. Birds usually begin to pass by our shores in April, with the largest numbers passing by in May. There are not a large number of spring records to draw on, however. On 29 April 2012, 20 birds were recorded on a pelagic trip out of Ucluelet; on 2 May 1970, 8 birds were tallied off Tofino;[48] and on 13 May 2001, 22 birds were seen off Tofino. In *The Birds of British Columbia*, mention is made of a flock of 50 birds off Ucluelet on 17 May 1949, and 66 birds at Esperanza Inlet on 28 May 1966,[111] these being among the larger numbers recorded in spring. However, on a pelagic trip off the central west coast on 8 May 2017, an estimated 2,000 birds were reported. That birds are still moving through in June was demonstrated when on 5 June 1999, during a northwesterly gale, 150 birds were seen from the south shore of Vargas Island with the aid of a spotting scope, and as late as 9 June in 2010, 200 birds were recorded offshore. Records for July are probably nonbreeders.

A map in *The Atlas of Pelagic Seabirds Off the West Coast of Canada and Adjacent Areas* is revealing. It shows 37 locations in our offshore waters where the species was recorded in spring. At 10 locations, from 1 to 10 birds were recorded, while at 2 locations numbers ranged between 10 and 100.[46] All other observations involved single individuals.

By mid to late August, the southward migration is well under way. Flocks of 200 birds were reported offshore on 25 August 2012, 12 September 2010, and 14 September 2013. An even larger flock of 300 birds was seen on 20 August 2011. An estimated 500 birds were seen on 13 September 1969, 22 km west of Tofino,[48] and again on 2 September 1984, at La Perouse Bank. An estimated 900 birds were seen at La Perouse Bank on 5 September 1982.[111] There is one report of an even larger number. On 28 August 1985, on a pelagic birding trip out of Bamfield, 2,000 Sabine's Gulls were reported.[26]

Lest the foregoing give the impression that Sabine's Gulls are to be found in abundance on almost any ocean voyage, encountering a large flock involves both timing and good luck. Most observations in fact involve only a few birds.

The height of the autumn migration likely occurs from late August to early October. The migration is over by the end of October. November records are rare.[217]

BONAPARTE'S GULL
Chroicocephalus philadelphia

STATUS: Generally an uncommon transient in spring, summer, and fall, though sometimes abundant offshore. Casual in winter.

This small and rather delicate gull breeds throughout much of Canada's boreal forest region, from western Quebec and northern Ontario to the Prairie provinces, south-central British Columbia, the Northwest Territories, the Yukon, and Alaska. In the east, it winters along the US Atlantic coast and throughout the Southeast. In the west, it winters along the Pacific coast, from south coastal British Columbia to Mexico. In our province, it breeds from the south-central interior northward, including the Peace River region, and across much of northern regions of the province. *The Birds of British Columbia* considers it a very abundant transient on the coast, and it can sometimes be very abundant on the Salish Sea and on the Strait of Juan de Fuca in winter.[111]

On the west coast, this bird occurs in far smaller numbers than on inside waters, although it passes northward in large flocks at irregular intervals. During 115 hours of migration watches on Clerke Point between 14 May and 27 June 1973, a total of 6,760 birds were counted, all in May. The estimated total northward movement was 30,700 birds. On 3 May, 250 Bonaparte's Gulls were counted in 10 minutes.[13] Most sightings, however, involve 1 to 5 birds seen during spring and fall. The spring movement occurs from early April through May

The Bonaparte's Gull has a black head in breeding plumage and is one of our smaller gulls. This bird is in nonbreeding plumage.

and possibly to mid-June. The two earliest spring dates are 11 April in 1999 and 8 April in 2016, with both sightings in Tofino. Large flocks have been recorded occasionally. On 3 May 1966, 82 birds were seen in Barkley Sound, and on 4 November 1979, 50 birds were recorded at Tofino. On 7 May 1982, 125 birds were seen at Cleland Island. More recently, on 29 April 2012, from 70 to 90 birds were estimated off Ucluelet during a pelagic birding trip, and on 10 May 2014, 33 birds were seen at the north end of Long Beach.

A record of 60 birds seen at Stubbs Island, Tofino, on 11 June 1980, demonstrates that spring migrants are still passing through then. Hatler et al. stated that "flocks of up to a hundred have been recorded at several locations in May and early June."[1] It should be pointed out that in some years birds are very scarce.

There have been a surprising number of sightings in the summer months, with 24 records in June and 20 in July. Birds seen from mid-June to mid or late July are likely nonbreeders and sightings usually involve 5 or fewer birds. The fall movement may begin as early as late July and continues into November. A record of 40 birds at Cape Beale on 30 July 1970 has been suggested as the vanguard of the fall movement.[1] The largest number of sightings in a single month (28) occurred in August. Two young birds-of-the-year were recorded at Chesterman Beach as early as 6 August in 2015.

The largest numbers ever recorded in our region were seen on 18 October 1987, when an estimated 650 birds were observed in Bedwell Sound. This raises the question of whether significant numbers pass through our area undetected because they frequent the inlets, the heads of which may be 20 mi from the outer coast and which are visited infrequently by observers. Birds may also be missed if they pass far out to sea. Nonetheless, numbers recorded in the west coast region are small compared with the flocks of thousands seen along the eastern shores of Vancouver Island.

We have records in all months of the year except February. Winter records are scarce, with two for December and single records for January and March.

FRANKLIN'S GULL
Leucophaeus pipixcan
STATUS: Casual vagrant from late May to late August.

Franklin's Gulls are rare in our region, though occasionally these birds show up on our coast in summer. Shown here is a juvenile.

This gull breeds in the Prairie provinces from Manitoba to Alberta, and in the northern United States from western Minnesota to northern Montana. It also breeds in western Oregon and eastern Idaho. After breeding, the species migrates south to the Gulf of Mexico, then southwest to the Pacific coast, where it winters from Central America south to Chile. In our province, it is considered an "uncommon to fairly common spring and autumn transient on the southwest coast."[111]

Our west coast region lies well outside its normal migration corridor, so sightings are few. To date we have a mere 6 records. Hatler et al. list a record of a specimen collected near Tofino on 29 June 1931,[1] but this was later identified as an immature Bonaparte's Gull and was not included in the provincial summary of 159 records through 1970.[218] The first record for the area occurred on 4 August 1972 when I observed an immature bird at Pachena Bay, near Bamfield.[111] No other birds were seen until 30 August 1977, when a juvenile was found at Stubbs Island, near Tofino, and 30 May 1983, when an adult was observed at Chesterman Beach. The following year, on 20 August 1984, a bird was recorded at the Arakun mudflats near Tofino. There were no further sightings for a period of 31 years, until 2015, when a juvenile was observed and photographed on 16 August at Chesterman Beach. The following year, a bird was seen by Ian Cruickshank on 2 August at Schooner Cove in Pacific Rim National Park. The 5 August records are undoubtedly fall transients, while the birds seen in May and June may represent nonbreeding individuals.

HEERMANN'S GULL
Larus heermanni

STATUS: Common in summer and early fall.

This gull was named after its discoverer, a little-known 19th-century American naturalist named Adolphus Lewis Heermann, who spent the years from 1849 to 1852 collecting specimens in California.

The Heermann's Gull is unusual not just for its uniform gray plumage, white head, and red bill but also for the fact that it is the only gull breeding south of the United States that visits Canada as part of a postbreeding dispersal. The population is currently estimated at 150,000 pairs, and 90% breed on a single island in the Sea of Cortez called Isla Rasa.[219] The rest breed in a few scattered colonies elsewhere in Mexican waters. After breeding, birds disperse and migrate as far south as Banderas Bay, Nayarit, and, rarely, to Guatemala. Northward they spend the summer along the US coast to southwestern British Columbia. The population has fluctuated greatly, from as high as 525,000 individuals in 2002[220] to as low as 55,000 pairs on Isla Rasa in 1975.[219]

In British Columbia, some birds travel up the Strait of Juan de Fuca into the Salish Sea, but the bulk of the visiting migrants spend the summer along the outer west coast of Vancouver Island, north to southern Clayoquot Sound. On the central west coast of Vancouver Island, birds usually begin arriving in

Heermann's Gulls breed in the Sea of Cortez and migrate north in early summer. Here we often see them standing on kelp beds.

early July, though in some years the earliest ones arrive in mid-June. Although Heermann's Gulls have occasionally been seen further up coast, north to Cape Scott and Triangle Island, and even (rarely) to Haida Gwaii,[221] they normally range only as far north as the southern half of Clayoquot Sound.

Heermann's Gulls are frequently seen standing on kelp beds or flying low over the water mainly during the months of August and September. The earliest arrival date on Cleland Island in 1970 involved an adult seen on 3 July. Roosting numbers increased to 21 on 27 July, peaked at 110+ on 7 and 13 August, and 5+ birds were last seen on 19 August (BCFWS).

Remarkably few are seen at Long Beach, nor do they travel up the inlets. Although uncommon even in Tofino harbour, they are common to abundant just 3 km to the west. Large flocks are often found at Monk's Rock, Wilf Rocks, and Cleland Island, and on a reef at the mouth of Father Charles Channel, where there are often ball-ups of small fishes. Some high numbers are as follows: 150 birds on 26 September 1983 at Chesterman Beach; 200 on 9 September 1987 at Stubbs Island; 200 on 10 September 1996 at Monk's Rock; 500 on 14 August 2002 at Cleland Island; and 300 on 11 September 2008 in waters near Tofino. There are also numerous records from points south, including Barkley Sound, the West Coast Trail, Port San Juan, and Jordan River, but not usually in the large numbers seen at Clayoquot Sound.

Birds begin to depart by mid-September or shortly thereafter, and all are gone by the end of October, earlier in most years. There is a single record after October. On 10 November 1983, a single bird was seen at Chesterman Beach.

MEW GULL
Larus canus

STATUS: Common to abundant in spring, fall, and winter. Uncommon in summer. Breeds.

This small gull is named for its voice, which sounds rather like a cat's mew. Known as Common Gull in Britain, it has a very large breeding range that extends from western Europe across Eurasia to Kamchatka. In North America, it breeds in most of Alaska, the Yukon, and Northwest Territories, and into northernmost Saskatchewan. In British Columbia, it breeds in the north and along the mainland coast, including Vancouver Island and Haida Gwaii.[222] It is considered common to abundant in spring, autumn, and winter on much of the south coast.

In our region, as elsewhere on the coast, Mew Gulls are common to abundant for much of the year. They prefer mudflats and sheltered waters, although small numbers are seen on Long Beach. In the protected waters near Tofino, particularly on the mudflats, large numbers may be seen from October to April. Congregations of up to 150 and even 200 birds may then be seen near the village. In April and May, birds disperse to breeding areas and numbers dwindle. The highest count I have, however, was on 2 May 2002, when an estimated 400 birds were seen on the Tofino mudflats. By mid-May, few birds remain; in some years, most birds are gone by early May. In June and July, most records on the mudflats or on the outer coast involve only a handful of birds. Two exceptions were 26 birds on 29 June 2012 on the Tofino mudflats, and 50 birds on 15 July 2002 at Stubbs Island. The latter may have been early returning postbreeding birds.

In 1969, birds were found nesting on Kennedy Lake,[223] both on islands on the main body of the lake and on small islands on Clayoquot Arm. The species has also been found breeding on Nahmint Lake as well as Kalmia Lake and Moneses Lake on Brooks Peninsula (BCNRS),[13] and may also breed on small lakes in the mountains. In the summer of 1995, I found a pair of Mew Gulls on a small lake on a saddle separating the Clayoquot Valley from the upper

Kennedy River valley at 586 m (1,922 ft) elevation. These birds were giving every indication of being a mated pair. As I was otherwise engaged at the time, I made no attempt to search for a nest. Mew Gulls usually nest on the ground or on hummocks/tussocks, but will occasionally nest above the ground in living trees.[111] Mew Gulls are also reported to nest at Hobbiton Lake in the Nitinat area.

In late summer, Mew Gulls begin arriving back on the outer coast throughout the month of August, with a significant increase in numbers by the end of the month, at least in some years. On 26 August 2014, 140 birds were counted at Stubbs Island. Numbers gradually increase through the month of September, and by late September or early October, numbers in the Tofino area have reached winter levels. On 30 September 2009, 178 Mew Gulls were counted in Tofino Harbour, which compares with counts made at that location in winter.

RING-BILLED GULL
Larus delawarensis

STATUS: Uncommon in spring, common in late summer and fall, casual in winter.

With a population estimated at 3 to 4 million birds, this may be the most populous gull in North America. Although often referred to as a "seagull" by the general public, this bird breeds on islands on inland waters, from Newfoundland and Labrador west through southern Quebec and Ontario and across the Prairie provinces to the south-central interior of British Columbia. In the United States, it breeds from the Great Lakes region west to Washington and Oregon.

In British Columbia, this bird has greatly expanded its range and numbers in the past half-century. In 1940, it was considered a transient in the interior of British Columbia and uncommon on the south coast. By the mid-1960s, it was considered "locally abundant, seasonally," and by 1968 was found breeding on a small island in Okanagan Lake. At the same time, the population was expanding continentally.[111] A similar expansion has occurred on Vancouver Island's west coast, albeit somewhat later. *Birds of Pacific Rim National Park* listed this species, with 43 records, as a rare migrant.[1] Up to that time, the largest number recorded at one time was six birds.

In our west coast region, Ring-billed Gulls today have been recorded in small numbers in all months of the year except for February. Although rare in winter, single birds were recorded in January of 2012 and 2013. Most sightings are made during the migration periods in spring and fall. Although a small number pass through in spring, by far the largest numbers are seen during the period from early July to November, the same period in which we see larger numbers of California Gulls on our shores. On 7 November 1987, 11 adults were seen at Stubbs Island, Tofino. Our highest counts were all made on the mudflats near Tofino in the month of September, and counts of 10 or more birds are not unusual. The two highest counts were 16 birds on 2 September 2009, and 21 birds, all adults, on 12 September 2008. Although most often seen on mudflats, they also frequent beaches and, less often, offshore rocky islands, where they may be found roosting among other gulls. Most sightings involve from 1 to 5 birds.

WESTERN GULL
Larus occidentalis

STATUS: Fairly common in fall, winter, and spring; locally common. Uncommon in summer.

In both shape and size, the Western Gull appears identical to the Glaucous-winged Gull and is very closely related to it. Hybrids between the two are commonly seen in the west coast region. Its breeding range extends along the Pacific coast of North America, from central Baja California north to central Washington. The mantles of birds in the southern portion of its range are considerably darker than those of birds in the north, and such southern birds, though rare here, have been seen on our shores on several occasions. Northern birds, on the other hand, are sometimes overlooked because the mantle is not as dark as expected. This is particularly true of second-year birds when the adult mantle is not yet complete. Birds with black wing tips and lighter mantles can be considered hybrids. While hybrids between Western Gulls and Herring Gulls have frequently been reported from the Salish Sea, they rarely occur on our west coast.

Western Gulls have been recorded in the west coast region in all months of the year, although they are most common in fall, winter, and early spring. In the past 15 years or so, birds have been seen to spend the winter in Tofino among the many Glaucous-winged Gulls that scavenge food pellets at a supply depot for salmon farms. A total of 70 birds were counted there in February and November of 2001, and 82 birds were recorded on 10 February 2008. In recent

Western Gulls breed along the US Pacific coast and disperse northward in summer and fall. This individual is an immature.

years, winter numbers in Tofino have been considerably lower, not exceeding 30 birds, and usually fewer than that. This is due to less spillage at the salmon farm facility. Like Glaucous-winged Gulls, Western Gulls disperse to feed on the mudflats of southern Clayoquot Sound at low tide, after which they gather with other gulls to rest at high tide.

With the approach of the breeding season, numbers begin to decline. Records suggest that most birds depart in March, though a few individuals stay on through April and May. A high number for April occurred on the 11th of that month in 1999, when 16 birds were seen at Stubbs Island. On Cleland Island, up to 6 subadults were seen frequently between 11 May and 4 August 1970 (BCFSW). Very few birds remain during the months of June and July. However, between 10 June and 25 July 1972, from 1 to 6 birds were observed on 21 separate days at Long Beach. All were second-year birds. On 29 July of that year, 21 immature or subadult birds were counted, signifying an increase in late summer. On 7 July 1971, Hatler reported 50 immature Western Gulls seen with California Gulls on Village Reef in Barkley Sound.[1] Such large numbers in summer are unusual, however. More recently, 12 birds were reported on 11 July 2008 at Seabird Rocks. A record of 10 birds at Pachena Bay on 2 August 2012 supports the observation of an increase in numbers at this time of year.

Sightings continue to increase throughout August and September. At Medallion Beach, Vargas Island, 13 birds were seen on 28 September 2008, and 12 birds on 5 September 2012. By October we begin to see larger numbers still. On 17 October 1998, 40 birds were counted on the roof of the BC Packers building in Tofino. Birds have reached their winter maximum by late October or early November.

CALIFORNIA GULL
Larus californicus

STATUS: Uncommon spring transient, fairly common in summer. Common and often abundant in late summer and fall. Rare in winter.

The California Gull breeds inland from Oregon and Idaho through Montana and North Dakota, north through Saskatchewan and eastern Alberta to the Northwest Territories. It breeds also in central Washington, and in British Columbia on Okanagan Lake and Fraser Lake in the central interior (BCNRS). On the BC south coast, it is a common to abundant migrant in spring and fall.

On Vancouver Island's west coast, we do not see a large movement in spring. Numbers recorded for that season include 18 birds seen on 29 March 2010; 40 on 18 April 2008; and 140 on 19 May 2010, all at Tofino. The largest number was recorded during a southeast gale on 25 March 2014 – an estimated 180 birds on Long Beach. This suggests that there are larger numbers of birds further out at sea. Small to modest numbers of second-year birds may be seen travelling up coast in June to spend the summer in west coast waters.

By the beginning of July, numbers begin to increase as adults and juveniles leave their breeding grounds in the central interior of the continent, including Saskatchewan and Alberta, and arrive on the coast. In most years, flocks numbering hundreds may be found by mid-July and thousands by the third week, although the timing varies from year to year. In 2013, concentrations remained relatively small at Long Beach throughout July.

California Gulls gather where creeks, sometimes even quite small ones, empty onto a beach. At Long Beach, one such location is at the mouth of Sandhill Creek (Combers); another is at the north end, below the Esowista Reserve. Some high numbers for Combers Beach include: 5,300 birds on 12 July 1982; 2,500 on 19 July 2004; 3,000 on 15 August 2010; 2,500 on 3 September 2010; and 900 on 21 September 2010. Small numbers of up to 50 birds also roost with other gulls on offshore islands such as Cleland Island, as on 11 and 17 July 1970 (BCFWS).

Even large numbers gather at the mouths of creeks along the West Coast Trail, such as at the Pachena, Darling, and Klanawa rivers. There exists an aerial photo of thousands gathered in late summer at the mouth of Carmanah Creek. California Gulls also gather in considerable numbers on the mudflats of southern Clayoquot Sound, on the Stubbs Island spit near Tofino, at Medallion Beach on Vargas Island, and on one occasion at the Long Beach Golf Course, where on 27 July 2000 about 900 birds were present. At Brooks Peninsula, 170 km north of Tofino, high counts were considerably lower, with 300 birds recorded on 3 July 1954, 340 on 12 August 1981, and 400 on 22 August 1981.[13]

By late September, birds on the west coast have usually declined to hundreds instead of thousands, and the decline continues through October and November. Occasionally an observation will defy that trend, as on 29 November 2001, when 250 birds were counted at Sandhill Creek. Still, such a high number is far from normal for that time of year. There are very few records for the period from December to March, though occasionally from 1 to 5 birds may be seen.

HERRING GULL
Larus argentatus

STATUS: Common transient in spring, late summer, and fall. Casual in June, rare in winter.

The Herring Gull has a wide distribution throughout the Northern Hemisphere, from Eurasia to Canada. As a breeder, migrant, or wintering bird, it may be seen in almost all regions of North America but the High Arctic. It breeds from New England, the Maritimes, and Labrador west through almost all of Canada and Alaska, except for the southern prairies and the mountain regions of the west. In British Columbia, it is known to breed in the central interior and in the north, but it does not breed on the coast.

On the west coast of Vancouver Island, Herring Gulls have been seen in all months of the year, though rarely in winter. Records collected since 1982 correspond closely with those in *Birds of Pacific Rim National Park*.[1] There is a spring movement in March, April, and May. It was thought then that this movement was minimal, but recent sightings show that it is much larger than previously suspected. On 10 April 2013, hundreds of Herring Gulls were seen among 1,400 gulls over Browning Passage that had been forced off the open ocean by a fierce headwind. The total number for that day was estimated at a minimum of 500 birds, but may have been much higher. A year later, during a southeasterly gale on 25 March, there were 250 Herring Gulls on Long Beach near Lovekin Rock, where the previous day there had been none, indicating that these birds had been forced off the ocean due to the inclement weather.

That Herring Gulls are commonly found many miles offshore has been verified by seabird researchers conducting pelagic bird surveys.[46] Indeed, in the west coast region, Herring Gulls are partial to the outside coast and are rarely seen over inside waters or on the Clayoquot Sound mudflats, even in late summer when other gulls congregate there in large numbers. Only when they are forced in by adverse weather conditions do we see them there.

Birds are still passing through in May, though in reduced numbers. An exception occurred on 11 May 2008, when 150 birds were observed flying over the south end of Vargas Island. The only land-based records after mid-May are two from Incinerator Rock, Long Beach: a single bird on Cleland Island between 10 and 20 July 1970, and up to 20 birds on offshore islets and reefs between 5 May and 14 August 1981 (BCFSW).[13] Two birds were seen on 10 June 2011, and one was recorded on 26 May 2015. A few birds are still seen in offshore waters in summer, particularly in the southern half of the west coast region.[111]

Records during July and most of August are rare, but by late August birds are being seen again. The southward movement continues throughout September and October, and into November. That a significant movement occurs as early as September is indicated by a record of 139 birds counted at Sandhill Creek on 9 September 2010, and 110 birds tallied at Chesterman Beach on 6 September 2011. In 2013, 81 Herring Gulls were found at Combers Beach (Long Beach) on 12 September, 150 birds on 14 September, and 129 birds on 18 September.

The migration continues throughout October and November, often unnoticed because birds are passing by either overhead or further out at sea. On 2 November 2012, 25 birds were observed on Chesterman Beach, forced down by strong headwinds, and during severe weather on 12 November 2015, 70 Herring Gulls were found resting on Long Beach, north of Sandhill Creek, while 45 more were found near the south end of Long Beach. As late as 29 November in 2012, nearly 100 birds were counted at Sandhill Creek. December sightings are scarce, but there is a record of hundreds of Herring Gulls passing over Chesterman Beach on 18 December 1982, and 50 birds at Pachena Bay on 7 December 1978. By late January, small numbers may again be seen on west coast beaches, possibly heralding the beginning of the spring movement.

The dominant subspecies in North America is *L. a. smithsonianus*. A second subspecies, the darker-mantled *L. a. vega* from eastern Asia and western Alaska, is occasionally reported elsewhere on the BC coast. There is thus far only a single record for our region. A specimen was collected at Henderson Lake on 27 November 1922 (MVZ 101280).[111]

ICELAND GULL
Larus glaucoides

STATUS: Uncommon migrant in spring, fairly common migrant in fall, and uncommon to locally common in winter.

Iceland Gulls breed from Greenland to Baffin Island and west of Hudson Bay, north to the High Arctic islands. Three subspecies are now recognized: *L. g. glaucoides*, *L. g. kumlieni*, and *L. g. thayerii*. The first two subspecies winter largely in the Atlantic region, while *L. g. thayerii* winters along Pacific shores from Yakutat, Alaska, to central Baja California. At one time, it was believed to be a subspecies of the Herring Gull, but in 1973 it was given full species status as Thayer's Gull. Recently, however, it was demoted by the American Ornithological Society to merely a subspecies of the Iceland Gull. Because the two eastern subspecies are rare in the west and have not yet been positively identified in our west coast region, the rest of this account will relate only to *L. g. thayerii*.

This subspecies is similar in appearance to the Herring Gull but can be differentiated from it by a number of features, including having less black in the primaries, a dark eye instead of a yellow eye, a somewhat smaller bill, and a more rounded head. However, these features are seen only when one is afforded a good look. For that reason, Iceland Gulls can easily be mistaken for Herring Gulls and overlooked.

The Birds of British Columbia lists the bird's status on Vancouver Island's west coast as common to abundant from mid-autumn to mid-spring.[111] Available records do not seem to support that, however. Of 134 recorded sightings, most involve 6 or fewer birds. There are only 8 records of 30 or more birds: 100 birds at Pachena Bay on 7 December 1978; 102 at Tofino on 18 March 1981; 100 at Long Beach on 7 April 1985; 600 along the North Shore of Barkley Sound on 28 December 1989; 30 at Sandhill Creek, Long Beach, on 16 September 2001; 300 at Chesterman Beach on 7 May 2008; 60 at Port Renfrew on 31 December 2011; and 72 at the mouth of Sandhill Creek, Long Beach, on 21 January 2013.

Significantly, three of the above records are from the month of December, and all of them are from more protected waters. Sea conditions on the outer coast in winter are often severe. It would make sense for wintering gulls to seek out quieter waters. Curiously, though, I could find only five records of birds seen in the protected waters of Clayoquot Sound. It appears that, like Herring Gulls, this species shuns the protected waters of inlets. Thayer's Gulls have been seen in all months of the year except for July. There is a single record for the month of June from Baeria Rocks in Barkley Sound, where three birds were seen on 22 June 2011.

Records suggest that the spring migration occurs from March to early May. While we do have February records, it remains unclear whether these are wintering birds or very early spring migrants. There are 9 records for March, 10 for April, and 5 for May. The largest count during the spring period was 300 birds at Chesterman Beach, Tofino, on 7 May 2008. The fall movement begins in late August. There are 2 records in August, 20 in September, 34 in October, and 13 in November.

As with Herring Gulls, most sightings have been made on beaches on the outer coast. Birds have been found in Barkley Sound in small numbers, although winter surveys in the sound could yet reveal large numbers similar to the 1989 count.

SLATY-BACKED GULL
Larus schistisagus
STATUS: Casual vagrant.

This large, dark-mantled gull breeds in northeastern Asia and western Alaska. It is similar in size and appearance to the Western Gull, but is 25% heavier. Adults have white subterminal spots at the ends of the primaries and a smudge through the eyes. The bill is noticeably less robust than that of the Western Gull. The species winters primarily in the western Pacific, but in recent decades it has been seen with increasing frequency in widely separate locations throughout North America, particularly on the Pacific coast. In the past decade, there have been a number of sightings on the BC south coast, including Qualicum Beach, Deep Bay, French Creek, Nanaimo, Duncan, Victoria, and Port Alberni on Vancouver Island. Some birds have been seen by multiple observers and others have been documented with photographs.

On Vancouver Island's west coast, the first confirmed sighting occurred on 14 October 2006, nearly 50 km west of Ucluelet, when an adult was seen by multiple experienced observers on a pelagic birding trip out of Tofino. The second sighting occurred at Amphitrite Point, Ucluelet, on 19 August 2012, when a bird was studied and well described by David La Puma and Michael Lazone. Three single-observer reports from the west coast have been omitted due to a lack of documentation, but could well be valid. This species likely occurs here more often than is currently recognized, and is probably overlooked on our coast due to its similarity in appearance to the Western Gull. I encourage birders to document any future sightings, preferably with a camera.

Despite having only two solid records for the region, this species will likely be seen here again, and is therefore considered casual rather than accidental.

GLAUCOUS-WINGED GULL
Larus glaucuscens
STATUS: Common resident, often abundant. Breeds.

This is the most common resident gull along the coast of the northeastern Pacific Ocean, its numbers eclipsed only by migrant California Gulls that appear in southwestern coastal British Columbia in late summer. Adults are usually easy to distinguish from other gulls by their large size, large bill, pinkish legs, and pale gray primaries. In the southern part of its range, it breeds readily with Western Gulls. Hybrid offspring are therefore common. The breeding range of this species stretches from western Alaska south to Washington. Birds nesting in Oregon are difficult to ascertain because they hybridize with Western Gulls. Glaucous-winged Gulls winter in all but the most northerly part of the breeding range. There is also a movement southward along the US coast and as far as the tip of the Baja California peninsula.

Glaucous-winged Gulls show little discrimination in what they eat, feeding on a wide variety of organisms in the intertidal zone and any fish small enough to swallow. They also scavenge, feeding on discarded garbage, dead beached mammals, and other marine debris. While Glaucous-winged Gulls are normally surface feeders, they do at times plunge into the water after fish. They often trail offshore fishing boats as well as inshore crab-boats for offal. It is not unusual to see a Glaucous-winged Gull standing with a sea star in its gullet, waiting for the lower half to digest before swallowing the rest. They will also eat shellfish, dropping them from a height in order to break them open, and no opportunity is missed to eat the eggs and young of other birds. They have even been known to pluck small migrant songbirds from the air. And near human habitation, if there is a garbage dump in the vicinity, all the better. Salmon farms and their supply depots have provided further feeding opportunities in the form of spilled food pellets. In other words, these gulls are opportunistic scavengers. Occasionally they are even seen plunging into the water in a shallow dive.

While they are mostly colony nesters, they will also nest alone on isolated islets and rocky headlands. Of the 28,953 pairs estimated to breed in British Columbia, 25% currently nest on the west coast of Vancouver Island at 43 sites. Historically, the species nested at 81 sites.[88] The two largest colonies, both located on the central west coast, are on Cleland Island and Florencia Island. At Cleland, a survey in 1988 found 1,687 nests, while at Florencia Island 346 were counted in 1982. Population size varies from year to year. Numbers at Sea Lion Rocks, for example, fluctuated from 131 pairs in 1967 to 175 pairs in 1973. Surveys of nesting sites are conducted at one's peril, for the parents will dive-bomb the intruder and will occasionally succeed in inflicting a nasty rap on one's head. Other sizable colonies exist at Triangle Island, Solander Island, Bunsby Island, Thornton Island off Kyuquot Sound, Great Bear Rock, and Seabird Rocks.[111]

In spring, Glaucous-winged Gulls will converge in large numbers on Pacific herring spawning locations. On 12 March 1982, a massive number of gulls converged on the mudflats across from Tofino harbour. With birds packed shoulder to shoulder and a large portion of the mudflat white with birds, my estimate was 20,000 birds. This herring run and others on which so much wildlife depends were unfortunately depleted due to short-sighted and ill-advised openings to commercial fishing, and today such large concentrations of gulls no longer occur in the Tofino area.

GLAUCOUS GULL
Larus hyperboreus

STATUS: Rare transient in spring, casual in fall and winter.

This large, pale gull is aptly named, for it breeds in the High Arctic regions of Eurasia and North America in the land that Greek mythology referred to as "Hyperborea," meaning "the lands that lie beyond the north winds." In the east, it winters on the Atlantic coast and the Great Lakes. On the Pacific coast, it winters from western Alaska south to the Columbia River, though occasionally as far south as Baja California.

Glaucous Gulls breed in the High Arctic. They have white primaries and a pink colour at the base of the bill. This bird is an immature.

On the BC coast, *The Birds of British Columbia* lists it as a "rare to uncommon winter visitant."[111] On the west coast of Vancouver Island, birds are seen somewhat less frequently. In 1978, *Birds of Pacific Rim National Park* listed 12 records.[1] Since then, there have been 21 additional occurrences. Combining all sightings, we have 1 record each for September and October; 2 records each for the months of November, December, and February; and 3 records for January. For March, records increase to 7. May has the largest number with 13 sightings, 2 of them involving two birds. There were only 3 sightings in April, but one of them involved four birds and occurred near the end of the month. There are no records for the months of June, July, and August.

The above records suggest that the movement on the west coast is somewhat contrary to that reported for the Salish Sea region. *The Birds of British Columbia* states that the main influx of wintering birds occurs in December, and by late March only a few remain.[111] Here on the outer coast, most sightings occur from March to May, with the latter being the busiest month by far. The birds we see here may be transients that have wintered along the US Pacific coast, and possibly the Salish Sea as well.

In addition to the foregoing, there are four records from offshore waters, one near Tofino, the rest from further south. Two birds were seen in February, one in March, and one in May.[46]

Since the Pacific herring runs were disrupted by commercial fishing in southern Clayoquot Sound, large congregations of gulls no longer occur here in spring, resulting in fewer sightings of this species.

CASPIAN TERN
Hydroprogne caspia
STATUS: Uncommon to fairly common visitor in spring and early summer. Rare in late summer.

With its blood-red bill, black crown, and shallow wing beats, the Caspian Tern is easy to distinguish from a gull, even at a considerable distance, and it usually announces its presence with a raucous cry. This is the world's largest tern and, like other terns, it feeds on small fish, which it catches by plummeting from a height. It breeds in colonies and has a widespread distribution throughout the globe.

In Eurasia, it has a discontinuous breeding distribution, from China to central Asia to northern Europe, and it winters from Australia to India and Africa. In North America, its discontinuous distribution is even more pronounced, with birds breeding in parts of Newfoundland, in the Great Lakes region, in the Prairie provinces, in the Northwest Territories, in Alaska, and in many locations in the American West, including coastal Washington. In British Columbia, birds breed at Fraser Lake in the central interior and recently on buildings in the Fraser River delta (BCNRS). There are many sight records from the southern interior, including the Cariboo-Chilcotin region, the Peace River region, and on the coast, north to Haida Gwaii.[150, 224] Western birds winter from southern California to southern Mexico.

In our west coast region, birds have been recorded from Port Renfrew in the south to Cape Scott and Triangle Island in the north. The first record was a bird collected on 19 August 1969 at Barkley Sound.[225] *Birds of Pacific Rim National Park* listed 21 records, with counts as high as 4 birds.[1] Today we have an additional 128 records since 1980. The highest recorded numbers were 24 birds on 3 July 1984; 21 on 12 June 1987; and 17 on 18 May 1996, all at Stubbs Island, Tofino. A total of 16 birds were seen off Carmanah Point on 16 June 1998. Further north, most records are of 1 or 2 birds. For example, 2 Caspian Terns were seen on Quineex Reef, off Brooks Peninsula, on 7 August 1981, and one was photographed flying (BC Photo 798) near the Bunsby Islands on 13 June 1982.[13]

Numbers have declined since then. Although Caspian Terns are still seen fairly often, a sighting exceeding 12 birds has occurred only once since 1998, and that was of 17 birds on 15 July 2011 at Port Renfrew. Most sightings are of 6 or fewer birds. Although breeding colonies are now established in the interior of the province and on the roof of a building in Richmond, this has resulted in fewer visitations to the west coast region.

In spring, first arrivals are usually seen in late April and seldom occur before the middle of the month. I could find only two records from the first half of April. On 13 April 2012, a single bird was seen at Stubbs Island, and on 4 April 1994, three were seen there. Sightings increase during May and June and begin to decline in July. There are only a few records for August and fewer still for September. On 3 September 1994, a single bird was seen at Tofino, and on 10 September 1989, one was seen at Chesterman Beach, Tofino. The latest bird ever recorded in autumn was on 23 September in 2014, first at Chesterman Beach and later at Long Beach.

Birds may be seen anywhere along the entire outer coast or over the Tofino mudflats, Browning Passage, and Tofino Harbour. There have also been several sightings in Barkley Sound. There are few records from north of the central coast, including Brooks Peninsula, Quatsino Sound, Triangle Island, and Cape Scott (BCFWS).

COMMON TERN
Sterna hirundo

STATUS: Rare transient in summer and fall. Casual in spring.

The breeding range of the Common Tern covers much of Eurasia and large areas of North America. In North America, the species breeds along the Atlantic coast from South Carolina to Labrador, and from the Maritimes west through the Great Lakes, northern Ontario, and the Prairie provinces, west to Alberta and southern parts of the Northwest Territories. The species winters along the Gulf Coast, the Caribbean, and the southern half of Mexico, Central America, and much of South America.

Common Terns do not breed in British Columbia but do occur as a frequent transient in both the southern interior and the south coast, where it is regarded as a common to abundant spring transient, and a very common to very abundant late summer and autumn transient.[111]

The earliest published record in the west coast region occurred on 21 September 1968, with a single bird at Grant Bay.[16] There is also a record of a bird on 29 November 1972, and two birds were seen at Tofino on 12 September 1974.[111] Although *Birds of Pacific Rim National Park* listed sightings of small terns in summer, Hatler et al. took a cautious approach and considered the species hypothetical for the national park reserve.[1] Since then, an additional 13 records of Common Terns have been added. Of those, 3 were in May, 1 in

Common Terns are seen infrequently but most often in offshore waters where they are sometimes mistaken for Arctic Terns.

July, 2 in August, and 7 in September. All but 3 of the sightings were in offshore waters. However, 2 birds were seen at Stubbs Island, Tofino, on 22 September 2001, and a single adult was seen there on 6 September 2016. A bird was also recorded at Amphitrite Point, Ucluelet, on 1 September 2012. Most of the offshore sightings involved single birds, but one May record involved 12 birds, the July record involved 7 birds, and an August record involved 10 birds.

Distinguishing between Common and Arctic Terns in the field can be a challenge even for experts, particularly on a moving boat, and small terns may sometimes be misidentified. It is worth noting that on the many pelagic bird surveys conducted out of Tofino, Common Terns were seen much more often than Arctic Terns.

ARCTIC TERN
Sterna paradisaea

STATUS: Rare spring and fall transient in offshore waters. Common further offshore.

The Arctic Tern is famous for its long-distance flight between its Arctic breeding grounds and its winter home on the Antarctic Ocean. It breeds extensively in northern regions, from Eurasia to Greenland, Canada, and Alaska. On the Pacific coast, Arctic Terns breed as far south as Baranof Island in southeast Alaska. In British Columbia, the species normally breeds only in the northwest corner of the province, from the Tatshenshini River east to Atlin Lake and south to the Spatsizi Plateau and Stewart.[111] A small number nested far south of their normal range in Puget Sound, Washington, in 1977 and 1978.[226] Recently, several disjunct breeding locations have been discovered in British Columbia. These include the Fireside/Liard River in north-central BC, Eagle Lake in the Chilcotin region,[227] and near Cortes Island at the north end of the Salish Sea (BCNRS).

For the west coast region, *Birds of Pacific Rim National Park* listed five records. Two of those involved birds that died in September 1971, one in Ucluelet Harbour and the other at Florencia Bay. The three others are sight records and therefore not entirely exempt from the possibility of error.

Small terns appear to be rare along the central west coast, and are seldom seen within 35 NM of shore. Over the past 20-year period, during 65 pelagic birding surveys in all months of the year, small terns were recorded on only seven occasions, two of which were close to shore while the rest were in pelagic waters. They were identified as Common Terns on six occasions and as Arctic Terns only once. That sighting occurred on 13 May 2001, when six Arctic Terns were reliably identified. Several more small terns were seen that day but could not be positively identified.

Marine bird studies by Vermeer et al., conducted off southwestern Vancouver Island, produced a very different result.[181] They reported that Arctic Terns were common in small numbers from July through September. The species, they said, was found at least 16 km from shore and became more common further seaward. Numbers at the shelf-break (the 200-fathom contour) peaked in August and September. They saw no Common Terns. It would seem that Arctic Terns come closer to shore off the mouth of Juan de Fuca Strait.

There have been reports of Arctic Terns on pelagic birding cruises out of Bamfield, Ucluelet, and Tofino. Three birds were reported offshore from Bamfield on 2 September 1984, and 6 on 21 May 2011. On 20 September 2015, 2 birds were reported by a large party of birders offshore from Ucluelet. An Arctic Tern was also reported by Bill Tweit and two others, who were conducting a transect off the mouth of Juan de Fuca Strait on 29 May 2004.[26] On a pelagic birding trip out of Tofino on 8 May 2017, 10 Arctic Terns were reported. Fifty small terns reported at Port San Juan in August 2015 as Arctic Terns is very intriguing, however the evidence falls short of eliminating the possibility of them being Common Terns.

Because of the difficulty of distinguishing between the two species in all but the most favourable circumstances, great care should be taken in the identification of all small terns. From July to September, Common Terns too may have blood-red bills without a black tip. For the reasons mentioned above, it is probably a good idea to treat reports of Arctic Terns with some skepticism. In order to better establish the status of this species in our region, I encourage birders on pelagic trips to photograph any small terns they suspect of belonging to this species.

ORDER COLUMBIFORMES

Pigeons and Doves   *Family Columbidae*

ROCK PIGEON
Columba livia

STATUS: Fairly common around human habitation. Breeds.

Rock Pigeons, formerly called Rock Doves, are native to areas of southern and western Europe, North Africa, and western Asia. In the British Isles, they nest on sea cliffs. It is from these that the feral Rock Pigeons have descended, and today they are found in towns and cities around the world. Wild Rock Pigeons in their native habitat are largely pale grey with two black bands on the wing. Many feral pigeons are likewise, but they also come in a variety of shades, ranging from white to sooty grey to nearly black. They tend to revert to their ancestral form over time. The population worldwide is estimated at 260 million birds.[228] So abundant are they in cities that it has created an ecological niche for Peregrine Falcons in some urban areas. Tall buildings provide the cliffs for nesting and Rock Pigeons provide the prey.

It is not entirely clear when Rock Pigeons first showed up on the west coast of Vancouver Island. *Birds of Pacific Rim National Park* mentions "a small band" of Rock Pigeons being seen in Ucluelet in January and February 1972, as well as a bird seen at a feeder in Tofino during the winter of 1972/73. Someone was raising them in Tofino late in the 1970s, and these may have provided the stock from which the current population has descended. Docks in the harbour provide nesting sites, and young flightless birds have been observed on the beams under the deck. This is probably the case in Ucluelet and other west coast villages as well.

In our region, Rock Pigeons appear to survive largely on birdseed at feeders. Without this subsidy, it is questionable whether any would survive here for long.

BAND-TAILED PIGEON
Patagioenas fasciata

STATUS: Fairly common spring migrant and summer visitor. Rare in fall, casual in winter. Breeds.

At 360 g in weight, this is North America's largest pigeon. It is also the closest living relative of the extinct Passenger Pigeon of the east. The Band-tailed Pigeon breeds extensively in the American Southwest, and from southern California and the Sierra Nevada north to southwestern British Columbia. The breeding range extends southward to the highlands of Mexico, to Central America, and, in South America, to northern Argentina. In winter, northern birds fly south to overwinter along the US coast. A few individuals overwinter in southwestern British Columbia, primarily when food is provided.

On the west coast of Vancouver Island, most first arrival dates for Band-tailed Pigeons are in April, but there are 6 records in March. They are: 8 March 1987 – 1; 20 March 1994 – 16; 17 March 2014 – 3; 9 March 2015 – 1; 31 March 2016 – 1; and 19 March 2017 – 5. All were recorded at Tofino at except for the last one, at Florencia Bay. Most first arrival dates range from 3 to 20 April. One pair of birds arrived at a Tofino feeder in April in six consecutive years. Their first arrival dates were 9 April 2009, 20 April 2010, 14 April 2011, 14 April 2012, 15 April 2013, and 8 April 2014.

In summer, Band-tailed Pigeons are often seen in areas where standing old-growth forest borders cut-over lands. Here the berries they seek are often abundant, while the forest provides shelter and mast. While these birds are wary and shy, they will readily come to backyard feeders for black sunflower seeds or grain, provided they feel safe. For that reason, I always feel greatly privileged to have these immaculately plumaged birds as my guests. When fed on the ground at a safe location, substantial numbers may gather. In the spring of 2014, as many as 60 to 70 birds were reported to congregate daily for food spread on the ground at one Tofino location.

Birds have been reported throughout the west coast region, from Jordan River in the south to Holberg in the north. The greatest number of reports by far originate in the southern half of the region. Whether this is entirely due to the presence of more observers in the south or to birds' greater abundance there is not clear at this time, but it is probably due to both. On Brooks Peninsula, 170 km north of Tofino, there are only five records during 48 different years of observation for 257 days throughout the year. From one to three birds were seen in May, July, and August.[13] Occasionally birds are seen on offshore islands, such as one flushed from Cleland Island on 11 July 1969 (BCFWS).

Since it is fairly common in the west coast region during spring and summer, it is evident that the species breeds here. Hard evidence for breeding remains somewhat sketchy, however. Young birds in the company of adults have been seen in Tofino, and there is a record of a half-grown nestling being found on the ground on 15 June 1972, after a tree was felled north of Tofino.[1]

On the south coast, the autumn migration is said to begin in late August and to peak in September.[111] This appears to be the case in our region as well, though perhaps somewhat earlier. Although sightings in September are scarce, two reports from Jordan River of 24 birds on 1 September 2013 and 14 birds on 8 September 2012 probably indicate a movement through that area. I could find only seven records for October, three of them from Jordan River and all but one in the first half of the month. There are two records of a bird seen in the month of December in Tofino, one on 8 December and the other on 29 December, both in 2001. This bird was probably tempted to stay late because food was available at a feeder.

EURASIAN COLLARED-DOVE
Streptopelia decaocto

STATUS: Common in spring, summer, and fall. Uncommon in winter. Breeding suspected.

The story of this pretty Eurasian dove is an interesting one. Originally its breeding range was limited to Asia, stretching from southern China to Turkey. By 1838 it was reported to have reached Bulgaria in Eastern Europe, and during the 20th century it colonized most of the rest of Europe. It was introduced to the Bahamas in the 1970s, and by the early 1980s it was colonizing nearby Florida. By the mid-1990s it was expanding rapidly throughout the United States and into southern Canada, with some birds reaching as far north as Alaska.[229]

The first verified sighting of Eurasian Collared-Doves in the west coast region occurred at Tofino in 2007, when a bird was photographed in a backyard. There

The Eurasian Collared-Dove is a relatively new arrival to our region. Originally from Asia, it has taken North America by storm.

were numerous sightings of from 1 to 3 birds the following year, with a maximum count of 6 on 13 June. In 2009, 12 birds were recorded on 17 May. A year later, a flock of 15 birds were counted on 20 May. On 10 July 2011, there was a count of 20 birds; on 13 November 2012, 30 birds. On 27 September 2013, and again on 17 May 2016, 40 birds were seen at Stubbs Island, near Tofino. The largest number recorded to date was 55 birds on 2 November 2014, at Tofino. Birds have often been seen at Ucluelet as well.

Although most Eurasian Collared-Doves depart in autumn, some have been known to overwinter when food is available. In Ucluelet, 8 birds were seen on 2 February 2010 and 13 on 30 December 2015. On 16 January 2015, 25 birds were seen at Stubbs Island, Tofino, and on 6 January 2016, 2 birds were recorded in Tofino.

As with several other invasive species, the Eurasian Collared-Dove gathers around human habitation. In much of North America, they breed near farm buildings and depend on crops or crop wastage to survive. In the west coast region, they rely almost entirely on the presence of bird feeders and it is doubtful that any would survive here without this helping hand. Be warned that if you choose to feed these birds, they may roost in nearby trees and their rather loud cooing at the crack of dawn may cause you to wish you hadn't. On the other hand, they are very attractive and have the added benefit of attracting raptors such as Merlins, Peregrine Falcons, Cooper's Hawks, and Northern Goshawks, all of which have been observed in pursuit of these birds.

No nests have been documented in the west coast region, as far as I know, but a family of four, including two newly fledged young, was seen near the airport on 26 June 2016.

WHITE-WINGED DOVE
Zenaida asiatica
STATUS: Casual vagrant in summer and fall.

Although the White-winged Dove breeds from Arizona southward, individuals occasionally make it this far north.

This dove of the tropical and subtropical regions has conspicuous white wing patches, making it easy to identify. It breeds from central South America north through Mexico and the Caribbean to southern Florida, Texas, and parts of New Mexico, Arizona, and southern California. A pair of birds, the first ever recorded in British Columbia, was seen in July 1918, just south of our area at French Beach, and one was collected (RBCM 4744).[111]

For the west coast region we have 5 records: 23 October to 5 November 1994, Ucluelet – 1 at a feeder (photo);[230] 17 to 26 November 1997, Tofino – 1 (photo);[230] 12 July 2004, Brooks Peninsula – 1 (photo);[231] 17 August 2005, Carmanah Point – 1 (photo);[232] 4 October 2010, Jordan River – 1; 17 June 2016, Ucluelet – 1 at a feeder (photo).

MOURNING DOVE
Zenaida macroura

STATUS: Rare migrant in spring, summer, and fall.

This rather delicate and lovely dove is named for its mournful call. It has by far the most widespread distribution of any native member of the family Columbidae in North America, breeding in southern Canada from coast to coast, south throughout all of the United States, much of Mexico, and the Caribbean. An isolated breeding population exists in Panama. The species winters south of its most northerly breeding areas. In British Columbia, it breeds in the southern interior north to Prince George, and also in the Fraser Valley and on southeastern Vancouver Island. Some birds winter on southeastern Vancouver Island, the Fraser Valley, and the southern interior,[111] while others may migrate south to Nevada and Arizona.

This dove prefers open and semi-open country, and the dense rainforests of the west coast region are therefore unsuitable as habitat. Nevertheless, Mourning Doves are recorded here periodically as transients, inevitably in open areas. In 1978, *Birds of Pacific Rim National Park* listed 10 records.[1] Since then there have been an additional 39 sightings. Mourning Doves are seen most often in May and September, with 12 records each. April and July had 2 sightings each, June had 7, August had 3, October had 6, and November had 4. There is a single record for December.

The earliest spring sighting involved two birds seen on 25 April in 2013 at Ucluelet. The latest occurred on 26 June in 1965, also near Ucluelet. In autumn, all sightings occurred between 5 September and 2 December. Sightings have been made at many additional locations, including Kapoose Creek, Bamfield, Long Beach, Tofino, the Long Beach Golf Course, South Bay, and the Long Beach Airport. The most northerly record occurred at Esperanza on 13 and 14 October 2012, and involved three birds.

There are two records for midsummer, one involving two birds on 14 July 2013, at Dodd Island in Barkley Sound, and one on 19 July 2013, when a single bird was seen at the airport. These dates are too late for the birds to be spring migrants and seem too early for fall. I can only think of categorizing them as summer vagrants, or perhaps nonbreeding wanderers.

Large numbers of these beautiful and delicate doves are still shot each year in pest control programs by the US Department of Agriculture. In 2015, the last year for which figures are available, 16,907 were killed.[233]

ORDER STRIGIFORMES

Owls *Family Strigidae*

WESTERN SCREECH-OWL
Megascops kennicottii
STATUS: Formerly an uncommon resident, now rare. Breeds.

The Western Screech-Owl is similar in appearance to the Eastern Screech-Owl, but has a very different voice, which can be described as an accelerating series of short whistled notes (creating a bouncing ball effect). This species is difficult to find by means other than voice, although once in a while one gets lucky, as I did when I encountered a family of owls in the Carmanah Valley in the early 1990s. It happened again a year later when I spotted an owl sitting at the entrance of a tree cavity in a dead snag at Spire Lake in the upper Kennedy River drainage.

This species breeds from British Columbia south to California, Arizona, New Mexico, western Texas, and Mexico. In British Columbia, it breeds in the southern interior, the Fraser Valley, and Vancouver Island, north along the coast to Prince Rupert and the Skeena River Valley, to Terrace and Hazelton. It is not found on Haida Gwaii. Birds on the coast are of the subspecies *M. k. kennicottii*, and apparently come in two morphs, a brown and a grey. I have personally never seen the grey, and all road kills I have seen have been brown.

On Vancouver Island's west coast, this species is a year-round resident. Records go back to 10 March 1936, when two males were collected at Quatsino (MVZ 101658-59).[111] *Birds of Pacific Rim National Park* listed 27 records.[1] Of those, 8 were recorded during the breeding season from May to August. D.F. Hatler heard birds on Turtle Island in Barkley Sound on 4 May and on 1 and 2 June 1972. On 1 June, three birds were vocalizing. On 20 June 1972, he also heard a bird on Effingham Island.[1]

There are two breeding records in the BC Nest Record Scheme.[234] On 21 June 1970, William Verbrugge found a live fledgling in the middle of the road that appeared to have collided with a vehicle near Kennedy Lake, and on 8 July 1979, students at the Bamfield Marine Station watched an adult feed a mouse to one of two fledged young, east of Bamfield.

In the years since then, birds have been recorded during the spring and summer months at other locations, such as the Clayoquot River valley on 11 August 1990, Ursus Creek on 26 May 1994, and Meares Island on 9 June

1994. In addition, a bird was observed in July 1985 on Thornton Island, off Kyuquot Sound. This owl was apparently subsisting on the Leach's Storm-Petrels that come and go from their nesting burrows in the dead of night. On a summer's evening in the early 1990s, in the Carmanah Valley, I observed a family of Western Screech-Owls sitting on a low branch just before sunset. Unfortunately, I could not find precise dates for the latter two observations. It is interesting that all of the summer sightings just mentioned occurred in old-growth forest.

Outside of the summer months, there are at least two other records from old-growth forests, one at Ursus Creek on 28 September 1992 and two birds in the Megin River Valley on 20 October 1993. Hatler et al. mentioned a report of birds seen in a red alder stand (second growth) near Kennedy Lake in the summer of 1973, where an employee of a logging company reported frequent sightings of Western Screech-Owls.[1] They also mentioned road kills, of which there were at least eight during the winters of 1971/72 and 1972/73. In the 1970s, it was not uncommon in winter to see one fly across the highway in front of a vehicle at night, and on a few occasions dead owls were picked up on the roadside. Road kills are of course a possible contributing factor in the subsequent decline of this owl in British Columbia.[235]

That screech-owls have declined in numbers locally on the BC south coast is well known among birders and ornithologists. On the central west coast of Vancouver Island, the last record I know of involving a living bird, prior to recent sightings, was on 29 December 2001, when a bird was seen on a Christmas Bird Count near Tofino. There are also two records from Carmanah Point, where a bird was recorded from 22 to 28 October 1997 and on 3 February 2002. Most of the blame for the bird's demise has been placed on Barred Owls, which are said to prey on screech-owls and which first appeared on Vancouver Island on 26 November 1969.[236]

The Barred Owl was first recorded in the west coast region on 29 May 1993, at Grice Bay, and by the year 2000 records were becoming much more frequent. The arrival of this new predator seems to correspond closely with the decline of screech-owls, as has been suggested elsewhere. However, several other factors should also be taken into account. Barred Owls are not the only predator to kill small owls. Other owls, especially the Great Horned Owl, are known to do so as well. The latter species is said to prefer the forest edge over the deep forest. Could the extensive logging that has occurred on Vancouver Island have favoured this large owl at the expense of the Western

Screech-Owl? Certainly, the removal of over 75% of the old-growth forest on Vancouver Island has not occurred without consequences for the inhabitants of that environment.

Collisions with motor vehicles may also take a toll during the year, but especially after birds disperse for the winter. What is curious is that sightings of birds in the headlights at night while motoring, as well as road kills, occurred mostly in the 1970s and appear to have become an uncommon or rare event long before Barred Owls came on the scene.

The Western Screech-Owl is currently regarded as threatened by the federal government (COSEWIC), and blue-listed by the BC government. Given the paucity of recent sightings, some fear that these birds may become endangered. However, an increase in records in recent years suggests that the situation is not as dire as was believed. On 22 May 2008, a bird was found at Woss Lake by Dan Tyson. The following month, Nigel Jackett found Western Screech-Owls at four locations south and southeast of Nimkish Lake, as well as a bird near Vernon Lake. Although these locations are somewhat outside our west coast region, sightings were subsequently recorded within its boundaries. On 4 July 2008, Nigel Jackett found a family of two adults and two juveniles in Carmanah Provincial Park.

Additional records emerged in subsequent years, with a bird heard by Bernard Schroeder in the Artlish River valley on 27 and 29 June 2011, and by Barb and Mike McGrenere along Caycuse Main on 10 July 2012. These were followed by three records for 2014. On 4 January, a bird was photographed in a backyard in Ucluelet by resident Helen Williams, and on 21 March, one (and possibly two) was heard at Carmanah by Bernard Schroeder. On 4 November 2014, a road-killed bird was picked up near Long Beach. Further confirmation that birds still survive in the old-growth rainforests of Clayoquot Sound came on 6 October 2015, when the Clayoquot Biosphere Trust, based in Tofino, made an audio recording of a Western Screech-Owl at the upper end of Sydney Inlet. On 13 September of the following year, the trust recorded two birds vocalizing at the same location. On 6 November, a bird was photographed at the base of Catface Mountain, northwest of Tofino.

The first six months of 2017 produced three records, all of them in Clayoquot Sound. On 18 May, a bird was found and photographed by Toby Theriault at Boat Basin, and three days later one was heard by Garret Beisel at the head of Clayoquot Arm of Kennedy Lake. On 11 and 12 June, two birds were heard by Ian Cruickshank calling at Boat Basin.

GREAT HORNED OWL
Bubo virginianus
STATUS: Uncommon resident. Breeds.

The Great Horned Owl is a fearsome predator of waterfowl, grouse, Red Squirrels, and many other species.

With razor-sharp talons and a powerful grip, this is a capable hunter, able to attack and kill sizable birds and mammals. The Eagle Owl of Eurasia is also in the genus *Bubo*, but the Great Horned Owl and Snowy Owl are the only representatives of the genus in North America. It breeds throughout the continent, except for the treeless northern tundra, where it is replaced by the Snowy Owl. Its range extends southward through Mexico, parts of Central America, and large areas of South America.

Appearance can vary considerably, depending on which region a bird inhabits. Great Horned Owls follow Gloger's Rule[237] in that birds inhabiting arid regions are lighter whereas those in humid regions are darker. Indeed, birds on the Pacific coast are the darkest of any in North America. Lightest is the subspecies found in the snowy regions of the north, *B. v. subarcticus*. As might be expected of a bird that is largely nocturnal, this owl is more often heard than seen. It hunts mostly at night but will sometimes hunt in the daylight hours.

The earliest record for this owl on the west coast is of a pair of birds seen or heard on 11 November in 1952, at Tofino.[111] This is not surprising, as the Tofino area, with its extensive mudflats and large duck population, is a particularly favourable environment for supporting these birds. Great Horned Owls have been heard on Meares Island on numerous occasions, including two fledged young with an adult recorded on 17 June 1984 (BCNRS files), indicating breeding on the island. The only other breeding record is from C.J. Guiguet during small mammal trapping on Sandford Island in Barkley Sound. On 9 August 1967, he heard an adult calling at night and later observed two fledged young (BCNRS).

Birds of Pacific Rim National Park listed 13 records.[1] Today that number stands at 44. Nearly all are from Long Beach, Tofino, and Meares Island, although on 11 August 1990, a bird was heard in the Clayoquot River valley.

That prolonged or severe rainfall can be a danger to this owl was demonstrated on 16 February 2011, when an adult was found in underbrush at Jensen's Bay, its plumage drenched after days of heavy downpour. Facing a cold night under a clear sky, the owl was captured and held in captivity for 24 hours. With its plumage dry and its hunger sated after a meal of supermarket chicken, the bird's strength and ferocity were restored and it was released back into the wild.

Little evidence exists regarding the type of prey this owl captures in our region, although the species is very opportunistic and capable of pursuing a wide variety of birds and mammals. For example, Great Horned Owls are known to fly 1.5 km from adjacent Brooks Peninsula to Solander Island to feed in the evening on Leach's Storm-Petrels (R. Wayne Campbell, personal communication). In the Tofino area, its diet undoubtedly includes waterfowl, which are abundant in the area. That it hunts Red Squirrels was revealed on 12 March 1992, when an adult Great Horned Owl clutching a dead Red Squirrel was surprised in the forest near the mouth of Sandhill Creek, at Long Beach. This occurred two or more hours before dusk, clearly indicating that it was hunting during daylight hours. The arrival of Barred Owls on this coast in the 1980s means that there is now more competition for small mammals such as the Red Squirrel. What effect, if any, this is having on the Great Horned Owl population is unknown. This is a powerful predator, however, capable of taking a great variety of prey. It is unlikely to disappear any time soon because of competition from a newly arrived upstart. Historically, the two species have coexisted wherever their ranges overlap.

SNOWY OWL
Bubo scandiacus

STATUS: Rare and irregular visitor in fall and winter.

This large owl of the northern tundra breeds across the Arctic regions of both Eurasia and North America. In an irruption year when food is scarce in the north, many birds migrate to southern Canada and the northern United States. In the Great Plains region, birds may be seen even in non-irruption years, but this occurs only occasionally on the BC coast. In the Fraser River delta and on southeastern Vancouver Island, the species may be fairly common during irruption years, though less so in the interior of the province. Most birds show up in November, although some birds arrive in October or even as early as September. There is a total of 21 records for the month of September in British Columbia.[238] A few birds may arrive as late as December.

On Vancouver Island's west coast, this handsome owl is seen much less often. The first recorded occurrence was in 1916, when a specimen was collected at Cape Beale (BCPM 2728).[111] The winter of 1916/17 was an invasion year, as were the winters of 1966/67, 1971/72, and 1973/74. *Birds of Pacific Rim National Park* lists 20 records for those years, 9 of them from the winter of 1973/74.[1] The winter of 1973/74 was also the period when Snowy Owls were reported at an unprecedented 11 different locations on the west coast of Vancouver Island between November and February. These sites included Triangle Island, Cape Scott,[4] Estevan Point, Vargas Island, Ahousat, Long Beach, Sandhill Creek, Florencia Bay, Amphitrite Point, Pachena Point, and Jordan River (BCFWS). Annual fluctuations in numbers, showing cyclic patterns for British Columbia from 46 years of Christmas Bird Counts between 1963 and 2008, have been published in *Wildlife Afield*.[238]

As elsewhere, most birds in our region were recorded in the months of November and December. The reason for the paucity of records after December may be twofold: a lack of suitable foraging habitat and the torrential rains we experience on the west coast make it difficult for birds to survive here for very long. At least six birds are known to have died or have been rescued over the years. Not only was a bird captured on Long beach in 1974 starving but the top of its feet were raw from the incessant rain.

More recently, birds have been recorded in fall in 1984, 1994, 1996, 2004, 2005, 2011, 2012, 2015, and 2016. In all, there are three January and four February records. The latest sighting ever recorded was a bird seen in Ucluelet on 10

March in 2015. Birds seen in February and March may be rare examples of birds surviving on this coast despite the wet weather. Admittedly, the bird seen in March may have come from further south.

Most sightings have occurred on beaches and in open areas such as at the Long Beach airport and golf course, though not always. A Snowy Owl was once observed by many local residents, perched in the rainforest at Chesterman Beach, its white plumage conspicuous and incongruous against the leafy green of western redcedar boughs.

In the irruption winter of 2012/13, at least five birds were seen from 12 November to 8 February. On the latter date, an individual was seen on the beach at Stubbs Island. A pellet that was examined contained only feathers, suggesting that the owl was surviving by feeding on birds. That Snowy Owls on the coast survive on a diet of birds was first discovered in the irruption year of 1973-74 in a study conducted on small rocky islands off southern Vancouver Island. By examining the pellets, researchers discovered that the bird's prey consisted of 22 species of birds, 16 of them water birds. The two birds most commonly taken were Horned Grebe and Bufflehead.[239] At Stubbs Island, both of those prey species are common, with Buffleheads often being abundant.

NORTHERN PYGMY-OWL
Glaucidium gnoma
STATUS: Uncommon resident. Breeds.

British Columbia's smallest owl, this species breeds throughout large areas of the American West, although large regions are devoid of these birds. It breeds also in the highland forests of Mexico, Guatemala, and Honduras. In Canada, it is found only in southeastern Alberta and the southern two-thirds of British Columbia, north to at least Williams Lake. On the coast, it has been found north to southeast Alaska and to Atlin Lake in British Columbia.

The Northern Pygmy-Owl is peculiar in that it has "eyes" in the back of its head – that is, it has spots resembling eyes, which are believed to fool or confuse birds that try to harass it. This owl is largely diurnal, though it is most active at dawn and dusk, when it hunts small mammals, birds, amphibians, and even large insects. It is very feisty for such a small bird and is known to occasionally take prey larger than itself. In January 2001, one was seen clutching a Varied Thrush, and in the Creston Valley in southeastern British Columbia,

The Northern Pygmy-Owl is more diurnal than most other owls. It is nevertheless a rare treat to see one during daylight hours.

a Mourning Dove, which weighs nearly twice as much as a Northern Pygmy-Owl, was killed and eaten.[240] Like other small owls, the Northern Pygmy-Owl is a secondary cavity nester.

In the west coast region, records go back to 28 May 1931, when a specimen was collected at Tofino (UBC 5603).[1] A few years later, on 17 September 1935, a specimen was also taken at Cape Scott (NMC 26069).[111] *Birds of Pacific Rim National Park* listed 4 additional records, including two by Richardson at Grant Bay in 1969.[16] Since then, another 41 records have been added, for a total of 47. Birds have been recorded in all months of the year, from Cape Scott and Holberg to Port San Juan and Jordan River. A few other locations include Long Beach, the Clayoquot Plateau, Brooks Peninsula, Nahmint Lake, Sidney Inlet, Megin Lake, Meares Island, Tofino, Ucluelet, Boat Basin, Moyeha River, the Kennedy Lake lowlands and Carmanah Point. It appears highly likely that this species inhabits the entire region, except perhaps forests at high elevation.

This small owl is more often heard than seen, and if observed at all is likely to be perched near the very top of a dead snag, sunning itself or surveying its surroundings. With hundreds of square kilometres of old-growth forest seldom visited by birders, this small and inconspicuous owl is undoubtedly much more common than records indicate.

New DNA evidence apparently supports splitting this owl into four separate species – the Northern, the Mountain, the Baja, and the Guatemalan pygmy-owls. If adopted by the American Ornithological Society, the Northern Pygmy-Owl will become *Glaucidium californicum*, with three or four geographical variations (subspecies). Currently, the birds that inhabit Vancouver Island are considered to be a distinct population (endemic) from those that inhabit the rainforest of the adjacent mainland coast, and have the name Vancouver Island Northern Pygmy-Owl (*G. g. swarthi*). Some question the validity of that designation, however.[241]

It has long been presumed that this species nests in the west coast region, but confirmation of breeding did not occur until 19 July 2016, when Ian Cruickshank observed two newly fledged young being fed at a location just north of Barkley Sound.

Although pygmy-owls are often associated with openings in the forest, it should be remembered that this unique owl has adapted to an island once covered almost entirely by forest except for alpine areas. How well this subspecies adapts to the conversion from old-growth forests to monoculture plantations remains to be seen. Fortunately, substantial tracts of original forest remain in the island's parks and in Clayoquot Sound.

BARRED OWL
Strix varia
STATUS: Uncommon resident. Breeds.

This large owl with round head and dark eyes was originally restricted to eastern North America. In Canada, it gradually spread westward through the Boreal Forest. In 1943, the first specimen for British Columbia was taken at Liard Crossing, and in 1946, the first nest was found in the province. In 1966, a Barred Owl turned up in the Lower Mainland in Surrey, and in 1969, the first one for Vancouver Island was recorded in Victoria.[236] By 1975, there were numerous records for eastern Vancouver Island, and in that same year the first breeding on the coast was recorded on Cortes Island when newly fledged young were photographed.[111]

In our west coast region, a Barred Owl was first recorded on 29 May 1993, at the head of Grice Bay in Pacific Rim National Park. Another bird was heard in the park in March 1995. On 28 and 29 June 2000, a bird was heard in the northwesternmost corner of Clayoquot Sound at the head of Sydney Inlet. Additional records soon followed, with birds heard or seen in the Tofino area on 16 February 2002, 27 September 2003, and 18 October 2003. On 12 October 2004, a bird was recorded at the Long Beach Airport. Many more records followed, indicating that the species was already well established.

Barred Owls are by nature birds of the deep forest. They prey on Red Squirrels, mice, and voles, though birds too may be taken when the opportunity presents itself. They are even known to catch fish on occasion. In a backyard at Chesterman Beach, one was reported doing just that in a shallow pool stocked with goldfish. They are also suspected of killing small owls, notably the Western Screech-Owl, which has greatly declined contemporaneously with the arrival of this much larger and more aggressive bird (see under Western Screech-Owl). Barred Owls, in turn, may fall prey to Great Horned Owls.

Breeding was indicated for the Tofino area when, in the summer of 2009, adult Barred Owls with young were reported on Stone Island by Sam Barwick. He has seen evidence that they continued to nest there in other years. Stone Island is located just north of Tofino harbour. Although Barred Owls may be seen or heard at any time of year, they are most often encountered in fall and winter. Tofino locals frequently report sightings of large owls without tufts, and it is not at all unusual to hear one at night through an open bedroom window, its rich baritone voice calling out, "*Who-who-Who-Whooooah,*" or "Who cooks for you? Who cooks for you?"

SHORT-EARED OWL
Asio flammeus

STATUS: Rare transient in fall, casual in winter and spring.

This diurnal owl of the open country has a wide breeding distribution throughout the Northern Hemisphere, from Eurasia to Alaska and the tundra regions of Canada. In North America, its breeding range also extends south to the Maritimes, southern Quebec, and southern Ontario, and to the Great Plains of both Canada and the United States. The species winters from southwest mainland British Columbia south throughout most of the United States, except for the southernmost regions.

In British Columbia, Short-eared Owls breed in the central interior of the southern half of the province, in the Peace River region, and formerly in the

Fraser Valley (R.W. Campbell, personal communication). The species winters locally in the central interior in low numbers, and on the Fraser River delta in fairly large numbers. It is also known to winter on southeastern Vancouver Island, although sparingly.

Whenever this lovely owl with its batlike flight is seen in our area, it is a treat, all the more because such opportunities are rare here. *Birds of Pacific Rim National Park* listed only 3 occurrences prior to 1978 and considered it "very rare."[1] *The Birds of British Columbia* lists 2 additional records for that early period, a bird at Triangle Island on 4 June 1974 and five birds at Long Beach on 3 November 1973. In addition, there are two noteworthy records from Cape Scott Park, both from Hansen Lagoon. One bird was seen hunting between 25 and 28 October 1973 and a single bird was observed flying on 17 May 1974.[4] Since then, 17 records have been added, all but 2 occurring in October and November. Most of these are from the period after 1995 when more active surveys were conducted. Records reveal that birds move through from late October through November. The earliest date was 3 October in 1996, and the latest was 13 December in 1978. The 1 additional spring record occurred on 18 March 1998, at the Long Beach Airport. Most sightings involve one bird, and occasionally two. On 29 November 1985 and on 31 October 2006, four birds were recorded at Grice Bay and the airport, respectively.

What these birds prey on while passing through is unknown, although since small mammals are scarce, they probably feed on birds. One individual seen by Doug Banks at the Long Beach Airport on 11 December 2016 was found to be feeding on a Northern Saw-whet Owl, which is considered to be a very rare visitor to the area.

BOREAL OWL
Aegolius funereus
STATUS: Casual visitor in fall and winter.

Known as Tengmalm's Owl in Britain, where it is a vagrant, and Boreal Owl on this side of the Atlantic, the North American name for it is apt, for it is truly a bird of the boreal forest. Its range stretches from Newfoundland and Labrador west throughout the Canadian boreal forest to Alaska. It also breeds in the Rockies south to Colorado, and has been found at high elevation at several other locations in the western United States. In British Columbia, its breeding range is not well known, though it has been seen at scattered locations throughout the province east of the Coast Mountains. It probably breeds in the north of the province, in the Rocky Mountains, and locally at high elevation elsewhere. It has been known to breed in at least three locations in British Columbia, including east of Okanagan Falls.[111]

There are three records for the west coast region. On 27 February 1993, a dead Boreal Owl was found as road kill near Tofino,[242] and on 3 October 1994, a bird was found on Triangle Island.[243] On 31 January 2009, a bird was found at Pachena Point lighthouse, for a third record. This bird may occur more often, but is rarely seen due to its secretive nature.

NORTHERN SAW-WHET OWL
Aegolius acadicus

STATUS: Casual visitor in spring, summer, and fall. Rare in the north of the region.

Only slightly larger than a Northern Pygmy-Owl, this is one of our smallest owls. Its breeding range extends from the northeastern United States and southeastern Canada westward through the boreal forest region to southern British Columbia, including southeastern Vancouver Island, south through forested regions of the western United States to the Sierra Madre of Mexico. On the coast, it breeds from Prince William Sound, Alaska, to southern California. In British Columbia, the species is known to breed in the Peace River region, on Haida Gwaii, and in the south-central interior north to Vanderhoof. It breeds also in the Fraser Valley and on southeastern Vancouver Island, where it is considered uncommon to rare.[111]

In our west coast region, this owl is very hard to find. I personally managed to view a living bird only in my 39th year of residency, and then only after being alerted to its presence by local resident Doug Banks, who had spotted the bird on his property. *Birds of Pacific Rim National Park* listed only 5 records, and 3 of those were dead specimens, presumably road kills.[1] Since then, only 14 additional records have been added: 5 November 1968, Vargas Island – 1; 16 November 1971, Long Beach – 1 (BC Photo 214);[41] 12 and 14 July 1979, Bamfield – 1; 15-19 April 1980, Cape Scott – 2; 27 March 1987, Bamfield – 1; 18 September 2004, west of Holberg – 1; 21 September 2004, north of Holberg – 1; 2 October 2004, Long Beach – 1 dead on Hwy 4; 17-18 February 2008, Lemmen's Inlet – 1 heard calling; 19 September 2008, Meares Island – 1; 4 November 2011,

The Northern Saw-whet Owl is named for one of its calls, which resembles the whetting of a saw. It is rarely seen in our region.

Jensen's Bay, Tofino – 1 (photo); November 2012, Tofino – 1 (photo); 30 December 2014, Tofino – 1 (photo); and 4 January 2017. In addition, there is a record of a juvenile found dead near the Long Beach Airport on 8 September 1972, and another dead bird in the clutches of a Short-eared Owl at the airport on 11 December 2016.

Whether or not this secretive species breeds in our region is currently unknown. The record of a bird in July is suggestive, as is the record of a juvenile in early September. It seems unlikely, however, as one would expect vocalizations to be heard from time to time. It is possible that habitat is more favourable for the species on the north end of the island. Guy Monty recorded two of the sightings listed above near Holberg, and noted seven additional sightings between Holberg and Port Hardy during the night of 21 September 2004. That section of road is mostly outside the west coast region, but only just. Of course, birds in September are likely to be migrants. Also interesting is his observation of "several birds" near Holberg between 17 and 27 May 2004.

Vehicular traffic is somewhat of a threat to this species. On the Lower Mainland, a study of road-killed owls showed that the Northern Saw-whet Owl was the second most frequently killed owl, with 88.9% ($n = 947$) found between November and February.[235] Like the Western Screech-Owl, this small owl may also be taken by larger owls, including the Barred, Great Horned, and Short-eared owls (see above).

ORDER CAPRIMULGIFORMES

Nightjars *Family Caprimulgidae*

COMMON NIGHTHAWK
Chordeiles minor
STATUS: Uncommon summer visitor. Breeds.

The Common Nighthawk belongs to a family called Caprimulgidae, which in the past was referred to as "goatsuckers." Members of this family are distinguished by an owl-like plumage, a very large mouth, and a tiny bill. All members of this family hunt flying insects, usually at night, and are neotropical. Three members of this family are normally found in Canada in summer, two of them in British Columbia. The Common Nighthawk is the most northerly, breeding in all provinces and territories in Canada with the exception of Nunavut. In British Columbia, it breeds throughout the province east of the Coast Mountains, but including the Fraser Valley, the south mainland coast, and all of Vancouver Island.[244] The species winters in South America.

In much of Canada, this bird is associated with warm summer nights, when the bird's nasal cries can be heard as it hunts airborne insects. They are not restricted to hunting at night, however, and are also seen in daylight hours. Because they seek out places with bare earth or gravel for nesting, they have adapted to nesting on gravel roofs of buildings in urban areas.

In our west coast region, this species has one of the shortest visitation periods of any summer visitor, usually arriving after 5 June and departing before the end of August, a window of about 12 weeks. *Birds of Pacific Rim National Park* listed 29 records.[1] In the many years since then, 56 additional sightings have been recorded, all but 6 after 1999 and 47 of them after 2006. I could find no records for the 1980s and only 5 for the 1990s. Since it is difficult to believe that this species could have been overlooked for so long, this suggests that there may have been a significant decline in our region for that period. In contrast, the years 2015 and 2016 alone produced 26 records. Combining all existing records, we have 50 in June, 17 in July, 18 in August, and 1 in September. Most sightings involved from one to four birds, but five birds were seen on three occasions and nine birds on one occasion.

Given the absence of warm summer evenings and the vagaries of wind and weather in the west coast region, it may be that this species has always been marginal here. Other than at the Long Beach Airport and on gravel logging roads closed to vehicular traffic and logging burns, there are few places suitable for nesting. Even unused logging roads become unsuitable as a nesting site once the trees on either side reach a certain height. Four birds seen flying north over the highlands at the upper end of Kennedy Lake on 18 June 2014 were suspected at the time of being late transients. However, the sparsely treed ridges surrounding the lake may provide suitable nesting habitat for this species.

Until recently, the only known nest for the central coast was found on a logging road near Kennedy Lake on 18 June and 4 July 1972.[1] A map in *The Birds of British Columbia* shows that a nest has also been found in the northern part of our region, though no details were given.[111] Not until 23 June 2016 was a third nest found, located between the Long Beach Golf Course and the airport. Just six days later, another nest was found nearby.

Although most birds have departed before the end of August, there is one late record. Three birds were observed at Ucluelet on 6 September 2015. Only four of our records are from the northern part of the west coast region. The Common Nighthawk occurs in low numbers on the west coast and appears to be marginal as a breeding bird.

ORDER APODIFORMES

Swifts *Family Apodidae*

BLACK SWIFT
Cypseloides niger

STATUS: Uncommon migrant and summer visitor, locally common in late summer. Rare in fall. Breeding likely but unconfirmed.

When seen, the Black Swift is inevitably viewed flying high overhead, alternately flapping, gliding, and banking in search of high-flying insects. Its tail is often spread fanlike, which makes it easy to distinguish from the Vaux's Swift.

This is perhaps our most enigmatic bird. It was unknown to science until 1857,[245] when a specimen was collected in Puget Sound, Washington. In the United States, a breeding site was not found until 1901, when a nest was located on a seacoast cliff near Santa Cruz, California.[246] It has since been found nesting at widely divergent locations throughout western North America, from

California and Colorado to western Montana, western Washington, and British Columbia. It nests also from southern Mexico to Panama and Venezuela. Our province appears to be its primary breeding range north of Mexico. Birds are seen throughout the southern half of British Columbia, north to Stewart and occasionally north to the Stikine River. Nests have been found at Vernon and at Clinton.[111] Its wintering grounds remained unknown until ornithologists planted geolocator chips on birds in 2006, and recaptured them in 2007 in order to recover the data. The data revealed that the species winters in the western Amazon region of Brazil.

In our west coast region, birds usually arrive in June and depart in September. The earliest arrival dates up to the year 2016 were 5 June in 2007, when 40 birds were observed over the airport at Long Beach; 8 June in 2013, when 33 birds were seen over the lower Kennedy River; and 1 June in 1995, when 12 birds were seen by Aziza Cooper over Taylor River, just outside our area. In 2015, Michael Shepard saw 18 birds over Gold River on 2 June. In 2016, those records were broken by a sighting of 2 birds over the lower Kennedy River on 23 May, and of 8 birds the next day. The arrival of this species is probably more weather-dependent than that of most other species. In May 2016, the weather was exceptionally fair.

In summer, particularly in August, birds are often reported from the Kennedy Lake region, which makes sense if birds are nesting in the mountains nearby. There are currently no nesting records from our west coast region, which is not surprising. These birds nest on damp, mossy cliff faces at inaccessible locations in the mountains, usually near waterfalls and sometimes behind them. They are also known to nest in sea caves dampened by sea spray, and may well do so in our region. On one occasion in early summer, a Black Swift was seen flying from the entrance of a large sea cave located just outside Hot Springs Cove in Clayoquot Sound. Unfortunately, this cave was visited daily by whale-watching boats and the resulting disturbance was probably too much for the bird, for it was never seen again. Some of the large sea caves located between Hot Springs Cove and Boat Basin may well provide suitable nesting sites for these secretive birds.

Black Swifts are seen infrequently during July. In 2014, a single bird was seen at the Long Beach Airport on 3 July, and 19 birds were seen there on 27 July. In 2015, 11 birds were observed at that location on 22 July. Sightings increase in August and September. *Birds of Pacific Rim National Park* listed 18 records for August and only 2 for September. Since then, an additional 15 sightings have been recorded in September, 4 of them after mid-month and the latest on 22 September in 1983, when 10 were seen over Tofino. That the southward movement occurs mainly in September is supported by records from the Rocky Point Bird Observatory near Sooke, where many September sightings have been reported. In the west coast region, there are no October records, though at Rocky Point, 5 birds were recorded as late as 7 October in 2011.

Due perhaps to a lack of information on the swift's biology and ecology and suggested declines in numbers in western Canada over the past three generations, the Committee on the Status of Endangered Wildlife in Canada (COSEWIC) declared the Black Swift endangered in 2015.[247] A count by George Bradd of 250 birds over the Alberni Valley on 10 August 2016 is therefore noteworthy.

VAUX'S SWIFT
Chaetura vauxi

STATUS: Uncommon spring migrant and summer visitor, locally common. Very rare in fall. Breeds.

This is one of four species of swifts that breed in Canada, and one of three species found in British Columbia. At 17 g in weight, it is also the smallest. It nests in dead snags, and frequently seeks out chimneys and natural crevices in old-growth western redcedars for shelter and as roost sites, where it congregates in large numbers. In Canada, it breeds only in British Columbia and southwestern Alberta. Along the Pacific coast, it is a summer visitor north to Juneau in southeast Alaska, and has been recorded over the Tatshenshini River. In the contiguous United States, it breeds east to western Montana and south to central California. It also breeds in the highlands of Mexico, Central America, and northern Venezuela, where it is a year-round resident. Northern birds winter in the species' southern range.

In the west coast region, the first birds usually arrive in mid-May or later, though there are several records earlier than that. On 10 May 1990, 8 birds were seen at Tofino, and on 8 May 1994, 4 birds were observed near Long Beach. The earliest recorded arrival date was 5 May in 2000, when 2 birds were seen in the Kennedy Lake lowlands. Birds continue to pass through until at least early June. On 5 June 2005, 60 birds were seen over the airport at Long Beach.

On the central west coast during the breeding season, birds are seen most often in the area of Kennedy Lake, often in the company of their larger cousin the Black Swift. Birds were seen entering and leaving trees near Kennedy Lake in 1968 and 1979,[1] and are often seen over the lower Kennedy River where there are many dead snags with cavities. Birds have been found inland throughout the region in June and July, including at the Little Nitinat River, Corrigan Creek, Sarita Lake, Burman River, and Conuma River, and near Holberg Inlet. In July 1985, while camped beside Megin Lake, I witnessed birds repeatedly skimming the surface of the lake, their breasts hitting the water, as they drank from the lake while remaining airborne. On the outer coast, in the summer of 1979, one individual was seen repeatedly flying low among the dead snags at Green Point, where it was likely nesting. Other locations on the outer coast where birds have been seen in June and July include Swan Lake, Ahousat, Ucluelet, Keeha Beach, the Long Beach Airport, and Jordan River.

Vaux's Swifts are seen most frequently in August, according to Hatler et al.,[1] who listed 14 records for that month alone, out of a total of 29. Since 1978, however, there have been more records in September than in any other month, mostly on the outer coast, because by then the southward migration has begun. A few records from the Long Beach Airport are as follows: 25 birds on 12 September 1982; 22 on 20 September 1983; 60 on 10 September 1985; 46 on 18 September 2004; and 18 on 11 September 2014. In 1992, 12 birds were seen at Megin Lake as late as 28 September.

An interesting record involving a large number of birds comes from Jordan River, where 980 birds were counted during a 52-minute period on 13 September 1984. This was said to represent only a small fraction of the total flight.[111] By the end of September, the southward movement is pretty much over. There are only two October records, one involving 2 birds seen at Tofino on 5 October 1986, and a very late record of a single bird on 22 October 1985, also at Tofino.

Because Vaux's Swifts nest in dead snags found in old-growth and mature riparian forests, this species has undoubtedly been impacted by the loss of nesting sites due to the extensive logging that has taken place in the west coast region in the past 60 years. It stands to reason that the continued liquidation of old forests will further reduce the available nesting habitat.

There are two schools of thought on how to pronounce the name of this species; "Vox's Swift," as an Englishman would pronounce it, or "Vo's Swift," as pronounced in France. Because William Sansom Vaux, after whom the bird was named, pronounced his name as "Vox," some argue it should be pronounced that way. Others argue that just because the man did not know how to pronounce his own name is no reason for everyone else to follow his lead. Perhaps the American Ornithological Society can resolve the matter.

Hummingbirds   Family Trochilidae

ANNA'S HUMMINGBIRD
Calypte anna

STATUS: Formerly a rare visitor in fall, winter, and spring, now locally fairly common. Uncommon in summer. Breeds.

The Anna's Hummingbird was not originally native to our province but expanded its range gradually northward from California, probably as early as 1944, when a hummingbird was observed wintering in Victoria.[111] By the early 1970s, there were many records for the Victoria area, due no doubt to the cultivation of the many flower gardens. The species is known to favour *Fuchsia* bushes and yellow jasmine, and is attracted by hummingbird feeders when available. Its current breeding range covers northern Mexico, parts of Arizona, California, Oregon, and Washington, north to southern British Columbia, including southern and eastern Vancouver Island (BCNRS files). It has wandered north along the coast as far as Anchorage, Alaska.[248]

The first Anna's Hummingbird recorded in our region, also a breeding record, was a female seen on a nest at Pachena Bay from 18 to 20 June 1973.[1] Unfortunately, full documentary evidence is lacking, but the species was recorded at Pachena Point on several occasions during the following winter. On 6 July 1974, a bird turned up at Triangle Island (BC Photo 398).[111] A second bird was seen less than a month later, on 2 August 1974, off Long Beach. On 23 May 1978, another bird was seen at Triangle Island, and on 2 June 1981, a bird was found in Tofino.

Although there were more occurrences after 1981, sightings remained rather sporadic. For 1982 and 1983, there are records in November and December, but I could find only two records for all of the 1990s, both in December. On 31 October 2004, a bird was seen in Ucluelet, and in November and December 2005, two or more birds were seen repeatedly in Tofino. This period seemed to herald a change, with more frequent sightings subsequently.

By 2009, there were at least three to four birds coming to feeders in Tofino, beginning in December. Since then there have been numerous records, largely due, I believe, to the proliferation of feeders local residents have put up to encourage hummingbirds to visit. Dates range from 2 October to 23 April, with occasional sightings even in summer. A bird was seen at Radar Hill on 9 June 2012. In October of that year, another bird was seen as far north as Esperanza. There have also been numerous sightings in Jordan River and Port Renfrew in recent years, with counts of up to four and five birds. Most observations have been made during spring and fall, but there have been a few occurrences in winter.

In 2013, a female was seen regularly at a feeder in Tofino throughout the spring and early summer. During this same period, an adult male was seen occasionally at a neighbouring feeder. On 1 July, a newly fledged young appeared at the feeder, and five days later, two young were observed in the company of an adult female, verifying that breeding was occurring in the village. A walk through part of the village of Tofino on 1 January 2016 produced five Anna's Hummingbirds. This pales in comparison with the 16 birds that were located in Ucluelet three days earlier by Ian Cruickshank. Clearly, the species is now well established on the west coast.

Anna's Hummingbirds have been known to hybridize with Rufous Hummingbirds on occasion.[249] From 5 April to 4 May 2010, a male Anna's × Rufous hybrid was seen daily "on territory" at a small park at the end of Third Street in Tofino.

RUFOUS HUMMINGBIRD
Selasphorus rufus

STATUS: Common in spring and summer. Breeds.

This is the only hummingbird adapted to living on the northwestern Pacific coast without relying on introduced garden shrubs and backyard feeders. Its breeding range is confined to the northwestern United States, British Columbia, western Alberta, and Alaska north to Cook Inlet. In our province, it is a common breeding bird throughout much of the province, with the exception of the extreme northeast, where it is less common as a breeder.[250] The species winters in western and southern Mexico.

Rufous Hummingbirds arrive on the west coast in early spring, just after the salmonberry flowers come into bloom.

In our west coast region, the arrival of the first ubiquitous Rufous Hummingbird in spring is eagerly awaited by rain-drenched residents. And while the bird's arrival may not be a harbinger of sunny skies and balmy weather, it is nevertheless a sure sign that spring has finally arrived. Rufous Hummingbirds are excellent flyers and do not hitch a ride on the backs of geese when migrating, as some people still believe. Rather, they time their arrival with the emergence of salmonberry flowers (*Rubus spectabilis*), in which they seek nectar. In the 13 years in which first arrival dates were recorded between 1992 and 2014, all dates fell between 20 March and 3 April. Despite the observation that salmonberry flowers often bloom earlier than in the past, this corresponds quite closely with the findings of Hatler et al.[1] In one recent year, the very first flowers were seen on 9 February rather than in early to mid-March. In 2015, after an unusually mild winter, the first Rufous Hummingbird, a female, arrived on 16 March, and the following spring a male on 14 March. Males are normally the first to arrive, with females arriving a week or two later.

Upon arrival, the males are quick to claim and defend territories. When not seen feeding on the nectar of salmonberry or salal flowers, they can be spotted perched on the very top of a small tree, from which they survey their domain for intruders, for they will vigorously defend their territory from all other males and are considered the most belligerent of all hummingbirds. Unlike most passerines, which advertise their territories in song, male Rufous Hummingbirds will fly straight up then do a rapid descent, as if trying to break the sound barrier. This dive is marked by a staccato series of notes. Like an aircraft at an airshow, the bird will pull out of the dive just before reaching the ground and zoom upward. Nests are usually built on the outer lower limbs of conifers or saddled on branches of tall shrubs. Materials include a variety of downy plant material that may be camouflaged with bits of lichen and reinforced with spider webs.

Wherever salmonberry or salal bushes are abundant, Rufous Hummingbirds are, naturally enough, also more common. An exception is Stubbs Island, near Tofino. There, despite a scarcity of salmonberry bushes, as many as 10 to 19 males have been found in April and May on less than 4.5 ha (10 acres). Ten males were counted there on 21 April 2011, and again on 8 May that year. Eleven males were present on 6 May 2012, and 19 males and 2 females on 12 April 2010. Whereas salmonberry bushes are scarce at this location, evergreen huckleberries (*Vaccinium ovatum*) are abundant, though I have no knowledge of whether Rufous Hummingbirds feed on these flowers. It is worth pointing out that, like many other hummingbird species, Rufous Hummingbirds do not feed on flower nectar alone but also consume insects.[251]

Males depart during the breeding season as they do not share incubation duties or help feed the young. They are said to head for alpine areas, following the flowers south. I have personally not seen evidence for this, but on a number of occasions birds have been seen flying rapidly south over the ocean. Females and young begin to thin out in late July and decrease rapidly until the end of the month, remaining in some years up to the end of the first week in August. After that, only an occasional bird is likely to be seen. The latest dates on which the species was recorded are 8 September in 1983, 9 September in 1985, 7 September in 1986, 8 September in 2001, and 1 September in 2011. There was a very late date of 19 September in 1970, and 20 September in 1974.[1] Perhaps the late migrants we see are from points much further north. There is a single record for October. On the 4th of that month in 2014, a juvenile or female was seen lingering at a feeder in Tofino. The most anomalous occurrence was a female or juvenile found at a feeder in Ucluelet by Ian Cruickshank on 29 December 2015, at a time when the temperature was dipping below 0°C at night.

As a defence against the onset of cold temperatures, Rufous Hummingbirds have the ability to reduce their body temperature from a normal 40-44°C (104-111°F) to 13°C (55°F). While in this state of torpor,[252] their heartbeat is reduced to as few as 50 beats per minute, compared with the normal 250. In flight, their heart rates can climb to an astonishing 1,250 beats per minute, or 21 beats per second!

ORDER CORACIIFORMES

Kingfishers   *Family Alcedinidae*

BELTED KINGFISHER
Megaceryle alcyon

STATUS: Common resident. Breeds.

With its slate-blue upperparts, large crested head, large bill, and white collar, the Belted Kingfisher is easily recognized and is a familiar sight across North America. "Belted" refers to the wide bluish band across the breast. Females and young birds have a rufous belt as well as the blue one. Its habitat includes streams, rivers, ponds, lakes, and coastal waters, where it may be seen sitting on a low perch from which it can survey the waters below, or dashing by at full throttle while emitting a raucous rattle. These birds also have the capability of hovering for a short time over the water, then plunging. The species nests in burrows in earthen banks, preferably near water.

Belted Kingfishers breed throughout Canada and the United States, except for the most northerly regions and much of the US Southwest. They winter throughout most of the United States, south to Central America and northern South America. Along the Pacific coast, birds winter north through British Columbia to Prince William Sound and Kodiak Island, Alaska.

In our region, Belted Kingfishers are seen most often along the shores of the marine environment, where small fishes are most abundant. However, they have also been found on lakes and rivers in the area, including Megin Lake on 28 September 1992, Ursus Creek on 26 May 1994, and along the lower Kennedy River on 13 June 2013. *The Birds of British Columbia* lists it as generally uncommon in the province and uncommon in winter on the coast, qualified as 1 to 6 individuals per day per locality.[111] By that definition, it is considered common

The Belted Kingfisher's presence is usually announced by a loud and raucous rattle. It is a fairly common resident on our coast.

in this book. In my personal files, there are 182 records from numerous locations in all months of the year. There seems to be no influx of birds from other regions in late summer and fall, though there may be some movement away from the exposed outer coast to more protected inside waters in autumn.

The factor that limits the population on the west coast is probably not availability of food but suitable locations for nesting, meaning a suitable earthen bank in which to dig a burrow. The eroded bank at Sandhill Creek, Long Beach, is an example of a nesting site used year after year, as are numerous steep banks along the West Coast Trail. The cliffs at Florencia Bay also have burrows that can be spotted from the beach. The Broken Group in Barkley Sound, on the other hand, with abundant food but few banks suitable for nesting, are eminently suitable habitat for kingfishers only outside the breeding season. According to Hatler et al., birds did not arrive there until early July in 1971 and 1972. Large areas of the coast would similarly be suitable for foraging but not for nesting. On the central west coast, human alteration of the landscape for road building and other construction purposes has inadvertently created new banks and thus new nesting sites.

During much of the year, Belted Kingfishers are easy to find in the harbours of the various west coast villages. Unfortunately, birds fly into large windows periodically, and when they do so at high speed, it is usually fatal.

ORDER PICIFORMES

Woodpeckers Family Picidae

RED-BREASTED SAPSUCKER
Sphyrapicus ruber

STATUS: Locally common in mountain valleys. On the outer coast, rare in spring and summer, uncommon in fall, and irregular in winter. Breeds.

The Red-breasted Sapsucker, formerly a subspecies of the Yellow-bellied Sapsucker, has a breeding range that is limited to the westernmost US states, from California to southeast Alaska. In Canada, it is found only in British Columbia, where it breeds widely, both on the coast and in the interior, but not in the southeast of the province and sparingly in the north. In September, birds move out of the interior and numbers on the east coast of Vancouver Island increase. The area encompassing the east coast of the island and the Fraser Lowlands is the centre of winter abundance in the province (R. Wayne Campbell, personal communication).

This attractive woodpecker is usually not easily found on the outer coast of our region. Walk into an old-growth forest, however, and evidence of its comings and goings is not hard to find in the form of rows of small holes drilled into the trunks of giant western redcedars and western hemlock. In winter, birds may also be seen clinging to the trunks of Sitka spruce; they do not drill holes in that species, but are likely seeking insect larvae under its scaly bark. When the temperature falls lower than usual, freezing the sap of trees in the mountains, these birds seek milder temperatures at low elevation near the coast.

In 1978, *Birds of Pacific Rim National Park* listed 23 records.[1] Since then a further 75 sightings have been recorded. Combining all records for the fall and winter periods, we have 14 in September, 20 in October, 5 in November, 11 in December, 15 in January, and 5 in February. What this appears to show is transients passing through in September and October, then declining in November. We see another small increase in numbers in winter when birds remaining on the island are pushed out of the mountains to the coast, though this occurs only in cold spells. There are only 7 records for spring and 21 for summer.

Red-breasted Sapsuckers are known to nest in the interior of the island, primarily in the southeastern region, but to a lesser extent in our region as well. On 24 June 1998, I observed two adults and one newly fledged young at low elevation in the Kennedy River valley. Reports of birds near Sutton Pass in May 2004 and August 2010 led me to conduct a survey in the upper Kennedy River valley during the breeding season in 2014, and I found four birds on a 4.5 km stretch of road from Sutton Pass to Spire Lake on 16 June. Returning to the area 10 days later, on 26 June, I observed an adult feeding one of its young, for a second breeding record for the valley. On 10 June the following year, walking the same stretch of road produced no fewer than seven birds, all adults. One was observed entering a nesting cavity. Another bird, surprisingly, was seen hawking insects like a tyrant flycatcher. There are also breeding records from Grice Bay, Bamfield, Kennedy Lake, and Port Alberni (BCNRS).

The valley bottom of the Upper Kennedy has a mix of deciduous and coniferous second growth, while on the slopes we find undisturbed climax forest containing a mixture of western hemlock, western redcedar, and a fairly high percentage of Douglas-fir, unusual for the west coast region and possibly indicative of drier conditions due to a rain shadow effect. It is not clear why birds are so much more common here in summer than near the outside coast, where they are rare. Birds have also been recorded during the June breeding season at other inland locations, such as Nahmint Lake, Flora Lake, Corrigan Creek, Harris Creek, and Norton Point on Holberg Inlet.

The only summer records I am aware of near the outer coast were recorded in the 1960s, when a bird was seen at the Green Point campground on 10 June 1967, and again on 13 and 17 August.[253] In the following year, one was seen at the same location on 2 August, and again on 18 August.[254] However, breeding was never confirmed. The only other birds seen near the outer coast in June were recorded at Winter Harbour, in the north of our region, on 16 June 2009 by Michael Shepard, and on 27 June 2013 by Brian Avent. Near Brooks Peninsula, a single bird was seen in red alders along the Klaskish River on 13 August 1981.[13]

DOWNY WOODPECKER
Picoides pubescens

STATUS: Rare transient in spring, summer, and fall. Very rare in winter. Breeding unconfirmed. Uncommon at Jordan River.

The Downy Woodpecker is the smallest of our woodpeckers. It breeds across the continent from coast to coast, with the exception of a large region bordering Mexico, and of the northern forest regions of Canada and Alaska, where it occurs sporadically. It does not occur at all in the tundra regions. In British Columbia, its breeding range covers the lower two-thirds of the province, where its status ranges from rare to locally fairly common.

In our west coast region, this woodpecker is not often seen. *Birds of Pacific Rim National Park* listed 11 records from December to June, with none recorded from July to November.[1] Since 1982, there have been 55 additional sightings in the west coast region, excluding Jordan River, covering all months. The largest number seen together was five birds on 26 November 1972, at Strawberry Island, Tofino, suggesting a family group.[1]

Unlike its larger cousin the Hairy Woodpecker, the Downy Woodpecker does not normally frequent the deep woods, but prefers forest edge and semi-open areas with scattered trees and shrubs. Deciduous woods are preferred over coniferous. The parking lots at Long Beach provide such conditions, and birds have been seen there on a number of occasions. In the Tofino/Long Beach area, birds have also been seen at the airport, the golf course, Chesterman Beach, the village of Tofino, the Grice Bay boat launch, Vargas Island, and Florencia Bay. There has been no evidence of breeding anywhere on the west coast (BCNRS). However, a nesting pair was reported in June 2008 just south of the mouth of Jordan River and outside the west coast region. A report of two birds at Holberg on 1 July 1978 is interesting for two reasons: it is the only record thus far from the northern half of the island, and it is also one of the few sightings recorded during the breeding period north of Jordan River.[111] Given the date, it could mean that the pair was breeding.

Downy Woodpeckers have been recorded in all months of the year, with the largest number in October and the smallest in July. A breakdown of all occurrences by month from Port Renfrew to Cape Scott is as follows: January – 5 records; February – 3; March – 6; April – 6; May – 5; June – 7; July – 1; August – 5; September – 7; October – 14; November – 2; and December – 5.

There are an additional 20 or more records from Jordan River, on our southern border, but these are not considered representative of the region as a whole and are not included here.

HAIRY WOODPECKER
Picoides villosus

STATUS: Uncommon spring and summer visitor on the outer coast. Rare in fall and winter. Uncommon to locally fairly common summer visitor in inland mountain valleys. Breeds.

This species looks very similar to the Downy Woodpecker but is considerably bigger, with a larger bill and larger voice. It is more an inhabitant of forest than

This male Hairy Woodpecker was found chiseling on a fallen log at Long Beach, searching for grubs to feed its youngster nearby.

the previous species, though the Hairy Woodpecker is also often seen in semi-open areas. This species breeds in forested areas across the continent, with the exception of some regions in the southwestern United States and the far north of Canada and Alaska. In British Columbia, it occurs in all regions of the province and is considered an uncommon resident in many areas. It should be noted that on coastal birds, the "white" of the underparts, tail, and face is dingy in appearance.

In the west coast region, *Birds of Pacific Rim National Park* listed 72 records and considered the species uncommon.[1] An additional 44 records were reported for the Brooks Peninsula region in 48 years between 1934 and 1984, mainly in mixed woodlands in the vicinity of the mouth of the Klaskish River. The species was recorded in all months except November to March.[13] Today, the Hairy Woodpecker continues to be listed as uncommon, but for the period from 1990 to the end of 2012, there are a mere 15 records in my files. During three years of intensive birding, only five birds were found, for an average of less than two sightings per year, which would qualify it as rare. The year 2013, on the other hand, produced 8 records and 2014 produced 4 records. It appears that the population experiences periodic fluctuations. Indeed, from 1975 to 1982, it was blue-listed in British Columbia, and numbers were also reported to be down south of the border, in Washington and Oregon. Evidence that the species is now considerably more common is provided by Ian Cruickshank. Between mid-May and the end of May 2016, he recorded this species at 12 locations between Tofino and Ucluelet. Keep in mind that most of us do not have the benefit of Ian's acute hearing.

That Hairy Woodpeckers nest in the west coast region has long been taken for granted, even if hard evidence is scarce. A map in *The Birds of British Columbia* shows two breeding symbols for northwestern Vancouver Island, indicating that breeding records exist for the Klaskish River and Chekleset Bay areas (BCNRS). A pair of nesting birds was also reported on 22 June 2008 at Jordan River. And on 22 May 2016, a young bird was observed begging from adults along the boardwalk to Schooner Cove.

Birds have also been reported from inland locations during the month of June, particularly from 2013 to 2015, by Michael Shepard. On 8 June 2013, he found a nest with young at Twaddle Lake in the upper reaches of the Gold River Valley (BCNRS). An exploratory trip that I undertook in the upper Kennedy River valley between Sutton Pass and Spire Lake on 16 June 2014 produced no fewer than six birds in two separate family groups. The first group appeared to be feeding in the red alders beside the road, although they occasionally darted into second-growth conifers. The second group was seen in young conifers more than 3 km away. Both families consisted of one adult and two young. Two surveys carried out in June of the following year found no birds. The habitat there is varied, with a mix of deciduous trees and second-growth conifers on the valley bottom, and old growth on the slopes, with a fairly high proportion of Douglas-fir present.

Combining all reported sightings going back to the 1930s, we have a total of 256 records. The vast majority since the 1960s are from the summer months, with 47 in June, 33 in July, and 29 in August. September and October have 10 records each, November has 9, and December 5. Note that numbers decline in each month after June and birds are scarce by December. Birds are seen only very occasionally in winter and early spring. There are 9 records for January, 3 for February, 7 for March, and 13 for April. Records soar to 39 in May. While having more sightings in the summer months is predictable because of the presence of more observers in the field, this does not explain the huge disparity in numbers between seasons. It seems likely, therefore, that many birds depart in fall and return in spring. It remains unknown whether birds spend the winter on the south end of Vancouver Island or fly further south. Hairy Woodpeckers are reported to be more common in the Victoria area in winter.

Little is known of the frequency of occurrence at higher elevations in our region, though there is no reason to suppose that these birds are absent. Indeed, on 2 October 2016, a Hairy Woodpecker was seen feeding on the cones of amabilis fir (*Abies amabilis*) above 750 m (1,460 ft) elevation on Mount Adder. Although this species can be elusive, when a concerted effort is made to find one by listening for its tapping in appropriate habitat, the searcher has a reasonable chance of success. More often, the species is encountered when you least expect it, such as when a bird is seen flying over a road, or when you unexpectedly hear its rather loud call while on a forest walk.

NORTHERN FLICKER
Colaptes auratus

STATUS: Fairly common in spring, summer, and fall. Locally common in winter. Breeds.

Northern Flickers are found in or near open areas. Red-shafted birds are common, while yellow-shafted birds are rare visitors.

The Northern Flicker has the largest breeding range of any woodpecker in North America, shunning only the most northern regions of the continent and southeastern California, southwestern Arizona, and much of Texas. It also inhabits large areas of Mexico. The species winters throughout nearly all of the United States and in the southernmost parts of Canada. This bird is more often seen in open areas than other woodpeckers, and it is not at all unusual to see one feeding on the ground. Northern Flickers are striking enough when perched, but even more so in the air, when they flash their brightly coloured flight feathers and white rump.

There are two easily identifiable subspecies, yellow-shafted and red-shafted birds. Eastern birds have yellow wings in flight, whereas western birds flash red. The two types were formerly considered separate species but were found to hybridize freely where their ranges overlap. The line where the two subspecies meet runs through the central Great Plains in the United States, and through Alberta and British Columbia in this country. In this province, yellow-shafted birds are found north of a line that runs approximately from Mount Robson Park to Vanderhoof and Stewart. Red-shafted birds are found south of that line.[111] Yellow-shafted birds and intergrades are occasionally seen in southwestern British Columbia, including Vancouver Island. For example, *C. a. auratus* and hybrid forms were reported at Grant Bay and Browning Inlet in March, April, October, and November.[16]

Northern Flickers are year-round residents of our west coast region, though favoured locations may shift somewhat with the seasons. The largest numbers are seen in fall and early winter. *Birds of Pacific Rim National Park* lists a sighting by Hatler of 8 to 10 birds on Vargas Island on 1 November 1968.[1] In later years, Christmas Bird Counts on 26 December 1982 and 29 December 2001 produced 10 and 9 birds, respectively. Stubbs Island, near Tofino, with its semi-open scrub habitat and with scattered trees, is the single most favoured location in fall and winter, with maximum counts of from 8 to 12 birds. Although it has not been verified, Northern Flickers probably feed on the fruit of the California waxmyrtle (*Myrica californica*), which proliferates there. Other locations where birds are often seen in fall and winter, though in smaller numbers, are the Long Beach Golf Course and adjacent airport. Further north, in the vicinity of Brooks Peninsula, birds have been reported frequently in all months but December.[13]

Northern Flickers are cavity nesters, though their excavation abilities are said to be weak. For this reason they often choose existing cavities, or trees where the wood is in a state of decay and is soft. Nesting has not been well documented in the west coast region, though in late June 1969, adults carrying food were seen entering a nest hole in a cedar snag near Kennedy Lake, and young could be heard. From their presence throughout the summer, it is quite clear that Northern Flickers nest on the central west coast. In spring, lone males can often be seen high up in a dead cedar snag, surveying their surroundings or advertising their presence by rapping the dry, resonant wood.

Although it is a fairly hefty bird with a weight of 130 g (4.6 oz), the Northern Flicker is not immune to danger from aerial predators and must stay alert.

Cooper's Hawks are rare on the west coast, but Sharp-shinned Hawks have been seen in active pursuit of Northern Flickers, and one was observed successfully taking a flicker by stealth (see under Sharp-shinned Hawk).

While red-shafted birds predominate in the west coast region, yellow-shafted birds or intergrades have been recorded in at least 10 separate years going back to 1983, multiple times in some years. Observations involving more than one bird occurred five times. On 9 November 1996, two such birds were seen on Stubbs Island, and on 12 January 2013, three birds were observed at the Long Beach Golf Course. On 1 December 2014, out of a flock of six birds at Florencia Bay, at least three birds were intergrades. Five days later in Tofino, two out of three birds were intergrades. Not all intergrades have yellow or amber wings in flight. Some may flash red wings but sport a black malar stripe and red nape crescent. An individual can even sport both a red malar stripe and a red nape. Many observations are fleeting and therefore indeterminate. The presence of yellow-shafted birds and intergrades in the west coast region can best be explained by an influx of birds from the interior and northern parts of our province.

That northern birds arrive here as early as late September is demonstrated by sightings of yellow-shafted birds or intergrades. A yellow-winged bird was seen on 26 September 1992 at Megin Lake, another on 26 September 2013 at Stubbs Island, Tofino, and two birds on 28 September 2016, also at Stubbs Island.

PILEATED WOODPECKER
Dryocopus pileatus

STATUS: Uncommon in spring and summer. Casual in fall, winter, and early spring.

Catching a glimpse of this large and conspicuous woodpecker with its contrasting black-and-white pattern and crimson crest is always a treat. And its wood-chiselling ability is as impressive as its appearance, for the large holes and gashes it leaves in the trunks of trees are far beyond the capability of any other of our woodpeckers. I once observed one drumming with full force on a concrete post. Only the specially constructed skull of a woodpecker could have cushioned a brain from such abuse.

The Pileated Woodpecker is a breeding resident throughout eastern North America, with the exception of the forests of the far north. Its range extends west through the Prairie provinces to British Columbia, western Montana, Idaho, Washington, Oregon, and northern California. There have been scattered sightings throughout most of British Columbia, but it is a breeding resident primarily in the southern half east of the Coast Mountains, and in the Fraser Lowlands and along southeastern Vancouver Island.

On the western half of Vancouver Island, Pileated Woodpeckers are usually hard to find, and it is clear that, unlike the southeastern part of the island, which was dominated by Douglas-fir forests, mature Pacific rainforest is not this bird's preferred habitat. When seen at all, this bird is most often viewed in flight as it travels from one location to another. Most records by far are based on its loud and distinctive drumming, which may be heard from as far as 2 km away. In the Tofino area, the drumming is most often heard coming from the old-growth forest on Meares Island. Birds have been seen and heard at numerous locations in the central coast region, including Grice Bay, Kennedy Lake, Ursus Creek, Megin Lake, Clayoquot River valley, and Long Beach. Elsewhere, birds have been recorded at St. Mary Creek, Cape Scott Park, on 21 May 1974,[4] in the vicinity of Klaskish River from 15 to 25 May 1974,[13] at the mouth of the Tahsish/Kwois River in Kyuquot Sound, and San Josef Bay in Cape Scott Provincial Park. There are also records from Barkley Sound to Port Renfrew and Jordan River in the south.

Pileated Woodpeckers have been recorded in all months of the year except, curiously, November and December. Records from January to March are also few, indicating that birds move out of the area for the winter. Most records are from the end of April to the end of August, suggesting that birds arrive here in spring from elsewhere. The greatest number of occurrences within a short period of time were recorded along the West Coast Trail in August 1972, suggesting that some areas of the west coast may be more suitable habitat than others. However, the extensive logging that was occurring in the nearby mountains at the time may have forced birds out of those areas.

Nesting in the west coast region is thus far unknown, although this species will probably be found nesting here eventually. If and when a nesting pair is found, it is likely to be in the interior of the island, where Douglas-fir is more common, such as the upper Kennedy River, the Nahmint Valley, or the San Juan River Valley. In July 2014, recently fledged young were found west of Gold Lake, just outside the eastern boundary of our region.[26]

ORDER FALCONIFORMES

Falcons   Family Falconidae

AMERICAN KESTREL
Falco sparverius

STATUS: Rare migrant in spring and fall, locally uncommon in fall. Casual in winter. Rare breeder.

This small, colourful falcon is familiar to rural people throughout much of Canada and the United States. Its breeding range covers most of the Western Hemisphere except for the Amazon rainforest and the treeless north of Canada. It is typically seen in open country, perched on fence posts and hydro poles, from which it hunts for mice, small birds, and large insects. This species nests primarily in tree cavities but will readily take to man-made nesting boxes. It winters throughout the United States, with the exception of the northern prairie states.

In British Columbia, it breeds in suitable habitat throughout much of the province east of the Coast Mountains, particularly in the southern half and in the Peace River region. It is also known to breed in the Fraser Valley and on eastern Vancouver Island, where it is considered an uncommon to fairly common summer visitor.[111]

In the west coast region, *Birds of Pacific Rim National Park* considered the American Kestrel a rare transient with 6 sightings in spring, 5 in fall, and 3 in winter.[1] Additionally, Richardson had recorded the species at Grant Bay in spring. Since 1978, there have been 82 additional sightings, nearly all in spring (31 sightings) and fall (48 sightings). In spring, 17 sightings were in April, 13 in May, and 1 in March. In fall, 3 sightings were in August, 25 in September, and 10 each in October and November. Most observations involved single birds, though 14 sightings involved two birds and 4 sightings were of three birds.

The vast majority of sightings were recorded at the Long Beach Airport, the birds being attracted to the large treeless area. Birds have also been recorded in subalpine areas on Steamboat Mountain (Clayoquot Plateau) and on Mount Klitsa. It seems likely that such habitat is used much more frequently than records indicate. Other locations where birds have been recorded include Bamfield, Tofino, Ucluelet, Chesterman Beach, Long Beach, and the mouth of the Tahsish/Kwois River in Kyuquot Sound, and Hansen Lagoon in Cape Scott Park on 15 May 1974.[4] There was one attempted nesting at the Long Beach

Airport, according to local resident Doug Banks, with at least one egg laid, although the attempt ended in failure.

There is a single record of a bird overwintering. On 15 January 2009 and again on 19 January, a female American Kestrel was observed on the beach at Florencia Bay, apparently feeding on small crustaceans commonly known as "beach hoppers." It was last seen on 11 March, indicating that it had successfully overwintered in the west coast's damp climate. The weather during this period was unusually favourable, however.

MERLIN
Falco columbarius

STATUS: Uncommon migrant in spring and fall, rare in winter, and very rare in summer. Breeds.

This small, fleet-winged falcon has a breeding range stretching from northern Europe and Siberia to Alaska and Canada, where it breeds in in virtually all regions except for most of Nunavut and the High Arctic. In the United States, it breeds on the northern Great Plains and in northern Washington. In British Columbia, nesting has been recorded at widely divergent south coastal (including Vancouver Island) and interior locations. The species winters on the US Atlantic coast, on the Great Plains, and along the Pacific Coast, from the southwestern corner of British Columbia south to northern South America.

On Vancouver Island's west coast, as elsewhere, the Merlin occurs primarily as a migrant. We often see it during the spring shorebird migration as it unexpectedly shoots by, low over the water at high velocity, its sharp eyes fixed on its intended prey. The Merlin, much more so than its larger cousin the Peregrine, uses stealth to catch its prey. Combining stealth with speed and manoeuvrability, this bird is deadly to small waders. Based on personal observations in Clayoquot Sound, the Merlin's success rate with shorebirds is much higher than that of the Peregrine Falcon.

Two subspecies are seen here, the dark, coastal Black Merlin, *F. c. suckleyi*, and the Taiga Merlin, *F. c. columbarius*, though it is not yet clear which is more common. In most cases, the observation is so fleeting that a determination cannot be made. There are 14 records of Taiga birds, involving eight individuals, as near as could be determined. A bird first photographed in Tofino on 23

November 2014 apparently overwintered, with sightings in February, March, and April. It was last seen on 20 April.

In spring, Merlins begin arriving by mid-April or shortly thereafter, and by early to mid-May most have passed through. Of 193 records since 1980, there were 32 sightings in April, 12 in May, 2 in June, and 5 in July. One of the July records involved an adult and newly fledged young observed at Swan Lake, just outside Pacific Rim National Park, on 30 July 2010. The first solid indication of breeding occurred in July 1971, when a Steller's Jay nest containing four Merlin young was found south of Barkley Sound.[255]

By August, especially during the second half of the month, southbound birds begin trickling through, and by September the movement is on in earnest. There are 15 records for August, 39 for September, and 47 for October. Birds continue to be seen occasionally after October, but by then the migration is largely over. Excluding the winter of 2014/15, when a bird overwintered, we have 18 records for November, 10 for December, 8 for January, 3 for February, and just 2 for March.

In most cases, Merlins are seen as single individuals, though occasionally two and even three birds have been recorded travelling together. Records in June and July likely represent breeding birds.

GYRFALCON
Falco rusticolus
STATUS: Casual transient in spring and fall.

This large falcon resembles a Peregrine but has broader wings and averages nearly twice the latter's weight. It comes in three colour morphs: dark brown, white, and grey. Gyrfalcons inhabit the tundra regions of Arctic Eurasia, Iceland, Greenland, and North America, where they hunt primarily for arctic hares and ptarmigan. Radio-tagging has recently enabled scientists to discover that some birds spend extended periods of time in winter living on the pack ice far from land between Iceland and Greenland, where they feed on seabirds. In Greenland, scientists found that Gyrfalcons will use the same cliffside nest site year after year. One site has been used for 2,500 years.[256]

While Gyrfalcons breed throughout Canada's Arctic regions, Yukon Territory and British Columbia are the only province or territory other than Quebec and Labrador where the species nests. This is understandable, given the high-elevation topography in these areas. In British Columbia, nests have been found in the Saint Elias Mountains, the vicinity of Atlin Lake, and south to the Spatsizi Plateau (BCNRS). Birds migrate south in some years and have been seen both in the interior and on the coast, including on Vancouver Island, where it is a rare visitor.

On the west coast, we had no records until 18 November 1991, when a grey juvenile in weakened condition was found at Chesterman Beach, Tofino. The bird died within hours but photos were taken of the specimen. Three years later, on 2 December 1994, a grey morph bird was reported at the Long Beach Airport by Rory Paterson. Five years later, on 4 May 1999, I saw a Gyrfalcon at the airport when one passed low overhead. Our fourth record is of a bird that died on a small island across from Tofino harbour in late November 2004. I was shown the carcass in mid-December to verify the identification. Like the others, it was a grey morph bird.

There have also been two unverified reports. A falcon reported at the airport on 20 September 1992 was described as a "dark morph Gyrfalcon." However, because juvenile Peale's Peregrines are both large and dark and there is no written description, the identification is considered uncertain. Another bird was reported on 13 January 2002, but also lacks documentation.

PEREGRINE FALCON
Falco peregrinus

STATUS: Fairly common migrant in spring and fall, rare in winter. Rare in summer outside breeding areas. Breeds at Triangle Island.

This sleek falcon has a reputation of being the fastest bird in the world. In straight flight, birds may achieve speeds of 65 to 70 mph, but in a stoop they can reach much greater speeds. This species has a global range. The only large islands it does not inhabit are Antarctica, New Zealand, and those in Canada's far north. Only a few other regions, such as the Sahara desert and tropical rainforest, are devoid of this species. In British Columbia, Peregrine Falcons formerly bred in the Okanagan Valley and today isolated pairs breed near Cache Creek, in the Cariboo-Chilcotin area, and East Kootenay (BCNRS). On the coast, it continues to breed in the southern Gulf Islands, northwestern

The Peregrine Falcon is known to be one of the fastest flying birds in the world. Shown here is a juvenile.

Vancouver Island, the mid-mainland coast, and especially Haida Gwaii, which, according to figures from the 1970s and 1980s, had a population estimated at 50 to 75 pairs.[111]

The coastal subspecies is known as Peale's Peregrine Falcon (*F. p. pealei*). It is larger and darker than other populations and breeds as far north and west as the Aleutian Islands and the Russian Commander Islands. Southward, it breeds on the San Juan Islands, the Columbia Gorge, the Olympic Peninsula, and urban areas of Seattle, Spokane, and Tacoma in Washington state.[257] During the breeding season, it feeds mainly on small seabirds such as alcids, storm-petrels, and kittiwakes, often nesting in close proximity to seabird colonies.[258] Surprisingly, this is actually of benefit to some seabirds. On Triangle Island, off Vancouver Island's northwest tip, researchers found that in the absence of nesting Peregrines, Bald Eagles would disturb and prey upon Common Murres and Pelagic Cormorants, causing incubating birds to flee. This in turn allowed gulls to swoop in and nab unattended eggs. When Peregrine Falcons were nesting nearby, however, they ferociously protected their territory and chased away other raptors, including even the much larger eagles, thereby protecting the seabird colony. Since Peregrines prefer smaller prey, murres and cormorants are not endangered by their presence.[259]

On their northward migration, Peregrines are often seen in pursuit of sandpipers at the Tofino mudflats. Given that Western Sandpipers travel in densely packed flocks containing thousands of birds, one would think it would be an easy matter for this powerful flyer to catch its prey. Not so. This falcon's success rate is in fact rather low, and most attempts end in failure. This seems to demonstrate that for its prey there is indeed safety in numbers. And even success can end in failure. On one occasion, I watched a Peregrine knock a Whimbrel out of the air and into the water. Before the Peregrine could recover the struggling bird, a Bald Eagle swooped in and snatched it from the water, to the vocal protests of the falcon. Peregrine Falcons are opportunist predators and use whatever hunting tactics are necessary to capture prey, even forcing birds up into the air for capture.[260]

Somewhat surprisingly, Peregrine Falcons will occasionally take prey much larger than themselves. On 8 October 2014, Tofino resident Doug Banks observed a Peregrine hitting a Greater White-fronted Goose, a bird three times as heavy, knocking it out of the air. In this case, the attack was not fatal and after swooping low over its downed prey, the Peregrine departed. Earlier in the season, the same observer watched two Peregrine Falcons harassing a Northern Harrier, apparently intent on bringing it down, but the harrier succeeded in evading its pursuers. This could explain the discovery of a harrier carcass consumed by a predator previously found at the Long Beach Airport. It was presumed to be the work of a Bald Eagle, but in light of the foregoing observation, the predator could well have been a Peregrine Falcon.

On the central west coast of Vancouver Island, Peregrines Falcons have been seen in all months of the year but occur most often during the spring and fall migration periods. While birds are seen occasionally during January, February, and March, the month of April sees a sharp increase, particularly in late April, corresponding with the arrival of shorebirds. Of 313 sightings recorded since 1980, 34 were in April and 35 in May. There is only a single record for June and 3 for July. By late August, birds begin to show up more frequently, and by September birds are moving through in numbers similar to April and May. The busiest month of the year is October, with 75 records. Two and even three individuals have been seen during a single bird walk. In November, with 37 records, birds have decreased back to September levels. We have 23 records for December and 17 for January. The northern subspecies, *F. p. tundrius*, is seen here, as well as the coastal *F. p. peali*, though it is not clear which is more common.

Peregrine Falcons have been reported in the vicinity of Brooks Peninsula, 180 km north of Tofino, in every month of the year since 1949.[13] In 1960, a pair bred on nearby Solander Island and it is suspected that a pair may be breeding in a Bald Eagle nest on the peninsula.[258]

ORDER PASSERIFORMES

Tyrant Flycatchers   Family Tyrannidae

OLIVE-SIDED FLYCATCHER
Contopus cooperi

STATUS: Uncommon migrant in spring and summer, rare in late summer and fall. Breeding highly likely but unconfirmed.

The Olive-sided Flycatcher prefers open or semi-open areas with dead snags from which it hawks for insects.

This is the largest of the flycatchers normally found on our coast. It is typically found sitting prominently atop a dead snag from which it pursues flying insects. Its song is a clear and unmistakable "quick-three-beers!" – or sometimes just "three-beers!" Its breeding range stretches from southern Labrador, the Maritimes, and parts of the New England states westward throughout the boreal forest region to Alaska and British Columbia (except Haida Gwaii), and south through forested regions of the American West to the Mexican border. It winters primarily in northern South America but also locally in Mexico and Central America.

In 1978, *Birds of Pacific Rim National Park* listed 30 records for the park region, though 11 of those probably involved a single bird at Swan Lake.[1] Since then, another 65 sightings have been added. The Olive-sided Flycatcher arrives on our shores in May, usually about mid-month, though there have been sightings a few days earlier than that. The earliest by far was a bird seen at Long Beach on 2 May in 1985. Combining all records and breaking them down by the month, we have 25 sightings in May, 25 in June, 11 in July, and 2 in August. The latest date a bird was ever recorded was 18 September in 2004, at the Long Beach Airport. Note that most sightings by far occur in May and June, when birds are most vocal. Those recorded in the month of May could include migrants, while those in June are likely mostly breeding birds. Our records come from numerous locations, though all but 3 are from the southern half of the west coast region. This is likely due primarily to the remoteness of the coast further north.

Preferred habitats during the breeding season are semi-open areas, often with dead snags and often in marshy, boggy, or swampy areas with standing water. The species may also use logged areas, clearcuts, and burns with some standing dead trees. Breeding is highly likely but remains unconfirmed for the west coast region.

During spring and autumn migration, birds may be found in a greater variety of habitats than during the nesting season. For example, on 25 May 2014, two birds were observed at the Long Beach Golf Course and another in a wooded area next to a building in Tofino.

Significant and widespread declines in Olive-sided Flycatcher populations in North America have been noted recently. This is significant for the species as 53% of the global population breeds in Canada. Consequently, this bird has been listed as threatened by the Committee on the Status of Endangered Wildlife in Canada.[261] Declines are also reported in British Columbia, but there is some concern that roadside routes do not adequately sample breeding habitats. For example, the Olive-sided Flycatcher is widely distributed on Vancouver Island but reaches its highest numbers in central portions in mixed coniferous forests at higher elevations, where the only access is via logging roads. During a decade of breeding bird survey routes here, there has been no decline; in fact, numbers have increased slightly.[262]

WESTERN WOOD-PEWEE
Contopus sordidulus

STATUS: Rare spring migrant and casual summer visitor. Casual migrant in fall.

While this species is rather similar to members of the genus *Empidonax*, it is larger and darker and can be most easily distinguished by its call. It breeds throughout much of western North America, from Alaska to Mexico and Central America, though at higher elevation in the south. It breeds east to western Manitoba and western Nebraska. In British Columbia, it breeds throughout the province east of the Coast Mountains, but also in the Fraser Valley and in the Salish Sea basin, including southeastern Vancouver Island. It winters in northwestern South America.

The Western Wood-Peewee is one of the least conspicuous inhabitants of the forest and usually comes to our attention only when heard. *Birds of Pacific Rim National Park* listed only three records. The first was seen by David F. Hatler on 21 May 1970.[1] None were seen or heard in the summer of 1972 during three months of intensive field work, which resulted in the bird being listed as very rare in summer.

The intervening years have brought the total number of sightings up to 29, only two of which were recorded north of Tofino. Based on available records, the spring migration occurs largely during the last two weeks of May and the first week of June. The only records earlier than that are both from April, with one bird seen on 22 April 1984 and another on 27 April 2008, both at Tofino. After the first week of June, birds have passed through. Indeed, in 44 years of observations, I encountered the species on only two occasions during the breeding season. On 17 July 1973, a bird was heard repeatedly at Sandhill Creek, Long Beach, and on 25 July 1994, a bird was found in Tofino. The species is thus far not known to nest in the west coast region.

Not until 2008 was the species reported again in summer. In that year, birds were reported by three observers from four locations in late June and July. One report was from the north end of Pacific Rim National Park, another was from Tsutsiat Falls, and the last two were from Port San Juan.[26] It seems curious that records during the breeding season are lacking in most years and then suddenly we have four in a single season. In 2016, a bird was heard singing on territory from 15 to 26 June, this time along the lower Kennedy River.

There are also 2 records for August and 1 for September, too few to accurately determine the timing of the fall movement, if any. The earliest occurred on

13 August and the latest on 11 September in 1983. A breakdown for the other months is as follows: April – 2 records; May – 8; June – 10; and July – 5. All birds were recorded at low elevation except for one bird recorded at about 305 m (1,000 ft) at the base of Clayoquot Plateau on 28 August 1990.

WILLOW FLYCATCHER
Empidonax traillii

STATUS: Generally uncommon, locally fairly common in spring and summer. Breeding highly likely but unconfirmed.

This flycatcher is slightly larger than the Pacific-slope Flycatcher and is easily distinguished from it visually by a number of features, including the white throat. It is most easily identified by its song, a burry "fitzbrew." Unlike the Western Wood-Pewee, the Willow Flycatcher's preferred habitat appears to be riparian areas near streams and swamps and bodies of fresh water, though it will sometimes inhabit shrubbery in drier areas. It breeds across the northern United States from Atlantic to Pacific. In western Canada, it breeds in the extreme south of the Prairie provinces as well as in western Alberta and southern British Columbia. In this province, it breeds in the southern interior, the Fraser Valley, and the Salish Sea basin, which is considered to be the centre of abundance for the species in the province.[263]

Birds of Pacific Rim National Park listed only five records.[1] Four of those were found during intensive surveys in June and July 1972, and the fifth was reported on 16 July 1975 at Bamfield. Hatler et al. listed the Willow Flycatcher's status as a "rare summer bird."[1] There are at least six additional coastal records north of Tofino, all in summer.[263]

Unaccountably, there are no records to be found between 1975 and 2004, a span of 29 years. However, I do recall hearing a bird at Megin Lake in July 1985. Since 2004, birds have been recorded on at least 39 occasions. From 6 June to 7 July 2004, a Willow Flycatcher was seen and heard in an area of dense shrubbery behind the club building at the Long Beach Golf Course. A bird was also reported in the Franklin River estuary on 4 July of that year.

In 2010, a bird was again seen and heard at the golf course from 6 to 13 July, and one was heard at Kennedy Lake on 24 June. There are six records from widely separated localities in 2011, and two records for 2012. In one of those, three males were heard singing at the airport on 9 June. There are seven records for 2013. On 6 June that year, five males were heard singing along the lower

Kennedy River by George Bradd. He reported that he had also encountered birds there in previous years. Additionally, birds were recorded at the Long Beach Airport on 9 June, 29 June, and 4 July 2013. In 2015, a bird (or birds) was heard singing at the airport from 30 May through June and July to 14 August; a bird was also heard there on 28 June and 22 July. The species has proven to be of regular occurrence along the lower Kennedy River, and undoubtedly breeds there.

The earliest date the species was recorded in spring was 23 May in 2016. All but one of our records are from the southern half of the island. The one exception was a bird recorded at the mouth of the Burman River, in Nootka Sound, on 28 June 2013. Given all of the sightings in recent years, I can only conclude that the species has either expanded in recent years or was overlooked in previous years.

HAMMOND'S FLYCATCHER
Empidonax hammondii

STATUS: Rare spring and fall migrant on the outer coast. Common summer visitor in river valleys. Breeding presumed but unconfirmed.

This species breeds from Alaska, the Yukon, and much of British Columbia, including Vancouver Island, south through forested areas of the western United States from the Rocky Mountains to Washington, Oregon, and northern California. It is largely absent from Arizona and New Mexico. In British Columbia, it breeds throughout the province, with the exception of most of the northeast.

Empidonax flycatchers are notoriously difficult to identify other than by voice, although identification can be done visually if one is afforded a close look. Most records, therefore, are based on vocalizations. Although Hammond's Flycatchers are said to nest in mid- to high-elevation forests throughout much of their range, on western Vancouver Island they can be found at low elevation in river valleys away from the outer coast. In Clayoquot Sound, there are summer records from June to August for Clayoquot Lake, Kennedy River, Ursus Creek, and Sydney River. On a survey in the upper Kennedy River valley on 5 June 2016, no fewer than 11 males were heard.

In Kyuquot Sound, there is a June record for Fair Harbour. There are also records from Zeballos, Gold River, and Burman River, and further north at Holberg.[26] In the south, the species has been found at numerous inland locations from Bamfield to Port Renfrew, particularly from late May through June. Northeast of the town of Gold River, it is found up to at least 300 m elevation, although it remains unclear whether it breeds much higher than that, as forays by hikers to higher elevations are usually made later in the summer, when birds have fallen silent.

On the outer coast, this flycatcher is encountered mainly during migration, though records are necessarily sparse, since migrating birds rarely vocalize and identifying them is not always possible. The earliest record for the region involved a bird on Cleland Island on 15 May 1969 (BCFWS). We now have 27 additional records from the outer coast, with 2 in April, 9 in May, 4 in June, 3 in July, 2 in August, and 7 in September. The records in June and July are surprising, especially considering that all those in June were recorded late in the month, suggesting that birds may occasionally breed on the outer coast.

Although proof of nesting is lacking for the west coast region, the fact that the species is widely distributed through our region throughout the month of June points to its being a regular and fairly common breeding bird in the west coast region.

PACIFIC-SLOPE FLYCATCHER
Empidonax difficilis

STATUS: Common in spring and summer. Uncommon in late summer and fall. Breeds.

Flycatchers in the genus *Empidonax* are difficult to distinguish from one another except by becoming very familiar with the field marks or by voice. Even experts can be stumped. Vocalizations are usually the surest way. This species used to be known as the Western Flycatcher until that species was split into the Cordilleran Flycatcher of the interior western United States and the Pacific-slope Flycatcher, which is found further west and further north. It breeds from northern Baja California north through the Pacific states to southern British Columbia, southwestern Alberta, and southeast Alaska. In our province, it breeds in the interior in the southern half of the province and on the coast, from the US border north to southeast Alaska, including Vancouver Island and Haida Gwaii.[263] It winters in Mexico.

This is the most common flycatcher in our west coast region. It can probably be found in low-elevation forest throughout the west coast region. Although small and inconspicuous, it can be located by listening for its call, a soft *pee-eet*, with a rising inflection, or its song, which sounds like *philip-pip* or *philip-pip-thsst*. The last part is very fine and not always made, and certainly not always heard. First arrival dates in spring are usually around mid-May. The years 2008 and 2012 were exceptions, with two birds recorded at Tofino on 27 April 2008 and 28 April 2012. In the vicinity of Gaultheria and Canoe lakes on Brooks Peninsula, the species has been recorded between 5 May and 15 August.[13] Occasionally it has been seen on small offshore islands, including Cleland Island on 11 May 1970 (BCFWS).

Birds on the coast have been found breeding from 6 May to 29 August.[263] One bird nested 7.62 m (25 ft) above the ground under the eaves of my small house in the woods. That nest was first found on 13 June 1992. According to notes made at the time, the incubation of three eggs began on 24 June. Three young were seen on 6 July, and only one remained on 14 July. The nest was empty on 15 July. With a reported incubation period of about two weeks, and the raising of the young requiring another two weeks, this seems too brief for a complete and successful nesting cycle.

It seems likely that birds begin moving south not long after the young have left the nest, though this is hard to prove since birds are silent in late summer. Certainly, most birds are gone well before the end of August. There are, however, a number of September records for the central west coast. These may be migrants from further north passing through, or they may be birds from a second nesting, which this species is known to do on occasion. These occurred on 14 September 2003, 25 September 2004, 26 September 2010, 4 September 2013, and 9 September 2016. There are also several late September records from Jordan River.

Little is known about how high in elevation these birds nest in the west coast region. According to *The Birds of British Columbia*, they nest up to 1,250 m elevation on the coast.[263] However, in our region there do not appear to be any high-elevation records that confirm this. Pacific-slope Flycatchers have often been found in river valleys during the breeding season. At both Clayoquot Lake and Sydney Inlet, this species and Hammond's Flycatchers were found to inhabit the same parcel of forest beside the water.

SAY'S PHOEBE
Sayornis saya
STATUS: Casual transient in spring, summer, and fall.

This flycatcher is one of three species in the genus *Sayornis*. It breeds throughout much of western North America, from Alaska, the Yukon, and western Northwest Territories south through much of western Canada and United States, except for the coast, and south through the interior of Mexico. In British Columbia, it breeds throughout the province east of the Coast Mountains, except for the extreme northeast. In the Fraser Lowlands and southeastern Vancouver Island, it is known only as a rare transient. There are several isolated records for Haida Gwaii.[263]

Vancouver Island's west coast lies well outside this bird's normal migration route, so records are few, as might be expected. We have 10 records, with a breakdown by month as follows: 2 records are in March, 1 in April, 2 in May, 1 in June, 3 in August, and 1 in September. In an interesting coincidence, we have 2 records for Stubbs Island on the same day in August exactly 91 years apart. All of our records, in chronological order, are: 25 August 1893, Stubbs Island, Tofino – 1;[264] 23 August 1976, Triangle Island – 1 (BC Photo 474); 25 August 1983, Stubbs Island, Tofino – 1; 23 March 2000, Carmanah Point – 1 (photo); 23 March 2006, Chesterman Beach, Tofino – 1; 1 June 2006, Carmanah Point – 1; 5 September 2010, Stubbs Island, Tofino – 1; 31 May 2012, Long Beach Airport – 1; 7 May 2015, Long Beach Airport – 1; and 2 April 2017, Ahousat – 1.

ASH-THROATED FLYCATCHER
Myiarchus cinerascens
STATUS: Casual vagrant in summer and fall.

This small, pale *Myiarchus* flycatcher is a bird of open forest and brushy habitat in arid and semi-arid regions. It breeds from central Mexico to the southwestern United States, including California, central Oregon, and extreme southern Washington. In British Columbia, the species is regarded as a very rare vagrant on the southwest coast, including southeastern Vancouver Island.

On Vancouver Island's west coast, we have six records from 1971 to 2014: two in June, one in August, one in September, and two in November. A bird was first observed on Vargas Island on 14 November 1971 by David Hatler.[1] Exactly one year later, on 14 November 1972, I saw a bird at the Millstream subdivision, near Ucluelet Inlet.[1] On 7 September 1983, a bird was seen at the mouth of Sandhill Creek, Long Beach, by Mike Shepard and others,[265] and on 23 August 1987, one was observed at Ucluelet.[263] The last two records are from opposite ends of our region. On 12 June 1994, a bird was seen on Triangle Island by Ian Jones and others,[266] and 20 years later, almost to the day, on 14 June 2014, a bird was seen at Jordan River by multiple observers on a Victoria Natural History Society field trip.

TROPICAL KINGBIRD
Tyrannus melancholicus
STATUS: Rare fall visitor.

As its name suggests, this large flycatcher is a bird of the tropics and subtropics. Its range extends from Argentina in the south to the deserts of northern Mexico. In the United States, it breeds only in southern Arizona and southern Texas. It winters somewhat south of its northernmost breeding range. Given this fact, one would not expect to see this bird in Canada. Inexplicably, a small number of birds fly in a northwesterly direction in fall and turn up along the Pacific coast of the United States from California to Washington and occasionally southwestern British Columbia, including Vancouver Island.

The first record for British Columbia occurred just south of our region, at French Beach, on 23 February 1923.[267] A second record, for both the province and Vancouver Island, occurred at Cadboro Bay in October 1972 (BC Photo 240).[268] The third record for the province and the first for the west coast region occurred in Tofino on 11 October 1976, when a bird was observed perched on a television antenna.[269] Since then, the total for our west coast region has risen dramatically, with well over 50 sightings. If multiple sightings of the same bird are eliminated, we are still left with a rather remarkable 30 or more records, exceeding by far the number of sightings for each of the other kingbirds that have occurred here. Those records involved at least 36 individuals seen in 22 separate years. Of those, 17 records are from Tofino, 3 from Ucluelet, 4 from Long Beach, 3 from Carmanah Point, 3 from Jordan River, 1 from Cheewat Beach, and 1 from Cape Scott. High counts were three birds on 23 October 1997

The Tropical Kingbird is very rare in Canada but more than 35 individuals have been recorded in our west coast region.

at Tofino; two birds on 5 October 1998 at Tofino; and two birds on 27 October 2001 at Carmanah Point. In 1985, birds were seen simultaneously at Ucluelet and Tofino, and at Long Beach shortly thereafter, indicating at least two, and possibly three, individuals.

On the central west coast, all sightings have occurred between 5 October and 23 November. In Tofino, individual birds have lingered for up to five weeks. In 1997, one or more birds were seen from 6 October to 23 October, and in 1998, an individual was present from 6 October to 16 November. Given the high number of sightings at this location, it appears that Tofino is the premier location for finding this species in Canada.

Occurrences on the west coast dropped off somewhat for a number of years but resumed in 2014 with a bird at Chesterman Beach on 18 October, and at Jordan River on 26 and 27 October, with additional sightings at Long Beach on 18 and 19 November. As an interesting footnote, the Jordan River bird was taken by a Merlin while under observation, and the bird at Long Beach was in the company of a Northern Mockingbird, which is also rare. In 2015, a bird was photographed at Cape Scott on 27 September, making this the earliest fall sighting ever recorded in the west coast region. Three weeks later, on 18 October, a bird was once again seen in Tofino. In 2016, a bird was seen hawking insects from telephone wires on Main Street from 28 October to 12 November, while two birds were found in the Ucluelet area on 13 November.

WESTERN KINGBIRD
Tyrannus verticalis
STATUS: Casual transient in spring, summer, and fall.

This bird is found in suitable habitat throughout most of the western United States, with the exception of the Pacific coast region. It breeds from northern Mexico to southern Canada, east to western Wisconsin, Kansas, and much of Texas. In British Columbia, it is a common bird of the southern interior, particularly the interior grasslands region. The species is reported to have expanded its range since the 1940s, apparently benefiting from agricultural expansion. It has bred in the Fraser Valley. On southeastern Vancouver Island, it is considered an uncommon spring transient and a very rare fall migrant. It was found breeding for the first time in 2016.[263] Western Kingbirds winter largely from Mexico to Costa Rica.

In our west coast region, the first Western Kingbird, a specimen, was recorded on 19 June 1909 at Ucluelet.[270] There were no further sightings for half a century until 16 May 1959, when a bird was seen at Jordan River perched on driftwood.[271] Four more sightings followed in the 1970s. Today we have a total of 18 records: 5 for May, 6 for June, 2 for July, and 5 for October. Birds seen in May, as well as a bird at Tofino on 3 June 1990 and two birds at Long Beach on 6 June 1994, are presumably wayward spring transients.

Our other June dates range from 12 to 22 June, which is quite late in the season for the birds to be spring migrants. On the west coast, however, the arrival of summer is considerably later than on southeastern Vancouver Island and some passerines arrive much later. Western Kingbirds seen on 9 and 14 July are more problematic, too late to be spring migrants and too early for fall. October dates, on the other hand, clearly represent fall transients. Fall dates range from 5 October to 23 October. Locations where sightings have occurred include Tofino, Ucluelet, the Long Beach Airport, Long Beach, Triangle Island, Bamfield, Carmanah Point, and Jordan River.

All records have involved single birds with two exceptions. Two birds were seen at Long Beach on 6 June 1994, and three birds were recorded at Jordan River on 20 May 2005. With Jordan River's close proximity to southern Vancouver Island, it is possible that Western Kingbirds will occur there somewhat more frequently than on the rest of the west coast.

EASTERN KINGBIRD
Tyrannus tyrannus
STATUS: Casual transient in spring and summer.

The Eastern Kingbird is aptly named, for it has an imperious nature and will attack even large predators such as the Red-tailed Hawk when they stray into its territory. It also has a colourful red-orange crown, though this is not always visible. Its breeding range covers much of North America, with the exception of the most northerly forests and the tundra regions, the most westerly parts of the continent, and the American Southwest. In British Columbia, Eastern Kingbirds breed widely in the southern half of the province east of the Coast Mountains, as well as in the Peace River region in the northeast. It also breeds sparingly in the Fraser Valley and locally on southeastern Vancouver Island (BCNRS). Eastern Kingbirds winter in South America, from Colombia through the western Amazon, south to Paraguay and northern Argentina.

In our west coast region, the Eastern Kingbird occurs only as a very rare vagrant. The first recorded sighting on the west coast occurred at Triangle Island on 5 July 1974.[272] *Birds of Pacific Rim National Park* listed only 2 records.[1] By 2015, that had increased to 16. All sightings occurred in the period from 17 May to 22 August. We have 2 records in May, 7 in June, 4 in July, and 3 in August. Locations where more than one bird has been seen include Pachena Point with 2 records, Carmanah Point with 4 records, and Tofino with 3 records. Bamfield, Long Beach, Long Beach Airport, Brooks Peninsula,[13] and Triangle Island all have 1 record each. The most recent sighting occurred on 4 June 2015, when a bird landed on a boat 35 km south of Ucluelet, rested awhile, then continued on its way.

SCISSOR-TAILED FLYCATCHER
Tyrannus forficatus
STATUS: Casual vagrant in spring, summer, and fall.

Like the kingbirds, to which it is related, this elegant bird with its ultra-long tail is a bird of open spaces, where it uses telephone wires, fences, fence posts,

The Scissor-tailed Flycatcher is a bird of the Great Plains of the southern Midwest. In our region it is a very rare visitor.

and other available perches from which to survey its surroundings and hawk for insects. Its breeding range is primarily the southern Great Plains of Kansas, Oklahoma, and Texas, but also western Louisiana, Arkansas, and barely into eastern New Mexico and Colorado. Its breeding range also extends across the Rio Grande into northeastern Mexico. The species winters in Central America. Although British Columbia is far north of its normal range, it occurs in this province occasionally as a vagrant.

This denizen of the warm, wide-open plains would seem to be quite out of place on our west coast, with its dense rainforest. However, in the summer of 1977, two independent reports were received from Tofino residents of a bird with a long forked tail that fit the description of a Scissor-tailed Flycatcher. Unfortunately, it was never confirmed and a record of the exact dates is lacking.

Today we have nine records, presumably involving six individual birds, plus one unconfirmed report. The first confirmed sighting for the region occurred on 16 May 1987, when Aziza Cooper found a juvenile on Long Beach at the mouth of Sandhill Creek (Combers Beach). It was photographed (BC Photo 1155) and was last seen on the following day.[273] A second bird, also a juvenile, was reported by Jacqueline Windh on 24 August 2003, at Chesterman Beach.[274] Ten days later, on 3 September, Brian Slater reported a bird, probably the same one, from the Millstream subdivision, northwest of Ucluelet.[274]

Additionally, there was a report of a bird at Florencia Bay on 28 June 2004. It was reported to Pacific Rim National Park staff by an unnamed birder, but was never seen by others, so it remains an unconfirmed single-observer sighting. A bird found at Botanical Beach Provincial Park on 19 May 2008 was seen by a number of observers until 26 May.[275] Less than a week later, on 2 June 2008, a bird that may have been the same individual was seen on Nootka Island by Jan Leina. On 28 June 2011, a bird was seen briefly at Carmanah Point by assistant lighthouse keeper Jerry Etzkorn.[276] There was also a sighting by Tom Maxie at San Josef Bay near Cape Scott on 2 and 3 June 2014 (a photograph shows it was an adult), and a sighting at Chesterman Beach, Tofino, on 12 June 2016 by Mike Wesbrook.

Shrikes   *Family Laniidae*

NORTHERN SHRIKE
Lanius borealis

STATUS: Rare fall transient. Casual in winter and spring.

This bird, with grey-and-white plumage and contrasting black wings, tail, and mask, is hard to mistake for any other, and is considered one of the true shrikes. There are 29 species worldwide, only 2 of which are found in North America. The second, the Loggerhead Shrike, is very rare in British Columbia. Shrikes are rather unusual in that they are carnivorous songbirds, feeding on prey ranging from earthworms[277] and large insects to mice, voles, and small birds. Northern Shrikes are sometimes called "Butcher Birds" after their practice of impaling prey on a thorn or a barbed-wire fence, and have been known to take birds as large as themselves. They inhabit open and semi-open areas.

The Northern Shrike is found in Eurasia as well as North America. In the latter, it breeds throughout the far north, from Labrador and northern Quebec west to the Yukon and Alaska. It winters in the northern United States and southern Canada. In British Columbia, it is known to breed only in the extreme northwest, though in winter it may be found throughout much of the province,

The Northern Shrike, sometimes called "Butcher Bird," is a passerine that preys on small rodents and small birds.

except for the far north. On southeastern Vancouver Island, it is an "uncommon to fairly common migrant and winter visitor."[263]

For our west coast region, *Birds of Pacific Rim National Park* listed only 5 records and it was considered rare in winter.[1] One of the earliest records involved an observation by Green Point resident Peg Whittington of a Northern Shrike chasing and capturing a shorebird in 1965 (BCFWS). Since 1978, there have been 55 additional sightings. By far the majority were seen in the months of October and November. There are 20 records for October, 17 for November, 6 for December, and 3 for January. The months of September, February, March, and April have 2 records each. There is a single record for May. A bird was observed at Carmanah Point on 31 May 1998. All sightings involved single birds, with the exception of two birds seen at the Long Beach Airport on 14 October 2008, and again on 11 October 2016.

In at least two years, birds successfully overwintered. In the winter of 1986/87, a bird wintered at the south end of Long Beach, with records from 15 December to 12 April. In the winter of 2008/09, a bird was seen at the Long Beach Airport from 13 November to 27 March. Virtually all sightings have been on beaches or at the airport, with the majority by far seen at the airport. There have also been sightings on Stubbs Island and a single sighting on Vargas Island.

Vireos   Family Vireonidae

CASSIN'S VIREO
Vireo cassinii

STATUS: Casual visitor in spring, summer, and fall. Rare transient in the south of our region.

In older bird books, the Cassin's Vireo is listed as Solitary Vireo. In 1997, this species was split it into three species: the Blue-headed Vireo of the east and north, the Plumbeous Vireo of the semi-arid regions of the American West, and the Cassin's Vireo of the Pacific coast and northwest, where it breeds from northern Baja California and coastal California to British Columbia, east to southwestern Alberta and western Montana. In British Columbia, it breeds primarily in the southern half of the province east of the Coast Mountains, but also further north in the Peace River region. It also breeds in the Fraser Valley and southeastern and southern Vancouver Island, where it is considered an uncommon to fairly common migrant and summer visitor. It is absent from Haida Gwaii.[277]

On the west coast, records for this species are rare. *Birds of Pacific Rim National Park* listed only 3 occurrences.[1] A bird was heard singing on the Goldmine Trail in Pacific Rim National Park on 16 July 1972, and another along the Willowbrae Trail the following day. On 18 and 20 May 1974, another Cassin's Vireo was seen and heard in Tofino. Since then the species has been recorded 10 more times: 1 May 1993, south end of Long Beach – 2 birds; 1 May 2000, Tofino – 1; 15 September 2006, Jordan River – 1; 19 September 2006, Tofino – 1; 11 April 2007, Jordan River – 1; 11-15 May 2008, Bamfield – 1; 13 August 2008, Port Renfrew – 1; 16 October 2011, Jordan River – 1; 1 September 2013, Jordan River – 3; and 19 September 2014, Jordan River – 2.

It is interesting, if not surprising, that of the last 10 records, half were found at Jordan River. This location borders the south end of the island, where the species is much more common. According to the online *Atlas of the Breeding Birds of British Columbia*, there have also been a few occurrences northeast and northwest of Gold River, though specific dates were not published.[278]

HUTTON'S VIREO
Vireo huttoni

STATUS: Fairly common in spring, summer, and fall. Rare in winter. Breeds.

This small vireo looks very similar to a Ruby-crowned Kinglet and can easily be overlooked. The Hutton's Vireo, however, has a heavier bill and white lores, and moves more slowly. The indication that this inconspicuous bird is in the neighbourhood is usually its call, a repeated *chuwee*, with a rising inflection. Hutton's Vireos are restricted to western North America, where they are divided into two separate populations. One population is resident from southern Arizona and New Mexico south through Mexico to Guatemala; the other is a resident of the western half of the three US coastal states and southwestern British Columbia. In our province, the species is largely restricted to the Fraser Valley, the Salish Sea basin, and Vancouver Island. It is a common breeder at low elevation over that same range (BCNRS).

For western Vancouver Island, there are numerous records for all months of the year. As might be expected, most records by far are from the outer coast or coastal plain, locations most often visited by birders, but there are enough records from further inland in mountain valleys to suggest that it is widespread throughout our region. The inland locations all span the time period from late April to late August, and include Ursus Creek, Tranquil Creek, upper Kennedy River, and Clayoquot Plateau, all in the Clayoquot Sound drainage.

East and south of Barkley Sound, birds have been recorded during the breeding period near Bamfield, Sarita Lake, Nitinat Lake, and Little Nitinat River, and at Corrigan Creek. In the late 1960s or early 1970s, birds were also recorded along the Klanawa River and the San Juan River.[1] At the north end of the island, birds have been recorded at Holberg and Holberg Inlet in late April, May, and June. They were also found along the Mahatta River in July and at Gold River in June. On the central west coast between Ucluelet and Tofino, Ian Cruickshank found birds at 15 locations during the second half of May 2016. There are only two confirmed breeding records for the west coast region (BCNRS). One nest was found at the north end of the island beside San Josef Main on 21 June 2005, and two adults were observed feeding three young. Another was found near Bamfield (see below).

Hutton's Vireos are usually encountered as single individuals or as pairs. Three birds have been recorded at times, including at Bamfield on 27 and 28 March 1993; near Long Beach on 14 October 2001; on Meares Island on 5 July

2011; at Jordan River on 31 October 2011; and at Tofino in mid-November 2014. As many as 5 birds were found at Jordan River on 3 December 2011 and again on 27 December that year. These last two records suggest a migratory movement. The largest number recorded on a single day occurred during a survey in the Bamfield area on 26 May 1991, when 22 birds were found and a nest was discovered.[48]

Winter records are scarce. I could find only 3 records for the central coast in December, 1 in January, 4 in February, and 2 in March. It appears that most birds move further south for the winter.

WARBLING VIREO
Vireo gilvus

STATUS: Fairly common in spring, summer, and fall. Breeds.

The Warbling Vireo breeds throughout much of the United States, and in the Sierra Madre of Mexico, but is absent from the southeastern states, most of Texas, southwestern Arizona, and southeastern California. In Canada, the species breeds in the southeast and in much of the west, from southwestern Manitoba through Saskatchewan. In British Columbia, it is found as a migrant and summer visitor throughout the province, mainly east of the Coast Mountains. On the coast, it is considered a fairly common migrant and summer visitor in the Salish Sea basin, including southeastern Vancouver Island. It is absent from Haida Gwaii.[263]

Birds of Pacific Rim National Park listed 15 records for the central west coast and considered the Warbling Vireo rare in summer.[1] Today there are well over 100 records, about half of them from the central coast and the rest from as far south as Jordan River, with scattered records north to Holberg Inlet. There is also a fall specimen record for Cape Scott, with a bird seen there on 15 September 1935 (NMC 26059). This was likely a migrant from the north. While records in the northwestern part of our region are scarce, this is probably due to a paucity of observers rather than an absence of birds. It should also be recognized that many occurrences simply go unrecorded because the species is fairly common.

The Warbling Vireo favours deciduous or mixed forests. Extensive logging on the island has resulted in large areas of regrowth in deciduous red alder, which has probably helped this species expand its population and range. Nearly all birds have been recorded in disturbed areas containing red alders or on the forest edge. Occasionally birds have been recorded in undisturbed original forest, though these too may contain alders. One such observation occurred in late May 1994, in the Ursus Creek valley, which is a tributary of the Bedwell River in Clayoquot Sound.

In spring, first arrivals are usually seen after mid-May, though occasionally earlier. There are two records for 9 May, one for 5 May, and one for 1 May. An unusually early sighting was recorded on 18 April 2004, in Tofino. Most birds were recorded as singles or pairs, but up to 5 have been recorded in spring, and up to 7 during migration in late summer. As many as 10 individuals were recorded by John Reynolds, 35 km northeast of Bamfield (north of Nitinat Lake) on 28 June 2011; two days later, he recorded 8 birds on the northern half of Nitinat Lake. Given the time of year, it is likely these birds were spread over a larger area, rather than being in a single flock. On a hike we undertook in the upper Kennedy River valley on 5 June 2016, Ian Cruickshank counted no fewer than 43 singing males. Although it seems obvious that the species breeds in the west coast region, there exists only a single breeding record, involving an observation of recently fledged young near Bamfield (BCNRS).

The timing of the fall movement is difficult to determine. Once the breeding season is over and young birds can fend for themselves, it seems likely they will begin to move on. There are only a few records for August but records in September are fairly numerous, almost all occurring on or before the 18th of the month. The latest record I could find was of a bird seen on 28 September in 1986, near Long Beach. Birds seen in September are likely migrants from further north.

RED-EYED VIREO
Vireo olivaceus

STATUS: Casual in spring, summer, and fall.

This vireo, with its dark crown, white eyebrow, and black eye-stripe, breeds throughout the eastern United States and most of the Midwest, and in Montana, Idaho, and Washington. In Canada, it breeds from the Maritimes to British Columbia, and north to the Northwest Territories. In this province, it breeds in the southern half of the province, north to the Skeena and Nass rivers and the Peace River region, and in the Taiga Plains of the northeast. On the coast, it breeds only in the Fraser Valley and the Salish Sea basin, including southeastern Vancouver Island.[263]

This bird is rarely encountered in our west coast region. The species was first recorded on 10 May 1970 at Tofino Inlet. On 12 June 1984, there was a second sighting at Chesterman Beach, Tofino. A third record involved three birds at Tofino on 13 September 1989.[263]

Jays, Magpies, Crows, and Ravens   Family Corvidae

GRAY JAY
Perisoreus canadensis

STATUS: Uncommon resident at high elevation. Uncommon at lower elevation in late summer. Breeding likely but not confirmed.

This is the famous "Whiskey Jack" of Canada's boreal forest region, and the only North American representative of the Old World jays. For many years, its official name was Canada Jay, until it was renamed by the American Ornithologists' Union. In 2016, the Gray Jay was selected as Canada's national bird. It is famous for its lack of fear of humans, and will often approach people camping, hoping for a handout. It is not unusual for one of these birds to perch on one's hand.

This species breeds throughout the northern forests, from the northern New England states, the Maritime Provinces, and Labrador westward throughout much of Canada, including the Northwest Territories and the Yukon, into Alaska and British Columbia. It also breeds at higher elevation from Idaho and eastern Montana south to New Mexico, and from Washington to northern California. In British Columbia, it breeds at lower elevation in the north, and in the subalpine forests further south, including on Vancouver Island.

In the west coast region, there are relatively few records. *Birds of Pacific Rim National Park* listed one sighting from the area of Sutton Pass in August 1969.[1] On 27 July 1986, I found three birds near the summit of Mount Klitsa, which is located on the eastern edge of our region, above Sproat Lake. Twenty-two years later, on 13 August 2008, Nigel Jackett also found three birds at that location. To the west of Mount Klitsa, a bird was seen by Garrett Beisel on Mount Pogo on 30 May 2015, and four birds were recorded by Frank Pinilla halfway between Mount Klitsa and Mount Pogo on 18 August 1997.[26]

Birds have also been seen in the months of May and June, before or during the breeding season. On 17 May 2005, a bird was again seen at Sutton Pass, and on 6 June 2012, one was observed by Radd Icenoggle along the Head Bay Road, northeast of Nootka Sound. The largest number of sightings were recorded by Michael Shepard in the Gold River Valley. In June and July of three consecutive summers, he recorded Gray Jays at five locations no fewer than eight times.[26] On one occasion, there were seven individuals, on another occasion eight. In the southern part of our region, southeast of Alberni Inlet and Barkley Sound, birds were found at three locations west of the Nitinat River in the summers of 2014 and 2015, again by Michael Shepard.[26] There are scattered records north of Tofino in summer, such as Browning Inlet, where F. Richardson reported two birds on 21 July 1968.[16]

That birds were found at relatively low elevation in June and July will probably be surprising to many readers, though they have long been known to descend in late summer. As mentioned earlier, birds have been seen at Sutton Pass on Highway 4, and on 27 August 1990, I saw a single bird in the forest at low elevation at the foot of Clayoquot Plateau Provincial Park, in the Kennedy River canyon. A year later, on 11 August, a bird was reported from Port San Juan. On 17 September 2016, birds were reported by Margaret Reine at two locations along the Wild Pacific Trail, Ucluelet.

It is interesting to note that most of our records are from two areas, the Gold River valley and the area from Mount Klitsa to Mount Pogo. Both of these areas are relatively accessible, though the higher elevations are not often visited. It seems likely, therefore, that the relatively low number of sightings in the west coast region is due primarily to a paucity of observers.

STELLER'S JAY
Cyanocitta stelleri

STATUS: Common in spring, summer, and fall. Uncommon to rare in winter. Breeds.

This handsome jay is restricted to western Canada, the western United States, and mountainous areas of Mexico. Its range overlaps only minimally with that of the Blue Jay, which is largely found east of the Rocky Mountains. For the most part, where Steller's Jays live, the Blue Jays do not. In British Columbia, it is widespread in the southern two-thirds of the province, north to the southern Peace River region in the east and the Nass River in the west, and sporadically

The Steller's Jay is a common denizen of the rainforest; in late summer and fall it is often ubiquitous on the outer coast.

elsewhere in the north. It is an uncommon to locally fairly common resident on the coast, including Vancouver Island.[263]

Steller's Jays are a familiar sight to visitors to Pacific Rim National Park, where birds are often seen by the roadsides, at campground picnic tables, and at Long Beach parking lots, for these birds eagerly seek handouts. Likewise, birds flock to backyard feeders after the breeding season. Up to a dozen jays have been seen at one apartment building in Tofino where several bird feeders were present. Steller's Jays tend to be bold and cheeky. Their fear of humans is minimal, and the only predators they fear are falcons and accipiter hawks, primarily the Sharp-shinned Hawk. Once the jay is aware of the hawk's presence, however, it is confident in its ability to avoid it and may even taunt its adversary. If caught, it will fight back vigorously.

Steller's Jays have been seen throughout our region in all months of the year, including the summer months, and though no nests have been found, they clearly breed, as newly fledged young are often seen in late summer (BCNRS). The species appears to be most common on the outer coast and is present as well on Brooks Peninsula year-round[13] and at Cape Scott. Birds have also been encountered at numerous other locations, including river valleys, and at higher elevation in the mountains. The species was recorded on the Clayoquot Plateau on 27 August 1990, on Halfpipe South on 1 September 2008, and on Mount Klitsa on 13 August 2008. Usually a single bird is seen, or two or three birds together.

When there is sufficient food, Steller's Jays will often congregate in larger groups, with 10 to 15 birds not being unusual. These larger congregations are most prevalent in late summer and fall, when "migrants" on Vancouver Island move down mountains and southward in autumn. Hundreds gather on the south end of the island in fall, apparently prevented by the 19 km expanse of ocean from continuing their passage southward.[279] Counts of 15 birds were made at Long Beach on 19 September 1984 and at Bamfield on 16 March 2009. On 7 September 2014, 17 birds were counted at Stubbs Island, 16 of which were seen together in a single wax-myrtle bush. On 24 December 2014, 26 Steller's Jays were seen together, feeding on the grass for worms or other delicacies at the Long Beach Golf Course. The highest counts of all were made at Jordan River, with 27 birds recorded on 19 December 2012 and 30 birds on 19 March 2013. The high numbers recorded there in late December and late March correspond with the decline of birds on the central west coast in winter and their reappearance in March. Such seasonal migrations are also known to occur in parts of the interior.

In the winter period (January/February), congregations larger than 3 are rarely seen. A review of 481 records showed that exceptions occurred on 4 January 2016, when 14 birds were seen at Florencia Bay, and two weeks later, on 19 January, when a loose congregation of 12 birds was found at the Long Beach Golf Course. Significantly, most birds had left the village of Tofino just a week or two earlier.

Steller's Jays are absent year-round from the Broken Group in Barkley Sound. During several years of fieldwork there, Hatler never encountered Steller's Jays. He postulated that this was due to some habitat deficiency rather than an inability to reach the islands.[1] As mentioned earlier, however, this species does show reluctance to cross an expanse of open water.

BLUE JAY
Cyanocitta cristata
STATUS: Casual vagrant in spring and fall.

This flamboyant bird with its raucous call is a widely distributed resident in the eastern United States, from the Midwest to Atlantic shores, and in Canada from the Maritimes through southern Quebec, southern Ontario, and large areas of the Prairie provinces. In British Columbia, it is an uncommon breeding resident in the Peace River region and a rare resident and breeder in the East and West Kootenay regions and the Chilcotin region (BCNRS). It is still considered rare or casual in coastal areas of the province (BCFWS).

We have 3 records for the west coast region: 10 April 1951, Clo-oose – 1;[263] 20 and 22 October 1977, Incinerator Point, Long Beach – 1 (BC Photo 486); and 14 October 1987, Tofino – 1.[280]

BLACK-BILLED MAGPIE
Pica hudsonia
STATUS: Casual vagrant.

This very handsome, long-tailed member of the corvid family is a breeding resident in much of the American and Canadian west, north into the Yukon and Alaska. It is not found in the most southerly areas of the American Southwest or the Pacific coast. In British Columbia, it is a breeding resident in the extreme northwest, in the Peace River region, and in the southern interior grasslands, where it is considered common. On the south coast, including Vancouver Island, it is a rare vagrant and formerly bred in the Lower Mainland (BCNRS).

On Vancouver Island's west coast, we have three records. On 28 April 1952, a bird was seen at Carmanah Point. There were no other occurrences until 40 years later, when on 29 May 1992 Rory Paterson saw a bird in Tofino. It is reported to have died a week later at MacKenzie Beach.[263] There was a third sighting on 21 June 2004, by Jim Hamilton at Cheewat Beach, along the West Coast Trail.

CLARK'S NUTCRACKER
Nucifraga columbiana
STATUS: Casual vagrant in fall, winter, and spring.

This member of the corvid family breeds at higher elevations throughout much of the western United States, north to the Rocky Mountains of western Alberta, and throughout the southern half of British Columbia east of the Coast Mountains. It subsists largely on the seeds of pine cones, especially ponderosa pine and high-elevation whitebark pine. Because those trees are not native to the coast, it is absent from Vancouver Island as a breeding bird. Although there have been a considerable number of sightings on the island over the years, the species is regarded as rare and erratic on southeastern Vancouver Island, and a very rare autumn and winter vagrant in our west coast region.[263]

For the west coast region, we have 10 records: 1 December 1935, Quatsino – 1 (CVMUBC 7444); 11 January 1976, Pachena Point – 1; 17 September 1977, Franklin Camp – 1; 11 November 1979, Jordan River – 1; 15 September and 14 October 1989, Tofino – 1; 24 September 1994, Klitsa Plateau – 1; 27 April 1996, Long Beach Airport – 1; 21 May 2007, San Juan Ridge – 1; 4 November 2009, Carmanah Point – 1; and 28 and 31 January 2010, Kootowis Creek and Kennedy Lake, respectively – 1.

NORTHWESTERN CROW
Corvus caurinus

STATUS: Common to abundant resident. Breeds.

This crow is adapted to survival on the Pacific coast, from northern Washington to the foot of the Alaska Peninsula. It survives largely by feeding in the intertidal zone. This intelligent bird is very adaptable, however, and also thrives in areas where human habitation dominates.

Its status as a species distinct from the American Crow of the interior of the continent is questioned by some, who regard it merely as a subspecies of the former. Those who know this bird intimately would likely consider that notion invalid. The Northwestern Crow is smaller, with a more nasal call than the American. Claims made in two prominent field guides that this bird's calls are lower are in my opinion incorrect, at least in our west coast region. Additionally, this species has unique vocalizations never heard in the American Crow, occasionally astonishing nonresidents, who report hearing a crow saying hello. That vocalization, though not remote from the imagined "hello," could more accurately be described as a soft, nasal falsetto "la-la." The Northwestern Crow differs from the American Crow in behaviour as well, with this species being exceedingly bold in the presence of humans.

This ubiquitous species is commonly found along the shore as well as on offshore islands throughout the entire west coast region. North of Tofino, it is also present year-round and seasonally gathers in small feeding aggregations such as 62 on Brooks Peninsula on 6 August 1981[13] and 16 at Hansen Lagoon in Cape Scott Park on 15 May 1974.[4] During the breeding season, Northwestern Crows disperse, but are particularly common along the outer coast and on small vegetated islands, rather than along the inlets. They hide their ground nests as best they can to avoid predation by their mortal enemy the Common Raven, often without success (see under Common Raven). It is estimated that at least 8 pairs nest on Cleland Island, with a maximum of 20 birds counted on 21 May 1969 (BCFWS).

Crows are major scavengers and predators in seabird colonies, where they have been reported to consume the eggs of cormorants and Glaucous-winged Gulls, particularly when the parent birds leave the nest due to disturbance by eagles or human visitors.[281] Crows undoubtedly consume the eggs of other breeding birds as well, such as those of Black Oystercatchers. And when afforded the opportunity, they will also kill and consume the newly hatched chicks of cormorants and the nestlings of storm-petrels as they emerge from their burrows. Such behaviour has been amply documented in a number of scientific papers. Being the opportunists they are, Northwestern Crows also feed on the eggs and chicks of many small birds.[263]

After the breeding season, and particularly in winter, Northwestern Crows gather in flocks late in the day and fly out to a roost, usually located on a small island. It is believed that they do this to avoid predation by Great Horned Owls. In Tofino, they have been known to gather in a flock of more than a thousand birds, which then heads over the water to Lennard Island. On 16 March 2004, several flocks totalling 1,300 birds were tallied from Chesterman Beach. The largest flock contained 900 birds. At dawn they again return to Tofino to disperse in search of food. There may be some movement out of the area in fall. Small flocks have been observed flying in a southeasterly direction in fall on occasion.

Members of this species are extremely clever and versatile when it comes to finding food. Local residents know better than to leave a bag of groceries unattended in the back of a pickup truck. And when the tide is out they feed on a variety of life in the intertidal zone. Crows are occasionally seen flying high in the air to drop a mollusc on rocks, pavement, drift logs, and even a parked car in order to break it open. On sandy beaches, they will dig out red worms, much as sandpipers do. On 20 January 2001, an estimated 350 crows were feeding on red worms near Sandhill Creek, Long Beach. Similarly, when the ground is wet in spring, they will sometimes hunt for earthworms in village parks alongside American Robins, from whom they may well have learned this practice.

Northwestern Crows are also known to feed on a variety of berries, including the fruit of California wax-myrtle (*Myrica californica*). The proliferation of fish farms in Clayoquot Sound has created another food source. At a supply depot and processing facility in Tofino, crows have been seen digging into leaking bags of fish pellets and competing with gulls for any spillage. There is little to fear about the continued survival of this adaptable and resilient little crow.

COMMON RAVEN
Corvus corax

STATUS: Common resident. Breeds.

The sociable and highly intelligent Common Raven can at times be seen engaging in "play" or recreational activity.

This very intelligent and adaptable bird has a widespread distribution in the Northern Hemisphere. In Eurasia, it breeds from eastern Siberia and China, west to Europe and south to the Arabian Peninsula and North Africa. In North America, it is a breeding resident throughout virtually all of Canada and Alaska, with the exception of southern Ontario and the Great Plains. While it has adapted even to the High Arctic islands, it is absent from most of the eastern United States, where it is found only in the Appalachians. It is a breeding resident throughout almost all of the American West and most of Mexico. In British Columbia, it is found throughout the province, and is seen even over metropolitan areas such as Vancouver and Victoria.

Twice as large as a Northwestern Crow and three times its weight, the Common Raven is easily distinguished from its small corvid relative by its size, wedge-shaped tail, and large bill and voice. Because both species are omnivorous, they compete with each other for food to some extent. Ravens therefore strive to reduce the crow population by searching out their nests in spring and early summer and devouring their eggs. Nor do they stop there. I once witnessed a raven killing all newly fledged young in the vicinity of a nest, though as far as I could see, none were eaten. When you hear the sound of very excited crows during the breeding season, chances are there is a raven nearby searching for their nests. The crows will harass the raven, but to no avail. Nothing will deter a raven from its mission of finding food and eliminating the competition in one stroke.

Ravens will also feed on seabirds that wash ashore, and if such a bird is alive but in a weakened state, the raven will not hesitate to use its large bill to hasten its demise. It is not uncommon to see a gull or alcid carcass on the beach, minus head and breast, or often just the head, a sure sign that a raven got there first. But they often eat the breast as well. Pinnipeds such as seals and sea lions washed up on a beach are another source of food. Unable to pierce the tough hide, they have to wait for eagles to do the preliminary work. By eating carrion, ravens also serve the useful function of helping to dispose of carcasses. So adaptable and opportunistic are these birds in their choice of food that I once watched a couple of ravens consuming sunflower seeds strewn on the sand for the benefit of other birds.

Although their nests are hard to find, evidence of nesting is revealed each summer by the raucous calls of the young clamouring for food after having left the nest. Let me assure you, the wailing of human infants is music to the ears by comparison. A nest was found at Chesterman Beach, Tofino, as far back as 15 May 1931, by Ian McTaggart-Cowan, who was conducting bird surveys in the area at the time.[1] A nest with three young was also reported from Kennedy Lake in the 1950s.[1]

Ravens are also quite playful and will spend hours cavorting over a beach on a westerly wind, at times flying in formation like jets at an airshow. At the mouth of Sandhill Creek, Long Beach, I have seen as many as 31 birds engaged in this kind of recreational activity. On 9 September 2010, I wrote in my notes: "One raven was hanging from a limb by its feet with its body and head pointing straight down while another looked on. Sort of like a human child who then calls out, 'Look at me, Ma.'" And on 13 April 2013, at Green Point, I wrote: "All were involved in what appeared to be play, hanging in the wind, plunging down occasionally and engaging each other. Two birds carried sticks with their feet, occasionally switching them to their beaks. One carefully placed the stick in a tree, presumably for future use." On 29 April 2015, similar "recreational" activity was occurring there, although this time the count was 47 birds, a record high number for that location, and possibly the area.

It is quite common to see a raven rolling over on its back momentarily in mid-flight, then rolling back again. On a brisk westerly wind, ravens will take advantage of the updrafts above a steep rise of the land such as we find at Green Point and Florencia Bay, and just hang in the wind. On two occasions, I watched a raven take stationary flying to a new level by grasping a small branch at the top of a tree with its bill and then just hanging there motionless. On another occasion, I watched a Raven swoop down on a wolf for no apparent reason and rap it on the back. Playful harassment? Probably.

Although ravens may be found in a wide variety of habitats, preferred areas in the west coast region appear to be mudflats and sandy beaches. These areas are likely to provide the greatest amount of food. Birds are often seen in the deep woods along the Rainforest Trail near Long Beach, although this location appears to be attractive as a gathering place and roost rather than a place to procure food. It is probably noteworthy that from here it is only a short flight to the mouth of Sandhill Creek, Long Beach, a favourite hangout, and also to the local garbage dump.

Larks   *Family Alaudidae*

HORNED LARK
Eremophila alpestris

STATUS: Casual transient in spring, rare in fall on the outer coast. Probably more common in alpine regions.

This is North America's only native lark. In Britain, it is known as Shore Lark. It inhabits treeless plains such as deserts, savannah, tundra, agricultural fields, and alpine meadows, and is found in suitable habitat throughout much of Eurasia and North America, including Mexico. There is even an isolated population in Colombia. In British Columbia, it breeds in large areas of the interior, from the US border to the Yukon, often at high elevation. It has been

The Horned Lark is a rare migrant in the west coast region, but is occasionally encountered on beaches and sand dunes in fall.

reported to nest up to 2,800 m. On eastern Vancouver Island and the Fraser River delta, it is an uncommon to locally common migrant and winter visitor. Four subspecies occur in British Columbia: *E. a. articola* (Pallid Horned Lark) is the most common and widespread; *E. a. merrilli* (Dusky Horned Lark) occurs mainly in the grasslands in the south-central interior; *E. a. hoyti* (Arctic Horned Lark) is found in the northeastern region; and *E. a. strigata* (Streaked Horned Lark) formerly nested on (and is extirpated from) southern Vancouver Island and the Fraser Valley.[263] Horned Larks winter from southern British Columbia to Mexico.

With its bold black markings on breast and head, the Horned Lark is easy to identify. Some variations in plumage occur, however, depending on the bird's origin. These variations range from birds with an all-yellow face and richly coloured upper parts to birds with an all-white face and drab upper parts. Some birds have both white and yellow on the head. While it is tempting to try to determine a bird's geographic origin based on appearance, keep in mind that considerable variation may occur even within a subspecies, and that one subspecies tends to gradually blend into another. Based on observations of birds with these variations in plumage, it appears that birds from two, and possibly three, populations pass through our area.

On Vancouver Island's west coast, this species is not often seen. In 1978, *Birds of Pacific Rim National Park* listed 3 records and considered it a very rare fall migrant.[1] Since then there have been an additional 22 sightings. Combining all existing records, we have 4 in spring and 18 in fall. In spring, we have 1 sighting each for the months of March and April, and 2 in May. In fall, 9 sightings were in September and 9 in October. Earliest and latest dates in spring were 17 March and 17 May, respectively. Earliest and latest dates in fall were 4 September and 29 October.

Horned Larks are usually encountered as single individuals or in pairs, with three notable exceptions. On 1 September 2008, 16 birds were recorded in the alpine zone on Halfpipe South, and two days later, on 3 September, 10 birds were observed on a nearby mountain with the distinctly unpoetic name of 5040. On 13 September 2013, 20 birds were reported from the Long Beach Airport. This is by far the largest flock ever recorded along the outer coast.

Because treeless habitat is limited on the west coast, sightings inevitably occur on beaches or in other open spaces. Six of our records are from Stubbs Island, and five from the airport. Two sightings are from Chesterman Beach, and there is one each from Tofino, Port Renfrew, and Carmanah Point. In view of the records from seldom-visited alpine areas in September, it seems likely that the species occurs there regularly at that time of year.

Swallows and Martins   *Family Hirundinidae*

NORTHERN ROUGH-WINGED SWALLOW
Stelgidopteryx serripennis

STATUS: Uncommon and local. Breeds.

Like the Bank Swallow, this rather drab swallow nests primarily in burrows in earthen banks. It breeds from southern Mexico north throughout the entire United States except southern Florida. In Canada, it breeds in the southeast, westward through the Great Plains to British Columbia, including Vancouver Island. In the interior of British Columbia, it breeds north to the Skeena River, and occasionally further north near the Yukon border.[263] On Vancouver Island's southeast coast it is a fairly common but local breeding bird. The species winters from the southern United States to Panama.

In our region, most records are from the central west coast. June records suggest that birds breed primarily in the southern half of the region, and then only at a few locations, such as Port San Juan, Pachena Bay, Long Beach, the Long Beach Airport, and the lower Kennedy River, and only occasionally elsewhere. Records from the northern half of our region are few, although there are records for the mouth of the Nasparti River on 6 August 1981[13] and a pair was suspected of nesting in a sand bank at Guise Bay in Cape Scott Park on 18-20 May 1974.[4] A map in *The Birds of British Columbia* indicates that birds have bred on the northern tip of Vancouver Island.[263] In 2014, Michael Shepard found two birds at Holberg in June and eight birds at Gold River in early July. A suitable breeding location is dependent primarily on the availability of a suitable nesting site, which for this species means an earthen bank.

First spring arrivals are usually seen between 20 April and early May. Spring sightings most often involve 1 or 2 individuals, but as many as 3 pairs have been seen together. The largest number on record was 12 birds on 16 July 1996, at the airport, where they are known to breed. At Long Beach, they are most often seen near Incinerator Rock and at Combers, where they nest in a bank at the mouth of Sandhill Creek. Birds are also seen in summer at the Pacific Rim National Park sewage pond and at Swan Lake.

After the young have left the nest, birds do not linger long but depart for points south. Birds usually leave before the end of July but may linger into early August. The two latest dates I have were recorded at the Long Beach Airport, with three birds on 25 August 2013 and three birds on 31 August 2017.

PURPLE MARTIN
Progne subis

STATUS: Casual spring and summer vagrant. Rare breeder.

This large swallow breeds throughout the eastern United States and southeastern Canada, as well as large areas of the Canadian Prairie provinces. It is absent from much of the western United States, but does breed locally in all states except for Nevada and Montana. It also breeds locally in Mexico. On the Pacific coast, it breeds from Baja California and parts of southern California north to southwestern British Columbia. It also breeds in areas of mainland Mexico. The species winters in South America.

In British Columbia, this colony nester breeds on the Sunshine Coast, in the Fraser Lowlands and on southeastern Vancouver Island, including the Canadian Gulf Islands. The population has fluctuated considerably over the years, reaching a low point of only 5 breeding pairs on Vancouver Island in 1985. A nest box program was begun in the Salish Sea basin in 1986, resulting in an increase to 200 pairs by 2002, 650 pairs in 2007, and 950 pairs in 2013. In 2015, a total of 1,100 pairs successfully raised 4,000 young.[282]

In our west coast region, this bird is rarely seen. *Birds of Pacific Rim National Park* did not list the species at all in 1978, but today we have nine records for the central west coast and a nesting record from Bamfield in 2014 (BCNRS). Our earliest sighting dates from 11 July 1979, when a bird was seen perched on hydro wires at the Crab Dock in Tofino.[263] No others were found for the next 23 years until 15 May 2002, when a second bird was observed in Tofino by George Bradd. On 7 June 2009, an adult female was seen at the Long Beach Airport, for a third record.

From this point on, several birds were recorded in fairly rapid succession. On 3 July 2011, a bird was found at the Botanical Gardens in Tofino by John Reynolds, and on 20 August 2012, two birds were seen at Tonquin Park, Tofino, by David La Puma and Michael Lanzone. Two years later, on 2 July 2014, I observed two birds flying above the floatplane pond at the Long Beach Airport, and photographed one of them. In 2015, a female was seen on 28 April, a second female on 5 June, and a third on 28 June, all at the airport. This increase in sightings on the west coast is undoubtedly a direct result of the expanding population in the Salish Sea basin. In June 2014, the first nesting on the west coast was recorded at Bamfield (BCNRS).

TREE SWALLOW
Tachycineta bicolor

STATUS: Uncommon to locally fairly common spring migrant and summer visitor. Breeds.

Swallows can be divided into three groups: mud nesters, burrow nesters, and cavity nesters. The Tree Swallow is a cavity nester. It breeds throughout North America from Atlantic to Pacific, with the exception of the far northern reaches of Canada and Alaska, and the southern United States. In the east, it winters from coastal Maryland south to the Gulf of Mexico, and in the west from southern California to northern South America.

In British Columbia, Tree Swallows breed in suitable habitat throughout the province, usually near water. It is a common to abundant migrant in many regions, including the south coast, where birds arrive as early as the second week of February. As with other swallows, this species arrives much later in our west coast region. Since 1997, all the earliest spring arrival dates but one are from 20 April or later. In 2002, a bird arrived on 19 April. There was a very early record of several birds at Kennedy Lake on 6 April 1969. An even earlier sighting, also at Kennedy Lake, occurred on 17 March in 1981.[263] Most records in our region involve from 1 to 10 birds. A single exception occurred on 22 April 2012, when 50 birds were seen at the Long Beach Airport. Further north, 15 birds, probably spring migrants, were foraging together at Hansen Lagoon in Cape Scott Park on 16 May 1974.[4] Only rarely does the Tree Swallow visit offshore islands (such as Triangle Island), where the Violet-green Swallow is the more common species (BCFWS).

Evidence for nesting on the west coast of Vancouver Island remained rather sparse for many years. The first nesting was recorded on 9 June 1960, when six eggs were found in a nest box by lighthouse keepers at Estevan Point, about 53 km northwest of Tofino. The nest had two nestlings on 14 July (BCNRS). On 5 August 1973, a bird was seen entering and leaving a hole in a dead tree at Bedwell River.[1] On 7 June 1979, a nest box at Bamfield contained five eggs (BCNRS). Another strong suggestion of nesting was recorded at the Long Beach Airport in 2013, when at least one bird was present from 3 May to 4 July, and two birds, a male and female, were seen on 23 and 24 May, with one bird entering a hole in a building. On 12 June, at least three birds were seen feeding nearby, with one believed to be a young bird. In 2009, two birds were also recorded at the airport as late as 4 July. On 8 June 2014, a male Tree Swallow was seen inhabiting a snag on the lower Kennedy River, very close to a potential nesting cavity.

Swan Lake, near the Tofino/Ucluelet junction, is another location where birds have been seen during the month of June. And in the Kennedy River drainage and lowlands there are several small lakes with potential as breeding sites, particularly Spire Lake, which has hundreds of standing dead snags in the water. In the spring of 2016, when three nesting boxes designed for Purple Martins were placed on columns supporting the bridge over the lower Kennedy River, they were immediately occupied by Tree Swallows. Further downriver, a pair even took up residence in a large nesting box built for Wood Ducks. A year later, when I erected a swallow box on the same bridge, it was already occupied by a pair of Tree Swallows by the following morning, suggesting that this species' numbers are limited largely by the availability of nest sites.

There is no noticeable fall movement in our region, and by mid to late July most summer birds are gone. I know of only one August record in recent years, although Hatler et al. listed four.[1] On 11 August 2013, a bird was seen in Ucluelet. There is one record later than that: on 12 September in 1983, four birds were seen at Chesterman Beach. These were likely migrants from points north passing through.

Tree Swallows are reported to feed on bayberries in their winter range in the southern United States, a custom unknown in any other swallow. The species, California wax-myrtle or Pacific bayberry (*Myrica californica*), is also very prevalent on the central west coast, from Ucluelet to Tofino, though no such activity has been observed here.

VIOLET-GREEN SWALLOW
Tachycineta thalassina

STATUS: A fairly common spring migrant and summer visitor. Breeds.

The breeding range of this exquisite little swallow is restricted to western North America, from central Mexico to central and western Alaska. In Canada, it breeds from southwestern Alberta west to the coast and north to the Yukon. It winters from coastal northern California south to northern Nicaragua. In British Columbia, it breeds in many regions of the province, from the south to the extreme north, but particularly in the southern half of the interior and the south coast. There are only a handful of nonbreeding records from Haida Gwaii.

Birds begin arriving in our region in early April, although the earliest birds may arrive in late March. Some early dates are 3 March 1991 (one at Carmanah Point),[263] 20 March 1974, 31 March 1987, 28 March 1996, 16 March 2011, 27 March 2012, and 29 March 2015. Poor weather can delay arrivals considerably. In 2013, no birds were seen until 23 April. Small numbers are frequently seen foraging over seabird colonies in spring. Up to four birds were present on Cleland Island from 12 May to 18 June 1970 (BCFWS).

This swallow is a cavity and crevice nester that in our west coast region nests mostly in buildings and in nest boxes from at least Jordan River north to Estevan Point (BCNRS). Hatler et al., however, mention a single nest found in a dead tree near Lost Shoe Creek on 4 May 1972.[1] On 8 June 2013, five birds were seen

Originally a tree-cavity nester, the Violet-green Swallow is most often seen in villages, having adapted to nesting in buildings.

on the lower Kennedy River. With no buildings in the neighbourhood, it is likely that birds in this area also nest in tree cavities. Likewise, on 16 June 2014, a bird was seen near Spire Lake in the upper Kennedy River, many miles from any buildings. The species was also suspected of nesting in rock crevices on Solander Island. On the central west coast, the species is seen most often in the villages of Tofino and Ucluelet, the airport at Long Beach, and Swan Lake, near the junction of Highway 4.

Once the young are out of the nest, they do not linger long. Records suggest that local birds depart in July, with a few lingering into August in some years. On 3 August 2010, a single bird was seen at Swan Lake and on 10 August 2011, 4 birds were still at the airport. On 18 August 1981, 5 birds were flying near a ridge near Cape Cook on Brooks Peninsula.[13] In both 2013 and 2014, the last bird of the season was recorded on 20 August. An interesting sighting occurred at the Long Beach Airport on 1 August 2010, when a remarkable 45 birds were counted. These were likely migrants passing through on their way south. The single record for the month of September occurred on 4 September 2012, when 3 birds were seen at the airport.

Because modern buildings offer fewer nesting opportunities for these swallows, those who value these attractive birds should consider building a nest box or two and attaching them to their house or outbuilding. All that's required is an unobstructed path in front of the box and a large open area. You'll have fewer mosquitos as well as the company of two very attractive birds.

BANK SWALLOW
Riparia riparia

STATUS: Casual vagrant in spring, summer, and fall. Accidental in winter.

Like the Northern Rough-winged Swallow, the Bank Swallow is a burrow nester, nesting in clay or earthen banks. However, whereas the former species usually nests as solitary pairs, the Bank Swallow nests in colonies. Its breeding range in Canada is much more extensive than that of the Northern Rough-winged Swallow, with birds breeding throughout much of the country except for the northern tundra. In British Columbia, it breeds throughout the province east of the Coast Mountains, though it is sparsely distributed in the north. It still breeds in the Fraser Valley (BCNRS) and has bred in Garibaldi Provincial Park, and is considered a rare migrant and summer visitor on the southeast side of Vancouver Island.[263]

The Bank Swallow was not recorded on the west coast of Vancouver Island until 11 September 1982, when I observed a bird at the mouth of Sandhill Creek, Long Beach.[263] No other birds were seen until the very unlikely date of 21 January 2004, when two birds were recorded on the west coast on the same day. One was seen at Carmanah Point lighthouse by Jerry Etzkorn, and the other, possibly the same bird, was seen at Chesterman Beach, Tofino. The Bank Swallow is a very rare vagrant on our west coast even in summer, so observing one in January is highly anomalous. However, 2004 was a year when swallows were also being reported in January at other locations on the south coast of British Columbia.

Since 2004, Bank Swallows have been recorded at the Long Beach Airport on 4 occasions. Three birds were seen on 9 July 2009, and single birds on 25 May 2014 and 7 August and 5 September 2017. A single bird was also recorded along the lower Kennedy River on 4 August 2016 by Ian Cruickshank. With 4 of the 8 occurrences recorded in the months of August and September, it appears that the species is most likely to occur during the southward migration.

BARN SWALLOW
Hirundo rustica

STATUS: Fairly common in spring and summer. Accidental in winter. Breeds.

Barn Swallows have become dependent on human dwellings, where they build clay nests under the eaves.

This swallow has an enormous breeding range. It is found across most of Eurasia, except for India, Southeast Asia, and the far north. It also breeds throughout most of North America except for the tundra regions. Eurasian and American birds differ slightly in appearance. The former are white-breasted and have a solid breast band, whereas adults of the latter have a tan wash and the breast band is incomplete. A Eurasian bird was recorded on a ship 150 km off Tasu Sound, Haida Gwaii, on 15 July 1960, and could occur again.[283] North American Barn Swallows winter from central Mexico south throughout Central and South America to Tierra del Fuego. They breed in suitable habitat throughout British Columbia. On the central and northern mainland coast, the species is sparsely distributed due to lack of buildings, but regularly frequents lighthouses.

On the central west coast, in the vicinity of Tofino, the first birds usually arrive in late April or the first week of May, much later than on southeastern Vancouver Island. There are five records for April, with the earliest two arrivals recorded on the 13th of the month in 1980 and 2014. The second earliest date is 17 April 2010. Most birds do not arrive until May. Observations by a number of observers at Jordan River in the spring of 2014 give a good indication of the sequence of arrival in the south of our region. Those records are as follows: 9 April – 2 birds; 13 April – 4; 26 April – 12; 4 May – 15; and 18 May – 30.[26]

Barn Swallows build open mud nests, thus nests are nearly always found using the shelter provided by a building, whether inside or under an overhang. Only rarely do they nest in natural situations such as caves, cliffs, or tree cavities. On the west coast, favourite nesting sites are located at all of the existing villages, where birds are sometimes known to nest under docks as well as in or on buildings. Another favourite location is the Long Beach Airport, where birds are attracted to the wide open spaces as well as the long floatplane pond, over which they frequently feed. There they nest in and around the hangar. In the 1970s, a favourite location was Stubbs Island, until the building they nested in was taken down. D.F. Hatler recorded the species several times in the Broken Group in Barkley Sound, with one nesting record.[1] On 23 June 1970, he observed 5 young-of-the-year on Cooper Island. He did not say whether or not these young were raised in a natural situation such as a tree nest cavity, but presumably the nests were on a building. Much more recently, David Pugh recorded 10 birds in Barkley Sound on 7 July 2012, though no exact location was given. Small numbers also nest on docks and buildings in Bamfield, and frequently on lighthouses, resorts, and floathouses along the outer coast (BCNRS). Barn Swallows frequently forage in spring and summer on offshore seabird islands and have attempted nesting on research cabins (BCFWS).

Barn Swallows are known to sometimes raise two broods, although whether they do so on the west coast with its more challenging climate is unknown. Judging by their early departures in recent years, this is unlikely. Records show that birds now depart the west coast for their winter home two to three weeks earlier than in the past. In 1980, 7 birds were recorded at Tofino on 26 September, and in 1987, 9 birds were seen on 23 September. The following year, 18 birds were counted on 19 September. The latest that migrants were ever recorded on the west coast was on 5 October in 1974, when two birds were seen at Port Renfrew.

Contrast those records with ones from the past six years of intensive surveys on the central west coast, when birds have been recorded in September on only three occasions, one occurring on 6 September 2017, when 7 birds were seen. Indeed, in 2011, birds were not seen after 10 August, with one exception, when two birds were recorded over Ucluelet Inlet on 18 September. In

2010, the last birds were seen on 3 August, in spite of the fact that regular counts were made in their preferred areas. A series of counts conducted at Jordan River by Cathy Carlson in 2014 demonstrates the build-up and decline of birds in late summer in the south of our region. They are as follows: 2 August – 20 birds; 8 August – 30; 15 August – 50; 4 September – 40; and 9 September – 16. Birds seen at Jordan River are likely from further north, although this has not been proven.

Swallows do not normally occur anywhere in Canada in winter, but, in a highly anomalous event, a Barn Swallow was observed at Long Beach on 23 January 2009, at a time when it should still have been in the tropics. Swallows were also being seen in the Victoria area during the same period. Presumably, unusually favourable weather triggered in these birds an impulse to migrate early, an impulse that almost certainly would have proven fatal unless the birds reversed direction, for a swallow is not likely to survive for long on the west coast in winter.

CLIFF SWALLOW
Petrochelidon pyrrhonota

STATUS: Casual migrant in spring and fall. Rare breeder.

Like the Barn Swallow, the Cliff Swallow builds a mud nest, though it is a more elaborate structure encased in a gourd. The species has a wide distribution in North America, breeding throughout much of the continent except for the southeastern United States, desert areas of California and Arizona, and the northern regions of Canada. It winters from Panama to northern Argentina. In British Columbia, Cliff Swallows breed in most areas of the province east of the Coast Mountains. On the coast, they normally breed only in the Salish Sea basin but are absent as a breeder on Haida Gwaii (BCNRS). There is, however, one nesting record for Port Hardy.

While the Cliff Swallow is a fairly common migrant and summer visitor to southeastern Vancouver Island, it is an infrequent visitor to our region. The earliest record for the west coast occurred on 2 May 1966, with the location listed as Clayoquot Sound. *Birds of Pacific Rim National Park* listed 4 additional records up to 1971.[1] There were no further reports until 12 September 1984, when a bird was observed near Tofino. Since then there have been 19 additional sightings, all of them after 2008 and involving from one to four birds. This increase in sightings may be the result of more time in the field and more reporting, rather than an increase in occurrence.

One of the records involved a pair of birds that built a nest under the eaves of a building at the Long Beach Airport in June 2009. The nest was abandoned on or about 9 June, after which the birds were no longer seen. It is suspected that nesting failed because this species cannot cope with the somewhat harsher weather conditions of the west coast. Strong winds are fairly common, as are fog and lower temperatures. Additionally, there is a lot of foraging competition from four other swallow species at the airport. Conditions may be somewhat better at Bamfield, where Ian Cruickshank found three pairs nesting on 3 June 2017. If fledged young result, it would be the first successful nesting recorded in the west coast region. Records of birds seen by John Reynolds in the Bamfield area in 2008 and 2015 suggest that birds may have nested there previously.

Most of our records have been in the months of May and June, with additional records in August and September. There is also one record in early July. Spring dates range from 29 April to 10 June. Late summer dates range from 1 August to 12 September and very likely represent southbound birds. Sightings have been made from Jordan River to Holberg and many points between, though most reports are from the central west coast.

Chickadees Family Paridae

CHESTNUT-BACKED CHICKADEE
Poecile rufescens

STATUS: Fairly common resident. Breeds.

This chickadee is restricted to western North America. It breeds from the Sierra Nevada and coastal redwood forests of California north to British Columbia, southeast Alaska and Prince William Sound. It also breeds in northern Idaho, western Montana, and southeastern British Columbia. In our province, the species is largely restricted to the coast and Coast Mountains, including the Fraser Valley, as well as east along southern portions of the province to the West Kootenays to Creston.[263] It occurs sporadically outside these regions.

This is the only chickadee that occurs on Vancouver Island. During the nonbreeding seasons, it is found from sea level to 2,200 m elevation,[263] and often travels with Golden-crowned Kinglets or even migrating warblers. In our west coast region, it has been seen in all months of the year at numerous

The Chestnut-backed Chickadee is the only member of its family found in Vancouver Island's forests.

locations and is believed to breed throughout the region up to 1,350 m elevation. On 28 June 1969, an adult was seen feeding young at Green Point, and on 20 June 1978, a pair was observed feeding young at the south end of Long Beach.[1]

Chestnut-backed Chickadees are cavity nesters. They will excavate their own cavities when the wood is soft enough, but will also use natural cavities or those excavated by others, as well as nest boxes. The time window in which this species breeds and rears its young appears to begin in mid-April and continues to early July. On 19 May 2008, two adults with four young were observed at a feeder in Tofino, and on 11 May 1999, an adult was seen feeding two newly fledged young at the Long Beach Airport. In 2003, four 4 newly fledged young were seen at Tofino as late as 8 July.

In fall and winter, these birds travel in family groups and often in larger flocks, which explains why they can be hard to find at this time of year. On 11 February 2013, a flock of 15 was recorded on Stubbs Island, Tofino. The two largest counts were made on 23 August 1972 (a flock of 39 birds near the San Juan River)[1] and 1 February 2015 (38 birds in a flock at Long Beach).

Although there are 155 records in total, that number is low in proportion to the actual number of sightings, for, as Hatler et al. pointed out, "most observers take this tiny bundle of energy for granted" and don't bother recording it.[1] *Birds of Pacific Rim National Park* listed it as common.[1] Although this small bird is far from conspicuous and can sometimes be hard to find, it should probably be considered a fairly common resident. Further north, on Brooks Peninsula, the species has also been recorded in all months, mostly along forest edges of beaches.[13]

Long-tailed Tits   Family Aegithalidae

BUSHTIT
Psaltriparus minimus

STATUS: Casual visitor in summer, fall, and early winter.

Bushtits are highly gregarious, and are almost always seen travelling in a flock. The Bushtit is largely a southern bird that has extended its range northward and arrived on southern Vancouver Island from the Lower Mainland only in the 1940s.[284] It breeds from Central America through Mexico, to the southwestern United States, north through Oregon and western Washington, and into southwestern British Columbia. In this province, it is a year-round resident in the lower Fraser Valley and southeastern Vancouver Island, and is considered common.

On the west coast of Vancouver Island, the situation is much different. Here the bird is outside its normal range and is rarely seen. The first sighting in our region occurred at Sarita River on 5 August 1965, when a "family group" was seen.[1] To date, we have 17 additional records, not including Jordan River. August has 7 records, followed by June with 3. July and December have 2 records each, and March, September, October, and November have 1 each. All records thus far are from the southern half of our region and no birds have been recorded north of Tofino.

It is curious that between 1988 and 2007, there is a 19-year span with no records whatsoever. It is also noteworthy that before 2008, no year had more than one record. In that year, however, there were two records, and by 2015, there were four sightings in a single year, raising the possibility that the Bushtit is currently in an expansionist phase. Time will tell whether the west coast climate and vegetation can adequately support this species.

Bushtits have been seen most often at Jordan River. Given the close proximity to Victoria, where it is common, this is not surprising. There were two records at Jordan River during the 1980s, with no further sightings until 13 December 2010, when a dozen birds were seen. There were three records in 2013, and another three in 2014.

Nuthatches   Family Sittidae

RED-BREASTED NUTHATCH
Sitta canadensis

STATUS: Uncommon to rare fall migrant and summer visitor. Casual in spring and winter.

This small nuthatch occurs either as a resident or seasonally in nearly all regions of North America north of the Rio Grande. Its breeding range includes most forested areas of Canada, much of the American West, and the northeastern United States. In British Columbia, it breeds throughout much of the southern two-thirds of the province east of the Coast Mountains. It is most common in the southern interior, however. In the coast region, it breeds in the Fraser Valley, the Sunshine Coast, and southeastern Vancouver Island, where it is considered uncommon to locally fairly common.[263]

In our west coast region, this species is much harder to find. *Birds of Pacific Rim National Park* listed 28 records and called it an "uncommon and irregular resident."[1] On Brooks Peninsula, the Red-breasted Nuthatch is "present in most months but recorded at irregular intervals,"[13] and there is a record of a bird at the San Jose River, Cape Scott Park, on 25 May 1974.[4] Searching personal files dating back to 1982, I found a mere 12 records for this species. An additional 48 records were found on eBird. Because this program is of fairly recent origin, most of those observations date from the last 10 years. With 61 records since 1982, a clearer picture of this bird's status can be formed. Breaking them down by month, we have 1 record for February, 2 for March, 3 for April, 2 for May, 11 for June, 4 for July, 11 for August, 11 for September, 9 for October, and 4 for November. There are only 3 records for December.

Note that most birds are recorded in late summer and fall, with 34 observations from August to November. It is significant that the largest number ever recorded, 17 birds, were seen in the extreme south of our region at Jordan River. The date was 2 September 2013. The next highest number, 13 birds, was recorded on 6 September 2017, near Grice Bay.

The relatively high number of birds recorded during the month of June, with a few in July, is a good indication that birds breed in our region, albeit sparsely. There are June records from the north shore of Barkley Sound, from Ucluelet, Long Beach, the Gold River area, Oktwanch River, Brooks Peninsula, Holberg Inlet, and Harris Creek, north of the San Juan River.

While spring records are rare, from 15 March to 8 April 1987, an individual was repeatedly heard at about 300 m elevation in original old-growth forest on

Meares Island. A bird was also seen along the Rainforest Trail near Long Beach on 7 February 2011. This was also in original old-growth forest. Whether these individuals were overwintering birds or migrants is unknown.

Despite a good many forays into wilderness areas in the 1980s and 1990s, I rarely encountered this species. There are, however, two records for June and two for July prior to 1974, including an observation of an adult seen entering a hole in a spruce snag near Long Beach on 13 June 1969.[1] This bird was believed to be feeding its young. Other summer records were from Stubbs Island near Tofino on 8 July 1960, and from Turtle Island and Chalk Island in Barkley Sound on 4 June 1973 and 10 July 1973, respectively.

Creepers   Family Certhiidae

BROWN CREEPER
Certhia americana

STATUS: Uncommon from May to December. Rare from January to April. Breeds.

Brown Creepers hunt for insects in the bark of trees. Unlike nuthatches, which climb headfirst down the trunk, this bird starts low and spirals upward. This species is the only member of its family – the Tree Creepers, or Certhiidae – in North America. This family is not to be confused with the Woodcreepers (Dendrocolaptidae) of tropical regions of Mexico and Central and South America.

Brown Creepers breed in forested regions throughout southern Canada, from Atlantic to Pacific, and in the northeastern United States and forested lands in much of the western United States. They also breed at high elevation in Mexico and northern Central America. In British Columbia, they breed throughout all but the most northern parts of the province. On the coast, they breed to Haida Gwaii and southeast Alaska, north and west to Anchorage.

Brown Creepers are very inconspicuous inhabitants of our west coast forests and tend to feed in the deep woods. They are therefore easily overlooked. Not only are these birds small, with brown upper parts that blend in with the colouration of tree bark, but their calls are thin and need good ears to be heard. It is notable that birders with acute hearing find birds much more often than those with less sensitive ears. In a two-week period in the second half of May 2016, Ian Cruickshank found birds in at least eight locations on the central west coast, suggesting that the species is considerably more common than records indicate. At Combers, Long Beach, he also saw fledglings on 29 May.

To date, we have 58 records in total, 54 of which were seen or heard from May to December. This suggests that most birds move out in winter and return in spring. However, given that observers spend much less time in the field from January to April, it is possible that the species is overlooked during those months. Campbell and Summers suggest that the Brown Creeper is probably a resident in the vicinity of Brooks Peninsula.[13] The species was also present in mixed coniferous forests at Guise Bay, Cape Scott, on 18 and 19 May 1974.[4] Richardson had sightings at Grant Bay in January 1969,[16] and a bird was found near Tofino when a deliberate search was made on 6 March 2015. Nevertheless, birds are not often found from January to April.

Breeding records are few, but breeding has been reported at three other locations by the online *Atlas of Breeding Birds of British Columbia* without specific details. Those locations are the Winter Harbour area, Ucluelet, and along the West Coast Trail. An adult with fledged young was also seen on Vargas Island, but the date was not recorded.

Although this species can potentially be found in almost any forest environment, two of the more favourable locations for searching for them on the central west coast are the trail that leads to Maltby Slough (yellow gate) near Cox Bay, and the trail behind the interpretive centre at the south end of Long Beach.

Wrens *Family Troglodytidae*

HOUSE WREN
Troglodytes aedon
STATUS: Casual in late summer.

This species breeds throughout most of the United States, with the exception of some of the most southerly regions. In Canada, it breeds from southern New Brunswick, southern Quebec, and southern and southwestern Ontario through the Great Plains region to British Columbia, where it breeds in the Peace River region, the southern interior, the Fraser Valley, and the Salish Sea basin. It is considered an uncommon migrant and summer visitor on southeastern Vancouver Island.[263] The species winters in the southern United States and Mexico.

On Vancouver Island's west coast, we had no records until 20 August 1987, when I was surprised to encounter a member of this species on the island's east-west divide at 1,500 m (4,920 ft) elevation, among the krummholz conifers in the subalpine zone of Big Interior Mountain, west of Della Lake. It remained our only record until 6 September 2000, when a second House Wren was found in dense scrub separating the Long Beach Airport from the golf course.

PACIFIC WREN
Troglodytes pacificus

STATUS: Common resident in spring, summer, and fall. Uncommon to rare in winter. Breeds.

The Pacific Wren may be small, but in spring and early summer its exuberant vocalizations announce its presence to the world.

The Pacific Wren breeds from the Sierra Nevada and coastal California north through Oregon, Washington, and British Columbia, north and west through coastal Alaska to the Aleutian Islands. It is found east to western Alberta and western Montana. In British Columbia, it breeds throughout the southern half of the province and the Coast Mountains, and along the entire coast.

The Pacific Wren was known as the Winter Wren until studies showed that eastern and western birds were reproductively isolated in areas where they overlapped. In other words, the two forms did not interbreed, indicating that they were separate species. Interestingly, if estimates based on genetic studies are correct, divergence between the eastern and western forms occurred as long as 4.3 million years ago.[285] Who could have guessed that two species so similar in appearance could be so far removed from each other?

On the west coast of Vancouver Island, this small brown bird is known to many residents only through its emphatic, effervescent song, because to say that this bird is visually inconspicuous is an understatement. But walk into almost any wooded area in spring, especially woods with old-growth characteristics, and it won't be long before this little wren's song will be heard – a vigorous jumble of notes and syllables, sometimes uttered nonstop for up to a minute or more. The singing usually begins in March and continues through May and June. In 2015, one very enthusiastic male was heard singing on a sunny day in late January. The male is reported to build several nests in its territory but leaves the lining of the nest, the interior decorating, to the female, as would any sensible male. Most nests are built in cavities, though Pacific Wrens also build globular nests that may be tucked among moss or inside hollow western redcedars. Nests are composed of "mosses, twigs, grasses, leaves, feathers, hair, plant fibres, rootlets, needles, shreds of rotten wood and similar soft debris." The wrens may also nest in large old stumps in second-growth forest and in clumps of mosses hanging from the outer branches of conifers. That nesting begins early has been shown by the emergence of fledged young before the end of May. Recently fledged young may also be found in August. On Brooks Peninsula, R.W. Campbell recorded 23 fledged young, all with natal down and yellow gapes, along the edge of a mixed coniferous forest from 5 to 15 August 1981.[13] The Pacific Wren is a regular breeding species on many offshore islands with dense vegetation. For example, the species has been recorded on Cleland Island from 11 May to 2 September, and a nest with young was found on 2 June 1969 (BCNRS).

Pacific Wrens have been seen (and heard singing) in all months of the year, although the highest numbers are observed in fall, early winter, and early spring, suggesting a migratory movement. It is interesting to note that most of the largest counts have been made in the extreme south of our region, as well as in the north. At Jordan River, 18 birds were counted on 19 December 2010 and 21 December 2012. On 11 November 2013, 17 birds were tallied at Mystic Beach. The largest fall number was recorded on 13 October 2012 at Esperanza, when 30 birds were counted. Further evidence that part of the population migrates is that on the central west coast, birds tend to become very scarce in January, February, and March. Among 114 records in my personal files, January sightings were recorded only in 2010, 2013, and 2015, and February records only in 2013 and 2015. We see a similar pattern in *Birds of Pacific Rim National Park*. It should be kept in mind, of course, that these small birds become very inconspicuous when not singing.

Numbers begin to rebound in spring. On 19 March 2013, 15 birds were recorded at Jordan River. The largest spring count made anywhere in our region was at Cape Scott, with 35 birds recorded on 26 April 2008.[26] These may have been transients on their way to Alaska.

The Pacific Wren resides largely in the understorey, close to the forest floor, making it particularly vulnerable to predation by house cats, both domestic and feral. The threat exists in and near villages, as well as in Pacific Rim National Park, where it is not uncommon for visitors to lose their pets while on holiday.

MARSH WREN
Cistothorus palustris

STATUS: Uncommon fall transient and winter visitor. Rare in spring.

During the breeding season, the Marsh Wren is an inhabitant of wetlands, from the New England states and Canadian Maritime provinces westward through the northern states and the Prairie provinces to British Columbia and much of the American West. The species winters largely in the southern United States and Mexico, but also along the Pacific coast, north to southern British Columbia, where it breeds in wetlands in the Columbia Valley north to Golden, the Creston Valley, the southern interior north to Vanderhoof, the Peace River region, and locally in the far northeast corner of the province. On the coast, it breeds in the Fraser Valley and on southeastern and central Vancouver Island, where it is considered a fairly common year-round resident.[263]

In our west coast region, the Marsh Wren is considerably less common and occurs as a fall transient and overwintering bird. *Birds of Pacific Rim National Park* listed only a single record.[1] The years since 1978 have brought an additional 66 sighting in 19 separate years, however. It is highly likely that Marsh Wrens can be found each and every winter when looked for. Ten of our sightings occurred in 2011, although these may have involved only two or three individuals. Records suggest they usually begin arriving in late August and depart in March or early April. The earliest fall dates were 1 September in 2004 at the

Long Beach Airport, 23 August in 2016 at Long Beach, and 28 August in 2016, with three birds at the airport.

Just when birds depart in spring is somewhat uncertain as we have few spring records. There is a spring date of 30 March 2011 at the Long Beach Airport, and an even later date at Bamfield, where a bird was recorded on 15 May 2008. There is not a single confirmed record for June or July, no doubt due to a lack of appropriate habitat such as marshes with cattails, which are rare on the west coast.

In winter, Marsh Wrens inhabit intertidal meadows such as those found at the head of Grice Bay, where they are found in tall sedge. They are also found in tall sedge with standing fresh water far from the marine environment, usually with dense shrubbery nearby. Besides Grice Bay, birds have been found at Stubbs Island, Jensen's Bay, and the Long Beach Airport. Once Marsh Wrens are found at a given location, they can usually be found there year after year. The largest number recorded at a single location was four birds at Jensen's Bay on 18 November 1982, five at the airport on 6 December 2016, and seven at the Grice Bay tidal meadows on 12 January 1979. Most sightings involve single birds.

BEWICK'S WREN
Thryomanes bewickii

STATUS: Casual fall vagrant. A regular fall migrant only at Jordan River.

This wren is a year-round resident in much of Mexico and the southwestern United States, from Texas, Arkansas, and Missouri west to California and western parts of Oregon and Washington, north to southwestern British Columbia, where it breeds throughout the Fraser Lowlands and the Sunshine Coast, and on the southeast side of Vancouver Island, where it is considered a fairly common resident.

In most of the west coast region, this bird is rarely encountered. Only at the extreme southern end of the region, at Jordan River, does it occur regularly. The first sighting for the west coast involved a bird seen at Port Renfrew on 5 October 1974. A second sighting occurred on 26 October 1986 at the Long Beach parking lot near Lovekin Rock. There is also a record from the northern half of our region, a bird seen at Esperanza Inlet on 14 October 2012.[26]

At Jordan River, there have been 14 occurrences in the past four years alone. Earlier sightings very likely occurred, but records are not readily available. The oldest record I could find is of a single bird recorded there on 30 November 1986. All subsequent records are also from the autumn period. The earliest date was 1 September in 2013, the latest on 21 December in 2012. Most records involved single birds, but two sightings involved two birds, and two involved four birds. Four birds were recorded on 8 September 2012 and 1 September 2014.

Dippers   *Family Cinclidae*

AMERICAN DIPPER
Cinclus mexicanus

STATUS: A widespread, fairly common resident along mountain streams. Breeds.

The American Dipper is an inhabitant of rivers and fast-moving mountain streams, where it has adapted to feeding underwater.

The American Dipper is unique in that it is North America's only aquatic songbird. It typically lives along fast-moving mountain streams, though occasionally it may be found on lakes. It feeds almost entirely on food found beneath the water's surface, and it does this by swimming underwater. Its diet is reported to consist largely of aquatic insects and their larvae, as well as small crayfish, salmon fry, and salmon eggs in season.

It is a breeding resident from British Columbia and western Alberta north to the Yukon and Alaska, and south through mountainous areas of the western United States, Mexico, and Central America. Throughout much of its range, it is a year-round resident, although in northern areas it is believed to be migratory to some extent.

In the west coast region, the American Dipper has been seen in numerous locations, including streams along the West Coast Trail, Juan de Fuca Trail, Kennedy River, Toquart Bay, Ursus Creek, Bulson Creek, Clayoquot River, Megin Lake, Clayoquot Plateau, Burman River, Sarita River, Little Nitinat River, Nasparti River, and Klaskish River. In addition, on 27 July 1987, a bird was observed on a small lake at 1,024 m (3,360 ft) on Mount Klitsa. Occasionally there are anomalous sightings at locations well away from fast-running streams, such as at Sandhill Creek, Long Beach, on 10 October 1982, and on a small beach at Felice Island, Tofino. A bird was even reported feeding on a reef 50 m from shore, southeast of Carmanah Point, by assistant lighthouse keeper Jerry Etzkorn. There are few records from the northwest of our region, though this is presumed to be due to an absence of observers rather than of birds. There is a record from Holberg, and breeding was confirmed on the Klaskish River, on 16 May 1978, when three nestlings were observed.[263]

Reliable and accessible locations for finding this bird on the central west coast are the Kennedy River (above the lake) and the Thornton Creek Fish Hatchery on Ucluelet Inlet in September and October. South of Port Renfrew, birds are often found at Loss Creek.

Kinglets *Family Regulidae*

GOLDEN-CROWNED KINGLET
Regulus satrapa

STATUS: Fairly common in summer and fall, rare to uncommon in winter and spring. Breeds.

With a length of 4 in and weighing only 6 g, this is one of the smallest birds in Canada. Only hummingbirds and bushtits weigh less. Its vocalizations are as thin as the bird is small, and observers need good ears to pick them up at a distance. This bird's preferred habitat is mixed coniferous forests from coast to coast, where it can be found gleaning insect life among the needles and cones. It often travels in the company of Chestnut-backed Chickadees and occasionally with warblers during migration periods.

The diminutive Golden-crowned Kinglet would go mostly unnoticed but for the thin, high notes that reveal its presence.

It breeds from the Maritimes and northern New England west through the boreal forest region to British Columbia, southern Yukon, and Alaska. It also breeds in forested regions of much of the western United States. The species winters from the Maritimes south throughout almost all of the United States except for North Dakota, eastern Montana, and Florida. In British Columbia, it breeds throughout the province (BCNRS). It winters in the southern interior and on the coast. In Alaska, it winters north to Cook Inlet.

In the BC interior, northern birds are reported to move south, but those in the south and on the coast may be year-round residents. At least that is the conventional wisdom, as there are records for every month. In our west coast region, most of the records are from summer and fall. Records from March and April are few and usually involve from 1 to 6 birds. Exceptions were 15 birds on 16 March 2009 at Bamfield, and 9 birds on 3 April 2001 at Cox Bay. Records from the months of May and June, which is presumably the breeding period, are even fewer, though 4 birds were seen at Guise Bay, Cape Scott, on 19 May 1974.[4]

Birds of Pacific Rim National Park lists breeding evidence as follows: 3 June 1973, juvenile female collected in Tofino (CVMUBC 8478); early June 1969, adult female feeding three young, Long Beach; 20 June 1972, two adults with two young, south end of Long Beach; and 20 July 1972, 10 to 12, including several immature birds, at Nettle Island. The latest breeding evidence is from 11 August in 2015, when an adult was observed feeding a newly fledged young. Additional records include two recently fledged young being fed by 2 adults at Bamfield on 21 June 1967; 1 adult feeding three young out of the nest in Lemmens Inlet on 2 July 1981; and one newly fledged young begging for food from 2 adults in Cape Scott Park on 30 June 1985 (BCNRS).

By early to mid-July Golden-crowned Kinglets gather in small flocks, with 12 birds at Port San Juan on 12 July 2008, 13 birds at Whyac-Nitinat on 15 July 2008, and 10 birds at Clark Island, Barkley Sound, on 17 July 2013. Even larger flocks are seen throughout August and September, and into the fall. On 29 August 2009, 25 birds were recorded at Juan de Fuca Park and on 23 September 2003, 20 birds were found in Pacific Rim National Park. A flock of 20 birds was also recorded near Incinerator Rock, Long Beach, on 3 October 2001. The largest numbers recorded in a single day occurred in the month of December, with 40 birds on 26 December 1982 and 27 birds on 29 December 2001, both in the Tofino area. These last two records were made during a Christmas Bird Count and probably involved several flocks. While those counts were high, the species was recorded on only six occasions during December.

By January, birds are seldom seen or heard, and I could find only 8 records for that month. One of those involved a large number. On 8 January 2011, 24 birds were recorded in Carmanah Valley. Although the evidence is hardly overwhelming, it does suggest there is a migratory movement through our region in fall and that few birds remain into January and February. Of 121 records listed in *Birds of Pacific Rim National Park*, only 6 were from January and 4 from February. Out of 70 records in my personal files, only 1 was from January and 2 from February. This raises the question of where these birds go in winter. Do they fly further south to Washington and Oregon, or do they retreat to the deep woods, where they are seldom seen? Mysteries still remain, and only additional observations will clarify their movements.

RUBY-CROWNED KINGLET
Regulus calendula
STATUS: Fairly common spring and fall migrant, rare in summer and winter. Rare breeder.

Though small and rather drab, the Ruby-crowned Kinglet is not entirely inconspicuous, for it draws attention to itself by its constant, almost frenetic activity as it flits among the branches. Only the Hutton's Vireo is similar in appearance, though it is a slower-moving bird with a thicker bill. This kinglet has a scarlet crown that is often not visible.

Its breeding range stretches across Canada, from the Maritimes to British Columbia, the Yukon, and Alaska. In the United States, it breeds in northern New England, the Great Lakes region, and parts of most of the western states, though not the Midwest. In our province, it breeds throughout the interior east of the Coast Mountains. It has bred on the north coast and may do so occasionally in the south. The species winters from the southeastern United States west to the Pacific Ocean and south to southern Mexico. In the west, it winters north to Washington and southern British Columbia, where it is considered uncommon to common in winter on southeastern Vancouver Island.[263]

In the west coast region, the spring movement begins in March with a few birds trickling in throughout the month. The main movement occurs from late March to late April. On 19 March 2013, 40 birds were seen at Jordan River, and on 21 March 2015, 8 birds were seen at Long Beach and 6 in Tofino. By the beginning of May, the spring movement is all but over. Two birds at Jensen's Bay, Tofino, on 3 May 2008, 4 at Fisherman Bay, Cape Scott, on 16 May 1974,[4] and 2 on Brooks Peninsula on 24 May 1981[13] are unusually late.

Although rare in summer, there are at least 8 records for the month of June. One dates back to 11 June 1972, when two birds were seen near Amphitrite Point. On 25 June 2011, two were also encountered near Bamfield. In addition, there are June records from near Gold River, Brooks Peninsula, the Zeballos River Valley, Nahmint Lake, and several other inland valleys. Given that migrants have largely passed through by the beginning of May, this raises the very real possibility that the species breeds at these locations. Breeding has been suggested near Port Renfrew and Port Alice.

By early to mid-September, birds begin to appear once again. Thanks to diligent observers who transcribe their records to eBird, we know that 16 birds were recorded on the southern edge of our region at Jordan River on 6 September 2013; 21 on 19 October 2013; 18 on 13 November 2010; 18 on 25 November 2012; and 19 on 19 December 2010. There are two early fall records: one on 15 August 1981 at Brooks Peninsula, and one on 27 August 1990 on the Clayoquot Plateau, although the elevation was not recorded.

Birds are usually seen singly or in pairs, though numbers of four or five are not unusual during the peak migration periods of April and October. The largest number seen together on the central west coast was nine at the Long Beach Airport on 12 October 2007.

Thrushes *Family Turdidae*

WESTERN BLUEBIRD
Sialia mexicana

STATUS: Casual fall migrant.

This bird, with its exquisite blue and orange plumage, breeds from southern British Columbia south to California, and east to western Texas and into the Mexican highlands. In British Columbia, it breeds primarily in the southern interior. It formerly bred in the Fraser Valley, and breeding populations have been reintroduced locally on eastern Vancouver Island (BCNRS). Today it is a rare migrant on southeastern Vancouver Island and a rare local summer and winter visitor.

On our west coast, we have three records. On 20 September 1935, a bird was seen at Cape Scott, and less than two weeks later, on 2 October, 12 birds were seen at Sea Otter Cove.[263] There is also one record for the central west coast, as indicated on a map in *The Birds of British Columbia*,[263] though it is not listed in the provincial records summary.

MOUNTAIN BLUEBIRD
Sialia currucoides

STATUS: Casual transient in spring, late fall, and winter.

This species breeds in open country across much of western North America. Contrary to what the name suggests, it is found on the prairies as well as in the mountains. Its breeding range stretches from New Mexico and Arizona north to our western provinces, the Yukon, and Alaska. It winters in the American Southwest, north to central Oregon.

In British Columbia, birds are reported to breed from valley bottoms up to 2,700 m (8,858 ft) elevation.[263] While their centre of abundance is in the Okanagan Valley and interior south-central grasslands, they may be found throughout much of the province east of the Coast Mountains. As a migrant, the Mountain Bluebird is sometimes fairly common in the Lower Mainland and is considered uncommon on southeastern Vancouver Island.[263]

In the west coast region, it is encountered much less frequently. Richardson recorded our first sighting at Grant Bay on 28 April 1969. Since then, there have been 12 additional sightings, 3 of them in 2017. Our records are as follows: mid-December 1971, MacKenzie Beach, Tofino – 1; 23 November 1972, Schooner Cove – 2; 5 January 1976, Long Beach – 1 (BC Photo 511); 27 April 1976, Long Beach – 1; 1 May 1997, Frank Island, Tofino – 1; 25 November 2001, Long Beach Airport – 4; 12 April 2003, Long Beach – 1; 27 December 2013, Long Beach – 1; 22 March 2016, Long Beach Golf Course – 1; 17 April 2017, Long Beach Golf Course – 1; 23 April 2017, Long Beach Airport – 3; and 25 April 2017, Long Beach Golf Course – 1. All our records occurred near sea level. In the interior of British Columbia, there is an annual fall passage at high elevation.

TOWNSEND'S SOLITAIRE
Myadestes townsendi

STATUS: Casual spring and fall migrant. Breeds.

This member of the thrush family is named after the 19th-century naturalist and collector John Kirk Townsend. It is an inhabitant of the western mountains and its breeding range stretches from the Sierra Madre of Mexico and much of the American West to the Alberta Rockies, British Columbia, the western Northwest Territories, the Yukon, and interior Alaska. It winters from southern British Columbia south to Mexico.

In British Columbia, Townsend's Solitaires breed widely in the interior of the province east of the Coast Mountains, especially in the southern half. The species is found most often between 500 and 1,800 m elevation.[263] On several occasions, it has been found breeding on Vancouver Island, and may do so regularly. In the Salish Sea basin, including eastern and southern Vancouver Island, it is considered an uncommon spring migrant.

On our west coast, this bird is seen only rarely in most years. It was not listed at all in *Birds of Pacific Rim National Park* but there are 2 records from before 1978. The oldest record dates back to 11 September 1943, when three birds were seen on the Clayoquot Plateau. The second was a bird seen at Florencia Bay on 5 April 1974. Since then, the species has been recorded on at least 31 additional occasions. It is seen most often in the month of April, with 19 records. We also have 2 records for March, 6 for May, and 2 for June. Two birds were seen on 11 April 1996 and a single bird on 3 May 2008, both of the latter sightings in the Tofino area. Our only fall sighting, aside from the aforementioned 1943 record, occurred on 25 November 1997. There is a single winter record. On 9 and 10

January 2017, a bird was seen and photographed in Tofino by Toby Theriault and her mother, Joanna Streetly. Of the 31 sightings, 8 occurred in the first half of 2017.

Townsend's Solitaires prefer open areas and avoid the deep woods entirely. Transient birds have been seen in Ucluelet, Tofino, Florencia Bay, the Long Beach Golf Course, Jensen's Bay, and the tidal meadows at Grice Bay. Birds have occasionally been encountered in the interior of the island during the summer breeding period. On 9 June 2013, a bird was seen at Oktwanch River, north of Muchalat Lake, and on 6 June 2014, another was seen at Corrigan Creek. It seems very possible that both these birds were on their breeding territory as the species is known to nest on central and southern Vancouver Island (BCNRS). The species has also been recorded on Brooks Peninsula in summer.

SWAINSON'S THRUSH
Catharus ustulatus

STATUS: Common summer visitor, rare fall migrant. Breeds.

If the song of the Hermit Thrush evokes a sense of mystery, the Swainson's Thrush speaks to us of summer, for on the west coast its song, more than any other, is the sound of summer. Walk down any woodland trail or any beach in June and its flutelike chimes spiralling upward are likely to be heard.

This thrush does not belong to the west coast region alone, however. It breeds in almost all forested regions of Canada, from the Maritimes and Labrador westward throughout the boreal forest to British Columbia, the Yukon, and Alaska. In the United States, it breeds from the Canadian border south to northern New Mexico, locally in Arizona, and along the Pacific coast to southern California. The species winters from Mexico to Argentina, although west coast birds winter from Mexico to Costa Rica. In British Columbia, it breeds throughout the province (BCNRS).

Swainson's Thrushes announce their arrival in spring with a single whistled note, which is usually first heard from 15 May to 24 May. In the 13 years in which first arrival dates were recorded on the central west coast, there were only two exceptions. In 2011 a bird was heard at Tofino on the remarkably early date of 5 May, and in 2010 the first bird was not heard until 26 May. Most birds arrive in late May or early June, and shortly after arrival commence

The spiraling flutelike song of the Swainson's Thrush represents the sound of summer to many west coast residents.

singing. On Brooks Peninsula, the species has been recorded from 26 May to 7 August.[13] This is much later than on southern and southeastern Vancouver Island, where birds arrive as early as April and, on rare occasions, in late March.

Swainson's Thrushes have been recorded in June throughout most of the west coast region, from Jordan River to Holberg and Triangle Island, supporting the contention that this is one of the most common breeding birds on the west coast. Despite this, and because of its secretive nature, few nests have been found. According to *Birds of Pacific Rim National Park,* an adult feeding two fledged young was observed at Long Beach on 27 July 1967, and a nest with four eggs was found on Cooper Island, Barkley Sound, on 23 June 1970.[1] Habitat preferences of this thrush are difficult to define, and tend to differ somewhat from that of its close relative the Hermit Thrush. Swainson's Thrushes are more often found in forests with large trees rather than scrub timber, and also tend to be near deciduous growth, particularly near beaches, in valley bottoms, and along water courses.

After the breeding season, birds fall silent, and since they are rather inconspicuous to begin with, this makes it difficult to determine just when they depart for their winter homes. In a 13-year period in which late dates were recorded, the latest dates ranged from 15 July in 2009 to 25 September in 2005.

During the years 2009, 2010, and 2014, no birds were seen or heard after July, despite the fact that surveys were carried out regularly. In the years 1990, 2003, 2004, and 2008, birds were recorded in August but not after. Our latest September dates were 7 September 1986, 9 September 1994, 25 September 2004, 19 September 2012, and 14 September 2014. Whether or not these September birds were late-departing resident birds or migrants from further north passing through is unknown, though I suspect the latter. We have only one report later than September. On 6 October 2013, a single bird was recorded at Jordan River.

HERMIT THRUSH
Catharus guttatus

STATUS: Fairly common in spring, fall, and winter. Uncommon in summer. Breeds.

In summer, the Hermit Thrush is an inconspicuous and seldom seen inhabitant of the forest. Spend some time hiking forest trails, however, and you may be lucky enough to hear its exquisite song, which, if heard well, is unforgettable. Its song is often described as ethereal, with a ventriloquial quality, although you need to be fairly close in order to appreciate the dazzling soliloquy to the full.

This species breeds in the northeastern United States, in much of the western United States, and in forested regions across Canada, from the Atlantic to the Pacific. In British Columbia, it breeds throughout the province, usually at higher elevation. The species winters in the southern United States and southward through Mexico into Guatemala. Along the Pacific coast, it winters north to the south coast of British Columbia.

In our region, Hermit Thrushes breed not only up to the subalpine zone but also down to sea level. You are not likely to hear it in summer at Long Beach, where Swainson's Thrushes prevail, but if you spend some time on headlands or in somewhat stunted coniferous forest, you may well hear its song. Just how its habitat requirements differ from those of its close cousin is difficult to define, but usually where one is, the other is not. This rule does not always apply, however. At two locations near Tofino, all four species of local thrushes have been heard singing at the same location at the same time, although this happens only in some years. On Brooks Peninsula, the Hermit Thrush is more common than the Swainson's Thrush, being recorded from 5 May through August.[13] Further north, at Cape Scott Park, the reverse is true.[4]

In summer, the Hermit Thrush is heard but rarely seen. In winter it can be seen along roadsides and especially near marine shores, but it is never heard. It is not unusual to see one or two among the drift logs on the beach, or on the edge of a parking lot at Long Beach. By late April and early May, an influx of spring migrants arrive, though this is not evident in all years. In both 1999 and 2000, 15 birds were counted on the first day of May at the Long Beach Golf Course. Six birds were counted there on 18 April 2001, and also on 27 April in both 2008 and 2010. After the first week of May, birds have departed for their breeding territories.

During the breeding period in June and July, there are records from many localities throughout the west coast region, indicating that this is a widespread breeder. On the central west coast, most have been recorded at or near sea level, though some have been recorded at high elevation. Virtually all low-elevation records are from old-growth coniferous forests, but a single record on 21 June 2011 involved a male singing in a second-growth tree plantation on the Long Beach coastal plain. Some locations on the central west coast where birds have been heard in summer include: Morpheus and Neilson Islands (across from Tofino harbour), Meares Island, the south side of Vargas Island between Long Beach and Florencia Bay, and the Rainforest Trail in Pacific Rim National Park. The only late summer record I have is from 27 August 1990, when a bird was heard singing on Steamboat Mountain, Clayoquot Plateau, although the elevation was not recorded. There are many other summer records scattered along the entire west coast of Vancouver Island (BCFWS). Although breeding is likely widespread, the only breeding records thus far are from the north end of our region.

There is no noticeable fall movement other than the appearance of birds at their winter locations. I have only two September records: 28 September 1992 at Megin Lake and 27 September 2012 at Stubbs Island. After mid-October, birds begin to be seen more frequently at all the usual winter locations.

AMERICAN ROBIN
Turdus migratorius

STATUS: Abundant migrant in spring, common in summer and fall. Uncommon in winter. Breeds.

Our largest thrush needs no introduction, as it is familiar to Canadians from coast to coast. Who has not stopped to listen to a robin's exuberant song emanating from the top of a tree, heralding the end a storm, or announcing a new morning? American Robins breed throughout almost all of Canada and the United States, except for the northern tundra regions and some areas in the southern United States. It breeds also at higher elevations in much of Mexico. The American Robin winters throughout most of the United States and northern Mexico. In eastern Canada, it winters from Nova Scotia to southern Ontario. In the west, it winters primarily in the southern interior of British Columbia and on the southwest coast. A few hardy birds winter north to Haida Gwaii.

Although a few American Robins winter on the west coast of Vancouver Island in most years, their numbers are small and most human residents may be unaware of their presence. In early winter, they sustain themselves largely by feeding on the berries of mountain-ash and those of various garden-variety shrubs. They prefer open areas, especially around human habitations.

American Robins are diurnal migrants and have the most visible migratory movement of any of the passerines. On the outer coast in spring, they may be seen by the dozens, and sometimes by the hundreds, on lawns and on beaches, seeking worms. The first spring migrants arrive in late February or early March in most years. On 4 March 2009, 70 birds were found at the Long Beach Airport. On 4 March 2010, 63 birds were counted there. The following year, birds arrived considerably later, with 32 birds at Tofino on 15 March.

In 2008, first arrivals were much earlier, with 14 seen in Tofino on 20 February and 28 on 29 February. Even when the vanguard arrives early, the rest usually continue to trickle in over a period of weeks, rather than arriving in a big rush, though sometimes numbers can increase very rapidly. In 2008, numbers at the airport had built up to 50 birds by 23 March. Three days later, there were 82, and two days after that, a remarkable 540 birds were counted at the nearby Long Beach Golf Course and another 79 birds at the airport, for a total of 619 birds.

Although the weather was not recorded that day, usually when such invasions occur, the weather consists of low overcast with rain or drizzle. At such times, robins can be seen on every bit of turf and lawn available. A "fallout" of American Robins occurred in 1999, with about 300 birds counted at the golf course on 5 May. Numbers at the golf course often top 100 birds around the peak of the spring season. The migration persists throughout the month of May, though numbers will have dropped off by mid-May. Surprisingly, as many as 87 birds were counted at the golf course as late as 23 May in 2012 and 51 on 1 June 2012.

As a common local breeder, American Robins continue to be seen and heard throughout the breeding season, mostly as single birds and pairs. This species prefers open areas in or near forests. They do, however, inhabit old-growth rainforest when trees are widely spaced and sunlight can reach the forest floor, which results in a bumper crop of berries. American Robins may be encountered almost anywhere in our region except for the deep forest and at high elevation.

After the breeding season, we begin to see the first flocks in early September. Whether these birds are gathering in preparation for the fall migration or are already migrating is not clear, though I suspect the latter. As early as 2 September in 2013, 23 birds were seen at Jensen's Bay. On 12 September 2010, 28 birds were observed at the airport, and on 19 September 2004, 60 birds were counted there. On 3 October 2004, there were 80 birds at the airport.

A few flocks continue to be seen through the month of October. On 17 October 2003 and 31 October 1998, a flock of 30 birds was seen at both the airport and at Tofino. On 21 October 1996, 78 birds were recorded at the airport, and on 31 October 2012, 48 birds were seen there. Occasional flocks are seen throughout November and into December, although the few birds encountered in December are likely attempting to winter rather than migrating. Even these birds may be pushed out in the event of a cold spell.

On Brooks Peninsula, small numbers are present in open areas along river mouths and beaches in all months except December and January.[13]

VARIED THRUSH
Ixoreus naevius

STATUS: Common in spring, fall, and winter. Uncommon in summer. Breeds.

This handsome thrush superficially resembles an American Robin but is smaller and has a band across the breast, and males have a slate-blue back. The wings are barred. It is restricted to the forests and mountains of the west. Its breeding range extends from western Alberta to the Pacific Ocean and up to the Yukon, western Northwest Territories, and most of Alaska. In the United States, it is found from western Montana and Idaho to Washington, western Oregon, and the northwestern part of California. In British Columbia, the species nests throughout most of the province, with the exception of the northeast and possibly the north-central region. It is most abundant during the breeding season in the southern one-third of the province, including Vancouver Island and on Haida Gwaii.

The handsome Varied Thrush can often be seen on roadsides in fall and winter, searching for worms among the leaf litter.

On Vancouver Island's west coast, Varied Thrushes are a common wintering bird on roadsides, in backyards, and in places where red alders grow. They spend much time at these locations turning over fallen leaves with their bills to expose food underneath. In fall, there is very little migratory movement evident even in October. Among 200 records in my files, I found only two October dates. By November, birds are being seen much more frequently, and they continue to be seen throughout the winter until late April or early May, when they depart for their nesting territories. On Brooks Peninsula, small numbers can be seen foraging along upper beaches near forest edges and in mixed forests in all months except December.[13]

On occasion, Varied Thrushes may be seen in considerable numbers, and nowhere more so than on Stubbs Island, near Tofino, where these birds feed on the berries of California wax-myrtle (*Myrica californica*). On 18 December 1983, an estimated 125 birds were present, and on 22 November 1996, 105 birds. In recent years, numbers were lower, but 41 birds were recorded on 3 January 2010.

For a brief period in spring, numbers in our region swell; perhaps local birds are joined by others from further south. At the Long Beach Golf Course, where a winter walk might produce 7 Varied Thrushes, an April walk is likely to produce twice that number. An influx of birds was witnessed on 14 April 2011, when a walk at both the airport and the golf course produced a combined total of 93 birds. Many of those were seen in flight, arriving from the south. On 17 March 2012, 22 birds were counted at the golf course.

In summer, this thrush is often hard to find. However, singing males have been heard during the breeding season at a number of locations, including islands very near Tofino. On 5 July 1999, a male was heard singing on the south side of Vargas Island, and on 29 June 2000 and July 2015, at Sydney Inlet. Most notably, on 21 June 2008, Varied Thrushes were heard singing at four locations near Tofino: Morpheus Island, Neilson Island, and two locations on Meares Island. A week earlier, one had been heard singing on Vargas Island as well. It is interesting to note that birds are not heard at these locations every year.

A nest containing three young was found at the Long Beach campground on 5 June 1969.[1] In that same account, David Hatler recounts finding three old nests in the Bedwell River valley in 1970, and seeing an adult feeding three fledged young on Vargas Island in 1968. Nesting has also been recorded near Bamfield, Zeballos, and Port Alice (BCNRS).

Catbirds, Thrashers, and Mockingbirds *Family Mimidae*

GRAY CATBIRD
Dumetella carolinensis

STATUS: Casual summer visitor. Very rare breeder.

The Gray Catbird is named for its catlike mewing calls. It breeds extensively in the eastern United States and southeastern Canada, the Great Plains, and the Rocky Mountain states. In British Columbia, it is considered an uncommon visitor and breeder in the southern interior, north to Quesnel. Small numbers breed in the Fraser Lowlands. On southeastern Vancouver Island, the species is considered casual.

The first sighting in the west coast region occurred on 24 June 1999, when a bird landed on a boat 6 NM west of Triangle Island and was photographed by Michael Force.[286] A second bird was observed and photographed at Little Beach, Ucluelet, on 20 July 2010, by resident George Fifield (personal communication). On 15 June 2016, a third catbird was discovered at the mouth of Sandhill Creek, Long Beach, by Ian Cruickshank. The same observer found another bird along the lower Kennedy River on 26 June and succeeded in recording its call. Exactly one month later, on 26 July, he heard a Gray Catbird calling from dense underbrush at the Long Beach Airport, and an hour or so later he saw and heard two adults, one of which was carrying food, indicating a breeding pair and constituting a first breeding record for Vancouver Island. Sightings of one or more adults continued until 6 August, after which they were absent. On 27 October 2016, a bird was photographed at Jordan River by Cathy Carlson.

BROWN THRASHER
Toxostoma rufum

STATUS: Casual fall vagrant.

The Brown Thrasher is not a regular inhabitant of the west coast but has occurred as a very rare visitor.

The Brown Thrasher breeds throughout the United States east of the Rocky Mountains. It breeds also in southeastern Canada, and from the Great Lakes westward across the prairies to the Rocky Mountains. Its preferred habitat is brushy open and semi-open country and forest edge. The species winters in the southeastern United States and along the Gulf Coast, west to the Rio Grande in Texas. British Columbia is outside its normal range, but it has occurred sporadically at widely scattered localities. It is considered accidental in the north and casual elsewhere, including the south coast.[287]

In the west coast region, we have three records, all from Long Beach. The first sighting was recorded by Susan Bennet and me at the mouth of Sandhill Creek on 17 and 21 November 1973.[287] This was only the fourth recorded occurrence for the province. There were no further records until 13 and 14 September 2006, when a bird was seen by George Bradd and others at the south end of Long Beach.[158] The third sighting occurred on 17 October 2013, when I found a bird at the Long Beach parking lot, near Lovekin Rock (BC Photo 4112).

SAGE THRASHER
Oreoscoptes montanus

STATUS: Casual spring transient.

This bird is widely distributed as a breeding bird in semi-arid regions throughout the western United States, but does not breed in the southernmost areas of the United States or on the coast. In Canada, its breeding range barely extends into southwestern Saskatchewan and into British Columbia, where it is found only in the southern Similkameen and Okanagan valleys, where it was considered uncommon in *Birds of the Okanagan Valley*[288] and locally rare in *The Birds of British Columbia*.[263]

One would certainly not expect to find this bird along our wet west coast, but we have three records. The first bird was seen by F. Richardson at Grant Bay on 8 May 1969.[16] The second sighting was by Jerry Etzkorn on 3 May 2005, at Carmanah Point, where it was photographed.[289] The third record was a bird I observed on 2 June 2010 at the Long Beach Airport.[290] There was also a seemingly reliable report of a Sage Thrasher seen in a logged-off area of the Walbran Valley in the late 1980s or early 1990s, but it lacks a precise date and written documentation.

NORTHERN MOCKINGBIRD
Mimus polyglottos

STATUS: Rare visitor, primarily in spring and early summer. Casual in winter.

This is one of the most widely known birds in the eastern and southwestern United States, after the American Robin. It has adapted well to human-altered

Northern Mockingbirds are only occasional visitors from the United States but are being seen more frequently.

rural and suburban areas, and it commonly nests near farm buildings and in residential backyards. It is very vocal during the breeding season and is an accomplished mimic. Its Latin name, in fact, means "many-tongued mimic." The breeding range of this species includes all of the eastern United States and parts of southeastern Canada, the southern half of the US Midwest, and the US Southwest, north to northwestern California. In British Columbia, it is mostly a rare visitor but it has nested at Princeton and at Ten Mile Point on southern Vancouver Island. It is an expansionist species and may in time become a regular breeding resident on southern and eastern Vancouver Island.[263]

In our region, Northern Mockingbirds are seen sporadically, usually in early summer, but also at other times of year. *Birds of Pacific Rim National Park* listed 20 records up to 1978.[1] It is unclear, however, how many individual birds were actually involved. One bird was present on Cleland Island from 22 to 30 May 1969 and again the following year from 13 June to 19 July (BCFWS). It is not unusual for a vagrant to follow the same route two years in a row. Hatler et al. mentioned other sightings at Tofino, Long Beach, Sandhill Creek (Combers), and at Pachena Point.[1] In addition, a bird was seen on Triangle Island, off the northwest tip of Vancouver Island on 22 August 1976.[272]

Since 1980, there have been 30 additional sightings involving 25 birds. There are 3 records for the 1980s, 9 for the 1990s, 8 for the period from 2000 to 2010, and 10 additional sightings up to the summer of 2017. Worth noting is the fact that more than half of all sightings occurred in the period from 30 May to 7 July. Surprisingly, birds have been recorded in three separate winters. In the winter of 1993/94, an individual overwintered in the Tofino area, apparently dividing its time between the village and the north end of Vargas Island, where it was fed by a resident couple. Five of our records are from Carmanah Point and 6 from Long Beach. The rest are from scattered locations along the central west coast. There is a second record for Triangle Island, with a date of 19 and 20 July 1986 (BC Photo 1117).

Starlings *Family Sturnidae*

EUROPEAN STARLING
Sturnus vulgaris

STATUS: Common resident on the central west coast. Further north, uncommon or rare in winter. Breeds.

If there is one underappreciated bird, it is the European Starling. Certainly, if a pair is nesting under the eaves of your roof and making a racket shortly after dawn when you're trying to sleep, then, yes, appreciation may be somewhat elusive. Although it is regarded as the rat of the bird world by some, if we take the time to observe it with fresh eyes, we may see a bird as beautiful and fascinating as any other.

European Starlings belong to an Old World family found in Eurasia and Africa. Some of its members are highly iridescent and spectacular in appearance. This species was first introduced to Central Park in New York City in the 1890s in order to bring to America birds mentioned in the works of William Shakespeare. Unfortunately, the introduction was successful – unfortunate because these birds compete with native birds for nesting sites. This has resulted in the decline of many native species that likewise seek out cavities for nesting, in trees, fence posts, and human habitations. It should be noted, however, that in some parts of its range, especially on southern Vancouver Island, the European Starling is a principal food of the Cooper's Hawk.

From that introduction of 60 birds in 1890, European Starlings, like the human invaders from Europe that preceded them, took the continent by storm.

By 1945, the first starlings had reached British Columbia. Three years later, the first nesting was recorded near 150 Mile House.[291] The species was first reported on Vancouver Island, at Victoria, in the winter of 1951/52, and on the west coast, at Pachena Point, in early May 1967.[292]

While this species is largely insectivorous, it is remarkably adaptable and has been known to feed on snails, earthworms, small frogs and lizards, and some fruits. On the west coast, birds are also seen feeding in the intertidal zone and on the fruit of California wax-myrtle. In spring, they are often seen on lawns, probably in search of earthworms and cranefly larvae (family Tipulidae). The potential for this species to multiply here appears to be limited primarily by the availability of nesting sites.

Starlings are year-round residents in the vicinity of Tofino and Ucluelet. However, sightings of flocks flying south over the airport at Long Beach in in the months of November and December suggest that part of the population leaves the area for a time. The largest flocks are seen in the fall, from October to December, and again in the early spring, in February and March. Elsewhere along the west coast, the species is of irregular occurrence. On Brooks Peninsula, it has been recorded only in May and June,[13] and at Grant Bay and Browning Inlet, it occurs in summer and occasionally in winter.[16] It also ventures to some offshore seabird islands in summer to feed; up to four birds were seen on Cleland Island from 12 to 26 June 1970 (BCFWS).

European Starlings have also been introduced to South America, Australia, New Zealand, South Africa, and the West Indies. Worldwide, their population is said to be as high as 100 million.[293] One way to counteract the negative effects of the starlings is to put up nesting boxes for swallows and wrens with entrance holes too small for the larger-bodied bird to enter.

Wagtails and Pipits *Family Motacillidae*

WHITE WAGTAIL
Motacilla alba
STATUS: Casual vagrant in spring and fall.

Wagtails are Eurasian ground-dwelling birds in the family Motacillidae. Compared with pipits, which belong to the same family, wagtails seem downright flamboyant, being either yellow-breasted or boldly marked in black and white. In the case of this species, the colour scheme is white, grey, and black, or sometimes just black and white. There are reported to be as many as 11 geographical variants, or subspecies, across its breeding range, which stretches from Iceland and western Europe eastward across Asia to China, Japan, and eastern Siberia. In North America, the subspecies *M. a. ocularis* is a rare but regular local breeder in western Alaska. The species winters from Southeast Asia and India to the Middle East and the northern half of Africa. Birds also winter in southern and western Europe.

In North America, this species is a very rare vagrant along the Pacific coast. It has been seen from California to British Columbia. On Vancouver Island's west coast, we have three records. On 24 May 1977, a bird was found at Pachena Point.[294] Eleven years later, on 11 September 1988, a bird was found at Jordan River by Keith Taylor.[263] A third record for our region occurred in 1996, when a White Wagtail spent from 30 April to 7 May on Triangle Island.[295] This bird was assigned to the subspecies *M. a. lugens*, sometimes referred to as the Black-backed Wagtail. This subspecies has a breeding range stretching from the Kamchatka Peninsula to Japan.

AMERICAN PIPIT
Anthus rubescens

STATUS: A fairly common spring and fall migrant. Casual in winter. Rare breeder.

Like the pipits of Eurasia, these are ground-dwelling birds that walk rather than hop, and that inhabit treeless plains and fields. When seen in southern regions, they are usually in flocks and can be identified in flight by their diagnostic undulating flight. This species breeds in the tundra regions of the north from Labrador to Alaska, and also inhabits the alpine regions of the west. In migration, birds may be seen in every province of Canada and in every state in the contiguous United States. They winter in the southern United States and Mexico, south to El Salvador, and along the Pacific coast north as far as southwestern British Columbia.

On Vancouver Island's west coast, spring passage was thought to occur from mid-April to mid-May. Until recently, the earliest recorded date was 13 April in 1984, but in 2016, two birds were found at the Long Beach Golf Course on 21 March, over three weeks earlier than usual, and again on 4 April, when six birds were found. It may be that in the past birds have been overlooked so early in the season.

Some of the largest numbers have been recorded at the Long Beach Golf Course and at the neighbouring airport, with 94 birds seen at these locations on 15 April 1984; 90 on 29 April 1996; 200 on 6 and 8 May 1999; 225 on 3 May 2001; and 60 on 21 April 2006. A flock of 86 birds at Cape Scott on 26 April 2008 is also noteworthy. The latest spring sighting occurred on 15 May in 2009.

American Pipits have been seen in alpine areas of Vancouver Island in summer, although evidence for nesting is sparse, with only two records. In the west coast region, nesting has thus far been recorded only near Gold River, although specific details for confirmation are lacking.[296]

The southward movement commences before mid-September and ends in late November or earlier. The earliest fall records are as follows: 3 birds at Stubbs Island on 9 September 1986; 2 at Stubbs Island on 10 September 2012; and 15 at the Long Beach Airport on 12 September 1982. In 2014, 8 birds were seen at the airport on 4 September, and 35 birds were seen there on 5 September. There are two August dates: a single bird was seen at Chesterman Beach, Tofino, on 31 August 1974, and one on Mount Klitsa on 13 August 2008. While most records are from September and October, there are also 12 records in November and 2 in December. A single bird was seen at Chesterman Beach on 4 December 1985, and another was recorded at the Long Beach Airport on 29 December 2014. Records in fall from alpine areas suggest that much of the movement occurs at high elevation.

Sightings are more frequent in fall than in spring, but flock size is smaller. Flocks of 45 birds have been recorded on three occasions at the Long Beach Airport: on 8 October 2003, 28 September 2010, and 16 September 2014. The largest flock recorded in fall consisted of 60 birds seen on 25 September 2016, also at the airport. Birds may also be found on beaches. The largest flock in fall consisted of 45 birds. This number was recorded on three dates at the airport: 8 October 2003, 28 September 2010, and 16 September 2014. On 29 September 2013, 28 birds were observed at Incinerator Rock, Long Beach.

The American Pipit has four subspecies, three in North America and one in eastern Asia, the latter being identifiable in the field. On 4 November 1995, I observed a pipit in Tofino that fit the description of the Asian subspecies, *A. r. japonicus,* also known as the Siberian Buff-bellied Pipit. The Tofino bird's most distinguishing feature was a white breast, heavily streaked with black. The American form always has some buff and lacks the heavy, black breast markings. This bird appeared injured around one eye and was lacking its tail. Unfortunately it disappeared in the time it took to fetch a camera. Two housecats in the yard next door were prime suspects in the disappearance. If true, this was a sad ending for a bird that had flown all the way from Asia.

Free-roaming domestic cats are a significant factor in the declining numbers of birds in North America. Two leading science and wildlife organizations recently estimated that house cats are responsible for the deaths of more than 1.4 billion birds annually in the United States alone.

Waxwings Family Bombycillidae

BOHEMIAN WAXWING
Bombycilla garrulus
STATUS: Casual vagrant in fall and winter.

The Bohemian Waxwing is larger and greyer than the familiar Cedar Waxwing of our west coast region. It has a very extensive range, breeding throughout the northern forests of Eurasia from Norway to eastern Russia. In North America, it breeds from the southern edge of Hudson Bay westward through the boreal forest to the Northwest Territories, the Yukon, Alaska, and British Columbia. The species winters south of its breeding range through much of western Canada and the northern half of the western United States. In British Columbia, it breeds throughout much of the province east of the Coast Mountains, particularly in the north, though breeding records are relatively scarce. In the south, its breeds at higher elevation. In the Salish Sea basin, it is considered "a very rare summer visitant" but "locally common in autumn and winter during some years."[263] This appears to apply to the Fraser Valley, however, and not to Vancouver Island.

On Vancouver Island's west coast, we have a mere five records. The first sighting was listed in *Birds of Pacific Rim National Park* as the sole record up to that time (1978).[1] It involved a single bird seen and photographed at Ucluelet by D. Foskett on 28 February 1975 (BC Photo 418). The second occurrence was on 10 October 1980, when four birds were seen at Granite Lake near Nitinat Lake. Two birds were seen in Tofino on 1 December 1985, and a single bird was recorded there on 7 December 1994. The latest occurrence was a bird seen on 6 June 1990 by staff of Pacific Rim National Park. These sightings represent the only known records of this rare and attractive bird on our west coast, though others will likely be seen on rare occasions.

CEDAR WAXWING
Bombycilla cedrorum

STATUS: Fairly common in late spring, summer, and early fall. Rare in winter. Breeds.

Masked and crested, Cedar Waxwings are easy to identify. In autumn they may be seen gorging on mountain ash berries.

Cedar Waxwings are named for the red, waxy substance on the ends of their secondaries. This rather delicate and beautiful bird is very widespread in North America, with a breeding range that covers the southern half of Canada and the northern United States from Atlantic to Pacific. It winters from extreme southern Canada south through the United States, Mexico, and Central America to Colombia. In British Columbia, it breeds primarily in the southern half of the province, including Vancouver Island, particularly in the dry interior, with the centre of abundance being the Fraser Valley and the Salish Sea basin. It is considered uncommon in winter on southeastern Vancouver Island and the Lower Mainland.

On our west coast, this species arrives rather late in spring. Among my first arrival records dating from 1983 to 2013, only seven are from the month of May, and of these, only one is earlier than mid-month. On 4 May 1996, 4 birds were seen on Stubbs Island, near Tofino. In contrast, in 2014 alone, there were six sightings in May, beginning with a single bird seen at the airport on 17 May. On 25 May, 34 birds were counted.

By June, sightings are frequent and small numbers may be seen throughout the breeding season, particularly near water. The species is particularly plentiful along the lower Kennedy River, with 12 birds counted on 12 July 2002, and 17 on 5 July 2013. They are also seen regularly at Swan Lake and at the Long Beach Airport. There are June records from numerous locations, from Jordan River in the south to Holberg in the north, indicating that this species breeds throughout the west coast region. It breeds along the entire coast wherever suitable habitat exists, especially second-growth deciduous shrubs bordering roads, highways, and riparian zones, from at least mid-June to mid-August. A nest containing five incubated eggs was found at Long Beach on 26 June 1967,[253] and three recently fledged young were being fed by adults at the same location on 10 August 1968.[254] Up to six birds were present daily on Brooks Peninsula from 27 June through 27 August 1981, where they were suspected of nesting.[13] Other confirmed breeding locations include Bamfield, Zeballos, and Port Alice (BCNRS).

It is difficult to pin down exactly when birds depart for points south. The following records suggest that the southward migration commences in early September and ends in early to late October. On 9 September 2012, 25 birds were seen at the airport, and on 19 September 2004, 13 birds were seen there. The largest flock ever recorded was on 13 September 2010, with 80 reported by Russell Cannings at the parking lot at Long Beach, a location very close to the previous two. A flock of 48 birds was seen at Chesterman Beach as late as 25 September in 2016. October records are few, though 17 birds were seen in Tofino on 9 October 1998. There is only a single record for November. On 15 November 1983, 5 birds were seen in Tofino.

Winter records are few, though we have several from Tofino. On 22 January 1985, a single bird was observed there, and in 2009, one was seen repeatedly between 11 December and 21 December, although this could be regarded as a very late fall migrant. In the winter of 2001/02, a small flock spent part of the winter in Tofino. Between 4 December and 20 January, from three to nine birds were seen on numerous occasions. They vanished after the 20th, perhaps because the winter supply of berries was depleted.

Longspurs and Snow Buntings Family Calcariidae

LAPLAND LONGSPUR
Calcarius lapponicus

STATUS: Uncommon fall transient. Casual in spring and early summer.

Longspurs are ground-dwelling birds adapted to living on treeless plains such as prairies and tundra. Of the four species found in North America, the Lapland Longspur is the only one that regularly occurs in our area. This species breeds on the Arctic tundra of both Eurasia and North America. In fall, it migrates south to escape the bitter cold and long nights of the far north. On migration and on its winter range, it seeks out prairies, farm fields, and other treeless areas, where it is often seen congregating in large flocks. It winters throughout much of the United States, except for the most southern regions and the more northerly Great Plains. In British Columbia, Lapland Longspurs have been seen in nearly all areas of the province as a transient. In the Fraser Lowlands and on southeastern Vancouver Island, the species is considered an uncommon and occasionally fairly common migrant and winter visitor.

On the west coast of Vancouver Island, this species is seen far less often. *Birds of Pacific Rim National Park* listed only 3 sightings and considered it a rare migrant.[1] Since then, 75 additional records have been added. In fall, birds normally occur from late September through the first week of November. However, there are two very early fall dates. In 1983, a single individual was seen at Chesterman Beach, Tofino, on 2 September, and in 2001, a bird was seen at Stubbs Island on 4 September. The latest fall date we have is 8 November in 1982, also at Stubbs Island. Of 66 fall records, 18 were in September, 42 in October, and 6 in November.

In our region, most sightings involve 1 or 2 individuals, although small flocks are not unusual. High counts are as follows: 14 birds on 17 October 1982, 18 October 1996, 19 October 2004, and 5 October 2014; 17 birds on 3 October 2013 and 5 October 2016; 19 birds on 20 October 2007; 28 birds on 4 October 2013; and 32 birds on 2 October 2013. Besides having the largest flock so far recorded, the year 2013 also had by far the most sightings of any year – a total of 14. The vast majority of sightings have occurred at two locations – Stubbs Island near Tofino, and the Long Beach Airport. Flocks seen at both locations within a two-day period, as in October 2013, were likely separate flocks.

Records in spring are sparse. Of the 75 sightings recorded since 1978, only 9 are from the spring period. There is 1 record for March, 1 for April, and 5 for May. There are also 2 records in June, with a single bird observed at Triangle Island on 13 June 1976, and a bird in full breeding plumage seen at the Long Beach Airport on 10 June 1982.

SNOW BUNTING
Plectrophenax nivalis
STATUS: Casual transient in fall and winter.

The Snow Bunting breeds in the far north and occurs in the region only as a very rare transient. It is usually seen on beaches.

This strikingly patterned bunting breeds on the tundra of Eurasia, Iceland, Greenland, and North America. In some cases, it also breeds somewhat further south at high elevation, including in the Tatshenshini region of British Columbia.[297] In winter, the species migrates south as far as Virginia, Missouri, and northern Utah. In British Columbia, Snow Buntings may be encountered as transients in all parts of the province in fall, winter, and spring. The main movement through the province, with flocks of hundreds reported, is in the vicinity of Fort St. John in the Peace River region.[298] On the Fraser River delta and on the southeast side of Vancouver Island, they are considered an uncommon to occasionally fairly common migrant.

On the west side of Vancouver Island, the species is seen much less frequently. *Birds of Pacific Rim National Park* listed only 6 records, with the oldest dating back to 8 February 1949, when resident M. Whittington reported it as "common" along the beach in front of her home on Long Beach.[253] Since 1978, there have been only 10 additional sightings, 3 of them from 1996, and 5 from 2014 and 2015. Most records involve single birds. Outside of the 1949 sighting, the largest number recorded was 4 birds on 9 October 1996, at Stubbs Island. All sightings but one have occurred in October and November, and nearly all sightings have been on beaches. Surprisingly, none have yet been observed at the Long Beach Airport.

Wood-Warblers   *Family Parulidae*

TENNESSEE WARBLER
Oreothlypis peregrina
STATUS: Casual fall vagrant.

This species was formerly in the genus *Vermivora*. It breeds in appropriate forest habitat throughout most of Canada, from Newfoundland to British Columbia, the Yukon, and the Northwest Territories. In British Columbia, it breeds primarily in the northeast, in the Peace River region, and in the central interior, but it has been found breeding in widely separate localities including the southeastern corner of the province (BCNRS). On the south coast, it is considered a casual migrant.[299]

On Vancouver Island's west coast, there have been four sightings, three of them by me. On 20 November 1982, an adult male was observed at close range at Radar Beach in Pacific Rim National Park.[300] The second sighting was of a bird in Tofino on 9 November 1983.[301] The third record, a juvenile, was observed at the south end of Long Beach on 6 September 2002. A bird was also seen at the Lovekin Rock parking lot at Long Beach on 5 May 1993, by Roger Burrows.

This species is likely to be seen again in our region as a fall migrant, even if sporadically. It has therefore been listed as casual rather than accidental.

ORANGE-CROWNED WARBLER
Oreothlypis celata

STATUS: Common spring and fall migrant, and common summer visitor. Casual in winter. Breeds.

The olive-green Orange-crowned Warbler is one of the most common wood-warblers in the west coast region.

It is probably fair to say that this yellow-green bird is the dingiest and least colourful of a rather spectacular group, the wood-warblers. It is also one of our most common warblers. Orange-crowned Warblers are more often detected by sound than by sight, their rising and falling trill a familiar sound from late April to the end of June. The species breeds right across Canada, from Labrador to British Columbia, and north to the Yukon and Alaska. It also breeds across most of the American West, south to northern Baja California and west to Texas. In British Columbia, it is very widespread and believed to breed in suitable habitat throughout the province. The species winters from the southern United States south to Guatemala and Belize.

The Orange-crowned Warbler is widely distributed along the entire length of the west coast region, where it is mainly a summer visitor. It has been recorded on Brooks Peninsula in mixed woodlands from 6 May to 27 August,[13] and is considered a summer resident at Grant Bay and Browning Inlet.[16] It also occurs on wooded offshore islands along the coast.

On the west coast of Vancouver Island, first arrival dates for eight out of ten years fell between 1 April and 25 April. The earliest first arrival date ever recorded, with one exception, was on 25 March in 1999. There is a single observation that precedes it by a full month: on 25 February 2014, a single bird was reported at Jordan River.

As with several other migratory passerines, this species can occasionally be seen in large numbers. On 17 April 2010, a total of 97 Orange-crowned Warblers were counted at a single location at Tofino after a weather system moved in overnight, and on 29 April 2012, 98 birds were tallied in a 15-minute period as they crossed a clearing at Jensen's Bay, Tofino. Breeding habitat may vary considerably, but this species is often seen near the ground in dense shrubbery. There are three breeding records. A nest with four eggs was found on Turtle Island on 24 May 1972, a young fledgling was caught by hand near the Ucluelet dump on 17 July 1971, and an adult was watched feeding two newly fledged young in small bushes at Bamfield on 19 June 1999 (BCNRS). During migration, they are usually seen higher in the trees, particularly in red alders.

The precise beginning of the fall movement is difficult to determine. There are numerous records for September, and this is probably when the main fall movement occurs. Numbers decline after early October, but individual Orange-crowned Warblers may linger well into October. Single birds have also been recorded in November in 1983, 1995, 1996, and 1998, and in December in 1983 and 1999. I have two dates in January that represent birds apparently overwintering in Tofino – 13 January 1987 and 26 January 2000. A follow-up date of 10 March 1987 provides evidence that at least one individual successfully overwintered.

NASHVILLE WARBLER
Oreothlypis ruficapilla

STATUS: Casual fall and winter vagrant.

This species has two populations, one in the east and one in the west. The eastern population breeds from the Maritimes and New England westward to central Saskatchewan. The western population breeds from California to Oregon, Washington, Idaho, western Montana, and British Columbia. In British Columbia, it breeds primarily in the Okanagan Valley but also east to the Creston Valley. It is considered a rare to locally uncommon transient on the southern mainland coast, and a rare transient on southeastern Vancouver Island.[299]

For Vancouver Island's west coast, we have 4 records, 3 of them listed in *Birds of Pacific Rim National Park*.[1] A Nashville Warbler was first seen at Maltby Slough, near Tofino, on 23 September 1972. A second bird was seen at Combers, Long Beach, on 31 December 1973 and 3 January 1974. There were no further sightings for 23 years, until 4 September 1997, when a bird was found at the sewage pond in Pacific Rim National Park. The fourth sighting occurred at Port Renfrew on 29 October 2014, when a bird was seen by three observers.

MacGILLIVRAY'S WARBLER
Geothlypis tolmiei

STATUS: Uncommon in spring and summer, locally fairly common. Rare in fall. Breeds.

This warbler is one of four species in the genus *Oporornis*, and one of three that have dark hoods and are similar in appearance. We need not fear mistaking one for another, however, as the others are not found here. The MacGillivray's Warbler is partial to low, dense vegetation and can therefore be quite elusive. The surest way to find one is to listen for singing males on territory during the breeding season. Its breeding range covers much of the western United States and southwestern Alberta, British Columbia, southeast Alaska, and southern Yukon. In British Columbia, it has been found throughout the province with the exception of Haida Gwaii, where it is absent, and much of the mainland coast, where it is a rather rare inhabitant. Its centre of abundance is southeastern British Columbia, but it is generally fairly common in the southern half of the province.[299]

On the west coast of Vancouver Island, MacGillivray's Warblers can be hard to find even during the breeding season unless you have good hearing and are in just the right habitat. This can vary from well-spaced climax forest with a lot of understorey made up of berry bushes, to clearings heavily overgrown with low shrubbery adjacent to second-growth forest. The species also inhabits logged areas some years after cutting, when shrubbery is prolific. From one to three birds were recorded in logging slash at Lost Shoe Creek on 13 occasions

The MacGillivray's Warbler is a skulker that can be difficult to find without hearing its song. Shown here is a juvenile.

between 19 May and 1 August 1972.[1] Hatler et al. listed the earliest arrival date as 16 May in 1972.[1]

Since then, there have been at least four earlier sightings in spring, three of them in 2014. A bird was recorded at Frederick Lake near Bamfield on 9 May 2008, and one was found at the garbage dump near Long Beach on 10 May 2014. A bird was also recorded the following day at Jordan River. The earliest spring date on record was 1 May in 2014, when two birds were found at the Long Beach Airport. Most birds arrive after mid-May, however, and sometimes well after. Such late arrivals should not be a surprise, as passerines tend to arrive much later on the west coast than they do on southeastern Vancouver Island.

Although singing males may be seen throughout the breeding season, there are only two confirmed breeding records for the west coast, one on the central west coast and another near Port Alice.

For the autumn period, there are seven dates after mid-September. The only records after September were on 12 October 1974 and 15 October 1982, at Long Beach. Birds seen after mid-September could be migrants from much further north. Local birds probably depart in August.

COMMON YELLOWTHROAT
Geothlypis trichas

STATUS: Locally common in spring and summer, uncommon in fall, casual in winter. Breeds.

The Common Yellowthroat has a widespread breeding range in Canada and United States, from the Atlantic to the Pacific, excluding only the most northerly forests and the tundra regions of Canada. In Alaska, it has been recorded north to Fairbanks. In British Columbia, it breeds in suitable habitat throughout much of the province with the exception of Haida Gwaii (one record), and possibly the islands off the mainland coast.

Find a shallow marshy area in spring or early summer almost anywhere, and chances are fairly good you will hear the *witchity-witchity-witchity* of a male Common Yellowthroat. Better yet, catch a glimpse of the handsome yellow-breasted male with his black mask as he skulks in thick vegetation, usually only a few feet above the ground, but occasionally proclaiming his territory well above the ground and in the open.

This bird has a strong association with wetlands in one form or other. On our west coast, this may be nothing more than standing water with lots of vegetation or, as is the case at the Long Beach Airport, dense stands of broom and berry bushes near wet areas. This species is commonly found along the slow-flowing lower Kennedy River in summer and undoubtedly breeds there. On 30 June 2015, a male and a female were observed carrying food. It has also been found in marshy vegetation around the shores of Kennedy Lake. At the Long Beach Airport, no fewer than 11 young birds were observed on 11 July 2015.

In spring, the first males arrive by the beginning of May or slightly earlier. The earliest records I have are 19 April in 1989 and 20 April in 1997. There is one earlier record from Jordan River, where a bird was recorded on 13 April in 2014. Determining when birds depart is more challenging. Although some birds probably leave in August, not long after the breeding season, birds continue to be seen throughout September and even to the end of October. Most of the southward movement probably occurs in September, and this appears to be supported by records from Jordan River, where most observations have occurred in that month. On 8 September 2012, as many as 10 birds were seen there by Jeremy Kimm and Jeremy Gatten. A high count of 32 birds was recorded by Ian Cruickshank at the Long Beach Airport on 28 August 2016. I could find only two records after October: 17 November 1982 and 10 November 1983,[300] both at Tofino. There is a single record that suggests overwintering: a female at Tofino on 15 February 1980 (BC Photo 540).

Most records are from near the outer coast or from the Kennedy Lake lowlands, but there are also two records in summer from the upper Kennedy River near Sutton Pass, a record from Zeballos River, and one from near Holberg. This suggests that the Common Yellowthroat is local but widely distributed, and that the species likely breeds in suitable habitat throughout the west coast region.

AMERICAN REDSTART
Setophaga ruticilla
STATUS: Casual fall vagrant.

This flamboyant wood-warbler has a widespread breeding range that covers most of eastern North America except for Florida and Canada's northern regions. It breeds throughout the northern Great Plains states west to Idaho and northeastern Oregon, and in Canada through the Prairie provinces to British Columbia, the Yukon, and the Northwest Territories. It winters from Baja California, western Mexico, and Central America to Peru. In British Columbia, it breeds widely throughout the interior, particularly the southern two-thirds of the province. In the Fraser Lowlands and southeastern Vancouver Island, it is considered a rare migrant and local summer visitor.[299]

There were no records for our region until 14 November 1972, when I spotted a female or juvenile near Ucluelet Inlet while keeping an Ash-throated Flycatcher under observation at the same location. It was subsequently photographed by Pacific Rim National Park naturalist Dudley Foskett (BC Photo 324). On 2 October 1997, a second American Redstart, a female, was observed and photographed at the west end of Main Street in Tofino. Because this species is likely to be seen again in the west coast region, albeit rarely, it is considered casual.

YELLOW WARBLER
Setophaga petechia
STATUS: Uncommon to fairly common migrant in spring, uncommon to locally common in summer. Common in fall. Casual in winter. Breeding suspected but unconfirmed.

The Yellow Warbler breeds throughout much of North America, including much of Mexico. In Canada, it is absent only from northern Labrador, northern

The Yellow Warbler breeds sparingly in our region. It is most common in September, when drab northern birds move through.

Quebec, most of Nunavut, and the Arctic islands. It winters from Mexico and the Caribbean to Brazil and Peru. In British Columbia, this species is believed to breed in suitable habitat throughout the province except Haida Gwaii. It is found in greatest abundance in the eastern parts of the province.

In our region, spring migration begins in mid-May or somewhat earlier. Earliest records since 1980 were as follows: 2 birds on 11 May in 1997 at Long Beach; 1 bird on 12 May in 2012 in Tofino; and 1 bird on 13 May in 2008 in Tofino. There is an unusually early record of a bird at McLean Point on 27 April 1972.[1]

The movement picks up steam in late May, and continues well into June in some years. Single birds seen in Tofino on 9 June 2008 and 12 June 2000 were clearly transients, even though local birds may quite possibly be breeding at this time. There are late June records from the Lovekin Rock parking lot at Long Beach, from the airport nearby, and from the Kennedy Lake lowlands, suggesting breeding at these locations. On 10 June 2015, 2 male Yellow Warblers were seen and heard singing in stands of willows along the upper Kennedy River, near Sutton Pass, apparently "on territory," and on 5 June 2016, 8 birds were recorded. Larger numbers have been found south of Barkley Sound. In 2011, 10 birds were found along the road to Bamfield by Jennifer Provencher, and Alan Burger found 9 birds east and northeast of Bamfield on the same day.

Lest the foregoing give the impression that this species is a common summer breeder throughout our region, it is worth noting that the only other locations where June birds have been recorded thus far are at Jordan River and Port San Juan, and along the road from Buttle Lake to Gold River. This bird's preferred habitat seems to be open deciduous forest with low vegetation, with a preference for willow during the breeding season. If such habitat is available, birds will likely be found, even in the north of our region.

The southward movement begins in August. In 2000, 2 birds were observed on 27 August, 6 on 28 August, and 18 on 3 September, all in Tofino and all believed to be transients. The earliest dates were 8 August in 1997 and 7 August in 2016, both on the central west coast. The main southward movement occurs in September and is the most conspicuous movement of any of the warblers. The largest flocks recorded are as follows: 45 birds on 13 September 1984, Tofino; 30 on 26 September 1984, Long Beach; 15 on 3 September 1996, Tofino; and 35 on 26 September 2008, Tofino.

In October, the movement drops off abruptly and sightings of more than two or three birds are rare, though they may continue throughout the month. Surprisingly, there are occasional sightings in November. Single birds were seen in Tofino from 3 to 15 November 2004, and on 1 to 7 November 2009. Two birds were seen on 21 November 2016, and again on 1 December. In 1995, a very hardy bird, and perhaps a foolish one, stayed in a Tofino backyard well into the winter. This was not a drab northern bird but a brightly coloured male. It was observed throughout November and December, and was last seen on 18 January 1996. Whether it then moved south or perished is unknown. When last seen, it was active and healthy and was still feeding on insects attracted to ivy blooms in a fruit tree. The end of the ivy blooming cycle likely forced the bird to move on.

The fall movement in the west coast region is not in accord with the movement reported elsewhere on the coast. At Rocky Point, on southern Vancouver Island, the peak of the Yellow Warbler migration is said to occur during the last two weeks of August, whereas here the main movement has yet to begin. The reason for this appears to be that birds pass through our region in two waves, a minor one in August, when birds of the bright yellow variety trickle through, and a much larger wave in September consisting largely of the drab northern birds. These drab birds are also seen in spring, but only infrequently. Perhaps, like Savannah Sparrows from Unalaska, the northern birds we see here have flown across the ocean from the Alaska Peninsula or the Aleutian Islands. Fishermen have often told of small yellow birds landing on their boats many miles offshore during fog, or when slash-burning darkened the sky in the 1970s.

CHESTNUT-SIDED WARBLER
Setophaga pensylvanica
STATUS: Casual vagrant in spring and fall.

This species breeds from the southern Appalachians, the northeastern United States, and southeastern Canada, including the Maritimes, west to central Alberta. In British Columbia, the species was first recorded on 29 May 1946 with a sighting at Knox Mountain in Kelowna.[302] Since then it has been seen occasionally at widely scattered locations. There is a single breeding record from east of Lillooet, in the interior (19 August 1998).[299] The species is considered very rare or casual anywhere in the province.

On the west coast of Vancouver Island, we have four records, three in autumn and one in spring. Three of the sightings occurred at the south end of Long Beach. The first bird was seen on 4 September 1993 at the interpretive centre parking lot.[303] The second sighting occurred at the same location on 7 June 2006, when a male in breeding plumage sang very briefly in full view of me, then disappeared into dense willows.[304] On 20 September 2011, George Bradd observed a juvenile female close to this same location, and on 15 September 2013, a juvenile landed on a boat during a pelagic birding trip. It was captured, viewed by all on board, photographed, and released.

BLACKPOLL WARBLER
Setophaga striata
STATUS: Casual transient in spring and fall.

This species breeds from the Maritimes and Labrador west throughout the boreal forest region to the Northwest Territories, the Yukon, and Alaska. In British Columbia, it occurs regularly in the northern two-thirds of the province east of the Coastal Mountains in summer, though breeding records are sparse. It is known to breed in the northwest corner of the province and in the Peace River region, but sightings during the breeding season are spread over most of northern British Columbia and in the southeast, from the town of Golden northward.[299] Blackpoll Warblers winter in northern South America. In spring, these warblers arrive in northern British Columbia and Alaska from the east.

In fall, birds fly east to New England and then embark on a 2,800 km nonstop flight south, over open ocean. They thus bypass southern British Columbia. However, *The Birds of British Columbia* points out that, whereas few birds are recorded in southern British Columbia or Washington and Oregon, a much larger number are reported in California in fall.[97] The authors speculated that a segment of the western population migrates nonstop over the Pacific Ocean. This would mean that some birds pass by our province far out to sea, and would explain the very occasional birds seen in our west coast region.

To date, we have five records, all but one occurring in September: 25 September 1972, Grice Bay (Pacific Rim National Park) – 1;[1] 18 June 1974, near Port Renfrew – 1;[299] 4, 5, and 8 September 1995, Triangle Island – 1 immature;[299] 16 September 1996, Wickaninnish sewage ponds (Pacific Rim National Park) – 1 immature;[299] and 15 September 2001, over the ocean off Ucluelet – 1.

PALM WARBLER
Setophaga palmarum
STATUS: Rare fall migrant. Casual in winter and spring.

The Palm Warbler is of course named for its winter home in the tropics, not its breeding habitat in the boreal forest regions of Canada. It breeds from the Maritimes and Newfoundland west through the boreal forest to Alberta and the Northwest Territories. In British Columbia, this species breeds only in the Peace River region and the northeast corner of the province. Palm Warblers winter in the southeastern United States, the Caribbean, the Yucatan Peninsula, and parts of Central America. Small numbers winter along the Pacific coast, from southern California north to Washington and occasionally southwestern British Columbia, including parts of Vancouver Island.[299]

In 1978, *Birds of Pacific Rim National Park* listed a single record (2 November 1973, BC Photo 323) for our west coast region and described its status as accidental.[1] Since then there have been 60 additional sightings in 22 separate years. A few records probably involved repeat sightings of the same bird. Most sightings have occurred in the months of October and November. There are 24 records for October and 16 for November, compared with only 3 September records. Moreover, 3 of the October records involved three individuals and a November record involved two birds. This suggests a small fall movement through our area. The 8 December records are presumed to be late fall migrants.

The earliest sightings in September were on the 19th of the month in 1988 and the 21st in 2010.

Records from 14 March 1983 and 14 February 1996 may represent overwintering birds. A bird recorded at the Long Beach Golf Course on 1 June 2012 was undoubtedly a late spring migrant. Most sightings have occurred in the village of Tofino, though there have been sightings at Stubbs Island, Long Beach, the Long Beach Golf Course/Airport area, and Ucluelet.

When seen, Palm Warblers are usually in low vegetation, or sometimes on the ground in semi-open areas. Birds seen in fall are rather drab, but their habit of tail wagging should be an immediate clue to their identity.

YELLOW-RUMPED WARBLER
Setophaga coronata

STATUS FOR AUDUBON'S WARBLER: Fairly common spring transient, uncommon summer visitor, rare fall transient. Casual in winter. Breeding likely but unconfirmed.

STATUS FOR MYRTLE WARBLER: Uncommon transient in spring, fairly common in fall. Generally rare in winter, but locally fairly common.

The Yellow-rumped Warbler can be divided into two easily identifiable subspecies known as the Myrtle Warbler and the Audubon's Warbler. Indeed, they were considered separate species for a long time, and may well be again in the future. The Myrtle Warbler breeds in the northeastern United States and across forested regions of Canada, from Newfoundland and the Maritimes west to the Rocky Mountains, the Northwest Territories, the Yukon, and Alaska. The Audubon's Warbler is confined to the west, from southeast Alaska and southwestern British Columbia south throughout most of the western states. It is absent from most of Arizona and California. Both subspecies move south in winter, though small numbers of Myrtle Warblers winter along the Pacific coast, north to Washington and southwestern British Columbia.

In British Columbia, the species breeds throughout most of the province east of the Coast Mountains. In the north, however, birds breed westward into the mountains and into southeast Alaska. The dividing line between breeding Myrtle Warblers in the northeast and Audubon's Warblers in the southwest runs approximately from Calgary, Alberta, to Atlin in the far northwest of British Columbia. Birds often interbreed where the two subspecies meet.[299]

In our region, the first spring arrivals are usually male Audubon's Warblers, resplendent in fresh breeding plumage. Local wintering Myrtle Warblers, on the other hand, are still in drab plumage at this time. Audubon's Warblers usually begin arriving in April, although there are records as early as March. The earliest arrival date is 14 March in 2000, in Tofino. There are also records for 24 March 1968, 26 March 2001, and 20 March 2016, all in Tofino, and several late March records from Jordan River. However, all March records that occur before the last few days of the month are exceptionally early. Most records are from April and the first week of May.

There are far fewer records of Myrtle Warblers as spring transients, but on 21 April 1999 and 29 April 2000, mixed flocks of 10 birds of both subspecies were seen at the Pacific Rim National Park sewage pond. The earliest spring record for a migrant Myrtle Warbler was 12 April in 2012 at the Long Beach Airport. The latest, also at the airport, was 22 May in 2011.

Male Audubon's Warblers heard singing in June and July are likely on territory and almost certainly represent breeding pairs. They have been seen and heard in those months at a number of locations, including the Long Beach Golf Course, Vargas Island, the Kennedy River lowlands, Harris Creek north of the San Juan River, Zeballos, Gold River, and Head Road, well west of Gold River. On Brooks Peninsula, the Audubon's Warbler has been recorded from 5 May through 13 August. It is suspected of breeding there in deciduous woodlands near river mouths.[13] Further north, in the vicinity of Grant Bay and Browning Inlet, the species is considered an occasional migrant.[16] Currently, the breeding range of this subspecies is regarded as being south of Brooks Peninsula. Any future breeding evidence from the west coast region will hopefully be documented. Other than singing males in June, the only evidence for breeding consisted of an adult and young seen at Swan Lake on 7 July 1972. This record was not accepted as confirmation of breeding by Hatler et al.[1] or *The Birds of British Columbia*.[299]

Birds seen and heard on Vargas Island in June, where they almost certainly breed, inhabit an open forest of shore pine (*Pinus contorta*) at low elevation. These are areas of poor drainage, often with standing water. The Long Beach Golf Course was built on similar habitat and remnant stands of shore pine are found there. If this is the preferred nesting habitat for the species, then there are fairly large areas on the west coast suitable for breeding, particularly in Clayoquot Sound and on the Hesquiat Peninsula.

It is difficult to determine exactly when local birds depart, though it is likely in August. The first northern birds begin arriving in late September and the movement continues through October and well into November. October appears to be the main migration period. On 14 October 1983, 30 birds were seen at Stubbs Island, and on 11 October 2012, 18 birds were counted at Tofino. Dates of 16 November 1982 at Tofino and 20 November 1982 at Radar Beach indicate that very late transients are still passing through then. All fall birds were Myrtle Warblers, except on two occasions: one Audubon's Warbler was seen on 11 November 2004 at Stubbs Island, and two were observed on 11 October 2012 accompanying a flock of Myrtle Warblers in Tofino.

There is a small wintering population of Myrtle Warblers on Stubbs Island, near Tofino, where they are found in an area containing stands of red alder and a profusion of wax-myrtle bushes, also known as Pacific bayberry. This is a unique situation in coastal British Columbia (R.W. Campbell, personal communication). By feeding on the waxy berries, Myrtle Warblers are able to survive the winter with minimal reliance on insects. The winter climate on the central west coast, it should be noted, is often the mildest (and wettest) in Canada, and insects in midwinter are not unusual. Myrtle Warblers have been seen here each winter since 1982, with counts varying from 6 to 30 birds. Due to the dense vegetation, any particular count likely does not take in all of the birds present.

BLACK-THROATED GRAY WARBLER
Setophaga nigrescens

STATUS: Rare migrant in spring and rare in early summer and fall. Breeding unconfirmed.

The Black-throated Grey Warbler breeds in suitable habitat throughout much of the western United States, from New Mexico north to western Wyoming and west to California, Oregon, and Washington. In British Columbia, the species breeds primarily in the Fraser Valley from Hope to Vancouver, and in the Salish Sea basin, including southeastern Vancouver Island. Black-throated Gray Warblers have been recorded over a much larger area, including the west coast, so the species may have a more extensive breeding range than is currently recognized. It is absent from Haida Gwaii and most of the central mainland coast (BCFWS).

Black-throated Gray Warblers were not proven to occur on southeastern Vancouver Island until 1927, although there is some evidence that they may have been present in Victoria as early as 1892. The species was scarce in the early part of the previous century, while today it is considered a fairly common migrant and summer visitor.

Until fairly recently, this bird was not often encountered in our west coast region. *Birds of Pacific Rim National Park* did not list this species at all, although at least two records existed prior to its publication in 1978. On 11 June 1961, 2 birds were seen at Carmanah Point,[299] and on 16 May 1969, a bird was seen at Grant Bay.[16] A published record of 10 birds reported from Tofino in May 1974 is considered suspect and is not accepted here. Such was the scarcity of this bird in our region that I did not see or hear one until 21 May 1996, 24 years after taking up residence on the west coast. There are, however, at least two records between 1969 and 1996. On 15 April 1980, one was recorded at Cape Scott Park, and on 15 August 1994, one was recorded near Ucluelet by Brian Slater. Admittedly, there may have been sightings during this period of which I have no knowledge.

After the mid-1990s, sightings became more frequent. A bird was recorded in Tofino on 11 August 1999, and another was found in the Kennedy Lake lowlands on 1 July 2002. From 31 May to 3 June 2004, one was seemingly on territory at the junction of the Radar Hill turnoff. Around this time, birds began to be encountered annually, with 1 or 2 records for each of the following eight years. Then in 2013, records jumped to 5 in a single year, and in 2014 there were 10 sightings. In 2016, there were 13 records before the end of June, some involving two and three birds. It seems clear that the species is gradually increasing and likely breeds here. This increase has likely been aided by the large-scale felling of old-growth forests, resulting in more deciduous trees. Birds have been found from Jordan River to Cape Scott.

There is a sighting that predates the very early spring sighting in April 1980 by more than a month. On the remarkably early date of 10 March in 2015, a male Black-throated Gray Warbler was seen in Tofino in the company of Chestnut-backed Chickadees and a male Townsend's Warbler.

TOWNSEND'S WARBLER
Setophaga townsendi

STATUS: Common spring transient and common breeding bird in late spring and early summer. Uncommon fall migrant. Breeds.

This exclusively western bird was named after the American naturalist and ornithologist John Kirk Townsend, who first collected this warbler in 1834-35. It was likely from one of his specimens that John James Audubon made his famous painting.

Members of the wood-warbler family are known for their colourful and often striking appearance, and this species does not disappoint. Indeed, a male Townsend's Warbler in breeding plumage, seen up close, is nothing short of stunning. It breeds from Oregon, Washington, Idaho, and western Montana north through western Alberta, British Columbia, the Yukon, and southeast Alaska. In British Columbia, it breeds widely throughout the province with the exception of the northeast. The species winters in two separate regions, one along the US coast from Washington to California, the other from western Mexico through Central America.

In our region, the first spring arrivals are usually seen around mid-April, though some have been recorded earlier. Single birds were first seen at Bamfield on 6 April 1991 and 12 April 1992. Two birds were recorded at Sombrio, south of Port Renfrew, and 3 at Jordan River on 5 April 2014. Two others were recorded at Port Renfrew on 9 April 2014. The earliest sighting ever recorded was on 10 March in 2015, in Tofino, but such an early date is highly unusual. A flight of 11 birds seen on 17 April 2010 at the Long Beach Golf Course and 2 in Tofino the same day suggest that a significant movement was already underway at that time.

The largest flight yet recorded in our region occurred on 21 April 2007, when an estimated 110 warblers passed by in minutes at the south end of Long Beach, most of them Townsend's Warblers. Two other large flights have been recorded. On 27 April 2013, 65 Townsend's Warblers passed by in a span of minutes near the mouth of Sandhill Creek, Long Beach, and two years later, again on 27 April, at least 50 were seen at the south end of Long Beach.

On the outer coast, the song of the males can be heard throughout May and June emanating from high up in the Sitka spruce trees adjacent to the beach. The song of the Townsend's Warbler has a number of variations, but can easily be distinguished by its quality. A sequence that sounds to my ears like *zeeya-zeeya-zeeya-zeeya-zit* is a common one. A bird survey conducted in the Combers area of Long Beach on 30 May 2016 demonstrates just how common the species can be during the breeding season. In a two-hour-and-forty-minute survey covering 2 km (1.24 mi), 24 singing males were logged by Ian Cruickshank.

While direct evidence of breeding is not easy to find, birds singing in June are presumed to be breeding birds on territory. There are at least four sightings that qualify as breeding records. On 7 July 1972, an adult with newly fledged young was observed at Grice Bay. Adults with young were seen on the Willowbrae Trail on 27 July 1972, and again in Tofino on 14 July 2001. An active nest found at Long Beach on 16 May 2015 was located 12 ft above the ground in a

Sitka spruce branch. While these birds favour the Sitka spruce zone along the outer coast in particular, they can also be encountered in the mountains and in river valleys. This species nests up to 1,200 m elevation on the coast.[299] In the first documented case of parasitism in this species, a female was seen feeding two fledgling Brown-headed Cowbirds on Blunden Island on 3 August 1968.[305]

Post-breeding departure, as usual, is hard to pin down, but by late July Townsend's Warblers are increasingly difficult to find, suggesting that they move out shortly after the young are fledged. A flight of seven birds travelling with other warblers on 2 August 1996 in Tofino seems to indicate that birds are already on the move then. There are also records of three birds on each of the following dates: 8 August 2010, 11 August 2015, and 17 August 2008. Birds seen in September and October are usually single individuals and appear to be merely stragglers. I could find only three records for October, all in the first week of the month, and there are no November records. There are, however, December records from Jordan River, at the southern tip of our region. From two to four birds were recorded in the month of December in 2010, 2011, and 2014. The latest date was 27 December in 2011, and involved four individuals.

Elsewhere along the coast, the Townsend's Warbler has been recorded on Brooks Peninsula, mainly in Sitka spruce forests, from 6 May to 17 August,[13] and is considered a summer resident in the vicinity of Grant Bay and Browning Inlet.[16]

WILSON'S WARBLER
Cardellina pusilla

STATUS: Common in spring and summer, uncommon fall transient, casual in winter. Breeds.

This species has a widespread breeding range in Canada. It is found in all regions except southern Ontario, the Great Plains, and the tundra regions of the far north. It also breeds in large areas of the western United States, primarily the north. In British Columbia, it breeds in suitable habitat throughout the province. The species winters from Mexico to Panama.

The Wilson's Warbler is one of the most common summer warblers in our region. The first spring arrivals usually show up in the last few days of April or in early May. The two earliest dates ever recorded were 12 April in 1971 in Tofino, and 19 April in 1989 at Combers Beach. Most birds arrive in May. As many as

15 birds were recorded at Port Renfrew on 9 May 2013 and 30 birds at Jordan River on 11 May 2013. They are usually easy to find during the months of May and June on roadsides where salmonberry bushes proliferate. Listen for the sharp call of the male, a rapid *ch-ch-ch-ch-ch*. If you watch for a few moments, you will likely spot him among the foliage. After the breeding season, birds fall silent and you will have to rely on sight alone. Although the Wilson's Warbler probably breeds along the entire west coast of Vancouver Island, there is only one confirmed breeding record. On 7 July 2002, an adult female was feeding two newly hatched young in a salmonberry bush near Bamfield (BCNRS).

Departure dates are almost impossible to determine with any accuracy. There are numerous records for July and August but only seven records for September, indicating that most birds depart in August. Volume 4 of *The Birds of British Columbia* lists an additional record of 20 birds at Tofino on 11 September 1971,[299] suggesting a significant movement on that date. For October, there are only two records – a bird seen on 25 October 1989 and one on 4 October 2010.

There is a surprisingly high number of records for November, all from Tofino: 17 November 1982, 16 November 1983, 11 to 25 November 2004, and 6 to 21 November 2016. There are also two records for December. From 4 to 8 December 1982, a bird was seen at Tofino, and on 3 December 1983, one was recorded at Jordan River. In Tofino, these very late birds survive by feeding on flies and bees attracted to flowering ivy. Indeed, the plentiful supply of food is undoubtedly the reason for their dallying. Local breeding birds are believed to move out during late July and August, and the birds we see in September or later are likely migrants from further north.

North of the central west coast, the Wilson's Warbler is widely distributed in the edges of forest openings, mainly as a summer visitor. It is present on Brooks Peninsula from 6 May to 19 August,[13] and is considered a summer resident in the vicinity of Browning Inlet.[16]

Sparrows and Towhees *Family Passerellidae*

AMERICAN TREE SPARROW
Spizelloides arborea

STATUS: Casual transient in spring and fall.

This is a bird of the far northern latitudes. It breeds along the edge of the tundra among scattered trees and shrubs from Labrador in the east across Canada to

Alaska and the Bering Sea. It winters in southern Canada from Nova Scotia to British Columbia, and in much of the United States with the exception of the south and the far west. In British Columbia, breeding is confined to the northern quarter of the province, where it nests at higher elevation. It is considered a rare migrant and winter visitor in the southern interior, in the Fraser Lowlands, and on southeastern Vancouver Island.[299]

On the west coast, this sparrow is encountered very infrequently. To date there are only four records: 3 November 1973, Sandhill Creek, Long Beach – 1 (BC Photo 678); 23 April 1987, 8 km northwest of Triangle Island – 1 landed on a boat; 29 October 1991, Stubbs Island, Tofino – 1; and 30 April 2006, Chesterman Beach, Tofino – 1.

CHIPPING SPARROW
Spizella passerina

STATUS: A casual vagrant except at Jordan River, where it is a rare transient in spring, casual in fall, and a rare breeder.

This species has a breeding range that covers much of North America except for parts of the American Southwest and the most northerly regions of Canada. In British Columbia, the species breeds throughout the interior of the province east of the Coast Mountains. On the coast, it breeds only in the Fraser Lowlands and along southeastern and southern Vancouver Island. The species winters in the southern United States, Mexico, and Central America. It has wintered on southern Vancouver Island.

For the west coast region, there are 30 records. Sixteen of these were recorded in Jordan River at the extreme south end of our region, which is not surprising. Most records are from the southern half of the region, with only two sightings from north of Tofino, both from Triangle Island: a bird was observed feeding in dry seaweed along the beach on 4 June 1976,[299] and another bird was seen on 4 and 11 August 1994.[26] The latter also happens to be our only August record. To break the records down by month, we have 1 record for the end of March, 8 for April, 6 for May, and 9 for June. Those recorded in early June are still considered spring migrants.

There is one other summer record. On 20 July 2014, five birds were seen at Jordan River. These included an adult seen carrying food to two fledglings. There have also been three sightings in September, and there is a single winter record. On 21 February 1996, a bird was seen at the Long Beach Golf Course.

It is not likely to have been overwintering, so it may have been an over-enthusiastic spring migrant that "jumped the gun," so to speak.

CLAY-COLORED SPARROW
Spizella pallida
STATUS: Casual vagrant in spring and fall.

This species breeds from southern Quebec, southern Ontario, and Michigan westward across the northern United States and the Canadian Prairie provinces to the Rocky Mountains and eastern British Columbia, and north to the Northwest Territories. In this province, Clay-colored Sparrows have expanded their range westward. The species breeds from the East Kootenays to the central interior and further north from the Peace River region to the northeast corner of the province. On the coast, it is considered a very rare spring and autumn vagrant,[299] with a single record of a bird overwintering near Victoria.[306]

In the west coast region, the species was first recorded at the Lovekin Rock parking lot at Long Beach on 6 and 30 October 1982 (BC Photo 809 1983).[265] Since then, there have been eight additional sightings from Carmanah Point to Cape Scott: 9-13 November 1986, mouth of Sandhill Creek Long Beach – 1, Linda Koch et al.;[152] 3 December 2000, Ucluelet – 1, Rob Worona;[307] 17 October 2004, Ucluelet – 1, Brian Slater; 28 and 29 September 2005, Cape Scott, J. Bradley and N. Johnston;[232] 10 September 2007, Kennedy Lake – 1, Mike Tabak; 29 November to 19 December 2011, Carmanah Point – 1, Jerry Etzkorn (BC Photo 4044); 14 September 2013, Ucluelet sewage pond – 1, John Reynolds and Rob Lyske; and 6 June 2014, Long Beach Airport – 1, A. Dorst. In addition, there have been two sightings at Jordan River, at the extreme south end of our region, both during the fall period.

LARK SPARROW
Chondestes grammacus
STATUS: Casual vagrant in spring, summer, and fall.

The breeding range of this handsome and distinctively marked sparrow extends throughout most of the western United States and the Midwest. In Canada, it breeds in southern areas of the Prairie provinces and in British Columbia. In our province, it breeds primarily in the Okanagan and Similkameen valleys of the southern interior. On the south coast, including Vancouver Island, it is considered a very rare transient in spring and fall.

On Vancouver Island's west coast, we have records involving 13 birds. The species was seen in all months from April to December. We have four records in spring, three in summer, and six in fall.

The first sighting occurred on 28 April 1975, when a Lark Sparrow was seen opposite the entrance to the Lovekin Rock parking lot at Long Beach (BC Photo 410). On 16 August the following year, a Lark Sparrow was recorded at Bamfield. Ten years later, on 2 July 1986, a male was found singing and apparently on territory at the Long Beach Airport. In 1994, a bird was present in Ucluelet from 22 November to 2 December. Two years later, one was seen and photographed in the village of Tofino from 21 to 25 October 1996. Another was seen there on 25 and 26 October 1998. On 29 May 2003, a bird was reported from Ucluelet.

Further records followed, with a sighting at Long Beach on 1 June 2006, at Carmanah Point on 24 August 2007, and at Jordan River on 26 May 2009. In 2013, a bird was seen and photographed at Stubbs Island, near Tofino, from 22 to 28 September. This bird appeared to be sustaining itself on the seeds of European varieties of dune grass growing on the island. Two weeks later, on 13 October, a juvenile bird was seen and photographed at Jordan River. On 13 May 2016, a Lark Sparrow was again seen on Stubbs Island.

LARK BUNTING
Calamospiza melanocorys

STATUS: Casual vagrant in spring, summer, and fall.

This is a bird of the open country of the Great Plains. Its breeding range stretches from northern Texas in the south to the Canadian Prairies in the north, where it breeds from the southwest corner of Manitoba across southern Saskatchewan to southeast Alberta. It is a vagrant anywhere west of the Rocky Mountains and is considered a very rare vagrant on the south coast, including Vancouver Island.

On the west coast of Vancouver Island, we have four records. On 28 August 2000, visiting birder Chris Siddle reported catching a glimpse of an interesting finch of unknown identity at the Pacific Rim National Park sewage pond. The bird was subsequently flushed from the long grass and identified as a Lark Bunting. Given the amount of white visible on the wings in flight, this was probably a young male. A second record for this species is of an adult female seen by Arthur Ahier at Tofino on 14 June 2004.[231] Our third record comes from Jordan River, where a female was found by Louis Haviland on 16 October 2011. A fourth sighting involved a female, discovered and photographed by Thomas Barbin at Botanical Beach, Port Renfrew, on 5 September 2016.

FOX SPARROW
Passerella iliaca

STATUS: Common in spring, summer, and fall. Uncommon to fairly common in winter. Breeds.

Shown here is the Sooty Fox Sparrow of the west coast. It is easily found in summer by listening for its melodious song.

Fox Sparrows have been divided into as many as 18 populations, or subspecies, with 11 of those occurring in British Columbia. More recently, however, the species has been divided into a complex of four distinctive types, three of them found in British Columbia. Based on genetic and behavioural studies, these could well be given full species status at some time in the future.[299] The Red (or Taiga) Fox Sparrow breeds in the boreal forest from the Maritimes and

Newfoundland right across Canada to northern British Columbia. The Slate-colored Fox Sparrow breeds in the American West and throughout the interior of British Columbia east of the Coast Mountains, while the Sooty Fox Sparrow breeds on the Pacific coast from Washington to Alaska.

On Vancouver Island's west coast, the resident bird is the Sooty Fox Sparrow. Walk the spruce fringe behind any beach in late spring or early summer and you won't get far before you hear its melodic song, for this is a common breeding bird in our region. In fact, on Vancouver Island it occurs regularly in summer only in far northern and western regions, including offshore islands.[308] So common is it on the west coast that on 4 June 1983, a total of 49 singing birds were counted between the south end of Long Beach and Tofino. While nests are difficult to find, newly fledged young (some being fed) have been seen at numerous locations, including Cleland Island, Brooks Peninsula, Solander Island, Triangle Island, and Long Beach. On Brooks Peninsula, 11 fledged young with short tails and natal down on the head were counted along drift logs between 5 and 14 August 1981.[13] Fledged young have been found as early as 22 May (1931) on Cleland Island (BCNRS).

Fox sparrows are most easily seen in fall and early winter, when they are scratching in the leaves behind beaches, or on the edge of parking lots and on roadsides. There is little evidence of transients from the north or the interior passing through in early fall. This is not surprising, given that the same is true for many other passerines, which pass over at night or bypass us altogether when they have favourable weather for flying. Only by observing a spike in numbers do we become aware that migrants are passing through.

With the exception of the summer count mentioned above, the month of December usually produces the highest numbers. On Christmas Bird Counts at Tofino, 16 birds were seen on 29 December 1987; 23 on 29 December 2001; and 16 on 26 November 2003. At a single location – the Lovekin Rock parking lot at Long Beach – 18 birds were recorded on 26 December 2012 and 17 on 1 January 2013. In the fall of 2012, birds were hard to find in November, but 5 were counted on 1 December. The very next day there were 19 birds and on 6 December there were 24, suggesting a sudden influx from elsewhere. Numbers gradually decline through January, suggesting that most birds depart for points south. In 2015, 8 birds were counted on 19 January, and by 25 January there was not a bird to be found. Only very low numbers persist through February and March in most years. In years when cold temperatures prevail, birds may dwindle much sooner.

Sooty Fox Sparrows from northern British Columbia and Alaska winter in Oregon and California. One would therefore expect to see a swelling of numbers in our area in spring as transient birds move through. However, records reveal only a modest increase in April, followed by a decline in May as birds disperse to their breeding territories. In 2008, numbers spiked on 8 April, in 2011 on 21 April, in 2012 on 11 April, and in 2014 during the last week of April.

Although three of the four types of Fox Sparrows have been recorded in the west coast region, only the Sooty is seen here regularly. The Red (or Taiga) Fox Sparrow was recorded in Tofino on 27 November 2010, and there had been one previous sighting in Tofino, although the date could not be found. A Slate-colored Fox Sparrow was observed and photographed at the Lovekin Rock parking lot at Long Beach on 30 March 2014. To date, this is our only record of the interior variety, though it is worth watching for as these birds likely occur from time to time.

DARK-EYED JUNCO
Junco hyemalis
STATUS: Common resident. Breeds.

There are as many as six geographical variants, or subspecies, of the Dark-eyed Junco. We need not go into all of them here, as only two occur in British Columbia: the Oregon Junco and the Slate-colored Junco. The latter breeds in forested areas throughout much of Canada except the southwestern half of British Columbia. The Oregon Junco was for many years considered a separate species. It breeds from California north to Washington, southern and western British Columbia, and the Rocky Mountains of western Alberta. It breeds commonly on Vancouver Island.

In the west coast region, Dark-eyed Juncos may be seen in all months of the year, although it is in fall that they are most common and conspicuous. During the summer months, they are on their breeding territories, which are usually in clearings ranging from clearcuts to bogs, forest edge, or even campgrounds. Anyone familiar with their song, a short trill, will have no difficulty finding them in appropriate habitat.

There is plentiful evidence that they breed in our area, particularly in the form of heavily streaked young seen in summer. On 26 June 2012, an adult was seen feeding a newly fledged young very close to home – on the balcony of my apartment in Tofino – and on 30 June 2015, young birds were observed near the lower Kennedy River. It appears that the species also nests at high elevation in the subalpine zone in the mountains. On 27 July 1986, I recorded

8 birds above 1,000 m elevation on Mount Klitsa, and on 13 August 2008, 18 birds were found there by Nigel Jackett. A small number of birds were also found on several other peaks in the area by the same observer, though somewhat later in September. Those peaks included 5040, Halfpipe South, and Steamboat Mountain, which is part of the Clayoquot Plateau.

By late September or October, Dark-eyed Juncos are being seen more frequently as they move out of their breeding territories and feed on roadsides or gather at backyard feeders. Before the end of November, they have settled into a winter territory. Flock size varies greatly, although most flocks contain fewer than 25 birds. Occasionally, flocks of 30 and even 45 birds have been recorded. An unusually large number, 65 birds, convened in a Tofino yard on 30 January 2009. This was likely due to the convergence of two or three flocks at a location where seed and grain had been spread on the ground. By April, birds begin to disperse and return to breeding territories; by late April or May, few, if any, remain.

Birds that arrive from afar in autumn may not be just local birds. This is demonstrated by the occasional appearance of a Slate-colored Junco among the Oregon subspecies. In Tofino, there are records of at least one individual in most years. This subspecies nests hundreds of miles away in the northwest and northeast of the province and northward.

Occasionally, a Slate-colored Junco will be found with white wing bars. In British Columbia, these have proven to be a variant that occurs in the population occasionally, rather than a member of the White-winged subspecies from the US Midwest.

WHITE-CROWNED SPARROW
Zonotrichia leucophrys

STATUS: Common migrant in spring and fall, locally common in summer. Locally fairly common in winter. Breeds.

White-crowned Sparrows breed from Labrador and northern Quebec west through northern parts of the boreal forests and the tundra regions to the Yukon and Alaska. They breed southward through western Alberta, British Columbia, and mountainous areas of the American West to northern New Mexico and California. They winter throughout much of the United States and northern Mexico, with the exception of parts of the northeastern states and the northern Midwest. In British Columbia, the species breeds throughout

The White-crowned Sparrow is a common breeding bird. In winter, adults and juveniles can be enticed to backyard feeders.

most of the province east of the Coast Mountains, in the Fraser Valley, and on Vancouver Island. On the coast, birds winter from southeast Alaska southward.

White-crowned Sparrows may be seen in our region in all months of the year. They breed in logged-over areas until the young trees attain a specific height, as well as in other semi-open habitat, including villages. This species is able to adapt even to urban areas. On several occasions, I have heard singing males in downtown Vancouver at the intersection of West Georgia and West Pender streets, apparently proclaiming a breeding territory in the shrubs of an office tower. Adult males on territory may also be seen in the centre of Tofino in some years.

White-crowned Sparrows are most evident during the spring migration period, when they are often seen in the company of Golden-crowned Sparrows, though they are usually outnumbered by the latter by 10 to 1, and usually much more. The largest number recorded in spring was 25 birds on 2 May 2000. The first migrants arrive in April, though the presence of wintering birds makes it difficult to determine exactly when. In 2010, there was a significant influx on 17 April, with 16 birds observed in Tofino and 10 birds at the Long Beach Golf Course. On 14 April 2011, 5 migrants were seen at the airport. In 2015, 3 newly arrived migrants were seen on 11 April at Long Beach.

If it is difficult to determine just when the northward movement begins, determining when it ends is even more so. This is due to the fact that the

White-crowned Sparrow is also a breeding resident. Northern birds probably pass through until mid-May, though perhaps later in some years. An observation of 10 White-crowned Sparrows at the Long Beach Golf Course on 29 May 2002 suggests that some migrants were still passing through at that late date.

Despite ample evidence of breeding, such as young birds seen in late summer, there are only two confirmed breeding records. However, there have been observations of territorial behaviour that strongly suggests nesting. An adult with young was seen by C.J. Guiguet on Stubbs Island on 13 July 1960, and an adult was seen feeding two recently fledged young in a bush at Bamfield on 2 July 2002 (BCNRS).

There is no pronounced movement in fall, at least not one that is readily apparent. However, a spike in numbers was observed at the Long Beach Airport on 9 September 2004, with 25 birds counted. Ten days later, on 19 September, 15 birds were tallied. In 2013, 17 birds were observed on 22 September. These numbers are significantly higher than usual, and while they might signify migrants passing through, it is more likely this boost in population is due to the presence of locally raised youngsters. Small numbers overwinter in Tofino and Ucluelet, and likely other villages as well. A flock of 21 birds seen in Tofino on 1 December 2016 had grown to 26 birds by 7 January and were undoubtedly overwintering. This also happened to be the largest flock ever recorded in winter. Members of this species, it should be noted, often mingle with Golden-crowned Sparrows during migration and in winter.

In spring, White-crowned × Golden-crowned hybrids have been seen on two occasions at a Tofino feeder. Since Golden-crowned Sparrows do not nest on Vancouver Island, the hybridization must have occurred much further north.

GOLDEN-CROWNED SPARROW
Zonotrichia atricapilla

STATUS: Common, often abundant, spring migrant. Uncommon in fall and winter, though may be locally fairly common.

This member of the genus *Zonotrichia* is exclusively western. Its breeding range extends throughout much of British Columbia east of the Coast Mountains, north and west to the Yukon and Alaska, and eastward into the western Northwest Territories and the Rocky Mountains of Alberta. Its preferred breeding habitat is shrubby open habitat, usually at higher elevation. There is a single isolated breeding record for southern Vancouver Island, near Sidney, at 21 m

Golden-crowned Sparrows are a common to abundant transient in spring, their plaintive song seemingly everywhere at times.

elevation.[309] The species winters from southwestern British Columbia south through western parts of Washington, Oregon, and California to northwestern Baja California.

The Golden-crowned Sparrow is well known to residents of the west coast, particularly devoted gardeners for whom these sparrows are a scourge each spring, nipping off the tender leaves of just-emerging garden vegetables. Long-time gardeners may therefore be more knowledgeable than field ornithologists as to just when the migration period begins and ends. Based on data over a period of several decades, a few early individuals may begin trickling in by mid-April or shortly thereafter. These can be distinguished from local wintering birds by their plumage. Migrants from further south are in breeding plumage, whereas local immature birds are not. The main movement from the south usually occurs during the last week of April and the first week of May, and often occurs as an inundation or "fallout" involving large numbers. For example, 50 birds were seen in Tofino on 26 April 1969, and 250 were estimated feeding along the beach at Grice Bay on 3 May 1974.

Fallout occurs when, during the peak of the migration, birds are forced down by a weather front that obscures the sun and stars, making navigation impossible. In our region, this is usually a southeasterly front with low scudding clouds, accompanied by rain or drizzle. On 29 April 1993, a fallout of 300 birds occurred in Pacific Rim National Park.[310] An even larger number was tallied on 5 May 1999 at the Long Beach Airport, when 261 Golden-crowned Sparrows were counted as they passed slowly by just above the ground. A count at the nearby golf course produced an additional 270 birds, for a total of 530 birds that morning. On 2 May 2000, 450 birds were counted at the golf course, and on 28 April 2008, an estimated 300 birds were in the immediate vicinity of my residence in Tofino.

Such moments are very impressive and memorable, as the air is filled with their song, and the excitement of these birds at being en route to their breeding territories is readily apparent.

Most sparrows will readily take sunflower seeds at feeders, and this species is no exception. Up to 50 birds have crowded onto my second-storey balcony after the deck has been seeded. These birds are also very trusting. Once, I inadvertently left the sliding glass door slightly ajar before leaving, and returned a short time later to find a dozen birds exploring all corners of the living room, appearing not the least bit discomfited by this alien environment. Their song, which consists of a pleasing but plaintive descending series of three notes, is described by a friend from the United Kingdom as sounding like *too-fat-to-fly, too-fat-to-fly.*

Records after the first week in May are scarce. The spring of 2008 was exceptional, with 35 birds still at the golf course on 14 May. The latest spring bird on the central west coast was one seen at the airport on 26 May in 2010. A bird on Triangle Island, seen in a scrub crabapple bush on 4 June 1974, was very unusual.[299] This species is entirely absent during the summer months, but by the third week of September or early October, the first birds appear once again, either on their way south or as winter residents. I have a single record of a bird earlier than that, recorded on 1 September 2004 at the airport.

Unlike the spring migration, the fall movement is inconspicuous with low numbers. Flocks are rarely larger than 12 birds and occasionally exceed 20. A record of 100 birds in Tofino on 9 September 1996 is exceptional. Another flock of 100 migrating birds was estimated on Lennard Island on 13 October 1976.[299] By late November or December, any birds still present can be presumed to be wintering birds. Although *Birds of Pacific Rim National Park* listed no winter records, there have been winter occurrences since at least 1979, and these are quite normal on the west coast, primarily in backyards and other semi-open areas such as the Long Beach Airport. Nearly all wintering birds are juveniles. Adults are rarely seen in winter.

Elsewhere on the west coast, such as in the vicinity of Browning Inlet, Golden-crowned Sparrows are not as common, and are considered only occasional spring and fall migrants.[16]

HARRIS'S SPARROW
Zonotrichia querula

STATUS: Casual vagrant in spring, fall, and winter. Accidental in summer.

This is the largest of the *Zonotrichia* sparrows and also the most boldly marked. Its breeding range lies west of Hudson Bay, beginning in northern Manitoba and running northwest across much of Nunavut and the Northwest Territories to the shores of the Beaufort Sea. It migrates through Canada's Prairie provinces to winter in the US Midwest, from southern South Dakota to Texas. Migrant birds stray widely, however, and have been recorded in all states and provinces. In British Columbia, the species has been seen in numerous locations at widely divergent points. It is considered a rare to uncommon winter visitor in the central interior and in the Salish Sea basin, including southeastern Vancouver Island.[299]

In our west coast region, Harris's Sparrows occur less frequently. *Birds of Pacific Rim National Park* listed only a single record, an immature at Chalk Island in the Broken Group, on 26 October 1972.[1] Since then, birds have been recorded in 10 additional years and have overwintered on at least three occasions. All dates in our region fall between 29 September and 23 March, with two exceptions. An adult was present at the feeder of Tofino resident Rory Paterson from 30 April to 15 May in 1993, and a bird was seen by Jerry Etzkorn at Carmanah Point on the very unlikely date of 26 June 2001. Most first arrival dates in fall are in November, and most of our visitors have been immatures.

WHITE-THROATED SPARROW
Zonotrichia albicollis

STATUS: Rare fall migrant. Casual in winter and spring.

For those who have spent time in Canada's north, the song of the White-throated Sparrow evokes the northern forests almost as strongly as the cry of the loon. This species breeds in the most northerly regions of the eastern United States west to Minnesota, and in the boreal forests of Canada from the Maritimes west to the Prairie provinces, the Northwest Territories, the southeastern Yukon, and northeastern British Columbia. In this province, it breeds in the

Taiga Plains of the northeast, the Peace River region, and central parts of the province, south to Quesnel. On southeastern Vancouver Island, it is considered an uncommon migrant and winter visitor.[299]

The first White-throated Sparrow recorded in the west coast region was seen in a meadow on Vargas Island on 14 November 1968. *Birds of Pacific Rim National Park* listed only one other record.[1] Since its publication in 1978, 32 additional birds have been recorded, 45 if records from Jordan River are included. One of the observations, recorded on 15 October 1981 at Chesterman Beach, involved 3 birds; another at Jordan River on 3 November 2011 involved 4 individuals. All other sightings but one were of single birds. Two birds were seen on Stubbs Island on 5 October 2016.

By far the majority of sightings have been in fall, with 7 records in September, 12 in October, 8 in November, and 4 in December. In 2015, an individual was seen daily at a feeder in Tofino from 24 November to 18 December. Winter records are scarce, with 3 sightings in January and one each in the months of February, March, April, and May. Only the summer months have no records. Most sightings have occurred in backyards and open areas with shrubbery in and around Tofino, although birds have also been sighted on Stubbs Island, at the Long Beach Airport, Cleland Island, Ucluelet, and Jordan River. One individual was recorded far offshore during a pelagic birding trip.

The only known occurrences north of the central coast were a bird observed and banded on Triangle Island on 2 October 1994 and one at Grant Bay on 8 November 1968.[16] It is unlikely that this absence of sightings in the northern half of our region is due to anything other than a paucity of observers.

VESPER SPARROW
Pooecetes gramineus

STATUS: Casual spring vagrant.

This rather drab ground-dwelling sparrow draws attention to itself when flushed by flashing white outer tail feathers. It is a bird of grasslands and sparsely vegetated fields. Its breeding range stretches across the northern half of the United States from coast to coast. In Canada, it breeds from Newfoundland west to the Prairie provinces and British Columbia. In this province, it is considered a common or fairly common breeding bird in the Columbia Valley and the Peace River region, and is very common in the dry interior grasslands. On the coast, it is considered a rare or very rare migrant. A few birds still breed at the airport in Cassidy south of Nanaimo (BCNRS). This is the coastal subspecies *P. g. affinis*.

In our region, we have five records, all in spring: 7 May 1969, south end of Long Beach – 1; 25 April 1981, south end of Long Beach – 1; 2 June 2001, Long Beach Airport – 1; 4-10 June 2002, Carmanah Point – 1; and 21 April 2006, Long Beach Golf Course – 1. Both sightings from the south end of Long Beach were in the sand dunes.

SAVANNAH SPARROW
Passerculus sandwichensis

STATUS: Common to abundant spring and fall migrant. Casual in winter. Breeds.

Savannah Sparrows are one of the most abundant transients. In fall, hundreds may be counted on beaches and grassy estuaries.

This bird of the grasslands breeds throughout North America except for the High Arctic islands and southern United States. In British Columbia, it breeds in suitable habitat throughout much of the interior of the province, as well as in the Fraser Valley and southeastern Vancouver Island. Savannah Sparrows winter through much of the southern United States southward, and on the west coast from Vancouver Island south to Guatemala.

The population that migrates through Vancouver Island's west coast region is the subspecies *P. s. sandwichensis,* which breeds on Unalaska Island at the eastern end of the Aleutian chain,[299] which lies some 2,600 km (1,600 mi) northwest of Vancouver Island. It appears that birds make the flight to and from Vancouver Island by taking a direct route over the Pacific rather than the much longer flight following the shore around the Gulf of Alaska. This would explain the overnight invasion of west coast beaches by hundreds of birds each year in September and October. When this occurs, it is inevitably after a period of clear skies, sometimes accompanied by a brisk wind from the northwest.

One location where large numbers convene in fall is Stubbs Island, near Tofino, where Savannah Sparrows feed on the seeds of several introduced varieties of European dune grass. On 19 September 2004, 300 birds were estimated there, and on 30 September 2013, 350 birds. An estimated 200 birds were recorded along the northern section of Long Beach on 20 September 1980, and about 250 birds at the Long Beach Airport on 11 October 1984.

In spring, such an inundation, or "fallout," is usually the result of a weather front interrupting the migration. Surveys conducted at the Long Beach Golf Course produced counts and estimates of 200 birds on 6 May 1999, 250 on 3 May 2001, 290 on 27 April 2008, and 132 on 11 May 2011. Birds generally begin arriving in late April, with the peak migration period occurring anywhere from late April to mid-May. By the end of the third week of May all birds have usually departed. On Cleland Island, migration counts were made in 1970. Thirty (the maximum number) were noted on 11 May, and the last bird was recorded on 6 June. For a four-year spring period from 1969 through 1972, the earliest arrival date was 19 April and the latest departure date was 30 May.

Extended periods of heavy fog in spring can be devastating for migrating Savannah Sparrows. On 2 and 3 May 1972, 57 passerines of five species were killed flying into the lighthouse at Cape Scott, in the northwest corner of the region. Of these, 30 (53%) were Savannah Sparrows and all were males, suggesting a sex-segregated migration.[311]

Fall migration usually commences during the last week of August or early September. First arrivals at Stubbs Island were seen on 30 August in 2014 and 26 August in 2016. In 2004, 60 birds were counted at the airport as early as 1 September, and in 2014, birds peaked at Stubbs Island on 5 September. Large numbers are usually not seen until mid-September or even into October. By late October, virtually all birds have departed. There is a late date of 20 birds on 31 October in 2010, at Jordan River. A very few individuals may linger to late November, and I have two records for December. On 6 December 1989, a bird was seen in Tofino, and on 1 December 2014, a single bird was observed on the beach at Florencia Bay. These were likely very late migrants. Overwintering birds are extremely rare. There is one record for Vargas Island on 10 January 1969,[299] and one record at the airport on 5 February 2001. As first suggested by Hatler et al., the fall migration generally occurs in two "waves."[1] In 2004, 100 birds were counted at the south end of Long Beach on 15 September; five weeks later, on 19 October, 300 birds were tallied at Stubbs Island. In 2014, the first wave peaked with 265 birds at Stubbs Island on 5 September; three weeks later, on 26 September, a second wave of 150 birds was observed at the same location.

As far back as 1972, birds had been heard singing at the Long Beach Airport during the month of June, raising suspicions that birds were breeding there. Breeding was confirmed on 14 June 2004, when an adult and newly fledged young were seen together. Since then, counts at the airport during the summer months indicate that a small population of Savannah Sparrows breeds there each year. In some years, a good number of young are seen in July and August.

Local birds occasionally overwinter. Resident airport birds appear to be slightly paler than the migrants, with less prominent streaking on the breast, sides, and face, indicating that they belong to the subspecies *P. s. brooksi*, which nests on the southeast side of Vancouver Island. Members of this subspecies are also the first to arrive in spring.

SONG SPARROW
Melospiza melodia

STATUS: Common in spring, summer, and fall. Uncommon in winter, though locally common. Breeds.

The Song Sparrow is one of Canada's most familiar birds – if not the bird itself, then at least its ebullient song. When breeding range and winter range are combined, it is found throughout most of North America, from Labrador, James Bay, and southern parts of the Northwest Territories to northern Mexico. In the west, it breeds from the Aleutian Islands of Alaska south to northwestern Mexico, and can be found wintering throughout the Pacific coastal region. In British Columbia, it breeds throughout the province, though in winter, birds of the northern interior migrate further south. Birds overwinter in parts of the southern interior, as they do on the coast.

On Vancouver Island's west coast, the Song Sparrow is a bird of the forest edge. It is found in all months of the year, though it is most conspicuous in fall and winter, when it may be seen at the edge of parking lots and other generally shrubby locations as well as at backyard feeders, particularly those close to the ground. Song Sparrows have been seen in numerous locations, from the coast to higher elevations in the mountains. Coastal Song Sparrows also feed in the intertidal zone, even dipping into a tide pool on occasion, and it is not unusual to see them on and under drift logs on beaches, where they probably seek out small crustaceans known to locals as "beach hoppers." It is a common breeding bird and is often seen in close proximity to the (Sooty) Fox Sparrow, particularly in fall. Coastal Song Sparrows are darker than those in other regions of North America. They are easily distinguished from Fox Sparrows by their streaked appearance.

The Song Sparrow is the most common sparrow on the west coast. Males are frequently heard singing in spring and early summer. Three males were heard singing as early as 21 February in 2015, at Stubbs Island. Newly fledged young may be seen from the end of May to early August. Flying young were seen as early as 30 May in 1972 on Cleland Island, though most nesting takes place in June and July. My notes from 21 July 2009 state that among 12 Song Sparrows observed at the Long Beach Airport, many were newly fledged young. A young bird fresh out of the nest was seen as late as 10 August in 2012.

Song Sparrows also breed on all offshore seabird islands with lush vegetation, especially tall grasses and dense shrubs, including Cleland Island, Solander Island, and Triangle Island. On Brooks Peninsula, two to three young in family flocks, some barely able to fly and still sporting natal down, could be found at the edge of the forest above drift logs between 5 and 14 August 1981.[13]

Numbers swell after the breeding season. While it is common to see from 1 to 7 birds on many or most bird walks, in late summer and fall one may see 12 or more birds, with the local adult population supplemented by juveniles. By late fall, migrants have arrived from elsewhere. Stubbs Island, near Tofino, with its low scrub and dune grass, is particularly favourable habitat for this species. A one-man count there on 26 December 2009 produced 24 birds, and on 12 December 2014, 29 birds. At the Long Beach Airport, high counts were 19 birds on 27 November 2015, and 20 birds on 6 December 2016. Counts of 20 or more birds have also been made in the southern extremity of our region at Jordan River. On 10 December 2013, a total of 30 birds were recorded there.

By mid-January, there is a noticeable decline in numbers in places where regular counts are conducted, such as at the airport, at Long Beach, and at Stubbs Island, suggesting that either most birds have moved further south or they have dispersed. Indeed, it can sometimes be difficult to find even one Song Sparrow at these locations in late January or February.

LINCOLN'S SPARROW
Melospiza lincolnii

STATUS: Uncommon spring and fall transient. Casual in winter.

Lincoln's Sparrows breed throughout almost all of Canada, except for the Great Plains and the tundra regions of the far north. They also breed in much of the American West and the southern half of Alaska. In British Columbia, they breed throughout much of the province, including northern Haida Gwaii, though not in the southern Coast Mountains, the southern mainland coast, or most of Vancouver Island. The species winters from coastal Washington southward to Honduras. A few birds winter in southwestern British Columbia.

This bird is unlikely to be noticed by the casual observer, as it is inconspicuous and tends to inhabit thickets of dense vegetation. Search for it in the right habitat in spring and fall and you may well find it. In spring, birds begin arriving in mid-April or just before, and pass through until about the 10th of May. The earliest arrival date I could find is 7 April in 2007 at Jordan River. There is an even earlier date of 27 March in 2009 at the Long Beach Airport, but this is so early that it could have been an overwintering bird. We have 22 records for April and 13 for May.

The southward migration commences by early September or the end of August in some years. The earliest fall dates that birds were recorded were 28 August in 2013 and 27 August in 2016. By the end of October, the fall movement is mostly over, though some birds linger into November and December. The movement through our region does not appear to be large, in any event. For the central west coast, we have 50 records for September, 29 for October, 13 for November, and 14 for December. Sightings usually involve from 1 to 3 birds, rarely larger numbers. There are two records involving 4 birds and two involving 6 birds, all of which occurred in September. The largest numbers recorded in a single count occurred at Jordan River in 2013, with 16 birds on 6 October and 20 birds on 12 October. Evidence for overwintering is sparse, but a bird was recorded on Stubbs Island on 6 January 2001, and at the Long Beach Airport on 15 and 20 January 2013, and on 3 January 2016. There is also one record each for February and March.

Locations on the central coast where Lincoln's Sparrows have been seen most frequently include backyards in Tofino and Ucluelet, the Long Beach Golf Course/Airport, and the parking lot at Long Beach. This species has also been recorded at Esperanza and Bamfield. Birds have been found at the north end of the island in the Nahwitti bog, just outside the west coast region, during the month of June, and are believed to breed there. To date, none have been recorded breeding within the boundaries of the west coast region.

SWAMP SPARROW
Melospiza georgiana

STATUS: Casual to rare fall migrant and winter visitor.

The Swamp Sparrow breeds in the northeastern United States and in suitable habitat across Canada, from Newfoundland and the Maritimes to Alberta and to British Columbia, where it was originally believed to be restricted to the northeastern part of the province. Since 1945, however, small numbers have been found breeding in the interior as far south as Dragon Lake (BCNRS). In November 1969, the first Swamp Sparrow was recorded on Vancouver Island near Victoria, and again in December 1974. In August 1972, it was recorded at Courtenay, 190 km northwest of Victoria. Since then, it has become a regular, if rare, migrant and winter visitor to the southeast side of Vancouver Island.[299]

The first sighting in the west coast region occurred on 29 September 1983, with a bird seen at the Lovekin Rock parking lot at Long Beach.[299] It was seen again on 20 October. On 8 December of the same year, a bird was seen at Jordan River by David Fraser and others. By the end of 2016, there had been sightings in 13 separate years. Nearly all involved single birds but two birds were recorded three times: at Stubbs Island on 2 December 2009, and at the Long Beach Airport on both 24 October 2012 and 17 December 2016.

Swamp Sparrows are not seen every year, but the frequency of sightings seems to be increasing. There are four records for the 1980s, one for the 1990s, four for the period from 2000 to 2010, and five for the first half of the subsequent decade. In the years when birds do show up, they usually arrive in late October. The first record for the west coast was also the only one recorded in September.

The next earliest arrival date was on 24 October in 2012. Birds have been recorded throughout the fall and winter, with the latest date being 19 February in 2013. Birds recorded in February are presumed to be overwintering, though birds seen in early January may still move further south.

This species prefers the forest edge or low scrub in semi-open areas. Locations where Swamp Sparrows have been seen on the central coast include the Lovekin Rock parking lot at Long Beach, the Long Beach Airport, Stubbs Island, and the village of Tofino. Large areas of scrub and new growth found in logged areas on the Long Beach coastal plain may also provide suitable habitat for this species in fall and winter, but have not been surveyed.

SPOTTED TOWHEE
Pipilo maculatus

STATUS: Common fall migrant, uncommon in winter and spring, rare in summer. Breeding unconfirmed.

The Spotted Towhee is one of six members of the towhee genus in North America north of Mexico, and is the western counterpart of the Rufous-sided Towhee of the east. They were for a time considered one species until they were split again. The Spotted Towhee breeds throughout most of the western United States and the highlands of Mexico, south locally to Guatemala. In Canada, it is restricted to southern Saskatchewan, southern Alberta, and southern British Columbia. Birds in the colder regions of their range move further south, but over most of its range the species is a year-round resident. In British Columbia, Spotted Towhees breed throughout much of the southern one-third of the province east of the Coast Mountains, but also including the Fraser Valley and southeastern Vancouver Island.

In our west coast region, Spotted Towhees have been recorded in every month of the year. They occur, however, primarily as fall migrants that arrive from late September through October and November. Whether these birds come from eastern Vancouver Island or the BC interior is not clear. By November or December they reach their maximum numbers. The largest number yet recorded on the central west coast was 12 birds on 26 November 2003 at Tofino. On two occasions, six birds were recorded at the parking lot at Long Beach, the first time on 7 December 2009 and the second time on 13 December 2013. In addition, 9 birds were tallied on a Christmas Bird Count in the Tofino area on 29 December 2001. Greater numbers have been seen at the extreme south end of our region at Jordan River, with 18 birds recorded on 6 and 12 October 2013, which is long before birds reach their peak on the central west coast.

Spotted Towhees follow the same pattern as several other species in the family Passerellidae, building up in numbers through the fall and becoming scarce in January. A few individuals will stay for the duration of the winter, particularly in villages if food is available at backyard feeders. Numbers seen on any single bird walk in winter do not usually exceed two or three birds. Records during the months of March, April, and May do not indicate any discernible upsurge in numbers, so any spring movement in our region likely only involves birds leaving the area.

Although most records are from the southern half of our region, there have been sightings in the northern half: 23 May 1974, Sea Otter Cove – 1;[4] 25 May 1974, San Josef Bay – 1;[4] 21 April 2004, San Josef River – 1;[26] 24 April 2004, Macjack River – 1;[26] 21 July 2007, Kyuquot – 1;[26] 22 April 2010, Nuchatlitz (Nootka Island) – 1;[26] and 4 July 2015, Raft Cove – 1.[26] The reason most of these sightings were recorded in spring and summer is that few people visit these far-flung locations at other times of year.

During the summer breeding season, Spotted Towhees are generally rare or absent. There are, however, June and July records from several locations near Long Beach, including Green Point, Incinerator Rock, the Long Beach Airport, and South Beach. There have also been summer sightings at Harris Creek near Port Renfrew, at Pachena Bay, at Port San Juan, and at Ucluelet. One bird spent the summer of 2003 in Tofino. These summer records raise the possibility that the species is a rare breeder in the west coast region.

Tanagers   *Family Thraupidae*

WESTERN TANAGER
Piranga ludoviciana

STATUS: Uncommon spring migrant and summer visitor, uncommon in late summer, rare in fall. Breeding suspected but unconfirmed.

The Western Tanager is the only member of this largely tropical and subtropical family to inhabit western Canada. It breeds in forested areas of much of the western United States, with the exception of southwestern Arizona and parts of California and New Mexico. In Canada, its breeding range covers much of British Columbia, northern Alberta, the southern Northwest Territories, and central Saskatchewan. It winters from northern Mexico to Costa Rica. In British Columbia, Western Tanagers breed in much of the province east of the Coast Mountains but also in the Fraser Valley and the Salish Sea basin. On southeastern Vancouver Island, it is considered a fairly common to common migrant and an uncommon to fairly common summer visitor.[299]

In our west coast region, Western Tanagers are most often seen in spring and early summer. *Birds of Pacific Rim National Park* listed only 3 records for the central west coast and 1 for northwestern Vancouver Island occurring on 25 August 1968 at Grant Bay.[16] The additional sightings for that period were from Gold River and the Tofino area.[1] Since then there have been 68 additional sightings. Of those, 1 was recorded in April, 20 in May, 27 in June, 6 in July, 4 in August, and 10 in September. Half of the September records are from Jordan River.

On the west coast, the first spring arrivals are considerably later than on the southeast side of the island, usually arriving after the middle of May. There are two records from Jordan River that are earlier, one on 9 May 2013, and the other on 11 May 2014. The earliest spring sighting ever recorded was on 27 April in 2015. Birds seen on the outer coast in May and early June are presumed to be migrants passing through. In recent years there have been a considerable number of sightings in the second half of June in valleys away from the coast, particularly in the region to the east and southeast of Barkley Sound, suggesting that birds are breeding in that region. In the interior, away from the coast, they are reported to have a strong association with old-growth Douglas-fir, while in the west coast region of Vancouver Island they were found in old-growth forests of Douglas-fir, western redcedar, western hemlock, Sitka spruce, and associated trees.[312]

Most records in our region involve single birds, though sightings of 2 or 3 birds are not unusual. Counts of 5 birds occurred on 1 June 2000 at Tofino, and on 1 June 2013 at Jordan River. The largest number ever recorded was 12 birds on 26 May 1978 at Lennard Island, near Tofino. Birds have been recorded throughout most of the region north to Quatsino Sound, though much more sporadically in the northern half. This may simply be due to fewer human visitations.

Cardinals, Grosbeaks, and Allies   Family Cardinalidae

ROSE-BREASTED GROSBEAK
Pheucticus ludovicianus

STATUS: Casual vagrant in summer, fall, and winter.

This large-beaked finch with its flashy scarlet bib has a breeding range that covers much of the northeastern United States and southeastern Canada. In the United States, its breeding range ends east of the 100th meridian. In Canada, its breeding range continues westward through the Prairie provinces to the foothills of the Rocky Mountains and into northeastern British Columbia and the Northwest Territories. The species winters from Mexico and Central America to Peru.

In British Columbia, it breeds primarily in the Peace River region and the Taiga Plains, but has been found breeding in the south-central interior. On the coast, it is seen occasionally in the Fraser Valley and southeastern Vancouver Island, where it is considered a very rare vagrant.

In our west coast region, we have six records. On 28 August 1995, a bird was captured on Triangle Island, banded, and released. On 23 November 1999, a second bird, an immature male, was seen near Ucluelet by Brian Slater,[313] and on 9-10 and 19 December 2001, an immature male was seen in Tofino.[314]

In 2005, no fewer than three birds were recorded. A second-year male was observed in Tofino on 8 February 2005 by Paul Levesque and Laurie Savard.[315] An adult male was seen by Jerry Etzkorn at Carmanah Point on 26 June,[316] and another adult male was seen by Jenny Bradshaw and others in Tofino on 14 November.[232]

BLACK-HEADED GROSBEAK
Pheucticus melanocephalus

STATUS: Uncommon visitor in spring and early summer. Casual in late summer. Breeding suspected but not confirmed.

Although closely related to the Rose-breasted Grosbeak of the east, the male Black-headed Grosbeak is strikingly different in appearance. In the US Midwest, the breeding range of the eastern bird ends and that of the western bird begins. The breeding range of the latter covers most of the western United States, except for southeastern California, western Arizona, and most of Texas. In Canada, it breeds in southernmost Alberta and southern British Columbia, including southeastern Vancouver Island.

In British Columbia, the Black-headed Grosbeak has expanded its range considerably since the 1940s. On the coast, it has been increasing since the 1960s.[299] It is a common migrant and summer visitor on southeastern Vancouver Island, north to Quadra Island and Sayward. It is also fairly common in the Alberni Valley and likely breeds there.

In our west coast region, the species was first recorded on 24 August 1951, when two birds were observed at Carmanah Point.[280] A second sighting, this time involving a single bird, was recorded on 9 August 1967 at Sanford Island near Bamfield, and a third on 23 August 1969 at Long Beach. Nearly five years later, on 20 June 1974, a bird was seen at Kennedy Lake.[299] Records were sparse for the next 16 years, but sightings began to increase beginning in 1991, with 5 records in the 1990s and 10 in the following decade. By 2011 and 2012, the species was recorded at least 10 times each year. Of 43 records, all but 7 occurred in the months of May and June. Those from 1951, 1967, and 1969 were all in August, and there are 3 records for September and one for October.

Black-headed Grosbeaks favour deciduous habitat, particularly red-osier dogwood (*Cornus sericea*), bigleaf maple (*Acer macrophyllum*), and black cottonwood (*Populus balsamifera*).[299] The latter two are not commonly available in our region, but the extensive cutting of coniferous forest has resulted in large areas of the west coast region being covered in deciduous red alder. Most sightings here have been in or near red alders. Males have been heard singing in June, apparently on territory, though up to now breeding has not been confirmed. Birds have been seen in Tofino, Ucluelet, Bamfield, Franklin River, Little Nitinat River, Burman River, Gold River, Long Beach, Grice Bay, Kennedy Lake, Juan de Fuca Trail, and Jordan River. Records are absent for the northern half of our region, with one exception. On 29 May 1993, Keith Riding observed a single bird at Cape Scott.

LAZULI BUNTING
Passerina amoena
STATUS: Casual spring vagrant.

This is a bird of the American West. It breeds in all US states west of the 100th meridian, though not in the most southerly areas of the Southwest. In Canada, its range extends north into southern Saskatchewan, southern Alberta, and British Columbia, where it breeds in the southern one-third of the province east of the Coast Mountains. It also breeds locally in the Fraser Lowlands. Its preferred habitat is open or semi-open brushy habitat. On southeastern Vancouver Island and the Lower Mainland, the species is considered a rare to uncommon summer visitor.

On Vancouver Island's west coast, we have 6 records: 1 June 1976, Cape Scott – 1;[299] 12 May 1995, Tofino – 1 (photo); 17-19 May 2001, Carmanah Point – 1 male; 25 May 2007, Carmanah Point – 1 female; 26 May 2007, Pacific Rim National Park sewage pond – 1 female; 27 May 2014, Tofino – 1 male (photo). There is also a photo of a male Lazuli Bunting taken in a backyard in Tofino in spring, but a precise date is lacking.

INDIGO BUNTING
Passerina cyanea

STATUS: Casual vagrant in spring, summer, and fall.

This is largely an eastern bunting. So striking is the all-blue plumage of the male that one does not tire of seeing this bird even in regions where they are common. Its breeding range covers nearly all of the eastern United States and the Midwest, and extends west to eastern Colorado and into New Mexico and Arizona. In Canada, it breeds from New Brunswick to southern Ontario, and barely into southern Manitoba and southeastern Saskatchewan. There have been occasional sightings in all states and provinces. In British Columbia, this species is a rare visitor to southern parts of the province. There is a single breeding record from near Creston.[299] The species winters from Central America and the Caribbean south to Colombia.

On the west coast of Vancouver Island, we have three records. On 5 May 2009, a male was observed and photographed at Florencia Bay by Bob Steventon. Three years later, on 2 June 2012, a male Indigo Bunting was seen at a remote location on Herbert Inlet in Clayoquot Sound by Ben Ronnenbergh. From his description, there was no mistaking its identity. The bird stayed for over a week and was last seen on 12 June. The following year, on 19 May 2013, a male Indigo Bunting was seen and photographed at a place called Ayi'saqh, in Hesquiat Harbour, by Steve and Karen Charleson. This location is just 33 km by air from the location of the previous year's sighting. There was an earlier report of a bird in Ucluelet in mid-January 2008, but documentation is lacking.

DICKCISSEL
Spiza americana
STATUS: Casual spring vagrant.

The breeding range of this species extends over the eastern United States, but only west of the Appalachians to the Midwest and southern Saskatchewan. It has been seen in various places in south-central and south coastal British Columbia as a casual vagrant.[299] It winters from Mexico to South America, where it sometimes gathers in enormous numbers in agricultural areas and may therefore be vulnerable to sudden calamity.

There were no records for our region until 3 June 1976, when a bird was flushed from the dune grass on Stubbs Island, Tofino (BC Photo 442).[174] This was our only record until 23 and 24 May 1993, when a male showed up at a feeder in Ucluelet (BC Photo 1812).[310] About two weeks later, from 2 to 7 June, a male, probably the same bird, was observed at a feeder in Tofino.[310] On 27 and 28 May 2006, a bird was seen at Jordan River by a number of observers.[317]

Blackbirds, Orioles, and Allies   *Family Icteridae*

YELLOW-HEADED BLACKBIRD
Xanthocephalus xanthocephalus
STATUS: Casual transient in spring, summer, and fall.

With the exception of the coast and northern boreal forest, the breeding range of this species covers much of western Canada and the western United States, as far east as the Great Lakes. In British Columbia, it breeds widely in the southern interior, east to the East Kootenay region and north to Vanderhoof. It also nests in the Peace River region. The only breeding known to occur on the coast has been at Iona Island near Vancouver (BCNRS). On southeastern Vancouver Island, the species is considered an uncommon migrant.

On Vancouver Island's west coast, we have 13 records. Seven occurred in spring, 4 in summer, and 1 in fall. All of our records are as follows: 16 May 1951, Carmanah Point – 1;[280] 12 August 1965, Bamfield – 1 male;[1] 6-7 May 1972, Ucluelet – 1 male;[1] 7 May 1972, Tofino – 1 male; 10 May 1975, Tofino – 1 female;[1] 16 May 1992, Ucluelet – 1;[310] 5 October 1997, Carmanah Point – 1 male; 17 May 1999,

Tofino – 1 female; 5 May 2000, Tofino – 1 male; 4 September 2004, Stubbs Island, Tofino – 1 female; 12 June 2010, Jordan River – 1; 30 August 2014, Stubbs Island – 2 immatures; and 5 June 2016, Tofino – 1.

Although most immature birds show enough yellow to be noticeable, some individuals have a very limited amount of yellow and could therefore be overlooked. However, this species is noticeably larger than the Red-winged Blackbird, with which it sometimes associates on Vancouver Island.

WESTERN MEADOWLARK
Sturnella neglecta
STATUS: Rare fall transient. Casual in spring, summer, and winter.

Although meadowlarks look very unlike other members in their family – blackbirds and orioles – they nevertheless are icterids. Meadowlarks are birds of the grasslands and are most often seen when flushed from the ground or perched on a roadside fence post in agricultural country or prairies. There are two species in North America, an eastern and a western bird. Although very similar in appearance, they have entirely different songs, that of the western bird being very melodious. Whereas the Eastern Meadowlark is absent from large areas of the western United States and entirely absent from western Canada, the Western Meadowlark's breeding range covers the western United States and the Midwest, east to the Great Lakes region.

In Canada, the species breeds throughout the Great Plains region to the Peace River. In British Columbia, it breeds locally in the Peace River region, but mainly in the southern one-third of the province east of the Coast Mountains, the Fraser Valley, and formerly southeastern Vancouver Island. It winters from interior and southwestern British Columbia south to Mexico. Western Meadowlarks were formerly a common breeding resident on southeastern Vancouver Island, but breeding has not been reported since 1977.[299] In the Salish Sea basin, it is considered uncommon to fairly common in winter.

In the west coast region, the species has occurred in all months of the year except August, albeit rarely in summer. *Birds of Pacific Rim National Park* listed 18 records for seven months.[1] Since then, there have been more than 50 additional sightings. Most involved single birds, but a few sightings involved two and even three birds. Three birds were seen on 4 November 1982 at Long Beach, and also on 31 October 2004 at the Long Beach Airport. The highest counts occurred on 16 and 26 October 2015, when a flock of five birds was seen at the airport.

Autumn is clearly the period in which one is most likely to encounter this species in our region. The vast majority of sightings have occurred in the month of October, with 21 records, followed by November, with 12. All other months had 3 sightings each, except for April, June, and July, with 1 sighting each, and August, with no records. Two locations, the Long Beach Airport and the Stubbs Island dunes, account for most of the sightings. Birds have also been seen along the southern section of Long Beach, which has dunes and dune grass, and at Incinerator Rock. In the south of our region, there are records from Carmanah Point and Jordan River. There is also a single record from Browning Inlet, located 220 km northwest of Tofino, of a bird on 8 November 1968.[16]

Birds sometimes stay for a prolonged period. In 2004, two birds were seen at the Long Beach Airport from 3 October to 15 November (44 days), and in the winter of 2000/01, one was seen at Carmanah Point from 22 November to 11 January (51 days). It appears that several birds overwintered in the winter of 2015/16: four Western Meadowlarks were seen at the airport on 14 December, and three remained on 24 December. After a period of no visits to the airport for months, surveys continued in March 2016. On the 22nd of that month, three birds were again seen. A year later, on 20 March, two Western Meadowlarks were seen at Incinerator Rock, Long Beach. These were almost certainly newly arrived migrants.

BULLOCK'S ORIOLE
Icterus bullockii

STATUS: Casual transient in spring and fall. Casual in winter.

The Bullock's Oriole is the western counterpart of the Baltimore Oriole of the east. For a time they were considered two subspecies under the name Northern Oriole, until they were split once again. Recent genetic studies have revealed that they are not as closely related to each other as they are to other species. The breeding range of the Bullock's Oriole covers much of Mexico and nearly all of the western United States, and extends into southern Alberta and southern British Columbia, north to the vicinity of Quesnel. The species winters from Mexico to Guatemala, and also sparingly in southern California and on the Gulf Coast. In this province, it is considered fairly common in summer in the interior grasslands. On the coast, it is an uncommon migrant and summer visitor, breeding locally in the Fraser Valley and on southeastern Vancouver Island north to Campbell River.

The species was first recorded on Vancouver Island on 26 August 1952, when a bird flew into the lighthouse at Carmanah Point[280] (RBCM 10057). With only a single record for our region up to 1978, *Birds of Pacific Rim National Park* listed it as accidental. Since then, Bullock's Orioles have been recorded in 15 separate years. Most sightings have occurred in Tofino, but there is one record each for the following locations: Ahousaht, Schooner Cove, Long Beach Airport, and Ucluelet Inlet. There are also three records for Jordan River. All records involve single birds, except for three individuals seen in Tofino on 25 May 1984. There are nine spring records, eight of them recorded in May. Birds seen on the west coast have all been juveniles or females.

For the autumn period, we have nine records, with most sightings in October and November. The earliest fall date was 10 September in 1982.[299] The latest date was 21 November in 1982, and probably involved the same bird. Occurrences in Tofino have dropped off since 2004, possibly due to the tourist boom, which has resulted in more buildings and less shrubbery downtown. The three records from Jordan River are all fairly recent, as is the sighting of a bird at Ahousaht.

In a highly unusual event, a bird overwintered in Tofino in 2000/01, surviving with the help of sunflower seeds, which it was observed shucking at a backyard feeder, and by deriving sustenance from fuchsia flowers, which are common in Tofino gardens. It was first seen on 30 October and observations continued throughout the winter, up to 2 April.

RED-WINGED BLACKBIRD
Agelaius phoeniceus

STATUS: Uncommon transient in spring and fall. Uncommon in summer, locally fairly common. Rare in winter. Breeding highly likely but unconfirmed.

The Red-winged Blackbird breeds across much of North America, including Mexico, though not in the more northerly regions of Canada. In British Columbia, it breeds at lower elevations throughout most of the interior of the province, though sparsely in the north. On the coast, it breeds in the Salish Sea basin, including southeastern Vancouver Island, where it is considered a "very common to very abundant resident."[299]

In our west coast region, this species is far less common. *Birds of Pacific Rim National Park* listed only 13 records for the region and considered it "a very rare non-breeding resident."[1] With the advantage of 38 additional years of observations, we have more than 10 times as many records, and if all sightings had been meticulously recorded, there would certainly be many more.

On the west coast, Red-winged Blackbirds are seen most often as migrants and winter visitors at feeders. Suitable breeding habitat is far from common, but birds can be found during the breeding season at a few locations, particularly on the central west coast, notably along the lower Kennedy River, where three birds were recorded on 12 July 2002. In the summer of 2013, eight birds were found there on 8 June, and seven birds on 5 July, strongly indicating that these birds were breeding. Eight birds were again seen there on 9 June and 12 July the following year. They have also been seen in summer at other locations in the region, including a small lake near Tofino Inlet and at Swan Lake, located near the junction of Highway 4. On 20 July 1970, two juveniles seen on Cleland Island may have been early migrants (BCFWS).

In spring, the first Red-winged Blackbirds usually arrive in April. Three birds were seen in Tofino on 7 April 1984; 17 at Swan Lake on 17 April 1994; 1 on 9 April 2011; and 1 on 5 April 2012. In 2013, a single bird showed up on 1 March at the Long Beach Golf Course, and 5 birds were recorded on 16 March at Bamfield. Further north, the species is considered an occasional migrant in spring in the vicinity of Browning Inlet, and at Cape Scott Park a male was present at Hansen Lagoon from 16 to 18 May 1974.[4]

After the breeding season, birds tend to disperse, showing up at new locations such as Stubbs Island, the Long Beach Golf Course, the adjacent airport, and the sewage pond near Long Beach. At Stubbs Island, near Tofino, birds gather to feed on the seeds of several species of introduced European dune grass and may arrive as early as at the end of the first week of August. Five birds were seen there on 8 August 1990 and 10 birds on 7 August 2013. In 2010, 8 birds were seen on 22 August. In some years, birds may linger at this location throughout October and into November. The latest date I have is 16 November in 2013. North of the central west coast, in the vicinity of Grant Bay/ Browning Inlet and Brooks Peninsula, the Red-winged Blackbird is more commonly seen in autumn. At the latter location, 2 to 3 juveniles were feeding with a flock of Brown-headed Cowbirds at the mouth of Nasparti River on 6 and 7 August 1981.[13]

Thanks to backyard feeders, particularly those where food is strewn on the ground, Red-winged Blackbirds have been known to winter in villages on the west coast, including Tofino, Ucluelet, Bamfield, and Port Renfrew. At Tofino,

11 birds were recorded on 6 January 1998; 8 on 1 February 1999; 24 on 12 January 2000; and 2 on 7 January 2002. No wintering birds have been recorded there in recent years, due to the shutdown of two major feeders in the village. Two birds were recorded at Bamfield on 16 February 2014; 7 at Port Renfrew on 13 February 2013; and 10 at Ucluelet on 27 December 2016.

Large numbers of Red-winged Blackbirds are killed annually in pest control programs in the United States. In 2009 alone, the US Department of Agriculture killed more than 4 million Red-winged Blackbirds, European Starlings, cowbirds, and grackles, primarily using poison.[318] In 2015, the official figure for Red-winged Blackbirds killed was 708,487.[233]

BROWN-HEADED COWBIRD
Molothrus ater

STATUS: Common transient in spring, and fairly common in summer. Casual in fall and winter. Breeds.

The Brown-headed Cowbird is parasitic – that is, like the Cuckoo of Eurasia, it does not build a nest of its own but lays its eggs in the nests of other birds, leaving the host bird to raise its young. Because cowbird eggs hatch sooner and the young are often larger, young cowbirds outcompete the nestlings of the host species. The young are known to push the other eggs out of the nest. As many as 220 bird species are known to have been parasitized by Brown-headed Cowbirds.[299]

Originally, this bird had a more restricted range, probably originating in the grasslands of the Great Plains, where it fed on insects and beetles kicked up by browsing Bison. After Europeans cleared the forests for settlements and agriculture, this bird spread far and wide, even to the west coast – or so it was believed. Recent evidence has shown, however, that birds in the interior of British Columbia are significantly different from those found in California and the Great Plains.[320] This suggests they have been there all along, although the population expanded with the arrival of cattle and horses. Today, the species' breeding range covers nearly the entire continent, except for the forests of the far north and the tundra regions.

In the east, it winters from the Great Lakes south to Florida and the Gulf of Mexico. In the west, it winters from Texas to California and Mexico, except for the Pacific coast, where it winters north to Washington and the southwest corner of British Columbia, including parts of Vancouver Island. In British

Columbia, this species breeds commonly in much of the interior east of the Coast Mountains, and probably does so in suitable habitat throughout the province. It a fairly common to locally very common migrant and summer visitor to the Fraser Lowlands and southeastern Vancouver Island.[299]

On Vancouver Island's west coast, Brown-headed Cowbirds begin arriving in late April. During eight years when arrivals were closely monitored, most first arrival dates fell between 16 April and 20 April, with all but one falling between 13 April and 23 April. Numbers in spring ranged from single birds to small flocks. Spring maximums varied from 10 to 36 birds and were recorded from the last few days of April to the beginning of June. As late as 2 June 2010, 21 birds were counted at the Long Beach Golf Course. This appears to represent the end of the spring migration period. Birds seen later than this can be presumed to be local summer visitors.

During June and July, cowbirds continue to be seen in smaller numbers. There are few records of parasitism on Vancouver Island's west coast, and all involve a host species feeding a recently fledged young cowbird. Species include Swainson's Thrush, Townsend's Warbler, Wilson's Warbler, Fox Sparrow, and Song Sparrow (BCNRS).

Evidence suggests that birds depart remarkably early and that well before September all birds have usually gone. The latest dates that birds were recorded on the west coast during four years of surveys were as follows: 24 July 2009, Long Beach Airport – 3 birds; 22 August 2010, Stubbs Island – 25; 10 August 2011, Long Beach Airport – 1; and 13 July 2012, Long Beach – 1. Twenty-five birds seen on Stubbs Island were likely transients passing through, as were 25 birds seen at the airport on 1 August 2010. From 1 to 13 cowbirds were recorded on Cleland Island from 3 July to 20 August 1970, with maximum count on 4 August (BCFWS). On Brooks Peninsula, small numbers were present from 2 to 25 August 1981, with a maximum of 16 birds feeding in tall grasses at the mouth of the Nasparti River on 6 and 7 August.[13] An exceptionally late sighting occurred on 31 October 2016, with 4 birds at a feeder in Ucluelet, and another individual across town at the sports field. Unseasonable storms throughout September and October likely interfered with their journey south.

Cowbirds do not normally overwinter, but one individual spent the winter of 1998/99 in Tofino. A record of a bird on 5 January 1998 at Tofino suggests that one probably overwintered in 1997/98 as well.

Juvenile Brown-headed Cowbirds have been known to fearlessly perch on people. This curious behaviour is likely related to their long association with bovines and ungulates. In agricultural country, it is not unusual to see birds astride cattle and horses.

RUSTY BLACKBIRD
Euphagus carolinus
STATUS: Casual spring and fall transient.

Adult male Rusty Blackbirds in breeding plumage are similar in appearance to Brewer's Blackbirds, but their habits and habitat requirements are very different. Whereas the Brewer's Blackbird is a bird of open fields, the Rusty Blackbird is associated with forests and wetlands. Its breeding range stretches across Canada's boreal forest region from the Maritimes and Labrador west to British Columbia, the Northwest Territories, the Yukon, and Alaska. The species winters throughout most of the eastern United States.

In British Columbia, they appear to breed widely throughout the province east of the Coast Mountains, though rarely in the south, and perhaps not in the north-central region. On Vancouver Island's southeast coast, it is considered a rare migrant, and a very rare vagrant in winter.[299]

On Vancouver Island's west coast, records are few. *Birds of Pacific Rim National Park* did not list the species, overlooking a bird recorded with two Brewer's Blackbirds in Tofino on 1 October 1976.[299] Today we have four more records: 4 October 1985, Megin River – 1 (RBCM 1042); 22 May 1987, MacKenzie Beach, Tofino – 1;[299] 2 April 1989, Tofino – 1;[299] 8 December 1990, Tofino – 1.

That no Rusty Blackbirds have been recorded in the west coast region since 1990 is probably a reflection of their overall status. The species has suffered a precipitous decline in the past 80 years. In the past 40 years alone, numbers have declined by 85 to 95%, and biologists have yet to determine the cause. Speculation ranges from habitat loss in their wintering grounds to poisoning in agricultural blackbird control programs, or changes in their breeding range due to the current warming period, or perhaps all of the above.

BREWER'S BLACKBIRD
Euphagus cyanocephalus
STATUS: Rare spring transient, uncommon transient in fall. Locally common in some years. Casual in summer and winter.

This ground-dwelling blackbird has a breeding range that covers much of western North America, from southern California and northern Arizona north to the southern Northwest Territories and east across the Prairie provinces to the Great Lakes. In British Columbia, it has been recorded in virtually all parts of the province east of the Coast Mountains, but breeding is limited mostly to the Peace River region and the southern half of the province. In the Fraser Valley and southeastern Vancouver Island, it is a common resident and is locally abundant in late summer, fall, and winter.[299] There is also an old record of 19 birds at Cape Scott, at the northern tip of Vancouver Island, on 30 September 1935.[299]

Brewer's Blackbirds are inhabitants of open country such as agricultural fields and meadows. The wooded west coast, therefore, does not provide much in the way of suitable breeding habitat. *Birds of Pacific Rim National Park* listed 9 records, all of them in spring and fall.[1] That trend has continued. Since 1978, there have been 50 additional records. In autumn, we have 22 sightings, with 18 in October and 4 in November. In spring, we have 13 records, 5 in March, 6 in April, and 2 in May.

Most sightings involved from 1 to 6 birds. Exceptions occurred on 26 October and 1 November 1994, when 51 and 60 birds, respectively, were counted in Ucluelet, where they frequented feeders in the area. A flock totalling 17 birds was again seen at the same location on 13 October 1997. No follow-up observations were ever made, so it is very possible that some of these well-fed birds overwintered. There were no confirmed winter sightings until 9 January 2013, when 2 males were seen at the Long Beach Golf Course, one an adult, the other an immature. They were last seen on 10 April, indicating that they successfully overwintered without relying on a feeder. Our one and only summer record occurred on 11 June 1989, when a bird was seen at the Long Beach Airport.

Nearly all records are from the central west coast, from Tofino to Ucluelet. There is one record from Bamfield and six from Jordan River.

COMMON GRACKLE
Quiscalus quiscula

STATUS: Casual vagrant in spring and summer.

Although the Common Grackle may appear black at a distance or under cloudy skies, when a bird is seen close-up in full sun, it is handsome indeed, with an iridescent deep-blue head and bronze back and wings.

The breeding range of this long-tailed blackbird extends throughout much of North America east of the Rocky Mountains, except for the most northerly boreal forest regions and tundra. It winters in most of the eastern United States, from southern Minnesota to Texas and from the New England states to Florida. In British Columbia, it is a breeding resident primarily in the northeast on the boreal plain, but recently it has been found breeding in Fernie and locally in the Chilcotin region.[310] The species is regarded as a very rare or casual vagrant in other areas of the province, including the south coast.

The scarcity of records in our region is consistent with the absence of this species elsewhere on the coast. In the west coast region, we have had only five occurrences. Tofino resident Rory Paterson had a Common Grackle at her feeder in Tofino from 20 to 24 May 1991.[319] There were no further records until 22 June 2000, when Marge Christianson saw one in Ucluelet on three consecutive days. On 14 May 2005, Jerry Etzkorn recorded a bird at Carmanah Point.[289] On 31 March 2006, I found a bird near the corner of Fourth and Campbell streets in Tofino.[317] Fourteen months later, on 25 May 2007, a Common Grackle, perhaps the same individual, was seen at the exact same street corner.

Finches and Allies   *Family Fringillidae*

BRAMBLING
Fringilla montifringilla
STATUS: Casual vagrant in spring and fall.

This Eurasian finch has a breeding range that stretches from northern Europe to eastern Asia. In North America, it breeds only in the western Aleutians, but it has been seen on the North American mainland as a rare wanderer from coast to coast. In British Columbia, it has been seen in numerous locations in the southern half of the province, with more records on the coast than in the interior.[299]

In the west coast region, we have three records. A bird visited a feeder at the home of Barbara and Barry Campbell at Chesterman Beach from 1 March to 25 March 1984 (BC Photo 903). Another bird visited Tofino from 28 October to 1 November 1998.[321] Ten years later, a bird was present in Ucluelet from 13 to 20 April 2008.[275]

EVENING GROSBEAK
Coccothraustes vespertinus
STATUS: Casual in all seasons.

This handsome, large-beaked finch breeds from the Maritimes westward through southern Canada to central Saskatchewan, northern Alberta, and interior British Columbia. It breeds throughout large areas of the western United States, from western Montana south through the Rocky Mountain states to New Mexico, Arizona, and the Sierra Madre of Mexico. Further west, it breeds from Washington to northern California.

In British Columbia, its breeding range is not well known. Like some of the other finches, its distribution is erratic and can vary considerably from year to year. However, its centre of abundance, both in summer and in winter, is the southern interior of the province. It is considered to be an uncommon to very common migrant and winter visitor on the south coast, but rare on western Vancouver Island.[299]

Birds of Pacific Rim National Park listed only 4 records and tentatively considered the Evening Grosbeak rare in winter.[1] I could find only 21 additional records, two of them dating back to the 1970s. This may seem surprising, considering that the species is fairly common in areas as close as the Alberni Valley. However, Evening Grosbeaks have an affinity for areas with Douglas-fir trees and bigleaf maples during the breeding season.[299] Most of our records involve fewer than 6 birds. The largest flocks recorded in our region consisted of 9 birds on 3 June 1969, at Tofino; 11 on 20 October 1983, at Chesterman Beach; 13 on 5 October 1986, at Jordan River; and 12 on 3 December 2011, also at Jordan River. A published report of 21 birds on 14 September 1984 at Tofino was in error.[299] Only 2 birds were counted. If previous records are included, we have 25 in total. Six records were in spring, 5 in summer, 12 in fall, and 2 in winter. (Early June records are considered spring transients here.) The only records north of Tofino are of a bird heard at San Josef Bay, Cape Scott Park, on 22 May 1974,[4] and an autumn record for Zeballos, details of which were not listed in *The Birds of British Columbia*.[299]

PINE GROSBEAK
Pinicola enucleator
STATUS: Casual in all seasons.

Pine Grosbeaks have a widespread breeding range in Canada, extending from the Maritimes and Labrador west through the northern forests to Alaska, and south throughout much of British Columbia. In the United States, they breed in the Rocky Mountains south to New Mexico, and also in the Sierra Nevada of California. In British Columbia, migration in fall is largely altitudinal and the Pine Grosbeak is fairly common and occasionally common at low elevation in the interior in winter.[299] In the Salish Sea basin, including the southeast side of Vancouver Island, it is occasionally fairly common at low elevation in winter.[299]

In our west coast region, this very attractive bird is rarely seen. *Birds of Pacific Rim National Park* listed only 5 occurrences, all of them from 1970 to 1974.[1] I know of only 6 additional sighting since then, and for one of those the date was not recorded (2 birds were reliably reported on the outskirts of Tofino in 2004). All existing records are as follows: winter of 1970, Ucluelet – 1;[1] 29 November 1971, Kennedy Lake – 15;[1] 27 January 1972, Ucluelet Inlet – 1;[1] 4 March 1972, McLean Point near Grice Bay – 1;[1] 5 and 22 January 1974, near Long Beach – 2;[1] 3 June 1990, Tofino – 1; upper Toquart River, 11 June 2004 – 2;[26] 1 September 2008, Halfpipe Mountain South – 3;[26] 14 June 2009, San Josef Recreation Site – 1;[26] and 30 December 2015, Chesterman Beach – 1.

This species may occur at high elevation in the west coast region more often than is currently realized.

GRAY-CROWNED ROSY-FINCH
Leucosticte tephrocotis

STATUS: Casual visitor in spring, summer, and fall. Rare summer visitor in alpine areas.

This finch breeds on the barren subalpine slopes of Alaska, the Yukon, western Northwest Territories, and British Columbia, as well as in the Rocky Mountains and the higher mountains of the western United States. It also breeds in the Aleutian Islands and islands in the Bering Sea. The species winters from southern British Columbia and the southwestern Great Plains south through much of the western United States to northern New Mexico and northeastern California. There are three identifiable populations or subspecies.

Because it nests at high elevation in remote and inhospitable places, its breeding range is not well known and few nests have been found in British Columbia. However, evidence such as adults feeding young have been seen in numerous locations. Gray-crowned Rosy-Finches are occasionally seen along roadsides in the interior, especially on high mountain passes during migration, when they often gather in large flocks. *The Birds of British Columbia* considers it an uncommon to fairly common winter visitor to the Salish Sea basin, including southeastern Vancouver Island.[299] It is considered a casual vagrant to Vancouver Island's west coast region.

For our region, we have 8 records: 21 November 1973, Schooner Cove (Pacific Rim National Park) – 1;[299] 15 April 1980, Cape Scott Provincial Park – 1;[299] 14 June 1981, Pogo Mountain – 2;[26] 1 March 1984, Tofino – 1 (BC Photo 903); 22-25 March 1984, Chesterman Beach – 1; 28 November 2006, Carmanah Point – 1; 28-29 September 2008, Clayoquot Plateau – 1;[26] and 13 August 2008, Mount Klitsa – 8.[26]

The three alpine locations mentioned here – Pogo Mountain, Clayoquot Plateau, and Mount Klitsa – are within a few kilometres of each other. Because so little time is spent exploring in the alpine zone, it is likely that this species is more common on the island than is currently recognized.

HOUSE FINCH
Carpodacus mexicanus
STATUS: Common resident. Breeds.

The House Finch originated in Mexico but has colonized most of the United States and southern Canada. It is common at feeders.

Although similar in appearance to the Purple Finch, the House Finch is easily distinguished when one becomes familiar with both. This finch was originally restricted to the American Southwest and Mexico. The release of caged birds resulted in the establishment of the species in the eastern United States and possibly elsewhere. Today the breeding range of the House Finch covers all of the contiguous 48 states except for southern Florida. In Canada, it breeds in the southernmost parts of the country from Nova Scotia to British Columbia. In this province, it breeds in the central interior at least as far north as Quesnel, as well as in the Fraser Valley and the Salish Sea basin, including southeastern and southern Vancouver Island.

The House Finch was unknown in this province until 1935, when a pair of nesting birds was found near Penticton. Only two years later, a pair was found nesting in Victoria.[322] Whether this species established itself on the island following the escape of captive birds or whether it came about through natural colonization is unknown. Throughout the 1940s, House Finches expanded and firmly established themselves on the island.[299]

In our west coast region, the species was first recorded at Carmanah Point on 13 January 1952.[280] On 31 March 1962, 5 birds were recorded at Tofino Inlet, and on 1 September 1968, 2 birds were seen in Tofino. A bird reached Triangle Island on 21 June 1976, and another was seen at Bamfield on 17 August 1977. There were no other sightings until 30 July 1983, when a single bird was seen in Tofino. There is an absence of records for the 1980s, but on 21 May 1996, 2 birds were observed in Tofino, and on 19 October 1996, 15 birds were counted. By 10 November of that year, 35 birds were found on Stubbs Island. Clearly, the species was now well established on the west coast. By 3 February 2001, numbers reached a peak, with a count of 65 birds, which has not been surpassed since.

House Finches adapt readily to human habitation when plenty of room is left for gardens and shrubs. In winter they rely on backyard feeders, and it is doubtful they would survive on the west coast without them. On 9 December 2013, 45 House Finches were counted at one Tofino feeder. At Stubbs Island, near Tofino, they also make use of the seeds provided by several European species of dune grass that are established there. As many as 39 birds were counted there on 23 October 2013.

It is not clear whether this species competes with House Sparrows or Purple Finches to any great degree other than at feeders. Besides Tofino and Stubbs Island, birds have been seen at Triangle Island, the Long Beach Airport, Tahsis, Gold River, Ucluelet, Bamfield, Port Renfrew, and Jordan River. Breeding evidence is sparse, though young birds still showing traces of natal down on the head have been seen at feeders in Tofino (BCNRS).

PURPLE FINCH
Carpodacus purpureus

STATUS: Common in spring, uncommon in summer, rare in fall, and uncommon to rare in winter. Breeds.

The Purple Finch is one of three finches in the genus *Carpodacus*, two of which occur in our region. The male is not actually purple; instead its plumage has a rich reddish hue with just a hint of purple. In spring, males are particularly red and may lack even that slight purple hue. Purple Finches are unusual in that both males and females sing. They breed in the northeastern United States and across Canada from coast to coast, from the Maritimes to British Columbia, the southern Northwest Territories, and southern Yukon. On the Pacific coast, the species breeds from southwestern British Columbia to southern California. In British Columbia, it has a broad though somewhat sparse breeding distribution east of the Coast Mountains, including the Peace River region.[250] Its centre of abundance is the Fraser Valley and the Salish Sea basin. In western North America, Purple Finches winter from Vancouver Island south through the coastal states to northern Baja California.

On the west coast of Vancouver Island, Purple Finches have been recorded in every month of the year but September, though records are scarce from August to January. Among 172 records collected on the central west coast since 1982, I could find only 3 records for the month of August, none for September, 7 for October, 3 for November, and 10 for December. In January, sightings increase to 13 records, February has 9, and March has 20. In April, sightings jump to 56. There are 25 records for May, 15 for June, and 11 for July. The scarcity of Purple Finches from August to January is puzzling, and just where birds go during this period is unclear. There are, however, several records in September from Jordan River and Port Renfrew.

When found at all in fall and winter, Purple Finches tend to be seen in flocks. In November and December 1982, flocks of 9 and 10 birds were seen in the Tofino area. In 1987, 26 birds were counted at the south end of Long Beach on 6 January, 15 were tallied at Tofino on 11 January, and 18 were counted there on 5 February. In most winters, however, birds are difficult to find. The first ones tend to reappear in March, with a noticeable influx in April, when we often hear their vigorous song emanating from the very top of a red alder tree. When fruit trees and decorative exotics are in bloom in April, these finches can often be found nipping the blossoms, which they appear to relish. By May, birds have dispersed to their breeding territories.

The Purple Finch occurs on our west coast in small numbers throughout the breeding period in May, June, and July. On 17 July 2012, a female appeared at a Tofino feeder, accompanied by a newly fledged young, thus confirming breeding. That some birds begin nesting in March was demonstrated by the appearance of a newly fledged young at the same feeder on 15 April 2015. Newly fledged young were also seen along the lower Kennedy River on 26 June 2016. June sightings have been recorded from Jordan River, Port Renfrew, Little Nitinat River, Pachena Bay, Bamfield, Ucluelet, Long Beach, and the lower Kennedy River. Indications are that Purple Finches breed throughout the southern half of the west coast region. Whether they do further north as well is currently unknown. I could find only two records from the northern half of the region. One of them was from 26 May 2014, at Holberg.

COMMON REDPOLL
Carduelis flammea

STATUS: Casual transient and winter visitor.

The Common Redpoll is a bird of the northern forest and tundra. It breeds in both Eurasia and North America. On this continent, its breeding range extends from Newfoundland and Labrador through northern Quebec, west to the Yukon, Alaska, and northwest British Columbia. The species winters southward into the rest of Canada and into the southern half of the United States. In British Columbia, it is known to nest only in the northwestern corner of the province, in the area of the Chilkat Pass and Alsek River.[299] In winter, it is seen throughout much of the province east of the Coast Mountains, and less commonly in the Fraser Valley. On southeastern Vancouver Island and the rest of the Salish Sea basin, it is considered a rare to uncommon migrant and winter visitor, though in some years it may be fairly common locally.

On Vancouver Island's west coast, this species was not listed at all in *Birds of Pacific Rim National Park*. This bird is indeed a rare visitor. In 44 years of birding in the west coast region, I have yet to see my first one. There have been a few sightings by others. The earliest was recorded on 27 December 1989, when a single bird was observed at a feeder in Tofino by Rory Paterson.[299] Other sightings by Rory at her feeder occurred on 6 December 1992, 22 May 1993, and 20 and 26 December 1994. The last three sightings all involved a single male, probably the same individual.

There is one additional record. A flock of 20 birds was observed by Ralph Crombie on 31 December 2012 at the end of Sharp Road, Tofino. There were two other reports, but their validity could not be assessed. At a distance, a flock of Pine Siskins could be mistaken for this species. The Common Redpoll is a bird that will show up here again, even if only very rarely.

RED CROSSBILL
Loxia curvirostra

STATUS: Irruptive. From uncommon to common to abundant. Sometimes absent. Breeds.

Red Crossbills feed on conifer cones and are usually seen in the tops of trees or passing overhead. Only adult males are red.

Red Crossbills are adapted to feeding on the seeds of conifer cones, hence the crossed mandibles, which are designed for extracting the seeds. Nine distinct variants, with different bill sizes and vocalizations, are recognized in North America. These appear to be reproductively isolated, though further study is needed. There is also a lot of plumage variation within this species, depending on sex and age. Very young birds are streaked and lack colour, while females vary from grey to drab olive-green to yellow-green. Juvenile males vary from yellowish to orange to pink. Only adult males have the red plumage.

Red Crossbills are irruptive and highly nomadic, leaving their home range when food is scarce for regions often far away, where food is more abundant. When times are good, they may breed in almost any month of the year.[323] Nestlings are able to survive cooling spells through episodes of torpor.

Red Crossbills have a wide distribution in the Northern Hemisphere, breeding throughout much of Europe and Asia as well as in North America. On this continent, the breeding range of the Red Crossbill stretches from the Maritimes and parts of New England across Canada to British Columbia, the Yukon, and southern Alaska. They breed also in large regions of the western United States, and at higher elevation in Mexico. In British Columbia, they may be found throughout the province but are scarce in the north.[299]

In our west coast region, this species has been recorded in every month of the year, though the frequency at which birds are seen can vary greatly. For example, I recorded the species only 3 times in 2009 and 17 times in 2012. Most observations involve fewer than 10 birds, but larger numbers are not unusual. Flocks of 35 were recorded on three occasions in 2012, and 40 were recorded on 16 July 2011. Fifty birds were seen at Vargas Island on 5 July 1999. Sixty birds were reported from Bamfield on 31 March 1985, and 250 birds on 8 August 2008. On 16 March of the following year, 350 birds were recorded at the same location. Elsewhere along the coast, Red Crossbills were abundant in Cape Scott Park between 17 and 25 May 1974, when flocks of 60 were at Hansen Lagoon on 17 May and 55 at Guise Bay on 18 May.[4] On Brooks Peninsula, flocks of up to 35 birds were recorded throughout the year.[13]

Large flocks are exceedingly difficult to estimate with any degree of accuracy, as I discovered on 19 June 2012 at Long Beach, when a very large flock passed overhead, momentarily filling the sky with birds. In the heat of the moment, an estimate of 1,500 birds did not seem far-fetched. However, even with that figure reduced by half, there would still have been 750 birds in the air. A flock of this size, it must be conceded, is highly unusual.

On the west coast, Red Crossbills are more often heard than seen. They are usually encountered in the treetops of the spruce fringe along the outer coast, feeding on the cones of Sitka spruce. This is not always the case. On 12 May 2012, for example, a small flock was observed in red alder trees, feeding on something within the unfurled leaves. The species has also been recorded in the mountains and river valleys of the west coast, though far less frequently than on the outer coast. This may be due to a paucity of observers rather than a scarcity of birds. Birds have been reported from Ursus Creek, Clayoquot Plateau, Sutton Pass, Mount Klitsa, Holberg, Gold River, Burman River, Tahsis River, Maggie Lake, and Little Nitinat River. That the species breeds in the west coast region, at least occasionally, was confirmed on 29 May 2014, when four newly fledged Red Crossbills were seen in a Sitka spruce tree at Incinerator Rock, Long Beach, with one of the young being fed by an adult.

Of the nine variants mentioned previously, the most common on our west coast is Type 3, which is associated with western hemlock. It has a small bill and a flight call described as *"tewp-tewp"* or *"jib-jib."* Type 10 is partial to Sitka spruce, and typically appears to be much less numerous. In flight it utters a high, musical bell-like *"whit."* Type 4 is common on the southeast side of Vancouver Island, where it is associated with Douglas-fir forest. Although thus far recorded in our region only from Jordan River, they are likely to be found in the interior of our region and in the San Juan River valley, where Douglas-fir is much more common. Type 1 is found mostly near the east coast of North America and is rare in the west. However, on 26 December 2014, the calls of eight birds of this variety were recorded at Tofino by Ian Cruickshank.

Very little is known about Type 7 (Enigmatic Crossbill), as it has been recorded in North America only a few times. On 1 May 2014, the flight calls of three birds believed to be of this type were recorded at the Long Beach Airport, also by Ian Cruickshank, and their identity was later verified by Matt Young of Cornell University. This was the first recorded occurrence for Type 7 in Canada. On 27 August 2016, Ian made yet another breakthrough when he heard and recorded the calls emitted by two Type 5 Red Crossbills near Ucluelet, which was their first recorded occurrence in British Columbia.

One additional variant has been recorded on Vancouver Island, albeit rarely. Type 2 is normally associated with the ponderosa pines of the southern interior and has a uniquely musical descending flight call. To date, it has not been recorded from the west coast region. Additional sound recordings are needed to clarify the status of these types in our region. I am indebted to Ian Cruickshank for enlightening me on these curious variants within this species.

WHITE-WINGED CROSSBILL
Loxia leucoptera

STATUS: Casual spring and summer visitor.

This crossbill is a widespread breeding bird in forested regions of Canada from coast to coast, but solid data are lacking for many areas, including British Columbia. According to *The Birds of British Columbia*, only a single nest had been located in the province up to 2001.[299] This is an irruptive species that follows the availability of food. Its distribution is therefore quite unpredictable. On the south coast of British Columbia, it is considered very rare, though at times it may be locally uncommon.

On Vancouver Island's west coast, this bird is seen very infrequently. The first record for the west coast occurred on 23 October 1956, when a dozen birds were seen at Alice Arm. There were no further sightings until July 1974, when birds were seen on Triangle Island on four occasions.[272] On the central west coast, at Tofino, 55 birds were spotted by local doctor Harvey Henderson on 1 May 1976, and were subsequently verified by me. In August 1981, this species was seen on three occasions on Brooks Peninsula: 3 birds on the 6th and 11th and 1 bird on the 13th with eight Red Crossbills.[13] In addition, there are records from Tofino in May 1991 and May 1996, though no details are given. Another bird was recorded at Tofino on 24 January 1995.

In 2008, White-winged Crossbills were reported from three locations along the West Coast Trail by Stuart Mackenzie. On 12 July, 12 birds were seen at Port San Juan. The following day, 10 birds were found in the area of Walbran Creek, and on 16 July, 6 birds were observed at Tsutsiat Falls. The latest sighting of this species occurred in early June of 2015, when Guy Monty reported a small flock of White-winged Crossbills at Knob Hill, at the north end of Vancouver Island. This brings the total number of sightings over the past 60 years to 13. Clearly, this species is very rare and erratic in the west coast region.

PINE SISKIN
Carduelis pinus

STATUS: Highly variable, from rare to common. Breeds.

This small finch has a widespread breeding range in Canada. It breeds in forested regions throughout the country from Newfoundland and Labrador to British Columbia and the Yukon. In the United States, it breeds in the extreme northeast, southern Alaska, and much of the West, south to western Mexico. In winter, it may be found in large areas of Mexico, virtually all of the United States, and the southern one-third of Canada.

In British Columbia, Pine Siskins breed widely throughout the province. In fact, the southeastern part of the province is reported to have the highest breeding density in North America. Birds banded in the eastern United States outside the breeding season have been recovered in British Columbia, indicating just how far this species may travel in search of food. The Pine Siskin is irregular and irruptive, following the supply of food. It may be seen commonly in one winter and not at all the next. Indeed, it may be seen in a given month, then not again for years. For example, on the central west coast, there are three records for February 1999, and no further records for that month until 2011. There are records for December 2001, then no further December records until 2012.

Pine Siskins eat a variety of food, including insects, willow catkins, and dandelion seeds, but subsist mostly on the seeds of conifers or, in our region, on the cones of red alders. When present, they may be seen in large flocks numbering from 50 to 150 birds. One flock seen on 22 October 2000 was estimated to contain 250 individuals. Flocks numbering in the thousands have been reported elsewhere. Pine Siskins can be readily induced to come to feeders for sunflower or thistle seeds. Be warned, however, that when feeding birds on a deck or on the ground, there is a danger of *Salmonella* contamination, which can kill them.

Pine Siskins were recorded in 14 of the past 23 years. Following is a breakdown of the number of years in which the species was recorded in a given month: January – 5 years; February – 3; March – 4; April – 7; May – 2; June – 2; July – 2; August – 3; September – 4; October – 5; November – 4; and December – 2. Keep in mind that there may have been numerous records during some of those months. All sightings but one were recorded at low elevation. On 27 August 1990, a Pine Siskin was recorded on Steamboat Mountain, Clayoquot Plateau, but the elevation was not recorded. Pine Siskins are reported to breed up to the subalpine zone.

My findings are somewhat at variance with the results outlined in *Birds of Pacific Rim National Park*, which listed by far the largest number of sightings during the summer months.[1] However, this can probably be attributed to the absence of observers during the winter period, as well as the unpredictable occurrence of the species. For example, from 19 June to 6 September 1967, Pine Siskins were recorded on seven occasions in the vicinity of Long Beach, twice in July, four times in August, and once in September.[253] The following year, from 3 June to 2 September, the species was rarely recorded but a pair was found nesting in Wickaninnish Park at Incinerator Point. The nest was saddled on a Sitka spruce bough 10 ft from the trunk and 15 ft above the ground. On 6 June 1968, an adult was carrying rootlets and other nesting material to the nest.[254] In 1981, flocks of up to 20 birds were recorded frequently on Brooks Peninsula between 5 May and 15 August.[13] The species was considered an occasional migrant by F. Richardson during his year in the vicinity of Grant Bay and Browning Inlet, northwestern Vancouver Island, from 15 July 1968 to 18

July 1969.[16] Further north, at Cape Scott, the Pine Siskin was regularly seen only between 16 and 21 May 1974. The maximum number was 6 birds at Guise Bay on 20 May.[4] Since then, only in 2008 and 2011 were Pine Siskin sightings fairly common here in summer.

As a defence against cold weather, siskins have the ability to store up to 10% of their body weight in food in their crops for the long winter nights. They also have the ability to raise their body temperature, which is already 40% higher than that of most small songbirds.

AMERICAN GOLDFINCH
Carduelis tristis

STATUS: Locally fairly common spring migrant and summer visitor. Rare in fall, casual in winter. Breeds.

This attractive lemon-yellow finch with its black crown and black wings is a welcome addition to any backyard feeder. Its breeding range covers most of the United States, with the exception of the southernmost states. In Canada, its breeding range stretches from the Maritimes to British Columbia, though mostly south of the boreal forest region. It winters primarily in the United States, though some winter in southeastern Canada. In British Columbia, its known breeding range is restricted to the south of the province, from west of the Rocky Mountains to southeastern Vancouver Island. It is a fairly common to very common migrant and summer visitor, and breeder, to the Salish Sea basin.[299]

This bird prefers open or semi-open areas, and may be seen along roadsides or in weedy fields. Such habitat is of course limited in our west coast region. Still, surprisingly large flocks have been seen here on occasion. A flock estimated at more than 100 birds was seen at Long Beach on 2 June 1968,[1] and on 12 May 2011, 70 birds were counted at a feeder in Tofino. Usually, however, flocks are much smaller, with 15 or fewer being the norm.

The first spring migrants usually arrive in the last week of April or the first week in May. In both 2014 and 2015, the first bird showed up on 10 April. In 2016, the first arrival date was 17 April. The earliest arrival date ever recorded was 1 April in 1977, with five birds seen at Lennard Island, near Tofino.[299] A bird seen in Tofino on 20 February and 6 March 2011 is believed to have been overwintering, undoubtedly with the help of backyard feeders. Peak numbers usually occur around mid-May.

Records on the west coast are concentrated in open areas, particularly around human habitation. There are summer records from all villages, from Tofino to Jordan River. Small numbers may also spend the summer on shrubby offshore islands like Cleland Island. Up to five birds (one male and four females) were present here from 23 May to 7 July 1970 (BCFWS). The only published records I could find north of Tofino are from Guise Bay in Cape Scott Park, where four were present from 15 to 19 April 1980, and from Brooks Peninsula/Solander Island area and Esperanza Inlet in spring (without details).[299] The most suitable breeding habitat on the west coast appears to be the wide, open brushy country at the Long Beach Airport, where birds may be seen throughout the summer.

Hatler et al. stated that sightings after the end of July are scarce.[1] While it may be true that some birds depart in July, surveys at the airport have revealed that in the first half of August, birds are fairly numerous. By mid-month, most birds have departed, though a few may linger to the end of the month. On 1 September 2004, eight birds were still present at the airport. Single birds or pairs may be encountered occasionally into October, November, and even December (one record).

American Goldfinches can be readily attracted to feeders with thistle seed or black sunflower seeds.

Old World Sparrows *Family Passeridae*

HOUSE SPARROW
Passer domesticus

STATUS: Uncommon to common in west coast villages. Rare elsewhere. Breeds.

Formerly known as the English Sparrow, this bird is an Old World sparrow. Its Latin name reflects its history of dwelling among human habitations. It was introduced from Europe to the United States in the period beginning in 1850 and ending in 1881. It was also introduced to Quebec City in 1868. Like the European Starling, it readily multiplied and expanded its range by colonizing towns, villages, and farms throughout the east, and gradually the west as well. It reached British Columbia between 1895 and 1898. Today it is found near human habitation in much of the province, though it is absent from large areas of the north.

Just when this sparrow first arrived on Vancouver Island's west coast is not entirely clear. The oldest record involved a bird seen at the Pachena Point lighthouse on 12 April 1975.[299] Five years later, on 10 May 1980, 7 birds were recorded at Tofino. By 26 November 2003, 35 birds had been counted in the village. The expansion of the population in Tofino may have been inadvertently aided by the installation of roofed street lamps, which provided the birds with not only warmth on cool winter nights but also a roof. Judging by the nesting material that could be seen protruding from beneath the rain guards, they nested there as well.

The year 2003 appears to have marked the maximum expansion of the population in Tofino. Since then, all sightings have involved fewer birds. The latest date on which more than a dozen birds were tallied was 27 October in 2010, with 14 individuals. House Sparrows may have declined for a number of reasons. The closing down of two major bird feeders and the replacement of the roofed street lamps with closed ones were undoubtedly significant factors. The arrival and proliferation of House Finches may also have introduced more competition for both food and nesting sites. While House Sparrows are capable of weaving a dome-shaped nest in a tree or a bush, they rarely do so, opting instead to build a nest in a building or a nesting box. House Sparrows have also been found in Port Renfrew, Bamfield, Ucluelet, Tofino, Gold River, Tahsis, and Holberg.

Visitors to Tofino can readily observe the symbiotic relationship between House Sparrows and humans at the Common Loaf Bakery, where a nesting box is conveniently located near the outdoor tables. The birds benefit from a readily available source of bread and pastry crumbs, and the management benefits from an inexpensive cleanup squad.

Somewhat ironically, House Sparrows are now on the threatened species list in England, the country of their origin, having declined by 50% in a 25-year period. However, as one of the most ubiquitous birds in the world, there is little danger of its extinction anytime soon, provided, of course, that human civilization, on which it depends, continues to survive. It is probably worth noting that the astronomically high numbers of Passenger Pigeons did not prevent their extinction.

ACCIDENTAL SPECIES

This section of species accounts is reserved for birds that are usually far from their normal range and, having occurred on the west coast only once or twice, are not expected again. If additional sightings occur, a bird's status may be elevated to casual.

Burrowing Owl

FALCATED DUCK
Mareca falcata

This strikingly handsome Asian bird breeds from southeastern Siberia to northern Mongolia and Japan. It winters from southern Japan east to China and Southeast Asia to northern India. In North America, it is a rare vagrant in the western Aleutian Islands and the Pribilof Islands and accidental in the western United States and Canada. Prior to 1994, there was a single record in Canada, from Swan Lake in Vernon, of a bird seen from 15 to 17 April 1932. It was regarded as an escaped bird, however, and the record was not accepted.[324]

On Vancouver Island's west coast, a single drake in full breeding regalia was discovered at the Tofino mudflats by Tofino resident Rory Paterson on 19 April 1994. The same bird was subsequently seen in three separate years by numerous birders, some of whom came from across the continent to see it. This individual, unlike the bird in 1932, has been accepted as a wild vagrant and is therefore the first record for both British Columbia and Canada. It was seen on the following dates: 19 to 22 April 1994;[325] 20 January to 28 March 1995;[326] and 27 January to 25 March 1996.[327]

TUFTED DUCK
Aythya fuligula

The male of this Eurasian species looks similar to a male Ring-necked Duck, but it has a visible tuft on the back of its head. It is a wanderer from Europe and Asia and has been seen at numerous locations on both the Atlantic and Pacific coasts. The first sighting south of Alaska was in California in 1948-49. The first occurrence in British Columbia was in 1961 on the south coast.[328] Since then, there have been numerous sightings in the Fraser River delta and a few on southern Vancouver Island, and it has been seen occasionally in the southern interior.[6]

There is a single record for our west coast region. On 10 May 2008, an adult male was observed and photographed at Port Renfrew by Rick Toochin.

ARCTIC LOON
Gavia arctica

The Arctic Loon is a Eurasian bird. It breeds throughout much of northern and central Eurasia, from Scotland and Norway to eastern Siberia. It winters in western and southern Europe, the Black and Caspian seas, and the Pacific Ocean from the Kamchatka Peninsula south to Hong Kong. It is similar in appearance to the Pacific Loon, but is noticeably larger and shows white flanks when on the water, which the Pacific Loon does not. The two were in fact considered a single species under the name "Arctic Loon" until they were split in 1985. Since the split, there have been only a few verified sightings of this loon in southern regions of North America.

On the British Columbia coast, there have been a number of reports, though at this writing there is only one verified record for the province. On 15 and 16 April 2012, a bird was photographed by Louis Havilland at the southern tip of our region at Jordan River.

SOLANDER'S PETREL
Pterodroma solandri

This bird, named after the Swedish botanist Daniel Solander, is also known as the Providence Petrel. In appearance it is very similar to the Murphy's Petrel. It is a burrow nester that breeds on only two islands off Australia, Lord Howe Island and Phillip's Island at Norfolk Island. From 1790 to 1793, a million birds were killed for food at Norfolk Island. By 1800, the species was entirely gone from there, though it did survive on Lord Howe Island. Estimates placed the population at 20,000 breeding pairs in the 1970s, and at 32,000 pairs in 2002. Fortunately, a small population has re-established itself at Norfolk Island. After the breeding season, birds head east over the Tasman Sea and north to the central Pacific Ocean. The population is currently estimated at around 100,000 birds.[329]

There were no reports of this species from North American waters until 20 May 1981, when seabird researcher R.L. Pitman reported it from Oregon waters, and shortly after also the very similar Murphy's Petrel off California.[330] As single-observer sightings without photos, these reports were not accepted at the time. In 1994, while conducting marine mammal and seabird surveys, BC birder Michael Force reported a Solander's Petrel 140 mi off the Oregon coast, and two more birds 180 mi off the coast in 1997. However, without photographic documentation, this species remained unconfirmed for North America.

On 6 October 2009, on a pelagic birding trip out of Tofino, Mike and Sharon Toochin, Roger Foxall, and Arthur Ahier saw a bird over Clayoquot Canyon, 28 NM offshore, that in the field was identified as a Murphy's Petrel. Although Murphy's Petrels had been sighted numerous times off the US west coast, this would have been the first verified record for Canada. Subsequent close examination of the several excellent photos taken by Sharon Toochin led them to conclude that it was probably a Solander's Petrel. The photos were sent to experts with first-hand experience with both species. The consensus was that this was indeed a Solander's Petrel, the first proven occurrence for North America.[331]

MAGNIFICENT FRIGATEBIRD
Fregata magnificens

The person who bestowed the name "Magnificent" on this bird had either observed the flamboyant male with its crimson neck sac inflated during the breeding season or was inspired by this bird's incredible ability to hang in the air on the flimsiest breeze. Magnificent Frigatebirds are birds of the tropics and subtropics and are found on both coasts of the Americas. On the Pacific coast, this bird's range stretches from Baja California to Ecuador. It is seen sporadically further north along the US coast.

In British Columbia, fishermen had over the years reported large, fork-tailed birds offshore on the tuna grounds. Those reports remained unconfirmed until 25 August 1981, when a Magnificent Frigatebird was photographed perched on a trolling pole at Langara Island, Haida Gwaii, for a first confirmed sighting in the province.[6] There have since been a number of reports from Vancouver Island, among them two from our west coast region. On 18 July 1997, an adult male was spotted at Cox Bay, Tofino, by Mike, Sharon, and Rick Toochin. Four years later, on 9 May 2001, a juvenile or subadult was seen off Flores Island, Clayoquot Sound, by tour-boat skipper Mike Woods (personal communication).

In addition to the above, there have also been reports of a bird 4 mi off Estevan Point in August 1969, and one off Tofino on 18 June 2001. This last report may have involved the same bird reported by Mike Woods in the previous month. With the proliferation of high-tech cameras of all sorts, we can expect future sightings to be photographed. Until then, this bird should probably be considered accidental on our coast.

AMERICAN BITTERN
Botaurus lentiginosus

American Bitterns breed from the Maritimes and the New England states westward across the continent to northern California, Oregon, Washington, and British Columbia. In this province, it breeds primarily east of the Coast Mountains, particularly in the dry interior, but also regularly in the Fraser Valley and the Salish Sea basin, including southeastern Vancouver Island (BCNRS). The species winters from the southern United States southward.

In our west coast region, there has been a single sighting. At the end of the first week of December 2015, George Fifield, an avid golfer, observed a large bird standing beside a pond near the eighth hole on the Long Beach Golf Course, and recognized it immediately as an American Bittern. The pond by the eighth hole is reported to contain small fish.

SNOWY EGRET
Egretta thula

Once hunted ruthlessly for their plumes to satisfy human vanity and enrich the fashion entrepreneurs, these birds are once again common in their former range. Though we tend to associate egrets with the tropics and subtropics, this species, like the Great Egret, nests quite far north. On the Atlantic coast, the Snowy Egret nests north to Maine, and in the Midwest to Wisconsin and North Dakota and even Manitoba. Further west, it breeds north to Idaho and eastern Oregon,[332] primarily at Malheur National Wildlife Refuge since the late 1800s. Western birds winter from California south to tropical regions. British Columbia is well north of its usual range, but very occasionally a wandering bird will venture north to this province, much to the delight of birders here. Records in this province remain few, however, and the species is considered casual.[6] All records thus far are from the southwest corner of the province.

In our west coast region, we had our first and only occurrence in the spring of 2011, when a Snowy Egret showed up on the Tofino mudflats at Jensen's Bay on 19 May. I first learned of it from Ralph Crombie during a telephone call in which he described a wolf sighting that morning and added, "Oh, by the way, there was a second egret here a while ago, small, with nice plumes, a dark bill, dark legs and yellow feet." It was referred to as a "second egret" because a Great

Egret had already been present there for some time. The Snowy Egret was subsequently seen by many other observers, sometimes feeding right next to the Great Egret, which was twice its size. One egret on the west coast was remarkable enough, but two species feeding side by side this far north was astonishing. This bird was last seen on 23 May.

BLACK-CROWNED NIGHT-HERON
Nycticorax nycticorax

This species has a widespread breeding range in the United States, breeding in every contiguous state, albeit marginally in some. In Canada, it is found from New Brunswick, southern Quebec, and southern Ontario in the east, and western Manitoba and southern Saskatchewan to Alberta in the west.

In British Columbia, the Black-crowned Night-Heron occurs sporadically in the southern interior and regularly on the southwest mainland coast. In recent years, the species has been a frequent resident, and occasional breeder on sloughs at the George C. Reifel Migratory Bird Sanctuary near the mouth of the Fraser River (BCNRS). On southern Vancouver Island, it is considered casual.[6] The only record for the west coast region is of a juvenile seen by Brian Slater at the Thornton Creek hatchery on Ucluelet Inlet from 14 to 17 August 2004.

BLACK-NECKED STILT
Himantopus mexicanus

This aptly named long-legged shorebird breeds throughout much of Mexico and large areas of the United States. It has a discontinuous range throughout much of the western United States and also breeds along the Gulf Coast, the lower Mississippi, and the Atlantic coast. The species winters from California and the Gulf Coast south to Argentina and Chile. In North America, this bird has been in an expansionist phase since the early 1970s and bred for the first time in Canada in 1977. Today it breeds regularly in southern Alberta and Saskatchewan.

In British Columbia, the species was first recorded in 1910 in the southeastern Cariboo and the first successful nesting occurred in the Thompson Valley in 2002. Today, seven nesting attempts are known in the province, four of them successful.[333] In 2012, the first breeding occurred on Vancouver Island when two pairs nested successfully on the Saanich Peninsula. For the west coast region, we have only a single record, dating back over 40 years. On 17 May 1974, a bird was observed and photographed by Robert A. Cannings at Hanson Lagoon, in Cape Scott Provincial Park (BC Photo 390).[4] At the time, there were only two earlier records for British Columbia.

BRISTLE-THIGHED CURLEW
Numenius tahitiensis

Bristle-thighed Curlew, 27 June 2010, Long Beach.

Although similar to the Whimbrel in appearance, this species has a very different distribution. It was first described in 1785 from Tahiti on Captain Cook's first voyage, hence the Latin name of *tahitiensis*. Cook and his men would have been incredulous had they been told that these birds fly north each spring over 8,000 km (5,000 mi) of trackless ocean to nest in western Alaska. The nesting grounds, however, would not be discovered until 1948.

On 31 May 1969, a Bristle-thighed Curlew was observed and collected at Grant Bay, northwestern Vancouver Island, by F. Richardson.[16] This was the first record for Canada. There were no further sightings for our west coast region until 24 June 2010, when Mrs. Daryl Johnson, camping at Greenpoint, Long Beach, with her family, observed a small flock of Whimbrels on the beach. Among them was a bird that looked somewhat different from the others. Consulting her field guide, she correctly identified it as a Bristle-thighed Curlew, for Canada's second confirmed sighting. The bird was photographed by her son on a cell phone shortly after, and later by others using telephoto lenses. It remained until the 27th of June.

CURLEW SANDPIPER
Calidris ferruginea

This sandpiper has been described as a more elegant version of a Dunlin. In breeding plumage, it is strikingly different from the latter, with a ruddy overall appearance. Juveniles look similar to the Dunlin, but with a more scalloped appearance on the back. In all plumages, the Curlew Sandpiper has a white rump that is conspicuous in flight. This species is reported to have suffered a 40% decline since 1975, possibly due to the effects of the current warming period.[334]

The Curlew Sandpiper breeds in northern Siberia and winters from Africa and Southeast Asia to Australia and New Zealand. In North America, it has shown up sporadically throughout much of the continent, including the east, where, strangely, it is seen more often than on the west coast. It has bred in western Alaska.[334] In *Shorebirds of the Pacific Northwest*, Paulson lists 21 records for the Pacific Northwest, including 8 from southern British Columbia,[133] 7 of which are listed in *The Birds of British Columbia*.[111]

For the west coast of Vancouver Island, we have two records. On 20 September 1987, a juvenile was seen at Long Beach by James Steele, and three years later, on 2 September 1990, a bird was seen at Chesterman Beach by Ian McLaren.[133]

CRESTED AUKLET
Aethia cristatella

This small to medium-sized auk breeds on islands in the Aleutian Islands and in the Bering Sea. It winters in the Bering Sea and in the Gulf of Alaska, south of the Alaska Peninsula.

Crested Auklet, 30 July 2013, Cleland Island (photo by Jason Feaver).

There are only three records for British Columbia, two of which were recorded off our west coast. In the winter of 1892/93, a specimen was taken off Kyuquot Sound (RBCM 11915).[111] The second record for the province was a bird seen and photographed south of our region at Rocky Point, Metchosin, in September and October 2003. The second sighting for our region occurred on 30 July 2013, when the skipper of a whale-watching boat, Orin Lawson, spotted a bird he did not recognize at Cleland Island. It was subsequently photographed (BC Photo 4137)[41] by another boat operator, Jason Feaver, and identified as an adult Crested Auklet. It was seen several more times in subsequent days.

BLACK TERN
Chlidonias niger

Like other terns, the Black Tern is a semi-colonial nester. It breeds in the marshes and shallow lakes of the interior of the mid-continent, from the Maritimes and southeastern Quebec westward through the northern United States and the Prairie provinces to Oregon, Washington, Alberta, the Yukon, and the interior of British Columbia east of the Coast Mountains. It has bred at Pitt Lake in the Fraser Valley, where it is considered a rare summer visitor. On southeastern Vancouver Island, it is considered casual. Black Terns winter along the Pacific coast from Jalisco, Mexico, to northern and western South America.

For the west coast of Vancouver Island, we have two records. A single bird was present at Grant Bay, in the northwest of our region, from 22 to 31 August 1968.[16] Twenty-four years later, on 6 September 1992, a bird in fall plumage was seen and photographed at Long Beach by Richard Clauke and S. Benoit.[324]

ORIENTAL TURTLE-DOVE
Streptopelia orientalis

Oriental Turtle-Dove, 18 August, 1992, Tofino.

This handsome Asian dove has a range stretching from Japan and China to Vietnam, India, and eastern Kazakhstan. It is of very occasional occurrence at the end of the Aleutian chain, where its status is considered casual.

The first occurrence for this species in Canada was in a backyard in Tofino on 18 August 1992, when it was first seen and correctly identified by Rory Paterson. It was photographed (BC Photo 1848)[41] and subsequently seen by many others until 25 August, after which it disappeared. A question is sometimes raised about provenance: was it an escaped bird or was it wild? There were no indications of this bird having been in captivity, although the date seemed somewhat early for a fall vagrant. A bird seen at the George C. Reifel Migratory Bird Sanctuary near the mouth of the Fraser River on 18 January 2010 was the second record for Canada.[335]

On 26 September 2013, twenty-one years after the first record at Tofino, I observed an Oriental Turtle-Dove on the beach at Stubbs Island, about 1.6 km (1 mi) across the water from where the first bird was seen in 1992. This apparent juvenile was extremely shy but was seen several times over the next few days by both Arthur Ahier and me. It was last seen on 2 October (BC Photo 4047). Two photos were submitted to the BC Bird Records Committee and the sighting was subsequently accepted.

YELLOW-BILLED CUCKOO
Coccyzus americanus

This is one of three North American cuckoos in the genus *Coccyzus*. The Yellow-billed Cuckoo breeds throughout the eastern United States and the Midwest, north into southern Ontario, west to southeastern Montana, and in the south to New Mexico, Arizona, and the highlands of Mexico. It breeds locally in widely scattered localities in all western states except Oregon and Washington.

In British Columbia, the Yellow-billed Cuckoo was considered accidental for many years. That was not always the case. From 1881 to 1927, there are as many as 30 reliable records, 3 of them from Vancouver Island at Victoria. After 1927, there were no records for 63 years. Then, on 5 July 1989, an emaciated but living bird was found in Victoria after being hit by a vehicle. This record heralded in an additional 18 occurrences up to the end of 2013, bringing the total for the province to 48. There is a single breeding record from Mount Lehman, in the central Fraser Valley, in 1904.[336]

There is a single record from the southernmost extremity of our west coast region. On 30 June and 1 July 2004, an adult was seen at Jordan River by Chris Saunders, Donna Ross, and Guy Monty.

BLACK-BILLED CUCKOO
Coccyzus erythropthalmus

The Black-billed Cuckoo breeds from the Maritime provinces (except Newfoundland) and the New England states west through the northern Midwest and the southern Prairie provinces to southeastern Alberta, Montana, and

Nebraska. In British Columbia, it is a very rare vagrant east of the Coast Mountains. On the coast, it is considered accidental.[111]

For our west coast region, there is one record. On 30 August 1986, a juvenile Black-billed Cuckoo was seen on Frank Island, Chesterman Beach, Tofino, by George Smith, Glen Gould, and Merrily Corder.[111,197]

BARN OWL
Tyto alba

Barn Owls are widespread globally and are found from Australia, Southeast Asia, India, Africa, and Europe to North and South America. In North America, the species breeds from the eastern United States and southern Ontario west to the Pacific coast and south to Mexico. It also breeds throughout Central and South America. In British Columbia, the Barn Owl is a rare resident in the south-central interior and is considered an uncommon resident in the Fraser Valley. On southeastern Vancouver Island, it is a rare resident, very rarely north to Campbell River.[111]

There is a single record for the west coast. On 2 December 2006, George Bradd found a dead and emaciated specimen in the possession of his dog at his residence near Cox Bay. A wing was saved and photographed.

BURROWING OWL
Athene cunicularia

This ground-dwelling owl is both nocturnal and diurnal. It is named for its ability to burrow into the ground in order to make a safe place to nest, although it usually relies on finding an abandoned mammal burrow. It breeds in suitable habitat in both North and South America. On this continent, it breeds from Mexico north through much of the American West to the Canadian Prairies. In the east, it breeds only in Florida. In British Columbia, the species nests in low numbers in the southern interior, and has nested in the Fraser River delta. There have been periodic sightings on southeastern Vancouver Island since the late 1920s, when Theed Pearse found the first one near Comox on 23 March 1927.[111]

There were no records for the west coast until 20 October 2013, when an owl flew into a window at the Common Loaf Bakery in Tofino. The bird was photographed shortly after by members of the Comox Valley Camera Club who happened to be visiting Tofino. Six days later, it was found in a small park a quarter-mile away, and on 27 November, it was rediscovered on the Tofino Hospital grounds by an observant young girl, Toby Theriault. The bird spent most of December living beneath a skateboard ramp near the community centre, and was last seen on 23 December, still looking quite healthy.

Information later emerged that the origin of this colour-banded female was the Nicola valley in the central interior of the province, where there is an active captive breeding program to restore the population in the wild. This bird had been born in captivity and had been released the previous April. Instead of migrating south in the fall, it flew west.

GREAT GRAY OWL
Strix nebulosa

This secretive owl breeds in Canada's north, from northern Ontario west through the boreal forest region to northern British Columbia, north to the Northwest Territories, the Yukon Territory, and Alaska. It also breeds in the Rocky Mountains south to northwestern Wyoming, and west to northeastern Oregon and the Cascade Mountains. In British Columbia, its known breeding distribution is far from complete, but it is known to breed in the southern interior, in the southern Rocky Mountains, and at several locations in the north of the province. This owl is largely sedentary but it does have occasional irruptions when part of the population disperses south.

The Great Gray Owl has only rarely been seen on Vancouver Island. On the west coast, we had our first occurrence in late January 1985, when a bird was seen in Pacific Rim National Park by park employee Dan Vedova. It was last seen on 28 February, when it was photographed. The following summer, I found a tuft of feathers that appeared to be from this species, among flood debris along the Megin River. The feathers were later verified by staff of the Royal BC Museum as being from a Great Gray Owl.

LESSER NIGHTHAWK
Chordeiles acutipennis

This is largely a bird of the tropics and subtropics. It breeds from Central America and Mexico north into the American border states, with its range in the west extending to northern California and southern Nevada. The species winters from the southern half of Baja California and southern Sonora to northern South America and eastern Brazil, west to Bolivia.

There were no records for the west coast region until 5 June 2006, when bird photographer Mike Yip snapped a photo of an adult male in flight 80 km (50 mi) west of Tofino. This was the second record for Canada and the first for British Columbia. A second bird was recorded on Vancouver Island on 28 May 2011, south of our region at Whiffin Spit, Sooke.[54]

EASTERN WHIP-POOR-WILL
Caprimulgus vociferus

This relative of the Common Nighthawk breeds throughout the eastern United States with the exception of the south. In this country, it breeds in southern Canada from the Maritimes west to southern Manitoba and southern Saskatchewan.

On 5 November 2001, a dead bird was picked up at Amphitrite Point by retired park naturalist Bill McIntyre, who suspected it to be a whip-poor-will. The bird had been dead for at least one week, and probably two or more. The specimen was given to me, and a decision was made to remove a wing and tail for positive identification. Although the bird was clearly a whip-poor-will, it was not obvious which of the two populations it belonged to, the one from eastern North America or the one from the American Southwest and Mexico. At that time, the two populations were considered separate subspecies but a taxonomic split was pending. If the bird proved to be from the east, it would be a new species for the province. If it was from the Southwest, it would be the Mexican Whip-poor-will (*C. arizonae*) and a new species for Canada.[337]

Eastern Whip-poor-will, 5 November 2001, Ucluelet.

The specimen was to be sent to California for identification but this did not occur due to permitting issues, and the specimen remains in Victoria, lost for now among hundreds of boxes in storage. In the meantime, a photo (BC Photo 3275)[41] that had been taken of the wing and tail was made available online to the birding community. Rather than resolving the issue, however, this only resulted in divided opinions on the matter. In 2014, the newly formed BC Bird Records Committee of the British Columbia Field Ornithologists weighed the evidence but took a cautious approach, reserving judgment on the bird's identity until such time as the specimen resurfaces and DNA samples can be taken.

When I compared measurements of the amount of white in the outer tail feathers, viewed from below, with those outlined in the literature, I found that they matched the eastern bird. Furthermore, the grey central tail feathers on the upper side of the tail lacked the brownish hue normally seen in *C. arizonae*, and were therefore a perfect match for *C. vociferus*. Confirmation of its identity came from Michel Gosselin, head of collections at the Canadian Museum of Nature in Ottawa. He concluded that the amount of white in the tail was beyond the range of the Mexican Whip-poor-will and stated "without reservation" that it was an eastern bird.

BLACK-CHINNED HUMMINGBIRD
Archilochus alexandri

This hummingbird is widely distributed throughout much of the west, from western Texas to California, north to western Montana, Idaho, and eastern Washington. In Canada, it is found only in the southern interior of British Columbia, where it nests primarily in the Okanagan Valley, often in human-associated habitat such as orchards and suburban gardens.[288] It is rarely recorded on the coast.

For our region, there is a single record. On 12-13 September 1994, an adult male Black-chinned Hummingbird was observed on Triangle Island by Martin K. McNicholl.[338]

COSTA'S HUMMINGBIRD
Calypte costae

This is a bird of the American Southwest. Its breeding range extends from central California and southern Nevada to southern Arizona, Baja California, and northwestern Mexico. The species winters in southern California, Baja California, and the western state of Sonora, Mexico. The species is seen very occasionally north to British Columbia. As of 2015, there have been 25 or more occurrences in the province.[339]

There are two records for the west coast region. On 21 April 1994, an adult male was seen on Triangle Island, off Vancouver Island's northern tip,[339] and on 7-8 April 2007, an adult male was found at Jordan River by Rick Toochin and subsequently photographed.[340] These remain the only records for our area.

BLACK PHOEBE
Sayornis nigricans

The Black Phoebe is one of three species in the genus *Sayornis* and is found largely in the tropics and subtropics. It breeds at higher elevation in the mountains of South America and Central America, north through Mexico to the southwestern United States. In the United States, it breeds from southwestern Texas, southern New Mexico, and southern Arizona through most of California, north to southernmost Oregon.

Although British Columbia is far north of its normal range, *The Birds of British Columbia*,[263] listed two records for the province, one from Marpole in south Vancouver and the other in Stanley Park. There have been two additional records from the Fraser Lowlands since then, and two sightings on southern Vancouver Island. By 2005, there had been 16 reports (verified and unverified) for the province.[197]

For Vancouver Island's west coast region, we have two records. On 24 April 2013, while searching for a vagrant shorebird reported at Long Beach, Saltspring Island resident Karen Ferguson and I were thrilled to find a Black Phoebe hawking insects at the mouth of Sandhill Creek, Long Beach. The bird was observed at close range through the use of binoculars and spotting scopes. Less than a year later, on 10 and 11 April 2014, a second Black Phoebe was observed in the west coast region, this one by Ewen and Barbara Brittain at their home beside Ucluelet Inlet.

GREAT CRESTED FLYCATCHER
Myiarchus crinitus

This species breeds throughout the eastern United States and southeastern Canada, as far west as central Saskatchewan to the Alberta border. *The Birds of British Columbia*[263] lists a handful of reports from within British Columbia, though most have been rejected due to inadequate documentation. On 29 and 30 September 1994, a Great Crested Flycatcher was observed on Triangle Island by Rick and Mike Toochin.[263] This was the first accepted record for the species in the province and the first for our region. Fifteen years later, on 5 July 2010, a Great Crested Flycatcher was seen along the lower Kennedy River by professional birding guide George Bradd (personal communication) and an unidentified client. It is accepted here because the observer was very familiar with both this species and the similar Ash-throated Flycatcher.

GRAY KINGBIRD
Tyrannus dominicensis

This large flycatcher from the tropics and subtropics looks rather like an Eastern Kingbird with an outsized bill. Its breeding range extends from northern South America and Central America through the islands of the Caribbean to Florida, and along a narrow coastal strip along the Gulf of Mexico. One would therefore not expect to find this bird in British Columbia. However, a specimen was collected at Cape Beal, near Barkley Sound, on 29 September 1889.[341] This remains the only record for British Columbia and the west coast of Vancouver Island.

PHILADELPHIA VIREO
Vireo philadelphicus

This species is similar in appearance to the Warbling Vireo but with darker crown and eye-line, and with the belly often yellowish in fall. It breeds from Newfoundland and the Maritimes west through the boreal forest region to, but not including, the Rocky Mountains, and north to the southern Yukon. In British Columbia, it breeds only in the Peace River region and the far northeast corner of the province. It migrates largely through the eastern half of the United States to winter from the Yucatan Peninsula in Mexico to Colombia.

Given its range, this is not a bird to be expected on our coast. However, on 13 September 2006, one was found by Rick Toochin at Jordan River at the extreme southern end of our region and subsequently photographed by Mike Bentley. It was last seen on 16 September.[195]

EURASIAN SKYLARK
Alauda arvensis

This species has a wide distribution throughout Eurasia but is not native to the Americas. The European subspecies, *A. a. arvensis,* was introduced to southern

Vancouver Island in 1903, and currently the small, sedentary population that nested at Victoria Airport in Saanich appears extirpated.[342]

In our west coast region, we have a single record. On 28 October 2004, a bird was seen and photographed at the extreme south end of our region at Jordan River by Ted Ardley and Rick Toochin.[195] This bird is not likely to be seen on the west coast again, and is therefore considered accidental.

BLUE-GRAY GNATCATCHER
Polioptila caerulea

This small bird with a long tail and conspicuous white outer tail feathers breeds throughout all of the eastern United States and into southern Ontario in the north and Mexico in the south. In the west, it breeds from Mexico north to western Wyoming, southern Idaho, and southern Oregon. Western birds winter in central and coastal California and Arizona, south through Mexico and Central America.

The Birds of British Columbia considered the species to be casual on the south coast and listed only three records between 1963 and 1994.[263] In recent years, birds have been seen in Victoria in 2007, 2011, and 2012, each time in the months of October, November, or December.

On Vancouver Island's west coast, we have three records, likely involving two birds, all in the Tofino area. On 30 December 1979, I had close-up looks at one as it flitted in bushes at the foot of First Street in Tofino. At that time, it was only the second record for the province. The seemingly unlikely date of December is consistent with other sightings in British Columbia, Washington, and Oregon. A second Blue-gray Gnatcatcher was found by Michael Shepard on 28 October 2016, just a city block's distance from where the first one was seen 37 years earlier. A third sighting, very likely the same individual as on 28 October, was made at nearby Stubbs Island on 11 November by Ian Cruickshank and Marcel and Toby Theriault.

SIBERIAN ACCENTOR
Prunella montanella

This species breeds in northern Siberia and winters in Southeast Asia. Occasionally it strays east to Alaska and very rarely to areas further south. It was first recorded in Alaska in 1927 and 1936 on islands in the Bering Sea. By the end of 1995, there were about 11 records for Alaska. Since then, the species has been recorded in the Pacific Northwest from Washington, Idaho, Montana, Alberta, and British Columbia. The first record for this province occurred on 5 July 1991 in Victoria, when a bird hit a window and was subsequently captured by a house cat.

Today there are six records for British Columbia, with one of those from our west coast region. On 20 September 1999, a bird was observed on a small island in the Nuchatlitz group, at the entrance to Esperanza Inlet, by David Shipway, who was kayaking in the area. His field notes and an accompanying drawing make a very convincing case that the bird belongs to this species. His notes are with the Biodiversity Centre for Wildlife Studies and are listed under BC Photo 2060.[41]

GRAY WAGTAIL
Motacilla cinerea

The Gray Wagtail has an enormous breeding range in Eurasia, from western Europe to the Kamchatka Peninsula. Birds in eastern Siberia are slightly larger in size, and are considered by some as a separate subspecies called *M. c. robusta*. The Gray Wagtail's breeding range extends to Korea and Japan. The species winters in much of Europe, northern and eastern Africa, India, and Southeast Asia. During spring migration, it is a very rare visitor to the western Aleutians, and is casual in the Pribilof Islands and St. Lawrence Island. It has been recorded in California, where it is accidental.

On 26 October 1994, assistant lighthouse keeper Jerry Etzkorn photographed an adult female Gray Wagtail at Carmanah Point[343] (BC Photo 3059).[41] This was the second record for Canada and the first for our region.

CHESTNUT-COLLARED LONGSPUR
Calcarius ornatus

This is a bird of the grasslands of the Great Plains, where it breeds from Manitoba to central Alberta, south to Montana, the Dakotas, and eastern Wyoming. Although British Columbia is well outside its normal range, there have been a number of verified reports from the province, including photos and specimens. Birds were also seen and photographed at Victoria on 24-25 October 2013 and 1 May 2015.

On our west coast, we have a single record. On 18 June 1972, David F. Hatler found and photographed a male in breeding plumage on the Faber Islets in Barkley Sound (BC Photo 224).[344]

SMITH'S LONGSPUR
Calcarius pictus

This little-known longspur is distinguished primarily by its buffy appearance. Only the male in breeding plumage is conspicuously marked with a black-and-white pattern on crown and face. It breeds on the Canadian tundra from James Bay west to Alaska. The species also breeds further south in the Wrangell Mountains of Alaska and the Chilkat pass area of extreme northwestern British Columbia. In migration, birds take an easterly route over the Great Plains to Oklahoma, northeastern Texas, and western Arkansas. They are only very rarely seen in southern British Columbia. In 1976, I was fortunate to see one outside our area on Cortes Island. There have been several reports from Vancouver Island. In our west coast region, there is a single record. On 18 October 1980, a bird was seen north of Bamfield by Keith Taylor.[299]

McKAY'S BUNTING
Plectrophenax hyperboreus

This species is closely related to the Snow Bunting, which it resembles. Its entire breeding range is restricted to two islands in the Bering Strait, and its population is believed to be under 6,000 birds. It winters on the west coast of Alaska, but there have been several sightings along the Pacific coast south of Alaska. One sighting was in Washington and one in Oregon.

On 12 February 1980, Pacific Rim National Park naturalist Barry Campbell found a bird at the south end of Long Beach and succeeded in photographing it.[299] This was the first record for Canada as well as for our west coast region.

NORTHERN WATERTHRUSH
Parkesia noveboracensis

This species breeds in forested regions throughout Canada, Alaska, and the northeastern United States. In the west, it breeds from northern Wyoming, western Montana, and northern Idaho to northeastern Washington and British Columbia. The species winters from Mexico to northern South America.

In British Columbia, it breeds in suitable habitat throughout much of the province east of the Coast Mountains. It is an uncommon migrant in the interior, and a very rare or casual transient on the coast. In our region, we have a single record. On both 24 and 26 August 1995, an individual was caught and banded on Triangle Island.[299]

BLACK-AND-WHITE WARBLER
Mniotilta varia

This species breeds throughout much of the eastern United States west to Texas, Oklahoma, and North and South Dakota. In Canada, it breeds from the Maritimes west through Quebec, Ontario, and the Prairie provinces, and through northern Alberta into the Northwest Territories. The species winters from the southeastern United States, the Caribbean, and northern Mexico south to northern South America.

In British Columbia, the species breeds in the Peace River region and in the northeast of the province. Elsewhere, there are scattered sightings of vagrant migrants at widely dispersed localities throughout the province, where its status is considered casual.[299] In our west coast region, we have two records. On 5 April 1977, an adult male was seen at Lennard Island, near Tofino,[299] and on 10 June 2017, a male was seen and photographed in Ucluelet by John Reynolds.

PROTHONOTARY WARBLER
Protonotaria citrea

This exquisite golden warbler with contrasting grey wings is a bird of the Carolinian forests of the eastern United States, where it inhabits lowland deciduous forests and swamps, particularly where old trees are present. Its range extends from Texas, Oklahoma, and Kansas east to Atlantic shores and north to Wisconsin and southern Ontario. The species winters from the Gulf Coast of Texas south to Central and South America.

There has been a measurable decline in numbers throughout its range since 1966. In Ontario, the only area of Canada in which this species breeds, numbers went from 40 or more breeding pairs in the 1980s to fewer than 12 pairs in 2008. It has been designated an endangered species in Canada and a recovery strategy is in place. A lack of suitable habitat is a major obstacle.

In British Columbia, with only six records, the species is considered accidental. The first occurrence for Vancouver Island was a window-killed bird in Victoria on 6 November 2001. The first occurrence for our west coast region came less than a year later, on 9 October 2002, when Tofino resident and birder Arthur Ahier found a Prothonotary Warbler feeding in red alder trees at Cox Bay, just outside Tofino. The bird was subsequently photographed.[345]

CONNECTICUT WARBLER
Oporornis agilis

This warbler is very similar in appearance to the MacGillivray's Warbler, which is a local breeder. The Connecticut Warbler, on the other hand, breeds only in the Peace River region and the northwest corner of British Columbia. Its breeding range stretches from Quebec, the northern Great Lakes region, and northern Ontario westward throughout the boreal forests to British Columbia. In late summer, it migrates to the eastern United States and from there to South America.

For the west coast region, *The Birds of British Columbia* lists a single record.[299] On 28 October 1994, a juvenile was found at Long Beach by John and Rick Toochin. This species differs from the MacGillivray's Warbler primarily by having an unbroken eye ring and being slightly larger. While its occurrence on the southwest coast was unprecedented, the species has been recorded to the south of us in all three US coastal states.

HOODED WARBLER
Wilsonia citrina

This bird's breeding range is restricted to eastern North America, where it nests in the deep deciduous forests of the Carolinian zone, particularly mature stands.

Its range in Canada is limited to southern Ontario, where it is considered threatened due to its small population and the absence of adequate habitat. The species winters in eastern Mexico, Central America, and islands in the Caribbean.

On 14 December 1989, I was alerted to the presence of a warbler by a chirp in the underbrush beside Campbell Street in Tofino, and succeeded in snapping a photo of a female Hooded Warbler, the first one recorded in British Columbia. It was last seen on 16 December.[346] Two others have since been seen in late fall on Vancouver Island, one at Duncan and one at Campbell River, and there are now several other records for the BC mainland. This remains the only record for the west coast region.

NORTHERN PARULA
Setophaga americana

This warbler breeds throughout much of the eastern United States and eastern Canada, from Nova Scotia and the Atlantic states west to southeastern Manitoba and the US Midwest. It is missing, however, from a wide belt south and east of the Great Lakes. The species winters from southern Mexico to Guatemala and Belize. British Columbia is far west of its normal range, but it has been periodically recorded in the province. On Vancouver Island, it has been found on eight occasions.

In the west coast region, it was seen for the first time on 15 June 2016 by Ian Cruickshank, who found a singing male on an island in the lower Kennedy River (Deer Bay) and recorded its song.

BAY-BREASTED WARBLER
Setophaga castanea

This species breeds from the Yukon and Northwest Territories south to northern Alberta and east to Quebec and the Maritime provinces. In British Columbia, it is an uncommon breeding bird in the northeast in the Peace River region. It has been seen as a casual vagrant elsewhere. It migrates southward mostly east of the 100th meridian to southern Central America, Colombia, and Venezuela.

On Vancouver Island's west coast, we have two records. On 10 to 13 October 1993, a juvenile was seen in Pacific Rim National Park by Michael Shepard and others.[347] Two years later, on 29 October 1995, a first-year bird was found in Tofino by Don Cecile.[348] It was subsequently photographed (BC Photo 1614).

PRAIRIE WARBLER
Setophaga discolor

Prairie Warbler, 28 September 2009, Tofino.

The breeding range of this distinctively marked warbler covers much of the eastern United States and the southern Midwest, with the exception of northernmost areas of New England. The species is absent from the northwestern United States, the northern Midwest, and southeastern Canada, except for a number of isolated breeding areas in southern Ontario and northwestern Michigan. It migrates directly south, then over the Gulf of Mexico to South America. Surprisingly, it is seen occasionally far to the west in coastal California, and has been seen on at least five occasions in British Columbia, including on at least two occasions in our west coast region.

The first sighting in the west coast region occurred on 29 May 1995, when an adult male was seen in Tofino by resident Rory Paterson. Although it was a single-observer sighting, a male in spring would seem to be unmistakable. Just over three months later, on 8 September 1995, an immature male was caught in a banding net on Triangle Island, located some 30 mi west of Cape Scott.[348] The third sighting occurred on 28 September 2009, when a juvenile Prairie Warbler took up a six-day residence in a small maple just outside my apartment window in Tofino. It was subsequently photographed and seen by numerous other observers until 3 October.[349]

CANADA WARBLER
Wilsonia canadensis

This species breeds from the Appalachians, New England, and the Maritimes west to the Great Lakes region and across the southern boreal forest region to British Columbia. In this province, Canada Warblers have been found breeding only in the northeastern part of the province in the Peace River region and on the Boreal Plains near Fort Nelson. The species migrates through the eastern and midwestern states to winter in northern South America. Western birds migrate east and then south.

The Birds of British Columbia lists only two records through 2000 for the province outside of the breeding range, one from the Fraser Valley and one from the extreme south end of our region.[299] On 2 and 3 December 1995, a bird was seen at Jordan River by Neil Hughes and others, and was photographed.[350]

GRASSHOPPER SPARROW
Ammodramus savannarum

Like others in its genus, the Grasshopper Sparrow is a bird that lives close to the ground. It nests in grasslands and in other habitat with low vegetation. Its breeding range extends across most of the eastern United States, southern Ontario, the Midwest, and the southern Prairie provinces. Further west, it breeds in coastal California, Nevada, Oregon, Idaho, Washington, and the interior grasslands of British Columbia, primarily the Okanagan Valley. On the coast, it is considered a casual summer and autumn vagrant in the Salish Sea basin.

For the west coast region, there is a single record. On 20 October 1996, a bird was observed on the beach at Jordan River by Keith Taylor.

YELLOW-BREASTED CHAT
Icteria virens

The Yellow-breasted Chat is the largest of the wood warblers. It breeds in suitable habitat throughout much of the United States. In Canada, it breeds in extreme southern Ontario, Saskatchewan, Alberta, and southern British Columbia. In this province, it breeds only in the Okanagan, Similkameen, and Creston valleys,[351] but has bred once in the Fraser Valley. It is considered a very rare vagrant elsewhere.

In our west coast region, we have had two occurrences. On 26 October 1950, a bird was recorded at Carmanah Point,[280] and on 21 August 1966, a bird was seen in Ucluelet.[299]

RUSTIC BUNTING
Emberiza rustica

The Rustic Bunting has a widespread breeding range across Eurasia, from northern Scandinavia east across central and northern Eurasia to Kamchatka and eastern Siberia. The species winters in southeastern China and Japan. It is a regular but very rare vagrant in the Aleutian Islands and western Alaska. It has also been recorded along the Pacific coast, south to California. The species was first reported in Canada when two birds were observed just west of Queen Charlotte (City), Haida Gwaii, on 26 October 1971.[352] Since then, there have been seven additional records for Canada, one in Saskatchewan and the rest on the BC coast.

The first sighting for Vancouver Island occurred on 25 November 1983, with a sighting at Jordan River by Vic and Peggy Goodwill. The bird was photographed (BC Photo 883)[41] and seen by numerous other observers until 20 February

1984, making it the first confirmed record for Canada.[353] The second record for our region occurred on 8 December 1990, when a bird showed up in the yard of Rory Paterson in Tofino. This bird was also photographed and seen by numerous observers. It was last recorded on 12 April 1991.[299]

PAINTED BUNTING
Passerina ciris

The male Painted Bunting boldly refutes everything that fashion-conscious people have taught us about the propriety of wearing matching colours. The male of the species sports the dazzling combination of a brilliant indigo-blue head atop a body with a crimson breast and a lime-green back. Its breeding range covers northeastern Mexico, Louisiana, Arkansas, Oklahoma, and Texas, and barely into New Mexico. There is also a breeding population along the southern Atlantic coast. This bird is therefore not to be expected in British Columbia, but there have been occurrences in the southern interior of the province, in Vancouver and on Vancouver Island, in central Saanich.

On the west coast, we have a single record. An adult male spent from 22 July to 28 July 2012 at a feeder behind the On the Inlet B&B in Ucluelet.[354] It was first observed by the residents of the property, Petra Arnold and her husband, and later by Jerry Herst and others. Given that a male Painted Bunting is highly unlikely to be mistaken for any other species and that it was seen by multiple observers, it is included here as a valid record.

BOBOLINK
Dolichonyx oryzivorus

This small, handsome blackbird nests in grasslands and agricultural fields from the New England states and Canadian Maritimes west to the Prairies, the central interior of British Columbia, and western Washington and western Oregon. It winters in southern South America. In the central interior of British Columbia, it is considered an uncommon to fairly common migrant and summer visitor. On southeastern Vancouver Island, it is considered a rare to very rare vagrant.

On Vancouver Island's west coast, we have two records. On 1 October 2002, a female or juvenile was observed at close range at the Carmanah Point Lighthouse Station by assistant lighthouse keeper Jerry Etzkorn,[345] and on 12 June 2016, a second bird, also a female, was found and photographed at the Long Beach airport by Ian Cruickshank.

ORCHARD ORIOLE
Icterus spurius

The breeding range of this species covers most of the eastern United States and extends north into southern Ontario, southern Manitoba, and southern Saskatchewan. Its migration route is directly south to Mexico, Central America, and the northern edge of South America.

There are two records for the west coast region. On the morning of 3 October 2009, a small group of birders who had travelled to Tofino to see a vagrant Prairie Warbler in a small maple tree in front of my Tofino apartment briefly saw what was believed to be a Bullock's Oriole land on a nearby balcony. Fortunately, the bird was photographed by a member of the group, because upon further scrutiny some time later, its identity proved to be a female or juvenile Orchard Oriole, a bird every bit as rare as the Prairie Warbler the group had come to see. Four years later, on 11 and 12 October 2013, having missed the first bird, I found and photographed a female Orchard Oriole (BC Photo 4113)[41] on Stubbs Island, less than 2 km from the location of the first sighting.[355]

BALTIMORE ORIOLE
Icterus galbula

Baltimore Orioles breed throughout much of the eastern United States and the Midwest. In Canada, the species breeds from Nova Scotia to the Great Lakes, and westward across the Great Plains to northwestern British Columbia. Elsewhere in British Columbia it is considered casual or accidental. There are several records for the south end of Vancouver Island.

For the west coast, we have a single record. On 7 January 2017, a juvenile Baltimore Oriole was observed and photographed northwest of Tofino at the village of Ahousaht, by Marcie Callewaert. This was all the more remarkable because the previous November, Marcie had photographed a juvenile Bullock's Oriole at the same location. The Baltimore Oriole was last seen on 17 January.

HYPOTHETICAL SPECIES

Hypothetical species are those birds that were reported but, lacking a photograph or other convincing evidence, are omitted from inclusion. Below is a list of birds that have been reported in the west coast region but have not been accepted here. A few reports are known to be invalid, while others may well be valid but were rejected due to insufficient evidence. In the absence of an active bird record committee in British Columbia for many years, the decision on whether to include or omit a record in this book rested solely with me. With a record committee now active in the province, such decisions will once again be determined by a panel of knowledgeable birders rather than by a single individual. As far as I can determine, none of the reports listed below has ever been officially accepted. With the remarkable advances in photographic technology in recent years, and the drop in cost, it has become easier than ever to photograph birds. I therefore encourage birders to carry a small camera at all times when birding to document any rarities they may encounter. Given the availability of this technology, the bar for accepting rare bird records may well be set higher, and documentation with photos could well become a requirement in future.

Garganey	Pacific Rim National Park sewage pond
Steller's Eider	Tofino
Common Eider	Botanical Beach, Port Renfrew
Streaked Petrel	Botanical Beach, Port Renfrew
Hawaiian Petrel	15 NM southwest of Cape Cook
Red-faced Cormorant	Botanical Beach and Tofino
Lesser Sand-Plover	Long Beach and Port Renfrew
Little Curlew	Chesterman Beach, Tofino
Spotted Redshank	Chesterman Beach, Tofino
Black-tailed Godwit	Tofino
Little Stint	Port Renfrew
Least Auklet	Off Cleland Island and northwest of Triangle Island

Kittlitz's Murrelet	Botanical Beach, Port Renfrew
Black-tailed Gull	Ucluelet Inlet and Tofino
Red-legged Kittiwake	Ucluelet
Three-toed Woodpecker	Tofino
Prairie Falcon	Long Beach Airport and Ucluelet
Fork-tailed Flycatcher	Flores Island
Veery	near Kennedy Lake
Eastern Yellow Wagtail	Long Beach Airport
Red-throated Pipit	Long Beach Airport
Ovenbird	Florencia Bay
Blackburnian Warbler	Ucluelet and Jordan River
Hermit Warbler	Klanawa River and Jordan River
Brewer's Sparrow	Port Renfrew
Hooded Oriole	Jordan River

While the birds listed above were excluded due to uncertainty in identification, there is no such uncertainty about a White-cheeked Starling, which was photographed at the Long Beach Golf Course on 27 April 2017. Its exclusion is therefore based entirely on uncertain provenance, a decision arrived at by the Rare Bird Committee of the BCFO. It will remain in a kind of ornithological limbo until such time (if ever) that a new sighting occurs in North America that is accepted.

White-cheeked Starling, 27 April, 2016, Long Beach Golf Course.

REFERENCES

A cloud of shorebirds takes to the air at Jensen's Bay, Tofino, during spring migration.

1. Hatler, David F., R. Wayne Campbell, and Adrian Dorst. Birds of Pacific Rim National Park. Occasional Paper No. 20. Victoria: British Columbia Provincial Museum, 1978. 194 pp.
2. US Fish and Wildlife Service. Waterfowl population status, 2015. Washington, DC: US Department of the Interior. https://www.fws.gov/migratorybirds/pdf/surveys-and-data/Population-status/Waterfowl/WaterfowlPopulationStatusReport15.pdf.
3. Deuel, Bruce E., and John Y. Takekawa. Tule Greater White-fronted Goose (*Anser albifrons elgasi*). In: W.D. Shuford and T. Gardali, eds. California bird species of special concern: a ranked assessment of species, subspecies, and distinct populations of birds of immediate conservation concern in California. Studies of Western Birds 1. Camarillo, CA: Western Field Ornithologists; Sacramento, CA: California Department of Fish and Game, 2008. pp. 74-78. https://nrm.dfg.ca.gov/FileHandler.ashx?DocumentID=10377.
4. Cannings, R.A. Natural history report: Cape Scott Park. Report No. 19. Victoria: British Columbia Parks Branch, 1975. 80 pp.
5. Reed, A., D.H. Ward, D.V. Derksen, and J.S. Sedinger. Brant (*Branta bernicla*). In: A. Poole and F. Gill, eds. The birds of North America, No. 337. Philadelphia: The Birds of North America, Inc., 1998. 32 pp.
6. Campbell, R. Wayne, Neil K. Dawe, Ian McTaggart-Cowan, John M. Cooper, Gary W. Kaiser, and Michael C.E. McNall. The Birds of British Columbia. Volume 1: non-passerines (introduction, loons through waterfowl). Victoria: Royal British Columbia Museum, 1990. 535 pp.
7. Mlodinow, Steven G., et al. Distribution and identification of Cackling Goose (*Branta hutchensii*) subspecies. North American Birds 2008; 62(3): 346. http://www.utahbirds.org/RecCom/IDhelp/Cackling_Goose-NAB.pdf.
8. Sibley, David. Distinguishing Cackling and Canada Goose. Sibley Guides; 2007. http://www.sibleyguides.com/2007/07/identification-of-cackling-and-canada-goose.
9. Hatler, D.F. An analysis of use, by waterfowl, of tideflats of southern Clayoquot Sound, British Columbia. Unpublished report. Canadian Wildlife Service, 1973.
10. US Fish and Wildlife Service. Giant Canada Goose, long believed extinct, rediscovered in Minnesota. Press release, 1 April 1963. https://www.fws.gov/news/ShowNews.cfm?ID=12DA0072-B899-63AB-14C509ECE07F10FF.

11 Edgell, M.C.R. Trans-hemispheric movements of Holarctic Anatidae: the Eurasian Wigeon (*Anas penelope* L.) in North America. Journal of Biogeography 1984; 11: 27-39.
12 Smith, M.R., P.W. Mattocks, and K.M. Cassidy. Breeding birds of Washington state. Volume 4 in K.M. Cassidy, C.E. Grue, M.R. Smith, and M.K. Dvornich, eds. Washington state gap analysis – final report. Publications in Zoology No. 1. Seattle: Seattle Audubon Society, 1997. 538 pp.
13 Campbell, R. Wayne, and Kenneth R. Summers. Vertebrates of Brooks Peninsula. In: Richard J. Hebda and James C. Haggarty, eds. Brooks Peninsula: an Ice Age refugium on Vancouver Island. Occasional Paper No. 5. Victoria: British Columbia Parks Branch, 1997. pp. 12.1-12.39.
14 Hunt, Davy. Pintail killed in Mississippi, banded in Japan. The Duck Hunter's Refuge; 2008. http://www.refugeforums.com/refuge/threads/pintail-killed-in-mississippi-banded-in-japan.596106/.
15 Blankenship, Devin. An amazing journey: California waterfowler bags pintail banded in Japan. Ducks Unlimited; n.d. http://www.ducks.org/hunting/reporting-leg-bands/an-amazing-journey.
16 Richardson, F. Birds of Grant Bay and Browning Inlet – northwest Vancouver Island, British Columbia; a year's phenology. Murrelet 1971; 52(3): 29-40.
17 Siddle, C. Summer season – British Columbia/Yukon region. National Audubon Society Field Notes 1994; 48: 240-42.
18 Hourston, A.S., and C.W. Haegele. Herring on Canada's Pacific coast. Canadian Special Publication of Fisheries and Aquatic Sciences, 48. Ottawa: Department of Fisheries and Oceans, 1980. 23 pp.
19 Surf Scoter (*Melanitta perspicillata*). Species status summary and information needs. Seaduck Joint Venture, March 2015. http://seaduckjv.org/wp-content/uploads/2014/08/SUSC-status-summary-March-2015-FINAL1.pdf.
20 Garner, M. Velvet, White-winged and Stejneger's scoters – photo guide. Birdwatch 2014; 260: 45-52.
21 Swick, Nate. #ABArare# – Common Scoter – California. American Birding Association; 2015. http://blog.aba.org/2015/02/abarare-common-scoter-california.html.
22 Swick, Nate. #ABArare# – Common Scoter – Oregon. American Birding Association; 2016. http://blog.aba.org/2016/11/abarare-common-scoter-oregon.html.
23 Population status of migratory game birds in Canada: November 2015. Canadian Wildlife Service Migratory Birds Regulatory Report No. 45. Environment and Climate Change Canada; 2015. https://www.ec.gc.ca/rcom-mbhr/default.asp?lang=En&n=9DB378FC-1.
24 Campbell, R. Wayne, Glenn R. Ryder, and Doug Innes. Breeding status of Common Goldeneye on the southwest coast of British Columbia including Vancouver Island. Wildlife Afield 2013; 11(1): 3-23.
25 British Columbia Vancouver Island Birds. https://groups.yahoo.com/neo/groups/BCVIBIRDS/conversations/messages/37690.
26 eBird Canada range map. http://ebird.org/ebird/canada/map.
27 Bellrose, F.C. Ducks, geese and swans of North America. Harrisburg, PA: Stackpole Books, 1976. 540 pp.

28 Campbell, R. Wayne. Two records of the Ruddy Duck nesting at Vancouver, British Columbia. Canadian Field-Naturalist 1968; 82(3): 220-21.
29 Martin, K., G.A. Brown, and J.R. Young. The historic and current distribution of the Vancouver Island White-tailed Ptarmigan (*Lagopus leucurus saxatilis*). Journal of Field Ornithology 2004; 75(3): 239-56.
30 Young, Vicky. Vancouver Island White-tailed Ptarmigan (*Lagopus leucurus saxatilis*) inventory. BC Conservation Corps, 2008. http://www.env.gov.bc.ca/wildlife/wsi/reports/4410_WSI_4410_RPT.PDF.
31 Reimchen, T.E., and S.D. Douglas. Feeding schedule and daily food consumption in Red-throated Loon (*Gavia stellata*) over the prefledging period. Auk 1984; 101: 593-99.
32 Burton, C.H. Southernmost breeding record of the Pacific Loon (*Gavia pacifica*) in British Columbia. Wildlife Afield 2006; 3: 144-46.
33 Delany, S., and D. Scott. Waterbird population estimates. Wageningen, Netherlands: Wetlands International, 2006.
34 Campbell, R. Wayne, Michael I. Preston, Linda M. Van Damme, David C. Evers, Anna Roberts, and Kris Andrews. Featured species – Common Loon. Wildlife Afield 2008; 5(1): 54-146.
35 Campbell, R. Wayne. Recent information on nesting colonies of Mew Gulls on Kennedy Lake, Vancouver Island, British Columbia. Syesis 1970; 3(1/2): 5-15.
36 Campbell, R. Wayne, Linda M. Van Damme, Mark Nyhof, and Patricia Huet. British Columbia nest record scheme 58th annual report – 2012 nesting season. Report No. 16. Victoria: Biodiversity Centre for Wildlife Studies, 2013. 112 pp.
37 Sibley, A.A. The Sibley guide to birds. New York: Alfred A. Knopf, 2007. 545 pp.
38 Muller, M.J., and R.W. Storer. Pied-billed Grebe (*Podilymbus podiceps*). In: A. Poole and F. Gill, eds. The birds of North America, No. 410. Philadelphia: The Birds of North America, Inc., 1999. 32 pp.
39 Munro, J.A. The grebes: studies of waterfowl in British Columbia. Occasional Paper No. 3. Victoria: British Columbia Provincial Museum, 1941. 71 pp.
40 Burger A.E. Status of the Western Grebe in British Columbia, March 1997. Wildlife Working Report No. WR-87. Victoria: Ministry of Environment, Lands and Parks, Wildlife Branch, 1997. https://pdfs.semanticscholar.org/7c71/7efa3d7f0be714e73c3d8f3ba414bc5b2343.pdf.
41 Wilson, S., E.M. Anderson, A.S.G. Wilson, et al. Citizen science reveals an extensive shift in the winter distribution of migratory Western Grebes. PLoS One 2013; 8(6): e65408. https://www.ncbi.nlm.nih.gov/pmc/articles/PMC3686804/.
42 Campbell, R. Wayne, and David Stirling. A photoduplicate file for British Columbia vertebrate records. Syesis 1971; 4: 217-22.
43 Laysan Albatross *Phoebastria immutabilis*. BirdLife International; 2017. http://datazone.birdlife.org/species/factsheet/22698365.
44 Laysan Albatross *Phoebastria immutabilis*. US Fish and Wildlife Service, Midway Atoll National Wildlife Refuge and Battle of Midway National Memorial; 2016. https://www.fws.gov/refuge/Midway_Atoll/wildlife_and_habitat/Laysan_Albatross.html.
45 Campbell, R. Wayne, and Michael G. Shepard. Laysan Albatross, Scaled Petrel and Parakeet Auklet: additions to the list of Canadian birds. Canadian Field-Naturalist 1973; 87(3): 179-80.

46 Kenyon, J.K., K.H. Morgan, M.D. Bentley, L.A. McFarlane Tranquilla, and K.E. Moore. Atlas of pelagic seabirds off the west coast of Canada and adjacent areas. Technical Report Series No. 499. Delta, BC: Canadian Wildlife Service, Pacific and Yukon Region, 2009. 308 pp.
47 Laysan Albatross *Phoebastria immutabilis*. In: Denlinger, L.M. Alaska Seabird Information Series. Unpublished report. US Fish and Wildlife Service, Migratory Bird Management, Nongame Program, Anchorage, 2006. pp. 3-4. https://www.fws.gov/alaska/mbsp/mbm/seabirds/pdf/laal.pdf.
48 Martin, P.W., and M.T. Myres. Observations on the distribution and migration of some seabirds off the outer coasts of British Columbia and Washington state, 1946-1949. Syesis 1969; 2: 241-56.
49 Campbell, R. Wayne, and Michael G. Shepard. Summary of spring and fall pelagic trips from Tofino, British Columbia. Vancouver Natural History Society Bulletin 1970; 150: 13-16.
50 *Phoebastria nigripes*. The IUCN Red List of Threatened Species; 2017. http://dx.doi.org/10.2305/IUCN.UK.2017-1.RLTS.T22698350A111620625.en.
51 Hawaiian Islands National Wildlife Refuge and Midway Atoll National Wildlife Refuge – annual nest counts through hatch year 2007. http://npawg.wikispaces.com/file/view/Albpopsummary2007final.pdf.
52 Carter, H.R., and Spencer G. Sealy. Historical occurrence of the Short-tailed Albatross in British Columbia and Washington, 1841-1958. Wildlife Afield, January–June 2014; 11(1): 24-38.
53 US Fish and Wildlife Service. Short-tailed Albatross recovery plan. Anchorage, AK: 2008. 105 pp. https://www.fws.gov/oregonfwo/documents/RecoveryPlans/ShortTailed_Albatross_RP.pdf.
54 Charlesworth, C. North American Birds, spring season – British Columbia. North American Birds 2011; 65: 504-5.
55 Wahl, T.R. Murphy's Petrel (*Pterodroma ultima*). In: T.R. Wahl, B. Tweit, and S.G. Mlodinow, eds. Birds of Washington: status and distribution. Corvallis: Oregon State University Press, 2005. p. 87.
56 Gillson, Greg. So you want to see a Murphy's Petrel? Oregon Seabirds; 2011. http://oregonseabirds.blogspot.ca/2011/06/so-you-want-to-see-murphys-petrel.html.
57 Bartle, J.A., D. Hu, J.-C. Stahl, P. Pyle, T.R. Simons, and D. Woodby. Status and ecology of gadfly petrels in the temperate North Pacific. In: K. Vermeer, T. Briggs, K.H. Morgan, and D. Siege-Causey, eds. The status, ecology and conservation of marine birds of the North Pacific. Special Publication. Ottawa: Canadian Wildlife Service, 1993. pp. 101-11.
58 Mottled Petrels in BC waters. British Columbia Rare Bird Alert; 2012. http://bcbirdalert.blogspot.ca/2012/03/mottled-petrels-in-bc-waters.html. Also: Washington Ornithological Society, Fall 2012 – Committee Meeting. http://wos.org/records/voting summary/fall-2012/.
59 Ainley, David G., and Bill Manolis. Occurrence and distribution of the Mottled Petrel. Western Birds 1979; 10(3): 113-23. https://www.westernfieldornithologists.org/archive/V10/10(3)%20p0113-p0124.pdf.

60 Adams Josh, Jonathan J. Felis, Peter Hodum, Valentina Colodro, Ryan Carle, and Verónica López. Migratory routes and at-sea threats to Pink-footed Shearwaters. Hobart, Tasmania, Australia: Agreement on the Conservation of Albatrosses and Petrels, 2016. https://pubs.er.usgs.gov/publication/70171462.
61 Committee on the Status of Endangered Wildlife in Canada. COSEWIC assessment and status report on the Pink-footed Shearwater *Puffinus creatopus* in Canada. Ottawa: COSEWIC, 2004. vii + 22 pp. http://www.registrelep-sararegistry.gc.ca/species/species Details_e.cfm?sid=819.
62 Žydelis, Ramūnas, Cleo Small, and Gemma French. June: the incidental catch of seabirds in gillnet fisheries: a global review. Biological Conservation 2013; 162: 76-88. https://www.journals.elsevier.com/biological-conservation/editors-choice/june-the-incidental-catch-of-seabirds-in-gillnet-fisheries.
63 del Hoyo, J., A. Elliot, and J. Sargatal. Handbook of the birds of the world. Volume 1: ostrich to ducks. Barcelona: Lynx Edicions, 1992.
64 Martin, P.W. Notes on some pelagic birds on the coast of British Columbia. Condor 1942; 44: 27-29.
65 Lavers, Jennifer L. Population status and threats to Flesh-footed Shearwaters (*Puffinus carneipes*) in South and Western Australia. ICES Journal of Marine Science 2015; 72(2): 316-27. https://academic.oup.com/icesjms/article/72/2/316/2801467/Population-status-and-threats-to-Flesh-footed.
66 Brooke, M. de L. Albatrosses and petrels across the world. Oxford: Oxford University Press, 2004.
67 Greater Shearwater *Puffinus gravis* (O'Reilly, 1818). Rare Birds of California. http://www.wfopublications.org/Rare_Birds/Greater_Shearwater.html.
68 Pearce, John M. First record of a Greater Shearwater in Alaska. Western Birds 2002; 33: 121-22. http://alaska.usgs.gov/products/pubs/2002/2002_Pearce_Western_Birds_33.pdf.
69 Greater Shearwater. Bird Web; n.d. http://www.birdweb.org/birdweb/bird/greater_shearwater.
70 Ratcliffe, Norman, and Christophe Barbraud. The first confirmed record of Great Shearwater *Puffinus gravis* for British Columbia. British Columbia Birds 2010; 20: 44-45. https://bcfo.files.wordpress.com/2013/08/grsh2010bcbirds.pdf.
71 British Columbia Field Ornithologists. BRC Round 5 Accepted Records, January 2015. http://bcfo.ca/brc-round-5-accepted-records-january-2015/.
72 Harper, P.C. Biology of the Buller's Shearwater (*Puffinus bulleri*) at the Poor Knights Islands, New Zealand. Notornis 1983; 30: 299-318.
73 Nichols, J.T. Tubinares off the north-west coast. Auk 1927; 44: 326-27.
74 Campbell, R. Wayne. First Canadian specimen of New Zealand Shearwater. Canadian Field-Naturalist 1971; 85(4): 329-30.
75 Buller's Shearwater *Ardenna bulleri*. BirdLife International; 2017. http://datazone.birdlife.org/species/factsheet/bullers-shearwater-ardenna-bulleri/text.
76 Marchant, S., and P.J. Higgins. Handbook of Australian, New Zealand and Antarctic birds. Volume 1: ratites to ducks. Melbourne: Oxford University Press, 1990. 7 vols.
77 BBC News. Tags record epic bird migration. BBC News, 8 August 2006. http://news.bbc.co.uk/2/hi/science/nature/5242360.stm.

78 Sooty Shearwater *Puffinus griseus*. In: Denlinger, L.M. Alaska Seabird Information Series. Unpublished report. US Fish and Wildlife Service, Migratory Bird Management, Nongame Program, Anchorage, 2006. pp. 7-8. http://www.fws.gov/alaska/mbsp/mbm/seabirds/pdf/sosh.pdf.

79 Ogi, H., A. Yatsu, H. Hatanaka, and A. Nitta. The mortality of seabirds by driftnet fisheries in the North Pacific. International North Pacific Fisheries Commission Bulletin 1993; 53: 499-518.

80 Guzman, J.R., and M.T. Myres. The occurrence of shearwaters (*Puffinus* sp.) off the west coast of Canada. Canadian Journal of Zoology 1983; 61: 2064-77.

81 Szabo, M.J. Short-tailed Shearwater. In: C.M. Miskelly, ed. New Zealand Birds Online; 2013. http://www.nzbirdsonline.org.nz.

82 Tweit, B., and D.R. Paulson. First report of the Washington Bird Records Committee. Washington Birds 1994; 5: 6-28.

83 Gillson, Greg. Manx Shearwater status in Oregon. Oregon Seabirds; 2009. http://oregonseabirds.blogspot.ca/2009/10/manx-shearwater-status-in-oregon.html.

84 Force, Michael, Ken Morgan, and Jukka Jantunen. Manx Shearwater in British Columbia; comments on a pioneering seabird. Wildlife Afield 2006; 3(1): 5-11. http://www.wildlifebc.org/pdfs/3_1_Force_Morgan_Jantunen.pdf.

85 BBC News. Bird is oldest in wild. BBC News, 25 April 2003. http://news.bbc.co.uk/2/hi/uk_news/wales/north_west/2976141.stm.

86 *Puffinus opisthomelas*. The IUCN Red List of Threatened Species; 2016. http://dx.doi.org/10.2305/IUCN.UK.2016-3.RLTS.T22698246A93673861.en.

87 Campbell, R. Wayne, and David Stirling. Notes on the natural history of Cleland Island, British Columbia, with emphasis on the breeding bird fauna. In: Report of the Provincial Museum of Natural History and Anthropology for the Year 1967. Victoria: Provincial Museum of Natural History and Anthropology, 1968. pp. HH25-HH43.

88 Rodway, Michael S., R. Wayne Campbell, and Moira J.F. Lemon. Seabird colonies of British Columbia: a history to 1990 (with current updates). Part 1: introduction and provincial summary. Wildlife Afield 2015; 21(2): 1-122.

89 *Hydrobates furcatus*. The IUCN Red List of Threatened Species; 2016. http://dx.doi.org/10.2305/IUCN.UK.2016-3.RLTS.T22698572A93690398.en.

90 *Hydrobates leucorhous*. The IUCN Red List of Threatened Species; 2016. http://dx.doi.org/10.2305/IUCN.UK.2016-3.RLTS.T22698511A86230533.en.

91 Mlodinow, S.G. Brown Booby (*Sula leucogaster*). In: T.R. Wahl, B. Tweit, and S.G. Mlodinow, eds. Birds of Washington: status and distribution. Corvallis: Oregon State University Press, 2005. p. 95.

92 Morgan, Ken, Scott Wallace, and Gary Krause. First record of a Brown Booby in British Columbia. British Columbia Birds 2009; 19: 13-15. https://bcfo.files.wordpress.com/2012/11/bcbvol19j.pdf.

93 Toochin R., Don Cecile, and Mike Ashby. Status and occurrence of Brown Booby (*Sula leucogaster*) in British Columbia. Ibis, Geography Department, University of British Columbia, 2015. http://ibis.geog.ubc.ca/biodiversity/efauna/documents/Brown_Booby-RTDCMA.pdf.

94 http://bcbirdalert.blogspot.ca/2013/.

95 Brandt's Cormorant *Phalacrocorax penicillatus*. In: Denlinger, L.M. Alaska Seabird Information Series. Unpublished report. US Fish and Wildlife Service, Migratory Bird Management, Nongame Program, Anchorage, 2006. pp. 23-24. https://www.fws.gov/alaska/mbsp/mbm/seabirds/pdf/asis_complete.pdf.

96 Stirling, D., and F. Buffam. The first breeding record of Brandt's Cormorant in Canada. Canadian Field-Naturalist 1966; 80: 117-18.

97 Carter, H.R., M.A. Lamberts, and D. Donnecke. Breeding of Brandt's Cormorant at Mandarte Island in 2013. Victoria Naturalist 2014; 70(3): 6. https://wildlife-species.canada.ca/bird-status/oiseau-bird-eng.aspx?sY=2014&sL=e&sB=BRAC&sM=p1.

98 Munro, J.A. Cormorants nesting on Bare Island, British Columbia. Condor 1928; 30: 327-28.

99 Lowe, R. Regional reports, Washington and Oregon. Pacific Seabirds 1997; 24: 89-93. Also: Myers, A.M., D.D. Roby, K. Collis, D.E. Lyons, and J.Y. Adkins. Diet composition of Double-crested Cormorants nesting at East Sand Island in the Columbia River estuary. Abstract. Pacific Seabirds 2002; 29: 56.

100 Adkins, J.Y., D.D. Roby, D.E. Lyons, K.N. Courtot, K. Colis, H.R. Carter, W.D. Shuford, and P.J. Capitolo. Recent population size, trends, and limiting factors for the Double-crested Cormorant in western North America. Journal of Wildlife Management 2014; 78: 1131-42.

101 Carter, H.R., P.N. Hébert, and P.V. Clarkson. Decline of pelagic cormorants in Barkley Sound, British Columbia. Wildlife Afield 2007; 4: 3-32.

102 *Pelecanus erythrorhynchos*. The IUCN Red List of Threatened Species; 2016. http://dx.doi.org/10.2305/IUCN.UK.2016-3.RLTS.T22697611A93624242.en.

103 Fannin, J. Check-list of British Columbia birds. Victoria: British Columbia Provincial Museum, 1891. 49 pp.

104 Blus, L.J., R.G. Heath, C.D. Gish, A. Belisle, and R.M. Prouty. Eggshell thinning in the Brown Pelican: implication of DDE. Bioscience 1971; 21: 1213-15.

105 Profita, Cassandra. Scientists discover California Brown Pelicans nesting in the Northwest. OPB News; 2014. http://www.opb.org/news/article/scientists-discover-california-brown-pelicans-nest/.

106 Checklist S18896364. eBird; 2014. http://ebird.org/ebird/view/checklist?subID=S18896364.

107 Campbell, R. Wayne, Michael G. Shepard, and Rudolf H. Drent. Status of birds in the Vancouver area in 1970. Syesis 1972; 5: 180-220.

108 Campbell, R. Wayne, and Wayne C. Weber. The Cattle Egret in British Columbia. Canadian Field-Naturalist 1977; 91(1): 87-88.

109 Wells, A.N. Green Heron at Chilliwack, British Columbia. Murrelet 1954; 35: 50.

110 Campbell, R. Wayne. The Green Heron in British Columbia. Syesis 1972; 5: 235-47.

111 Campbell, R. Wayne., Neil K. Dawe, Ian McTaggart-Cowan, John M. Cooper, Gary W. Kaiser, and Michael C.E. McNall. The birds of British Columbia. Volume 2: diurnal birds of prey through woodpeckers. Victoria: Royal British Columbia Museum, 1990. 632 pp.

112 Campbell, R. Wayne, Michael I. Preston, Linda M. Van Damme, and Diann MacRae. Feature species – Turkey Vulture. Wildlife Afield 2005; 2: 96-116.

113 Shepard, M.G. British Columbia birds – spring and summer, 1974. Discovery 1975; 3: 32-38.
114 Campbell, R. Wayne, and F.J. Edward (Ted) Hillary. Two instances of Osprey capturing a Meadow Vole in British Columbia. Wildlife Afield 2009; 6(2): 153-54.
115 US Fish and Wildlife Service. Queen Charlotte Goshawk (British Columbia distinct population segment) (*Accipiter gentilis laingi*). Threatened and Endangered Species; May 2012. http://www.fws.gov/alaska/fisheries/endangered/goshawk/pdf/QC_goshawk_factsheet_v2.pdf.
116 McLaren, Erica. Northern Goshawk Population Inventory for Vancouver Island, British Columbia, 1994-1998. In: L.M. Darling, ed. Proceedings of a conference on the biology and management of species and habitats at risk, Kamloops, BC, 15-19 Feb., 1999. Volume 1. Victoria: Ministry of Environment, Lands and Parks; Kamloops, BC: University College of the Cariboo, 2000. pp. 251-62. http://www.env.gov.bc.ca/wld/documents/ce02mcclaren.pdf.
117 Northern Goshawk *Accipiter gentilis laingi* Recovery Team. Recovery strategy for the Northern Goshawk (*Accipiter gentillis laingi*) in British Columbia. Victoria: Ministry of Environment, 2008. http://www.env.gov.bc.ca/wld/documents/recovery/rcvrystrat/northern_goshawk_rcvry_strat_200508.pdf.
118 Committee on the Status of Endangered Wildlife in Canada. COSEWIC assessment and status report on the Northern Goshawk *Accipiter gentilis laingi* in Canada. Ottawa: COSEWIC, 2013. x + 56 pp. http://www.sararegistry.gc.ca/virtual_sara/files/cosewic/sr_autour_palombes_northern_goshawk_1213_e.pdf.
119 Beebe, F.L. Field studies of the Falconiformes of British Columbia. Occasional Paper No. 17. Victoria: British Columbia Provincial Museum, 1974. 163 pp.
120 US Fish and Wildlife Service. Queen Charlotte Goshawk Status Review, 2007. 169 pp. https://www.fws.gov/alaska/fisheries/endangered/pdf/goshawk_status_review.pdf.
121 Parrish, Julia K. Common Murre demography on Triangle Island, 1995. Unpublished report, 1996. http://www.env.gov.bc.ca/bcparks/eco_reserve/anne_er/common_murre_demography.pdf.
122 Helzer, Chris. 2014 Sandhill Crane migration – Platte River, Nebraska. The Prairie Ecologist; 2014. http://prairieecologist.com/2014/03/31/2014-sandhill-crane-migration-platte-river-nebraska/.
123 The Ad Hoc Eastern Population Sandhill Crane Committee. Management plan for the eastern population of Sandhill Cranes. 2010. 36 pp. http://www.fwspubs.org/doi/suppl/10.3996/042015-JFWM-035/suppl_file/042015-jfwm-035.s5.pdf?code=ufws-site.
124 Mattocks, P.W. The spring season – northern Pacific coast region. American Birds 1985; 39: 34-344.
125 Woodford, Riley. Alaska's stately Sandhill Cranes. Alaska Fish and Wildlife News, November 2008. Alaska Department of Fish and Game. http://www.adfg.alaska.gov/index.cfm?adfg=wildlifenews.view_article&articles_id=409.
126 Campbell, R. Wayne. The American Avocet (*Recurvirostra americana*) in British Columbia (1908-1970). Syesis 1972; 5: 173-78.
127 Campbell, R. Wayne. British Columbia wildlife – summer report 1987. BC Naturalist 1987; 25(3): 6-7.

128 Groves, S. Aspects of foraging in Black Oystercatchers (Aves: Haematopodidae). PhD dissertation, University of British Columbia, 1982. 123 pp.
129 Page, G.W., and R.E. Gill. Shorebirds in western North America: late 1800s to late 1990s. Studies in Avian Biology 1994; 15: 147-60.
130 Tessler, David F., et al. Black Oystercatcher (*Haematopus bachmani*) conservation action plan, Version 1.1. International Black Oystercatcher Working Group, Alaska Department of Fish and Game, Anchorage; US Fish and Wildlife Service, Anchorage; Manomet Center for Conservation Sciences, Manomet, MA, 2010. 115 pp. http://www.whsrn.org/sites/default/files/file/Black_Oystercatcher_Conservation_Action_Plan_10_02-28_v1.1.pdf.
131 Andres, B.A., P.A. Smith, R.I.G. Morrison, C.L. Gratto-Trevor, S.C. Brown, and C.A. Friis. Population estimates of North American shorebirds, 2012. Wader Study Group Bulletin 2012; 119(3): 178-94.
132 Campbell, R. Wayne, Michael G. Shepard, Bruce A. MacDonald, and Wayne C. Weber. Vancouver birds in 1972. Publication No. 5. Vancouver: Vancouver Natural History Society, 1974. 96 pp.
133 Paulson, Denis. Shorebirds of the Pacific Northwest. Vancouver: UBC Press; Seattle: Seattle Audubon Society, 1993. 406 pp.
134 Sangster, G., A.G. Knox, A.J. Helbig, and D.T. Parkin. Taxonomic recommendations for European birds. Ibis 2002; 144(1): 153-59.
135 Richardson, S.A. Snowy Plover (*Charadrius alexandrinus*). In: T.R. Wahl, B. Tweit, and S.G. Mlodinow, eds. Birds of Washington: status and distribution. Corvallis: Oregon State University Press, 2005. pp. 134-35.
136 Ward, P.R.B. Further record of Snowy Plover in BC. Discovery 1973; 2: 80-81.
137 Siddle, C. The spring season – British Columbia/Yukon region. American Birds 1991; 45: 486-89.
138 Bain, M., and M. Holder. Cross Canada round-up: April and May 1996. Birders Journal 1996; 5: 106-7.
139 Charlesworth, C. Winter and spring season – British Columbia. North American Birds 2010; 64: 100-3.
140 Dec 18 – Snowy Plover – Pacific Rim National Park. British Columbia Rare Bird Alert; 2014. http://bcbirdalert.blogspot.ca/2014/12/dec-18-snowy-plover-pacific-rim.html.
141 Vancouver Island. British Columbia Rare Bird Alert; n.d. http://bcbirdalert.blogspot.ca/p/vancouver-island.html.
142 Pearson, S.F., C. Sundstrom, B. Hoenes, and W. Ritchie. Washington State Snowy Plover population monitoring, research, and management: 2013 nesting season research progress report. Olympia: Washington Department of Fish and Wildlife, Wildlife Science Division, 2014. http://wdfw.wa.gov/publications/01625/wdfw01625.pdf.
143 Lauten, David J., et al. The distribution and reproductive success of the Western Snowy Plover along the Oregon Coast – 2016. https://ir.library.oregonstate.edu/xmlui/bitstream/handle/1957/60174/2016%20SNPL%20monitoring%20report.pdf?sequence=1.
144 Campbell, R. Wayne. Semipalmated Plover breeding at Vancouver, British Columbia. Murrelet 1972; 53(1): 11-12.

145 Sims, Jim, and R. Wayne Campbell. New breeding locations for Semipalmated Plover in the Chilcotin region of central British Columbia. Wildlife Afield 2009; 6(1): 36-39.

146 Campbell, R. Wayne. Featured species – Semipalmated Plover. Wildlife Afield 2004; 1(1): 10-16.

147 Campbell R. Wayne. Wickaninnish Provincial Park, summer 1967. Unpublished report. Parks Branch, Victoria, 1967.

148 Center for Conservation Biology. Migrant Whimbrel tracked on 5,000 kilometer, transcontinental flight. Press release, 2008. http://www.ccbbirds.org/2008/06/02/migrant-whimbrel-tracked-on-5000-kilometer-transcontinental-flight/.

149 Campbell, R.W., and R.W. Nelson. Long-billed Curlew records for Haida Gwaii (Queen Charlotte Islands), British Columbia. Wildlife Afield 2011; 8(1): 117-19.

150 Siddle, C. Birds of north Peace River (Fort St. John and vicinity), British Columbia, 1975-1999. Part I (introduction and nonpasserines: waterfowl through woodpeckers). Wildlife Afield 2010; 7: 84.

151 Mattocks, P.W., and E.S. Hunn. Spring migration – northern Pacific coast region. American Birds 1983; 37: 903-6.

152 Mattocks, P.W., and B. Harring-Tweit. The autumn migration – northern Pacific coast region. American Birds 1987; 41: 478-82.

153 Bain, M., and P. Holder. Cross Canada round-up: August and September 1993. Birders Journal 1993; 2: 222-25.

154 Cecile, D. Fall season – British Columbia & Yukon. North American Birds 2004; 58: 129-30.

155 Thompson, Andrea. Bird makes longest non-stop flight. LiveScience; 1 October 2007. http://www.livescience.com/1894-bird-longest-stop-flight.html.

156 Shepard, M.G. Spring season: March 1 – August 31, 1999 – British Columbia. North American Field Notes 1999; 53: 318-19.

157 Cecile, D. Spring season – British Columbia–Yukon. North American Birds 2001; 55: 342-46.

158 Cecile, D. Fall season – British Columbia. North American Birds 2007; 61: 124-26.

159 Charlesworth, C. Summer season – British Columbia. North American Birds 2010; 64: 636-37.

160 Gibson, Daniel D., and Brina Kessel. Geographic variation in the Marbled Godwit and description of an Alaska subspecies. Condor 1988; 91: 436-43. https://sora.unm.edu/sites/default/files/journals/condor/v091n02/p0436-p0443.pdf.

161 Butcher, G.S., and D.K. Niven. Combining data from the Christmas Bird Count and the Breeding Bird Survey to determine the continental status and trends of North American birds. New York: National Audubon Society, 2007.

162 Campbell, R. Wayne, and Glenn R. Ryder. Earliest occurrences of Ruddy Turnstone in interior British Columbia. Wildlife Afield 2014; 11(1): 57-59.

163 Smith, W.G., R.W. Campbell, and D.A. Demarchi. The food habits of a population of Black Turnstones and Rock Sandpipers wintering in southern British Columbia. Wildlife Afield 2015; 12(1): 21-28.

164 Red Knot roselaari type. Species at Risk Public Registry; 2017. http://www.registrelep-sararegistry.gc.ca/species/speciesDetails_e.cfm?sid=982.

165 Senner, S.E., and B.J. McCaffery. Surfbird (*Aphriza virgata*). In: A. Poole and F. Gill, eds. The birds of North America, No. 266. Philadelphia: Academy of Natural Sciences; Washington, DC: American Ornithologists' Union, 1997. 20 pp.

166 Bowling, J. Autumn migration – British Columbia/Yukon region. North American Field Notes 1998; 52: 111-13.

167 Bain, M., and D. Shanahan. Cross Canada round-up: August and September 2000. Birders Journal 2000; 9: 214-17.

168 Cecile, D. Winter season – British Columbia. North American Birds 2007; 61: 314-15.

169 Handel, Colleen M., and Robert E. Gill Jr. Wayward youth: trans-Beringian movement and differential southward migration by juvenile Sharp-tailed Sandpipers. Arctic 2010; 63(3): 273-88. http://arctic.journalhosting.ucalgary.ca/arctic/index.php/arctic/article/view/1492/1471.

170 Moskoff, W., and R. Montgomerie. Baird's Sandpiper (*Calidris bairdii*). In: A. Poole and F. Gill, eds. The birds of North America, No. 661. Philadelphia: The Birds of North America, Inc., 2002. 20 pp.

171 Smith, A.L. COSEWIC assessment and status report on the Buff-breasted Sandpiper *Tryngites subruficollis* in Canada. Ottawa: COSEWIC, 2012. 44 pp.

172 *Calidris subruficollis*. The IUCN Red List of Threatened Species; 2017: http://dx.doi.org/10.2305/IUCN.UK.2017-1.RLTS.T22693447A111804064.en.

173 Campbell, R. Wayne, and Patrick T. Gregory. The Buff-breasted Sandpiper in British Columbia with notes on its migration in North America. Syesis 1976; 9: 123-30.

174 Crowell, J.B., and H.B. Nehls. The fall migration – northern Pacific coast region. American Birds 1976; 30: 112-17.

175 Campbell, R.W. British Columbia wildlife – spring [autumn] report. BC Naturalist 1991; 29(3): 6-8.

176 Butler, Robert W., and R. Wayne Campbell. The birds of the Fraser River delta: populations, ecology, and international significance. Occasional Paper No. 65. Ottawa: Canadian Wildlife Service, 1987. 73 pp.

177 Iverson G.C., S.E. Warnock, R.W. Butler, M.A. Bishop, N. Warnock. Spring migration of Western Sandpipers along the Pacific coast of North America: a telemetry study. Condor 1995; 98: 10-21. https://sora.unm.edu/sites/default/files/journals/condor/v098n01/p0010-p0021.pdf.

178 Jehl, R. Joseph Jr., Joanna Klima, and Ross E. Harris. Short-billed Dowitcher (*Limnodromus griseus*). In: P.G. Rodewald, ed. The birds of North America. Ithaca, NY: Cornell Lab of Ornithology, 2001. https://birdsna.org/Species-Account/bna/species/shbdow.

179 Vermeer, K., D.A. Manuwal, and D.S. Bingham. Seabirds and pinnipeds of Sartine Island, Scott Island group, British Columbia, 1974 and 1975. Murrelet 1976; 57: 14-16.

180 Mattocks, P.W. The spring season – northern Pacific coast region. American Birds 1985; 39: 340-44.

181 Vermeer K., R. Hay, and L. Rankin. Pelagic seabird populations off southwestern Vancouver Island. Canadian Technical Report of Hydrography and Ocean Sciences No. 87. Ottawa: Minister of Supply and Services Canada, 1987. iii + 26 pp. http://www.dfo-mpo.gc.ca/Library/106598.pdf.

182 Common Murre *Uria aalge*. In: Denlinger, L.M. Alaska Seabird Information Series. Unpublished report. US Fish and Wildlife Service, Migratory Bird Management,

Nongame Program, Anchorage, 2006. pp. 57-58. http://www.fws.gov/alaska/mbsp/mbm/seabirds/pdf/comu.pdf.
183 Hipfner, J.M. Population status of the Common Murre *Uria aalge* in British Columbia, Canada. Marine Ornithology 2005; 33: 67-69. http://www.sfu.ca/biology/wildberg/NewCWEPage/papers/HipfnerMarOrnithol05.pdf.
184 Parrish, J.K., and S.G. Zador. Seabirds as indicators: an exploratory analysis of physical forcing in the Pacific Northwest coastal environment. Estuaries 2003; 26: 1044-57.
185 Ainley, D.G., and T.J. Lewis. The history of Farralon Island marine bird populations, 1854-1972, Point Reyes Bird Observatory, Bolinas, California 94924. 1973. https://sora.unm.edu/sites/default/files/journals/condor/v076n04/p0432-p0446.pdf.
186 Campbell, R. Wayne, John G. Ward, and Michael G. Shepard. A new Common Murre colony in British Columbia. Canadian Field-Naturalist 1975; 89(3): 244-48.
187 Vallée, A., and R.J. Cannings. Nesting of the Thick-billed Murre, *Uria lomvia*, in British Columbia. Canadian Field-Naturalist 1983; 97: 450-51.
188 Marbled Murrelet. National Park Service; 2015. https://www.nps.gov/redw/learn/nature/marbled-murrelet.htm.
189 Ryder, Glen R., R. Wayne Campbell, Harry R. Carter, and Spencer G. Sealy. Earliest well-described tree nest of the Marbled Murrelet: Elk Creek, British Columbia, 1955. Wildlife Afield 1983; 9(1): 49-48.
190 Blood, Donald. Marbled Murrelet. Victoria: British Columbia Ministry of Environment, Lands and Parks, 1998. 6 pp. http://www.env.gov.bc.ca/wld/documents/murrelet.pdf.
191 Bertram, D.F., M.C. Drever, M.K. McAllister, B.K. Schroeder, D.J. Lindsay, and D.A. Faust. Estimation of coast-wide population trends of Marbled Murrelets in Canada using a Bayesian hierarchical model. PLoS One 2015; 10(8): e0134891. http://journals.plos.org/plosone/article?id=10.1371/journal.pone.0134891.
192 Marbled Murrelet *Brachyramphus marmoratus*. In: Denlinger, L.M. Alaska Seabird Information Series. Unpublished report. US Fish and Wildlife Service, Migratory Bird Management, Nongame Program, Anchorage, 2006. pp. 65-66. http://www.fws.gov/alaska/mbsp/mbm/seabirds/pdf/mamu.pdf.
193 Committee on the Status of Endangered Wildlife in Canada. COSEWIC assessment and status report on the Marbled Murrelet *Brachyramphus marmoratus* in Canada. Ottawa: COSEWIC, 2012. xii + 82 pp. http://publications.gc.ca/site/archivee-archived.html?url=http://publications.gc.ca/collections/collection_2013/ec/CW69-14-238-2012-eng.pdf.
194 Sanger, G.A. New northern record for Xantus' Murrelet. Condor 1973; 75: 253.
195 Cecile, D. Fall season – British Columbia. North American Birds 2005; 59: 133-34.
196 Dorst, A. A noteworthy record of Xantus' Murrelet near Tofino, British Columbia. Wildlife Afield 2007; 4: 68-70.
197 Toochin, R., Paul Levesque, and Jamie Fenneman. Rare birds of Vancouver Island. Unpublished report, 2013. http://ibis.geog.ubc.ca/biodiversity/efauna/documents/RareBirdRecordsofVancouverIslandXZA.pdf.
198 del Hoyo, J., A. Elliott, and J. Sargatal. Handbook of the birds of the world. Volume 3: hoatzin to auks. Barcelona: Lynx Edicions, 1996.

199 Gaston, A.J. The Ancient Murrelet: a natural history in the Queen Charlotte Islands. London: T. and A.D. Poyser, 1992. 267 pp.
200 Sealy, S.G., and R.W. Campbell. Post-hatching movements of young ancient murrelets. Western Birds 1979; 10: 25-30.
201 David, Rachel. Bird flies 16,000-kilometer Pacific circuit for no clear reason. New Scientist, 7 August 2015. https://www.newscientist.com/article/dn28018-bird-flies-16000-kilometre-pacific-circuit-for-no-clear-reason/.
202 Cassin's Auklet *Ptychoramphus aleuticus*. In: Denlinger, L.M. Alaska Seabird Information Series. Unpublished report. US Fish and Wildlife Service, Migratory Bird Management, Nongame Program, Anchorage, 2006. pp. 71-72. http://www.fws.gov/alaska/mbsp/mbm/seabirds/pdf/caau.pdf.
203 Harfenist, Anne. Cassin's Auklet, *Ptychoramphus aleuticus*. Accounts and Measures for Managing Identified Wildlife – Accounts V, 2004. http://www.env.gov.bc.ca/wld/frpa/iwms/documents/Birds/b_cassinsauklet.pdf.
204 CBC News. Cassin's Auklets found washed up near Tofino. CBC News, 6 January 2015. http://www.cbc.ca/news/canada.
205 Welch, C. Mass death of seabirds in western US is "unprecedented." National Geographic, 2015. http://news.nationalgeographic.com/news/2015/01/150123-seabirds-mass-die-off-auklet-california-animals-environment/.
206 Burger, Alan E. Beached bird surveys in British Columbia, 1986-1997. Report to the Nestucca Trust Fund, 31 August 2002. Unpublished report, 2002. http://web.uvic.ca/~mamu/pdf/Burger%20BBS%20report%202002.pdf.
207 Charlesworth, C. Winter and spring season – British Columbia. North American Birds 2010; 64: 100-3.
208 Carter, Harry. R., Alan E. Burger, Peter V. Clarkson, Yuri Zharikov, Michael S. Rodway, Spencer G. Sealy, R. Wayne Campbell, and David F. Hatler. Historical colony status and recent extirpations of burrow-nesting seabirds at Seabird Rocks, British Columbia. Wildlife Afield 2012; 9(1): 13-48.
209 Rodway, M.S., and M.J.F. Lemon. British Columbia seabird inventory. Report no. 7: northern mainland coast. Technical Report Series No. 121. Delta, BC: Canadian Wildlife Service, 1991.
210 Blight, Louise K., and John L. Ryder. Predation of Rhinoceros Auklet eggs by a native population of *Peromyscus*. Condor 1999; 101: 871-76.
211 Rhinoceros Auklet *Cerorhinca monocerata*. In: Denlinger, L.M. Alaska Seabird Information Series. Unpublished report. US Fish and Wildlife Service, Migratory Bird Management, Nongame Program, Anchorage, 2006. pp. 81-82. http://www.fws.gov/alaska/mbsp/mbm/seabirds/pdf/rhau.pdf.
212 Rodway, M.S., M.J.F. Lemon, and K.R. Summers. British Columbia seabird colony inventory: report #4 – Scott Islands. Census results from 1982 to 1989 with reference to the Nestucca oil spill. Technical Report Series No. 86. Delta, BC: Canadian Wildlife Service, 1990. 109 pp.
213 Tufted Puffin *Fratercula cirrhata*. In: Denlinger, L.M. Alaska Seabird Information Series. Unpublished report. US Fish and Wildlife Service, Migratory Bird Management, Nongame Program, Anchorage, 2006. pp. 85-86. https://www.fws.gov/alaska/mbsp/mbm/seabirds/pdf/tupu.pdf.

214 Rodway, M.S., and M.J.F. Lemon. British Columbia seabird colony inventory: report #5 – West Coast Vancouver Island. Technical Report Series No. 94. Delta, BC: Canadian Wildlife Service, 1990. 87 pp.
215 Black-legged Kittiwake *Rissa tridactyla*. In: Denlinger, L.M. Alaska Seabird Information Series. Unpublished report. US Fish and Wildlife Service, Migratory Bird Management, Nongame Program, Anchorage, 2006. http://www.fws.gov/alaska/mbsp/mbm/seabirds/pdf/blki.pdf.
216 Maunder, J.E., and W. Threlfall. The breeding biology of the Black-legged Kittiwake in Newfoundland. Auk 1972; 89: 789-816. http://www.sealifebase.org/References/FBRefSummary.php?ID=80123&database=FB.
217 Wahl, T.R. Sabine's Gull (*Larus sabini*). In: T.R. Wahl, B. Tweit, and S.G. Mlodinow, eds. Birds of Washington: status and distribution. Corvallis: Oregon State University Press, 2005. pp. 187-88.
218 Campbell, R. Wayne, and Robert G. Foottit. The Franklin's Gull in British Columbia. Syesis 1972; 5: 99-106.
219 Burger, J., and M. Gochfeld. Laridae (gulls). In: J. del Hoyo, A. Elliott, and J. Sargatal, eds. Handbook of the birds of the world. Barcelona: Lynx Edicions, 1996. pp. 572-623.
220 *Larus heermanni*. The IUCN Red List of Threatened Species; 2017. http://dx.doi.org/10.2305/IUCN.UK.2017-1.RLTS.T22694296A112274330.en.
221 R. Wayne Campbell, Michael I. Preston, Spencer G. Sealy, Bob Hansen, and Michael G. Shepard. Featured species – Heermann's Gull. Wildlife Afield 2006; 3(2): 152-204.
222 Rodway, M.S., James A. Sedgwick, and N.C. Sedgwick. First record of Mew Gulls breeding in the Queen Charlotte Islands, British Columbia. Northwestern Naturalist 1993; 73: 61-62.
223 Campbell, R. Wayne. Recent information on nesting colonies of Mew Gulls on Kennedy Lake, Vancouver Island, British Columbia. Syesis 1970; 3(1/2): 5-15.
224 Campbell, R. Wayne. Status of the Caspian Tern in British Columbia. Syesis 1971; 4(1/2): 185-90.
225 Schick, W.J. First British Columbia specimen record of Caspian Tern. Syesis 1970; 3: 187.
226 Manuwal, D.A., P.W. Mattocks, and K.O. Richter. First Arctic Tern colony in the contiguous United States. American Birds 1979; 33: 144-45.
227 Campbell, R. Wayne, Jim Sims, Phil Ranson, and Sandy Proulx. Two disjunct breeding locations for Arctic Tern in British Columbia. Wildlife Afield 2009; 6(1): 15-19.
228 *Columba livia*. The IUCN Red List of Threatened Species; 2016. http://dx.doi.org/10.2305/IUCN.UK.2016-3.RLTS.T22690066A86070297.en.
229 Scheidt, S.N., and H.S. Hurlbert. Range expansion and population dynamics of an invasive species: Eurasian Collared-Dove (*Streptopelia decaocto*). PLoS One 2014; 9(10): e111510. http://journals.plos.org/plosone/article?id=10.1371/journal.pone.0111510.
230 Bowling, J. Autumn migration – British Columbia/Yukon region. North American Field Notes 1998; 52: 111-13.
231 Cecile, D. Summer season – British Columbia. North American Birds 2004; 58: 587-88.
232 Cecile, D. Fall season – British Columbia. North American Birds 2006; 60: 124-26.

233 Conniff, Richard. America's wildlife body count. Sunday Review, New York Times, 17 September 2016. https://www.nytimes.com/2016/09/18/opinion/sunday/americas-wildlife-body-count.html?_r=0.
234 Campbell, R. Wayne, Linda M. Van Damme, Mark Nyhof, and Patricia Huet. British Columbia Nest Record Scheme 58th annual report – 2012 nesting season. Report No. 16. Victoria: Biodiversity Centre for Wildlife Studies, 2013. 112 pp.
235 Preston, M.I., and G.A. Powers. High incidence of vehicle-induced owl mortality in the Lower Mainland and central Fraser Valley, British Columbia. Wildlife Afield 2006; 39 (supplement): 15-23.
236 Stirling, D. A sight record of the Barred Owl on Vancouver Island. Murrelet 1970; 51: 19.
237 Lynch, W. Owls of the United States and Canada: a complete guide to their biology and behavior. Vancouver: UBC Press, 2007. 256 pp.
238 Campbell, R.W., and Michael I. Preston. Featured species – Snowy Owl. Wildlife Afield 2009; 6(2): 173-255.
239 Campbell, R. Wayne, and Michael McCall. Winter foods of Snowy Owls at Victoria, British Columbia. Journal Wildlife Management 1978; 42(1): 190-92.
240 Scott, L. Northern Pygmy-Owl preys on Mourning Doves at Creston, British Columbia. Wildlife Afield 2007; 4: 76-78.
241 Wink, M., A-Aziz El-Sayed, H. Sauer-Gürth, and J. Gonzalez. Molecular phylogeny of owls (Strigiformes) inferred from DNA sequences of the mitochondrial cytochrome b and the nuclear RAG-1 gene. Ardea 2009; 97: 581-91.
242 Siddle, C. The summer season – British Columbia/Yukon. American Birds 1993; 47: 1141-43.
243 Bowling, J. The fall migration – British Columbia/Yukon region. North American Field Notes 1995; 49: 87-92.
244 Campbell, R. Wayne, Martin K. McNicholl, R. Mark Brigham, and Janet Ng. Featured species – Common Nighthawk. Wildlife Afield 2006; 3(1): 32-71.
245 Kennerly, C.B.R. Description of a new species of *Cypselus*, collected on the Northwest Boundary Survey. Proceedings of the Academy of Natural Sciences of Philadelphia 1857; 9: 202.
246 Vrooman, A.G. Discovery of the egg of the Black Swift. Auk 1901; 18: 394-95.
247 Kirk, D.A. COSEWIC assessment and status report on the Black Swift *Cypseloides niger* in Canada. Ottawa: COSEWIC, 2015. 50 pp.
248 Anchorage area rarity – Anna's Hummingbird. Anchorage Audubon Society, 2015.
249 Banks, R.C., and N.K. Johnson. A review of North American hybrid hummingbirds. Condor 1961; 63: 3-28.
250 Phinney, M. Spring & summer birds of Dawson Creek, 1991-1995. Wildlife Report No. 4. West Vancouver, BC: Wild Bird Trust of British Columbia, 1998. 50 pp.
251 Calder, W.A. Rufous Hummingbird (*Selasphorus rufus*). In: A. Poole and F. Gill, eds. The birds of North America, No. 53. Philadelphia: Academy of Natural Sciences; Washington, DC: American Ornithologists' Union, 1993. 20 pp.
252 Bucher, T.L., and M.A. Chappel. Ventilatory and metabolic dynamics during entry into and arousal from torpor in *Selasphorus* hummingbirds. Physiological Zoology 1992; 65: 978-93.

253 Campbell, R. Wayne. Summer naturalist report, Wickaninnish Provincial Park – 1967. Report for British Columbia Ministry of Recreation and Conservation, Parks Branch, Victoria, 1967. 163 pp.
254 Campbell, R. Wayne. Summer naturalist report, Wickaninnish Provincial Park – 1968. Report for British Columbia Ministry of Recreation and Conservation, Parks Branch, Victoria, 1968. 104 pp.
255 Beebe, F.L. Field studies of the Falconiformes of British Columbia. Occasional Paper No. 17. Victoria: British Columbia Provincial Museum, 1974. 163 pp.
256 Burnham, K.K., W.A. Burnham, and I. Newton. Gyrfalcon *Falco rusticolus* post-glacial colonization and extreme long-term use of nest sites in Greenland. In: R.T. Watson, T.J. Cade, M. Fuller, G. Hunt, and E. Potapov, eds. Gyrfalcons and ptarmigan in a changing world. Volume 2. Boise, ID: Peregrine Fund, 2011. http://peregrinefund.org/subsites/conference-gyr/proceedings/123-Burnham.pdf.
257 Anderson, C.M., and S.G. Herman. Peregrine Falcon (*Falco peregrinus*). In: T.R. Wahl, B. Tweit, and S.G. Mlodinow, eds. Birds of Washington: status and distribution. Corvallis: Oregon State University Press, 2005. 436 pp.
258 Campbell, R.W., M.A. Paul, M.S. Rodway, and H.R. Carter. Tree-nesting Peregrine Falcons in British Columbia. Condor 1977; 79: 500-1.
259 Hipfner, J. Mark, Kyle W. Morrison, and Rachel Darvill. Peregrine Falcons enable two species of colonial seabirds to breed successfully by excluding other aerial predators. Waterbirds 2011; 34(1): 82-88. http://www.bioone.org/doi/abs/10.1675/063.034.0110.
260 Campbell, R. Wayne. Hunting tactics of a Peregrine Falcon on Black Turnstones. Condor 1976; 77(4): 485.
261 Committee on the Status of Endangered Wildlife in Canada. COSEWIC assessment and status report on the Olive-sided Flycatcher *Contopus cooperi* in Canada. Ottawa: COSEWIC, 2007. 25 pp. http://www.registrelep-sararegistry.gc.ca/document/dspHTML_e.cfm?ocid=6356.
262 Campbell, R.W., and T.N. Campbell. Breeding bird surveys on the southwest coast of British Columbia: 2011 final report. Report for Western Forest Products Ltd., Campbell River, BC, 2011. 32 pp.
263 Campbell, R. Wayne, Neil K. Dawe, Ian McTaggart-Cowan, John M. Cooper, Gary W. Kaiser, Michael C.E. McNall, and G.E. John Smith. The birds of British Columbia. Volume 3: passerines (flycatchers through vireos). Vancouver: UBC Press, 1997. 693 pp.
264 Macoun, J., and J.M. Macoun. Catalogue of Canadian birds. Ottawa: Department of Mines, Geological Surveys Branch, 1909. 761 pp.
265 Hunn, E.S., and P.W. Mattocks. The autumn migration – northern Pacific coast region. American Birds 1983; 37: 214-18.
266 Bain, M. Cross Canada round-up: June and July 1994. Birders Journal 1994; 3: 173-74.
267 Kermode F. The Lichtenstein Kingbird on Vancouver Island. Condor 1928; 30: 251.
268 Crowell, J.B., and H.B. Nehls. The fall migration – northern Pacific coast region. American Birds 1974; 28: 93-98.
269 Mattocks, P.W., and E.S. Hunn. The autumn migration – northern Pacific coast region. American Birds 1978; 32: 245-50.

270 Rand, A.L. On some British Columbia birds. Canadian Field-Naturalist 1943; 57: 60-63.
271 Stirling, D. Sight records of unusual birds in the Victoria area for 1959. Murrelet 1960; 41: 10-11.
272 Vermeer, K., K.R. Summers, and D.S. Bingham. Birds observed at Triangle Island, British Columbia, 1974 and 1975. Murrelet 1976; 57: 35-42.
273 Campbell, R. Wayne. British Columbia wildlife – summer report 1987. BC Naturalist 1987; 25(3): 6-7.
274 Cecile, D. Fall season – British Columbia and Yukon. North American Birds 2004; 58: 129-30.
275 Cecile, D. Spring season – British Columbia. North American Birds 2008; 62: 93-95.
276 Charlesworth, C. Summer season – British Columbia. North American Birds 2011; 65: 77-78.
277 Van Damme, Linda M. Field observation of a Northern Shrike preying on Meadow Vole in the Creston Valley, British Columbia. Wildlife Afield 2011; 8: 111-13.
278 Davidson, P.J.A., R.J. Cannings, A.R. Couturier, D. Lepage, and C.M. Di Corrado, eds. Atlas of the breeding birds of British Columbia, 2008-2012. Delta, BC: Bird Studies Canada, 2014. http://www.birdatlas.bc.ca/e.
279 Stewart, A.C., and M.G. Shepard. Steller's Jay invasion on southern Vancouver Island, British Columbia. North American Bird Bander 1994; 19: 90-95.
280 Irving, E.B. Birds at Carmanah Point. Victoria Naturalist 1953; 10: 19-22; 28-31.
281 Verbeek, N.A.M. Egg predation by Northwestern Crows; its association with human and Bald Eagle activity. Auk 1982; 99: 347-52.
282 Western Purple Martin Foundation. http://www.saveourmartins.org/.
283 McTaggart-Cowan, Ian, and Gary McTaggart-Cowan. The Amur Barn Swallow off British Columbia [note in From Field and Study]. Condor 1961; 63(5): 419. https://sora.unm.edu/sites/default/files/journals/condor/v063n05/p0419-p0419.pdf.
284 Meugens, A.L. Coast Bushtit extending its range. Victoria Naturalist 1945; 2: 26.
285 Toews, David P.L., and Darren E. Irwin. Cryptic speciation in a Holarctic passerine revealed by genetic and bioacoustic analyses. Molecular Ecology 2008; 17(11): 2691-2705.
286 Shepard, M.G. The winter season – British Columbia – Yukon region. North American Field Notes 1999; 53: 423-24.
287 Campbell, R. Wayne. Brown Thrasher on the west coast of British Columbia. Canadian Field-Naturalist 1974; 88(2): 225.
288 Cannings, R.A., R.J. Cannings, and S.G. Cannings. Birds of the Okanagan Valley, British Columbia. Victoria: Royal British Columbia Museum, 1987. 632 pp.
289 Cecile, D. Spring season – British Columbia. North American Birds 2005; 59: 482-83.
290 Charlesworth, C. Summer season – British Columbia. North American Birds 2010; 64: 636-37.
291 Jobin, L. European Starling in central British Columbia. Condor 1952; 54: 318.
292 Campbell, R. Wayne. European Starling at Pachena lightstation. Victoria Naturalist 1968; 24(5): 55.

293 Common Starling *Sturnus vulgaris*. BirdLife International; 2017. http://datazone.birdlife.org/species/factsheet/22710886.
294 Godfrey, W.E. The birds of Canada. Revised ed. Ottawa: National Museum of Canada, 1986. 595 pp.
295 Burger, A.E., and H. Knechtel. Vagrant Black-backed Wagtail at Triangle Island: the second record for British Columbia. Birders Journal 1996; 5: 303-4.
296 Davidson, P.J.A. American Pipit *Anthus rubescens*. In: P.J.A. Davidson, R.J. Cannings, A.R. Couturier, D. Lepage, and C.M. Di Corrado, eds. Atlas of the breeding birds of British Columbia, 2008-2012. Delta, BC: Bird Studies Canada, 2015. http://www.birdatlas.bc.ca/accounts/speciesaccount.jsp?sp=AMPI&lang=en.
297 Campbell, R. Wayne, and Brigitta M. Van Der Raay. First breeding record of the Snow Bunting for British Columbia. Wilson Bulletin 1985; 97(1): 128-29.
298 Siddle, C. Birds of north Peace River (Fort St. John and vicinity), British Columbia, 1975-1999. Part 2 (passserines: flycatchers through Old World sparrows). Wildlife Afield 2010; 7: 143-280.
299 Campbell, R. Wayne, Neil K. Dawe, Ian McTaggart-Cowan, John M. Cooper, Gary W. Kaiser, Andrew S. Stewart, and Michael C.E. McNall. The birds of British Columbia. Volume 4: passerines, wood-warblers through Old World sparrows. Vancouver: UBC Press, 2001. 739 pp.
300 Campbell, R.W. Wildlife atlases progress report. BC Naturalist 1983; 21(1): 4-5.
301 Campbell, R.W. Wildlife atlases progress report – winter 1983-84. BC Naturalist 1984; 22(2): 6-7.
302 Campbell, R. Wayne. Earliest confirmed records of Chestnut-sided Warbler (*Setophaga pensylvanica*) for British Columbia and the Pacific Northwest. Wildlife Afield 2015; 12(1):78-81.
303 Siddle, C. Autumn migration – British Columbia/Yukon region. National Audubon Society Field Notes 1994; 48: 240-42.
304 Cecile, D. Summer season – British Columbia. North American Birds 2006; 60: 568-69.
305 Friedman, H. Host relations of the parasitic cowbirds. Bulletin 233. Washington, DC: United States National Museum, 1963. 276 pp.
306 Campbell, R. Wayne. Clay-colored Sparrow over-wintering on Vancouver Island, British Columbia. Wildlife Afield 2012; 9(2): 211-14.
307 Cecile, D. Fall season – British Columbia. North American Birds 2001; 54: 93-94.
308 Preston, M.I., and R.W. Campbell. Evaluation of trends in monitoring birds during summer bird surveys on coastal British Columbia. Westcam Consulting Services Report for Weyerhaeuser, Victoria, 2002. 42 pp.
309 Campbell, R. Wayne. Golden-crowned Sparrow breeding on Vancouver Island. Canadian Field-Naturalist 1975; 89(2): 175-76.
310 Siddle, C., and J. Bowling. The spring season – British Columbia/Yukon. American Birds 1993; 47: 445-47.
311 Hatler, David F., and R. Wayne Campbell. Notes on spring migration, including sex segregation, of some western Savannah Sparrows. Syesis 1975; 8: 401-2.
312 Bryant, A.A., J.-P.L. Savard, and R.T. McLaughlin. Avian communities in old-growth and managed forests of western Vancouver Island, British Columbia. Technical Report Series No. 167. Delta, BC: Canadian Wildlife Service, 1993. 115 pp.

313 Shepard, M.G. Fall migration – British Columbia–Yukon region. North American Field Notes 2000; 54: 93-94.
314 Cecile, D. Winter season – British Columbia–Yukon region. North American Birds 2002; 56: 212-14.
315 Cecile, D. Winter season – British Columbia–Yukon region. North American Birds 2005; 59: 212-14.
316 Cecile, D. Summer season – British Columbia. North American Birds 2005; 59: 642-43.
317 Cecile, D. Spring season – British Columbia. North American Birds 2006; 60: 424-25.
318 Jonsson, Patrik. Bye bye blackbird: USDA acknowledges a hand in one mass bird death. Christian Science Monitor, 20 January 2010. http://www.csmonitor.com/USA/Society/2011/0120/Bye-Bye-Blackbird-USDA-acknowledges-a-hand-in-one-mass-bird-death.
319 Campbell, R.W. British Columbia wildlife – summer report 1991. BC Naturalist 1992; 30(1): 8-10.
320 Jaramillo, Alvaro. Blackbirds, orioles and allies. The Sibley guide to birdlife and behaviour. Toronto: Alfred A. Knopf and Random House of Canada, 2001. 588 pp.
321 Shepard, M.G. The winter season – British Columbia–Yukon region. North American Field Notes 1999; 53: 198-99.
322 Cowan, I. McT. The House Finch at Victoria, British Columbia. Condor 1937; 39: 225.
323 Campbell, R. Wayne. Autumn nesting of Red Crossbill in British Columbia. Wildlife Afield 2012; 9(2): 201-3.
324 Brooks, A. The occurrence of the Falcated Duck (*Eunetta falcata*) in Okanagan, British Columbia. Murrelet 1932; 13: 92. Also: Brooks, A. Additions to the distributional list of the birds of British Columbia. Condor 1942; 44: 33-34.
325 Bowling, J. Spring migration – British Columbia/Yukon region. North American Field Notes 1994; 48: 332-34. Also: Paterson, A. The Tofino Falcated Teal. Birders Journal 1994; 3: 240-41.
326 Bowling, J. The winter season – British Columbia–Yukon region. North American Field Notes 1995; 49: 184-89.
327 Bowling, J. The winter season – British Columbia–Yukon region. North American Field Notes 1996; 50: 208-13.
328 Hughes, W.M. Sight record of the Tufted Duck at Vancouver, British Columbia. Canadian Field-Naturalist 1963; 77: 62-63.
329 *Pterodroma solandri*. The IUCN Red List of Threatened Species; 2017. http://www.iucnredlist.org/details/22698042/0.
330 Bailey, S., P. Pyle, and L. Spear. Dark *Pterodroma* petrels in the North Pacific: identification, status, and North American occurrence. American Birds 1989; 43: 400-15.
331 Gillson, G. Solander's Petrel in British Columbia. Oregon Seabirds; 2009.http://oregonseabirds.blogspot.ca/2009/10/solanders-petrel-in-british-columbia.html.
332 Toochin, Rick. Status and occurrence of Oriental Turtle-Dove (*Streptopelia orientalis*) in British Columbia, 2017. http://ibis.geog.ubc.ca/biodiversity//efauna/documents/ORTD-article-RT.

333 Gyug, Les W., and Jason T. Weir. American Avocet and Black-necked Stilt breeding status and population trends at Kelowna, British Columbia, 1997-2015. British Columbia Birds 2017; 27: 13-17.
334 Holmes, R.T., and F.A. Pitelka. Breeding behavior and taxonomic relationships of the Curlew Sandpiper. Auk 1964; 81: 362-79.
335 Oriental Turtle Dove in Delta. Vancouver Sun, 18 January 2010. http://vancouversun.com/news/community-blogs/oriental-turtle-dove-in-delta.
336 Campbell, R. Wayne, et al. An updated account of the Yellow-billed Cuckoo in British Columbia, 1881-2013: status and distribution, first breeding, habitat and conservation. Wildlife Afield 2014; 11(2): 190-231.
337 Dorst, A. Whip-poor-will (*Caprimulgus vociferus*): a new species for British Columbia. Wildlife Afield 2006; 3: 16-17.
338 Bowling, J. Fall, 1994 – British Columbia/Yukon region. American birds. National Audubon Field Notes 1995; 48: 332-34.
339 Toochin, R., and Don Cecile. Status and occurrence of Costa's Hummingbird (*Calypte costae*) in British Columbia. http://ibis.geog.ubc.ca/biodiversity/efauna/documents/CostasHummingbird-RT-DC-g.pdf.
340 Cecile, D. Winter season – British Columbia. North American Birds 2007; 61: 314-15.
341 Fannin, J. A preliminary catalogue of the collections of natural history and ethnology of the Provincial Museum, Victoria, British Columbia. Victoria: British Columbia Provincial Museum, 1898. 196 pp.
342 Campbell, R. Wayne, Linda M. Van Damme, and Stephen R. Johnson. Sky Lark (*Alauda arvensis*). In: A. Poole and F. Gill, eds. The birds of North America, No. 286. Philadelphia: Academy of Natural Sciences; Washington, DC: American Ornithologists' Union, 1997. 20 pp. Also: R.W. Campbell, personal communication.
343 Etzkorn, Jerry, and Janet Etzkorn. Gray Wagtail (*Motacilla cinerea*): a new species for British Columbia. Wildlife Afield 2004; 1: 64-65.
344 Hatler, D.F. Chestnut-collared Longspur in British Columbia. Canadian Field-Naturalist 1973; 87: 66.
345 Cecile, D. Fall season – British Columbia and Yukon. North American Birds 2003; 57: 105-6.
346 Siddle, C. The winter season – British Columbia and Yukon. American Birds 1990; 44: 312-17.
347 Bain, M. Cross Canada round-up – October and November 1993. Birders Journal 1993; 2: 281-82.
348 Bowling, J. The autumn migration – British Columbia/Yukon region. North American Field Notes 1996; 50: 99-105.
349 Charlesworth, C. Fall season – British Columbia. North American Birds 2010; 64: 103-5.
350 Campbell, R. Wayne, Michael I. Preston, Mark Phinney, Chris Siddle, and John Deal. Featured species – Canada Warbler. Wildlife Afield 2007; 4(1): 91-155.
351 Campbell, R. Wayne, and Ed McMackin. Status of the Yellow-breasted Chat in the Creston Valley, British Columbia. Wildlife Afield 2006; 3(1): 17-21.
352 Crowell, J.B., and H.B. Nehls. The fall migration – northern Pacific coast region. American Birds 1972; 26: 107-11.

353 Hunn, E.S., and P.W. Mattocks. The fall migration – northern Pacific coast region. American Birds 1984; 38: 236-40.
354 Charlesworth, C. Summer season – British Columbia. North American Birds 2012; 66: 721.
355 Campbell, R. Wayne. Report of the Wildlife Data Centre: 1 January to 30 June 2014. Wildlife Afield 2014; 11(1): 79-90.

INDEX

Anna's Hummingbird

A

Accentor, Siberian, 512-13
Accipiter
  cooperii, 174
  gentilis, 175
  striatus, 172
Actitis macularius, 250
Aechmorphorus
  clarkii, 127
  occidentalis, 125
Aegolius
  acadicus, 322
  funereus, 321
Aethia
  cristatella, 501
  psittacula, 275
Agelaius phoeniceus, 473
Aix sponsa, 64
Alauda arvensis, 511
Albatross
  Black-footed, 130-32
  Laysan, 128-30
  Short-tailed, 133-34
Ammodramus savannarum, 520
Anas
  acuta, 74
  crecca, 77
  platyrhynchos, 73
Anser
  albifrons, 46
  caerulescens, 43
  canagicus, 46
  rossii, 45
Anthus rubescens, 420

Antigone canadensis, 189
Aquila chrysaetos, 169
Archilochus alexandri, 509
Ardea
  alba, 163
  herodias, 161
Ardenna
  bulleri, 141
  carneipes, 139
  creatopus, 138
  gravis, 140
  grisea, 142
  tenuirostris, 144
Arenaria
  interpres, 214
  melanocephala, 215
Asio flammeus, 320
Athene cunicularia, 506
Auklet
  Cassin's, 274-75
  Crested, 501-2
  Parakeet, 275-76
  Rhinoceros, 276-78
Avocet, American, 192
Aythya
  affinis, 84
  americana, 80
  collaris, 81
  fuligula, 495
  marila, 83
  valisineria, 79

B

Bartramia longicauda, 205

Bittern, American, 498
Blackbird
  Brewer's, 477-78
  Red-winged, 473-75
  Rusty, 477
  Yellow-headed, 470-71
Bluebird
  Mountain, 405-6
  Western, 405
Bobolink, 521-22
Bombycilla
  cedrorum, 423
  garrulus, 422
Bonasa umbellus, 108
Booby, Brown, 151-52
Botaurus lentiginosus, 498
Brachyramphus marmoratus, 267
Brambling, 479
Brant, 50-53
Branta
  bernicla, 50
  canadensis, 57
  hutchinsii, 53
Bubo
  scandiacus, 316
  virginianus, 314
Bubulcus ibis, 164
Bucephala
  albeola, 95
  clangula, 96
  islandica, 98
  scandiacus, 316
Bufflehead, 95-96
Bunting
  Indigo, 469
  Lark, 447-48
  Lazuli, 468-69
  McKay's, 514
  Painted, 521
  Rustic, 520-21
  Snow, 426-27
Bushtit, 392
Buteo
  jamaicensis, 181
  lagopus, 184

Butorides virescens, 165

C

Calamospiza melanocorys, 447
Calcarius
  lapponicus, 425
  ornatus, 513
  pictus, 514
Calidris
  acuminata, 221
  alba, 223
  alpina, 225
  bairdii, 228
  canutus, 216
  ferruginea, 501
  himantopus, 222
  mauri, 235
  melanotos, 232
  minutilla, 229
  ptilocnemis, 226
  pugnax, 220
  pusilla, 234
  subruficollis, 230
  virgata, 218
Callipepla californica, 107
Calypte
  anna, 329
  costae, 509
Canvasback, 79-80
Caprimulgus vociferus, 507
Cardellina pusilla, 443
Carduelis
  flammea, 485
  pinus, 489
  tristis, 491
Carpodacus
  mexicanus, 482
  purpureus, 484
Catbird, Gray, 414-15
Cathartes aura, 165
Catharus
  guttatus, 409
  ustulatus, 407
Cepphus columba, 266
Cerorhinca monocerata, 276

Certhia americana, 394
Chaetura vauxi, 327
Charadrius
    alexandrines, 200
    semipalmatus, 201
    vociferus, 203
Chat, Yellow-breasted, 520
Chickadee, Chestnut-backed, 390-92
Chlidonias niger, 502
Chondestes grammacus, 446
Chordeiles
    acutipennis, 507
    minor, 324
Chroicocephalus philadelphia, 284
Cinclus mexicanus, 400
Circus hudsonius, 170
Cistothorus palustris, 398
Clangula hyemalis, 93
Coccothraustes vespertinus, 480
Coccyzus
    americanus, 504
    erythropthalmus, 504
Colaptes auratus, 340
Collared-Dove, Eurasian, 307-9
Columba livia, 305
Contopus
    cooperi, 350
    sordidulus, 352
Coot, American, 188-89
Cormorant
    Brandt's, 152-54
    Double-crested, 154-55
    Pelagic, 155-57
Corvus
    caurinus, 374
    corax, 376
Cowbird, Brown-headed, 475-76
Crane, Sandhill, 189-92
Creeper, Brown, 394-95
Crossbill
    Red, 486-88
    White-winged, 488-89
Crow, Northwestern, 474-76
Cuckoo
    Black-billed, 504-5
    Yellow-billed, 504
Curlew
    Bristle-thighed, 500-1
    Long-billed, 208-9
Cyanocitta
    cristata, 372
    stelleri, 370
Cygnus
    buccinator, 61
    columbianus, 63
Cypseloides niger, 325

D

Dendragapus fuliginosus, 110
Dickcissel, 470
Dipper, American, 400-1
Dolichonyx oryzivorus, 521
Dove
    Mourning, 310
    White-winged, 309
Dowitcher
    Long-billed, 240-42
    Short-billed, 238-40
Dryocopus pileatus, 342
Duck
    Falcated, 495
    Harlequin, 86-88
    Long-tailed, 93-94
    Ring-necked, 81-83
    Ruddy, 106-7
    Tufted, 495
    Wood, 64-65
Dumetella carolinensis, 414
Dunlin, 225-26

E

Eagle
    Bald, 177-81
    Golden, 169-70
Egret
    Cattle, 164-65
    Great, 163-64
    Snowy, 498-99
Egretta thula, 498
Eider, King, 86

Emberiza rustica, 520
Empidonax
　difficilis, 355
　hammondii, 354
　traillii, 353
Eremophila alpestris, 378
Euphagus
　carolinus, 477
　cyanocephalus, 477

F

Falco
　columbarius, 345
　peregrinus, 347
　rusticolus, 346
　sparverius, 344
Falcon, Peregrine, 347-50
Finch
　House, 482-83
　Purple, 484-85
Flicker, Northern, 340-42
Flycatcher
　Ash-throated, 358-58
　Hammond's, 354-55
　Great Crested, 510
　Olive-sided, 350-51
　Pacific-slope, 355-56
　Scissor-tailed, 361-63
　Willow, 353-54
Fratercula
　cirrhata, 279
　corniculata, 278
Fregata magnificens, 497
Frigatebird, Magnificent, 497
Fringilla montifringilla, 479
Fulica americana, 188
Fulmar, Northern, 134-36
Fulmarus glacialis, 134

G

Gadwall, 70
Gallinago delicata, 242
Gavia
　adamsii, 119
　arctica, 496
　immer, 117
　pacifica, 115
　stellata, 113
Geothlypis
　tolmiei, 430
　trichas, 432
Glaucidium gnoma, 317
Gnatcatcher, Blue-gray, 512-13
Godwit
　Bar-tailed, 210-11
　Hudsonian, 209-10
　Marbled, 211-14
Goldeneye
　Barrow's, 98-100
　Common, 96-98
Golden-Plover
　American, 196-97
　Pacific, 197-99
Goldfinch, American, 491-92
Goose
　Cackling, 53-56
　Canada, 57-61
　Emperor, 46
　Greater White-fronted, 46-50
　Ross's, 45
　Snow, 43-45
Goshawk, Northern, 175-77
Grackle, Common, 478-79
Grebe
　Clark's, 127-28
　Eared, 124-25
　Horned, 122-23
　Pied-billed, 125-22
　Red-necked, 123-24
　Western, 125-27
Grosbeak
　Black-headed, 467-68
　Evening, 480
　Pine, 480-81
　Rose-breasted, 467
Grouse
　Ruffed, 108-9
　Sooty, 110-11

Guillemot, Pigeon, 266-67
Gull
  Bonaparte's, 284-86
  California, 293-94
  Franklin's, 286-87
  Glaucous, 299-300
  Glaucous-winged, 298-99
  Heermann's, 287-89
  Herring, 294-96
  Iceland, 296-97
  Mew, 289-90
  Ring-billed, 290-91
  Sabine's, 283-84
  Slaty-backed, 297-98
  Western, 291-93
Gyrfalcon, 346-47

H

Haematopus bachmani, 192
Haliaeetus leucocephalus, 177
Harrier, Northern, 170-72
Hawk
  Cooper's, 174
  Red-tailed, 181-84
  Rough-legged, 184
  Sharp-shinned, 172-74
Heron
  Great Blue, 161-63
  Green, 165
Himantopus mexicanus, 499
Hirundo rustica, 387
Histrionicus histrionicus, 86
Hummingbird
  Anna's, 329-30
  Black-chinned, 509
  Costa's, 509
  Rufous, 330-33
Hydroprogne caspia, 301

I

Icteria virens, 519
Icterus
  bullockii, 472-73
  galbula, 522-23
  spurius, 522

Ixoreus naevius, 412

J

Jaeger
  Long-tailed, 261-62
  Parasitic, 260-61
  Pomarine, 258-59
Jay
  Blue, 372-73
  Gray, 369-70
  Steller's, 370-72
Junco, Dark-eyed, 450-51
Junco hyemalis, 450

K

Kestrel, American, 344-45
Killdeer, 203-4
Kingbird
  Eastern, 361
  Gray, 511
  Tropical, 358-59
  Western, 360
Kingfisher, Belted, 333-34
Kinglet
  Golden-crowned, 401-3
  Ruby-crowned, 403-4
Kittiwake, Black-legged, 281-82
Knot, Red, 216-18

L

Lagopus leucura, 111
Lanius borealis, 363
Lark, Horned, 378-80
Larus
  argentatus, 294
  californicus, 293
  canus, 289
  delawarensis, 290
  glaucoides, 296
  glaucuscens, 298
  heermanni, 287
  hyperboreus, 299
  occidentalis, 291
  schistisagus, 297
Leucophaeus pipixcan, 286

Leucosticte tephrocotis, 481
Limnodromus
  griseus, 238
  scolopaceus, 240
Limosa
  fedoa, 211
  haemastica, 209
  lapponica, 210
Longspur
  Chestnut-collared, 513-14
  Lapland, 425-26
  Smith's, 514
Loon
  Arctic, 496
  Common, 117-19
  Pacific, 115-17
  Red-throated, 113-15
  Yellow-billed, 119-20
Lophodytes cucullatus, 100
Loxia
  curvirostra, 486-88
  leucoptera, 488-89

M

Magpie, Black-billed, 373
Mallard, 73-74
Mareca
  americana, 72
  falcata, 495
  penelope, 71
  strepera, 70
Martin, Purple, 381-82
Meadowlark, Western, 471-72
Megaceryle alcyon, 333
Megascops kennicottii, 311
Melanitta
  americana, 92
  deglandi, 90
  perspicillata, 88
Melospiza
  georgiana, 463
  lincolnii, 462
  melodia, 460
Merganser
  Common, 102-4
  Hooded, 100-1
  Red-breasted, 105-6
Mergus
  merganser, 102
  serrator, 105
Merlin, 345-46
Mimus polyglottos, 416
Mniotilta varia, 515
Mockingbird, Northern, 416-18
Molothrus ater, 475
Motacilla
  alba, 419
  cinerea, 513
Murre
  Common, 262-64
  Thick-billed, 265
Murrelet
  Ancient, 272-73
  Marbled, 267-70
  Scripps's, 270-71
Myadestes townsendi, 406
Myiarchus
  cinerascens, 357
  crinitus, 510

N

Night-Heron, Black-crowned, 499
Nighthawk
  Common, 324-25
  Lesser, 507
Nucifraga columbiana, 373
Numenius
  americanus, 208
  phaeopus, 205
  tahitiensis, 500
Nutcracker, Clark's, 373-74
Nuthatch, Red-breasted, 393-94
Nycticorax nycticorax, 499

O

Oceanodroma
  furcata, 148
  leucorhoa, 150
Oporornis agilis, 516
Oreoscoptes montanus, 416

Oreothlypis
  celata, 428
  peregrina, 427
  ruficapilla, 429
Oriole
  Baltimore, 522-23
  Bullock's, 472-73
  Orchard, 522
Osprey, 167-69
Owl
  Barn, 505
  Barred, 319-20
  Boreal, 321-22
  Burrowing, 505–6
  Great Gray, 506
  Great Horned, 314-15
  Northern Saw-whet, 322-24
  Short-eared, 320-21
  Snowy, 316-17
Oxyura jamaicensis, 106
Oystercatcher, Black, 192-94

P

Pandion haliaetus, 167
Parkesia noveboracensis, 515
Parula, Northern, 517
Passer domesticus, 492
Passerculus sandwichensis, 458
Passerella iliaca, 448
Passerina
  amoena, 468
  ciris, 521
  cyanea, 469
Patagioenas fasciata, 306
Pelecanus
  erythrorhynchos, 157
  occidentalis, 159
Pelican
  American White, 157-59
  Brown, 159-60
Perisoreus canadensis, 369
Petrel
  Mottled, 137
  Murphy's, 136
  Solander's, 496-97

Petrochelidon pyrrhonota, 389
Phalacrocorax
  auritus, 154
  pelagicus, 155
  penicillatus, 152
Phalarope
  Red, 247-49
  Red-necked, 245-47
  Wilson's, 244-45
Phalaropus
  fulicarius, 247
  lobatus, 245
  tricolor, 244
Pheucticus
  ludovicianus, 467
  melanocephalus, 467
Phoebastria
  albatrus, 133
  immutabilis, 128
  nigripes, 130
Phoebe
  Black, 509-10
  Say's, 357
Pica hudsonia, 373
Picoides
  pubescens, 336
  villosus, 337
Pigeon
  Band-tailed, 306-7
  Rock, 305-6
Pinicola enucleator, 480
Pintail, Northern, 74-77
Pipilo maculatus, 464
Pipit, American, 420-22
Piranga ludoviciana, 465
Plectrophenax
  hyperboreus, 514
  nivalis, 426
Plover
  Black-bellied, 195-96
  Semipalmated, 201-3
  Snowy, 200-1
Pluvialis
  dominicus, 196
  fulva, 197

squatarola, 195
Podiceps
  auritus, 122
  grisegena, 123
  nigricollis, 124
Podilymbus podiceps, 120
Poecile rufescens, 390
Polioptila caerulea, 512
Pooecetes gramineus, 457
Porzana carolina, 186
Progne subis, 381
Protonotaria citrea, 515
Prunella montanella, 512
Psaltriparus minimus, 392
Ptarmigan, White-tailed, 111-13
Pterodroma
  inexpectata, 137
  solandri, 496
  ultima, 136
Ptychoramphus aleuticus, 274
Puffin
  Horned, 278-79
  Tufted, 279-81
Puffinus
  opisthomelas, 147
  puffinus, 146
Pygmy-Owl, Northern, 317-19

Q

Quail, California, 107-8
Quiscalus quiscula, 478

R

Rail, Virginia, 185-86
Rallus limicola, 185
Raven, Common, 376-78
Recurvirostra americana, 192
Redhead, 80
Redpoll, Common, 485-86
Redstart, American, 433
Regulus
  calendula, 403
  satrapa, 401
Riparia riparia, 386
Rissa tridactyla, 281

Robin, American, 410-12
Ruff, 220-21

S

Sanderling, 223-25
Sandpiper
  Baird's, 228
  Buff-breasted, 230-31
  Curlew, 501
  Least, 229-30
  Pectoral, 232-33
  Rock, 226-27
  Semipalmated, 234-35
  Sharp-tailed, 221-22
  Solitary, 251-52
  Spotted, 250-51
  Stilt, 222
  Upland, 205
  Western, 235-38
Sapsucker, Red-breasted, 335-36
Sayornis
  nigricans, 509
  saya, 357
Scaup
  Greater, 83-84
  Lesser, 84-85
Scoter
  Black, 92-93
  Surf, 88-90
  White-winged, 90-92
Screech-Owl, Western, 311-13
Selasphorus rufus, 330
Setophaga
  americana, 517
  castanea, 517
  coronata, 438
  discolor, 518
  nigrescens, 440
  palmarum, 437
  pensylvanica, 436
  petechia, 433
  ruticilla, 433
  striata, 436
  townsendi, 441

Shearwater
  Black-vented, 147-48
  Buller's, 141-42
  Flesh-footed, 139-40
  Great, 140-41
  Manx, 146-47
  Pink-footed, 138-39
  Short-tailed, 144-45
  Sooty, 142-44
Shoveler, Northern, 68-69
Shrike, Northern, 363-65
Sialia
  currucoides, 405
  mexicana, 405
Siskin, Pine, 489-91
Sitta canadensis, 393
Skua, South Polar, 257-58
Skylark, Eurasian, 511-12
Snipe, Wilson's, 242-44
Solitaire, Townsend's, 406-7
Somateria spectabilis, 86
Sora, 186-87
Sparrow
  American Tree, 444-45
  Chipping, 445-46
  Clay-colored, 446
  Fox, 448-50
  Golden-crowned, 453-55
  Grasshopper, 519–20
  Harris's, 456
  House, 492-93
  Lark, 446-47
  Lincoln's, 462-63
  Savannah, 458-60
  Song, 460-62
  Swamp, 463-64
  Vesper, 457-58
  White-crowned, 451-53
  White-throated, 456-57
Spatula
  clypeata, 68
  cyanoptera, 67
  discors, 65
Sphyrapicus ruber, 335
Spiza americana, 470

Spizella
  pallida, 446
  passerina, 445
Spizelloides arborea, 444
Starling
  European, 418-19
  White-cheeked, 525
Stelgidopteryx serripennis, 380
Stercorarius
  longicaudus, 261
  maccormicki, 257
  parasiticus, 260
  pomarinus, 258
Sterna
  hirundo, 302
  paradisaea, 303
Stilt, Black-necked, 499-500
Storm-Petrel
  Fork-tailed, 148-49
  Leach's, 150-51
Streptopelia
  decaocto, 307
  orientalis, 503
Strix
  nebulosi, 505
  varia, 319
Sturnella neglecta, 471
Sturnus vulgaris, 418
Sula leucogaster, 151
Surfbird, 218-20
Swallow
  Bank, 386
  Barn, 387-89
  Cliff, 389-90
  Northern Rough-winged, 380-81
  Tree, 382-84
  Violet-green, 384-86
Swan
  Trumpeter, 61-63
  Tundra, 63-64
Swift
  Black, 325-27
  Vaux's, 327-29
Synthliboramphus
  antiquus, 272

scrippsi, 270

T

Tachycineta
  bicolor, 382
  thalassina, 384
Tanager, Western, 465-66
Tattler, Wandering, 252-53
Teal
  Blue-winged, 65-67
  Cinnamon, 67
  Green-winged, 77-79
Tern
  Arctic, 303-5
  Black, 502-3
  Caspian, 301-2
  Common, 302-3
Thrasher
  Brown, 415-16
  Sage, 416
Thrush
  Hermit, 409-10
  Swainson's, 407-9
  Varied, 412-14
Thryomanes bewickii, 399
Towhee, Spotted, 464-65
Toxostoma rufum, 415
Tringa
  flavipes, 255
  incana, 252
  solitaria, 251
  melanoleuca, 254
  semipalmata, 255
Troglodytes
  aedon, 395
  pacificus, 396
Turdus migratorius, 410
Turnstone
  Black, 215-16
  Ruddy, 214-15
Turtle-Dove, Oriental, 503-4
Tyrannus
  dominicensis, 511
  forficatus, 361
  melancholicus, 358
  tyrannus, 361
  verticalis, 360
Tyto alba, 505

U

Uria
  aalge, 262
  lomvia, 265

V

Vireo
  cassinii, 365
  gilvus, 367
  huttoni, 366
  olivaceus, 368
  philadelphicus, 511
Vireo
  Cassin's, 365
  Hutton's, 366-67
  Philadelphia, 511
  Red-eyed, 368-69
  Warbling, 367-68
Vulture, Turkey, 165-67

W

Wagtail
  Gray, 513
  White, 419-20
Warbler
  Bay-breasted, 517-18
  Black-and-white, 515
  Black-throated Gray, 440-41
  Blackpoll, 436-37
  Canada, 519
  Chestnut-sided, 436
  Connecticut, 516
  Hooded, 516-17
  MacGillivray's, 430-31
  Nashville, 429-30
  Orange-crowned, 428-29
  Palm, 437-38
  Prairie, 518-19
  Prothonotary, 515-16
  Tennessee, 427
  Townsend's, 441-43

Wilson's, 443-44
Yellow, 433-35
Yellow-rumped, 438-40
Waterthrush, Northern, 515
Waxwing
  Bohemian, 422-23
  Cedar, 423-24
Whimbrel, 205-8
Whip-poor-will, Eastern, 507-8
Wigeon
  American, 71
  Eurasian, 72-73
Willet, 255
Wilsonia
  canadensis, 519
  citrina, 516
Woodpecker
  Downy, 336-37
  Hairy, 337-40
  Pileated, 342-43
Wood-Pewee, Western, 352-53
Wren
  Bewick's, 399-400
  House, 395-96
  Marsh, 398-99
  Pacific, 396-98

X

Xanthocephalus xanthocephalus, 470
Xema sabini, 283

Y

Yellowlegs
  Greater, 254-55
  Lesser, 256-57
Yellowthroat, Common, 432-33

Z

Zenaida
  asiatica, 309
  macroura, 310
Zonotrichia
  albicollis, 456
  atricapilla, 453
  leucophrys, 451
  querula, 456

Printed and bound in Canada by Friesens
Set in Myriad and Devanagari by Artegraphica Design Co. Ltd.
Text design: Irma Rodriguez
Copy editor: Frank Chow
Cartographer: Eric Leinberger